Franchising

Practice and precedents in business format franchising

Franchising

Practice and precedents in
business format franchising

John N Adams, LLB, MIEX
Barrister, Professor of Commercial Law, University of Kent

K V Prichard Jones, BA
Solicitor

Third edition

Butterworths
London, Dublin, Edinburgh
1990

United Kingdom	Butterworth & Co (Publishers) Ltd, 88 Kingsway, LONDON WC2B 6AB and 4 Hill Street, EDINBURGH EH2 3JZ
Australia	Butterworths Pty Ltd, SYDNEY, MELBOURNE, BRISBANE, ADELAIDE, PERTH, CANBERRA and HOBART
Canada	Butterworths Canada Ltd, TORONTO and VANCOUVER
Ireland	Butterworth (Ireland) Ltd, DUBLIN
Malaysia	Malayan Law Journal Sdn Bhd, KUALA LUMPUR
New Zealand	Butterworths of New Zealand Ltd, WELLINGTON and AUCKLAND
Puerto Rico	Equity de Puerto Rico, Inc, HATO REY
Singapore	Malayan Law Journal Pte Ltd, SINGAPORE
USA	Butterworth Legal Publishers, AUSTIN, Texas; BOSTON, Massachusetts; CLEARWATER, Florida (D & S Publishers); ORFORD, New Hampshire (Equity Publishing); ST PAUL, Minnesota; and SEATTLE, Washington

All rights reserved. No part of this publication may be reproduced in any material form (including photocopying or storing it in any medium by electronic means and whether or not transiently or incidentally to some other use of this publication) without the written permission of the copyright owner except in accordance with the provisions of the Copyright, Designs and Patents Act 1988 or under the terms of a licence issued by the Copyright Licensing Agency Ltd, 33-34 Alfred Place, London, England WC1E 7DP. Applications for the copyright owner's written permission to reproduce any part of this publication should be addressed to the publisher.

Warning: The doing of an unauthorised act in relation to a copyright work may result in both a civil claim for damages and criminal prosecution.

© Butterworth & Co (Publishers) Ltd 1990

A CIP Catalogue record for this book is available from the British Library.

ISBN 0 406 13790 0

Typeset by Kerrypress Ltd, Luton
Printed and bound in Great Britain by Mackays of Chatham, PLC, Chatham, Kent

Preface to third edition

The last edition of this book appeared in early 1987. Since then, many legal developments have taken place necessitating this new edition. As a consequence of the EEC block exemption and Court of Justice decision in *Pronuptia*, Chapter 2 has been largely rewritten. The Copyright, Designs and Patents Act 1988 has also required a substantial reworking of Chapter 3. Indeed every chapter of the book has needed fairly substantial changes in the light of developments in the law. Finally, the precedents have been extensively revised to take account, amongst other things, of the provisions of the block exemption. We have also added new precedents which we think readers will find useful. The 'core franchise' agreement is designed to cover a fairly recent development in this country: the 'bolting together' of a number of separate franchises belonging to the franchisor to form a 'package' suitable for a particular site.

As with the previous editions we have tried to make the book 'user friendly'. The subject involves consideration of a large number of areas of law, some of very great complexity. To help the reader to pursue detailed points which may not be covered in a text of this length, we have tried to supply as much bibliographical information as to the leading texts as possible. We have also tried to help the reader with the more complex areas by providing checklists.

July 1990

John N Adams
Ken Prichard Jones

Preface to first edition

The aim of this book is to provide a guide to the legal problems involved in business format franchising. However, to the extent that many of the problems of business format franchising are, from the point of view of the franchisor, simply those of intellectual property licensing generally, it should also be of assistance to those advising on ordinary licence agreements. We have tried to produce a work which will be of help both to those advising franchisors, and to those advising franchisees, and one which is convenient to use. Because there are very many areas of law involved, and some of them quite complex, we have tried to save the practitioner's time by providing introductory summaries, checklists and source material at the relevant points in the text. The inclusion of source material may also be of particular assistance to overseas readers.

In order to keep the book within a manageable length, we have tried to confine discussion to the core of any franchise agreement, the licence of the intellectual property rights, and the *particular* problems which are involved in business format franchising. Thus, for example, planning laws in practice create many difficulties, but because they are not peculiar to franchising and are adequately dealt with in monographs, we do not deal with them. Precedents for leases are commonly needed but are generally available and are therefore not included (we include some particular clauses). By contrast, some areas such as competition law, may not appear to give rise to many problems in practice for the average franchise business, but because they *do* give rise to peculiar problems they are dealt with at length (and furthermore there is at present no available work dealing comprehensively with the competition law problems of licensing). Again, in the precedents chapter, we have included precedents we think are useful in the special context of franchising. Precedents are things about which people tend to have strong views, having developed their own particular styles. We do not imagine we will please everyone but we hope at any rate we have provided a useful basis from which people can work. We have tried, as far as we are able, to warn of possible dangers, and to explain why we have adopted particular forms of clause.

As the state of the art is more developed in the United States, fairly extensive use is made of American cases and materials, with an attempt to draw out differences in United Kingdom law. We hope that this will be helpful, particularly for those advising American chains thinking of operating in the United Kingdom. Various parts of the tax section should be helpful in this respect also.

To our knowledge, this is the first legal monograph on franchising to be published in the United Kingdom. Martin Mendelsohn's *Guide to Franchising* is a valuable introduction for both lay readers and lawyers, but there is no text dealing specifically with the law. Writing the first book in any area presents special difficulties. At least we hope to have alerted the reader to the principal problems, and to have

Preface

provided a basis for discussion of what we believe to be an increasingly important area of law.

1 August 1981

John N Adams
Ken Prichard Jones

Acknowledgments

The authors would like to thank the British Franchise Association, Danielle Baillieu, Prof John Birds, Mark Heselden, Prof Martin Mendelsohn, and Dr Frank Wooldridge for the kind assistance they have provided with various parts of this edition. Full responsibility for errors and omissions, however, is, of course, the authors'.

Contents

Preface to third edition v
Preface to first edition vii
Acknowledgments ix
Table of statutes xv
Table of cases xxiii

Introduction 1
The use of the EEIG and the SE for the purposes of franchising 3
Competition policy 4
Why franchise? 5
The British Franchise Association 8
Streetwise Franchising 16

Chapter 1 Franchising as a legal concept 17
Introduction 17
The distinctive features of franchising 17
The licence of the trade name, etc and goodwill of the business 18
The franchisor's liability for the acts and defaults of his franchisees 31
Franchisor's liability under the Consumer Protection Act 1987 43
Relationship of the franchisor and franchisee inter se 44

Chapter 2 Competition law 51
Introduction 51
Common Market competition law 55
Summary of the block exemption 57
Agreements not within the block exemption 69
Domestic competition law 89
Restraint of trade at common law 90
Fair Trading Act 1973 and Competition Act 1980 100
Forms legislation 107
Restrictive Trade Practices Act 1976 107
Resale price maintenance 110

Chapter 3 Setting up the franchise business: intellectual property 112
Introduction 112
Choice of the name for the franchise business 113
Protecting the package 118
Protection of intellectual properties abroad 158
Procedural aspects of licensing of intellectual property 162

xi

Contents

Chapter 4 Tax problems 166
Introduction 166
Royalties 166
Value added tax 170
Know-how 174
Outlets 175
Finance 180
Corporation tax and advanced corporation tax 189
Investment risk 191

Chapter 5 Setting up the franchise business: some other considerations 238
Introduction 238
The operating manual 239
Safeguard trade secrets and know-how if possible by non-legal strategies 239
Supply of the initial equipment, etc 240
Ties 240
Consumer Credit Act 1974 243
The franchise premises 244
Preliminary contract 253
Territorial rights 254
The initial fee 255
Continuing fees or royalties 255
Liability of the franchisor to his franchisees 256
Franchisor's liability to third parties for acts and defaults of the franchisee 257
Liability of the franchisor to third parties for his own acts and defaults 260
Insurance 261
Minimum turnover clauses and minimum royalty payments 262
Goodwill 262
Licence under the Consumer Credit Act 1974 262
Data Protection Act 1984 263
Training 263
Further periods of training 264
Advertising 264
Annual meeting and franchisees' club 265
Minimum wages provisions 265
Vehicles used in the franchised business 266
Death or incapacity of the franchisee 267
Sale of the franchised business 267
Pre-printed replies to preliminary enquiries 267

Chapter 6 Acting for the prospective franchisee 268
Introduction 268
Preliminary enquiries 268
Replies to preliminary enquiries 277

Chaper 7 Control of unfair and fraudulent trading 286
Introduction 286
British Code of Advertising Practice 288
Remedies for misrepresentation 289
Trade Descriptions Act 1968 291
Persistent unfair conduct 295

Consumer Credit Act 1974 296
Pyramid selling 297
Financial Services Act 1986 301
Companies Act 1985 and Insolvency Act 1986 301
Protection against harassment 301
Equitable relief 302
Disclosure laws 303
Conclusion 307

Chapter 8 Precedents 308
Introduction to precedents 308
 1 Franchise agreement—master form 316
 2 Franchise application form 371
 3 Letter to prospective franchisee enclosing application form 373
 4 Confidentiality agreement 373
 5 Prospectus inviting subscriptions for shares in company franchisee 376
 6 Letter to Inland Revenue applying for clearance under ICTA 1970, s 54 389
 7 Letter to Office of Fair Trading re restrictions on franchisor relating to territory 390
 8 Board Minutes of franchisor company concerning letter to the Office of Fair Trading 390
 9 Franchise purchase agreement 391
10 Shareholders'/directors' covenant letter 393
11 Deed of guarantee 394
12 Leasehold covenants in lease of premises to be used for franchisee's operations 396
13 Licence agreement of site 397
14 Letter to accompany application to the court 400
15 Sales report by franchisee 401
16 Stationery text 401
17 Development area agreement 402
18 Licence and agency agreement 404
19 Core franchise 408

Appendix 1 Franchise agreement 413

Appendix 2 Guidelines laid down by the Trade Marks Registry, August 1984 417

Appendix 3 Commission notice of 3 September 1986 419

Appendix 4 Commission regulation (EEC) No 4087/88 423

Appendix 5 Text of the court's judgment in *Pronuptia* 432

Appendix 6 SP 1/90 Company residence 442

Appendix 7 The registration of Restrictive Trading Agreements (EEC Documents) Regulations 1973 (SI 1973/950) 447

Index 449

Table of statutes

References in this Table to *Statutes* are to Halsbury's Statutes of England (Fourth Edition) showing the volume and page at which the annotated text of an Act may be found. Paragraph numbers in **bold** type indicate where the section of an Act is set out. Page references in *italic* type refer to Ch 8 and the Appendices.

	PARA
Banking Act 1979 (4 *Statutes* 457)...	4.112
Business Names Act 1985 (48 *Statutes* 165)............	1.53, 2.22, 5.44, 5.45, 6.24, *323, 354*
s 1(1), (2)	6.24
2(2)...........................	6.24
4	6.24
(1)(a),(b)	6.24
(5).........................	6.24
5, 7............................	6.24
8(1)	6.24
Capital Allowances Act 1990	4.78
Capital Gains Tax Act 1979 (42 *Statutes* 620)	
s 15(1).........................	4.98
(a), (b)....................	4.98
(2), (3)	4.98
(4), (5)	4.98, 4.121
(8)–(10)	4.98
17	4.121
(2)...........................	4.121
19	4.71, **4.72**, 4.75, 4.76, 4.86, 4.87, 4.96, 4.108
(1)..........................	4.71
20	**4.73**, 4.86, 4.108
(1)(c)..........	4.71, 4.72, 4.75, 4.76
(d)	4.71, 4.75, 4.76, 4.87
25	4.72, **4.74**, 4.75, 4.86, 4.87, 4.96, 4.108
(1)..........................	4.71
26	4.71, 4.86
136	4.108
149c (1), (2), (6)	4.47
157(2).........................	4.64
Sch 7, para 8	4.64
Companies Act 1948	
s 95	*366*
154	1.02
Companies Act 1981	
s 119(5)........................	3.05, 6.24
Companies Act 1985 (8 *Statutes* 107)................	*377, 384, 385*
s 83	*376*

	PARA
Companies Act 1985—*contd*	
s 309, 319–322..................	1.62
330–346	1.62
736	1.02
741(2)........................	1.62
Company Directors Disqualification Act 1986	
s 6, 7..........................	1.62
22(5)..........................	1.62
Competition Act 1980 (47 *Statutes* 463)...........	2.04, 2.72, 2.122, 5.06, 5.38
s 2(1).........................	2.127, 2.132
(2)..........................	**2.133**
(3)–(5)	2.135
(6)..........................	**2.128**
(b)	2.135
3	2.126, 2.127
(4),(10)	2.138
4	2.127, 2.138
5	2.126, 2.127, 2.138, 2.139
6	2.127
7	2.127
(6)..........................	2.138
8–10	2.127
14	2.139
33(1).........................	2.128
Sch 2.........................	2.135
Consumer Credit Act 1974 (11 *Statutes* 15)............	4.28, 4.112, 6.03, 7.44, 7.56, *308, 330*
s 8	5.56, 6.21
(1)–(3)	7.29
11(1)(a), (b)...................	7.30
(2)..........................	7.30
12(a), (b).....................	7.30
15	5.56, 6.21
16(5).........................	6.21
19	**5.14**, 7.29
21	6.21
23(3).........................	5.57, 6.21
48, 49.......................	5.57, 6.21
56(1), (2)	7.29

XV

Table of statutes

	PARA
Consumer Credit Act 1974—*contd*	
s 61	7.32
67–69	7.29
75(1)–(3)	7.30
123, 124	7.33
145	5.56, 6.21
(1), (2)	7.31
149	7.31
189	5.56, 7.29
(1)	6.21
Consumer Protection Act 1987 (39 Statutes 188)	
s 2(1)	1.56, 5.51
(2)(b)	1.36, 1.44, 1.56, 5.51
(4), (5)	1.56, 5.51
5	1.56, 5.51
Copyright Act 1911 (24 Statutes 146)	
s 11	3.14
Copyright Act 1956 (11 Statutes 236):	4.80
s 3(1)(c)	3.86
9(8)	3.81
19(3)	3.143
Copyright, Designs and Patents Act 1988	4.80
s 1(1)	3.80
(2)	3.89
(3)	3.91
2	3.80
3(1)	4.94
4(1)	3.81
(a)	3.80, 3.81
(b)	3.80, 3.105
(2)	3.105
5(1)	3.14
9	3.107
(11)	3.85
10	3.107
11(1)	3.85
12(1)	3.84, 3.87
15	3.87
16(1)	3.82
(5)(b)	3.14
17(2), (3)	3.81
(4)	3.14
22	3.82
51	3.81, 3.86, 3.103, 3.105
(1)	3.81, 3.88, 3.103
(3)	3.105A
52	3.84, 3.87, 105A
(2)	3.84
53(1)(a)	3.105A
90(3)	3.85, 3.88
213	3.102
(2)	3.107
(3)	3.102
(b)	3.105A
(4)	3.102
226	3.107
236	3.103
265(1)	3.91, 3.105A
(3)	3.91

	PARA
Copyright, Designs and Patents Act 1988—*contd*	
s 269	3.77, 3.105A
Sch 1 para 12	3.86, 3.100
Sch 3 para 5	3.107
Data Protection Act 1984 (6 Statutes 831)	364
Defective Premises Act 1972 (31 Statutes 195)	
s 1, 4	5.50
Fair Trading Act 1973 (47 Statutes 125)	2.04, 2.123, 7.28, 7.34
s 6(1)	2.123
7(1)	2.123
9	2.123
34(1)–(3)	7.28
48, 49, 84	2.125
118	7.38
(1)(c)	7.42
(2)	7.39
(4)	7.42
119(1), (2)	7.37, 7.41
120	7.41
137(1)	2.128
Finance Act 1965	
s 22(3)	4.71
Finance Act 1972	
s 74(1)(a)	4.53
Finance Act 1977	
s 42	4.64
Finance Act 1980	
s 14(1)	4.12
28(1)(a)	4.53
37	4.50, 4.52
80	4.121
Finance Act 1981 (43 Statutes 856)	
s 53(1), (2)	4.51
54(1)	4.50
56(2)–(4), (6), (7)	4.51
80	4.121
(1), (3), (4)	4.121
81	4.121
Finance Act 1983	4.29
Sch 5 para 22, 23	4.51
Finance Act 1984 (5 Statutes 337)	4.106, 4.107
s 82	4.70
Finance Act 1985	
s 50(2), (3)	4.23
65(3)(a)	4.92
Finance Act 1986	
s 15	4.37
Finance Act 1987	
s 11	4.12
13	4.08
19	4.09
Sch 2	4.09
Finance Act 1988	
s 11	4.09
14	4.08
32	4.46

Table of statutes

	PARA
Finance Act 1988—*contd*	
s 50	4.34
51(1)(b)	4.33, 4.36
66	*442*
(1)	*446*
Sch 7	*442*
para 1, 5	*443*
Sch 14	4.09, 4.12
Finance Act 1989	
s 47	4.53
115(2)	4.156
Sch 12 para 12, 13	4.53
Finance (No 2) Act 1987 (43 *Statutes* 1453)	
s 83, 95	4.57
Financial Services Act 1986 (30 *Statutes* 254)	
s 1(1), (2)	7.46
3	4.28
Sch 1	7.46
Franchises Act RSA 1980 (Alberta)	7.64
c.F-17	7.03
Harmful Business Practices Act 1988 (South Africa)	7.67
Income and Corporation Taxes Act 1970 (42 *Statutes* 385)	
s 54	*389*
268A (1)(a), (c), (g)	4.64
(2), (4)	4.64
482	4.68
Income and Corporation Taxes Act 1988 (44 *Statutes* 1)	4.104
s 4	4.02
6(1)	4.22
(2)	4.22, 4.55
(3), (4)	4.22
7(2)	4.55
8(1)	4.55, 4.56, 4.60
(2)–(6)	4.56
9	4.60
(1)	4.55
10(1)	4.56
11	4.06
13	4.153
14(1)–(3)	4.55
Schedule A	4.16, 4.18, 4.22, 5.18
s 15	4.22
(1)	4.16, 5.18
18(1)(a)	4.02
(3)	4.09, 4.60, 4.63
Schedule D	4.02, 4.09, 4.21
Case I	4.02, 4.09, 4.22, 4.60, 4.63
Case III	4.02, 4.53
Case IV	4.63
Case V	4.60, 4.63
Case VI	4.89, 4.93
s 19(1), (2)	4.02
24	5.18
(1)	4.16
25	4.17, 4.22
26	4.17

	PARA
Income and Corporation Taxes Act 1988—*contd*	
s 28	4.17
(1)	4.22
29	4.17
(1)	4.22
30	4.17
31(1)	4.22
34	4.19, 5.18
(1)	4.16, 4.21
(2), (3)	4.17
(4), (5)	4.16
35	4.18, 4.19
(2)(a), (b)	4.18
37	4.16
(5), (6)	4.16
38	4.16
43(1), (3)	4.23
52	4.16
65(1)	4.60
(a), (b)	4.60
74(n)	4.63
87	4.24
(1)(a)	4.19, 4.24
(2), (3)	4.19
(9)(a)	4.19
111	1.60
116	4.141
209	4.55, 4.63, 4.155
(2)(a), (e)	4.155
210–211	4.55
231(1), (3)	4.58
238(1)	4.55, 4.58
(5)	4.55
239(3)	4.56
246(1)–(4)	4.55
254	4.55
264	4.36
276	4.02
289	4.30, 4.34, 4.36, 4.37, 4.39, 4.40, 4.41, 4.42, 4.43, 4.44
290(2)	4.37
290A	4.33, 4.36
292	4.44
293(1)	4.36
(2)	4.36
(a)	4.36
(3), (5)	4.36
(6)	4.38
(7), (8)	4.36
294	4.36, 4.40
(2)(a)–(c)	4.40
(3)	4.34
(5)	4.34, 4.41
(8)	4.41
295	4.40
296	4.34
296(1)	4.34
(a), (g)	4.43
(2)	4.44

xvii

Table of statutes

	PARA
Income and Corporation Taxes Act 1988—*contd*	
s 297(2)(a)–(c)	4.32, 4.42
(d)	4.42
(e)–(g)	4.32, 4.42
(h)	4.42
(j)	4.32
(3)	4.42
(a), (b)	4.32
(12)	4.36
298(1)(a)	4.36
(3)	4.42
(6)(a),(b)	4.32
299	4.47
(1)	4.36
(a)	4.39
(5)	4.39
307(8)	4.40
337	4.62
(2)	4.04
(3)	4.63
338	4.61, 4.62
(3)	4.63
(a)	4.04, 4.06, 4.63, 4.153
(b)	4.63
(4)	4.04
(a)	4.04, 4.06, 4.63, 4.153, 4.155
(5)(a)	4.153
339	4.61, 4.62
340	4.62, 4.153
(1)(a)–(c)	4.63
(2)	4.155
343	4.69
348	4.02, 4.09
(1)	4.06
(2)(a)	4.153
349	4.02, 6.03, *309*
(1)	4.06, 4.23, 4.50, 4.89
(a)	4.02, 4.04, 4.06, 4.09, 4.112
(2)	4.63, 4.112
(3)(a), (b)	4.63
350	4.02
(1), (3)	4.23, 4.50, 4.63
(4)	4.02, 4.04, 4.63, 4.157
(a)	4.23, 4.50
352	4.02
353	4.53
(1)(b)	4.53
(3)(b)	4.53
360	4.53
(1)	4.53
(b), (c)	4.53
(3)	4.53
386(3)	4.92
393(2)	4.22
402(3), (4)	4.110
403	4.110
(10), (11)	4.110
405(1)–(6)	4.110

	PARA
Income and Corporation Taxes Act 1988—*contd*	
s 406(1)–(8)	4.110
408	4.110
409(5)–(8)	4.110
411(3)–(9)	4.110
413(2), (5)	4.110
414(1), (2)	4.97
416	4.65, 4.140
417	4.54
424	4.53
(4)(a)	4.53
431	4.98
441(8)	4.98
473(2)(a)	4.98
524(1)	4.89
530(1), (6), (7)	4.14, 4.24
531	4.24, **4.92**
(2)	4.14, 4.21, 4.93
(3), (4), (7)	4.93
(8)	4.24
533(1)	4.78
(7)	4.14, 4.24, 4.84, 4.92
534, 535	4.94
536	4.05, 4.06, 4.86
537A(1)–(6)	4.95
574	4.50
(1), (3)	4.50
575	4.50
576(1)–(3)	4.50
(4)	4.50
(c)	4.50
(5)	4.50
663(2)	4.98
Pt XV Ch III (ss 671–682)	4.127
s 677(2)(b)	4.123
(6)	4.123
686	4.123
687(3)	4.98
703	4.67
704	4.67
(c)	4.67
739	4.115, 4.121, 4.125
740(1)	4.125
747	4.65, 4.75, 4.121, 4.138
(1)–(3), (6)	4.99
748	4.75, 4.102, 4.103, 4.121, 4.138
(1)(a), (c), (d)	4.99
(7)	4.99
749	4.75, 4.121, 4.138
(3), (5)	4.99
750	4.75, 4.121, 4.138
(2)	4.99
751	4.75, 4.121, 4.138
(6)	4.99
752	4.75, 4.99, 4.121, 4.138
753	4.75, 4.121, 4.138
754(1)–(9)	4.75, 4.121, 4.138
755	4.75, 4.99, 4.121
756	4.75, 4.121

Table of statutes

	PARA
Income and Corporation Taxes Act 1988—*contd*	
s 756(1)	4.138
757(1)–(7)	4.98
758–761	4.98
762	4.98, 4.121
763, 764	4.98
765	4.108
766(1)–(4)	4.108
767(1)–(6)	4.108
770	4.70, 4.71, 4.76, 4.86, 4.87
(1)	4.70, 4.75, 4.86, 4.94
(2)(a)	4.70, 4.75, 4.86, 4.94
(b), (d)	4.86, 4.94
(3)	4.86, 4.94
772	4.70
773	4.70, 4.71
(1), (2)	4.70, 4.86, 4.94
(3)	4.86, 4.94
(4)	4.70, 4.86, 4.94
790	4.60, 4.116
(4)	4.60
(5)(a)	4.60
(12)	4.61
811	4.61
818	4.06
828	4.40, 4.41
834(1)	4.149
838	4.65
840	4.65, 4.70, 4.140
Sch 1 para 9	4.53
Sch 13 para 1	4.56
Sch 16	4.02
para 2	4.04, 4.157
3	4.157
4	4.04, 4.157
Sch 19 para 7	4.50
Sch 24	4.99
para 1	4.99
5, 7	4.100
Sch 25	4.99, 4.102, 4.106
Pt I para 4	4.103
Pt II	4.99
para 5	4.102
6	4.102, 4.103
7, 9	4.102
Pt III, IV	4.99
Sch 26	4.99
Sch 29	4.39, 4.55, 4.64, 4.71, 4.75, 4.99, 4.108, 4.121, 4.123, 4.138
Independent Broadcasting Authority Act 1973	7.08
Inheritance Tax Act 1984 (43 *Statutes* 1068)	
s 94(1)	4.97
(2)(a)	4.97
94(4)	4.97
95–102, 160	4.97

	PARA
Insolvency Act 1986 (4 *Statutes* 717)	
s 214(2), (7)	1.62
251	1.62
Interpretation Act 1978 (41 *Statutes* 899)	
s 5	2.128
Sch 1	2.128
Landlord and Tenant Act 1927 (23 *Statutes* 60)	5.25
s 1	5.29
2(1)(b)	5.30
19(1)	5.22, 5.34
Landlord and Tenant Act 1954 (23 *Statutes* 142)	5.18, 5.25, 5.26, 6.08, *310, 316, 361*
s 23(1)	5.26
24	5.25, 5.26, *396, 399, 400*
(1)	5.26
25–28	5.25, 5.26, 5.27, *396, 399, 400*
30	5.27
(2)	5.27
37	5.28
38(1)	5.26
(4)	5.25, 5.26, *400*
43(2)	5.26
Lanham Act (USA)	
s 1051, 1127	1.26
Law of Property Act 1969	5.26
s 11	5.28
Limited Partnerships Act 1907 (32 *Statutes* 662)	1.51, 4.28
s 6(1)	1.50, 1.52
Magistrates' Courts Act 1980 (27 *Statutes* 157)	
s 32	7.27
Misrepresentation Act 1967 (27 *Statutes* 724)	7.09
s 2(1)	**7.10**
(2)	7.13
National Insurance Act 1965	
s 1(2)	1.34
Partnership Act 1890 (32 *Statutes* 636)	
s 1	1.47
2	1.50
(2), (3)	1.50
4(2)	1.46
5	1.41, 1.47, 1.48
14(1)	1.41
30	2.103
45	1.47
Patents Act 1977 (33 *Statutes* 127)	3.110, 3.112, 3.126, 3.128
s 1(1)	3.111
(2)	3.111
(c)	3.111
5	3.126
7	3.113
7(1), (2), (4)	3.129
8(1)	3.129
12	3.129

Table of statutes

	PARA
Patents Act 1977—*contd*	
s 23	3.112
25	3.106
30(4)	3.144
33(1)	3.144
44	5.11
(3)	5.11
(4)	5.12
(6)	5.11
51	2.139
60(4)	2.80
67(1)	3.144
68	3.144
69(1), (2)	3.130
77	3.126
(1)	3.110, 3.112
78–85	3.126
89	3.127
130(1)	3.144
Sch 1, 3, 4	3.112
Patents, Designs and Marks Act 1986 (48 *Statutes* 174)	1.18, 3.22, 3.25, 3.36, 3.37
s 2(3)	3.133
Sch 2 para 3, 5, 11	3.133
Patents, Designs and Trade Marks Law (Guernsey) 4/11/1922	4.82
Prevention of Fraud (Investments) Act 1958 (30 *Statutes* 126)	7.46
Protection from Eviction Act 1977 (23 *Statutes* 302)	
s 2	7.48
3	7.48
(2)	7.48
Registered Designs Act 1949 (33 *Statutes* 74)	3.78
s 1	3.105A
(3), (4)	3.91
6(4)	3.90
8	3.77, 3.105A
(1), (2)	3.100
(5)	3.89
14(1)	3.131
19	3.146
(4)	3.146
Resale Prices Act 1976 (47 *Statutes* 386)	2.04, 2.72, 2.150, 3.89, 3.107
s 9(2)	2.15
Restrictive Trade Practices Act 1956:	447, 448
Restrictive Trade Practices Act 1968	
s 5(2)	2.147
7(1)(a)	2.147
Restrictive Trade Practices Act 1976 (47 *Statutes* 321)	1.02, 1.46, 2.04, 2.92, 2.117, 2.128, 2.133, 2.150, 2.151, 3.107, 5.18, 5.38, 6.06, *309, 314, 322, 324, 325, 335, 341*
s 1(3)	2.148

	PARA
Restrictive Trade Practices Act 1976—*contd*	
s 6	2.144, 2.147, 2.148
7	2.147
9(3)	2.142, 2.148, 2.151
11	2.144, 2.147, 2.148
12	2.147
18	2.148
21(2)	2.143
25	2.146
35	**2.146**, 2.147, 2.148
(1)(b)	2.149
(2)	2.149
43(1)	1.02, 2.136, 2.142, 2.147
Sch 2 para 5	2.146
Sch 3 para 4	3.136
5	3.89
Road Traffic Act 1988	
s 192(1)	5.68
Road Traffic Regulation Act 1984 (38 *Statutes* 180)	
s 142(1)	5.68
Sale of Goods Act 1893	7.28
Securities Act 1983 (Quebec)	7.03, 7.64
Sherman Act (USA)	
s 1	2.02
Statute of Monopolies (1623)	51
Supply of Goods and Services Act 1982 (39 *Statutes* 161)	7.28
Taxes Management Act 1970 (42 *Statutes* 259)	
s 78, 83	4.23
Theft Act 1968 (12 *Statutes* 484)	
s 16	7.22
Trade Descriptions Act 1968 (39 *Statutes* 41)	1.56, 5.51
s 1	7.19
2(1)	7.19
(g)	3.17
3(4)	3.17
4	7.19
(2)	7.19
5	7.19
14	**7.20**, 7.21, 7.22
(1)	7.22
(b)	3.17, 7.21
(3)	7.22
18	**7.26**
24	**7.24**, 7.25
25	**7.24**
39(1)	7.19
Trade Disputes Act 1906	1.35, 1.57
Trade Marks Act 1883	
s 70	1.08
Trade Marks Act 1905	
s 3	1.07, 1.11
22	1.08
Trade Marks Act 1938 (48 *Statutes* 43)	1.56, 4.50, 5.51
s 4(1)(b)	3.37
s 5(2)	3.37

Table of statutes

Trade Marks Act 1938—*contd*	PARA
s 8	3.04
9	3.25, 3.35
(1)(a)	3.34
(d)	3.29
(e)	3.34, 3.48
10	**3.36**
11	3.39, 3.50, 4.81
16	3.35A
17	1.13
(1)	*418*
(2)	3.39, 4.81
(4)	3.47
20	3.50
22(1)	1.10, 1.22
(2)	1.22
23(2), (2A)	3.43
26(1)(a), (b)	3.24, 3.138
(3)	3.138
28	1.10, 3.137, 4.150, *419*
(1)	**1.18**, 3.137, 3.138, 3.140
(2)	3.138, 4.150
(3)	3.136
(4)	3.140
(5)	3.12
(6)	1.08, 1.13, 3.12, *417*
(12)	1.20, 3.12
29(1)(a)	3.45
(b)	1.13, 3.12, 3.45, *417*
(4)	3.45
30(1)	3.43
32	1.24, 3.138
42(3)	3.40
s 62	1.11, 4.150

Trade Marks Act 1988—*contd*	PARA
68	*418*
(1)	1.08, 1.10, 3.22
Trade Marks (Amendment) Act 1984 (48 *Statutes* 156)	1.15, 1.18, 3.20, 3.22, 3.25
Trade Marks Law 1958 (Jersey)	4.82
Trade Marks Registration Act 1875	
s 2	1.08
Trade Practices Act 1974 (Aust)	7.03
Unfair Contract Terms Act 1977 (11 *Statutes* 214)	5.43, 5.45, 7.09
s 2	5.43
(1)	5.43
3	5.43
8	**7.14**
11(1)	7.14, 7.15
13	5.43
Sch 1 para 1	5.43
Uniform Limited Partnership Act (USA)	
s 7	1.52
Value Added Tax Act 1983 (48 *Statutes* 598)	
s 2(5)	4.08
7	4.09
14(2)	4.09
16	4.08
39(7)	4.12
44	4.08
Sch 1	4.08
para 1	4.08
Sch 5, 6	4.08
Sch 7 para 12	4.12

Table of cases

Decisions of the European Court of Justice are listed both alphabetically and numerically. The numerical Table follows the alphabetical.

PARA

A

AEG-Telefunken Agreement, Re (EC Commission Decision 82/267) OJ L117, 30.4.82, p. 15, [1982] 2 CMLR 386; on appeal AEG-Telefunken AG v EC Commission: 107/82 [1983] ECR 3151, [1984] 3 CMLR 325, ECJ . . 2.71
AIRCO Trade Mark [1977] FSR 485 . . . . 3.24
AOIP/Beyrard, Re (EC Commission Decision 76/29) OJ L6, 13.1.76, p.8, [1976] 1 CMLR D14 . . . . 2.14, 2.49
ARG/Unipart, Re (EC Commission Decision 88/84) OJ L45, 18.2.88, p. 34, [1988] 4 CMLR 513 . . . . 2.71
Ad-Lib Club Ltd v Granville [1971] 2 All ER 300, 115 Sol Jo 74, [1972] RPC 673, [1971] FSR 1 . . . . 2.114, 3.54
Adam v Newbigging (1888) 13 App Cas 308, [1886-90] All ER Rep 975, [1886-90] All ER Rep Ext 1465, 57 LJ Ch 1066, 59 LT 267, 37 WR 97, HL . . . 1.49
Adler v Upper Grosvenor Street Investment Ltd [1957] 1 All ER 229, [1957] 1 WLR 227, 101 Sol Jo 132, 168 Estates Gazette 731 . . . . 5.22, 5.34
Advocaat Zwarte Kip, Re (EC Commission Decision 74/432) OJ L237, 29.8.74, p.12, [1974] 2 CMLR D79 . . . . 2.80
Allen (W H) & Co v Brown Watson [1965] RPC 191 . . . . 3.54, 3.59
Allen & Hanburys Ltd v Generics (UK) Ltd [1988] 2 All ER 454, [1989] 1 WLR 414, 133 Sol Jo 628, [1988] 1 CMLR 701, ECJ, apld, [1988] 3 All ER 1057n, [1989] 1 WLR 414, HL 2.79, 2.80
American Greetings Corpn's Application, Re, (Re Holly Hobbie Trade Mark) [1983] 2 All ER 609, [1983] 1 WLR 269, 127 Sol Jo 51, [1984] RPC 329; on appeal [1983] 2 All ER 609, [1983] 1 WLR 912, 127 Sol Jo 424, [1984] RPC 329, [1983] FSR 581, CA; affd [1984] 1 All ER 426, [1984] 1 WLR 189, 128 Sol Jo 99, [1984] RPC 329, [1984] FSR 199, [1985] EIPR 6, HL . 1.05, 1.08, 1.13, 1.14, 1.20, 3.12, 3.137
Amoco Australia Pty Ltd v Rocca Bros Motor Engineering Co Pty Ltd [1975] AC 561, [1975] 1 All ER 968, [1975] 2 WLR 779, 119 Sol Jo 301, PC . . 2.101
Amp Inc v Utilux Pty Ltd [1972] RPC 103, [1971] FSR 572, HL . . . 3.92
Anciens Établissements Panhard et Levassor, SA des v Panhard Levassor Motor Co Ltd [1901] 2 Ch 513, [1900-3] All ER Rep 477, 70 LJ Ch 738, 85 LT 20, 50 WR 74, 17 TLR 680, 45 Sol Jo 671, 18 RPC 405 . . . . . 3.57
Anheuser-Busch Inc v Budejovicky Budvar Narodni Podnik, Budweiser Case (1984) 128 Sol Jo 398, [1984] LS Gaz R 1369, [1984] FSR 413, CA . . 3.53, 3.56
Annabel's (Berkeley Square) v Schock [1972] RPC 838, [1972] FSR 261, CA . 3.64, 3.69
Apple v Standard Oil 307 F Supp 107 (1969) 1.40, 1.42
Aristoc Ltd v Rysta Ltd [1945] AC 68, [1945] 1 All ER 34, 114 LJ Ch 52, 172 LT 69, 61 TLR 121, 89 Sol Jo 10, 62 RPC 65, HL 3.23
Aspro-Nicholas Ltd's Design Application [1974] RPC 645 . . . . 3.91
Association des Centres Distributeurs Edouard Leclerc v Thouars Distribution SA [1984] 1 CMLR 273 . . . . 2.72
Athans v Canadian Adventure Camps Ltd (1977) 80 DLR (3d) 583 . . 3.16
Athletes Foot Marketing Associates Inc v Cobra Sports Ltd [1980] RPC 343 . 3.56
Attwood v Lamont [1920] 3 KB 571, [1920] All ER Rep 55, 90 LJKB 121, 124 LT 108, 36 TLR 895, 65 Sol Jo 25, CA 2.121

Table of cases

PARA

B

BBC v Talbot Motor Co [1981] FSR 228	3.54, 3.59
BMW's Agreement, Re (EC Commission Decision 75/73) OJ L29, 3.2.75, p.1, [1975] 1 CMLR D44	2.55, 2.71
BP Oil v Mabe 370 A 2d 554 (1977)	1.33, 1.37
Baker v Gibbons [1972] 2 All ER 759, [1972] 1 WLR 693, 116 Sol Jo 313	2.116
Bank of America National Trust and Savings Association's Trade Mark, Re [1977] FSR 7	3.24
Bartram & Sons v Lloyd (1903) 88 LT 286, 19 TLR 293; revsd (1904) 90 LT 357, 20 TLR 281, CA	7.50
Baskins-Robbins Ice Cream Co v Gutman [1976] FSR 545	3.56
Baylis (Inspector of Taxes) v Gregory [1986] 1 All ER 289, [1986] 1 WLR 624, 130 Sol Jo 16, [1986] STC 22, [1986] LS Gaz R 200; on appeal [1989] AC 398, [1987] 3 All ER 27, [1987] 3 WLR 660, 131 Sol Jo 1124, [1987] STC 297, [1987] LS Gaz R 2362, CA; affd [1989] AC 398, [1988] 3 All ER 495, [1988] 3 WLR 423, 132 Sol Jo 1120, [1988] STC 476, [1988] NLJR 219, [1988] 34 LS Gaz R 49, HL	4.67
Beck v Arthur Murray 54 Cal Rptr 328 (1966)	1.42
Beck v Kantorowicz (1857) 3 K & J 230	7.50
Becke v Smith (1836) 2 M & W 191, 2 Gale 242, 6 LJ Ex 54	2.147
Beckett v Kingston Bros (Butchers) Ltd [1970] 1 QB 606, [1970] 1 All ER 715, [1970] 2 WLR 558, 134 JP 270, 114 Sol Jo 9, 68 LGR 244, [1970] RPC 135, [1970] FSR 41	7.25
Beckham v Exxon Corpn 539 SW 2d 217 (1976)	1.33
Bennett v Bennett [1952] 1 KB 249, [1952] 1 All ER 413, [1952] 1 TLR 400, CA	2.119
Bernardin (Alain) et Cie v Pavilion Properties Ltd [1967] RPC 581, [1967] FSR 341	3.56
Beswick v Beswick [1968] AC 58, [1967] 2 All ER 1197, [1967] 3 WLR 932, 111 Sol Jo 540, HL	2.147
Billops v Magness Construction 321 A 2d 196 (1978)	1.42
Bismag Ltd v Amblins (Chemists) Ltd [1940] Ch 667, [1940] 2 All ER 608, 109 LJ Ch 305, 163 LT 127, 56 TLR 721, 84 Sol Jo 381, 57 RPC 209, CA	3.37
Bocardo SA v S & M Hotels Ltd [1979] 3 All ER 737, [1980] 1 WLR 17, 123 Sol Jo 569, 39 P & CR 287, 252 Estates Gazette 59, CA	5.22, 5.34
Bolton (H L) (Engineering) Co Ltd v T J Graham & Sons Ltd [1957] 1 QB 159, [1956] 3 All ER 624, [1956] 3 WLR 804, 100 Sol Jo 816, 168 Estates Gazette 424, CA	4.105
Bond v Pittard (1838) 2 M & W 357, 1 Horn & H 82, 7 LJ Ex 78, 2 Jur 183	1.50
Boot Tree Ltd v Robinson [1984] FSR 545	1.22
Bostitch Inc v McGarry and Cole Ltd [1964] RPC 173	3.141
Bostitch Trade Mark [1963] RPC 183	1.11, 3.45, 3.137
Bowden Wire Co Ltd v Bowden Co Ltd (No 2) (1913) 30 RPC 609	1.11
Bowden Wire Ltd's Trade Marks, Re, Bowden Wire Co Ltd v Bowden Brake Co Ltd (1913) 30 RPC 45; on appeal 30 RPC 580, CA; affd (1914) 31 RPC 385, HL	1.08, 1.09
Brasserie de Haecht SA v Wilkin-Janssen: 48/72 [1973] ECR 77, [1973] CMLR 287, CMR 8170, ECJ	2.58, 2.61, 2.64, 2.67
Brasserie de Haecht SA v Wilkin: 23/67 [1967] ECR 407, [1968] CMLR 26, CMR 8053, ECJ	2.57, 2.64
Brauerei A Bilger Söhne GmbH v Jehle: 43/69 [1970] ECR 127, [1974] 1 CMLR 382, CMR 8076, ECJ	2.63, 2.64
Bray v Ford [1896] AC 44, [1895-9] All ER Rep 1000, 65 LJQB 213, 73 LT 609, 12 TLR 119, HL	7.50
British Airways Board v Taylor [1976] 1 All ER 65, [1976] 1 WLR 13, 140 JP 96, 120 Sol Jo 7, [1976] 1 Lloyd's Rep 167, HL	7.22
British Leyland Motor Corpn Ltd v Armstrong Patents Co Ltd [1986] RPC 279, [1982] Com LR 240, [1983] FSR 50; affd [1984] 3 CMLR 102, 128 Sol Jo 659, [1986] RPC 279, [1984] FSR 591, [1984] LS Gaz R 2225, CA; revsd [1986] AC 577, [1986] 1 All ER 850, [1986] 2 WLR 400, [1986] ECC 534, 130 Sol Jo 203, [1986] RPC 279, [1986] 2 FTLR 8, [1986] NLJ Rep 211, [1986] LS Gaz R 974, [1986] FSR 221, HL	3.80, 3.82, 3.102, 3.105

Table of cases

	PARA
British Milk Products Co's Application, Re [1915] 2 Ch 202, 84 LJ Ch 819, 113 LT 925	3.26
British Northrop Ltd v Texteam Blackburn Ltd [1974] RPC 57	3.80
Broad & Co v Cast Iron Drainage Co [1970] FSR 363	3.37
Broad & Co Ltd v Graham Building Supplies Ltd [1969] RPC 286	3.37
Brock (H N) & Co Ltd, Re [1910] 1 Ch 130, 79 LJ Ch 211, 101 LT 587, sub nom Re Trade Marks Nos 224722, 230405 and 230407 26 TLR 100, 26 RPC 850, CA	3.04, 3.38
Bronbemaling and Heidemaatschappij, Re (EC Commission Decision 75/570) OJ L249, 25.9.75, p.27, [1975] 2 CMLR D67	2.49
Brown Shoe Co v United States 370 US 294 (1962)	2.02
Buchanan v Canada Dry 226 SE 2d 613 (1976)	1.32, 1.42
Burberrys v J C Cording & Co Ltd (1909) 100 LT 985, 25 TLR 576, 26 RPC 693	3.54
Burroughs AG and Delplanque & Fils Agreement, Re (EC Commission Decision 72/25) OJ L13, 17.1.72, p.50, [1972] CMLR D67	2.49
Butler v Board of Trade [1971] Ch 680, [1970] 3 All ER 593, [1970] 3 WLR 822, 114 Sol Jo 604	3.118

C

C & A Modes Ltd v C & A (Waterford) Ltd [1978] FSR 126, [1976] IR 148	3.56
C's Application, Re (1919) 37 RPC 247	3.111
CBS United Kingdom Ltd v Charmdale Record Distributors Ltd [1981] Ch 91, [1980] 2 All ER 807, [1980] 3 WLR 476, 124 Sol Jo 741	3.107, 3.143
CICRA v Régie Nationale des Usines Renault: 53/87 (5 October 1988, unreported)	2.90
Cadbury-Schweppes Pty Ltd v Pub Squash Co Pty Ltd [1981] 1 All ER 213, [1981] 1 WLR 193, 125 Sol Jo 96, [1981] RPC 429, [1980] 2 NSWLR 851, PC	3.16, 3.53, 3.59
Campari-Milano OJ C198, 19.8.77, p.3	2.50
Caparo Industries plc v Dickman [1990] 1 All ER 568, [1990] 2 WLR 358, 134 Sol Jo 494, 6 BCC 164, [1990] 12 LS Gaz R 42, HL	5.49
Carroll's Application, Re (1899) 16 RPC 82	3.26
Cawthorn v Phillips Petroleum 124 So 2d 517 (1960)	1.40
Centrafarm BV v American Home Products Corpn: 3/78 [1978] ECR 1823, [1979] 1 CMLR 326, CMR 8475, [1979] FSR 189, ECJ	2.80, 2.85
Centrafarm BV v Winthrop BV: 16/74 [1974] ECR 1183, [1974] 2 CMLR 480, [1975] FSR 161, CMR 8247, ECJ	2.80
Centrafarm BV and Adriaan De Peijper v Sterling Drug Inc: 15/74 [1974] ECR 1147, [1974] 2 CMLR 480, CMR 8246, [1975] FSR 161	2.79, 2.80
Central Rly Co of Venezuela (Directors etc) v Kisch (1867) LR 2 HL 99, 36 LJ Ch 849, 16 LT 500, 15 WR 821	7.50
Champagne Heidsieck et Cie Monopole SA v Buxton [1930] 1 Ch 330, 99 LJ Ch 149, 142 LT 324, 46 TLR 36, 47 RPC 28	2.80, 3.107
Chemidus Wavin Ltd v Société pour la Transformation et l'Exploitation des Résines Industrielles SA [1976] 2 CMLR 387; affd [1978] 3 CMLR 514, [1977] 5 WWR 155, [1977] FSR 181, CA	2.56, 2.115
Cheryl Playthings Ltd's Application, Re [1962] 2 All ER 86, [1962] 1 WLR 543, 106 Sol Jo 286, sub nom Rawhide Trade Mark [1962] RPC 133	3.39
Chevron Oil v Sutton 515 P 2d 1283 (1973)	1.32
Children's Television Workshop Inc v Woolworths (NSW) Ltd, Muppets Case [1981] RPC 187, [1981] 1 NSWLR 273	1.23, 1.27, 3.73
City and Westminster Properties (1934) Ltd v Mudd [1959] Ch 129, [1958] 2 All ER 733, [1958] 3 WLR 312, 102 Sol Jo 582	7.16
Clegg v Fishwick (1849) 1 Mac & G 294, 19 LJ Ch 49, 1 H & Tw 390, 15 LTOS 472, 13 Jur 993, 84 RR 61	7.49
Coca-Cola Bottling Co v Coca-Cola Co 269 F 796 (1920)	5.05
Coca-Cola Trade Marks [1986] FSR 472	3.16, 3.35A, 3.60
Coco v A N Clark (Engineers) Ltd [1969] RPC 41, [1968] FSR 415	3.120, 4.84
Coe v Esau 377 P 2d 815 (1963)	1.40, 1.42
Coleman v Chrysler 525 F 2d 1338 (1975)	6.05, 7.02

Table of cases

	PARA
Coles (J H) Pty Ltd v Need [1934] AC 82, 103 LJPC 13, 150 LT 166, 50 RPC 379, PC	1.24, 1.27, 2.114
Collier (R H) & Co Ltd's Applications for Registration of Designs, Re (1937) 54 RPC 253	3.80
Colquhoun (Surveyor of Taxes) v Brooks (1889) 14 App Cas 493, [1886-90] All ER Rep 1063, 59 LJQB 53, 61 LT 518, 54 JP 277, 38 WR 289, 5 TLR 728, 2 TC 490, HL	4.60
Commercial Plastics Ltd v Vincent [1965] 1 QB 623, [1964] 3 All ER 546, [1964] 3 WLR 820, 108 Sol Jo 599, CA	2.105, 2.121
Compatibility Research Ltd v Computer Psyche Co Ltd [1967] RPC 210	3.54
Computerland, Re (EC Commission Decision 87/407) OJ L222, 10.8.87, p. 12, [1989] 4 CMLR 259	2.15, 2.38, 2.75
Continental National Bank of Boston v Strauss 32 NE 1066 (1893)	1.52
Continental TV v Sylvania 433 US 36 (1977)	2.03
Corelli v Wall (1906) 22 TLR 532	3.15
Coty v United States Slicing Machine Co 373 NE 2d 1371 (1978)	1.32
Courtauld v Legh (1869) LR 4 Exch 126, 187, 38 LJ Ex 124, 20 LT 496	2.147
Cox v Coulson [1916] 2 KB 177, 85 LJKB 1081, 114 LT 599, 32 TLR 406, 60 Sol Jo 402, CA	1.50
Cox v Hickman (1860) 8 HL Cas 268, 30 LJCP 125, 3 LT 185, 7 Jur NS 105, 8 WR 754, sub nom Wheatcroft v Hickman 9 CBNS 47	1.46
Cranleigh Precision Engineering Ltd v Bryant [1964] 3 All ER 289, [1965] 1 WLR 1293, 109 Sol Jo 830, [1966] RPC 81	3.118
Crittendon v State Oil 222 NE 2d 561 (1966)	1.42
Croft v Day (1843) 7 Beav 84	3.04
Cullen v BMW 531 F Supp 555 (1982)	1.32
Customglass Boats Ltd v Salthouse Bros Ltd [1976] 1 NZLR 36, [1976] RPC 589	3.70

D

Daiquiri Rum Trade Mark [1969] RPC 600, HL	3.43
Davey v Shawcroft [1948] 1 All ER 827, 112 JP 266, 64 TLR 289, 92 Sol Jo 297, 46 LGR 272	2.128
Davide Campari-Milano SpA Agreement, Re (EC Commission Decision 78/253) OJ L70, 13.3.78, p. 69, [1978] 2 CMLR 397	2.44
Davidson Rubber Co Agreements, Re (EC Commission Decision 72/237) OJ L143, 23.6.72, p.31, [1972] CMLR D52, [1972] FSR 451	2.49
Davis v New England College of Arundel [1977] ICR 6, 11 ITR 278, EAT	1.34, 1.57
Davis (J & S) (Holdings) Ltd v Wright Health Group Ltd [1988] RPC 403	3.91, 3.104
Davis (Clifford) Management Ltd v WEA Records Ltd [1975] 1 All ER 237, [1975] 1 WLR 61, 118 Sol Jo 775, CA	2.101, 2.103
Davis's Trade Marks, Re, Davis v Sussex Rubber Co [1927] 2 Ch 345, 97 LJ Ch 8, 137 LT 714, 44 RPC 412, CA	3.04, 3.38
De Beers Consolidated Mines Ltd v Howe (Surveyor of Taxes) [1905] 2 KB 612, 74 LJKB 934, 93 LT 63, 54 WR 9, 21 TLR 578, 5 TC 198, CA; affd [1906] AC 455, 75 LJKB 858, 95 LT 221, 22 TLR 756, 50 Sol Jo 666, 5 TC 198, 13 Mans 394, HL	4.105
De Bussche v Alt (1878) 8 Ch D 286, [1874-80] All ER Rep 1247, 47 LJ Ch 381, 38 LT 370, 3 Asp MLC 584, CA	7.49
Dee Corpn plc's Applications [1989] FSR 266; affd sub nom Dee Corpn plc, Re [1989] 3 All ER 948, CA	1.16, 3.24
Deere & Co, Re (EC Commission Decision 85/79) OJ L35, 7.2.85, p.58, [1985] 2 CMLR 554	2.58, 2.69
Dehydrating Process Co v A O Smith Corpn 292 F 2d 653 (1961)	2.02
De Mattos v Gibson (1858) 4 De G & J 276, 28 LJ Ch 165, 32 LTOS 268, 5 Jur NS 347, 7 WR 152; on appeal (1859) 4 De G & J 276, 28 LJ Ch 498, 33 LTOS 193, 5 Jur NS 555, 7 WR 514	1.67
Demo-Studio Schmidt v EC Commission: 210/81 [1983] ECR 3045, [1984] 1 CMLR 63, ECJ	2.71
Denison Mattress v Spring-Air 308 F 2d 403 (1962)	0.04

Table of cases

PARA

De Norre v NV Brouwerij Concordia: 47/76 [1977] ECR 65, [1977] 1 CMLR 378, CMR 8386, ECJ 2.57
Dent v Turpin (1861) 2 John & H 139, 30 LJ Ch 495, 4 LT 637, 7 Jur NS 673, 9 WR 548 . . . . 1.23
Derry v Peek (1889) 14 App Cas 337, [1886-90] All ER Rep 1, 58 LJ Ch 864, 61 LT 265, 54 JP 148, 38 WR 33, 5 TLR 625, 1 Meg 292, HL . . . 7.09
Deutsche Castrol Vertriebsgesellschaft mbH, Re (EC Commission Decision 83/205) OJ L114, 29.4.83, p.26, [1983] 3 CMLR 165 . . . . 2.57
Deutsche Grammophon GmbH v Metro-SB-Grossmärkte GmbH & Co KG: 78/70 [1971] ECR 487, [1971] CMLR 631, CMR 8106, ECJ . . . 2.90
Deutsche Philips GmbH, Re (EC Commission Decision 73/322) OJ L293, 20.10.73, p.40, [1973] CMLR D241 . . . . 2.72
Diehl KG's Application [1969] 3 All ER 338, [1970] 2 WLR 944, 114 Sol Jo 336, [1968] FSR 571, [1970] RPC 435 . . . . . 1.21, 1.24
Distillers Co Ltd v EC Commission: 30/78 [1980] ECR 2229, [1980] 3 CMLR 121, [1980] FSR 589, CMR 8613, ECJ 2.73, 2.74
Distillers Co plc, Re (EC Commission Notice dated 14th September 1983) [1983] 3 CMLR 173 . . . . 2.73
Division of Triple T Service Inc v Mobil Oil 304 NYS 2d 191 (1969) . . 7.54
Dobie & Sons Ltd's Trade Mark, Re (1935) 52 RPC 333 . . . 1.08
Dockrell v Dougall (1899) 80 LT 556, 15 TLR 333, CA 3.15
Dorling v Honnor Marine Ltd [1965] Ch 1, [1964] 1 All ER 241, [1964] 2 WLR 195, 107 Sol Jo 1039, [1963] 2 Lloyd's Rep 455, [1964] RPC 160, CA . . 3.92
Dorsic v Kirtin 96 Cal Rptr 528 (1971) 1.32
Drexel v Union Prescription Centers 582 F 2d 781 (1978) . . . 1.32, 1.50
Dunhill (Alfred) v Sunoptic SA and C Dunhill [1979] FSR 337, CA . 3.64, 3.69
Dunlop Pneumatic Tyre Co Ltd v Selfridge & Co Ltd [1915] AC 847, [1914-15] All ER Rep 333, 84 LJKB 1680, 113 LT 386, 31 TLR 399, 59 Sol Jo 439, HL . 1.67
Dunlop Rubber Co Ltd v Dunlop [1921] 1 AC 367, [1920] All ER Rep 745, 90 LJPC 140, 124 LT 584, 37 TLR 245, HL 3.15
Dupont de Nemours (Deutschland) GmbH, Re (EC Commission Decision 73/196) OJ L194, 16.7.73, p.27, [1973] CMLR D226 . . . . . 2.72

E

Eastman Photographic Materials Co Ltd v Comptroller-General of Patents Designs and Trade Marks, Solio Case [1898] AC 571, 67 LJ Ch 628, 79 LT 195, 47 WR 152, 14 TLR 527, 15 RPC 476, HL 3.27
Eastman Photographic Materials Co Ltd v John Griffiths Cycle Corpn Ltd and Kodak Cycle Co Ltd, Re Trade Mark No 207006 (1898) 15 RPC 105 . 3.69
Eilbeck (Inspector of Taxes) v Rawling [1982] AC 300, [1981] 1 All ER 865, [1981] 2 WLR 449, 125 Sol Jo 220, [1981] STC 174, 54 TC 101, [1981] TR 123, HL . 4.67
Elida Gibbs Ltd v Colgate-Palmolive Ltd [1983] FSR 95 . . . . 3.59
Elkins v Husky Oil Co 455 P 2d 329 (1969) 1.40
English and Irish Church and University Assurance Society (No 2), Re (1863) 1 Hem & M 85, 2 New Rep 107, 8 LT 724, 11 WR 681 . . . . 1.46
Esso Petroleum Co Ltd v Harper's Garage (Stourport) Ltd [1968] AC 269, [1967] 1 All ER 699, [1967] 2 WLR 871, 111 Sol Jo 174, 201 Estates Gazette 1043, HL . 1.40, 2.94, 2.97, 2.98, 5.09, 5.18
Esso Petroleum Co Ltd v Mardon [1976] QB 801, [1976] 2 All ER 5, [1976] 2 WLR 583, 120 Sol Jo 131, 2 BLR 85, [1976] 2 Lloyd's Rep 305, CA . 7.09, 7.12, 7.27
Etablissements Consten SARL and Grundig-Verkaufs-GmbH v EEC Commission: 56, 58/64 [1966] ECR 299, [1966] CMLR 418, CMR 8046, ECJ . 2.79
Eurofix-Bauco v Hilti (EC Commission Decision 88/138) OJ L65, 11.3.88, p. 19, [1988] 4 CMLR 489 . . . . 2.90
European Sugar Cartel, Re (EC Commission Decision 73/109) OJ L140, 26.5.73, p.17, [1973] CMLR D65 . . . . 2.90
Eurymedon, The. See New Zealand Shipping Co Ltd v A M Satterthwaite & Co Ltd
Evans Medical Supplies Ltd v Moriarty (Inspector of Taxes) [1957] 3 All ER 718, [1958] 1 WLR 66, 102 Sol Jo 67, 37 TC 540, [1957] TR 297, 36 ATC 277, 51 R & IT 49, HL 4.14, 4.93

Table of cases

	PARA
Exchange Telegraph Co Ltd v Gregory & Co [1896] 1 QB 147, [1895-9] All ER Rep 1116, 65 LJQB 262, 74 LT 83, 60 JP 52, 12 TLR 19, CA	3.118
Exxon Corpn v Exxon Insurance Consultants International Ltd [1982] Ch 119, [1981] 2 All ER 495, [1981] 1 WLR 624, 125 Sol Jo 342, [1982] RPC 69; affd [1982] Ch 119, [1981] 3 All ER 241, [1981] 3 WLR 541, 125 Sol Jo 527, [1982] RPC 69, CA	3.14, 3.69, 3.80, 3.83, 3.88, 4.80

F

Faccenda Chicken Ltd v Fowler [1985] 1 All ER 724, [1984] ICR 589, [1984] IRLR 61, [1985] FSR 105; affd [1987] Ch 117, [1986] 1 All ER 617, [1986] 3 WLR 288, [1986] ICR 297, [1986] IRLR 69, 130 Sol Jo 573, CA	2.104, 2.107, 3.120, 3.122
Farah Trade Mark [1978] FSR 234	3.30
Fawcett v Whitehouse (1829) 1 Russ & M 132, 8 LJOS Ch 50	7.50
Featherstonhaugh v Fenwick (1810) 17 Ves 298, [1803-13] All ER Rep 89, 31 WR 318	7.49
Federal Comr of Taxation v United Aircraft Corpn (1943) 68 CLR 525	1.10, 1.27, 5.43
Ferguson v Donovan [1929] IR 489	4.60
Ferguson v John Dawson & Partners (Contractors) Ltd [1976] 3 All ER 817, [1976] 1 WLR 1213, [1976] IRLR 346, 120 Sol Jo 603, 8 BLR 38, [1976] 2 Lloyd's Rep 669, CA	1.34, 1.57
Fidelman-Dansiger v Statler Management 136 A 2d 119 (1957)	1.42
Fine Cotton Spinners and Doublers' Association Ltd and John Cash & Sons Ltd v Harwood Cash & Co Ltd [1907] 2 Ch 184, 76 LJ Ch 670, 97 LT 45, 23 TLR 537, 14 Mans 285, 24 RPC 533	1.23
Fonderies Roubaix-Wattrelos SA v Société nouvelle des Fonderies A Roux and Societe des Fonderies JOT: 63/75 [1976] ECR 111, [1976] 1 CMLR 538, CMR 8341, [1976] FSR 397, ECJ	2.63
Ford of Europe Inc and Ford-Werke AG v EC Commission: 228, 229/82 [1984] ECR 1129, [1984] 1 CMLR 649, ECJ	2.72
Fortner v United States Steel 394 US 495 (1969)	2.02
Fraser v Evans [1969] 1 QB 349, [1969] 1 All ER 8, [1968] 3 WLR 1172, 112 Sol Jo 805, CA	3.118
Fraser v Thames Television Ltd [1984] QB 44, [1983] 2 All ER 101, [1983] 2 WLR 917, 127 Sol Jo 379	3.118
Fromont v Coupland (1824) 2 Bing 170, 9 Moore CP 319, 3 LJOSCP 237	1.49
Furniss (Inspector of Taxes) v Dawson [1984] AC 474, [1984] 1 All ER 530, [1984] 2 WLR 226, 128 Sol Jo 132, [1984] STC 153, 55 TC 324, HL	4.67

G

GE Trade Mark, Re [1970] RPC 339, [1970] FSR 113, CA; revsd [1973] RPC 297, sub nom General Electric Co v General Electric Co Ltd [1972] 2 All ER 507, [1972] 1 WLR 729, 116 Sol Jo 412, HL	3.04, 3.137
GEMA, Re (EC Commission Decision 71/224) OJ L134, 20.6.71, p.15, [1971] CMLR D35	2.90
Gaines Animal Foods Ltd's Application for Trade Mark [1958] RPC 312	3.39
Galloway v Hallé Concerts Society [1915] 2 Ch 233, [1914-15] All ER Rep 543, 84 LJ Ch 723, 113 LT 811, 31 TLR 469, 59 Sol Jo 613, [1915] HBR 170	7.53
Garden Cottage Foods Ltd v Milk Marketing Board [1984] AC 130, [1983] 2 All ER 770, [1983] 3 WLR 143, [1983] 3 CMLR 43, 127 Sol Jo 460, [1984] FSR 23, [1983] Com LR 198, HL	2.91
Gerofabriek NV, Re (EC Commission Decision 77/66) OJ L16, 19.1.77, p. 8, [1977] 1 CMLR D35	2.72
Gianaclis' Trade Mark, Re (1889) 58 LJ Ch 782, 6 RPC 467	3.26
Gibbs and Houlder Bros & Co Ltd's Lease, Re, Houlder Bros & Co Ltd v Gibbs [1925] Ch 575, [1925] All ER Rep 128, 94 LJ Ch 312, 133 LT 322, 41 TLR 487, 69 Sol Jo 541, CA	5.19
Gizzi v Texaco 437 F 2d 303 (1971)	1.32, 1.42
Glamorgan County Quarter Sessions v Wilson (Surveyor of Taxes) [1910] 1 KB 725, [1908-10] All ER Rep 812, 79 LJKB 454, 102 LT 500, 74 JP 299, 26 TLR 351, 5 TC 537	4.02

	PARA
Gleeson and Gleeson Shirt Co Ltd v H R Denne Ltd [1975] RPC 471, [1975] FSR 250, CA	4.80
Goldberg v Kolloman Instruments 191 NE 2d 81 (1963)	1.56, 5.51
Golden Chemical Products Ltd, Re [1976] Ch 300, [1976] 2 All ER 543, [1976] 3 WLR 1, 120 Sol Jo 401	7.41
Golden Pages Trade Mark [1985] FSR 27	3.24
Goldsoll v Goldman [1914] 2 Ch 603, 84 LJ Ch 63, 112 LT 21, 59 Sol Jo 43; affd [1915] 1 Ch 292, [1914-15] All ER Rep 257, 84 LJ Ch 228, 112 LT 494, 59 Sol Jo 188, CA	2.121
Goodyear Italiana SpA, Re (EC Commission Decision 75/94) OJ L38, 12.2.75, p.10, [1975] 1 CMLR D31	2.71
Grace v Smith (1775) 2 Wm Bl 998	1.50
Grainge v Wilberforce (1889) 5 TLR 436	1.25, 1.27
Greene v Church Comrs for England [1974] Ch 467, [1974] 3 All ER 609, [1974] 3 WLR 349, 118 Sol Jo 700, 29 P & CR 285, 232 Estates Gazette 195, CA	5.22, 5.34
Gregson v Cyril Lord Ltd [1962] 3 All ER 907, [1963] 1 WLR 41, 106 Sol Jo 899, CA	5.27
Grey v IRC [1958] Ch 375, [1958] 1 All ER 246, [1958] 2 WLR 168, 102 Sol Jo 84, [1957] TR 293, 36 ATC 296; revsd [1958] Ch 690, [1958] 2 All ER 428, [1958] 3 WLR 45, 102 Sol Jo 469, [1958] TR 165, 37 ATC 136, CA; affd [1960] AC 1, [1959] 3 All ER 603, [1959] 3 WLR 759, 103 Sol Jo 896, [1959] TR 311, 38 ATC 313, HL	1.25, 1.27
Grohe, Re (EC Commission Decision 85/44) OJ L19, 23.1.85, p. 17, [1988] 4 CMLR 612	2.71
Grosvenor Place Estates Ltd v Roberts (Inspector of Taxes) [1961] Ch 148, [1961] 1 All ER 341, [1961] 2 WLR 83, 105 Sol Jo 87, 39 TC 433, [1960] TR 391, 39 ATC 442, CA	4.02
Gunston v Winox Ltd [1921] 1 Ch 664, 90 LJ Ch 288, 125 LT 295, 37 TLR 361, 65 Sol Jo 310, 38 RPC 40, CA	3.92

H

Haelon Laboratories Inc v Topps Chewing Gum 202 F 2d 866 (1953)	3.16
Halsall v Brizell [1957] Ch 169, [1957] 1 All ER 371, [1957] 2 WLR 123, 101 Sol Jo 88, 168 Estates Gazette 642	1.67
Hambro v Shell Oil Co 674 F 2d 784 (1982)	2.03
Hammerton v Earl of Dysart [1916] 1 AC 57, 85 LJ Ch 33, 113 LT 1032, 80 JP 97, 31 TLR 592, 59 Sol Jo 665, 13 LGR 1255, HL	0.01
Hammond (Marc A) Pty Ltd v Papa Carmine Pty Ltd [1978] RPC 697	3.37
Harrington v Victoria Graving Dock Co (1878) 3 QBD 549, 47 LJQB 594, 39 LT 120, 42 JP 744, 26 WR 740	7.50
Harrods Ltd v R Harrod Ltd (1923) 40 TLR 195, 41 RPC 74, CA	3.69
Harrods Ltd v Schwartz-Sackin & Co Ltd [1986] FSR 490	3.16, 3.59
Hasselblad (GB) Ltd v EC Commission: 86/82 [1984] ECR 883, [1984] 1 CMLR 559, ECJ	2.73
Heatons Transport (St Helens) Ltd v Transport and General Workers' Union [1973] AC 15, [1972] 3 All ER 101, [1972] 3 WLR 431, [1974] ICR 308, [1972] IRLR 25, 116 Sol Jo 598, 14 KIR 48, HL	1.31
Hedley Byrne & Co Ltd v Heller & Partners Ltd [1964] AC 465, [1963] 2 All ER 575, [1963] 3 WLR 101, 107 Sol Jo 454, [1963] 1 Lloyd's Rep 485, HL	5.49, 7.09, 7.11, 7.27
Helmore v Smith (No 2) (1886) 35 Ch D 449, 56 LJ Ch 145, 56 LT 72, 35 WR 157, 3 TLR 139, CA	3.122
Henderson v Radio Corpn Pty Ltd (1960) SRNSW 576, 77 WN 585, sub nom Radio Corpn Pty Ltd v Henderson [1960] NSWR 279	3.65
Hensher (George) Ltd v Restawile Upholstery (Lancs) Ltd [1976] AC 64, [1974] 2 All ER 420, [1974] 2 WLR 700, 118 Sol Jo 329, [1975] RPC 31, [1974] FSR 173, HL	3.86, 3.103
Hickson (Oswald), Collier & Co v Carter-Ruck [1984] AC 720n, [1984] 2 All ER 15, [1984] 2 WLR 847n, 126 Sol Jo 120, CA	2.116

Table of cases

	PARA
Hilti AG, Re (EC Commission Notice of 2nd September 1985, IP (85) 374) [1985] 3 CMLR 619	2.90
Hoffman-La Roche & Co AG v Centrafarm Vertriebsgesellschaft Pharmazeutischer Erzeugnisse mbH [1984] 2 CMLR 561	2.84
Hoffmann-La Roche & Co AG v Centrafarm Vertriebsgesellschaft Pharmazeutischer Erzeugnisse mbH: 102/77 [1978] ECR 1139, [1978] 3 CMLR 217, CMR 8466, ECJ	2.80, 2.84, 2.90
Holiday Inns v Newton 278 SE 2d 85 (1981)	1.32
Holloway v Holloway (1850) 13 Beav 209	3.04
Holly Hobbie Trade Mark, Re. See American Greetings Corpn's Application, Re	
Holt's Trade Mark (1896) 13 RPC 16	3.26
Holzman v De Escamilla 195 P 2d 833 (1948)	1.52
Hong Kong Caterers v Maxim's Ltd (1983) unreported	3.24
"Hospital World" Trade Mark [1967] RPC 595	3.24
Hydrotherm Gerätebau GmbH v Compact de Dott Ing Mario Andreoli & CSAS: 170/83 [1984] ECR 2999, [1985] 3 CMLR 224, ECJ	2.79

I

IBM Personal Computer, Re (EC Commission Decision 84/233) OJ L118, 4.5.84, p. 24, [1984] 2 CMLR 342	2.71
IPC Magazines Ltd v Black and White Music Corpn, Judge Dredd Case [1983] FSR 348	3.72, 3.74
Imperial Group Ltd v Philip Morris & Co [1984] RPC 293	3.70
Infabrics Ltd v Jaytex Shirt Co (1978) [1984] RPC 405, [1978] FSR 451; on appeal sub nom Infabrics Ltd v Jaytex Ltd [1980] Ch 282, [1980] 2 All ER 669, [1980] 2 WLR 822, 124 Sol Jo 309, [1984] RPC 405, [1980] FSR 161, CA; revsd [1982] AC 1, [1981] 1 All ER 1057, [1981] 2 WLR 646, 125 Sol Jo 257, [1984] RPC 405, [1981] FSR 261, HL	3.78, 3.82
IRC v Duke of Westminster [1936] AC 1, [1935] All ER Rep 259, 104 LJKB 383, 153 LT 223, 51 TLR 467, 79 Sol Jo 362, sub nom Duke of Westminster v IRC 19 TC 490, 14 ATC 77, HL	4.67
IRC v Garvin [1981] 1 WLR 793, 125 Sol Jo 398, [1981] STC 344, [1984] TC 24, [1981] TR 213, HL	4.67
IRC v Henry Ansbacher & Co [1963] AC 191, [1962] 3 All ER 843, [1962] 3 WLR 1292, 106 Sol Jo 899, [1962] TR 281, 41 ATC 293, HL	2.147
IRC v Muller & Co's Margarine Ltd [1901] AC 217, [1900-3] All ER Rep 413, 70 LJKB 677, 84 LT 729, 49 WR 603, 17 TLR 530, HL	3.54, 3.55, 3.60, 4.85
IRC v National Book League [1957] Ch 488, [1957] 2 All ER 644, [1957] 3 WLR 222, 101 Sol Jo 553, 37 TC 455, sub nom National Book League v IRC [1957] TR 141, 36 ATC 130, 50 R & IT 603, CA	4.02, 4.153
IRC v Plummer [1980] AC 896, [1979] 3 All ER 775, [1979] 3 WLR 689, 123 Sol Jo 769, [1979] STC 793, 54 TC 1, [1979] TR 339, HL	4.67
IRC v Regent Trust Co Ltd [1980] 1 WLR 688, 124 Sol Jo 49, [1980] STC 140, 53 TC 54, [1979] TR 401	4.123
Interlego AG v Tyco Industries Inc [1989] AC 217, [1988] 3 All ER 949, [1988] 3 WLR 678, 132 Sol Jo 698, PC	3.14, 3.84
International Combustion Ltd v IRC (1932) 16 TC 532	4.02
Irish, Re, Irish v Irish (1888) 40 Ch D 49, 58 LJ Ch 279, 60 LT 224, 37 WR 231, 5 TLR 39	3.122

J

Jamieson & Co v Jamieson (1898) 14 TLR 160, 42 Sol Jo 197, 15 RPC 169, CA	3.04
Jeffrey (Inspector of Taxes) v Rolls-Royce Ltd [1961] 2 All ER 469, [1961] 1 WLR 897, 105 Sol Jo 404, 40 TC 443, [1961] TR 73, 40 ATC 56, CA; affd sub nom Rolls-Royce Ltd v Jeffrey (Inspector of Taxes) [1962] 1 All ER 801, [1962] 1 WLR 425, 106 Sol Jo 261, 40 TC 443, L(TC) 2006, [1962] TR 9, 41 ATC 17, HL	3.119, 4.93
Jirna Ltd v Mister Donut of Canada Ltd (1970) 13 DLR (3d) 645; revsd (1971) 22 DLR (3d) 639 (Ont CA); affd (1973) 40 DLR (3d) 303 (Can SC)	7.50, 7.51

	PARA
Johnson and Johnson, Re (EC Commission Decision 80/1283) OJ L377, 31.12.80, p.16, [1981] 2 CMLR 287	2.54
Jourdan (Charles), Re (EC Commission Decision 89/94) OJ L35, 7.2.89, p. 31, [1989] 4 CMLR 591	2.15, 2.44
Junghans GmbH, Re (EC Commission Decision 77/100) OJ L30, 2.2.77, p.10, [1977] 1 CMLR D82	2.46, 2.71
Junior Books Ltd v Veitchi Co Ltd [1983] 1 AC 520, [1982] 3 All ER 201, [1982] 3 WLR 477, 126 Sol Jo 538, 21 BLR 66, [1982] Com LR 221, [1982] LS Gaz R 1413, 1982 SLT 492, HL	1.63

K

Kabel-und Metallwerke Neumeyer AG and Etablissements Luchaire SA Agreement, Re (EC Commission Decision 75/494) OJ L222, 22.8.75, p.34, [1975] 2 CMLR D40	2.49
Karo Step Trade Mark, Re [1977] RPC 255	1.21, 1.24, 1.27
Keener v Sizzler Family Steak House 597 F 2d 453 (1979)	2.02
Kentucky Fried Chicken v Diversified Packaging 549 F 2d 368 (1977)	2.02
Keurkoop BV v Nancy Kean Gifts BV: 144/81 [1982] ECR 2853, [1983] 2 CMLR 47, CMR 8861, [1982] Com LR 212, [1983] FSR 381, ECJ	2.80
King Features Syndicate Inc v O and M Kleeman Ltd [1940] Ch 806, [1940] 3 All ER 484, 109 LJ Ch 353, 163 LT 201, 56 TLR 937, 58 RPC 57, CA; revsd [1941] AC 417, [1941] 2 All ER 403, 110 LJ Ch 128, 165 LT 98, 57 TLR 586, 58 RPC 207, HL	3.14, 3.81
Kingston, Miller & Co Ltd v Thomas Kingston & Co Ltd [1912] 1 Ch 575, 81 LJ Ch 417, 106 LT 586, 28 TLR 246, 56 Sol Jo 310	1.23
Klarmann (H) Ltd v Henshaw Linen Supplies [1960] RPC 150	3.92
Knox v Boyd 1941 JC 82	7.21
Kodak, Re (EC Commission Decision 70/332) OJ L147, 7.7.70, p.24, [1970] CMLR D19	2.71
Kohl (Theodor) KG v Ringelhan and Rennett SA: 177/83 [1984] ECR 3651, [1985] 3 CMLR 340, ECJ	2.80, 2.82
Krehl v Baskin-Robbins Ice Cream Co 664 F 2d 1348 (1982)	2.03
Kuchta v Allied Builders 98 Cal Rptr 588 (1971)	1.42
Kugler v AAMCO Automatic Transmissions 460 F 2d 1214 (1972)	2.02

L

LB (Plastics) v Swish Products [1979] RPC 551, [1977] FSR 87; on appeal [1979] RPC 597, [1978] FSR 32, CA; revsd [1979] RPC 611, [1979] FSR 145, HL	3.81, 3.86, 3.107
Lacteosote Ltd v Alberman [1927] 2 Ch 117, 96 LJ Ch 305, 137 LT 319, 43 TLR 336, 71 Sol Jo 451, 44 RPC 211	1.08
Lancôme SA v Etos BV: 99/79 [1980] ECR 2511, [1981] 2 CMLR 164, CMR 8714, ECJ	2.71
Lego Systems A/S v Lego M Lemelstrich [1983] FSR 155	3.64, 3.70
Lilley v Elwin (1848) 11 QB 742, 17 LJQB 132, 11 LTOS 151, 12 JP 343, 12 Jur 623	2.103
Linoleum Manufacturing Co v Nairn (1878) 7 Ch D 834, 47 LJ Ch 430, 38 LT 448, 26 WR 463	1.11
Lord Strathcona SS Co v Dominion Coal Co [1926] AC 108, [1925] All ER Rep 87, 95 LJPC 71, 134 LT 227, 42 TLR 86, 16 Asp MLC 585, 31 Com Cas 80, PC	1.67
L'Oréal NV v De Nieuwe AMCK PVBA: 31/80 [1980] ECR 3775, [1981] 2 CMLR 235, CMR 8715, ECJ	2.71
Lovegrove v Nelson (1834) 3 My & K 1, 3 LJ Ch 108	1.49
Löwenbräu München v Grünhalle Lager International Ltd [1974] 1 CMLR 1, 118 Sol Jo 50, [1974] RPC 492, [1974] FSR 1	2.83
Lucas (T) & Co Ltd v Mitchell [1974] Ch 129, [1972] 3 All ER 689, [1972] 3 WLR 934, 116 Sol Jo 711, CA	2.120, 2.121
Lyngstad v Anabas Products [1977] FSR 62	3.64, 3.73

Table of cases

	PARA

M

MFI Warehouses Ltd v Nattrass [1973] 1 All ER 762, [1973] 1 WLR 307, 137 JP 307, 117 Sol Jo 143, [1973] Crim LR 196	7.21
Mabe v BP Oil 356 A 2d 304 (1976)	1.42
McCulloch v Lewis A May (Produce Distributors) Ltd [1947] 2 All ER 845, 92 Sol Jo 54, 65 RPC 58	3.63
McDonald's Hamburgers Ltd v Burgerking (UK) Ltd [1986] FSR 45, 4 Tr L 226; revsd [1987] FSR 112, CA	3.60
Macsi Informatique Sàrl v Apple Computer Inc (1988) ECC 374	2.71
Mair v Wood 1948 SC 83, 1948 SLT 326	1.46
Manus Akt v R J Fullwood and Bland Ltd (1948) 65 RPC 329; on appeal [1949] Ch 208, [1949] 1 All ER 205, [1949] LJR 861, 66 RPC 71, CA	1.10, 1.12, 3.138, 3.141
Martin v Routh (1964) 42 TC 106, [1964] TR 277, 43 ATC 277	4.22
Marwell v Sheraton Inns (1981) Bus Franchise Guide (CCH) P1 7626	1.32, 1.50
Mason v Provident Clothing and Supply Co Ltd [1913] AC 724, [1911-13] All ER Rep 400, 82 LJKB 1153, 109 LT 449, 29 TLR 727, 57 Sol Jo 739, HL	2.120, 2.121
Massam v Thorley's Cattle Food Co (1880) 14 Ch D 748, 42 LT 851, 28 WR 966	1.07
Massey v Crown Life Insurance Co [1978] 2 All ER 576, [1978] 1 WLR 676, [1978] ICR 590, [1978] IRLR 31, 13 ITR 5, 121 Sol Jo 791, CA	1.34, 1.57
Maxim's Ltd v Dye [1978] 2 All ER 55, [1977] 1 WLR 1155, [1977] 2 CMLR 410, 121 Sol Jo 727, [1977] FSR 364	3.56
Maxwell v Hogg (1867) 2 Ch App 307, 33 LJ Ch 433, 16 LT 130, 31 JP 659, 15 WR 467	3.59
Megevand, Re, ex p Delhasse (1878) 7 Ch D 511, 47 LJ Bcy 65, 38 LT 106, 26 WR 338, CA	1.49
Meikle v Maufe [1941] 3 All ER 144, 85 Sol Jo 378	3.85
Merlet v Mothercare plc (1984) 128 Sol Jo 614, [1986] RPC 115, [1984] FSR 358, [1984] LS Gaz R 1926; affd [1986] RPC 115, CA	3.80, 3.81
Metric Resources Corpn v Leasmetrix Ltd [1979] FSR 571	3.56
Michael (John) Design plc v Cooke [1987] 2 All ER 332, [1987] ICR 445, 131 Sol Jo 595, [1987] LS Gaz R 1492, CA	2.105, 2.118
Mills v Mills [1963] P 329, [1963] 2 All ER 237, [1963] 2 WLR 831, 107 Sol Jo 214, CA	2.147
Milsen v Southland Corpn 454 F 2d 363 (1971)	2.02
Mobil Oil v Rubenfield 339 NYS 2d 623, 370 NYS 2d 943 (1972)	7.54
Molyslip Trade Mark, Re [1978] RPC 211	1.20, 3.137
Montreal v Montreal Locomotive Works Ltd [1947] 1 DLR 161	1.34
Moodie v IRC [1990] 1 WLR 1084, [1990] STC 475	4.67
Moore v Davis (1879) 11 Ch D 261, 27 WR 335	1.49
Morrish v Hall (1863) 2 New Rep 448, 8 LT 697, 27 JP 470, sub nom R v Morrish 32 LJMC 245, 10 Jur NS 71, 11 WR 960	5.31
Motor Lodge Trade Mark [1965] RPC 35	3.28
Mouson & Co v Boehm (1884) 26 Ch D 398, sub nom Mouson (J G) & Co v Boehm, Re Boehm's Trade Mark 53 LJ Ch 932, 50 LT 784, 32 WR 612	3.138
Muppets Case. See Children's Television Workshop Inc v Woolworths (NSW) Ltd, Muppets Case	
Murphy v Holiday Inns 219 SE 2d 874 (1975)	1.32, 1.33, 1.36, 1.50
Musker (Inspector of Taxes) v English Electric Co Ltd (1964) 41 TC 556, [1964] TR 129, 43 ATC 119, HL	4.93
My Kinda Bones Ltd v Dr Pepper's Store Co Ltd [1984] FSR 289	3.54, 3.59

N

Navarro v Moregrand Ltd [1951] WN 335, [1951] 2 TLR 674, 95 Sol Jo 367, CA	1.31
Nederlandsche Banden-Industrie Michelin NV v EC Commission: 322/81 [1983] ECR 3461, [1985] 1 CMLR 282, ECJ	2.90
Neilson v Horniman (1909) 26 TLR 188, CA	3.143
Nelson v International Paint 734 F 2d 1084 (1984)	1.32
New Jersey v Lawn King 417 A 2d 1025 (1990)	2.03

Table of cases

PARA

New Zealand Shipping Co Ltd v A M Satterthwaite & Co Ltd [1975] AC 154, [1974] 1 All ER 1015, [1974] 2 WLR 865, 118 Sol Jo 387, sub nom The Eurymedon [1974] 1 Lloyd's Rep 534, PC 5.44
News International plc v Shepherd (Inspector of Taxes) [1989] STC 617 . . . 4.67
Newstead (Inspector of Taxes) v Frost [1978] 2 All ER 241, [1978] 1 WLR 511, 122 Sol Jo 33, [1978] STC 239, L(TC) 2658, 53 TC 525, [1977] TR 301; on appeal [1979] 2 All ER 129, [1978] 1 WLR 1441, 122 Sol Jo 813, [1979] STC 45, L(TC) 2702, 53 TC 525, [1978] TR 221, CA; affd [1980] 1 All ER 363, [1980] 1 WLR 135, 124 Sol Jo 116, [1980] STC 123, L(TC) 2774, 53 TC 525, [1980] TR 1, 130 NLJ 136, HL 4.60, 4.67
Nicholls v Stretton (1847) 10 QB 346, 11 Jur 1008 . . . . . . 2.116
Nichols v Arthur Murray Inc 248 Cal App 2d 610 (1967), 56 Cal Rptr 728 . 1.32, 1.36, 1.50
Nocton v Lord Ashburton [1914] AC 932, [1914-15] All ER Rep 45, 83 LJ Ch 784, 111 LT 641, HL 7.50
Noddy Subsidiary Rights Co Ltd v IRC [1966] 3 All ER 459, [1967] 1 WLR 1, 110 Sol Jo 674, 43 TC 458, [1966] TR 237, 45 ATC 263 . . . . . 4.150
Nordenfelt v Maxim Nordenfelt Guns and Ammunition Co [1894] AC 535, [1891-4] All ER Rep 1, 63 LJ Ch 908, 71 LT 489, 10 TLR 636, 11 R 1, HL . . 2.96, 2.105
Norris, Re, ex p Reynolds (1888) 4 TLR 452, 5 Morr 111, CA 7.42
North Shore Toy Co v Stevenson [1974] RPC 545 . . . . . 1.24, 1.27
Northern v McGraw-Edison & Co 542 F 2d 1336 (1976) 1.32
Nungesser (L C) KG v EC Commission: 258/78 [1982] ECR 2015, [1983] 1 CMLR 278, CMR 8805, ECJ 2.49

O

OSCAR Trade Mark, Re [1979] RPC 173 . . . . 3.14
Oberlin v Marlin American Corpn 596 F 2d 1322 (1979) 1.36
Office Overload Ltd v Gunn [1977] FSR 39, CA . . 2.108, 2.112, 2.118
Ogilvie v Kitton (Surveyor of Taxes) 1908 SC 1003, 5 TC 338 . . . . 4.60
Omega Watches, Re (EC Commission Decision 70/488) OJ L242, 5.11.70, p.22, [1970] CMLR D49 . . . . 2.71
Ortega v General Motors 392 So 2d 40 (1980) 1.32, 1.50
Ottermeyer v Baskin 625 P 2d (1981) 1.32
Ozer Properties Ltd v Ghaydi (1987) 20 HLR 232, [1988] 1 EGLR 91, [1988] 03 EG 87, CA 7.48

P

PIZZA Trade Mark [1975] RPC 349 . . . . 3.28
Pan Press Publications Ltd's Applications, Re (1948) 65 RPC 193 . . . 1.10
Pao On v Lau Yiu Long [1980] AC 614, [1979] 3 All ER 65, [1979] 3 WLR 435, 123 Sol Jo 319, PC 5.44
Parfums Marcel Rochas Vertriebs-GmbH v Bitsch: 1/70 [1970] ECR 515, [1971] CMLR 104, CMR 8102, ECJ 2.58, 2.59
Parke, Davis & Co v Probel: 24/67 [1968] ECR 55, [1968] CMLR 47, CMR 8054, [1968] FSR 393, ECJ 2.79, 2.80, 2.81, 2.90
Parnass/Pelly Ltd v Hodges [1982] FSR 329 . . . . 3.56
Parsons (H) (Livestock) Ltd v Uttley Ingham & Co Ltd [1978] QB 791, [1978] 1 All ER 525, [1977] 3 WLR 990, 121 Sol Jo 811, [1977] 2 Lloyd's Rep 522, CA . 7.12
Patchett v Oliver [1977] 5 WWR 299 . . . . 7.51
Pearl Assurance plc v Shaw [1985] 1 EGLR 92, 274 Estates Gazette 490 . 5.22, 5.34
Penney (J C) Co Inc v Punjabi-Nick (otherwise Punjabi Narain) [1979] FSR 26 . 3.56
Penryn Corpn v Best (1878) 3 Ex D 292, 48 LJQB 103, 38 LT 805, 42 JP 629, 27 WR 126, CA 0.01
Petrofina (Great Britain) Ltd v Martin [1966] Ch 146, [1966] 1 All ER 126, [1966] 2 WLR 318, 109 Sol Jo 126, [1966] Brewing Tr Rev 145 . . 2.94, 2.98, 5.09
Pharmon BV v Hoechst AG: 19/84 [1985] ECR 2281, [1985] 3 CMLR 775, ECJ . 2.80
Philippart v William Whiteley Ltd, Re Philippart's Trade Mark Diabolo [1908] 2 Ch 274, 77 LJ Ch 650, 99 LT 291, 24 TLR 707, 25 RPC 565 . . . 3.27
Phillips v Crown Central Petroleum 602 F 2d 616 (1979) 2.03

xxxiii

Table of cases

	PARA
Photovest v Fotomat 606 F 2d 704 (1979)	2.02
Pinto v Badman (1891) 7 TLR 317, 8 RPC 181, CA	1.08
Pitman's Application [1969] RPC 646, [1969] FSR 355	3.111
Pittsburgh Corning Europe, Re (EC Commission Decision 72/403) OJ L272, 5.12.72, p.35, [1973] CMLR D2	2.61, 2.67
Planck (Con) Ltd v Kolynos Inc [1925] 2 KB 804, 94 LJKB 923, 133 LT 798	3.92
Plowman (G W) & Son Ltd v Ash [1964] 2 All ER 10, [1964] 1 WLR 568, 108 Sol Jo 216, CA	2.116
Poiret v Jules Poiret Ltd and Nash (1920) 37 RPC 177	3.57
Port Line Ltd v Ben Line Steamers Ltd [1958] 2 QB 146, [1958] 1 All ER 787, [1958] 2 WLR 551, 102 Sol Jo 232, [1958] 1 Lloyd's Rep 290	1.67
Powell's Trade Mark, Re [1893] 2 Ch 388, CA; affd sub nom Powell v Birmingham Vinegar Brewery Co [1894] AC 8, 63 LJ Ch 152, 70 LT 1, 58 JP 296, 10 TLR 84, 6 R 52, 11 RPC 4, HL	1.07
Price v Esso Petroleum Co Ltd (1980) 255 Estates Gazette 243, CA	5.27
Price's Patent Candle Co, Re (1884) 27 Ch D 681, 54 LJ Ch 210, 51 LT 653	3.26
Principe v McDonald 631 F 2d 303 (1980)	2.03
Printers and Finishers Ltd v Holloway [1964] 3 All ER 731, [1965] 1 WLR 1, 109 Sol Jo 47, [1965] RPC 239	2.104, 3.118, 3.120
Pritchard v Briggs [1980] Ch 338, [1978] 1 All ER 886, [1978] 2 WLR 317, 122 Sol Jo 96, 35 P & CR 266, 244 Estates Gazette 211; revsd [1980] Ch 338, [1980] 1 All ER 294, [1979] 3 WLR 868, 123 Sol Jo 705, 40 P & CR 1, CA	5.34
Procureur de la République v Giry and Guerlain SA: 253/78 and 1-3/79 [1980] ECR 2327, [1981] 2 CMLR 99, CMR 8712, ECJ	2.71
Prontaprint plc v Landon Litho Ltd [1987] FSR 315	2.108, 2.110, 2.111, 2.112
Pronuptia, Re (EC Commission Decision 87/17) OJ L13, 15.1.87, p. 39, [1989] 4 CMLR 355, [1989] FSR 416	2.15, 2.38, 2.44
Pronuptia de Paris GmbH, Frankfurt am Main v Pronuptia de Paris Irmgard Schillgalis, Hamburg: 161/84 OJ C191, 19.7.84, p.11, [1986] 1 CMLR 414, ECJ	2.08, 2.28
Prym-Werke (William) KG and Beka Agreement, Re (EC Commission Decision 73/323) OJ L296, 24.10.73, p.24, [1973] CMLR D250	2.14
Pussy Galore Trade Mark [1967] RPC 265	3.45

Q

Quad-L v Tastee Freez 528 NE 2d 1107 (1988)	1.32

R

R v Poor Law Comrs, Re Whitechapel Union (1837) 6 Ad & El 34, 2 Nev & PKB 8, Nev & PMC 303, Will Woll & Dav 440, 6 LJMC 114, 1 JP 195, 1 Jur 428	2.147
R v Sunair Holidays Ltd [1973] 2 All ER 1233, [1973] 1 WLR 1105, 137 JP 687, 117 Sol Jo 429, 57 Cr App Rep 782, [1973] Crim LR 587, CA	7.22
RAI/UNITEL, Re (EC Commission Decision 78/516) OJ L157, 15.6.78, p. 39, [1978] 3 CMLR 306	2.14
RLM Associates v Carter Manufacturing Corpn 248 NE 2d 646 (1969)	7.54
Radio Corpn Pty Ltd v Henderson. See Henderson v Radio Corpn Pty Ltd	
Ramsay (W T) Ltd v IRC [1982] AC 300, [1981] 1 All ER 865, [1981] 2 WLR 449, 125 Sol Jo 220, [1981] STC 174, 54 TC 101, [1982] TR 123, HL	4.67
Ravenseft Properties Ltd's Application [1978] QB 52, [1977] 2 WLR 432, 120 Sol Jo 834, sub nom Ravenseft Properties Ltd v Director General of Fair Trading [1977] 1 All ER 47	2.98, 2.101, 5.18
Raymond (A) & Co and Nagoya Rubber Ltd Agreement, Re (EC Commission 72/238) OJ L143, 23.6.72, p.39, [1972] CMLR D45	2.49
Rea v Ford Motor Co 355 F Supp 842 (1972)	6.05, 7.02
Ready Mixed Concrete (London) Ltd v Cox (1971) 115 Sol Jo 143, 10 KIR 273	1.34, 1.35, 1.57
Ready Mixed Concrete (South East) Ltd v Minister of Pensions and National Insurance [1968] 2 QB 497, [1968] 1 All ER 433, [1968] 2 WLR 775, 112 Sol Jo 14	1.34, 1.61

Table of cases

PARA

Reckitt & Colman Products Ltd v Borden Inc [1990] 1 All ER 873, [1990] 1 WLR 491, [1990] 16 LS Gaz R 42, HL 3.35A, 3.53, 3.60, 3.104
Redgrave v Hurd (1881) 20 Ch D 1, [1881-5] All ER Rep 77, 57 LJ Ch 113, 45 LT 185, 30 WR 251, CA 7.13
Regal (Hastings) Ltd v Gulliver (1942) [1967] 2 AC 134n, [1942] 1 All ER 378, HL . 7.49
Reohorn v Barry Corpn [1956] 2 All ER 742, [1956] 1 WLR 845, 100 Sol Jo 509, 167 Estates Gazette 604, CA 5.27
Reuter (R J) Co Ltd v Mulhens [1954] Ch 50, [1953] 2 All ER 1160, [1953] 3 WLR 789, 97 Sol Jo 762, 70 RPC 235, CA 3.35A, 3.54
Reuter/BASF AG, Re (EC Commission Decision 76/743) OJ L254, 17.9.76, p.40, [1976] 2 CMLR D44 . . . . 2.14, 2.49
Reynolds v Skelly Oil Co 287 NW 823 (1939) 1.40
Robb v Green [1895] 2 QB 1, 64 LJQB 593, 72 LT 686, 59 JP 695, 44 WR 26, 11 TLR 330, 39 Sol Jo 382; affd [1895] 2 QB 315, [1895-9] All ER Rep 1053, 64 LJQB 593, 73 LT 15, 59 JP 695, 44 WR 25, 11 TLR 517, 39 Sol Jo 653, 14 R 580, CA 3.122
Rocher (Yves), Re (EC Commission Decision 87/14) OJ L8, 10.1.87, p. 49, [1988] 4 CMLR 592 . . . . 2.15, 2.35
Rolls Razors Ltd v Rolls (Lighters) Ltd (1949) 66 RPC 137; on appeal 66 RPC 299, CA 3.62
Rolls-Royce Ltd v Jeffrey (Inspector of Taxes). See Jeffrey (Inspector of Taxes) v Rolls-Royce Ltd
Rowland v Mitchell, Re Rowland's Trade Mark [1897] 1 Ch 71, 66 LJ Ch 110, 75 LT 498, 13 TLR 84, 41 Sol Jo 111, 14 RPC 37, CA 3.35A
Russell v Scott [1948] AC 422, [1948] 2 All ER 1, [1948] LJR 1265, 64 TLR 297, 92 Sol Jo 424, 30 TC 375, [1948] TR 205, 41 R & IT 281, HL . . . 4.67

S

SABA, Re (EC Commission Decision 76/159) OJ L28, 3.2.76, p.19, [1976] 1 CMLR D61 . . . . 2.71
SABA, Re (No 2) (EC Commission Decision 83/672) OJ L376, 31.12.83, p. 41, [1984] 1 CMLR 676 . . . . 2.71
Saunders v Vautier (1841) Cr & Ph 240, [1835-42] All ER Rep 58, 4 Beav 115, 10 LJ Ch 354, 54 RR 286 . . . . 1.25, 1.27
Schroeder Music Publishing Co Ltd v Macaulay [1974] 3 All ER 616, [1974] 1 WLR 1308, 118 Sol Jo 734, HL 2.101, 2.103
Schuler (L) AG v Wickman Machine Tool Sales Ltd. See Wickman Machine Tool Sales Ltd v L Schuler AG
Scruttons Ltd v Midland Silicones Ltd [1962] AC 446, [1962] 1 All ER 1, [1962] 2 WLR 186, 106 Sol Jo 34, [1961] 2 Lloyd's Rep 365, HL 5.44
Seager v Copydex Ltd [1967] 2 All ER 415, [1967] 1 WLR 923, 111 Sol Jo 335, [1967] RPC 349, CA 3.120, 4.84
ServiceMaster, Re (EC Commission Decision 88/604) OJ L332, 3.12.88, p. 38, [1989] 4 CMLR 581 . . . . 2.15, 2.42
Shaver v Bell 397 P 2d 723 (1964) 1.40
Shell-Mex and BP Ltd v Manchester Garages Ltd [1971] 1 All ER 841, [1971] 1 WLR 612, 115 Sol Jo 111, 218 Estates Gazette 285, CA 1.37, 5.19
Shell UK Ltd v Lostock Garage Ltd [1977] 1 All ER 481, [1976] 1 WLR 1187, 120 Sol Jo 523, CA 2.101
Shepherd (Inspector of Taxes) v Lyntress Ltd [1989] STC 617 . . . 4.67
Sheraton Corpn of America v Sheraton Motels Ltd [1964] RPC 202 . . 3.56, 3.58
Sherman v Texas Oil Co 165 NE 2d 916 (1960) 1.40, 1.42
Shrewsbury (Countess) v Earl of Shrewsbury (1907) 23 TLR 224, CA . . 4.02
Siegel v Chicken Delight 311 F Supp 847; affd 448 F 2d 43 (ND Cal 1970) . 2.02, 2.149
Silvola v Rowlett 272 P 2d 287 (1954) 1.52
Sinclair (John) Ltd's Trade Mark, Re [1932] 1 Ch 598, 101 LJ Ch 239, 146 LT 417, 49 RPC 123, CA 1.08
Singer Machine Manufacturers v Wilson (1877) 3 App Cas 376, 47 LJ Ch 481, 38 LT 303, 26 WR 664, HL 3.54
Singleton v International Dairy Queen 332 A 2d 160 (1975) . . . 1.32, 1.42

xxxv

Table of cases

	PARA
Sirdar Ltd Agreement, Re (EC Commission Decision 75/297) OJ L125, 16.5.75, p.27, [1975] 1 CMLR D93	2.80
Sirena Srl v Eda Srl: 40/70 [1971] ECR 69, [1971] CMLR 260, CMR 8101, ECJ	2.80, 2.90
Sky Petroleum Ltd v VIP Petroleum Ltd [1974] 1 All ER 954, [1974] 1 WLR 576, 118 Sol Jo 311	7.53
Slates v International House of Pancakes 413 NE 2d 457 (1981)	1.32, 1.33
Smith, Kline & French Laboratories Ltd v Sterling-Winthrop Group Ltd [1975] 2 All ER 578, [1975] 1 WLR 914, 119 Sol Jo 422, [1976] RPC 511, [1975] FSR 298, HL	3.35A
Snook v London and West Riding Investments Ltd [1967] 2 QB 786, [1967] 1 All ER 518, [1967] 2 WLR 1020, 111 Sol Jo 71, CA	4.67
Sobrefina SA's Trade Mark Application [1974] RPC 672	3.92
Société de Vente de Ciments et Bétons de l'Est SA v Kerpen and Kerpen GmbH & Co KG: 319/82 [1983] ECR 4173, [1985] 1 CMLR 511, ECJ	2.56
Société Technique Minière v Maschinenbau Ulm GmbH: 56/65 [1966] ECR 235, [1966] CMLR 357, CMR 8047, ECJ	2.57
Solar Thomson Engineering Co Ltd v Barton [1977] RPC 537, CA	3.80
Solio Case. See Eastman Photographic Materials Co Ltd v Comptroller-General of Patents Designs and Trade Marks, Solio Case	
Solle v Butcher [1950] 1 KB 671, [1949] 2 All ER 1107, 66 (pt 1) TLR 448, CA	2.56
Sotnick v IRC (1990) Times, 9 May	4.67
Southern v How (1616-18) J Bridg 125, Cro Jac 468, Poph 143, 2 Rolls Rep 26	1.06
Spalding & Bros v A W Gamage Ltd (1915) 84 LJ Ch 449, 113 LT 198, 31 TLR 328, 32 RPC 273, HL	3.67
Spelling Goldberg Productions Inc v BPC Publishing Ltd [1981] RPC 283, [1979] FSR 494	3.14
Spices, Re (EC Commission Decision 78/172) OJ L53, 24.2.78, p.20, [1978] 2 CMLR 116	2.71
Spiers v Mackinnon (1929) 14 TC 386, 8 ATC 197	4.60
Spur Oil Ltd v R (1980) 22 February, doc 80-5948	4.106
Standard Cameras Ltd's Application (1952) 69 RPC 125	3.26
Standard Oil Co v United States 221 US 1 (1910)	2.100
Stanford v Dairy Queen Products 623 SW 2d 797 (1981)	1.32
Stannard v Reay [1967] RPC 589	3.54
Star Industrial Co Ltd v Yap Kwee Kor (t/a New Star Industrial Co) [1976] FSR 256, PC	1.22, 1.27, 3.54
Stekel v Ellice [1973] 1 All ER 465, [1973] 1 WLR 191, 117 Sol Jo 126	1.49
Stephens v Yamaha Motor Co 627 P 2d 439 (1981)	1.32
Stevenson (or Stephenson) Jordan and Harrison Ltd v MacDonald and Evans (1951) 68 RPC 190; revsd [1952] 1 TLR 101, 69 RPC 10, CA	3.119, 3.121, 4.83
Strata Mercella (Abbot of) Case (1591) 9 Co Rep 24a	0.01
Stringfellow v McCain Foods (GB) Ltd [1984] FSR 199; revsd 128 Sol Jo 701, [1984] RPC 501, CA	1.27, 3.53, 3.54, 3.64, 3.65, 3.141
Susser v Carvel Corpn 206 F Supp 636 (1962); on appeal 332 F 2d 505 (1964)	2.02, 5.05
Sutton & Co v Grey [1894] 1 QB 285, 63 LJQB 633, 69 LT 673, 42 WR 195, 10 TLR 96, 38 Sol Jo 77, 9 R 106, CA	1.50
Swedish Central Rly Co Ltd v Thompson [1924] 2 KB 255, [1924] All ER Rep 710, 93 LJKB 739, 131 LT 516, 68 Sol Jo 575, 9 TC 342, CA; affd [1925] AC 495, [1924] All ER Rep 710, 94 LJKB 527, 133 LT 97, 41 TLR 385, 9 TC 342, 4 ATC 163, HL	4.105
Sykes v Sykes (1824) 3 B & C 541, 5 Dow & Ry KB 292, 3 LJOSKB 46	1.06, 3.04

T

Tarzan Trade Mark [1970] FSR 245, [1970] RPC 450, CA	3.28
Tastee Freez International Ltd's Application to Register a Trade Mark [1960] RPC 255	3.28
Tavener Rutledge Ltd v Trexapalm Ltd, Kojak Case (1975) 119 Sol Jo 792, [1977] RPC 275, [1975] FSR 479	3.72

Table of cases

	PARA
Taylor's Central Garages (Exeter) Ltd v Roper [1951] WN 383, 115 JP 445, sub nom Roper v Taylor's Central Garages (Exeter) Ltd [1951] 2 TLR 284	7.21
Telephone Apparatus Manufacturers' Application, Re (1962) LR 3 RP 462, [1963] 1 WLR 463, 107 Sol Jo 271, sub nom Automatic Telephone and Electric Co Ltd's Application, Re [1963] 2 All ER 302, CA	5.18
Terrapin (Overseas) Ltd v Terranova Industrie CA Kapferer & Co: 119/75 [1976] ECR 1039, [1976] 2 CMLR 482, CMR 8362, ECJ	2.80
Tesco Supermarkets Ltd v Nattrass [1972] AC 153, [1971] 2 All ER 127, [1971] 2 WLR 1166, 135 JP 289, 115 Sol Jo 285, 69 LGR 403, HL	7.25
Tetra Pak 1 (BTG licence), Re (EC Commission Decision 88/501) OJ L272, 4.10.88, p. 27, [1988] 4 CMLR 881	2.90
Texaco Ltd v Mulberry Filling Station Ltd [1972] 1 All ER 513, [1972] 1 WLR 814, 116 Sol Jo 119	2.101
Tolley v J S Fry & Sons Ltd [1931] AC 333, [1931] All ER Rep 131, 100 LJKB 328, 145 LT 1, 47 TLR 351, 75 Sol Jo 220, HL	3.15
Trade Mark Mac No 458654, Re, Macleans Ltd v Lightbrown & Sons Ltd (1937) 54 RPC 230	1.08
Transocean Marine Paint Association, Re (EC Commission Decision 67/454) OJ L163, 20.7.67, p.10, [1967] CMLR D9	0.10, 2.76
Transocean Marine Paint Association OJ L351, 21.12.88, p. 40	2.52
Turton v Turton (1889) 42 Ch D 128, 58 LJ Ch 677, 61 LT 571, 54 JP 151, 38 WR 22, 5 TLR 545, CA	3.04
Turvey v Dentons (1923) Ltd [1953] 1 QB 218, [1952] 2 All ER 1025, [1952] 2 TLR 996, 96 Sol Jo 852, [1952] TR 471, 31 ATC 470, 45 R & IT 772	4.02

U

UPDATE Trade Mark [1979] RPC 166	3.24
Union Texas International Corpn v Critchley (Inspector of Taxes) [1990] STC 305, CA	4.156
United Brands Co v EC Commission: 27/76 [1978] ECR 207, [1978] 1 CMLR 429, CMR 8429, ECJ	2.90
United States v Arnold, Schwinn & Co 388 US 365 (1967)	2.03
United States v Carroll Towing Co Inc 159 F 2d 169 (2nd Circ 1947)	1.56, 5.51
United States v Jerrold Electronics 187 F Supp 545 (1960)	2.02
United States v Silk 331 US 704 (1946)	1.57

V

Vaessen/Moris, Re (EC Commission Decision 79/86) OJ L19, 26.1.79, p.32, [1979] 1 CMLR 511	2.14, 2.49, 2.50, 2.61, 2.66
Van Zuylen Frères v Hag AG: 192/73 [1974] ECR 731, [1974] 2 CMLR 127, CMR 8230, [1974] FSR 511, ECJ	2.80, 2.82
Vereniging ter Bevording van de Belangen des Boekhandels v Eldi Records BV: 106/79 [1980] ECR 1137, [1980] 3 CMLR 719, CMR 8646, ECJ	2.59
Visa Trade Mark [1985] RPC 323	3.24
Vitamins Ltd's Application, Re [1955] 3 All ER 827, [1956] 1 WLR 1, 100 Sol Jo 14, [1956] RPC 1	3.39
Völk v Vervaecke: 5/69 [1969] ECR 295, [1969] CMLR 273, CMR 8074, ECJ	2.68
Volvo (AB) v Erik Veng: 238/87 [1989] 4 CMLR 122	2.90

W

Walker West Developments Ltd v Emmett (1978) 252 Estates Gazette 1171, CA	1.50
Warnink (Erven) BV v J Townend & Sons (Hull) Ltd [1979] AC 731, [1979] 2 All ER 927, [1979] 3 WLR 68, 123 Sol Jo 472, [1980] RPC 31, [1979] FSR 397, HL	1.22, 3.53, 3.54, 3.64, 3.68
Waugh v Carver (1793) 2 Hy Bl 235	1.41, 1.50
Weiner v Harris [1910] 1 KB 285, [1908-10] All ER Rep 405, 79 LJKB 342, 101 LT 647, 26 TLR 96, 54 Sol Jo 81, 15 Com Cas 39, CA	1.49
Wells Fargo Trade Mark, Re [1977] RPC 503	3.24

Table of cases

	PARA
Wessex Dairies Ltd v Smith [1935] 2 KB 80, [1935] All ER Rep 75, 104 LJKB 484, 153 LT 185, 51 TLR 439, CA	2.116
Weston Trade Mark [1968] RPC 167, sub nom Re Sangamo-Weston's Application (1968) 112 Sol Jo 270	3.137
Westre v De Buhr 144 NW 2d 734 (1966)	1.40
Wham-O Manufacturing Co v Lincoln Industries Ltd [1985] RPC 127 (NZCA)	3.91, 3.103
Wheatley v Bell [1984] FSR 16	3.123
Whelan v Alfred Leney & Co Ltd [1936] AC 393, [1936] 1 All ER 468, 105 LJKB 197, 154 LT 537, 52 TLR 329, 80 Sol Jo 284, 20 TC 321, HL	4.22
Wickman Machine Tool Sales Ltd v L Schuler AG [1972] 2 All ER 1173, [1972] 1 WLR 840, 116 Sol Jo 352, CA; affd sub nom Schuler (L) AG v Wickman Machine Tool Sales Ltd [1974] AC 235, [1973] 2 All ER 39, [1973] 2 WLR 683, 117 Sol Jo 340, [1973] 2 Lloyd's Rep 53, HL	6.11, 7.53
Wimpey (George) International Ltd v Rolfe (Inspector of Taxes) [1989] STC 609	4.61
Windsurfing International, Re (EC Commission Decision 83/400) OJ L229, 20.8.83, p.1, [1984] 1 CMLR 1	2.49
Wombles Ltd v Wombles Skips Ltd [1977] RPC 99, [1975] FSR 488	3.73

Y

York Trade Mark, Re [1984] RPC 231; revsd [1984] RPC 231, HL	3.29, 3.30
Young v Timmins (1830-31) 1 Cr & J 148, 331, 1 Tyr 15, 9 LJOS Ex 4	2.103

Decisions of the European Court of Justice are listed below numerically.
These decisions are also included in the preceding alphabetical Table.

56, 58/64: Etablissements Consten SARL and Grundig-Verkaufs-GmbH v EEC Commission [1966] ECR 299, [1966] CMLR 418, CMR 8046, ECJ	2.79
56/65: Société Technique Minière v Maschinenbau Ulm GmbH [1966] ECR 235, [1966] CMLR 357, CMR 8047, ECJ	2.57
23/67: Brasserie de Haecht SA v Wilkin [1967] ECR 407, [1968] CMLR 26, CMR 8053, ECJ	2.57, 2.64
24/67: Parke, Davis & Co v Probel [1968] ECR 55, [1968] CMLR 47, CMR 8054, [1968] FSR 393, ECJ	2.79, 2.80, 2.81, 2.90
5/69: Völk v Vervaecke [1969] ECR 295, [1969] CMLR 273, CMR 8074, ECJ	2.68
43/69: Brauerei A Bilger Söhne GmbH v Jehle [1970] ECR 127, [1974] 1 CMLR 382, CMR 8076, ECJ	2.63, 2.64
1/70: Parfums Marcel Rochas Vertriebs-GmbH v Bitsch [1970] ECR 515, [1971] CMLR 104, CMR 8102, ECJ	2.58, 2.59
40/70: Sirena Srl v Eda Srl [1971] ECR 69, [1971] CMLR 260, CMR 8101, ECJ	2.80, 2.90
78/70: Deutsche Grammophon GmbH v Metro-SB-Grossmärkte GmbH & Co KG [1971] ECR 487, [1971] CMLR 631, CMR 8106, ECJ	2.90
48/72: Brasserie de Haecht SA v Wilkin-Janssen [1973] ECR 77, [1973] CMLR 287, CMR 8170, ECJ	2.58, 2.61, 2.64, 2.67
192/73: Van Zuylen Frères v Hag AG [1974] ECR 731, [1974] 2 CMLR 127, CMR 8230, [1974] FSR 511, ECJ	2.80, 2.82
15/74: Centrafarm BV and Adriaan De Peijper v Sterling Drug Inc [1974] ECR 1147, [1974] 2 CMLR 480, CMR 8246, [1975] FSR 161	2.79, 2.80
16/74: Centrafarm BV v Winthrop BV [1974] ECR 1183, [1974] 2 CMLR 480, [1975] FSR 161, CMR 8247, ECJ	2.80
63/75: Fonderies Roubaix-Wattrelos SA v Société nouvelle des Fonderies A Roux and Société des Fonderies JOT [1976] ECR 111, [1976] 1 CMLR 538, CMR 8341, [1976] FSR 397, ECJ	2.63
119/75: Terrapin (Overseas) Ltd v Terranova Industrie CA Kapferer & Co [1976] ECR 1039, [1976] 2 CMLR 482, CMR 8362, ECJ	2.80
27/76: United Brands Co v EC Commission [1978] ECR 207, [1978] 1 CMLR 429, CMR 8429, ECJ	2.90
47/76: De Norre v NV Brouwerij Concordia [1977] ECR 65, [1977] 1 CMLR 378, CMR 8386, ECJ	2.57

Table of cases

PARA

102/77: Hoffmann-La Roche & Co AG v Centrafarm Vertriebsgesellschaft Pharmazeutischer Erzeugnisse mbH [1978] ECR 1139, [1978] 3 CMLR 217, CMR 8466, ECJ 2.80, 2.84, 2.90

3/78: Centrafarm BV v American Home Products Corpn [1978] ECR 1823, [1979] 1 CMLR 326, CMR 8475, [1979] FSR 189, ECJ 2.80, 2.85

30/78: Distillers Co Ltd v EC Commission [1980] ECR 2229, [1980] 3 CMLR 121, [1980] FSR 589, CMR 8613, ECJ 2.73, 2.74

253/78 and 1-3/79: Procureur de la République v Giry and Guerlain SA [1980] ECR 2327, [1981] 2 CMLR 99, CMR 8712, ECJ 2.71

258/78: L C Nungesser KG v EC Commission [1982] ECR 2015, [1983] 1 CMLR 278, CMR 8805, ECJ 2.49

99/79: Lancôme SA v Etos BV [1980] ECR 2511, [1981] 2 CMLR 164, CMR 8714, ECJ 2.71

106/79: Vereniging ter Bevording van de Belangen des Boekhandels v Eldi Records BV [1980] ECR 1137, [1980] 3 CMLR 719, CMR 8646, ECJ . . 2.59

31/80: L'Oréal NV v De Nieuwe AMCK PVBA [1980] ECR 3775, [1981] 2 CMLR 235, CMR 8715, ECJ 2.71

144/81: Keurkoop BV v Nancy Kean Gifts BV [1982] ECR 2853, [1983] 2 CMLR 47, CMR 8861, [1982] Com LR 212, [1983] FSR 381, ECJ . . . 2.80

210/81: Demo-Studio Schmidt v EC Commission [1983] ECR 3045, [1984] 1 CMLR 63, ECJ 2.71

322/81: Nederlandsche Banden-Industrie Michelin NV v EC Commission [1983] ECR 3461, [1985] 1 CMLR 282, ECJ 2.90

86/82: Hasselblad (GB) Ltd v EC Commission [1984] ECR 883, [1984] 1 CMLR 559, ECJ 2.73

107/82: AEG-Telefunken AG v EC Commission [1983] ECR 3151, [1984] 3 CMLR 325, ECJ 2.71

228, 229/82: Ford of Europe Inc and Ford-Werke AG v EC Commission [1984] ECR 1129, [1984] 1 CMLR 649, ECJ 2.72

319/82: Société de Vente de Ciments et Bétons de l'Est SA v Kerpen and Kerpen GmbH & Co KG [1983] ECR 4173, [1985] 1 CMLR 511, ECJ . . 2.56

170/83: Hydrotherm Gerätebau GmbH v Compact de Dott Ing Mario Andreoli & CSAS [1984] ECR 2999, [1985] 3 CMLR 224, ECJ 2.79

177/83: Theodor Kohl KG v Ringelhan and Rennett SA [1984] ECR 3651, [1985] 3 CMLR 340, ECJ 2.80, 2.82

19/84: Pharmon BV v Hoechst AG [1985] ECR 2281, [1985] 3 CMLR 775, ECJ . 2.80

161/84: Pronuptia de Paris GmbH, Frankfurt am Main v Pronuptia de Paris Irmgard Schillgalis, Hamburg OJ C191, 19.7.84, p11, [1986] 1 CMLR 414, ECJ . 2.08, 2.28

53/87: CICRA v Régie Nationale des Usines Renault (5 October 1988, unreported) . 2.90

238/87: AB Volvo v Erik Veng [1989] 4 CMLR 122 . . . . . 2.90

xxxix

Introduction

0.01 The use of the word 'franchise' to cover commercial concessions seems to have originated in the United States[1] where it is currently used in relation to three different marketing systems:

(1) manufacture under licence of patented or proprietary products, eg mattresses, soft drinks, together with a licence to apply the licensor's trademark to the goods so produced;

(2) distributorship agreements, eg for motor cars and petrol;

(3) contractual licences under which the franchisee is permitted to carry on business under a trade name, etc belonging to the franchisor, and under which the franchisor controls the way in which the franchisee does business and provides continuing advice and assistance to the franchisee in this connection. The businesses are, however, separate.

It is this third type of franchising, sometimes known as 'business format' franchising[2] which is the subject of this book[3]. The use of the same word to cover three different marketing systems (and other things besides) is perhaps unfortunate. However, although the use of another word to cover 'business format' operations might have been preferable, the word has now passed into popular usage in this connection, and appears in the names of the various trade associations[4]. Business format franchising is capable of being applied to very many different types of business including manufacture under licence and distributorships.

1 'Franchise' (Norman French 'fraunchise') has a technical meaning at common law. It is a royal privilege or branch of the Crown's prerogative, subsisting in the hands of a subject either by grant or prescription. Franchises are of two classes: (1) those originally forming part of the Crown's prerogative and exercisable therefore by the sovereign before being granted to a subject, eg wrecks, royal fish, forests; and (2) those which can only be created by granting them to a subject, eg fairs, markets, etc. The owner of the franchise has the right of preventing all other persons from interfering with its exercise. It differs from a monopoly in that it is coupled with a duty. A monopoly is merely the right to exclude all others without any duty to meet the needs of the public. 2 Blackstone's Commentaries 37: *Case of the Abbot of Strata Mercella* (1591) 9 Co Rep 24a; *Penryn Corpn v Best* (1878) 3 Ex D 292, CA; *Hammerton v Earl of Dysart* [1916] 1 AC 57, HL.
2 Also 'turnkey' or 'chain style' franchising.
3 A more exact characterisation of this type of franchise is given in Chapter 1.
4 Details of the British Franchise Association are given in para 0.16, post.

0.02 In the popular mind 'franchising' tends to be associated with fast food—hamburgers, soft ice-cream, etc. As we observed above, however, the system can be, and has been applied to a very wide variety of activities indeed: fast printing, car tuning, estate agency and dance instruction, to name but a few[1]. These moreover are only the most 'visible' end of the business, the types of franchise dealing directly

0.03 Introduction

with consumers. Many franchises do not deal with members of the public as consumers at all, but exist to provide services to industry, for example, employment agencies and industrial drain cleaning operations. Indeed franchising is, in principle, suitable for any type of business which can be reduced to a system, or systems, which can be learned relatively easily. This of course is one of its drawbacks, because one of the key features of it is that outlets are 'cloned'.

1 See generally: Martin Mendelsohn, *Guide to Franchising* (4th edn, 1984) (Pergamon); Baillieu *Streetwise Franchising* (1988) (Hutchinson Business) p 139 et seq.

0.03 An account of the way in which this form of marketing has emerged, may be helpful in understanding the reasons why it is so popular at the present time. From the franchisee's point of view, the great advantage over opening up a business entirely on his own account, is that he can shelter behind the umbrella of a large organisation. The grouping of independent businessmen in co-operative ventures, has, of course, a long history. In some respects it may be thought to resemble the regulated company which became common with the expansion of foreign trade in the sixteenth century. Each member of such companies traded with his own capital on his own account, and his liability was entirely separate from that of the other members. On the other hand, as in franchising, each member of the company was bound to obey a common code of conduct[1]. The *raison d'être* for such companies, however, from the point of view of the individual members was quite different from that of the modern franchise operation. They combined to exploit monopolies granted to the company by the Crown. Whilst the statutory monopolies in the form of trade marks and copyright owned by the franchisor might at first sight suggest an anology, this would be misleading. From the point of view of the individual franchisees, the grouping with others to exploit these monopolies serves to enable them to compete more effectively with large organisations operating in similar fields. This aspect of franchising is reflected in the growth of the 'voluntary group or chain' in the United Kingdom.

1 See Carr 'Select Charters of Trading Companies' Selden Society Vol. 23.

0.04 The growth of voluntary groups or chains of independent businesses has been a feature of the grocery trade in the United Kingdom in the last three decades or so, and it is spreading into other fields. It is a means of improving the competitiveness of small businesses against the multiple stores[1]. The usual scheme is that a chain of wholesalers associate to supply an otherwise independent group of retailers, who operate under a uniform name 'Spar', 'Mace', etc. The fundamental difference between this and franchising is the informality of the association between the businesses. Generally it does not depend on a contract. In fact the group is largely held together purely through economic convenience. An institution which provides a more formal legal framework to much the same end, is the *groupement d'intérêt économique* introduced in France by the Ordinance of 23 September 1967: Article 1 provides:

> 'Deux ou plusieurs personnes physique ou morale peuvent constituer entre elles, pour une durée déterminée, un groupement d'intérêt économiques en vue de mettre en oeuvre tous les moyens propres á faciliter ou à développer l' activite' économique de ses membres, à améliorer ou à accroître les résultats de cette activité.[2]'

1 See *Denison Mattress v Spring-Air* 308 F 2d 403 (1962).

2 'Two or more individuals or legal persons may agree between themselves to form for a specified term, a *groupement d'intérêt économique*, to facilitate or develop the economic activities of the members, or to improve or increase the profits or benefits of such activities'.

0.05 The GIE is a legal entity separate from its members. It operates under its own name and has its own directors. It can contract as a legal entity with third parties, and indeed one of the objects in establishing it is to facilitate such things as bulk buying (which may be of considerable importance in the franchising context). It is not possible to fit franchising in its entirety into the GIE framework as it exists at present, however[1]. In the first place the management of the GIE is subject to some control by the members. That of course may not be any bad thing looked at from the viewpoint of the individual franchisees, but it may be rather less acceptable to franchisors[1]. Another problem is that there are difficulties in providing for new members, although it might be possible to overcome these. The most serious objection, however, is that all the members of the GIE are individually responsible for the whole of its debts without limitation, and creditors may recover from any one or more members[2]. Nevertheless, the concept is an interesting one for it does provide a legal framework for the combination of individual businesses into a single entity, without the loss of their independence.

1 See Guyenot & Valletta (1975) 4 Anglo-Am LR 331.
2 Art 4.

The use of the EEIG and the SE for the purposes of franchising

0.06 Business entities and professional firms within the Community have become increasingly aware of the existence of the EEIG, and of its possible use as a vehicle for co-operation, in the last year or so. It has thus been used as a vehicle for co-operation between law firms in different Member States. Accountancy firms have also displayed some interest in its potentialities. The EEIG (European Economic Interest Grouping), was much inspired by the French *groupement d'intérêt economique*. The EEIG is intended to facilitate or develop the economic activities of its Members, and to improve or increase the results of those activities. Its purpose is not to make profits for itself. Unlike most forms of co-operation based upon a contractual relationship, the use of the EEIG is facilitated by the fact that (depending on the Member State), the grouping may have its own legal personality and in any event, has its own capacities[1].

1 See Regulation (EEC) 2137/85 of 25 July 1985 (OJL 199/1, 31.7.85), Article 1(2) and (3).

0.07 Although one must not of course be dogmatic, and one must recognise that there may be a certain publicity value in the use of this form, it would not seem that the EEIG has an other than limited value for the purpose of franchising. As already pointed out, a grouping cannot make profits for itself[1], and its activities must be no more than an alliance to those of Members'[2]. In addition, it may not exercise a power of management or supervision over its Members' own activities[3], and its Members have joint and several liability which is unlimited for its debts and other liabilities of whatever nature[4]. These factors may discourage the use of the grouping to a widespread extent for the purpose of 'concessions'. Furthermore, in use it may well not accord particularly satisfactorily with the exercise of leadership

0.08 Introduction

by the franchisor. Thus Article 12 of the Regulation provides that no one Member may hold the majority of the votes.

1 Regulation, Article 3(1).
2 Ibid.
3 Ibid, Article 3(2).
4 Ibid, Article 24(1).

0.08 However, subject to the above reservations, one cannot entirely exclude the use of the grouping in franchising. It may be employed for the purpose of holding marks and other forms of intellectual property, providing common transport services, and acting as a central purchasing agency. It should be remembered that the activities of certain groupings may well be subject to the competition laws of the EEC, and that negative clearance may sometimes have to be requested, or advantage taken of existing exemptions, when using a grouping.

0.09 The draft statute for a European Company (SO), which is accompanied by a complementary Directive, is not yet in force. It is doubtful whether, if it is enacted in the near future, it will prove of much assistance to persons wishing to set up or continue franchising operations. Like the grouping (but perhaps to an even greater extent), the European company would be governed by a complex legal regime. This would differ in each Member State. Furthermore, the compulsory character of worker participation might be thought unsuitable by certain enterprises. Individuals would not make use of the SE, and the provisions governing formation are very complex. It is hoped that the SE will come into being, but for all the reasons indicated, it is unlikely to be much used in the present field. It is thought that franchise operations will continue to be principally governed by contractual arrangements for some time in the future.

Competition policy

0.10 The idea behind the voluntary group, the GIE and the EEIG, namely the encouragement of co-operation which increases competition, corresponds with the policy of the European Commission[1]. In the Notice of 29 July 1968 on co-operation agreements[2] the Commission said: 'The Commission welcomes co-operation amongst small and medium-sized enterprises when such co-operation enables them to work more rationally and increase their productivity and competitiveness on the larger market. The Commission considers that it is its task to facilitate co-operation amongst small and medium-sized enterprises in particular[3]'. The decision in the *Transocean Marine Paint Association*[4] provides an illustration of this policy. In that case a number of independent paint manufacturers combined to exchange information and market paint made to an identical formula under the same trade mark. Exemption was granted by the Commission under Article 85.3[5] on the ground that the arrangement facilitated marketing with a resulting benefit to the consumers of the relevant products. Consistently with this the Commission has adopted a generally favourable view of franchising in the block exemption which it promulgated in 1988[6]. In the present context, recital (7) of the exemption is worth quoting at length:

> 'Franchise agreements as defined in this Regulation normally improve the distribution of goods and/or the provision of services as they give franchisors the possibility of establishing a uniform network with limited investments, which may assist the entry of new competitors on the market, particularly

in the case of small and medium-sized undertakings, thus increasing interbrand competition. They also allow independent traders to set up outlets more rapidly and with higher change of success than if they had to do so without the franchisor's experience and assistance. They have therefore the possibility of competing more efficiently with large distribution undertakings. As a rule, franchise agreements also allow consumers and other end users a fair share of the resulting benefit, as they combine the advantage of a uniform network with the existence of traders personally interested in the efficient operation of their business. The homogeneity of the network and the constant cooperation between the franchisor and the franchisees ensures a constant quality of the products and services. The favourable effect of franchising on interbrand competition and the fact that consumers are free to deal with any franchisee in the network guarantees that a reasonable part of the resulting benefits will be passed on to the consumers.'

1   See eg Working Document DG4 IV/471/85-EN.
2   See also First Report on Competition Policy, April 1972, 1–58 and subsequent Reports passim.
3   Para I. This same policy is reflected in the encouragement of concentrations of undertakings—see 'Memorandum on the Problem of Concentration' in the Common Market Competition Series, Study No 3 (Brussels 1966).
4   [1967] OJ L163/67, [1967] CMLR D9, and see Ninth Report on Competition Policy, April 1980, 60–61.
5   See para 2.69 et seq.
6   Regulation 4087/88 OJ 28 December 1988 L359/46—see Appendix 4.

Why franchise?

0.11 The tendency of small independent traders to group together then is a general feature of the business world today, and one that is actively promoted by governments. It does not, however, explain why franchisors choose to market through franchised outlets. The usual reason given for this, and one mentioned in the recital quoted above, is that it is a convenient way of raising capital. Certainly this was an important element in the emergence of the distributorship which was one of the precursors of business format franchising. The earliest recognisable form of the modern distributorship began in the United States after the Civil War when the Singer Sewing Machine Company instituted a manufacturer/retailer distribution system[1]. In the inter-wars period franchised distributorship[2] agreements were to become a general feature of the automobile industry. Indeed Ford was able to extricate itself from financial difficulties in 1921 by off-loading inventory on to its distributors[3]. As well as raising capital, a reason for adopting the system in the motor trade was the general need for purchasers to trade-in their existing model against a new one. It is difficult to see how any other system could have coped with this peculiar feature of the industry[4]. Petrol companies adopted franchised distribution principally for other reasons (which also motivate modern franchisors): the belief that the franchisee as owner of his own business would achieve better sales, and the desire to avoid labour problems[5]. Soft drink manufacturing and bottling franchises, the rapid growth of which was also a feature of the inter-wars period were primarily a result simply of the problems of shifting large quantities of liquid over great distances economically[6]. This period also saw the beginnings of 'chain style' operations[7].

1   Andrew B Jack 'The Channels of Distribution for an Innovation: The Sewing Machine

0.12 Introduction

Industry in America. 1860–1865' in *Explorations in Entrepreneurial History* (New York, 1957) (Macmillan).
2 Franchised distribution systems of this sort, as noted in para 0.01, differ from business format franchising in that a much lesser degree of control is exercised by the 'franchisor' and less business assistance is provided to the franchisee.
3 See S Macaulay *Law and the Balance of Power: The Automobile Manufacturers and their Dealers* (New York, 1966) (Russell Sage Foundation).
4 Alfred P Sloan Jr *My Years with General Motors* (Garden City, New York, 1964) (Doubleday & Co) p 283.
5 John G Mclean & Robert Haigh *The Growth of Integrated Oil Companies* (Boston, 1954) (Division of Research, Graduate School of Business Administration, Harvard) p 72.
6 Ben Ginsberg *Let's Talk Soft Drinks* (Springfield, Mo, 1960) (Mycroft Press) p 35.
7 Taylor W Meloan *The Old and New of Franchise Marketing*, American Marketing Association, Proceedings of Fall Conference 1966, ed Richard M Hans (Chicago, 1966) p 214.

0.12 'Business format' franchising may obviously, in relation to a particular business, have for the franchisor the same sort of attractions as these earlier forms. What needs some explanation, however, is the distinctive feature of the business format franchise: the close and continuous control exercised by the franchisor. Whilst the raising of capital may be an important reason for franchising, rather than distributing directly through company-owned outlets, it must be recognised that it is not necessarily a cheap way of raising capital. It can be argued that the profits made by the franchisee (which in theory might have accrued to the franchisor in a wholly owned system) have to be added back to ascertain the true cost of borrowing to the franchisor. This is one possible explanation of the tendency observed in the United States for some franchise operations to move towards vertical integration once the business has grown sufficiently to raise its own capital[1]. Not all operations exhibit this tendency, however. If the raising of capital were of itself the heart of the matter, arguably a cheaper way of doing it would be to offer the prospective franchisee a portfolio in the whole business, and make him manager of an outlet. A risk minimising franchisee ought to prefer this, since if his outlet fails, he does not lose his whole investment. He ought accordingly to expect and receive a lower rate of return since the return does not have to cover the same risk of capital. The franchisee's risk of capital is the key to the whole enterprise, however. Franchisees prefer it, since they believe that if they work hard they will secure a high return. Franchisors prefer it because they believe that the franchisees will work harder, which in turn will benefit them more in the long run than distribution through managers[2]. It is a particularly suitable strategy to adopt in the case of businesses where employee behaviour is difficult to monitor. This would explain why franchising seems to have developed first in the catering industry. In business format franchising, the franchisor retains similar controls over the franchised outlet, as over a managed outlet. The reality is that it is a kind of managed outlet, in which the franchisee risks his capital[3]. The risk of capital is itself a control device. When working properly the arrangement benefits all parties. The franchisor gets a better return because the franchisee, whose capital is at risk, works hard to make a success of the business. The franchisee gets a high return on his capital without the risks and difficulties involved in starting a business of his own. The public benefit because they get a better and more reliable service.

1 See Oxenfeldt & Kelly 'Will Successful Franchise Systems Ultimately Become Wholly-Owned Chains?' (1970) 43 Journal of Retailing 19; Lillis Narayana & Gilman 'Competitive Advantage Over the Life Cycle of a Franchise' (1976) 40 Journal of Marketing 77. There are other reasons for this, of course, in particular, in certain types of business the need to

respond rapidly to market changes makes franchising inevitable — changing the course of a franchise operation is rather like altering course in an ocean liner, it takes a long time!

2   The survival of very many profitable tenancies in the licensed trade suggests that brewers think along the same lines—in this case of course there will not generally be the same degree of capital commitment by the licensee as in a true franchise, nor the same degree of control.

3   This view of the arrangements could perhaps be of some importance in relation to competition policy — as to which see chapter 2, post.

0.13   The boom in this style of franchising in the United States began in the early 1950s. By the mid-1960s over-saturation of the market had begun to lead to failures. The most famous of these was the failure of the Minnie Pearl Chicken System. By 1969 this franchisor had sold 1800 franchises, but opened only 161 stores, all of which eventually failed[1]. Franchise fever died down in the more sober economic climate of the 1970s. Nevertheless, because as we shall see, the system can offer real advantages to both parties, the 1970s was a period of steady growth of franchising in the United States. American franchisors also increasingly turned their attentions overseas. The 1980s was a period of rapid growth in the United Kingdom, both of American and other overseas chains, and of indigenous enterprises.

1   'Franchising: Too Much Too Soon' Business Week, 27 June 1970, p 54.

0.14   In the United Kingdom, business format franchising seems to have begun at about the same time as in the United States. Certainly, there is at least one pre-war operation still in existence. However, in spite of some expansion in the 1950s, the real growth began only in the last twenty years or so. Ironically, in the United Kingdom, this growth may actually have been accelerated by the recession of the early 1980s, because of the number of people with capital by way of redundancy payments wishing to set up their own businesses. Such people regrettably were (and still are) often the target of less scrupulous operators[1]. This must be a matter for concern, and it may be that there is need for specific legislation, of the sort which has been introduced in the United States[2] and some other countries. The United Kingdom trade association, the British Franchise Association, provides some safeguard against sharp practice, but its effectiveness in this respect must depend to a large extent on general public awareness that reputable operators should belong to it.

1   See Harold Brown *Franchising: Trap for the Trusting* (1969) (Little, Brown) Baillieu *Streetwise Franchising* (1988) (Hutchinson Business).
2   See para 7.56 et seq.

0.15   Further information about the industry can be obtained from the following publications:

Business Format Franchising
The Economist Intelligence Unit
40 Duke Street
London W1M 5DG
071-493 6711

Euromonitor—Franchising
87–88 Turnmill Street
London EC1M 5QU

Euromonitor—Franchising in the European Economy

0.16 *Introduction*

Franchise Directories and Magazines
Franchise Manual & Directory
Franchise World
Bob Riding
James House
37 Nottingham Road
London SW17 7EA
081-767 1371

Jordan's—UK Franchising—A Financial Survey
Jordan House
Brunswick Place
London N16EE
071-253 3030

Keynote Report—Franchising
Keynote Publications Ltd
28–42 Banner Street
London EC1Y 8QE
071-253 3006

The Mintel Report 1987, Opportunities in Franchising
Mintel Publications Ltd
Kae House
7 Arundel Street
London WC2R 3DR

The Power Report
Franchising: The Industry and the Market (Changes in Scale & Structure—1984–1986),
Michael Power
Power Research Associates
17 Wigmore Street
London W1H 9LA
071-580 5816

The British Franchise Association

0.16 The British Franchise Association (BFA) was formed in 1977 by a number of leading British and international companies engaged in the distribution of goods and services through independent outlets under franchisee and licensee agreements. Its aims include establishing a clear definition of the ethical franchising standards to assist members of the public, press, potential investors and government bodies in differentiating between sound business opportunities and suspect investment offers.

The BFA Code of Ethics[1] adopted in accordance with clause 3(2)(a) of the Memorandum of Association reflects the Code established by the International Franchise Association, and is as follows:

(1) The BFA's Code of Advertising Practice shall be based on that established by the Advertising Standards Association and shall be modified from time to time in accordance with alterations notified by the ASA.

The BFA will subscribe fully to the ASA Code unless, on some specific issue, it is resolved by a full meeting of the Council of the BFA that the ASA is acting

The British Franchise Association 0.16

against the best interests of the public and of franchising business in general on that specific issue. In that case the BFA will be required to formally notify the ASA, setting out the grounds for disagreement.

(2) No member shall sell, offer for sale, or distribute any product or render any service, or promote the sale or distribution thereof, under any representation of condition (including the use of the name of a 'celebrity') which has the tendency, capacity, or effect of misleading or deceiving purchasers or prospective purchasers.

(3) No member shall imitate the trademark, trade name, corporate identity, slogan or other mark or identification of another franchisor in any manner or form that would have the tendency or capacity to mislead or deceive.

(4) Full and accurate written disclosure of all information material to the franchise relationship shall be given to the prospective franchisees within a reasonable time prior to the execution of any binding document.

(5) The franchise agreement shall set forth clearly the respective obligations and responsibilities of the parties and all other terms of the relationship, and be free from ambiguity.

(6) The franchise agreement and all matters basic and material to the arrangement and relationship thereby created, shall be in writing and executed copies thereof given to the franchisee.

(7) A franchisor shall select and accept only those franchisees who, upon reasonable investigation, possess the basic skills, education, personal qualities, and adequate capital to succeed. There shall be no discrimination based on race, colour, religion, national origin or sex.

(8) A franchisor shall exercise reasonable surveillance over the activities of his franchisees to the end that the contractual obligations of both parties are observed and the public interest safeguarded.

(9) Fairness shall characterise all dealings between a franchisor and its franchisees. A franchisor shall give notice to its franchisee of any contractual breach and grant reasonable time to remedy defaults.

(10) A franchisor shall make every effort to resolve complaints, grievances and disputes with its franchisees with good faith and good will through fair and reasonable direct communication and negotiation.

The BFA publishes a booklet for its members, providing more detailed guidance on how it expects them to behave, and also on what they should expect of franchisees and consultants. This will be referred to at various points in this book[2].

The BFA is rigorous in investigating applications for membership. The qualifications for membership are as follows:

(1) Members shall be actively engaged in the franchise system of distribution of goods and services.

(2) Members shall have established and be operating an ethical franchise network which shall be based on sound business principles, and providing a genuine and adequate service to both franchisee and consumer.

(3) Members will be required to demonstrate to the Accreditation Committee the intention to provide, on a continuing basis, the service offered to the franchisee and, where relevant, to the public. The viability of the operation, both with respect to the franchisee and the franchisor, must also be demonstrated.

(4) Members will be required to satisfy the Accreditation Committee that the systems established by the member company are adequate to protect both the public and the franchisee, where money is advanced in anticipation of the service to be provided at a future date.

(5) The member company shall give an absolute undertaking that it will subscribe

0.16 Introduction

to the Code of Ethics adopted by the British Franchise Association. This Code of Ethics draws heavily on the Code established by the International Franchise Association and on the Code of Advertising Practice established by the British Advertising Standards Authority (ASA). Members also shall have completed the following Declaration:

> We, the applicant company . . . . Ltd, give our undertaking that we are prepared at all times to subscribe to the Code of Ethics adopted by the British Franchise Association. We declare, to the best of our knowledge and belief, that the franchise system we offer is based on sound business principles and provides a viable and ethical business opportunity for the franchisee and a genuine end-product or service for the consumer. It is our belief that the systems we operate, satisfactorily protect both the franchisee and the consumer and, accordingly, we hereby apply for membership of the British Franchise Association:
>
> (signed etc)

Company and service information together with references from three established franchisees must also be provided with the application. Copies of current contracts and licences together with promotional literature, must also be submitted. Application forms, together with other information can be obtained by writing to:

The Admissions Secretary,
British Franchise Association,
75a Bell Street,
Henley-on-Thames,
Oxon, RG9 2BD
The telephone number is:
(0491) 578049/578050

The BFA provides a 'forum' for the interchange of information and franchising expertise amongst members and the public, through an advisory information service designed to assist potential franchisees in making a value judgment prior to selecting a final investment. The BFA also gives members advice on their franchises and organises exhibitions for prospective franchisees to attend and talk to franchisors. A National Franchise Exhibition is held each year in October at the Kensington Exhibition Centre, London, organised by the Dresswell Group. Future objectives include establishing approved education programmes, a move towards standardisation in franchising agreements, and acting as a common voice in liaison with government bodies where legislation exists or is likely to be formulated. The BFA acts as a 'spokesman' for responsible franchising. Activities organised by the BFA include meetings for the interchange of information and expertise, and seminars and conferences covering topics of interest to members and the public. It also maintains high level contact with overseas franchise associations, and nominates delegates to attend international seminars and report on them to all members.

The British Franchise Association 0.16

In order that a framework should exist for the resolution of disputes, the BFA has established an arbitration scheme to be administered by the Chartered Institute of Arbitrators. Details of the scheme are as follows:

The Chartered Institute of Arbitrators British Franchise Association Arbitration Scheme

Rules

(1987 Edition)

These Rules provide an inexpensive and informal method of resolving disputes between franchisors and franchisees which the parties cannot resolve amicably between themselves. The Rules will apply to arbitrations commenced under the Scheme after 1 May 1987.

Introduction

(1) In these Rules:
  (i) 'The Institute' shall mean the Chartered Institute of Arbitrators of 75 Cannon Street, London EC4N 5BH.
  (ii) 'the BFA' shall mean the British Franchise Association of 75a Bell Street, Henley on Thames, Oxon RG9 2BD.
  (iii) 'the Arbitrator' shall mean a sole and independent arbitrator appointed by the President or Vice-President of the Institute in an arbitration under this Scheme.
  (iv) 'the Franchisor' shall mean a company firm or person who is the franchisor in respect of any agreement under which a dispute arises and is referred to arbitration under this Scheme.
  (v) 'the Franchisee' shall mean a company firm or person who is the franchisee in respect of any agreement under which a dispute arises and is referred to arbitration under this Scheme.
  (vi) 'the costs of the arbitration' shall mean the total of the Arbitrator's fees and expenses, the Institute's administrative costs, and the cost of any independent examination under Rule 8(iv).
  (vii) 'costs in the reference' shall mean legal or other costs incurred by a party in connection with an arbitration under this scheme.

(2) The Franchisee may apply for arbitration under this Scheme as an alternative to court action. He must decide at the outset whether to use this Scheme or to seek his remedy through the Courts. If he uses this Scheme he will not be able to start again with court action, because awards made under the Scheme are final and binding on the parties.

(3) (i) Application for arbitration must be made on the prescribed application form which may be obtained from the BFA.
  (ii) A deposit of £150 is payable by each party when an application for arbitration is submitted. These deposits may be refunded or may be applied in whole or in part towards defraying the costs of the arbitration, at the discretion of the Arbitrator.

(4) (i) The application form should be completed by the Franchisee and returned to the BFA with the Franchisee's deposit.

0.16 *Introduction*

(ii) The BFA will then refer the application form to the Franchisor, to be completed and returned to the BFA with the Franchisor's deposit.

(iii) The Franchisor's agreement to arbitration is necessary for the application to proceed. The BFA will encourage the Franchisor to agree, but he is not obliged to do so. If the Franchisor does not agree to arbitration, he is required to inform the BFA accordingly. The Franchisee's deposit will be returned and he may seek his remedy through the Courts.

Institution of Arbitration Proceedings

(5) Provided the application form has been signed by both parties and is accompanied by the appropriate deposits, it will be forwarded to the Institute by the BFA with the deposits.

(6) The arbitration commences for the purposes of these Rules when the Institute despatches to the parties written notice of acceptance of the application. The notice sent to the party making the claim will be accompanied by a claim form.

Procedure

(7) General

Subject to any directions issued by the Arbitrator the procedure will be as follows:

(i) The Franchisee is required, within 28 days of receipt of the claim form, to send the completed form, together with any supporting documents in duplicate, to the Institute. The Franchisee is also required to notify the Institute at this stage if he requests an attended hearing. (The Franchisee may not, without the consent of the Institute, claim an amount greater than specified on the application for arbitration.)

(ii) A copy of the claim documents will be sent by the Institute to the Franchisor, who is required, within 28 days of receipt of the documents, to send to the Institute his written defence to the claim together with any supporting documents in duplicate. (The Franchisor may include with his defence a counterclaim in respect of any balance of payment alleged to be due on the contract between the parties, or in respect of any other matter notified to the Franchisee before the Franchisee applied for arbitration.)

(iii) A copy of the defence documents will be sent by the Institute to the Franchisee, who is entitled to send to the Institute any written comments which he wishes to make on the defence documents within 14 days of their receipt. Such comments should be in duplicate. They must be restricted to points arising from the Franchisor's defence, and may not introduce any new matters or points of claim.

(iv) The President or a Vice-President of the Institute, at such stage of the proceedings as the Institute considers appropriate, will appoint the Arbitrator, taking into account the nature of the dispute and the location of the Franchisee's trading premises. The Institute will notify the parties of the Arbitrator's appointment.

(v) The Arbitrator may in his discretion call the parties to an attended hearing, and shall do so if the Franchisee has so requested in accordance with Rule 7(i). Subject to that, the Arbitrator will make his award with reference to the documents submitted by the parties.

(vi) The Arbitrator will send his award to the Institute for publication. Unless the parties otherwise agree the Arbitrator's reasons will be set out or referred to in his award.

(vii) The Institute will notify the parties when it has received the award from the Arbitrator, and will also notify the Franchisor of any costs of the Arbitrator payable under Rule 11. On payment of such costs, the Institute will publish the award by sending copies to each of the parties. In normal circumstances the Institute will also send a copy to the BFA.

(viii) After publication of the award the Institute will return the Franchisee's deposit in whole or in part if so directed by the Arbitrator.

(ix) Unless directed otherwise in the award, within 21 days of despatch by the Institute to the parties of the copy award, payment shall be made of any monies directed by the award to be paid by one party to the other. Such payment shall be made by the party liable direct to the party entitled, and not through the Institute.

(x) If either party has sent original documents in support of its case to the Institute that party may within six weeks of publication of the award request the return of those documents. Subject to that, case papers will be retained by the Institute and may in due course be disposed of in accordance with the Institute's policies from time to time.

(8) Supplementary

(i) Attended hearings shall be conducted in private at a place to be notified to the parties by the Institute on behalf of the Arbitrator, who shall use his best endeavours to take into account the convenience of the parties. The parties may attend a hearing in person or be represented by an employee (but not a person employed to give legal advice) unless the Arbitrator agrees they may be legally represented.

(ii) The Arbitrator may, through the Institute, request the provision of any further documents/information which he considers would assist him in his decision. If the documents/information are not supplied to the Institute within such time as it prescribes, the Arbitrator will proceed with the reference on the basis of the documents already before him.

(iii) Where in the opinion of the Arbitrator it is desirable, he may make an examination of the subject matter of the dispute without holding an attended hearing. The parties shall afford the Arbitrator all necessary assistance and facilities for the conduct of this examination.

(iv) Where, in the opinion of the Arbitrator, it is desirable that independent examination of the subject matter of the dispute be made, an independent examiner will be appointed by the Institute to make such examination and a written report thereon. The parties shall afford the examiner all necessary assistance and facilities for the conduct of this examination and copies of his report shall be sent by the Institute to the parties who will then be given 14 days in which to comment thereon.

(v) If the Franchisee does not furnish his claim within the time allowed and does not remedy his default within 14 days after despatch to him by the Institute of notice of that default, he will be treated as having abandoned his claim. The arbitration will not proceed and the Franchisee's deposit will be returned less the Institute's administrative costs to date. The Franchisor's deposit will be returned in full.

(vi) If the Franchisor does not furnish his defence within the time allowed and does not remedy his default within 14 days after despatch to him by the Institute of notice of that default, the Arbitrator will be appointed and

0.16 *Introduction*

subject to any directions he may give the dispute may be decided by him by reference to the documents submitted by the Franchisee.

(vii) If a party fails to attend or be represented at an attended hearing the Arbitrator shall either make an award ex parte, or, if he so decides, adjourn the hearing for such time as he considers reasonable and serve notice on the party failing to attend that the matter will be dealt with ex parte at the adjourned hearing.

Costs

(9) The Franchisor shall be responsible for the costs of the Arbitration less any amount which the Arbitrator may order the Franchisee to pay but the Franchisor shall in any event be responsible for not less than two-thirds of the costs of the Arbitration. Where the arbitration is conducted on the basis of documents only, the Arbitrator will not order the Franchisee to pay a contribution to the costs of the Arbitration in excess of £150 unless he considers the application by the Franchisee to have been frivolous or vexatious. In the case of an attended hearing, if the costs of the Arbitration exceed £300 the Arbitrator may order the Franchisee to pay part of such excess in addition to the sum of £150 (or more if he considers the application frivolous or vexatious).

(10) The Arbitrator may order the Franchisor to pay some or all of the Franchisee's costs in the reference and may order the Franchisee to pay up to one-third of the Franchisor's costs in the reference.

(11) The Franchisor agrees to pay to the Institute within 14 days of notice from the Institute of receipt of the Award and of the amount of the costs of the Arbitration, a total sum equal to the costs of the Arbitration less the amount of any deposits ordered to be utilised towards payment of the fees and expenses. This is without prejudice to any right which the Franchisor may have to recover from the Franchisee a contribution to the costs of the arbitration or the Franchisor's costs in the reference, ordered in the Arbitrator's award to be paid by the Franchisee.

Miscellaneous

(12) The arbitration shall be conducted in accordance with the law of England.

(13) The Institute reserves the right to appoint a substitute Arbitrator if the Arbitrator originally appointed dies or is incapacitated or is for any reason unable to deal expeditiously with the dispute. The parties shall be notified of any substitution.

(14) Awards made under the Scheme are final and binding on the parties. Subject to the right of a party to request the Institute to draw the Arbitrator's attention to any accidental slip or omission which he has power to correct, neither the Institute nor the Arbitrator can enter into correspondence regarding awards made under the Scheme.

(15) Rights of application or appeal (if any) to the Courts are as under the relevant Arbitration Acts provided that the special costs provisions of the Scheme shall not apply to any such application or appeal.

(16) Neither the Institute nor the Arbitrator shall be liable to any party for any act or omission in connection with any arbitration conducted under these Rules save that the Arbitrator (but not the Institute) shall be liable for any conscious or deliberate wrongdoing on his own part.

The British Franchise Association 0.16

The Chartered Institute of Arbitrators
International Arbitration Centre
75 Cannon Street
London EC4N 5BH
Telephone 071-236 8761
Telex: 893466 CIARB G

The Chartered Institute of Arbitrators British Franchise Association Arbitration Scheme
Application for Arbitration

To: The Chartered Institute of Arbitrators
    (to be submitted through the British Franchise Association)

(1) .... Franchisee
of .... Phone: ....
                          and
.... Franchisor
of .... Phone: ....

Hereby apply to the Chartered Institute of Arbitrators for the following dispute to be referred to arbitration under the Rules of the British Franchise Association Arbitration Scheme for the time being in force for determination by an Arbitrator appointed for that purpose by the Institute.

(2) The dispute has arisen in connection with the following:

....
....
....
....

(NOTE: Only an outline is required here to enable the dispute to be identified by the parties. The Franchisee will be asked to submit his specific claim in detail as soon as the arbitration request has been accepted by the Institute.)

(3) We, the parties to this application, are each in possession of the current (1987) Rules of the Scheme. We agree to be bound by these Rules (or any amendment thereof for the time being in force that may be notified to us) and by the Award of the Arbitrator appointed to determine the dispute.

(4) A cheque for the sum of £150* in respect of the Franchisee's deposit, and a cheque for the same amount in respect of the Franchisor's deposit are enclosed.

We agree to the disposal of these deposits in accordance with the Rules of the Scheme.

Signed .... Date ....
    (Franchisee)

Signed .... Date ....
    (Franchisor)

*Cheques should be in favour of:
'The Chartered Institute of Arbitrators'

0.16 *Introduction*

In establishing the Scheme BFA is not requiring all franchisees to agree to adopt arbitration. The Scheme is available to those who wish to use it. However, the Code of Ethics clearly requires franchisors to seek to resolve disputes amicably and BFA expects members to endeavour to do so. BFA recognises that it takes co-operation and willingness by both parties to resolve disputes in this way and if a franchisee will not co-operate there is nothing the franchisor or BFA can do.

1   This is under review at the time of writing.
2   Martin Mendelsohn *The Ethics of Franchising* A British Franchise Association Guide (1987).

Streetwise Franchising

0.17   This body has been set up specifically to assist and support franchise owners and those who wish to take up franchises. Further details of it are given at para 6.14.

Chapter 1
Franchising as a legal concept

Introduction

1.01 In this chapter we attempt to define and analyse the nature of franchising for legal purposes. The continuing control by the franchisor over the way in which the franchisee operates the business is the most significant feature of the arrangement. The object of it is to preserve strict uniformity between outlets, and thereby preserve and enhance the goodwill associated with the name, mark, etc. The element of control immediately poses the problem as to whether a franchise 'network'[1] is one business or many. It will be suggested that there may not be a single answer to this question. For some purposes the operation may be treated as a single entity. In relation to competition law, for example, a case could be made for this. For other purposes, it would seem that the franchisor and franchisee ought to be considered to be carrying on separate businesses. This is particularly the case with regard for example to taxation and National Insurance.

1 As to how franchise networks are in fact treated under the various competition laws in operation in this country, see Ch 2.

The distinctive features of franchising

1.02 The British Franchising Association define a franchise as:

'A contractual licence granted by one person (the franchisor) to another (the franchisee) which:
   (a) permits or requires the franchisee to carry on, during the period of the franchise, a particular business under or using a specific name belonging to or associated with the franchisor; and
   (b) entitles the franchisor to exercise continuing control during the period of the franchise over the manner in which the franchisee carries on the business which is the subject of the franchise; and
   (c) obliges the franchisor to provide the franchisee with assistance in carrying on the business which is the subject of the franchise (in relation to the organisation of the franchisee's business, the training of staff, merchandising, management or otherwise); and
   (d) requires the franchisee periodically, during the period of the franchise, to pay the franchisor sums of money in consideration for the franchise, or for goods or services provided by the franchisor to the franchisee; and
   (e) is not a transaction between a holding company and its subsidiary (as defined in section [736] of the Companies Act [1985])[1] or between subsidiaries

1.03 *Franchising as a legal concept*

of the same holding company, or between an individual and a company controlled by him.'

This definition may be compared with that of the International Franchise Association:

'A franchise operation is a contractual relationship between the franchisor and franchisee in which the franchisor offers or is obliged to maintain a continuing interest in the business of the franchisor in such areas as knowhow and training; wherein the franchisee operates under a common trade name, format or procedure owned by or controlled by the franchisor, and in which the franchisee has or will make a substantial capital investment in his business from his own resources.'

1 The original reference is to the Companies Act 1948, s 154. This exclusion ought to be borne in mind when deciding whether or not to adopt this scheme either as a method of avoiding the need to furnish particulars under the Restrictive Trade Practices Act 1976 (see s 43(1)) or for other reasons. The name sometimes given to such an arrangement is 'branchising'.

1.03 These definitions have in common the following features:

(1) a franchise involves a contractual relationship between the parties under which one party (the franchisor) licences the other party (the franchisee) to carry on business under a name, etc owned or associated with the franchisor;

(2) control by the franchisor over the way in which the franchisee carries on that business;

(3) provision of assistance to the franchisee by the franchisor in running the business;

(4) the businesses are however separate: the franchisee provides and risks his own capital.

The significant differences between the two definitions are that the British Franchising Association's expressly excludes the theoretical possibility of a single once and for all payment by the franchisee to the franchisor, and excludes transactions between holding companies and their subsidiaries. In using the words 'trade name, format or procedure' the IFA gives a wider definition of the basic right purchased by the franchisee, though the BFA's definition must be intended to include the possibility of a business operating purely under a trade mark, symbol or format.

1.04 There are four principal problems which need to be considered: (1) the effect of the licence of the trade name and mark; (2) the potential liability of the franchisor to third parties for the acts and defaults of the franchisee; (3) the relationship of the parties inter se; and (4) how the arrangement is to be regarded for the purposes of competition law. Competition law is considered in Ch 2; in the following pages we consider the first three problems.

The licence of the mark, trade name, etc and the goodwill of the business

Introduction

1.05 The two basic ingredients of a franchise are the licence to the franchisee to operate under a trade name etc associated with the franchisor, and the franchisor's continuing control over the way in which the franchisee does business. The result is a uniformity between outlets calculated to lead the public into believing they are dealing with a single business rather than many. The public do not in general distinguish between franchise operations and vertically integrated operations. The goodwill attaches to the mark, trade name, and distinctive 'get up' which serves to distinguish the operation as a whole from competing businesses. In general the public do not realise that outlets are separately owned, and operate only under licence from the franchisor. The control exercised by the franchisor in conjunction with this licensing serves to promote this by ensuring the uniformity of product the customers associate with the mark, trade name etc and thereby the goodwill of the business is built up. This idea of a single goodwill built up by a number of independent businesses operating under licence, is one which would have startled our ancestors for whom goodwill was essentially something built up and associated with a particular manufacturer or trader, a view reflected in the development of trade marks law in the last century. On the assumption that in order to see where we are, it is sometimes quite helpful to know where we have come from, it is worth considering briefly how the concept of a trade mark emerged in the nineteenth century, and how that concept was to affect the development of trade mark licensing in this country. As the *Holly Hobbie* case[1] showed, the ghosts of the past are not quite laid to rest, even today.

1 [1984] RPC 329.

Registered trade marks and licensing

1.06 Although it is generally said that the law of trade marks is a nineteenth century creation[1], the *use* of marks goes back very much further[2]. In the middle ages a distinction was made between production marks which indicated the origin of goods, and proprietary marks or merchants' marks[3]. The purpose of merchant marks was to provide proof of ownership[4]. By contrast an important function of the medieval production mark was to facilitate the establishing of liability, eg under the Assize of Bread[5]. The translation of a production trade mark from a liability into an asset, a mark of quality, seems first to have occurred in relation to the collective marks of the cloth trade, and the marks of the cutlery makers. A case arose in 1452 before the Mayor and Aldermen of the City of London on the right to use a double crescent mark. That case is significant in showing that by this period marks had become of sufficient value to be the subject of litigation for their restoration, and the notion of property in a mark had developed to the point where it might descend to a widow, so long as she remained in the business[6]. Nevertheless, producers' trade marks were unlikely to acquire importance as valuable symbols of goodwill as long as producer and consumer were in close contact[7]. For the most part therefore, the development in importance of trade marks is a function of the industrial revolution, and we would not expect the law to develop very much before the eighteenth century therefore[8]. It now seems probable that nineteenth century developments were built on eighteenth century foundations[9]. It may well be, although at present admittedly it is a matter of pure speculation, that proprietary marks too had come to bear a goodwill aspect where members of the public came to associate them with a particular merchant's skill in selection. At all events, the terminology of proprietary marks survived[10] the decline of the original purpose. Indeed, in the early eighteenth century the two tended to be

1.07 Franchising as a legal concept

confused, suggesting that by then goodwill may have become a central feature of both[11].

1 Kerly *Law of Trade Marks*, ed White and Jacob (10th edn) (Sweet and Maxwell) 1-03 (most of this historical material is omitted from the 11th edn). Although the first reported case is *Sykes v Sykes* (1824) 3 B & C 541, actions seem not to have been unusual in the eighteenth century. Presumably, as usual, people did not bother to report the commonplace—see Adams 'The Intellectual Property Cases in Lord Mansfield's Court Notebooks' (1987) 8 Jo Leg Hist 18.
2 See Schechter *Historical Foundations of Trade Mark Law* (1925) (Columbia University Press)—the use of marks goes back to prehistoric times in fact.
3 Op cit pp 20-21.
4 Op cit Ch II
5 Op cit Ch III.
6 Op cit pp 108-109.
7 Op cit pp 129.
8 *Southern v How* (1617) Poph 143, J Bridg 125 (the exact date of the case is uncertain, possibly it was 15 Jac I) is usually given as the starting point. Schechter describes it as a tenuous link between the medieval and the modern period.
9 See Adams 'The Intellectual Property Cases in Lord Mansfield's Court Notebooks' (1987) 8 Jo Leg Hist 18.
10 See the definition of 'trade mark' in Tomlin's *Law Dictionary* (1820)—one of the very few early attempts.
11 See Giles Jacob *Lex Mercatoria* (1718) pp 26-27.

1.07 The view of a trade mark which emerged was that it was something used in relation to goods which either might be taken as a warranty that they had come from a particular manufacturer[1], or which gave 'an indication to a purchaser... of the *trade source* from which the goods come or the trade hands through which they pass on their way to the market[2]. This way of thinking was embodied in section 3 of the Trade Marks Act 1905 which for the first time provides a statutory definition of a trade mark[3]:

> 'A "trade mark" shall mean a mark used or proposed to be used upon or in connexion with goods for the purpose of indicating that they are the goods of the proprietor of such trade mark by virtue of manufacture, selection, certification, dealing with, or offering for sale.'

1 *Massam v Thorley's Cattle Food Co* (1880) 14 Ch D 748, per James LJ.
2 *Powell's Trade Mark* [1893] 2 Ch 388 at 403-404, per Bowen LJ.
3 Earlier attempts contained in the 1862 Trade Marks Bill never reached the statute book. The equivalent words were '... used by any person to denote any chattel... to be a thing of the Manufacture, Workmanship, Produce or Merchandise of such person'.

1.08 When we consider this definition and the history of trade marks, we will understand why the assignment or transmission of marks independently of goodwill was not considered to be possible. The Trade Marks Acts in fact contained an express prohibition against the assignment and transmission of marks in gross[1]. Even so, the statutory prohibition on assignment or transmission[2] in gross was unnecessarily widely drawn. Section 22 of the 1905 Act provided that a trade mark when registered might be assigned only in connection with the goodwill of a business for which it had been registered. In *John Sinclair Ltd's Trade Mark*[3], Carreras Ltd owned a mark which they had used only in connection with particular cigarettes. They purported to assign it to the plaintiffs with such goodwill as attached to the particular mark. It was held that the assignment was bad. The requirement that a mark could be assigned only in connection with the goodwill of the business

The licence of the mark, trade name, etc and the goodwill of the business 1.09

concerned[4] required at least the assignment of Carreras' whole business in cigarettes[5]. As Fry LJ observed in *Pinto v Badman*[6] '[a trade mark] can be assigned if it is indicative of origin, when the origin is assigned with it. It cannot be assigned when it is divorced from its place of origin, or when, in the hands of the transferee, it would indicate something different to what it indicated in the hands of the transferor[7]. So long as trade marks continued to be regarded in this way, licensing could not be permitted. Indeed, until the 1938 Act, it was arguable that this was the case[8]. The leading authority was the House of Lords decision in *Re Bowden Wire Ltd's Trade Marks, Bowden Wire Co Ltd v Bowden Brake Co Ltd*[9]. Because this case has never actually been declared no longer to be good law, and indeed has been cited in recent times[10] on the important question of what amounts to 'trafficking'[11] in a mark, it is necessary to consider it at some length.

1   Trade Marks Registration Act 1875, s 2; Trade Marks Act 1883, s 70; Trade Marks Act 1905, s 22.
2   These terms were not defined until the 1938 Act, s 68(1) of which defines 'assignment' as meaning assignment by act of the parties and 'transmission' as meaning transmission by operation of law, devolution on the personal representative of a deceased person, and any other mode of transfer not being an assignment.
3   [1932] 1 Ch 598, 49 RPC 123, CA.
4   1905 Act, s 22.
5   See also *Lacteosote Ltd v Alberman* [1927] 2 Ch 117, 44 RPC 211; *Dobie & Sons Ltd's Trade Mark* (1935) 52 RPC 333; *Re Trade Mark Mac No 458 654, Macleans Ltd v Lightbrown & Sons Ltd* (1937) 54 RPC 230.
6   (1891) 8 RPC 181, CA.
7   Ibid at 194.
8   The 1883 Act appeared to permit licensing. When coupled with s 70 however, which forbade transmission in gross, it was arguable that the Act section conferred no such permission—*Re Bowden Wire Ltd's Trade Marks, Bowden Wire Co Ltd v Bowden Brake Co Ltd* (1913) 30 RPC 45; on appeal 30 RPC 580 at 587, CA.
9   (1914) 31 RPC 385, HL.
10 *Holly Hobbie Trade Mark* [1984] RPC 329.
11 Within the meaning of s 28(6).

1.09   The plaintiffs were the proprietors of a patent granted in 1896 for a type of wire used for cycle brakes—similar to that used at the present day. The wire was known as 'Bowden wire'—indeed at the present day 'Bowden cable' is used as a generic name of this type of brake cable. In 1903 the plaintiffs registered a trade mark for cycle brakes consisting of a picture of a coil of their wire with the word 'Bowden' enclosed therein. The defendants were duly licensed by the plaintiffs to make cycle brakes using the patent. The necessary cable for the brakes was to be supplied by the plaintiffs and the remainder, the levers, etc, by the defendants. The whole mechanism was to have the 'Bowden' trade mark applied to it. In 1904 the plaintiffs registered the same mark, in respect of cycle accessories other than brakes and accessories for motor cycles, motor cars and other road vehicles and proceeded to make and apply the mark to such articles. After the expiration of the licence and the patent, the defendants continued to use the mark in connection with cycle brakes, and also to use it on motor cycle brakes using the same principle. The plaintiffs sought to restrain this, and the defendants applied to have both registrations expunged. The judge at first instance held that the marks were distinctive and that the defendants had no right to continue to use the mark after expiry of the licence. He granted the plaintiffs an injunction. The case eventually came before the House of Lords who held that the marks were not distinctive, and must be removed from the register. In a crucial passage, with reference to

1.10 *Franchising as a legal concept*

the setting up and licensing of the defendant company by the plaintiffs, Lord Dunedin said ' . . . in so acting, I think it is free from doubt that the [plaintiffs] really vitiated their own trade mark as registered. It was an attempt to assign a trade mark in gross, a thing which cannot be done. By registration they affected to tell the public that goods in the class and of the description specified, marked with the registered mark, were their goods; that is to say, manufactured, or at least put on the market by them. But in reality, with their assent, the mark was, in practice, adhibited to goods which were not put on the market by them, but manufactured by or which were of composite manufacture and put on the market by the [defendants]'[1]. Similar views are to be found in Lord Shaw's speech: 'A trade mark . . . is simply an intimation upon the goods that they are the goods of the owner of the mark'[2].

1 (1914) 31 RPC 385, HL.
2 Ibid, at 395.

1.10 Following the recommendations of the Goschen Committee[1] the 1938 Act introduced a provision for the registration of users[2]. The definition of a 'trade mark' accordingly was altered by the 1938 Act. It provides that a 'trade mark' is:

'. . . a mark used or proposed to be used in relation to goods for the purpose of indicating, or so as to indicate, a connection in the course of a trade between the goods and some person having the right either as proprietor or as registered user to use the mark[3]'.

Furthermore the assignment provisions were amended making it clear that notwithstanding any rule of law to the contrary, a registered trade mark should be, and should be deemed always to have been, assignable and transmissible either in connection with the goodwill of a business or not[4]. As a result of these changes, it was at least arguable that Bowden had ceased to be good law—a view expressed by Wynn-Parry J in the *Pan Books* case[5]. Unfortunately, in *Manus Akt v RJ Fullwood and Bland Ltd* [6] the Court of Appeal chose to distinguish it. In *Manus* the plaintiffs were a Swedish company manufacturing milking machines in Sweden, sold in this country under the name 'Manus' or 'Manus the Gold Metal Milking Machine'. 'Manus' was a registered trade mark in this country. The defendants were the sole selling agents here. After war broke out in 1939, it became impossible to continue to import the machines from Sweden, and a licence was granted to manufacture the machines in this country for the remaining period of the patent and to mark the machines 'Manus'. After the expiry of the licence, the defendants continued to make and sell machines under the name 'Manus'. The plaintiffs sought to restrain this, and the defendants counter-claimed for removal of the mark from the register. The plaintiffs obtained an injunction. At first instance Harman J distinguished *Bowden* on the ground that the agreement was not a licence to use the mark 'Manus'— the defendants apparently being ignorant that this was a trade mark[7], rather it was an agreement to keep the word 'Manus' as a trade name alive. Evershed LJ on appeal, appeared to take the same view. With respect, however, this distinction is untenable. The knowledge of the defendants is irrelevant: had they attempted to use the name 'Manus' without the licence they could have been restrained, as indeed eventually they were, because it would have been an infringement of the mark. The agreement whatever its object therefore had *effect* as a licence of the trade mark[8].

22

The licence of the mark, trade name, etc and the goodwill of the business 1.11

1   Cmd 4568, para 123.
2   Section 28.
3   Section 68(1).
4   Section 22(1).
5   *Re Pan Press Publications Ltd's Applications* (1948) 65 RPC 193 at 200.
6   [1949] Ch 208, 66 RPC 71, CA.
7   (1948) 65 RPC 329.
8   A licence being simply an authority to do something which could otherwise be wrongful or illegal—see *Federal Comr of Taxation v United Aircraft Corpn* (1943) 68 CLR 525.

1.11 Would the outcome of the *Bowden* case be different at the present day? An important point in the *Bowden* case was that all of the goods marked with the Bowden trade mark, whether made by the plaintiff or the defendant, used Bowden wire. Would that be sufficient to establish a connection in the course of a trade between the proprietor and the goods? On the facts of the case, the answer would seem to be 'no'. The plaintiffs in the *Bowden* case failed in a separate passing off action[1]. The reason why they failed was because they had no rights in the words 'Bowden wire'. After the expiry of the patent, as Warrington J observed, it was open to all the world to sell and use the wire and call it Bowden wire[2]. The words 'Bowden Control' applied by both the plaintiffs and the defendants in advertisements for their goods, simply indicated a system of using Bowden wire. They indicated nothing about the origin of the goods save that during the continuance of the patent, the wire would have had to be of the plaintiff's manufacture. The problem was that there was nothing about the use of the mark which ensured that the goods were in some way those of the plaintiff[3]. Indeed it would appear that at the relevant time the terms 'Bowden wire' or 'Bowden cable' had become purely descriptive[4]. By contrast, in the *Manus* case, goodwill attached to the mark, and the goods bearing the mark were associated with the plaintiffs. Nothing in the licensing agreement was calculated to destroy that association: the goods had to be manufactured according to the plaintiffs' patented design and the word 'Manus' applied to them. Section 62 of the 1938 Act expressly provides that the use of a mark in relation to goods shall not be deemed likely to cause deception or confusion on the ground only that a different form of connection in the course of a trade now exists between the proprietor and the goods, than existed formerly. At all events, although it may well be that *Bowden* is still to be regarded as correct on its own facts, the licensing of unregistered users of registered marks[5] has been repeatedly recognised by the courts in cases subsequent to *Manus*. In the well known *Bostitch* case[6] Lloyd-Jacob J observed:

'[A proprietor's] mark only becomes vulnerable . . . if he permits its use in a manner which is calculated to deceive or cause confusion. The test of his actions is in consequence this: has he authorised such use of the mark as to deprive it of its very reason of existence, namely, as a mark which should distinguish his goods from the goods of other makers?'[7]

1   (1913) 30 RPC 609.
2   Ibid at 617–618
3   See 1905 Act, s 3, para 1.07; ante
4   See (1913) 30 RPC 609. In the same way as eg 'lino'. See *Linoleum Manufacturing Co v Nairn* (1878) 7 Ch D 834.
5   As to the licensing of unregistered marks, see para 1.22, post.
6   *Bostitch Trade Mark* [1963] RPC 183.
7   Ibid, at 197.

1.12 *Franchising as a legal concept*

1.12 In the *Bostitch* case itself, the proprietors had in general only authorised the manufacture of machines from essential components supplied by themselves, only the non-essential components were to come from other sources. Furthermore, in supplying all the relevant working drawings, manufacturing and assembly data and specimen components for reproduction it was held that Bostitch were imposing their identity upon the articles produced therefrom. The controls contained in the authorisation were more rigorous than those in the *Manus* case[1], where the licence merely provided for the manufacture of the machines in accordance with the patent and the affixing thereto of the mark, 'Manus'.

1 [1949] Ch 208, 66 RPC 71, CA.

1.13 What licensing of marks is permissible, and what is not, must now be considered in the light of *Holly Hobbie Trade Mark*[1]. The appellants in that case, the American Greetings Corporation, neither used nor intended to use the *relevant* marks themselves[2]. Accordingly, they accompanied their applications with registered user agreements under section 29(1)(b). Each such agreement contained comprehensive quality control provisions. It was held that the character merchandising[3] activities of the appellants amounted to 'trafficking' within the meaning of section 28(6), that is, dealing in the trade mark as a commodity in its own right and not primarily for the purpose of identifying or promoting merchandise in which the proprietor of the mark was interested. Mere ability to control quality was not enough to establish the necessary 'connection in the course of trade' required by the Act. Lord Brightman, cited Lord Loreburn's dictum in *Bowden Wire*[4]:

> 'The object of the law is to preserve for a trader the reputation he has made for himself, not to help him in disposing of that reputation as of itself a marketable commodity, independent of his goodwill, to some other trader. If that were allowed, the public would be misled, because they might buy something in the belief that it was the make of man whose reputation they knew, whereas it was the make of someone else . . . In this case the appellants parcelled out the right to use their trade mark as if they had been dealing with a patent.'

Lord Brightman went on to deal with the introduction of registered users following the Goschen Committee's recommendations[5]. He was prepared to accept that character merchandising has become a widespread trading practice, and might well be perfectly harmless in that it deceives nobody. Nevertheless, he held that the merchandising activities of the appellants amounted to 'trafficking' and registration of their marks must accordingly be refused. What then are the implications of this decision for franchising?

1 [1984] RPC 329.
2 They did however themselves use the mark on other goods, and separate applications under s 17 in respect of these succeeded.
3 'Character merchandising' is the use in marketing or advertising of goods of a fictional personality or situation eg Mickey Mouse, Batman. 'Personality merchandising' involves the true identity of an individual eg a tennis player or pop star. The distinction is crucially important for legal purposes, though in reality some might say that in the case of some personalities the distinction between fiction and real life is somewhat blurred. Character merchandising is dealt with at para 3.09, post.
4 Para 1.08, ante.
5 [1984] RPC 329 at 356.

The licence of the mark, trade name, etc and the goodwill of the business 1.16

1.14 In the first place, it is important to remember that the *Holly Hobbie* case was concerned with the registrability of marks and the interpretation of certain statutory provisions relevant to this. It was not concerned with unregistered marks to which the registered user provisions of the 1938 Act do not of course apply. The position in relation to unregistered marks is considered later[1]. In relation to registered marks, it is obvious that licensing is permissible provided the proprietor's activities do not amount to 'trafficking'.

Lord Brightman in *Holly Hobbie* did not deal with franchising as such. He did say that no difficulty would have arisen in respect of goods which the appellants themselves manufactured or bought in the market[2], and as noted above[3], the appellants did succeed in registering marks in respect of such goods. Most franchisors do trade themselves through company owned outlets, and to this extent would clearly be entitled to register trade marks. Would their franchising activities endanger these registrations? Almost certainly not. Although the question was not discussed in the House of Lords, in the Court of Appeal Dillon LJ said[4] that an instance where the granting of a registered user's licence would be convenient and proper would be 'where a proprietor grants franchises to local distributors to market the proprietor's goods under the proprietor's mark or to make up and market under the mark goods according to the proprietor's formula or patent'. This dictum clearly embraces both distribution and manufacturing franchises, and in relation to these because in franchising the control involved in the continuing relationship between the parties is absolutely crucial, and it may be asserted with confidence that the connection in the course of a trade between the owner of the mark, the franchisor, and the goods will be preserved, and consequently the goodwill associated with the mark. Indeed it may be suggested that franchising (in the sense in which this word is used in this book) represents an ideal in the way of quality control, to be aimed at in *all* trade marks licensing[5]. To put it another way, if marks are endangered by franchising, it is difficult to see what licensing would be permissible.

1 Para 3.52, post.
2 [1984] RPC 329 at 351.
3 Para 1.13, n 2, ante.
4 [1984] RPC 329 at 343.
5 This view is supported by *Michaels on Trade Marks* (1982) (ESC) 5.4.

Registered service marks and licensing

1.15 Up to this point we have discussed the problem of trade mark licensing, because historically in the United Kingdom marks were only registrable in respect of goods. The Trade Marks (Amendment) Act 1984 has introduced service mark registration. The Act came into operation on 1 October 1986—a much overdue reform. We must accordingly now extend the discussion to service marks. Since the difference between goods and services from an economic point of view, involves special problems in relation to licensing, it is necessary at this point to consider this.

1.16 From an economic point of view, goods franchises can be divided into three types:
 (1) those where the franchisee distributes goods made and marked by or for the franchisor—the ordinary distributorship but with the additional controls characteristic of business format franchising;

1.17 *Franchising as a legal concept*

(2) those where the franchisee manufactures the goods under licence—similar to an ordinary manufacturing licence, but again with the additional controls associated with business format franchising;

(3) those which deal in goods made and marked by other people with their own marks, eg sports shoes. In this case, although it might be thought that the dominant element was the retail services provided by the shop, in practice, shops register in respect of goods, and apply their marks to such items as the bags used to carry away the goods. In point of fact the International Classification makes no express provision for marks in respect of retail services, and presumably this practice will continue in view of the decision in *Re Dee Corpn*[1].

1 [1989] FSR 266—see para 3.24.

1.17 The feature which is common to all service franchises is that there is only one market level: the distribution level. With the qualification that there is only one market level possible, the closest analogy to service franchises is manufacturing franchises. The *Holly Hobbie* decision is relevant to the meaning of 'trafficking' generally, but the way in which it is to be applied to service mark licensing is not altogether clear. The trafficking objection arguably has less force here because in the nature of things, the product is inevitably furnished to the public by the licensee, and the quality control provisions therefore are the *only* connection in the course of a business which *can* exist between the proprietor and the services. It is also arguable that the words 'course of business' which is the expression used in section 68 in relation to services, implies something different from 'connection in the course of trade' which is the expression used in the definition of marks used in relation to goods. On the other hand, the analogy of manufacturing licences is not inappropriate, if we regard the services as products. On this view, *Holly Hobbie* (which itself involved manufacturing licences) would be applicable to service franchises. It seems reasonably clear however, that even on this view, as with true goods franchising, *Holly Hobbie* should not cause difficulty for true service franchising.

1.18 The registered user provisions are applied to service marks by the Trade Marks (Amendment) Act 1984. Section 28(1) is amended to read:

'28(1) Subject to the provisions of this section, a person other than the proprietor of a service mark[1] may be registered as a registered user thereof in respect of all or any of the services in respect of which it is registered and either with or without conditions or restrictions.

The use of a service mark[1] by a registered user thereof in relation to services with the provision of which he is connected in the course of business and in respect of which for the time being the *mark* remains registered and he is registered as a registered user, being use such as to comply with any conditions or restrictions to which his registration is subject, is in this Act referred to as the "permitted use" thereof.'

1 Substituted by the Patents, Designs and Marks Act 1986.

1.19 For the same reasons that we argued that franchising represents the ideal to be aimed at in the way of quality control in relation to trade mark licensing, it can be argued that it represents the ideal in relation to service mark licensing.

The licence of the mark, trade name, etc and the goodwill of the business 1.22

If the franchising of service marks endangers them, it is difficult to see what licensing would be permissible.

Sub-licensing of registered trade marks and service marks

1.20 The situation frequently arises, especially where an overseas franchisor is proposing to enter the United Kingdom market through a master franchisor, that the franchisor is not the proprietor of the relevant marks. In this circumstance it is frequently proposed that the franchisor should become the licensee of the marks and should grant sub-licences to his franchisees. This arrangement must be avoided at all costs. In the first place, because there is no privity of contract between the proprietor and the franchisees, the proprietor has no direct way of enforcing quality control terms against them[1]. Whilst in a direct licence it is probably unobjectionable that quality supervision is delegated to third parties[2], because in that situation there is a possibility of direct action against a licensee who fails to meet his obligations, in the case of sub-licensees there is not this possibility. For this reason, apart from anything else, the proprietor could expose himself to the argument that he is 'trafficking' in his marks as defined in *Holly Hobbie*[3]. Moreover, it is certainly arguable that section 28(12) which provides that 'Nothing in this section shall confer on a registered user of a mark any assignable or transmissible right to the use thereof' has a public interest aspect, and is not simply there for the protection of registered proprietors[4].

1 For those having to pick up the pieces when an operation has been set up on this basis (unfortunately not unknown), a 'long shot' argument might be that the whole arrangement constitutes a 'network contract', in relation to which the priority doctrine does not apply—see Adams and Brownsword *Privity and the Concept of a Network Contract* [1990] Legal Studies 12—and at para 1.63.
2 See *Molyslip Trade Mark* [1978] RPC 211 at 219.
3 [1984] RPC 329 at 356–357.
4 See Registrar's decision in *Holly Hobbie*.

How to avoid the need to sub-licence

1.21 In order to avoid the need for the franchisor to sub-license to his franchisees, two alternative strategies may be adopted. In the first place, the franchisor can become proprietor of the United Kingdom marks. This strategy could be appropriate where the franchisor is a wholly owned subsidiary of an overseas franchising company[1]. The alternative course is for the franchisor to be appointed agent by the proprietor of the marks, for the purpose of negotiating and granting licences of them. This latter strategy would also be appropriate where the United Kingdom franchisor is dealing with the proprietor of the marks at arm's length[2].

1 But it is a dangerous strategy otherwise—see *Diehl KG's Application* [1969] 3 All ER 338, [1970] RPC 435. Compare however, *Karo Stap Trade Mark* [1977] RPC 255.
2 See Precedent 18.

The licensing of unregistered marks, trade names etc

1.22 Section 22(1) of the Trade Marks Act 1938, which makes marks assignable and transmissible either in connection with the course of a business or not, applies only to registered marks. Unregistered marks can be assigned only with the goodwill

1.23 *Franchising as a legal concept*

of a business[1] or with a registered mark used in the same business (s 22(2)). The principal source of protection for unregistered marks is the action for passing off. A key requirement for the success of a plaintiff in a passing off action is that there is goodwill attaching to his mark or name which the defendant's misrepresentation is calculated to damage[2]. Consequently, for a franchisor who is licensing an unregistered name or mark[3], the question of ownership of the goodwill generated by the franchisees is crucial. If the goodwill were to accrue to the franchisees alone, the protection of passing off would be available to the franchisees, but not to the franchisor. We will now attempt to analyse the problem of ownership of the goodwill on the basis of the little authority which exists.

1   *Star Industrial Co Ltd v Yap Kwee Kor (a New Star Industrial Co)* [1976] FSR 256, PC. See also *Boot Tree Ltd v Robinson* [1984] FSR 545.
2   *Erven Warnink BV v J Townend & Sons (Hull) Ltd* [1979] AC 731, [1980] RPC 31 at 85, HL—see para 3.53, post.
3   After the introduction of the registration of service marks, fewer marks will need to remain unregistered. However, there are always likely to be some marks which for one reason or another are not registered.

1.23 The goodwill associated with the trade name and marks (registered and unregistered), etc is built up by the franchisor *and* the individual franchisees. If a licensor did not monitor quality, and a licensee built up a reputation in the mark by controlling quality, it would be unfair that the licensee who had built up the goodwill associated with the mark should see it transfer to the licensor at the end of the licence. The same thing would apply to other distinctive insignia which fulfil similar functions to trade marks and are protected by copyright, etc. In the case of franchising however where the franchisor fulfils a central role in building up the goodwill by controlling all his franchisees, there would not appear to be this objection. On the contrary, it seems reasonably clear that for this reason the goodwill accrues to the franchisor[1]. In order to illustrate this, let us suppose for the sake of argument that a chain were to be started involving no true intellectual property rights at all, but merely a trade name, ie at the outset there is no real licence because there is nothing to licence[2]. The chain prospers. To the public it is not a collection of separate businesses, but a single business providing a uniform product. It is the *control* exercised by the franchisor which ensures that uniformity. Consequently it would appear that to the extent that goodwill in this way is built up and associated with the name of the franchisor, it belongs to the franchisor, and to that extent the name becomes the property of the franchisor vis-à-vis the franchisees. The franchisees will each have particular goodwills attaching to their outlets of course of which they can dispose, subject to the terms of the agreement[3]. Were we to take the view that the goodwill in the name accrued to the franchisees there would be nothing to stop them from terminating their 'licences' and continuing to carry on business under the name: the 'licence' being no licence at all. The obligation that the 'franchisees' follow the 'franchisor's' procedures would also then cease. Indeed the whole agreement could be void for want of consideration on the part of the franchisor, unless the business advice provided by the franchisor were construed to be the consideration—an interpretation which in effect reduces the transaction to a sort of business consultancy which could be terminated anyway subject to the payment of compensation. Were that to happen the control over quality which was the public's safeguard would disappear. There would exist simply a chain of separate businesses, each operating under the same name[4], but doing as they liked with resulting confusion for the public. Consequently, so long as

The licence of the mark, trade name, etc and the goodwill of the business 1.25

it can be shown that the franchisor's control is a crucial element in preserving the uniformity of product offered by the chain, the goodwill which is the subject of existing and future licences of the name should, it is submitted, belong to the franchisor. What applies to a business name simpliciter applies also where a bundle of property rights including trade marks is licensed.

1   *Children's Television Workshop Inc v Woolworths (NSW) Ltd* [1981] RPC 187.
2   See eg *Fine Cotton Spinners and Doublers' Association Ltd and John Cash & Sons Ltd v Harwood Cash & Co Ltd* [1907] 2 Ch 184 at 190; *Kingston, Miller & Co Ltd v Kingston & Co Ltd* [1912] 1 Ch 575.
3   See Precedent 1 clause 10.4, post.
4   Each presumably able to maintain a separate passing off action—see eg *Dent v Turpin* (1861) 2 John & H 139.

1.24 This view, that the goodwill generated by the franchise business as a whole accrues to the franchisor, even in the absence of a provision in the agreement requiring the franchise to hold goodwill generated on trust for the franchisor[1] gains support from the Privy Council decision in *J H Coles Pty Ltd v Need*[2]. In that case the appellant carried on business under the trade name of 'J H Coles 3d 6d and 1s Stores'. It entered into an agreement whereby the respondent would at his own expense open up a shop under the same style, and purchase the stock from the appellants. The licence was later terminated, but the respondent continued to do business under the same style. It was held that the trade names were still distinctive of the licensor, and the respondent might therefore be restrained from using them. Although in this case the franchisor initially had goodwill in the name and clearly therefore had something to licence, it is significant that the Privy Council do not seem to have thought that the effect of the licence was to fragment that goodwill. A reasonable explanation is that because the licensee was required to purchase his stock from the licensor, the licensor controlled quality. The goods emanated from the licensor, as much as they did when sold in the licensor's own shops[3].

1   See para 1.25.
2   [1934] AC 82, 50 RPC 379 (Aust). See also *North Shore Toy Co v Stevenson* [1974] RPC 545 (NZ) and *Karo Step Trade Mark* [1977] RPC 255 distinguishing *Diehl KG's Application* [1969] 3 All ER 338, [1970] RPC 435. The result in the *Diehl* case seems to have turned on the peculiar circumstances of the trade mark registration, for a UK distributor of a German company's goods was allowed initially to register the German company's mark in the UK. The court refused to exercise its discretion under Trade Marks Act 1938, s 32 to substitute the German company at a later date.
3   [1934] AC 82 at 89, 50 RPC 379 at 387, 388, per L Wright. The fact that the licensee had been obliged to buy elsewhere because of the licensor's inability to supply did not affect the position on the facts.

1.25 Usually a clause is inserted in the franchise agreement under which the goodwill is held in trust for the franchisor. There would appear to be no difficulty with the concept of a trust of goodwill[1] nor where there is a master franchisee with a clause in the master franchise agreement whereby the master franchisee holds such goodwill in trust for the ultimate franchisor: you can have a trust of a trust[2].

1   *Scott on Trusts* (4th edn) 82.4
2   *Grainge v Wilberforce* (1889) 5 TLR 436, 437 per Chitty J; *Grey v IRC* [1958] Ch 375, 382 for Upjohn J. Arguably in such a case the 'middle men' would 'drop out' leaving the fiduciary relationship between the franchisees and the ultimate franchisors under the rule in *Saunders v Vautier* (1841) 4 Beav 115. The ultimate franchisor ought to be able to obtain a

1.26 Franchising as a legal concept

declaration that the goodwill is vested in it. These clauses are inserted *ex abundanti cautela:* if the argument set out above is correct, there is nothing to hold in trust, but if goodwill accrues to the franchisee, there is. The separate goodwill of the outlet benefits the franchisee on disposal—see Precedent 1 clause 10.4.

Conclusion

1.26 We have felt obliged to deal with the problems of licensing registered and unregistered marks and trade names at some length, because there intellectual properties lie at the heart of franchising. As we have said, franchising ought to represent the ideal in permissible licensing. The fact that any uncertainties persist in this regard, is an unfortunate product of the survival of outmoded concepts. As in so many things, we seem to have been unnecessarily conservative in our approach to marks, and have created problems where none need have existed had we been more prepared to revise our concepts about the way in which marks in fact function in the modern world. A good summary of the function of trade marks law today was provided by Senator Pepper, the Chairman of the Senate Subcommittee reporting on the Lanham Bill[1]. He said that a mark protects the public so that in purchasing a product bearing the mark it will get the product it asks for and wants; and second, where the owner of the mark has spent energy, time and money in presenting the product to the public, he is protected in his investment from its misappropriation by pirates and cheats[2]. The emphasis placed by the Senator on the protection of the public is, it is submitted, very proper, and in the case of well run franchises, the marks do ensure that the public gets the products it wants.

1   The Lanham Act is the basis of United States trade marks law—15 USCA, §§1051 et seq.
2   The definition of trade mark actually contained in the Lanham Act seems to reflect an older view, §1127 ' . . . any word, name, symbol or device or any combination thereof adopted or used by a merchant to identify his goods and distinguish them from those manufactured or sold by others'.

1.27 To summarise our position on this important question, in *Stringfellows*[1] it was argued, citing *Star Industrial v Yap Kwee Kor*[2], that in absence of a registered mark, the licensing of marks was not possible. Two questions were confused here, can you licence? And, can you assign?

(1) You cannot *assign* in gross, because without goodwill, you cannot sue in passing off.

(2) You can license, because a licence is simply a permission to do that which is unlawful—*Federal Comr of Taxation v United Aircraft Corpn*[3].

(3) The crucial question is: to whom does the goodwill accrue if an unregistered mark is licensed?

    (a) There is a 'trust of goodwill' clause:
       (i) Goodwill can be held on trust[4].
       (ii) Where there is a master agreement, a trust upon a trust, benefiting the ultimate franchisor via the master franchisor, is possible[5]. Under the rule in *Saunders v Vautier*[6] the master franchisor ought to be able to obtain a declaration that the goodwill is vested in it[7].
    (b) There is no such clause: in this case, the exercise of proper quality control by the franchisor would itself appear to ensure that it accrues to the franchisor[8].

If the licensing of unregistered marks is not possible, violence would therefore be done to basic property concepts.

(4) There is nothing problematic at the present day in the franchising context about the licensing of trade marks or other insignia which function in the same way to distinguish the franchise chain from competitors, since the control exercised by the franchisor serves to preserve the necessary 'connection in the course of trade' between him and the mark, etc.

(5) That control serves to ensure that the goodwill in the marks, etc accrues to the franchisor and not to the individual franchisees.

1 [1984] RPC 501.
2 [1976] FSR 256.
3 (1943) 68 CLR 525.
4 *Scott on Trusts* (4th edn) para 82.4.
5 *Grainge v Wilberforce* (1889) 5 TLR 436; *Grey v IRC* [1958] Ch 375.
6 (1841) 4 Beav 115.
7 See *Grainge v Wilberforce* (1889) 5 TLR 436 at 437.
8 *Children's Television Workshop Inc v Woolworths ('Muppets')* [1981] RPC 187; *J H Coles v Need* [1934] AC 82. Also *North Shore Toy Co v Stevenson* [1974] RPC 545; *Karo Step Trade Mark* [1977] RPC 255.

The franchisor's liability for the acts and defaults of his franchisees

Introduction

1.28 Franchising, as we have said, bears a double aspect. From the point of view of the parties themselves, the chain consists of independent businesses. From the point of view of third parties, however, there is only one business with a number of outlets. Each franchisee owes to the public the normal duty of care imposed by law, as well as the duties imposed by his contracts with his customers. The franchisor also owes both the franchisee and members of the public a duty of care[1]. A further and interesting question is, however, whether in the absence of negligence on his own part, the franchisor could be held liable for the acts and defaults of his franchisee[2]—especially in contract, which is a risk the franchisor may not readily be able to cover by insurance. This is a question of some difficulty.

1 See para 5.49, post.
2 Atiyah *Vicarious Liability* (1967) (Butterworths) Chs I and II.

1.29 It is argued in the following sections that the franchisor could in such a case be held liable to third parties. The argument focuses on the essentially distinctive features of a franchise operation, namely, the control exercised by the franchisor over the franchisee, and the impression cultivated in the mind of the public that the chain is one business. The traditional jurisprudential categories under which for these purposes the relationship of the parties might be categorised are: (1) master and servant; (2) principal and agent; and (3) independent contractors. However, it cannot be overemphasised that franchising is a comparatively recent phenomenon, and we would argue that such a novel relationship needs a novel approach. One of the underlying reasons traditionally given for imposing vicarious liability on a master for a servant's act is the control exercised by the master over the servant[1]. A further reason is the tendency of the public to identify employees with their employers[1]—liability under the doctrine of agency by estoppel is justified by a similar

1.30 Franchising as a legal concept

principle. In the case of a true agency, so far as the question of a principal's liability to third parties for acts of an agent done in the course of his employment is concerned, it is by no means clear what the difference is between an agent and a servant[2]. It is submitted that the control exercised by a franchisor over a franchisee, and the impression cultivated in the minds of the public that the operation is one business, could justify the franchisor being held liable to third parties as a consequence of the franchisee's acts, *independently of how the relationship of the franchisor and franchisee inter se is characterised*. Indeed, the peculiar nature of franchising *requires* that the question of the franchisor's liability to third parties be treated separately from the question of how we characterise the relationship of the parties inter se. Consequently, although in the following sections the question of the franchisor's liability to third parties is considered under the traditional heads of master and servant, and principal and agent, this scheme is adopted principally to demonstrate that there may be drawn from each of these areas of law, grounds for holding the franchisor liable to third parties for acts and defaults of the franchisee. The question of the nature of the relationship of the parties inter se is considered in para 1.57, post.

1 Atiyah *Vicarious Liability* (1967) (Butterworths) Chs I and II.
2 See *Bowstead on Agency* (15th edn, 1985) (Sweet and Maxwell), pp 18–19.

Vicarious liability

1.30 For the purposes of determining the question of liability to third parties, the relationship between an individual franchisee and the franchisor could conceivably be treated as analogous to that of master and servant. Whilst obviously the relationship between a franchisee and the franchisor cannot literally be so characterised, it is submitted that the same sorts of considerations which have imposed vicarious liability on a master could nevertheless apply.

In the case of an individual franchisee, if the relationship between the parties were in fact that of master and servant, a number of important consequences would in fact follow: not only would the franchisor be liable vicariously to third parties, but the law of master and servant would regulate the relationship of the parties inter se and their liability to pay tax and National Insurance contributions would be affected. In English law, however, the relationship of the parties *inter se* almost certainly is not that of master and servant[1]. If it were, that would of course settle the question of vicarious liability. The fact that they are not master and servant inter se does not, however, necessarily mean that the franchisor might not be held vicariously liable for the acts and defaults of his franchisees.

1 See para. 1.57, post.

The confusion between vicarious liability and agency liability

1.31 In principle, 'the dichotomy of servants and independent contractors is based on the degree of control exercised by the master or employer, and is principally relevant to determine his liability for torts of physical damage to person and property caused by others. The terminology of agency is based on the idea that one person may be bound by acts which he has authorised another to do, and is principally relevant to contract and the disposition of property, though it is sometimes used in analysing tort situations and has many other applications in the law'[1]. In practice, vicarious liability and liability under agency law tend to become confused. Indeed, in many cases, the terminology tends to be used interchangeably. In America in fact the law of agency and the law of master and servant have tended to merge[2]. In discussing liability to third parties, English courts have held that in determining the liability of a master for his servant and a principal for his agent, the test is the same, ie whether the servant or agent was acting within the scope of the authority conferred by the master or principal[3]. Furthermore, it is certainly arguable that to some extent vicarious liability is justified by the same considerations which underlie agency by estoppel and ostensible authority, ie the expectations which might reasonably be aroused in the minds of third parties. Professor Atiyah writes, 'There can be little doubt that the man in the street tends to personify a group of this kind [employees and company] which has an identifiable unity, and to think in terms of corporate liability . . . "they ought to pay"'[4]. Professor Glanville Williams similarly writes, 'There is no doubt that the notion of group unity is a powerful reason for general acceptance of vicarious liability'.[5] The idea that vicarious liability may in part be based on a similar principle to agency by estoppel seems reasonable[5]. However, it is also clearly based on other principles: you do not have to know that the van which runs you over is driven by X's servant. The question of degree of control has traditionally been a part of the test for the existence of a master and servant relationship, and is also one of the justifications traditionally given for imposing vicarious liability[6]. Clearly the controls exercised by the franchisor over the franchisee could (all other things being equal) justify a court in holding the franchisor liable on grounds which could be independent of the fact that the idea is inducted in the minds of third parties, by virtue of those controls, that the operation is a unity. The question is, what sort of controls? Professor Atiyah[7] points out that an independent contractor is usually controlled only by specification: he will often be required to work to plans and supervised to ensure that he does so satisfactorily. It is controls which go further than this which give rise to vicarious liability. This test raises some nice questions in relation to franchising.

1 *Bowstead on Agency* (15th edn, 1985) (Sweet & Maxwell) p 386 et seq.
2 See Restatement Agency, §§1 and 2, Comments; 62 Am Jur 2d Private Franchise, §16.
3 *Heatons Transport (St Helens) Ltd v Transport and General Workers Union* [1973] AC 15, [1972] 3 All ER 101, HL. See also *Navarro v Moregrand Ltd* [1951] 2 TLR 674 at 690, CA, per Denning LJ.
4 *Vicarious Liability* (1967) (Butterworths) pp 19–20.
5 (1957) 20 MLR 234.
6 See Atiyah, op cit Chs 1 and 2.
7 Op cit p 42.

The American case law

1.32 Before we consider the few relevant English authorities, it is helpful to consider some of the American cases[1]. Sometimes in these cases the controls *as such* exercised by the franchisor over the franchisee seem to have been considered important[2], at other times it was the impression created in the mind of the third party that seems to have weighed most[3]. Examples of controls which seem of themselves to have been important in establishing liability are: regulation of the franchisee's hours of operation[4]; laying down methods for preparing or furnishing to the public the franchised goods or services going beyond mere specification[5]; the portions to be served[6]; detailed regulation of methods of operating; specifying the inventory to be carried[7]; and limiting the franchisee's choice of suppliers[8]. Other controls which

1.32 Franchising as a legal concept

have been held relevant in establishing liability have included the control over hiring and firing of staff; benefits; promotions; uniforms and training of the franchisee's employees; the prices charged to customers; record keeping and accounting methods; and right to inspect books and premises to check on compliance[9]. Control over all advertising by the franchisee, whether local or national, and requiring payments to be made to a national advertising fund have also been held relevant[10]. The right to control the location of the premises and their layout, decor and furnishings has also been held relevant[11]. Other matters taken into account have included termination provisions and the franchisor's broad discretionary powers over the franchisee[12]. It must be observed that many of these matters seem equally, or more relevant, to liability under some estoppel or holding out principle, but as we have observed above, the distinction between the two bases of liability is blurred. Others however do not seem particularly relevant to either head. Thus the duty of the franchisee to follow certain record keeping accounting procedures, and the franchisor's right to inspect books and premises to check on compliance, would simply seem to be an aspect of licensing arrangements generally. Types of controls which seem more particularly relevant to establishing some estoppel or holding out principle of liability on the part of the franchisor have included: requirements that the franchisee display particular signs[13]; requirements as to store appearance[14]; requirements as to packaging[15]; requirements as to employees' uniforms[16]. What these cases really underline is the fact that American courts have not generally attempted to step beyond the traditional categories of master and servant or principal and agent, and tried to analyse the true basis of a franchisor's liability to third parties.

1   See Borchard and Ehrlich 69 TMR 109 (1979); Behringer and Otte 19 Am Bus LJ 109 (1981); Kirkland 50 UNKCLR 241 (1982); Monica 49 Mo LR 309 (1984).
2   Eg *Northern v McGraw-Edison & Co* 542 F 2d 1336 (1976); *Drexel v Union Prescription Centers* 582 F 2d 781 (1978); *Ottermeyer v Baskin* 625 P 2d (1981). Compare *Coty v United States Slicing Machine Co* 373 NE 2d 1371 (1978); *Slates v International House of Pancakes* 413 NE 2d 457 (1980); *Quad-L v Tastee Freez* 528 NE 2d 1107 (1988).
3   *Singleton v International Dairy Queen* 332 A 2d 160 (1975); *Drexel v Union Prescription Centers* 582 F 2d 781 (1978). *Chevron Oil v Sutton* 515 P 2d 1283 (1973).
4   Eg *Dorsic v Kirtin* 96 Cal Rptr 528 (1971).
5   Eg *Singleton*, ante; *Drexel*, ante.
6   Eg *Singleton*, ante.
7   Eg *Drexel*, ante.
8   Eg *Singleton*, ante. Compare *Stanford v Dairy Queen Products* 623 SW 2d 797 (1981); *Nelson v International Paint* 734 F 2d 1084 (1984); *Slates*, ante.
9   Eg *Nichols v Arthur Murray Inc* 56 Cal Rptr 728 (1967); *Singleton*, ante; *Drexel*, ante. Compare *Murphy v Holiday Inns* 219 SE 2d 874 (1975); *BP Oil v Mabe*, ante; *Coty*, ante; *Holiday Inns v Newton* 278 SE 2d 85 (1981).
10   Eg *Nichols v Arthur Murray Inc*, ante. Compare *Murphy v Holiday Inns*, ante.
11   Eg *Nichols v Arthur Murray Inc*, ante; *Billops v Magness Construction* 391 A 2d 196 (1978), ante; *Stanford*, ante.
12   Eg *Singleton*, ante; *Drexel*, ante; Compare *Murphy v Holiday Inns*, ante; *Marwell v Sheraton Inns* (1981) Bus Franchise Guide (CCH) P1 7626 at 12533; *Slates*, ante; *Stanford*, ante.
13   *Buchanan v Canada Dry* 226SE 2d 613 (1976); *Gizzi v Texaco* 437 F 2d 303 (1971); *Wood v Holiday Inns*, ante; *Drexel*, ante. Compare *Ortega v General Motors* 392 So 2d 40 at 44 (1980); *Stephens v Yamaha Motor Co* 627 P 2d 439 at 440 (1981); *Cullen v BMW* 531 F Supp 555 (1982).
14   *Drexel*, ante.
15   *Drexel*, ante; *Singleton*, ante.
16   *Chevron Oil*, ante; *Singleton*, ante.

1.33 Matters held relevant in establishing that the franchisor was not liable to a third party have included the fact that the franchisee received no salary or commission from the franchisor but paid only a rent computed by reference to sales of a tied product[1]; set his own prices[2]; retained profits from his franchise[3]; paid his own business expenses or taxes[4]; hired and fired his employees or controlled their wages and conditions of work[5]; received no reports from franchisees[5]; and finally that he set his own hours of operation[6]. The common knowledge that certain classes of trades are independent seems to have been relevant in some of the cases cited above involving petrol filling stations.

1 *BP Oil v Mabe* 370 A 2d 554 (1977).
2 *Beckham v Exxon Corpn* 539 SW 2d 217 (1976).
3 *BP Oil*, ante; *Beckham*, ante.
4 Ibid. This seems simply to beg the question.
5 *BP Oil*, ante; *Murphy v Holiday Inns* 219 SE 2d 874 (1975); *Ortega v General Motors* (above); *Slates v International House of Pancakes* 413 NE 2d 457 (1981).
6 *BP Oil*, ante.

The English case law

1.34 These lists derived from the American cases should not be used as checklists in drafting agreements. It is clear that English courts will always look at all the circumstances of the case. This is established by the case of *Ready Mixed Concrete (South East) v Minister of Pensions and National Insurance*[1], which is one of the few English cases having a bearing on the matter. Ready Mixed had entered into a type of franchise agreement for the delivery of their concrete in owner driven concrete mixer trucks bearing Ready Mixed's name. The contract declared that the owner driver of the trucks was an independent contractor, and that he would at his own expense carry concrete for the company is consideration of a payment at mileage rates. The vehicle which the driver was to make available to the company for this purpose was to be purchased by the driver and operated under the company's insignia (including a special driver's uniform). The driver had to obtain the necessary carrier's licence and to insure and maintain the vehicle at his own expense. The driver was restricted to carrying for the company and had to keep accounts in the manner approved by the company. It was held that the driver was not an 'employed person' within the National Insurance Act 1965, s 1(2). Mackenna J reached this conclusion on the basis that the declaration in the contract that the driver was an independent contractor was irrelevant. The inference was a conclusion of law based on the parties' respective rights and duties under the contract. A contract of service existed where: (1) the servant agreed to do work in consideration of a wage or other remuneration; (2) he agreed that he would be under the control of the other party sufficient to make him master; (3) the other provisions of the contract were consistent with its being a contract of service. The obligation to do work subject to the other party's control was not invariably a sufficient condition of a contract of service, if the other provisions of the contract were inconsistent with it being a contract of service, and that in this connection it was relevant to consider who owned the assets or bore the financial risk[2]. This approach has been approved in other cases[3]. In *Massey v Crown Life Insurance Co* Lord Denning MR expressed the view that where the situation is doubtful or ambiguous, it is open to the parties themselves to stipulate in the agreement what the relationship shall be[4]. Of course, the court may hold that the relationship is not doubtful or ambiguous and ignore whatever is stipulated in the contract.

1.35 Franchising as a legal concept

1 [1968] 2 QB 497, [1968] 1 All ER 433.
2 This follows dicta of L Wright in *Montreal v Montreal Locomotive Works Ltd* [1947] 1 DLR 161 at 170.
3 *Ready Mixed Concrete (London) Ltd v Cox* (1971) 10 KIR 273; *Ferguson v John Dawson & Partners (Contractors) Ltd* [1976] 3 All ER 817, [1976] 1 WLR 1213, CA; *Davis v New England College of Arundel* [1977] ICR 6, EAT; *Massey v Crown Life Insurance Co* [1978] 2 All ER 576, [1978] 1 WLR 676, CA.
4 *Massey v Crown Life Insurance Co* [1978] 1 WLR 676 at 680. See also per Lawton LJ at 682.

1.35 Although the *Ready Mixed* case is a useful authority on the question of the relationship of the parties inter se, it is submitted that it ought not to be relied on on the question of vicarious liability. Neither it, nor any of the cases approving it, involved this issue. In *Ready Mixed Concrete (London) Ltd v Cox*[1] it is true that a third party was involved, but the issue was whether or not under the Trade Disputes Act 1906 a trade union could claim immunity from liability it would otherwise have incurred. On the question of vicarious liability, the incidence of financial risk which was thought relevant in *Ready Mixed Concrete (South East) Ltd v Minister of Pensions and National Insurance* in establishing that the parties were not master and servant, could be used along with other factors to justify the imposition of liability to third parties on the franchisor. It has been argued above, that the franchisee's risk of his capital is in part a control device. It helps to ensure that the franchisee will use his best endeavours and will conform to 'the method'[2] in circumstances where his conduct would be difficult to monitor. In this regard it is simply one of the devices (and an important one) designed to preserve the quality of service by which the goodwill of the operation is built up. As suggested above[3], if it were a mere capital raising device, the franchisor and franchisee would arguably either prefer to sell and buy shares in the whole chain, or alternatively, as in the case of dealerships, the franchisor would not bother to exercise much in the way of continuing control over the franchisees beyond monitoring their performance.

1 (1971) 10 KIR 273.
2 As to which, see para 0.12.
3 Para 0.12.

How are English courts likely to approach the question?

1.36 It is difficult to predict how a court will approach the matter. It might be that the court, while prepared to hold a franchisor liable to a third party, would wish to lay down criteria which would serve to distinguish ordinary trade marks licences and the like in order to make it clear that in such cases there is no question of vicarious liability on the part of the licensor to third parties. It might in this respect wish to make a distinction between controls always necessary to preserve the goodwill associated with a mark, and those which go further[1]. The American case of *Nichols v Arthur Murray Inc*[2] provides an illustration of this approach[3]. Under the agreement in this case, the franchisor exercised the following controls: the right to control the employment of all personnel of the franchisee; the right to fix the minimum tuition rates to be charged; the right to designate the location of each dance studio and its decor and layout; the right to pay off all complaints made by third parties against the enterprise and recover indemnity therefore from the franchisee; and the right to require the franchisee to honour unused dance lessons purchased from other franchisees. It was considered that many of the controls (the judge did not specify which, but presumably he was not simply referring to the accounting provisions) were not related to the protection of the trade name, and the relation of principal and agent was held to exist. The problem with this approach is that it is difficult to make a rational distinction between the two: the controls exercised by the franchisor over the franchisee in general are designed to preserve and enhance the goodwill associated with the mark.

1   On the other hand, in the United States at any rate, there is something of a trend towards holding trade mark licensors liable also—see Germain 'Tort Liability of Trademark Licensors' 69 TMR 128 (1979) (and note Consumer Protection Act 1987, s 2(2)(b)).
2   248 Cal App 2d 610 (1967), 56 Cal Rptr 728.
3   See also *Murphy v Holiday Inns* 219 SE 2d 874 (1975); *Oberlin v Marlin American Corpn* 596 F 2d 1322 (1979). For a critique of this approach see Monica 49 Mo LR 309, 317 (1984).

1.37   A court might also wish to lay down criteria which would distinguish the traditional tied public-house arrangement, or 'solus' filling station agreement. It might do this by drawing a distinction based on the fact that these frequently involve leases: the relationship of the parties is landlord and tenant[1]. It is submitted that this approach would be mistaken. The relationship of landlord and tenant does not preclude the existence of a master and servant relationship, and it could draw a somewhat arbitrary distinction between franchisors who lease premises from their franchisors and those who do not. It would be better to draw a distinction based on the fact that in the case of these older arrangements, the nature of the relationship is well known[2].

1   See *BP Oil v Mabe* 370 A 2d 554 (1977). In this country, the licensing of petrol stations is also common—see *Shell-Mex and BP Ltd v Manchester Garages Ltd* [1971] 1 All ER 841.
2   See para 1.33, ante.

1.38   It is quite possible that the franchisor could be held liable to third parties under the principles of agency law. Two possibilities need to be considered: first of all agency by estoppel or holding out; second the possibility that a true agency, a partnership, exists between the parties.

Agency by estoppel or holding out

1.39   Although the franchise agreement is likely to contain a term providing that the franchisee is not the franchisor's agent, the franchisor may nevertheless become liable in contract to third parties under the so-called 'agency by estoppel'[1] principle: 'where a person, by words or conduct, represents or permits it to be represented that another person is his agent, he will not be permitted to deny the agency, with respect to anyone dealing, on the faith of such representation, with the person so held out as agent, even if the relationship of principal and agent has not arisen . . .'[2].

1   This term is somewhat controversial—see Stoljar *Law of Agency* (1961) (Sweet and Maxwell) Chs 2 and 3 et seq.
2   *Bowstead on Agency* (15th edn, 1985) (Sweet and Maxwell), p 90.

1.40   The crucial question is, what is sufficient to amount to such a representation? Most cases in English law have been concerned with apparent, or ostensible, authority, ie cases where the agency already had *some* authority and acts by the

1.41 Franchising as a legal concept

agent outside that authority have been held to bind the principal. The principles applicable in both cases appear to be the same[1]. The existence of types of 'franchise' operations where franchisors have not in the past been thought to be liable to third parties in relation to filling stations or tenanted public-houses, is not a real safeguard for new operations in other fields. Those older operations could be treated as special cases depending on general public knowledge as to what they are[2]. This certainly has been the view of some American courts in the case of gasoline stations[3].

1 *Bowstead* loc cit. This is different from the view expressed in Restatement 2d Agency, §8, Comment d where agency by estoppel is treated as essentially a principle of the law of torts. See also ibid §§8B and 141.
2 See, eg *Esso Petroleum Co Ltd v Harper's Garage (Stourport) Ltd* [1967] 1 All ER 699 at 730–731, per Wilberforce L. See also para 1.33, ante.
3 *Reynolds v Skelly Oil Co* 287 NW 823 (1939); *Cawthorn v Philips Petroleum* 124 So 2d 517 (1960); *Sherman v Texas Oil Co* 165 NE 2d 916 (1960); *Coe v Esau* 377 P 2d 815 (1963); *Shaver v Bell* 397 P 2d 723 (1964); *Westre v De Buhr* 144 NW 2d 734 (1966): *Apple v Standard Oil* 307 F Supp 107 (1969); *Elkins v Husky Oil Co* 455 P 2d 329 (1969).

1.41 It is possible that the franchisor might be held liable simply by virtue of the fact that he allows a name associated with him to be used as the name of the franchised business. In this respect the question is the same as in the case of partnership by holding out[1]. As Eyre CJ observed in the old case of *Waugh v Carver*[2] 'if [a man] will lend his name as a partner, he becomes, as against all the rest of the world, a partner, not upon the ground of the *real* transaction between them, but upon principles of general policy, to prevent frauds to which creditors would be liable' [emphasis added]. The fact that the losses of a business may be borne by another is quite immaterial if the lending by a party of a name justifies the belief that he is willing to be responsible to those who may be induced to trust him for payment[3].

1 See Partnership Act 1890, s 14(1). The question as to whether or not the relationship could be a true partnership and thus the normal partner's agency under section 5 of the Act exist, is considered in para 1.48, post.
2 (1793) 2 Hy Bl 235.
3 *Lindley on Partnership* (15th edn, 1984) (Sweet and Maxwell) p 112 et seq.

1.42 The heart of the matter is the expectation aroused in the minds of third parties, and it is quite reasonable for third parties to assume that by virtue of the fact that advertising, notepaper, billheads, etc all carry a name associated with the franchisor, they are dealing with a single entity: the franchisor. Such reliance is obviously capable of making the franchisor liable in contract as well as in tort. There appear to be no relevant English authorities. In the United States some courts have in fact taken the view that the carrying on of a business under the name and insignia of another could be sufficient to fix that other with liability[1]. Other courts have taken the view that something more is required[2]. If any general conclusion may be drawn it is that in the cases involving gasoline stations where the nature of the relationship of the parties is fairly well known, the courts tend to require more than mere use of name and insignia. In cases where the true nature of the enterprise with which the third party dealt was not a matter the third party could reasonably be supposed to know, use of a name and insignia alone might be sufficient.

1 See para 1.32 ante, and especially *Fidelman-Danziger v Statler Management* 136 A 2d 119 (1957); *Beck v Arthur Murray* 54 Cal Rptr 328 (1966); *Gizzi v Texaco* 437 F 2d 303 (1971); *Kuchta v Allied Builders* 98 Cal Rptr 588 (1971); *Singleton v International Dairy Queen* 332 A

The franchisor's liability for the acts and defaults of his franchisees 1.46

2d 160 (1975); *Buchanan v Canada Dry* 226 SE 2d 613 (1976); *Billops v Magness Construction* 391 A 2d 196 (1978).
2 Eg *Sherman v Texas Oil Co* 165 NE 2d 916 (1960); *Coe v Esau* 377 P 2d 815 (1963); *Crittendon v State Oil* 222 NE 2d 561 (1966); *Apple v Standard Oil* 307 F Supp 107 (1969); *Mabe v BP Oil* 356 A 2d 304 (1976).

1.43 It is possible though probably unlikely that English courts might be prepared to hold a franchisor liable on the basis of the use of the franchisor's name and insignia alone. For the reasons explained above, such liability could be in either contract or tort. The nature of franchise operations is not a matter of common knowledge in this country outside the old-established areas of petrol stations and tied public-houses. In practice, in a true franchise as opposed to dealerships, there will always be controls. These controls of themselves, by ensuring uniformity between outlets, can contribute to the misunderstanding induced in the minds of third parties about the nature of the business, and therefore are to be taken into account in deciding whether or not any estoppel arises. So far as the public at large are concerned, there is only one business. A court is likely to have considerable sympathy with a plaintiff who asserts that he thought he was dealing with a single business with a number of branches. The control exercised by the franchisor is also relevant in relation to his possible vicarious liability, to the extent as we have seen that the doctrine is based on underlying policy considerations different from agency by estoppel.

1.44 It may be thought that this line of argument has potentially far-reaching consequences in relation to trade mark licensing and the like. We have already suggested[1] that a central element in the concept of a trade mark is the expectation aroused in the mind of the public that the goods are vouched by the trade mark owner to be of a particular quality. To the extent that this induces reliance on the part of a member of the public, it would seem reasonable that the licensor should be held liable for damage suffered in consequence of such reliance, whether in contract or in tort[2]. On the other hand, as we have already suggested, a court might choose to draw a distinction between the controls necessary to preserve the goodwill associated with the mark and those which go further[3]. We have already suggested that it may be difficult to do this rationally.

1 Para 1.11 et seq.
2 And see the Consumer Protection Act 1987, s 2(2)(b)—see para 5.51 post. A similar argument could also be applied in relation to celebrity name licensing, to the extent that this implies to the public that the celebrity is in some way vouching the goods.
3 See para 1.32, ante.

Partnership

1.45 In the previous section we considered the possibility that the franchisor could become liable to third parties on a principle of estoppel or holding out. There is also however the possibility that a true contract of agency may be held to exist. It may be held that the relationship between the parties is in reality that of partners.

1.46 Partnership law is essentially a branch of agency law[1]. As Lord Cranworth observed in the leading case of *Cox v Hickman*[2]: 'It is often said that the test, or one of the tests, whether a person not ostensibly a partner, is nevertheless, in contemplation of law, a partner, is, whether he is entitled to participate in the

1.47 Franchising as a legal concept

profits. This no doubt, is in general, a sufficiently accurate test; for a right to participate in profits affords cogent, often conclusive evidence, that the trade in which the profits have been made, was carried out in part for or on behalf of the person setting up such a claim. But the real ground of liability is, that the trade has been carried on by persons acting on his behalf. When that is the case, he is liable to the trade obligations, and entitled to its profits, or to a share of them. It is not strictly correct to say that his right to share in the profits makes him liable to the debts of the trade. The correct mode of stating the proposition is to say that the same thing which entitles him to the one makes him liable to the other, namely, the fact that the trade has been carried on on his behalf, ie that he stood in relation of principal towards the persons acting ostensibly as the traders, by whom the liabilities have been incurred, and under whose management the profits have been made'.

1 *Re English and Irish Church and University Assurance Society (No 2)* (1863) 1 Hem & M 85. The position in Scottish law is different: a partnership is for certain purposes treated as a legal entity—Partnership Act 1890, s 4(2); *Mair v Wood* 1948 SC 83 at 86. This would not appear to affect the application of antitrust legislation. The Restrictive Trade Practices Act 1976 and EEC law clearly apply to agreements between firms which may well be joint venturers or partners.
2 (1860) 8 HL Cas 268 at 306.

1.47 The law of partnership was codified by the Partnership Act 1890. Section 1 of that Act defines a 'partnership' as 'the relation which subsists between persons carrying on a business[1] in common with a view of profit'. If the relationship is held to exist each partner is an agent of the firm and section 5 of the Act provides:

'Every partner is an agent of the firm and his other partners for the purpose of the business of the partnership; and the acts of every partner who does any act for carrying on in the usual way business of the kind carried on by the firm of which he is a member bind the firm and his partners, unless the partner so acting has in fact no authority to act for the firm in the particular matter, and the person with whom he is dealing either knows that he has no authority, or does not know or believe him to be a partner.'

1 Every trade, occupation or profession—section 45.

1.48 Normally, it will not matter much whether or not a true partnership exists. If there is liability by estoppel or holding out a third party may claim. The point is however that even if there were no holding out, if a true partnership existed between the parties, section 5 would apply and the franchisee would be the franchisor's agent. It will be argued in the following sections that there could be held to be a true partnership between the franchisor and franchisee. The crux of the matter again is the view we take of the significance of the control exercised by the franchisor. Unfortunately, this aspect of partnership law is lacking in English authorities.

1.49 The basis of a partnership is an agreement, express or implied. It is this which distinguishes agency by estoppel or partnership by holding out from a true agency or partnership. It is necessary therefore that for a true partnership to arise there must be some dealing between the parties from which the necessary consent[1] to become a partner may be implied. It follows from this that the individual franchisees, who in the nature of things do not deal with one another are not partners. No franchisee is constituted agent for the other. The franchisor and franchisee who are in contractual relationship with one another, however could be partners. The fact that the franchisor is a corporation does not matter, nor does it matter that the franchisee may be. Partnerships can exist between legal persons, legal and natural persons, or between partnerships for that matter[2]. Nor does the fact that the capitals are separately owned matter[3]. Furthermore, it is clear that it is the substance of the agreement which matters. If that is held to amount to a partnership, simply to describe it as something else will be of no effect[4]. It follows that 'no partnership' clauses will have little bearing on the matter.

1 See *Lovegrove v Nelson* (1834) 3 My & K 1.
2 *Lindley on Partnership* (14th edn, 1979) (Sweet & Maxwell) p 65.
3 *Fromont v Coupland* (1824) 2 Bing 170.
4 *Adam v Newbigging* (1888) 13 App Cas 308 at 315. See also *Re Megevand, ex p Delhasse* (1878) 7 Ch D 511, CA; *Moore v Davis* (1879) 11 Ch D 261; *Weiner v Harris* [1910] 1 KB 285 at 290, CA; *Stekel v Ellice* [1973] 1 WLR 191 at 199.

1.50 The mere payment of a royalty to the franchisor based on *gross* takings will not of itself make the franchisor a partner[1]. The reason for this is that a person taking a share thus computed is not thereby agreeing to share the losses which have to be taken into account in computing profits[2]. In the unlikely event of a franchisor agreeing to take a royalty based on *net* takings, the position could be different. That would appear to amount to a sharing of profits which is prima facie evidence of a partnership[3]. This rule applies even though the agreement contains a clause whereby one party agrees to indemnify the other against losses[4]. In the normal set-up the financial arrangements between the parties are unlikely to give rise to a partnership. The rules for guidance in determining the existence of a partnership contained in section 2, are not the end of the matter however. The arrangement as a whole between the parties has to be considered. The most significant element here is the control exercised by the franchisor over the way in which the franchisee runs the business. Although there seems to be no directly relevant English authority relating to general partnerships, there is the rule relating to limited partnerships that if a limited partner takes part in the management of the partnership business he shall be liable for all debts and obligations of the firm incurred while he so takes part in the management as though he were a general partner[5]. It is submitted that the circumstances in which a limited partner's intervention in the business serve to turn him into a general partner, could also serve to make a franchisor a general partner. However, on the assumption that the franchisor is not otherwise a partner, there is one important difference: a limited partner is *already* a partner of sorts. He simply changes his status from a limited to general partner by intervention. Could a franchisor *become* a partner by virtue of the controls he exercises? The answer to this seems to lie in the underlying reason for the intervention rule in the case of a limited partnership. There appears to be no authority on this in English law.

1 Partnership Act 1890 s 2(2). *Sutton & Co v Grey* [1894] 1 QB 285, CA; *Cox v Coulson* [1916] 2 KB 177, CA. American case law accords with this; see *Nichols v Arthur Murray Inc* 248 Cal App 2d 620 (1967), 56 Cal Rptr 728; *Murphy v Holiday Inns* 219 SE 2d 874 (1975); *Drexel v Union Prescription Centers* 582 F 2d 781 (1978); *Ortega v General Motors* 392 So 2d 40 (1980); *Maxwell v Sheraton Gardens Inn* [1981] Bus Franchise Guide (CCH) 91, 7626 at 12, 553.
2 It is not absolutely essential however that the parties agree to share losses for a partnership to be found to exist—see *Walker West Developments v Emmett* (1978) 252 Estates Gazette 1171, CA.

1.51 *Franchising as a legal concept*

3   Partnership Act 1890, s 2(3). *Grace v Smith* (1775) 2 Wm Bl 998; *Waugh v Carver* (1793) 2 Hy Bl 235.
4   *Bond v Pittard* (1838) 2 M & W 357.
5   Limited Partnerships Act 1907, s 6(1).

1.51 The origin of the modern limited partnerships is the *commenda*, which was common all over Europe in the Middle Ages[1]. In its original form, this was a partnership in which a person provided capital to a trader, who repaid the lender with a share of the profits. The lender was liable only to the extent of the capital invested by him. This institution was the ancestor of the *société en commandite* of French law[2]. The *société en commandite* was the model for the Limited Partnerships Act 1907. It is relevant therefore to consider the reason for the intervention rule in French law. In modern French law the reason for the rule is the protection of third parties. A distinction is drawn between *gestion externe* and *gestion interne*. The first renders the *commanditaire* liable to third parties, and is based on the fact that such intervention is likely to induce in their minds a misapprehension as to his true status[3]. In other words, it turns out to be similar to the agency by estoppel or holding out rule[4].

1   Holdsworth *History of English Law* Vol VIII, pp 195 et seq.
2   Pothier *de Société* §§60 and 102; Code de Commerce, Arts 23–33.
3   See Ripert *Traité Elementaire de Droit Commercial* (9th edn 1977). In German law a non-trading partner can be active in managing the business without incurring liability— H Wurdinger *German Company Law* p 228.
4   See para 1.39, ante.

1.52 American courts, however, in construing a provision virtually identical to section 6(1) of the Limited Partnership Act 1907[1], have tended to focus rather on the fact of control of itself[2]. They have drawn a distinction between on the one hand 'mere observation or that incidental supervision and advice which a person having capital invested in a concern would naturally give to an enterprise in which perhaps the greater part of his fortune was invested'[3], and on the other hand actively directing or managing the business[4]. Thus, directing which crops were to be planted on a farm, and requesting and obtaining the resignation of a partner as manager and his replacement by another, were facts taken into account in holding a limited partner liable[5]. Merely to render services without an element of control seems to be unsufficient[6]. The stress on control rather suggests an underlying policy consideration similar to that which seems in part to underlie the doctrine of vicarious liability. The idea that a person who intermeddles in a business should carry part of the burden of the losses seems to be a basic one and certainly existed before modern theories of vicarious liability and agency[7].

1   Uniform Limited Partnership Act. §7.
2   Though holding out seems to have been a factor in some cases—see *Russell v Warner* 217 P 2d 43 (1950).
3   *Continental National Bank of Boston v Strauss* 32 NE 1066 (1893).
4   See generally *Rowley on Partnership* (1960) §53.7.
5   *Holzman v De Escamilla* 195 P 2d 833 (1948).
6   *Silvola v Rowlett* 272 P 2d 287 (1954).
7   Emile Szlechter *Le Contrat de Société en Babylonie, en Grèce et à Rome* (1947) section 4.

1.53 It is difficult, given the absence of English authorities, to predict how English courts will view the matter. If they were to stress the control aspect as such, presumably all the internal arrangements between the franchisor and franchisee would be taken into consideration, quite independently of whether or not they were calculated to mislead third parties about the true nature of the arrangement. If on the other hand they were to stress that it is the impression given to third parties which matters, they would look at those elements of the agreement likely to induce third parties to believe that they are dealing with the franchisor. It must now be borne in mind however that the Business Names Act 1985 makes certain disclosure requirements in respect of business names. In some cases these could well have the effect of negativing any allegation of holding out by the franchisee. These provisions are dealt with in paras 5.45 and 6.24, post. Indeed, it is submitted that in practice courts are likely to consider both. Although different policy considerations may be seen to underlie liability by virtue of control, and liability by virtue of estoppel, in any given case the two are not likely to be very clearly separable, for controls which ipsi facto justify liability, are likely also to contribute to the expectations of third parties.

Conclusion

1.54 There could be held to be a true partnership between the parties, depending on the view a court took of the significance of the controls exercised by a franchisor over a franchisee. It is clear that the court will look beyond the descriptions of the parties and statements contained in the agreement, and consider whether or not the relationship taken as a whole amounts to a partnership.

1.55 To the extent that liability is founded on estoppel or holding out, the question is simply one of reliance, whether the cause of action is contract or tort. Did the third party embark on the course of conduct during which he suffered the damage as a result of the belief induced in his mind that he was in fact dealing with the franchisor? To the extent that the basis of liability is the control exercised by the franchisor over the franchisee simpliciter, liability will depend on the usual master and servant test, which is whether the act was done in the normal course of the servant's employment. In the context of franchising this would become the question as to whether or not the act was committed in the normal course of the business franchised. Again, the question is the same whether the cause of action is contract or tort.

Franchisor's liability under the Consumer Protection Act 1987

1.56 This Act is supposed to implement the EEC Product Liability Directive[1], by imposing upon manufacturers and certain other persons in the distribution chain, strict liability for defective products. Whether it actually does implement the intentions of the drafters of the Directive, and indeed whether it introduces simply a species of negligence liability[2], is a matter of some debate. At all events, our principal concern here is how it might apply in the franchising context. Liability is imposed by the Act upon the following persons:
   (a) the producer of the product;
   (b) any person who, by putting his name on the product or using a trade mark or other distinguishing mark in relation to the product, has held himself out to be the producer of the product;

1.57 Franchising as a legal concept

(c) any person who has imported the product into a member State from a place outside the member State in order, in the course of any business of his, to supply it to another[3].

Subsections (a) and (c) are clear enough, (b) is the problem. A person whose name is put on a product whether by himself or by a licensee, is clearly within subsection (b), but it then goes on to refer to '*a* trade mark' [emphasis supplied], and could be read as imposing liability on the proprietor, or the licensee. Arguably the former is the right interpretation, since the licensee who manufactures goods and applies the licensor's mark, would in any case be liable under subsection (a), and the section clearly contemplates joint liability.[4] Suppliers of products other than persons falling under the above subsection, can also incur liability, if they fail upon a reasonable request to do so to identify their own suppliers[5]. Liability under the Act is for death or personal injury, or damage to property exceeding £275 caused by the defective product[6]. It is unclear whether or not negligence principles of remoteness of damage apply to liability incurred under the Act. The moral of the above is, that where the franchise involves the distribution of goods, whether supplied by the franchisor, or by the franchisee under the franchisor's marks[7], both parties should carry product liability insurance.

1   85/374.
2   At least negligence in the Learned Hand sense—see *United States v Carroll Towing Co Inc* 159 F 2d 169 (2nd Circ 1947). Strict liability properly understood is a species of loss distribution—*Goldberg v Kollsman Instruments* 191 NE 2d 81 (1963).
3   Section 2(1).
4   Section 2(5).
5   Section 2(4).
6   Section 5.
7   The Act does not, apparently, require the mark to be applied to the product, simply to be used in relation to it—s 2(2)(b). By contrast, a trade name apparently has to be on the product itself—(ibid). No doubt the draftsman chose the wording to echo the Trade Marks Act 1938, and the Trade Descriptions Act 1968, but in the present context the choice was hardly felicitous.

Relationship of the franchisor and franchisee inter se

Master and servant

1.57 In the first place the relationship between the franchisor and franchisee might be characterised as that of master and servant. We suggested in the previous section that the criteria for determining the relationship of the parties inter se were not *necessarily* the same as those determining the vicarious liability of the franchisor to third parties, and indeed we would argue that they *ought* not to be. However, it is conceivable that the kind of controls which in the American cases discussed above[1] were held sufficient to establish vicarious/agency liability, might be held to be relevant to showing that the relationship of the parties inter se is *in fact* that of master and servant. The fact that the franchisee may own the assets of his outlet and bear the financial risks, should not in the present context be made too much of. If, however, our argument is accepted that the question of liability to third parties, and the question of the relationship of the parties inter se are different, there is no reason why the same fact should not be regarded differently in answering each question. To put it another way, the idea behind having the franchisee risk his capital, is that he will thereby work harder to make a success of his outlet. It is one of the controls therefore which go towards building up the goodwill of the operation. The very basis of that goodwill, the idea of good and uniform quality between outlets, depends on the public viewing the chain as an entity rather than separate businesses. That image could provide a justification for holding franchisors liable to third parties. However, the same thing, the separate risk of capital by the franchisee, equally well could be said to justify treating the parties as independent businesses for the purposes of such things as taxation and National Insurance. The *Ready Mixed Concrete* case[2] provides valuable guidance on the question of the relationship of the parties inter se. In that case the issue was liable for payment of National Insurance contributions, but equally it could be said to justify treating the parties as independent businesses for tax purposes. MacKenna J observed, 'It is true that the company are given special powers to ensure that he runs his business efficiently, keep proper accounts and pays his bills. I find nothing in these or any other provisions of the contract inconsistent with the company's contention that he is running a business of his own. A man does not cease to run a business on his own account because he agrees to run it efficiently or to accept another's superintendence'.

Amongst the matters thought relevant in determining that the driver and owner of the ready-mixed lorry was an independent contractor were, in addition to the incidence of financial risk and chance of profit: (1) freedom to decide when and how the vehicle would be maintained; (2) freedom to employ another to drive in his place; and (3) freedom to purchase fuel or other requirements. Obligations thought to be consistent with the status of the franchisee as an independent contractor included: (1) the duty to make the vehicle available during the contract period; (2) the duty to repair and maintain it; and (3) the duty to employ a competent driver in the event of his absence. The payment of the franchisee was on the basis of so much per mile for the quantity of concrete delivered. This case was followed in *Ready Mixed Concrete (London) Ltd v Cox*[2], where the issue was a trade union's exemption under the Trade Disputes Act 1906 from liability for inducing a breach of contract. It is clear from these cases that it is not what the parties choose to call themselves, but the agreement taken as a whole, which matters[3]. The trend of these cases is generally away from the former emphasis on the control test in determining the relationship of the parties inter se[4]—a test which however we have argued is of considerable importance on the question of liability to third parties. Where the relationship is doubtful, it may be open to the parties to stipulate what their relationship is[5].

1 Para 1.32.
2 (1971) 10 KIR 273.
3 See also *Ferguson v John Dawson & Partners (Contractors) Ltd* [1976] 3 All ER 817, [1976] 1 WLR 1213; *Davis v New England College of Arundel* [1977] ICR 6, EAT; *Massey v Crown Life Insurance Co* [1978] 2 All ER 576, [1978] 1 WLR 676, CA.
4 See also *United States v Silk* 331 US 704 (1946).
5 *Massey v Crown Life Insurance Co*, ante, at 680 and 682, per Denning MR, Lawton LJ.

Conclusion

1.58 The relationship between the parties could, by virtue of the controls exercised by the franchisor over the franchisees, be held to be that of master and servant. However, in this context the fact that the franchisees separately risk their capitals may, and indeed we would argue should, all other things being equal, be taken to indicate that they are not.

1.59 Franchising as a legal concept

Partnership

1.59 We have already discussed the question of whether or not for the purposes of agency liability a partnership may exist, and reference should be made to that section[1]. Our conclusion was that the relationship between the franchisor and each franchisee could be held to be a partnership, though the relationship of the franchisees between themselves probably was not. Even if the substance of the agreement were held not to be a true partnership, there is no reason why the relationship of the parties inter se should not at least be regulated on the analogy of partnership law. This is of importance in relation to the obligation of good faith. The implications of this will be considered later[2].

1 Paras 1.45 et seq, ante.
2 Paras 7.49 et seq, post.

1.60 Another consequence of holding that a true partnership existed would of course be in relation to taxation. Although a partnership is not for this purpose an entity, the rights and liabilities of the partnership being simply those of the individuals concerned, special provisions apply[1]. This could conceivably result in a franchisor being held liable in the event of the non-payment of tax on the insolvency of a franchisee. Again, however, it is to be hoped that the question of the relationship of the parties inter se for the purposes of revenue law, VAT, National Insurance contributions etc, will be treated separately from the question of the relationship to third parties. It is submitted that the approach adopted in the *Ready Mixed* case on the former question is the right one[2].

1 Income and Corporation Taxes Act 1988, s 111.
2 Para 1.34, ante.

1.61 Whether or not our argument is accepted that the question of the franchisor's liability to third parties for acts and defaults of his franchisees is to be treated separately from the question of the true nature of the relationship inter se, it is obvious that controls of the sort which have been held relevant to holding the franchisor liable to third parties should be avoided as far as possible. A court might well hold them to be relevant in establishing what the relationship between the parties in fact is. Reference should be made to the previous discussion for guidance on provisions to avoid[1]. The *Ready Mixed* case[2] should also be referred to.

1 Paras 1.34 et seq and 1.57 et seq, ante.
2 [1968] 2 QB 497, [1968] 1 All ER 433.

Franchisor as shadow director of corporate franchisee

1.62 A franchisor could incur liability as a 'shadow director' of a corporate franchisee. The Companies Act 1985[1] defines 'shadow director' as 'a person in accordance with whose directions or instructions the directors of the company are accustomed to act' (however, a person is not deemed a shadow director by reason only that the directors act on advice given by him in a professional capacity). The scope of this provision is not clear. On a literal reading, a franchisor could be held to be a 'shadow director' unless the advice given by it to the franchisee were held to have been given in a professional capacity, though this exclusion may be limited to advisers such as solicitors and accountants, whose situation is clearly distinguishable in that their clients do not have to follow the advice they give. A further possible distinction which might be made is between merely having the contractual right to direct (which in a sense covers most persons with whom a company contracts), and actually intervening in the internal running of a company. The most likely circumstance in which the latter could occur, is where the franchisor's own personnel are put into the franchisee company to assist in its running. Shadow directors have a duty to have regard to the interests of the company's employees[2]. Shadow directors are also treated as directors for the purposes of other provisions of the Act[3]. A disqualification order can be made against a shadow director[4]. Shadow directors also incur liability under the Insolvency Act 1986[5]. As well as becoming liable to a fine in respect of the offences specified in Chapter X of the Act, the franchisor could find itself liable to make a contribution to the insolvent company's assets. This could happen where at some time before the commencement of the winding up the franchisor knew or ought to have concluded that there was no reasonable prospect that the company would avoid going into insolvent liquidation[6].

1 Section 741(2).
2 Section 309.
3 Sections 319, 320–322, 330–346.
4 Company Directors Disqualification Act 1986, ss 6, 7 and 22(5).
5 Section 251.
6 Section 214(2) and (7). A shadow director is treated as a 'connected person' for the purposes of Parts I–VII of the Act.

Franchise operations as network contracts

1.63 Up to this point, we have contemplated the franchisor as a single entity. In practice, as the diagram at para 5.45 illustrates, separate companies may be set up to own the intellectual properties and to provide the management services. These companies may operate under a head UK master franchisee company, which in turn may be responsible to a foreign company. The rigid adherence of English law to the doctrine of privity of contract could be a particular inconvenience if a member of the network wishes to sue another member with whom it does not have privity of contract. The effective demise of *Junior Books*[1] has exacerbated this problem. The most likely situation in which such problems might arise, is where the consultancy services company and the intellectual property holding company go into liquidation. Together, they constituted from the franchisee's point of view 'the franchisor'. Could the franchisee sue the master franchisor direct? The doctrine of privity says not. However, to the extent that the series of contracts constitute a network contract, it is arguable that the privity rule might not bar the franchisee from remedy[2]. A network contract is:

(1) A contract forming part of a set of contracts.
(2) The set of contracts has the following characteristics:
    (i) there is a principal contract (or, there are a number of principal contracts) within the set giving the set an overall objective,
    (ii) other contracts (secondary and tertiary contracts and so on) are entered into, an object of each of which is—directly or indirectly—to further the attainment of this overall objective, and
    (iii) the network of contractors expands until a sufficiency of contractors are obligated, whether to the parties to the principal contract or to other contractors within the set, to attain the overall objective.

There are four basic privity problems. These are as follows:

1.64 *Franchising as a legal concept*

P1. Can a person enforce a contract to which he is not a party? For example, could a franchisee sue on a term in the master franchise agreement requiring the master franchisee to provide proper management services?

P2. Can a person set up a defence based on the terms of a contract to which he is not a party in order to answer a claim brought by a person who is a party to the relevant contract? For example, could the master franchisee rely on an exemption clause in the contract between a franchisee and the management company if sued by the franchisee?

P3. Can a contracting party set up a defence based on the terms of his own contract in order to answer a claim brought by a person who is not a party to the relevant contract? For example, could the master franchisee rely on an exemption clause in the contract between itself and the management company?

P4. Can a contracting party enforce his own contract against a person who is not a party to the relevant contract? For example could a master franchisee which has provided computer software to the management company under the terms of a 'shrink wrap' licence, enforce the terms of that licence against a franchisee who is in breach of them? Could a trade mark holding company enforce the terms of a head licence against a franchisee who is a sub-licensee?

In a properly set-up franchise, the solution to many of these questions will have been anticipated, eg by agency contracts. Sometimes, however, things are not so well organised. In this case the only option may be a frontal assault on the privity doctrine. The concept of a network contract could provide the ammunition for such an assault. To the extent that our franchise operation is a network contract, and we would argue that it is a paradigm case, the doctrine of privity would not apply between the members of the network. The following situations can be envisaged.

1 *Junior Books v Veitchi* [1983] 1 AC 520, [1982] 3 All ER 201—see Adams and Brownsword 'From *Jarvis* to *Junior Books*; Tortuous and Tortious Constructions' [1989] 5 Constr LJ 3.
2 See Adams and Brownsword 'Privity and the Concept of a Network Contract' [1990] Legal Studies 12.

(1) P1: A franchisee (A) sues a master franchisee (C) for breach of the contract between the master franchisee (C) and the management company (B).

1.64 According to our proposal A, as a member of the network, has the right to enforce the contract between B and C. Procedurally, what we are doing is putting A in B's shoes for the purposes of holding C to his contractual obligations. Thus, where A's ordinary avenue of contractual recourse fails, particularly where B becomes insolvent, A is permitted to intervene directly in B's contract with C. This, we suggest, is analogous to those rules which permit an undisclosed principal to intervene directly in his agent's contracts.

(2) P2: A franchisee (A) sues a master franchisee (C) either: (a) for negligence (C's duty of care arising independently of the contract between the management company (B) and the master franchisee (C))[1] or (b) for breach of the contract between the management company (B) and the master franchisee (C)[2]. The master franchisee (C) in either case, defends by setting up terms in the franchise agreement between the franchisee (A) and the management company (B) (these terms, of course, being intended to protect the master franchisee (C)).

1.65 Case (a) seems to be relatively straightforward. The basis of the contract between A and B includes protection for C. A has assented to this risk. In principle, it is only fair that A's action against C should be limited by the terms of the contract between A and B[3]. Case (b) is slightly more difficult. A is intervening in the contract between B and C, and there is nothing in this particular contract to defeat or restrict A's claim. However, it would be transparently unfair if A could thus outflank terms to which he has assented. Accordingly, in case (b), A's enforcement of the contract between B and C is subject to any limitations accepted by A. In both versions of P2, therefore, the question of whether A has accepted a particular risk is critical.

1 Eg based on an erroneous market research report provided by the master franchisee on which the franchisee alleges it relied notwithstanding clear evidence in the agreement that it understood the report was not to be relied on.
2 Eg where it is the master franchisee's failure to observe its obligations under the contract with the management company which has led to the liquidation of the management company.
3 For a critique along these lines see Battersby (1975) 25 Univ Toronto LJ 371.

(3) P3: A franchisee (A) sues a master franchisee (C) either: (a) for negligence of the master franchisee's duty of care arising independently of the contract between the management company (B) and the master franchisee (C), or (b) for breach of the contract between the management company (B) and the master franchisee (C); the master franchisee (C) in either case, defends by setting up terms in the contract between the management company (B) and itself (C).

1.66 Case (a) is a difficult one. If a strict privity approach is adopted, C's defence fails. Given that the basis of the contract between B and C includes protection for C, this seems unfair to C. Our network contract proposal opens up the possibility of C's defence succeeding. This protects C's legitimate interests, but we must be sure that it does not involve any unfairness to A. The key to this seems to be A's knowledge. In line with our thinking on P2, if A has assented to the risk, it is only fair that he should be held to it. So, to tackle case (a) under P3, we must stipulate clear rules concerning the knowledge—both of the existence of contracts and of their particular terms—to be attributed to network contractors. Three approaches might be taken:

(i) a test based on actual knowledge: network contractors are not to be taken as knowing unless they actually do know;

(ii) a test based on reasonable constructive knowledge (network contractors are deemed to have such knowledge as it is reasonable to expect of contractors in a particular kind of network), supplemented by any additional actual knowledge; or,

(iii) a test based on perfect constructive knowledge: in other words, network contractors are deemed to know about all the contracts, and all the terms of such contracts, as comprise their particular network.

Test (i) is fairest; test (iii) is most certain; but we imagine that test (ii) will make most appeal as a compromise between the demands of justice and certainty. There is room for debate about this, but we offer test (ii) as the appropriate ground rule. Accordingly, where case (a) under question P3 arises, we propose that C should be permitted the defence provided that A is deemed (in accordance with test (ii)) to have assented to the terms.

1.67 Franchising as a legal concept

(4) P4: A master franchisee or trade mark licensor sues a franchisee with whom it is not in privity of contract, for breach of the terms of its own management contract or licence.

1.67 The concept of acquiring property subject to burdens is well known in the context of restrictive covenants in land, where enforceability depended[1], in part, upon the defendant's actual or constructive knowledge of the covenant[2]. The analagous idea of acquiring chattels subject to burdens was recognised by the Privy Council, in *Lord Strathcona SS Co v Dominion Coal Co*[3]. Notwithstanding the criticism of this case by Diplock J in *Port Line Ltd v Ben Line Steamers Ltd*[4], it is submitted that the case is correct and, reliance on *Dunlop Pneumatic Tyre Co Ltd v Selfridge & Co Ltd*[5] is misplaced. Another doctrine of land law, namely that a person cannot take the benefits of a deed, without accepting its burdens[6], might also be applied by analogy to the present context.

1 Ie pre-1926.
2 Eg could a master licensee (C) enforce the terms eg of a trade mark or copyright licence between itself and a master franchisee (B) against a franchisee (A)?
3 [1926] AC 108—following the dictum of Knight Bruce LJ in *De Mattos v Gibson* (1858) 4 DeG & J 276 at 282.
4 [1958] 2 QB 146 at 168.
5 [1915] AC 847.
6 *Halsall v Brizell* [1957] Ch 169, [1957] 1 All ER 371.

To summarise

1.68 To the extent that a franchise operation is a network contract, the doctrine of privity ought not to be applied unquestioningly in actions between the different legal persons which constitute the network.

Chapter 2
Competition law

Checklists are to be found at paras 2.76, 2.140, 2.144, 2.151

INTRODUCTION

2.01 Although at the present day, competition laws are generally viewed in the context of economic theories about the way in which various forms of business practice, broadly labelled 'anti-competitive', interfere with and distort the free market, it must be remembered that antipathy towards monopolies long predates modern economic theory. Abuses arising from the grant of monopolies by James I eventually resulted in a Bill being agreed by a joint committee of both Houses of Parliament, which was enacted on 25 May 1624. It was an exception of this Act, the Statute of Monopolies, from which our patent system developed[1]. A lesson of considerable practical importance can be learnt from this historical episode: it is that competition laws are not merely to be understood in the light of (often conflicting) economic theory. They are a response to what at any time is felt to be fair and just in business practice. A franchisor who ignores this aspect, does so at his peril. This said, it must also be observed that the scope for disgruntled franchisees and others to take action through private suit is, at present, much more limited in the United Kingdom than it is in the United States where triple damages anti-trust suits[2] have been a considerable problem, occasionally leading to the wrecking of chains. Nevertheless, competition laws must not be ignored either at the outset, when setting up a franchise business, or during its operation. The more successful an operation, the more potential it has to run into competition law problems and, by the same token, the greater the potential for damage to it. Although, as explained above, some of the problems could not occur here, it is worth looking at some American cases briefly for the light they shed on provisions franchisees found irksome and courts objectionable.

1 See *Hulme* (1896) 12 LQR 141, (1897) 13 LQR 313, (1900) 16 LQR 44, (1902) 18 LQR 290, (1907) 23 LQR 348; *Davies* [1934] LQR 86 and 260; Adams and Averley 'Journal of Legal History' (1986) 7 Jo Leg Hist 156.
2 The triple damages concept seems to have been taken from the Statute of Monopolies.

2.02 The trade marks, etc, owned by the franchisor were regarded as tying items to bring into play the Sherman Act[1]. The evil which the American courts perceived was clearly stated in *Susser v Carvel*[2]. The fundamental economic evil in a tying arrangement deemed unlawful under the anti-trust laws lies in the ability of a producer who possesses market dominance in one particular product to impose upon his vendor the obligation to purchase other products as to which the producer possesses no market dominance and the consequent foreclosure to other producers of the non-dominant products of such markets for this merchandise. *Siegel v Chicken Delight*[3] is one of the key cases[4] and provides a very good illustration. The franchisees

2.03 *Competition law*

in that case were required to purchase paper packaging, cookers, fryers and food preparation mixes from the franchisor at a price which the franchisor sought only to justify by arguing that it was an accounting device for payment for use of the trade mark. The court formed the view, however, that it was rather a device for concealing the true royalty payments demanded of the franchisees. The court pointed out that a simple royalty was just as convenient a method of payment without any of the anti-competitive effects. It ruled that 'tie-ins' were a per se violation of the Sherman Act and could be justified on only four grounds: (1) quality control for the protection of trade mark goodwill[5]; (2) the needs of a new business[6]; (3) the franchisor's need to secure the supply of the initial equipment and subsequent suppliers; and (4) an accounting device where less restrictive devices cannot reasonably be used[7]. Since the franchisor failed to establish any of these things, the tie-ins were held to be unjustified. It is worth noting, however, that one of the consequences of this litigation was the virtual collapse of a once successful chain.

1   15 USC, 1.
2   332 F 2d 505 at 511 (1964). First instance decision 206 F Supp 636 (1962).
3   311 F Supp 847; affd 448 F 2d 43 (ND Cal 1970).
4   See also *Fortner v United States Steel* 394 US 495 (1969); *Milsen v Southland Corpn* 454 F 2d 363 (1971); *Kugler v AAMCO Automatic Transmissions* 460 F 2d 1214 (1972); *Photovest v Fotomat* 606 F 2d 704 (1979); Compare, eg *Kentucky Fried Chicken v Diversified Packaging* 549 F 2d 368 (1977); *Keener v Sizzler Family Steak House* 597 F 2d 453 (1979).
5   *Susser v Carvel Corpn*, ante; *Chock Full O'Nuts Corpn* [1973–76 Transfer Binder] Trade Reg Rep (CCH) [20,441 (FTC 1973) at 20,346]; *Howard Johnson Co* [1976–79 Transfer Binder] Trade Reg Rep (CCH) [21,577] (FTC 1979). See also outside franchising context, *United States v Jerrold Electronics* 187 F Supp 545, 559–60 (1960); *Dehydrating Process Co v AO Smith Corpn* 292 F 2d 653, 656 (1961).
6   *United States v Jerrold Electronics Corpn*, ante; *Brown Shoe Co v United States* 370 US 294, 330 (1962).
7   Really the four defences reflected the more general proposition stated above, that there must be a sound business reason for the tie—see *Kugler v AAMCO Automatic Transmissions*, ante.

2.03 Franchisees ought to get the return on their capital they have bargained for, bearing in mind the risks. The truth is that some of the American cases involved franchisees who had been misled by the apparently low royalty payments stipulated. The franchisor's true royalty was concealed behind the 'tie-ins'. It is submitted that this does not necessarily involve an anti-trust problem, but rather a consumer protection problem of much the same order as the statement of true rates of interest in consumer credit transactions. It is interesting to note that in the early 1980s there began to be signs that American courts were changing their views in line with the prevalent economic fashions, and in particular those associated with the 'Chicago' school[1] of economists. *New Jersey v Lawn King*[2] was a significant decision in this respect. That case involved dealer and distributorships of lawn care products. The distributors were required to purchase grass seed, chemicals and equipment from Lawn King, and the dealers to purchase these items from the distributors. The court ruled first that the purchasing requirements should be reviewed under the rule of reason rather than a per se rule[3], and second that the purchasing requirements might serve legitimate business purposes other than quality control or protection of trade mark goodwill. The New Jersey Supreme Court in effect held the purchasing requirements were not a tie at all, ie it rejected the traditional two product analysis of trade marks and tied items. The court held that this analysis was inappropriate for franchising. It did not consider whether the purchasing requirements were necessary for the successful operation of the franchise, nor whether quality could have been adequately controlled through specification. Interestingly enough the court did not define a 'franchise system' or explain why Lawn King was one. The view implicity in *New Jersey v Lawn King*, of the franchise as a single product, was also adopted in *Principe v McDonald*[4], where the trade mark, lease and other elements making up the McDonald system were held to be parts of a single 'bundle of benefits'. '[T]he very essence of a franchise is the purchase of several related products in a single competitively attractive package'[5]. *Siegel v Chicken Delight* was distinguished as involving a different type of franchising, described by McDonald's as 'rent-a-name', although on the facts of that case it is difficult to see how it could be so described. The limits of this 'single bundle' approach were not spelled out in either of these cases and it would be unsafe to conclude that they represent a wholesale legitimation of 'tie-ins'. In particular the failure to characterise the nature of a true franchise, to which the doctrine is to be applied, creates uncertainty. However, to the extent that they may present a trend towards a more realistic approach to competition policy, they are to be welcomed.

1 See Weston 15 ICC 269 (1984).
2 417 A 2d 1025 (1990).
3 Following in the direction set by *Continental TV v Sylvania* 433 US 36 (1977) which overruled *United States v Arnold, Schwinn & Co* 388 US 365 (1967) on per se point.
4 (1980) 631 F 2d 303. Compare *Krehl v Baskin-Robbins Ice Cream Co* 664 F 2d 1348 (1982); *Hamro v Shell Oil Co* 674 F 2d 784 (1982).
5 *Phillips v Crown Central Petroleum* 602 F 2d 616, 627 (1979); cited *Principe v McDonald*, ante, at 309.

2.04 United Kingdom competition laws at the moment[1] are of two sorts: those which attempt to designate particular *forms* of business practice thought to be anti-competitive, and those which focus on the anti-competitive *effects* of business practices. The 'forms' approach was adopted in the legislation consolidated in the Restrictive Trade Practices Act 1976 (to which we may add the legislation consolidated in the Resale Prices Act 1976 since the approach is much the same). The 'effects' approach is adopted by Article 85(1) of the Treaty of Rome and the Competition Act 1980. These are the four pieces of legislation which are most relevant for practical purposes, although for completeness, we must also consider the monopoly provision of the Fair Trading Act 1973 and Article 86 of the Treaty of Rome. The common law doctrine of restraint of trade is also of considerable practical importance. As will be explained, the basis of that doctrine is not entirely clear, though it does to some extent take into account the context and the effects of a particular restraining covenant. For our purposes the important difference between the 'forms' legislation and the 'effects' legislation is that the first applies only to agreements under which the parties accept particular restrictions: if they do not, they are not subject to it, even though the effects may be anti-competitive. The 'effects' legislation by contrast concentrates on the anti-competitive consequences of business practices, without attempting to provide an exhaustive catalogue of the form they may take. English lawyers tend to feel most at home with the 'forms' approach. The solution to the problem presented by it is, essentially, careful drafting. The solution to the problems presented by the 'effects' category is of quite a different order. The lawyer's role here is to avoid drafting agreements which produce, when they are acted upon, anti-competitive effects. That involves a consideration of the economic consequences of the provisions of different kinds of franchise agreement.

1 They are likely to be changed to assimilate them to EEC law in the foreseeable future—see para 2.92.

2.05 Competition law

2.05 Those who emphasise predictability as a necessary element in a just legal system will find loosely drafted competition laws unsatisfactory. Certainly, from the point of view of predictability the 'forms' approach was fairly satisfactory. In this respect, the Treaty of Rome and Competition Act are much less so. In view of what we have said, in considering the possible effects of any particular agreement, the draftsman would be well advised not to direct his attention solely to possible economic effects (which may be open to argument anyway), but also to consider whether particular terms may produce conduct which is likely to be thought unfair either to the franchisees or to the public at large.

2.06 Franchising raises acutely a basic problem of anti-trust law: what do we take for this purpose to be the economic unit? Is the franchise network to be regarded as a single entity or rather as a group of separate though connected businesses? The Restrictive Trade Practices Act gives a clear answer to this. It simply adopts a 'counting of heads' approach[1]. As we shall see, the answer for the purposes of Article 85(1)[2], and possibly also the Competition Act[3], is more ambivalent, and it is likely that the policy pursued under any legislation following the White Paper will resemble that of the Commission[4].

1 Para 2.14, post.
2 Paras 2.15 et seq, post.
3 Para 2.128, post.
4 See Cm 727.

2.07 The heart of any business format franchise is (1) the intellectual property owned by the franchisor; (2) the business system developed by the franchisor. In essence, these are the things which a franchisee will be seeking the right to use by entering into the franchise agreement.

2.08 Two types of competition law problems are inherent in this basic franchise 'package'. Because they exist under national laws, all forms of intellectual property have a tendency to insulate markets. This aspect of the matter is considered in para 2.77 et seq. A problem peculiar to franchising, however, is the requirement that the franchisee follow, exactly, the franchisor's business system. This requirement, which in turn is intended to secure absolute uniformity of outlets, has its own potential competition law problems. Whilst one of the main advantages of franchising is that the franchisee acquires the right to operate under a name or mark which can be promoted centrally on behalf of all the franchisees in the network, so that franchising is from this point of view, a mechanism for promoting competition, it must not be supposed that every aspect of the system allegedly necessary to preserve uniformity of outlet will automatically, because it is designated a part of the business system, be treated uncritically as necessary for the image and promotion of the system. In particular, unnecessarily restricting the franchisees' purchasing of materials used in the franchise, will be apt to infringe competition laws. Moreover, it is to be remembered that, franchisees who have to pay large sums of money for supplies which they can obtain more cheaply elsewhere than from the franchisor, quickly become disgruntled. It is worth bearing in mind in this connection the warning we gave at the outset, that historically competition laws are not merely to be understood in the light of economic theory (indeed they long predate it), they have also been a response to what has been felt to be fair and just in business practice[1]. It was no doubt a sense of injustice which spurred Frau Schillgalis into the actions which culminated in the *Pronuptia* Case[2]. Had she felt that her franchisors were behaving as she thought they should, it is highly unlikely that that case would ever have seen the light of day.

1 See para 2.01, ante.
2 Case 161/84 *Pronuptia de Paris GmbH, Frankfurt am Main v Pronuptia de Paris Irmgard Schillgallis, Hamburg* [1986] 1 CMLR 414 see para 2.16 post.

2.09 Franchisees may not resent having to buy overpriced widgets from the franchisor, when the benefits of the franchisor's system are first becoming apparent, but once they have learned the system, any such restraint is likely to seem irksome. The usual response to this is that 'tie-ins' are a very good way of accounting between franchisor and franchisee, especially as the franchisee will be setting against the VAT it collects, the input tax it pays so that monitoring is straightforward. This of course is true, and it is also true that in many franchises, the franchisee does not wish to obtain widgets elsewhere, because the price reflects the benefit of the franchisor's buying in bulk. In this happy situation there is really no need for a legal tie. That must be the situation to be aimed at, unless there are business reasons such as the preservation of secret formulae, or the use of the franchisor's trade mark in relation to the goods, which necessitate a tie (and in the latter case a certain degree of free purchasing can usually be permitted if the franchisor is using a number of suppliers). Otherwise, the rule must be to leave franchisees unrestricted and to preserve quality and standards by specification.

2.10 Another frequent source of problems is restraint of trade. It follows from what was said at the outset[1], namely, that franchising is only suitable for business systems which can be 'cloned', that the systems must be relatively simple and easily learned. A franchisee whose term is coming to an end (for whatever reason), may well feel able to operate a similar business independently, and of course it is a fundamental principal of the common law that skills, as opposed to trade secrets, learned in the course of a trade, must be freely exploitable. Any clause seeking to restrain this is likely to be struck down as an unreasonable restraint of trade. It is in the nature of franchising that secrets in the true sense[2] are hardly ever involved. Nevertheless, the franchisor has legitimate interests deserving of protection, and so long as the franchisor imposes restraints which go no further than protecting those legitimate interests, there should be no difficulty.

1 Para 0.02.
2 As to the criteria to be applied in determining what is a trade secret see para 3.118 et seq.

2.11 In the following section, we deal with the principal competition law problems to which franchising gives rise.

Common Market competition law

Basic principles

2.12 One of the principal objects of the Treaty of Rome is to promote freedom of trade between Member States. This principal is embodied in Articles 30 and 34. These provide as follows:

2.13 Competition law

ARTICLE 30
'Quantitative restrictions on imports and all measures having equivalent effect shall, without prejudice to the following provisions, be prohibited between Member States.'

ARTICLE 34(1)
'Quantitative restrictions on exports, and all measures having equivalent effect, shall be prohibited between Member States.'

This policy is furthered by the competition Articles, 85 and 86, and the proviso to Article 36 which qualifies the protection of national intellectual property rights for the same reason.

2.13 The text of Article 85(1) is as follows:

'1 The following shall be prohibited as incompatible with the common market: all agreements between undertakings, decisions by associations of undertakings and concerted practices which may affect trade between Member States and which have as their object or effect the prevention, restriction or distortion of competition within the common market, and in particular those which:
(a) directly or indirectly fix purchase or selling prices or any other trading conditions;
(b) limit or control production, markets, technical development, or investments;
(c) share markets or sources of supply;
(d) apply dissimilar conditions to equivalent transactions with other trading parties, thereby placing them at a competitive disadvantage;
(e) make the conclusion of contracts subject to acceptance by the other parties of supplementary obligations which, by their nature or according to commercial usage, have no connection with the subject of such contracts.'

2.14 It is clear that an individual can be an 'undertaking' for the purposes of Article 85(1). The word is not defined by the Treaty of Rome, possibly because the drafters of the Treaty wished to give the European Court of Justice and the Commission as wide a jurisdiction as possible in promoting inter-Member trade, and the Commission has taken the view that an individual involved in the commercial exploitation of a talent[1] or intellectual property[2] may be an undertaking. It is reasonable to suppose in fact that any individual engaged in commercial activity is an undertaking for the purposes of Article 85(1)[3]. Franchisees, whether individual or corporate, are therefore undertakings.

1 *RAI/UNITEL* OJL 157, 15.6.78, p. 39; [1978] 3 CMLR 306.
2 *Re Vaessen/Moris* OJL 19, 26.1.79, p. 32; [1979] 1 CMLR 511.
3 See also eg *Re AOIP/Beyrard* OJL 6, 13.1.76, p. 8; OJL 254, 17.9.76, p. 40; [1976] 1 CMLR D 14; *Reuter/BASF AG* [1976] 2 CMLR D 44. In *Re William Prym-Werke KG and Beka Agreement* OJL 296, 24.10.73, p. 24; [1973] CMLR D 250, it seems to have been assumed that a German limited partnership was an undertaking.

The application of EEC law to franchise agreements

2.15 The application of EEC competition law to business format franchise agreements was somewhat speculative before the decisions in *Pronuptia*[1], *Computerland*[2] and *Yves Rocher*[3], which involved goods franchises, and

ServiceMaster[4] which involved a service franchise. As a result of these cases, the block exemption[5], and the more recent decision in *Charles Jourdan*[6], the position is now somewhat clearer.

1 OJ 1987 L13/37.
2 OJ 1987 L222/12.
3 OJ 1987 L8/49.
4 OJ 1988 L332/38.
5 Regulation 4087/88 1988 L359/46.
6 1989 OPJ 35/31.

2.16 *Pronuptia* involved the well-known franchise specialising in the sale and hire of wedding attire. The goods bearing the 'Pronuptia' trade mark (about two-thirds of the goods traded through the network) had to be ordered from the franchisor. The European Court ruled as follows:

(1) The compatibility of distribution franchise agreements with Article 85(1) depended upon the clauses contained in such agreements and on their economic context.

(2) Clauses which were essential for preventing the know-how transferred and the assistance provided by the franchisor from benefiting competitors did not constitute restrictions on competition within Article 85(1).

(3) Clauses which provided the control necessary for the preservation of the identity and reputation of the distribution network which was symbolised by the brand name did not constitute restrictions of competition within Article 85(1).

(4) Clauses which resulted in a partitioning of markets between franchisor and franchisees or between franchisees constituted restrictions on competition within Article 85(1).

(5) The notification by a franchisor to a franchisee of recommended prices was not a restriction of competition provided that there was not a concerted practice between the franchisor and the franchisees, or among the franchisees with a view to those prices being applied in practice.

(6) Distribution franchise agreements containing clauses resulting in a division of markets between franchisor and franchisee or among franchisees were capable of affecting trade between Member States.

The court in that case was unable, because the agreements had not been notified, to consider the question of exemption under Article 85(3) on the basis that the overall effect of the agreements was to further competition.

2.17 The Commission, however, considered this aspect in *Yves Rocher, Computerland,* and *ServiceMaster.* Unfortunately, it tended to treat as matters for exemptions, clauses which the Court appeared to consider not to infringe Article 85(1) at all, moreover it appears to have paid little attention to the Court's view that regard must be had to the particular economic context. The position under Regulation 4087/88 is that certain clauses will be regarded as infringing Article 85(1), but may benefit from the block exemption.

Summary of the block exemption

2.18 The block exemption is unclear in some important respects. As noted below, it also differs from the court's views in *Pronuptia,* and, at the end of the day, it is the court which creates the law not the Commission. The present Commissioner for competition policy, Sir Leon Brittan, is known to favour a less interventionist

2.19 *Competition law*

approach to competition policy, and it may be that the defects in the present exemption will produce in the foreseeable future a further revision in an attempt to reduce the Commission's workload. We propose to proceed as follows: we will attempt a summary of its principal provisions in simple language; we will then offer a commentary dealing with some of the more important points which arise in practice; finally we will provide notes on individual clauses in the precedents. In the block exemption, the Commission distinguishes three types of franchise: industrial franchises, involving the manufacturing of goods; distribution franchises, involving the sale of goods; and service franchises, involving the supply of services. It is important to note at the outset that the block exemption only covers franchises for the retail distribution of goods and services[1]. These are franchise agreements whereby one of the parties supplies goods or provides services to end users[2]. Industrial franchise agreements, consisting of manufacturing licences based on patents, technical know-how, trade marks etc are not covered (though they may benefit from other block exemptions)[3]. The Regulation covers agreements whereby a combination of goods and services are provided to end users eg where goods are processed or adapted to fit the specific needs of customers. It also applies to cases where the relationship between the franchisor and franchisee is created through a master franchisee. It is often the case that the marks, etc, are held by a separate company from the franchisor[4]. The franchisor is appointed agent to appoint the franchisees licence of such works. It is believed that such an arrangement would not take the agreement outside the Regulation (which applies only to agreements between two undertakings), because the actual franchise agreement itself is made only between the franchisor and the franchisee. A master franchise agreement itself can fall within the Regulation[5]. It does not cover wholesale franchise agreements[6].

1 Article 1.
2 Id.
3 See para 2.48.
4 See para 5.45.
5 Article 1(3)(c).
6 Recital (5) and Art 1(3)(a).

Restatement of block exemption

2.19 (1) Regulation 4087/88, Recital 5, Article 2 contains a list of restrictions of competition in these agreements which are exempted. These are[1]:

(a) sole and exclusive terms and regard to the franchise territory;

(b) an obligation on master franchises not to conclude franchise agreements with third parties outside their territory;

(c) an obligation for the franchisee to exploit the franchise only from the contract premises;

(d) restraints on the franchisee seeking customers outside his territory;

(e) an obligation not to sell or use in the course of providing services goods competing with the franchise goods (this obligation may not be imposed, however, in respect of spare parts or accessories).

1 For actual text see Appendix 4.

2.20 Following the usual pattern of block exemptions, Article 3 then sets out a list of 'white clauses'. These are clauses which are permissible in so far as they are necessary to protect the franchisor's industrial and intellectual property, or

Summary of the block exemption 2.21

to maintain the common identity and reputation of the franchised network. The obligations which may be imposed on franchisees, and which have conditional clearance, are as follows:[1]

(a) to sell or use exclusively goods meeting the franchisor's objective quality specifications;

(b) to sell only goods manufactured by the franchisor or designated suppliers, where it would be impractical, owing to the nature of the goods, to apply objective quality specifications;

(c) not to compete with other franchised outlets in the business (including the franchisor's), and for a reasonable period after termination (which may not exceed one year) in the territory where the franchisee exploited the franchise;

(d) not to acquire financial interests in competitors, which would provide influence over them;

(e) to sell the goods which are the subject-matter of the franchise only to end users, to other franchisees or to resellers within other distribution channels supplied by the manufacturer of the goods or with its consent;

(f) to use their best endeavours to sell the goods or provide the services, including minimum range stocks and turnover requirements, as well as customer warranty services;

(g) to pay advertising contributions to the franchisor and to carry out advertising as approved by the franchisor.

1 Article 3(1). For the actual text see Appendix 4.

2.21 Other clauses listed in Article 3(2) have unconditional clearance, and in the event that the obligations referred to fall within the scope of Article 85(1), they are also exempted.[1] These are[2]:

(a) confidentiality requirements as to know-how[3] both during the course of the agreement and after termination;

(b) feedback of information requirements, by which the franchisee is required to communicate its experience in exploiting the franchise and to permit the franchisor and other franchisees to benefit from that experience by granting non-exclusive licences;

(c) requirements that franchisees provide assistance in pursuing infringers;

(d) requirements that franchisees use know-how[4] licensed by the franchisor only in exploiting the franchise, and not to use it after termination (until presumably it becomes generally known in the trade in question);

(e) requirements that franchisees attend training courses arranged by the franchisor;

(f) requirements that franchisees use the franchisor's business methods (which will be set out in the manual);

(g) requirements that franchisees adhere to the franchisor's standards eg of cleanliness, presentation and quality control:

(h) requirements that franchisees allow the franchisor to carry out spot checks;

(i) prohibitions on the change of the location of the franchise without the franchisor's prior consent;

(j) prohibitions on assignment without the franchisor's consent.

1 Article 3(3).
2 Article 3(2). For the actual text see Appendix 4.
3 As to the meaning of 'know-how', see para 2.34.
4 Ibid.

2.22 Competition law

2.22 Article 4 then sets out conditions for exemption to apply[1]:

(a) the franchisee must be free to obtain the goods which are the subject of the franchise from other franchisees, where such goods are also distributed through another network of authorised distributors, the franchisee must be free to obtain goods from them;

(b) where the franchisee must honour guarantees for the goods, it must honour similar guarantees from other suppliers of the goods within the EEC;

(c) the franchisee must be required to indicate its status as an independent undertaking (in the UK this obligation is usually complied with in any event because of the requirements of the Business Names Act 1985)[2].

1 For actual text see Appendix 4.
2 See para 6.24.

2.23 The 'black list' is contained in Article 5. The following will prevent the exemption from applying[1]:

(a) market sharing agreements whereby undertakings producing goods or providing services which are identical, or are considered by users as equivalent (ie they are goods or services in respect of which there is in the economist's phrase 'consumer substitutability'), enter into franchise agreements with each other in respect of such goods or services;

(b) foreclosing the possibility of the franchise obtaining equivalent goods from other suppliers (note it is *equivalent* goods, as noted above tie-ins are permissible if it is the only practical way of ensuring goods meet the franchisor's specifications);

(c) foreclosing supplies, ie where the franchisor refuses for reasons other than the protection of its intellectual property, or maintaining the identity and reputation of the franchised network, to designate third party suppliers;

(d) a ban on post-termination use of the know-how once it has become generally known or easily accessible[2];

(e) resale price maintenance, or maximum price maintenance it would seem[3] (recommended prices are permitted unless this was to amount to a concerted practice);

(f) no challenge clauses in respect of intellectual property of the franchisor (though the agreement can be made to terminate on a challenge);

(g) prohibitions on the supply of users resident outside the territory (though, as noted above, the franchisee can be restrained from actively seeking customers outside his territory).

1 For actual text see Appendix 4.
2 See para 2.34 below.
3 See para 2.151.

2.24 Agreements within the conditions provided by the Regulation need not be notified. Agreements which do not, must be notified, but by Article 6 are subject to the opposition procedure.

2.25 The benefit of the exemption can be withdrawn if the effect of parallel networks established by competing manufacturers or distributors is to restrict competition, if the goods or services enjoy a *de facto* monopoly in a substantial part of the EC, if the franchisor or franchisees prevent end users from access to parallel imports or otherwise isolate markets within the EC, if there is evidence of horizontal concerted practices to maintain prices, and if there are unjustified controls over franchises for reasons other than the protection of the franchisor's legitimate trading interests[1]. The exemption is to continue in force until 31 December 1999.

1 Article 8.

Two recent decisions

2.26 In addition to the block exemption and the earlier *Computerland* case, two more recent decisions shed light on the Commission's thinking. In *ServiceMaster* the agreement involved a pure service franchise. The Commission took the view that for the purposes of competition law, service franchises can be assimilated to distribution franchises. However, this basic assimilation does not prevent the Commission from taking into account in individual cases certain specificities relating to the provision of services. The agreement in that case contained a prohibition against franchisees setting up outlets in other Member States, and against actively seeking customers outside their territory. The Commission exempted the agreement from the application of Article 85(1), because the agreements fulfilled all the conditions of Article 85(3). In particular, the franchisees were free to provide services to unsolicited customers resident outside their own territory.

2.27 The other case is *Charles Jourdan*. Charles Jourdan manufactures and distributes shoes, leather goods and handbags. Its main activity, however, is the production and sale of shoes, particularly in the medium and top quality range. Its share of the French market in these is 1 per cent, and of the Community market it is negligible. If the relevant market is medium and top quality shoes, on the other hand, its share is 10 per cent of the French market, and 2 per cent of the Community market. The distribution of Charles Jourdan goods is carried on through four types of outlet: branches; franchised shops, franchised counters in department stores; and traditional retailers. The two types of franchise are operated under agreements containing the following clauses: restrictions on personal and transfer; exclusive territory; provision of management assistance and know-how; licence of intellectual property subject to the exclusive right of Charles Jourdan to determine the use made of it; right of inspection by the franchisor; up-front fees and continuing fees; obligations on the part of the franchisees not to deal in competing products; and recommended prices. The franchisees were free to purchase Charles Jourdan goods from the group, from a Group branch shop, from another member of the network, whether a franchisee, or retailer. This freedom extended to purchasers from distribution outlets in other Member States. The Commission took the view that the combined effect of such provisions in the franchise agreements was to improve the distribution of Charles Jourdan products. The pressure of competition within the sector and the freedom of consumers to purchase the products at any shop within the network will tend to force franchisees to pass on to consumers a reasonable share of the advantages resulting from rationalised distribution. The standard form franchise agreements contained only restrictions that were indispensable to the attainment of these benefits. The franchisees were in competition with one another, since they were allowed to sell to any consumer within or outside their allotted territory, and were free to set their selling price. All the conditions for the application of Article 85(3) were thus met and, accordingly, the Commission granted individual exemption.

Commentary[1]

2.28 Those familiar with the Restrictive Trade Practices Act should be warned: the block exemption should not be approached like a checklist. It provides guidance only. Moreover, in some respects the exemption does not follow the court's decision in *Pronuptia*[2], and it must be remembered that, at the end of the day, it is the court which creates law, not the Commission, though the Commission's thinking on particular matters is obviously of importance to those drafting franchise agreements. It must also be borne in mind that the exemption makes no distinction between new franchises and established franchises, even though it is arguable that restrictions ought to be permitted in a new franchise network which might be objectionable in an established one.

1 See also Korah *Franchising and the EEC Competition Rules Regulation 4087/88 (1989)* (ESC Oxford).
2 Case 161/84 [1986] 1 CMLR 414.

The Recitals

2.29 Those trained in the common law tradition may be tempted to skip the Recitals. They must be considered, however, because they contain matters crucial to the understanding of the Exemption. We will consider some of the more important provisions of the Recitals.

2.30 Recital (6) states that franchise agreements, as defined in the Regulation, may in particular affect intra-Community trade where they are concluded between undertakings from different Member States, or where they form the basis of a network which extends beyond the boundaries of a single Member State. Quite a number of franchises are local, and for commercial and cultural reasons are unlikely to expand outside their national market. In the case of such franchises, Article 85(1) is unlikely to be infringed though, as *Pronuptia* made clear, regard must always be had to the whole economic context. Thus if widgets are made all over the EEC, the agreements under which a franchise network, specialising in buying widgets and tailoring them to the special needs of the UK consumer, operated, would clearly infringe Article 85(1) if the franchisees were obliged by the franchisor to buy UK made widgets. It is also to be borne in mind that many networks do not exceed the guidelines of 5 per cent market share and an overall turnover of 200 ECUs, of the Notice on Agreements of Minor Importance, and consequently do not infringe Article 85(1)[1].

1 See para 2.68—for text see Appendix 3.

2.31 Recital (9) defines the obligations restrictive of competition which may appear in franchise agreements as follows:

> 'This Regulation must define the obligations restrictive of competition which may be included in franchise agreements. This is the case in particular for the granting of an exclusive territory to the franchisees combined with the prohibition on actively seeking customers outside the territory. The same applies to the granting of an exclusive territory to a master franchisee combined with the obligation not to conclude franchise agreements with third parties outside the territory. Where the franchisees sell or use in the process of providing services, goods manufactured by the franchisor or according to its instructions

and or bearing its trade mark, an obligation on the franchisees not to sell, or use in the process of the provision of services, competing goods, makes it possible to establish a coherent network which is identified with the franchised goods. However, this obligation should only be accepted with respect to the goods which form the essential subject-matter of the franchise. It should notably not relate to accessories or spare parts for these goods.'

2.32 Recital (12) states that to guarantee that competition is not eliminated for a substantial part of the goods which are the subject of the franchise, it is necessary that parallel imports remain possible. Therefore, cross-deliveries between franchisees should always be possible. Furthermore, where a franchise network is combined with another distribution system, franchisees should be free to obtain supplies from authorised distributors. Where franchisees have to honour guarantees for the franchisor's goods, this obligation should also apply to goods supplied by the franchisor, other franchisees or other agreed dealers.

Definitions (Article 1(3))

2.33 These, inter alia, define the field of application of the exemption. For this purpose the key terms are 'franchise' and 'franchise agreement':
Article 1(3)(a) provides:

> '"franchise" means a package of industrial or intellectual property rights relating to trade marks, trade names, shop signs, utility models, designs, copyrights, know-how or patents, to be exploited for the resale of goods or the provision of services to end users'.

Article 1(3)(b) provides:

> '"franchise agreement" means an agreement whereby one undertaking, the franchisor, grants the other, the franchisee, in exchange for direct or indirect financial consideration, the right to exploit a franchise for the purposes of marketing specified types of goods and/or services; it includes at least obligations relating to:
> —the use of a common name or shop sign and a uniform presentation of contract premises and/or means of transport,
> —the communication by the franchisor to the franchisee of know-how,
> —the continuing provision by the franchisor to the franchisee of commercial or technical assistance during the life of the agreement'.

2.34 Although the requirement that the franchisor communicate 'know-how' to the franchisee, would appear at first sight to limit the application of the exemption severely because many franchises do not involve any know-how in the technical sense, 'know-how' is defined in Article 1(3)(f) to mean 'a package of non-patented practical information, resulting from experience and testing by the franchisor, which is secret, substantial and identified'. 'Testing' in the franchisor's pilot scheme presumably suffices, but if there are only untested ideas as would be the case if there has been no pilot scheme, the initial franchise agreements would appear not to fall within the definition, and therefore to be outside the block exemption. 'Secret' simply means 'not generally known or easily accessible'[1]. It is the corpus of information which matters, it is not necessary that each component should be unknown and unobtainable outside the franchisor's business[2]. Given the limitations on the possibility of preventing former franchisees from using much of the

2.35 Competition law

information they acquire as franchisees[3], it would appear that this ought to be read as not being generally known outside the trade in question, otherwise the scope of the exemption will practically be limited to know-how in the technical sense, which is clearly not what is intended. The know-how must be useful to the franchisee in that it is capable of improving its competitive position by improving its performance, or helping it to enter the market[4]. It must be identified, ie described sufficiently, for example, in the manual to make it possible to verify that it fulfils the criteria of secrecy and substantiality[5].

1 Article 1(3)(g).
2 Ibid.
3 See para 2.107 et seq.
4 Article 1(3)(h).
5 Article 1(3)(i).

2.35 The use of the word 'marketing' in Article 1(3)(b) indicates that the exemption applies where the franchisee will hire goods to customers, or sell as agent (as in *Yves Rocher*)[1].

1 Case 87/14 [1988] 4 CMLR 592.

2.36 It seems likely that the indents in Article (1)(3)(b) are cumulative (they are in the French text), so that to come within the exemption, the franchise agreements must exhibit all of these characteristics.

2.37 Having indicated the field of application of the Regulation, we will deal with some of the more common points which arise.

(1) Restrictions accepted by the franchisor

2.38 Under Article 2(a) and (b), the exemption provided for in Article 1 applies to undertakings on the part of the franchisor not to:
 (i) grant the right to exploit all or part of the franchise to third parties;
 (ii) itself to exploit the franchise, or market the goods or services which are the subject-matter of the franchise under a similar formula [ie presumably marketing the specified goods[1] or services using a marketing formula similar to that used in the franchise];
 (iii) itself to supply the franchisor's goods, ie 'goods produced by the franchisor or according to its instructions, and/or bearing the franchisor's name or trade mark'[2] to third parties. The franchisor must, it seems, be free to supply to third parties not operating under the franchise formula.
 It appears that all or any of these restrictions may be included, for Article 1(1) exempts agreements which include 'one or more of the restrictions listed in Article 2'.

1 See Art 1(3)(b)—these may include goods made by various manufacturers. See also *Computerland* Case 87/407 [1989] 4 CMLR 259; *Pronuptia* Case IV/30.937 [1989] FSR 416.
2 Article 1(3)(d).

Summary of the block exemption 2.42

(2) Franchisee restraints

(i) Seeking customers

2.39 By Article 2(d) a restraint on the franchisee seeking customers outside its territory for the goods or services which are the subject-matter of the franchise are exempted. It is unclear whether this restriction can extend to spare parts and accessories. The specific mention of such goods appears only in Article 2(e)[1]. A literal reading of the exemption would suggest that the prohibition can extend to spare parts and accessories. However, there must be instances where competition between franchisees in spare parts and accessories would improve the consumer's position, without undermining the competitive thrust of the franchise. It may therefore be unwise to rely on too literal a reading.

1 See below—see also Recital 9.

(ii) To operate only from the franchised premises

2.40 The franchisee may be restrained from exploiting the franchise other than from the contract premises[1]. A restraint on changing the location of the contract premises without the franchisor's consent[2] falls outside Article 85(1) altogether[3].

1 Article 2(c). This includes transport used for the exploitation of the franchise—Art 1(3)(e).
2 If consent is unreasonably withheld, the benefit of the exemption may be withdrawn—Art 8(e).
3 Article 3(2)(i), *Pronuptia* para 19, but a restraint on opening a second shop within an exclusive territory needs exemption—*Pronuptia* para 24. The effect of Art 2(c) appears to be to give this exemption.

(iii) Not to compete with other members of the network

2.41 The obligation not to compete with other members of the franchise network during the term, and for up to one year afterwards *in the territory where it has exploited the franchise*[1] is whitelisted. This appears also to whitelist non-competition with company owned outlets. It is believed that a clause drafted along the lines of that suggested in Precedent 1 clause 5 would generally comply with this article. Obviously, during the term, clauses within Article 2(c) (obligation of the franchisee to exploit the franchise only from the contract premises) and Article 2(d) (obligation of the franchisee not to seek customers outside its territory), help to achieve the same result and Article 2 is not qualified by the need to show that the obligation is necessary to protect the franchisor's intellectual property etc.

1 Article 3(1)(c). *Pronuptia* para 16—without this restraint the franchisor's know-how might benefit competitors directly or indirectly. The court, however, in *Pronuptia* took a less restrictive view of post-term restraints.

(iv) Restrictions on persons with whom they may deal

2.42 Franchisees may be restrained from selling the goods which are the subject of the franchise[1] otherwise than by retail. They must be free to supply other franchisees[2] within the network and resellers within other channels of distribution supplied by or with the consent of the manufacturer[3]. Franchisees may not be

2.43 Competition law

restrained from selling to customers outside the franchised territory[4] (though they can be restrained from soliciting them outside their territory)[5]. These limits on exclusivity may be a problem for some kinds of goods distribution franchise.

1 In *Servicemaster* Case 88/604 [1989] 4 CMLR 581 an obligation not to sell home care products without the consent of the franchisor and only to the franchisee's customers was cleared.
2 Article 4(a) makes freedom to obtain goods from other franchisees a condition of the exemption.
3 Article 3(1)(e). See *Yves Rocher* para 46.
4 Article 5(g).
5 Article 2(d), para 2.39, ante.

(v) Exclusive dealing

2.43 Restraints on the franchise handling competing goods are exempted by Article 2(e). Although the Article reads as though it were limited to the franchisee manufacturing, or selling or using competing goods in the course of the provision of services, it seems fairly clear that a comma has been omitted after 'sell', otherwise the second part of the exemption, which makes it clear that such exclusivity does not apply to spare parts, where either the subject-matter of the franchise is the sale[1] of goods or their use in the provision of services, makes no sense at all.

A 'best endeavours' clause, cleared by Article 3(1)(f), can achieve a similar effect to an exclusive dealing clause.

The exclusive dealing obligation may not be imposed in respect of spare parts or accessories. The meaning of the latter terms are unclear; floppy disks and cassette ribbons are fairly clearly either accessories or spare parts for computers, but what about shoes and jewellery forming part of a wedding dress design as an ensemble?— or relishes for hamburgers[2]?

1 Not hire of goods.
2 It might, of course, be argued that the hamburgers and the particular relishes chosen by the franchisor to go on them form a unit, and it is that unit which the customer wants, not the hamburger with any old relish.

(vi) Approved sources and quality controls

2.44 Franchisors often wish to tie, because this can be a convenient way of accounting for fees and, bearing in mind VAT, it is an easy way to police royalties. Ties relating to goods manufactured by the franchisor or [designated][1] third parties are whitelisted by Article 3(1)(b) only where it is impracticable, owing to the nature of the goods which are the subject matter of the franchise, to apply objective quality specifications. In *Pronuptia* approved sources were said to be justified when there were too many franchisees to monitor. However, such terms appear to be blacklisted by Article 5(b) and (c). By Article 5(b) provisions whereby the franchisee is prevented from obtaining supplies of goods of equivalent quality to those of the franchisor are blacklisted, and by Article 5(c) refusal by the franchisor to designate other suppliers for reasons other than protecting the franchisor's intellectual property or maintaining the common identity and reputation of the network are blacklisted. By Article 3(1)(a) an obligation to sell or use only goods matching the franchisor's objective quality criteria is whitelisted, only so far as this is necessary to protect the franchisor's intellectual property or to maintain the common identity or reputation. It would appear that third parties must be free to supply the franchisee with goods of equivalent quality to those offered by the franchisor. Presumably third parties who make the franchisor's goods, or apply its trade mark, cannot be restrained from selling into the territory. Putting these provisions together we may draw the following conclusions:

(1) a tie of special recipe substances in eg a food or drink franchise, would be justified where this is necessary to protect the franchisor's secret recipe. Such a tie was allowed by the Commission in *Campari Milano*[2].

(2) In retailership franchises, where franchisees are selling a variety of goods bearing the trade marks of various manufacturers, it is possible to require the franchisee to obtain the franchisor's prior approval of new lines, but such approval must be given if the lines match the franchisor's objective criteria. Such a provision was allowed in *Computerland*[3] and in *Servicemaster*[4]. In some cases the requirement that the criteria should be objective may cause difficulties. However, provided that the criteria can be shown to be an attempt to fulfil the commercial necessity for preserving the quality of goods or services provided by the network, it is believed that the requirements of the exemption will be satisfied. If, on the other hand, the provisions are a mere sham to preserve unnecessary ties, they will be outside the exemption.

(3) Ties of the core of goods connected with the essential object of the franchise such as those in *Pronuptia*, or *Charles Jourdan*[5] are permissible. As we have seen, by Article 2(e) the franchise may be prevented from selling goods competing with the franchisor's which are the subject matter of the franchise[6]. This obligation may not however be imposed in respect of spare parts or accessories.[7] By Article 3(1)(b), in so far as it is necessary to protect the franchisor's intellectual property or to maintain the common identity and reputation of the network, the franchisee may be required to sell goods manufactured by the franchisor or designated third parties where it is impracticable owing to the nature of the goods which are the subject matter of the franchise, to apply objective quality specifications. In *Charles Jourdan*[8] there was an obligation on the franchisee, unless otherwise authorised by the franchisor, in view of the nature of the products concerned (fashion goods) and in order to preserve the consistency of the brand image, to order the goods *connected* with the essential object of the franchise business exclusively from the franchisor or designated suppliers. The franchisee might, however, purchase the goods in question from any other franchisee, franchise-corner retailer or traditional retailer belonging to the Charles Jourdan network. Recital 9, however, restricts the tie to goods *forming* the essential subject-matter of the franchise. By contrast, in *Pronuptia*[9], the Court said:

> 'It may in certain cases—for instance, the distribution of fashion articles—be impractical to lay down objective quality specifications. Because of the large number of franchisees it may also be too expensive to ensure that such specifications are observed. In such circumstances a provision requiring the franchisee to sell only products supplied by the franchisor or by suppliers selected by him may be considered necessary for the protection of the network's reputation. Such a provision may not, however, have the effect of preventing the franchisee from obtaining those products from other franchisees.'

In other words, the Court adopted a less restrictive attitude than the Commission, and there may be cases where franchisors will wish to notify and rely on this.

The 'blacklist' Articles 5(b) and (c) (foreclosing suppliers) are both subject to Article 2(e). Article 5(c) is not, however, subject to Article 3(1)(b). The effect of

2.45 *Competition law*

this is that if the franchisor refuses, for reasons other than protecting its intellectual property, or maintaining the common identity and reputation of the network to designate third parties as authorised manufacturers, then the agreement is outside the exemption.

1 Not presumably third parties 'designed' by the franchisor!—which is what the English text says.
2 Case 78/253 [1978] 2 CMLR 397, and, reading Art 3(1)(b) with the preamble to Article 3(1), which clears the obligations listed in so far as they are necessary to protect the franchisor's intellectual property or the common identity and reputation of the network, this type of tie appears to be cleared.
3 Para 23(vi).
4 Para 17.
5 Case 89/94 [1989] 4 CMLR 591. See also *Pronuptia* Case IV/30.937 [1989] FSR 416 where a right to vet, *ex post facto* peripheral goods stocked by franchisee to ensure their quality was held by Commission not to infringe Article 85(1).
6 As to meaning of this term see para 2.38 at n 1, ante.
7 As to the meaning of which see para 2.43, ante.
8 Para 28.
9 Para 21.

(vii) Confidentiality

2.45 Article 3(2)(a) clears unconditionally terms whereby the franchisee is obliged not to disclose to third parties the know-how provided by the franchisor, and the franchisee may be held to this obligation after termination. By Article 3(2)(d), we will recall, the franchisee may be restrained from using know-how other than for the purpose of exploiting the franchise, and again can be held to this after termination of the agreement. We will recall that 'know-how' is defined in a broad, rather than a technical sense[1]. However, a restriction on the use and disclosure of know-how in the technical sense, is obviously much stronger than one relating to know-how in the broader sense, and it is to be borne in mind that the common law doctrine of restraint of trade, prevents a franchisee from being limited in applying ordinary skills which he acquires in operating the franchise, once the agreement is terminated[2]. It is believed that the suggested restraint of trade clause[3] would satisfy the requirements of the exemption.

1 Article (1)(2)(g)—see para 2.34.
2 See para 2.10.
3 Precedent 1 clause 5.

Obligations having a narrower scope than those mentioned in the exemption

2.46 It might be expected that obligations of the same type, but narrower in scope than those cleared or exempted by the Regulation would *a fortiori* fall within its terms. This may not be the case: there is no express provision for this and, certainly in relation to the exclusive sale exemption[1], it has been held that such agreements fall outside its terms[2]. Consequently, agreements, for example, granting partial exclusivity will have to be notified.

1 Regulation 83/83 (replacing regulation 67/67).
2 See *Junghans* [1977] 1 CMLR D82. See also 17th Report on Competition Policy para 28.

The opposition procedure

2.47 As noted above, agreements which do not fall within the guidelines contained in Articles 2 and 3 of the exemption, may benefit from the opposition procedure. In order to do so, they must fulfil the conditions laid down in Article 4, and not fall within the scope of Article 5. The agreement must be notified to the Commission, and it will be exempted, unless the Commission does not oppose exemption within six months. The six months runs from the date of receipt of notification by the Commission, or the date of the postmark if notification is sent by registered post. Express reference to Article 5 must be made in the notification, and complete information must be furnished with it[1]. Where agreements were notified prior to the coming into force of the Regulation (1 February 1989), the opposition procedure can be invoked by submitting a communication to the Commission referring expressly to Article 6 and to the notification. Member states can oppose exemption within three months of notification being forwarded to them. The information furnished to the Commission must be treated by it as confidential[2].

The question has been raised as to whether the Commission's adoption of this procedure is ultra vires[3]. It is also unclear whether agreements are valid in the period between notification and the end of the six months' period[4]. The moral is to try to thread agreements through the block exemption whenever possible.

1 As to procedure on notification, see para 2.58.
2 Article 7.
3 Kerse *EEC Antitrust Procedure* (2nd edn, 1988) (European Law Centre para 2.42; Korah *Franchising and the EEC Competition Rules Regulation 4087/88* (1989) (ESC) para 7.5.1.
4 *Korah* para 7.1.

Agreements not within the block exemption

2.48 The block exemption is limited in its application to franchises which supply goods or services to end users. In the nature of things, because there can be only one market level in relation to the provision of services, ie the distribution level, the Regulation appears to be applicable to all service franchises. However, in relation to franchises involving the manufacture or distribution of goods, it is obviously possible to envisage franchises which do not supply end users. A manufacturing franchise, might, for example, supply wholesale or retail traders, a master distribution franchise might supply, for example, franchisees selling to end users, and a wholesale warehouse franchise might supply the branded goods of various manufacturers and selectors, for example, to the members of a voluntary chain. How are such franchises likely to be treated? So far as the third type of franchise is concerned, to the extent that the warehouse is dealing in goods in which there is strong inter-brand competition, and it is supplying outlets which are in competition with other sources of the same goods, it is unlikely that there would be any problems in relation to Article 85(1), even if each warehouse is restricted to the supply of outlets in its own territory. Manufacturing and master distribution franchises, on the other hand, are more problematic. Although, like all franchising, they can be regarded on the one hand as being a way of improving competition, they could certainly have the features which the court and the Commission have found objectionable in relation to ordinary manufacturing licences and distribution agreements. The safe advice must be to stay within the guidelines which have emerged in relation to them[1]. The possibility that such agreements may come within another block exemption is expressly recognised in Recital 9, though in *Pronuptia* the court, without

2.49 Competition law

giving very satisfactory reasons, held that Regulation 67/67 (the old block exemption on distributorships) was not applicable to franchise agreements[2]. There is also the problem that the patent and know-how block exemptions do not appear to contemplate the licence as being ancillary to a trade mark licence as it always will be in franchising[3].

1   See para 2.49 et seq below.
2   See *Pronuptia* para 28 et seq.
3   Regulation 2849/84, Art 2(6) and Recital 10; Regulation 556/89 Art 1(7) and Recital 2.

Manufacturing licences

2.49 Clearly, ordinary manufacturing licences, as well as franchised manufacturing licences can lead to the rapid diffusion of technology throughout the EEC, and thus increase inter-brand competition. Some sort of territorial prohibition for licensees may, however, be indispensable in order to persuade licencees to invest in the technology. This in turn, has the potential to insulate individual markets. In the *Maize Seed Case*[1] the court took the view that a licensor could grant territorial exclusivity without falling within Article 85(1), so long as it did not grant absolute territorial protection by preventing export into the relevant territory altogether. The Commission, on the other hand, continued to consider most manufacturing licences as being caught by Article 85(1) and requiring exemption. It did, however, recognise a degree of territorial protection in the patent block exemption[2] by allowing a five year restriction on passive sales, and a restriction on active sales for the length of the patent. In *Pronuptia*, as we have seen, the court indicated that provisions which maintain the identity and reputation of the franchise network, and restrictions which are ancillary to franchise agreements, might not come within Article 85(1) at all. Although the block exemptions may suggest otherwise, it is possible to argue on the basis of the court's decisions that certain manufacturing licences are not caught by Article 85(1). Relevant considerations might be the novelty of the technology, together with the possibility of its rapid dissemination through the market which franchising could in certain circumstances provide. It is also to be borne in mind that with regard to some types of technology there may be a 'naturally' localised market[3]. A situation could be envisaged of a franchise based on a technological development where it would be feasible for each franchise to satisfy only a localised set of buyers, and yet the overall effect of the dissemination of the technology would be to increase inter-brand competition. Such a situation would be rare, however. A more likely situation is that even without direct distribution restrictions, there is the possibility in manufacturing franchises of achieving an insulation of markets. Suppose X wants widgets to be manufactured in the United Kingdom and France. He may be able to ensure that United Kingdom widgets are not exported to France and vice versa by licensing[4] small producers who individually lack the capacity to indulge in exports and who have no incentive to do so anyway if local demand is good. By making the various licences exclusive, and thereby preventing himself from licensing further manufacturers and promoting thereby an export trade in widgets, X would be in breach of Article 85(1). In the *Davidson Rubber* case there was this possibility[5]. 'Non-competition' and 'no-challenge' clauses may also assist in preserving market insulation in such cases[6]. A manufacturing network which had such a restrictive effect could arise accidentally through the capital market attracting only small firms at the outset. The licensor would usually not be allowed to continue to keep the markets insulated in perpetuity

Agreements not within the block exemption 2.52

and restrictions on him granting further licences would almost certainly be held to be in breach of Article 85(1).

1 Case 258/78 *LC Nungesser KG v Commission* [1982] ECR 2015, [1983] 1 CMLR 278.
2 Regulation 418/8503 OJ 1983 L53/5.
3 Eg where only one buyer requires a product and only one licensor is able and willing to market it—for example, special car components as in *Re Raymond & Co and Nagoya Rubber Ltd Agreement* [1972] CMLR D45.
4 The existence of intellectual property rights such as patents will in practice be an essential part of this strategy of course.
5 See *Re Davidson Rubber Co* OJ L143, 23.6.72, p. 31, [1972] CMLR D 52. See also *Re Burroughs-Delplanque* OJ L13, 17.1.72, p.50; [1972] CMLR D 67; *Re Kabelmetal's Agreement* OJ L222, 22.8.75, p.34; [1975] 2 CMLR D40; *Re Bronbemaling and Heidemaatschaappij* OJ L249, 25.9.75, p.27; [1975] 2 CMLR D67.
6 *Re Reuter-BASF* AG OJ L254, 17.9.76, p.40; [1976] 2 CMLR D44; *Re AOIP/Beyrard* OJ L6, 13.1.76, p.8; [1976] 1 CMLR D14; *Re Vaessen Moris* [1979] 1 CMLR 511. Case 83/400 *Re Windsurfing International* OJ L229, 20.8.83, p.1; [1984] 1 CMLR 1.

2.50 So much for restrictions operating at the distribution level. The features of all kinds of manufacturing licences, however, most likely to give rise to problems in relation to Article 85(1) are of course 'tie-ins'. In order to justify these to the Commission it would appear that a very good reason must be adduced, such as that satisfactory results cannot be achieved by specification[1], or that they are necessary to preserve trade secrets[2].

1 *Vaessen Moris* [1979] 1 CMLR 511—the 'tie-in' in this case was not justified. See also Block Exemption reg 419/85 OJ 1985 L 53/5. *Re Windsurfing International*, ante.
2 *Campari-Milano* OJ C198, 19.8.77, p.3.

The patent and know-how block exemptions[1]

2.51 Where patents or know-how are involved, regard should be had to the provisions of the relevant block exemption in drafting a manufacturing franchise agreement[2]. For the reasons given in the previous paragraph, it is not sufficient merely to treat the agreement through the 'white list' and to avoid 'black list' clauses; the possible *de facto* insulation of markets by a network of agreements must also be considered.

Given the views expressed in *Pronuptia* about the non-application of the block exemption on distributorships to franchising agreements, and the fact that the trade mark licence is required to be ancillary to the know-how, not vice-versa[3], it would appear to be advisable to notify even agreements complying with the provisions of these two block exemptions.

1 For detailed guidance on these see Korah *Patent Licensing and EEC Competition Rules* (1989) (ESC Oxford); *Know-how Licensing Agreements and the EEC Competition Rules Regulations 556/89* (1989) (ESC Oxford).
2 The possibility of franchise agreement falling outside the franchise block exemption benefiting from other block exemptions is expressly mentioned in Recital (4) of the franchise block exemption. The patent block exemption is contained in Regulation 2349/84 OJ 1984L 219/5, the know-how block exemption in Regulation 556/89, OJ 1989 L61/1. Mixed know-how and patent licences can be accommodated within the know-how block exemption.
3 See Regulation 556/89 Recital 2, and see Article 1(3).

2.52 In the last analysis, if the overall effect of the network of agreements is to improve inter-brand competition, rather than restricting or destroying competition, following the logic of *Pronuptia*[1] it would appear that at least as a fall back position, it ought to be possible to argue that the agreements are not caught by Article 85(1) at all[2].

1 And note the renewal of the example in *Transocean Marine Paint Association* OJ L 351 21.12.88, p.40.
2 See para 2.17.

Selective distribution agreements

2.53 Selective distribution systems can produce much the same anti-competitive effects as exclusive supply terms and a selective distribution policy will always be a feature of business format distributorships. The effects of selective distribution policies have been considered in a number of cases and certain features commonly found in them have been held not to infringe Article 85(1) at all. In order to avoid unnecessary repetition, however, these are dealt with after Article 85(3), since qualitative criteria have been accepted in certain circumstances as a basis for exemption[1].

1 Paras 2.71 et seq, post.

Price restrictions

2.54 Price restrictions, whether directly or indirectly[1] maintained, have an obvious tendency to insulate markets in *all* types of franchising and are objectionable. Maximum price terms could have the effect of removing the incentive to sell from a cheap market into a more expensive one, and in principle could therefore infringe Article 85(1). However, recommended prices are not a restriction unless the conduct of the parties indicates a concerted practice[2].

1 Case 80/1283 *Re Johnson and Johnson* OJ L377, 31.12.80; p 16; [1981] 2 CMLR 287.
2 *Pronuptia*, ante.

Termination provisions

2.55 Termination provisions have the potential to increase the observance of objectionable restrictions in all types of franchise agreements[1]. However, in the franchising block exemption Article 5(f) permits agreements being made to terminate on a challenge to the validity of the franchisor's intellectual property, this is also the case under the patent licensing block exemption[2] and the know-how block exemption[3].

1 *Re BMW's Agreement* OJ L29, 3.2.75, p 1; [1975] 1 CMLR D44.
2 1984 L219/15.
3 1989 L61/1 Article 3(4).

Effect of infringement of Article 85(1)

2.56 Any agreement prohibited by Article 85(1) is automatically void. It is void *ab initio*. This does not necessarily mean that the whole agreement is void. This is of course a matter for the municipal[1] courts. So far it is unclear whether or not English courts will approach the matter along the lines of the 'blue pencil' rule[2]. In *Chemidus Wavin Ltd*[3] only Buckley LJ seems to have thought that it would not. Area restrictions as we have seen may infringe Article 85(1), and it could well be that if these restrictions were severed, the franchisee would find himself paying the same rate of royalties with no territorial guarantee. This would seem to be unfair, and it may be that the franchisees' interests would be better served by a holding that the agreements as a whole were void. The probable outcome of that would be a renegotiation by the parties of the terms of the agreement. Since the alternative could be the collapse of the chain, the franchisor is likely to agree new contracts. If an agreement were to be held to be entirely void it is a difficult question whether or not any lump sums paid to the franchisor might be recovered. If the agreements have actually operated, it would be difficult to argue that the consideration has wholly failed, and given the nature of the mistake, it is difficult to argue that it is money paid under a mistake of fact[4].

1 Case 319/82 *Société de Vente de Ciments et Bétons de L'Est SA v Kerpen and Kerpen GmbH & Co KG* [1983] ECR 4173, [1985] 1 CMLR 511, ECJ.
2 See paras 2.119 et seq, post.
3 [1976] 2 CMLR 387; affd [1978] 3 CMLR 514, CA.
4 Although the distinction between mistakes of law and mistakes of fact is a fine one—*Solle v Butcher* [1950] 1 KB 671, [1949] 2 All ER 1107, CA.

Agreements are not considered in isolation

2.57 Although the effect on inter-Member trade of any individual franchise agreement is unlikely to be significant, it is clear that the Commission and the Court of Justice will not look at individual agreements in isolation. This seemed to follow from the *Société Technique Minière* case[1] and was accepted in the *Brasserie de Haecht SA* case[2]. In the latter case a brewery lent money to cafe proprietors. In return the borrowers agreed to purchase their supplies of beer, drinks and lemonade exclusively from the Brasserie. The ties were to last until the debts were paid off plus a further two years. The question was, were the tying agreements void under the Treaty? The court ruled that whilst any one agreement might not be inconsistent with the Treaty, they might be so when considered in their economic and legal context, ie having regard to other agreements made by the Brasserie as well as those made by other Belgian brewers. If Belgian brewers made a widespread practice of exacting such ties, it would restrict the possibility of eg German brewers selling to Belgium. The implication of the *Brasserie de Haecht SA* case then is that the purposes of Article 85(1), is the effect on inter-Member trade which restrictions in the agreements entered into by the franchisor with his franchisees are *likely* to have overall, when considered in the context of the particular market in which the restrictions operate. It is to be noted that there has been a move away from the *Société Technique Minère* doctrine that an agreement is capable of affecting trade between Member States if there is a sufficient *degree of probability* that it will have an effect. It is sufficient if agreements have the potential. This approach is implicit in *Pronuptia*[3].

1 Case 56/65 *Société Technique Minière v Maschinenbau Ulm GmbH* [1966] ECR 235, [1966] CMLR 357, CMR 8047.
2 Case 23/67 *Brasserie de Haecht SA v Wilkin* [1967] ECR 407, [1968] CMLR 26, CMR 8053; Case 47/76 *De Norre v NV Brouwerij Concordia* [1977] ECR 65, [1977] 1 CMLR 738; *Re Deutsche Castrol* OJ L114, 29.4.83, p 26; [1983] 3 CMLR 165, CMLR 378, CMR 8386, ECJ.
3 See paras 2.16 et seq, ante.

Notification of new agreements, negative clearance and exemptions

Regulation 17, Article 4

2.58

'1 Agreements, decisions and concerted practices of the kind described in Article 85(1) of the Treaty which come into existence after the entry into force of this Regulation and in respect of which the parties seek application of Article 85(3) must be notified to the Commission. Until they have been notified, no decision in application of Article 85(3) may be taken.'

Informal advice on the need to notify an agreement can be obtained by writing to the Commission. The advice given will be entirely unofficial of course. Formal notification should be made on Form A/B[1]. Copies must be filed[2], together with copies of the supporting documents, which may be certified copies[3]. Both negative clearance[4] and exemption under Article 85(3) can be applied for on the same form, and generally should be[5]. It is not necessary to notify each franchising agreement, but only the standard form which will be, or is, being used[6].

1 See Regulation 27. One copy is required by the Commission and one each for the competent authorities in every Member State. For procedure see para 2.59 below
2 Regulation 27, Art 2(1) as amended by Regulation 1699/75.
3 Regulation 27, Art 2(2).
4 Under Regulation 17, Art 2. It is granted on the basis that there is no ground for action under Arts 85 or 86.
5 Case 85/79 *Re Deere & Co* OJ L35, 7.2.85, p 58; [1985] 2 CMLR 554. If negative clearance only is applied for, exemption cannot be given.
6 Case 1/70 *Parfums Marcel Rochas Vertriebs-GmbH v Bitsch* [1970] ECR 515, [1971] CMLR 104, CMR 8102; Case 48/72 *Brasserie de Haecht SA v Wilkin-Janssen* [1973] ECR 77, [1973] CMLR 287, CMR 8170.

(i) Completing Form A/B[1]

2.59 The questions are grouped under six headings, not all of which may be relevant to a particular agreement. It is essential that the form be completed with care: if wrong or incomplete information is given exemption may be refused, and immunity from a fine may not be secured.

In the case of standard form contracts such as franchise agreements, it is only necessary to attach the text of the standard form to Form A/B. Information relating to the names and addresses of all the undertakings to the agreement need not be supplied under Heading I, *Information regarding parties*. In *Parfums Marcel Rochas Vertriebs-GmbH V Bitsch*[2], the court said 'Because of its very nature, a standard contract, on being notified, draws the Commission's attention to the economic and legal context in which an agreement of this kind subsists'. The Commission may obtain further information if it requires it under Regulation 17, Art 11. Agreements in the form of the contract notified, subsequently concluded, enjoy the benefits of notification.

Heading III contains questions regarding *inter alia* the *Means of achieving the aims of the agreement*. The court indicated in *Vereniging ter Bevording van de Belangen des Boekhandels v Eldi Records BV*[3] that where the full text of an agreement is annexed to the form, the agreement will be properly notified even though only some of the clauses are quoted on the form, provided that the description given there constitutes a fair and accurate record of the provisions which at the time were considered the most important, and there is no intention evident merely to notify part of the agreement.

Heading IV requires the facts and reason as to why Article 85(1) is considered inapplicable to be given. If negative clearance is not being sought, this part of the form need not be completed. If it is being sought question (b) should be answered in the affirmative.

Heading V is relevant to exemption under Article 85(3). It is usually necessary to attach an annex showing how the agreement satisfies the conditions of Article 85(3)[4]. The guidance provided by the *Pronuptia* case[5], and the *Yves Rocher* case[6], is helpful in this regard.

Heading VI, which asks whether further supporting arguments are to be produced in relation to the questions under the previous headings, should be noted.

The form may be signed by representatives on behalf of the undertakings concerned, but written proof of the representative's authority to act must be supplied. Since only one party to an agreement need submit it, the submission by the franchisor of the standard form will suffice. The franchisees do not need to notify in addition.

Form A/B can be obtained from the Commission of the European Communities, 8 Storey's Gate, London SW1 (tel: 01-222 8122) or from Directorate General for Competition, Rue de la Loi, 200, B-1049 Brussels, Belgium.

1 See generally C Kerse 'EEC Antitrust Procedure' ELC (2nd edn, 1988) s 2.21 et seq.
2 Case 1/70 [1970] ECR 515, [1971] CMLR 104, CMR 8102, ECJ.
3 Case 106/79 [1980] ECR 1137, [1980] 3 CMLR 719, CMR 8646, ECJ.
4 Para 2.69, post.
5 Para 2.16, ante. The case is helpful, even though the question of exemption did not arise.
6 OJ 1987 L8/49.

2.60 If the agreement is subject to registration under the Restrictive Trade Practices Act 1976[1], the information required by the Registration of Restrictive Trading Agreements (EEC Documents) Regulation 1973[2] must be sent to the Director General of Fair Trading.

1 See para 2.141 et seq. post.
2 (SI 1973 No 950)—see Appendix 7.

(ii) Consequences of failure to notify

2.61 Note: *for reasons of space, pre-accession agreements, ie agreements in existence on 1 January 1973, are not dealt with. Special provision has been made for these in relation to notification and reference should be made if necessary to the standard works.*[1]

(1) There is no protection from the imposition of a penalty for breach of Articles 85 and 86[2]. A notified agreement is protected from the time of notification until a decision under Article 85(3)[3]. More usually, instead of making a decision under Article 85(3), the Commission sends out a 'comfort letter', informing the person notifying that it is closing its file on the matter[4]. If an agreement were to be held to be excused notification, but not granted exemption under Article 85(3), theoretically a fine could be imposed. In practice this is unlikely since the object of Regulation 17, Art 4(2) is to discourage unnecessary notification and the imposition of a fine would be somewhat counter to this policy[5].

(2) If the agreement is notifiable, no clearance can be granted under Article

2.62 Competition law

85(3) unless it is notified. Furthermore, exemption can only be retroactive to the date of notification. If on the other hand, an agreement is excused notification under Regulation 17, Art 4.2(2), the court can nevertheless grant retrospective clearance[6], ie the rule which prevents the court's decision from taking effect prior to the date of notification[7] is inapplicable. Consequently the main danger of failing to notify a notifiable agreement is that, even though the agreement may obtain clearance, there will automatically be a period when it will have been technically void. Such voidness can be pleaded by a party sued under the agreement[8].

1 For the position with regard to agreements existing on 1 January 1973, see Bellamy and Childs *Common Market Law of Competition* (3rd edn 1987) (Sweet & Maxwell) para 11.039 et seq. We are concerned only with new agreements.
2 See *Re Pittsburgh Corning Europe* OJ L272, 5.12.72, p 35; [1973] CMLR D2.
3 Provided the information notified was not incorrect or misleading—Regulation 17.15(1).
4 See [1983] OJ C 295/6.
5 In *Vaessen-Moris* OJ L 19, 26.1.79, p 32; [1979] 1 CMLR 511, however, the reason why the Commission did not impose a fine was that Moris's firm was small and obtained its sole return from the sale of the tied items.
6 Regulation 17.6(2).
7 Regulation 17.6(1).
8 Case 48/72 *Brasserie de Haecht SA v Wilkin-Janssen* [1973] ECR 77, [1973] CMLR 287, CMR 8170, ECJ, *Pronuptia* para 2.16, ante.

(iii) Agreements excused notification

2.62 Regulation 17, Art 4(1) contains the requirements that new agreements be notified. Article 4(2) however excuses certain agreements from the need for notification.

'2. Paragraph 1 shall apply to agreements, decisions or concerted practices where:
(1) the only parties thereto are undertakings from one Member State and agreements, decisions or practices do not relate either to imports or to exports between Member States;
(2) not more than two undertakings are party thereto, and the agreements only:
(a) restrict the freedom of one party to the contract in determining the prices for or conditions of business on which the goods which he has obtained from the other party to the contract may be resold: or
(b) impose restrictions on the exercise of the rights of the assignee or user of industrial property rights—in particular patents, utility models, designs or trademarks—or of the person entitled under a contract to the assignment, or grant, of the right to use a method of manufacture or knowledge relating to the use and to the application of industrial processes;
(3) they have as their sole object:
(a) the development of uniform application of standards or types; or
(b) joint research and development; or
(c) specialisation in the manufacture of products, including agreements necessary for the achievement thereof;
(i) where the products which are the object of specialisation do not, in a substantial part of the common market, represent more than 15% of the volume of business done in identical products, or those considered by the consumers to be similar by reason of their characteristics, price and use, and
(ii) where the total annual turnover of the participating undertakings does not exceed 200 million units of account.
These agreements, decisions and practices may be notified to the Commission.'

Agreements not within the block exemption 2.65

2.63 The first point to be noted is that it is possible for an agreement to have the potential of voidness under Articles 85(1) and yet be exempt from notification. This interpretation was reached in the *Bilger*[1] and the *Fonderies Roubaix*[2] cases.

1 Case 43/69 *Brauerei A Bilger Söhne GmbH v Jehle* [1970] ECR 127, [1974] 1 CMLR 382, CMR 8076, ECJ.
2 Case 63/75 *Fonderies Roubaix-Wattrelos SA v Société Nouvelles des Fonderies Roux* [1976] ECR 111, [1976] 1 CMLR 538, CMR 8341.

2.64 The meaning of the words 'relate to imports/exports' in Article 4.2(1) was considered in the *Bilger* case[1]. The facts of *Brauerei Bilger* were similar to the *Brasserie de Haecht SA* case. Bilger, a German brewery, made loans to Jehles who ran a number of establishments for the retail sale of beer in Germany. In return Jehles undertook only to sell Bilger's beers. This was an agreement between parties from one Member State, and therefore complied with the first requirement of Article 4.2(1). The second requirement however is that the agreement should not 'relate either to imports or exports between Member States'. Although the agreements might affect trade between Member States[2], the court held that they did not relate to exports or imports between Member States. Consequently, the agreement did not require notification. In the *Fonderies Roubaix* case the court went even further in holding that Article 4.4(2) applied 'where the marketing envisaged by the agreement takes place solely within the territory of the Member State to whose law the undertakings are subject even if the goods in question have at an earlier stage been imported from another Member State'. It would appear therefore that the court takes the view that the agreement must relate directly to exports or to imports eg an agreement between two undertakings that they will export to or import from only certain Member States. The *Bilger* case involved 'tie-ins', but the same reasoning must apply to area restrictions, which as we have already pointed out may affect inter-Member trade. It must be said that the distinction between 'agreements affecting' and 'agreements relating to' is difficult to justify rationally. Every agreement which might affect such trade must surely 'relate to' it—and that in principle includes agreements of the *Bilger* sort[2]. Consequently, the cautious advice would be that if an agreement could affect trade, it ought to be notified. It was also held in *Bilger* that an agreement qualifying as non-notifiable remained valid until its nullity was established by an appropriate tribunal. This view was rejected in *Brasserie de Haecht SA v Wilkin-Janssen*[3], however. Both notifiable and non-notifiable agreements are therefore void ab initio.

1 Case 43/69 *Brauerei A Bilger Söhne GmbH v Jehle* [1970] ECR 127, [1974] 1 CMLR 382, CMR 8076, ECJ.
2 Case 23/67 *Brasserie de Haecht SA v Wilkin* [1967] ECR 407, [1968] CMLR 26, CMR 8053, ECJ.
3 Case 48/72 [1973] ECR 77, [1973] CMLR 287, CMR 8170, ECJ.

2.65 Article 4.2(2) relates only to agreements to which not more than two undertakings are parties. Would franchising chains which consist of a network of identical agreements be considered to be agreements between two undertakings for the purposes of Article 4.2(2)? The answer suggested by *Parfums Marcel Rochas* and other cases is, 'yes'. In that case Rochas entered into several standard form contracts, with concessionaires in France, which prohibited exports. The court concluded that the existence of parallel standard form contracts did not matter, they were nevertheless concluded between two parties: an interpretation confirmed by Regulation 153/62.

2.66 *Competition law*

2.66 It would appear that an agreement may qualify to be excused notification under any of the sub-paragraphs of paragraph 2[1] (on the other hand the provision within sub-paragraphs (2) and (3) are alternative).

1 *Vaessen/Moris* OJ L19, 26.1.79, p 32; [1979] 1 CMLR 511.

(iv) Negative clearance

Regulation 17, Article 2

2.67

'Upon application by undertakings or associations of undertakings concerned, the Commission may certify that, on the basis of the facts in its possession, there are no grounds under Article 85(1) or Article 86 of the Treaty for action on its part in respect of an agreement, decision or practice.'

Any franchise agreement may be notified for clearance[1], and until a 'comfort letter' is sent[2], or a ruling is given the parties are protected from fines from the date of notification[3]. When clearance is given, it can be retrospective[4].

If the court should eventually refuse clearance, the civil consequence is that the agreement is void ab initio[5].

1 For the procedure see para 2.58 et seq, ante.
2 See [1982] OJ C 343/4.
3 Regulation 17.15(5) Not before *Re Pittsburgh Corning Europe* OJ L 272, 5.12.72, p 35; [1973] CMLR D2.
4 Regulation 17.6.
5 Case 48/72 *Brasserie de Haecht SA v Wilkin-Janssen* [1973] ECR 77, [1973] CMLR 287, CMR 8170, ECJ.

(v) Minor agreements

2.68 In the Notice of 3 September 1986[1], the Commission again affirms its policy of promoting economically desirable co-operation between small and medium-sized undertakings. It goes on to state that agreements whose effects on trade are negligible do not fall within Article 85(1). Only those agreements are prohibited which have an appreciable impact on market conditions, in that they appreciably alter the market position, ie the sales outlets and supply possibilities of non-participating undertakings and of consumers[2]. Probably the 5 per cent market share or 200 million units of account thresholds set out in the Notice will be considered to be those of the chain as a whole[3]. The problem, when trying to apply this guidance to franchising, is that it is not possible (usually) to be certain when drafting agreements that a network of them will not exceed the limits. The other practical problem with these Guidelines, is to determine the relevant market. Thus, as noted above, Charles Jourdan has a negligible share of the French and Community markets in shoes, but if the market is medium and top quality shoes, the share rises to 10 per cent of the French market, and 2 per cent of the Community market, so that its agreements would be outside the guidelines. Agreements within the guidelines do not have to be notified[3].

1 [1986] OJ C 231/2—see Appendix 3, post.
2 See Case 5/69 *Völk v Vervaecke* [1969] ECR 295, [1969] CMLR 273, CMR 8074.
3 See para 2.24 ante.

(vi) Exemption under Article 85(3)

2.69 An agreement outside the block exemption, and which is not granted negative clearance may nevertheless be granted individual exemption under Article 85(3) provided that the agreement has been notified for exemption. In practice, a 'comfort letter' is a more likely outcome than individual exemption. Such a letter indicates that the Commission is closing its file on the relevant case. Although such letters have no formal status within the framework of the EEC competition law, they are generally relied on in practice, and provisionally, if the matter subsequently came before the court or the Commission, would be taken into consideration in deciding whether or not it was appropriate to impose a fine. Unfortunately, it would appear that such a letter would not have the effect of validating provisions requiring exemption, so that they will remain unenforceable in a national court as contrary to Article 85(1). As we have pointed out, both negative clearance, and exemption can and should be applied for at the same time on Form A/B[1]. An application for negative clearance alone under Regulation 17, Art 2 does not count as notification under Regulation 17, Art 4 and does not provide a legal basis for exemption under Article 85(3)[2]. Agreements exempted from notification under Regulation 17, Art 4.2 may also be granted exemption under Article 85(3). Article 85(3) provides:

> 'The provisions of paragraph 1 may, however, be declared inapplicable in the case of:
> any agreement or category of agreements between undertakings; any decision or category of decisions by associations of undertakings; any concerted practice or category of concerted practices;
> which contributes to improving the production or distribution of goods or to promoting technical or economic progress, while allowing consumers a fair share of the resulting benefit, and which does not:
> (a) impose on the undertakings concerned restrictions which are not indispensable to the attainment of these objectives;
> (b) afford such undertakings the possibility of eliminating competition in respect of a substantial part of the products in question.'

1 Para 2.58: *Re Deere & Co* OJ L35, 7.2.85, p 58; [1985] 2 CMLR 554.
2 See para 2.58, ante.

2.70 The agreement must therfore fulfil four conditions in the view of the Commission:
(1) it must contribute to improving the production or distribution of goods or to improving technical or economic progress; and
(2) it must allow consumers a fair share of the resulting benefit; and
(3) it must impose no further restrictions than are indispensable to the attainment of these objectives; and
(4) it must not afford such undertakings the possibility of eliminating competition in respect of a substantial part of the products in question.

Selective distributorships

2.71 The problem with any particular network of franchise agreements which is outside the block exemption is whether or not the interference with the free movement of goods can be justified, ie are the markets artificially divided? The

2.72 Competition law

problem, we will recall, is largely likely to arise in connection with selective distributorships, but could also arise in the case of manufacturing franchises[1]. Certainly in the case of distributorships qualitative criteria have been accepted where they appeared to be necessary. For example the Commission has accepted the need to have competent staff to sell such things as photographic equipment[2], watches and clocks[3]. The need to keep an adequate store of spares and trained staff able to do repairs has also been accepted in the case of motor cars[4]. Computers need an adequate after-sales back-up service, and this too justifies the operation of a selective distribution system[5]. In some types of distributorships, allowing improperly qualified people to handle goods could, of course, present a real risk to consumers, resulting in additional expense and even injury to the consumer. A requirement that an adequate range of lines of electronic equipment be stocked was accepted in *Re SABA*[6]. Minimum target turnover requirements were also accepted in *Re SABA*, and in *Demo-Studio Schmidt v EC Commission*[7] a requirement that shops open at certain hours, and a refusal to accept part-time outlets in the interests of good customer service was held not to infringe Article 85(1). The point of these examples is that it was possible to demonstrate that at the time these supply limitations served a useful and beneficial purpose. They were not simply arbitrary and a way of limiting competition. The fact that some restriction in price competition is inherent in any selective distribution system has been accepted, so that competition in the quality of services provided is lawful, but only to the extent it can be strictly justified[8]. Exclusive sale and purchasing requirements, which in distribution franchising are crucial because they compel the franchisee to put his best efforts behind the line and prevent him from using the guidance and advice received from the franchisor to promote other lines, have also been granted exemption[9], and in the light of *Pronuptia* this would certainly seem to be acceptable, provided that it did not lead to artificial division of markets[10].

1 Paras 2.49 et seq; 2.53 et seq.
2 *Re Kodak* OJ L 147, 7.7.70; p 24; [1970] CMLR D 19.
3 *Re Omega Watches* OJ L 242, 5.11.70, p 22; [1970] CMLR D 49; *Re Junghans GmbH* OJ L 30, 2.2.77, p 10; [1977] 1 CMLR D 82.
4 *Re BMW's Agreement* OJ L 29, 3.2.75, p 1; [1975] 1 CMLR D 44.
5 *Re IBM Personal Computer* 84/233 [1984] 2 CMLR 342; *Macsi Informatique Sàrl v Apple Computer Inc* (1988) ECC 374 (held not to infringe Article 85(1))—Court of Appeal, Paris.
6 OJ L 28, 3.2.76, p 19; [1976] 1 CMLR D 61; Case 83/672 [1984] 1 CMLR 676.
7 Case 210/81 [1983] ECR 3045, [1984] 1 CMLR 63, ECJ.
8 Case 107/82 *AEG Telefunken AG v EC Commission* [1983] ECR 3151, [1984] 3 CMLR 325, ECJ see also Case 82/267 *Re AEG-Telefunken Agreement* OJ L117, 30.4.82, p 15 [1982] 2 CMLR 386. Exemption was granted in *Agreement Between Austin Rover Group and Unipart* [1988] 4 CMLR 513 where it was possible to show that the relevant restrictions were essential to improve the distribution of the goods in question.
9 Eg *Re Goodyear Italiana SpA* OJ L 38, 12.2.75, p 10; [1975] 1 CMLR D 31. Cf *Re Spices* OJ L 53, 24.2.78, p 20; [1978] 2 CMLR 116.
10 In addition to the cases cited under the text above, the following may be helpful in providing guidance as to what is helpful and what is not in selective distributorships; Case 99/79 Lancômbe SA v Etos [1980] ECR 2511, [1981] 2 CMLR 164, CMR 8714, ECJ; Case 31/80 *L'Oreal NV v De Nieuwe AMCK PVBA* [1980] ECR 3775, [1981] 2 CMLR 235, CMR 8715, ECJ. Cases 253/78 and 1-3/79 *Procureur de la Republique v Giry and Guerlain SA* [1980] ECR 2327, [1981] 2 CMLR 99, CMR 8712, ECJ; *Re Grohe* [1988] 4 CMLR 612.

2.72 *Pronuptia* gave a limited sanction to the notification by a franchisor of recommended prices and this policy is continued in the block exemption. The limits of that sanction should be noted however; there must not be a concerted practice

Agreements not within the block exemption 2.74

between the franchisor and franchisees with a view to these prices being applied in practice. Obviously both minimum price terms, and a minimum advertised prices policy, have the potential to affect trade between States. Such price fixing is expressly mentioned in Article 85(1)(a), but could there be a case for exemption under Article 85(3)? The chief argument in favour of minimum resale prices in distribution arrangements, is that they serve to protect those with high promotion costs, etc., from the 'free rider'[1] and there is some evidence that the court may now be prepared to take account of this[2]. However, clearly they can also reduce competition at the distribution level and help to preserve oligopoly[3]. Although directly imposed *resale* price maintenance is not generally possible in the United Kingdom because of the Resale Prices Act 1976[4], a successfully operated policy of minimum advertised prices could have the same effect. Such a policy may be investigated now under the Competition Act 1980[5], however. So far as Article 85(1) is concerned, it falls clearly within the wording of sub-paragraph (a). To the extent that goods are involved which are imported, re-imported or exported, it is likely to be found as objectionable as directly imposed price maintenance. To the extent that the policy is purely national, it may also be objected to, at least if the market share of the goods concerned is significant[6].

1 See Cases 228/229/82 *Ford of Europe Inc and Ford-Werke AG v EC Commission* [1984] ECR 1129, [1984] 1 CMLR 649; *Association des Centres Distributeurs Edouard Leclerc v Thouars Distribution SA* [1984] 1 CMLR 273.
2 See para 2.73 post.
3 See eg *Re Dupont de Nemours (Deutschland) GmbH* OJ L 194, 16.7.73, p 27; [1973] CMLR D 226; *Re Deutsche Philips GmbH* OJ L 293, 20.10.73, p 40; [1973] CMLR D 241.
4 See para 2.150.
5 See para 2.126 et seq.
6 *Re Gerofabriek NV* OJ L 16, 19.1.77, p 8; [1977] 1 CMLR D 35—see, however, First Report on Competition Policy, 1972, 55.

2.73 A clause giving a national distributor the right to control the advertising of dealers was objected to in *Hasselblad (GB) Ltd v EC Commission*[1]. In franchising, the public are taught to recognise outlets where they will receive a standard range of goods and service both pre-sale and after-purchase. It is this which gives the peculiar emphasis to the 'free rider' problem. If third parties are allowed to import and sell the same goods, this will destroy the association of goods and their ancillaries and outlets in the minds of the public, and will result, presumably, in the destruction of the franchise operation. Where advertising and promotion are done ordinarily (ie outside the business format context) by a manufacturer, arguably this is not so much of a problem (even though he may have to invest more in advertising in some countries than others). Ultimately, in theory, the markets should balance out and the supply/demand curves intersect at their natural point of balance, resulting in a free market price. In business format franchising, the franchisees themselves pay[2] substantially towards the advertising because it promotes *their* business. Their investment both in capital (including fitting out of premises, etc.) and in advertising will simply be lost.

1 Case 86/82 [1984] ECR 883, [1984] 1 CMLR 559, ECJ. Case 30/78 *Distillers Co Ltd v EC Commission* [1980] ECR 2229, [1980] 3 CMLR 121, CMR 8613, ECJ; *Re Distillers Co plc* [1983] 3 CMLR 173.
2 The sum will often be specifically allotted to this purpose.

2.74 A further line of argument may be developed from this, for it leads us to focus on the operation as a whole. It ought to be possible to argue under Article

2.75 Competition law

85(3) that restrictions which are imposed to preserve the chain as a whole should be exempted[1]. In appropriate cases, it may be possible to show that this may benefit the consumer, for the elimination of such competition may be justified on the ground that such competition might lead to the disappearance of weaker links in the chain and thereby a worsening of service to the public. If F1 makes 75 per cent of his earnings from the part of his territory adjoining F2 and F2 takes that 75 per cent, F1 may go out of business and leave the remaining 25 per cent unserved. Consequently, even though F1 and F2 may be in different countries, and therefore the restriction clearly affects inter-Member trade, it could be justified under Article 85(3), though of course regard would be had to the whole economic and legal context[2].

1 See block exemption Recitals (8) (9) and (10) *Pronuptia* para 15 et seq.
2 Case 30/78 *Distillers Co Ltd v EC Commission* [1980] 3 CMLR 121 at 146 et seq.

2.75 We have focused on exemption for selective distributorships because they are the most problematic (franchises distributing goods manufactured and marked by a variety of manufacturers[1] are less problematic[2]. The same sorts of argument can be applied to 'manufacturing' franchises, however. The extent to which the public end up by paying more as a result of goods being marketed through a business format chain, of course, very much depends on the level of inter-brand competition. Savings on distribution costs may well result in them paying less. Allowing third parties deliberately to import goods at artificially low prices in order to break up the chain, and gain an entry to the market, could eventually lead to the consumer paying higher prices.

1 See *Computerland* OJ 1987 L222/12.
2 See para 2.48.

2.76 It is also to be noted that the Commission may be prepared to tolerate restrictions which are imposed to enable small businesses to penetrate the market[1], and this could well justify restrictions up to the time the chain secures a reasonable market share.

1 *Re Transocean Marine Paint Association* OJ L 163, 20.7.67, p 10; [1967] CMLR D 9; fourth renewal 21 December 1988 OJ L 351/40.

Agreements not within the block exemption 2.76

COMMON MARKET COMPETITION LAW—CHECKLIST

Note: this checklist must not be used mechanically. As explained above, the whole economic context both at the outset, and when the network has achieved a significant market share need to be considered.

Does the agreement involve the supply of goods or services to end users?

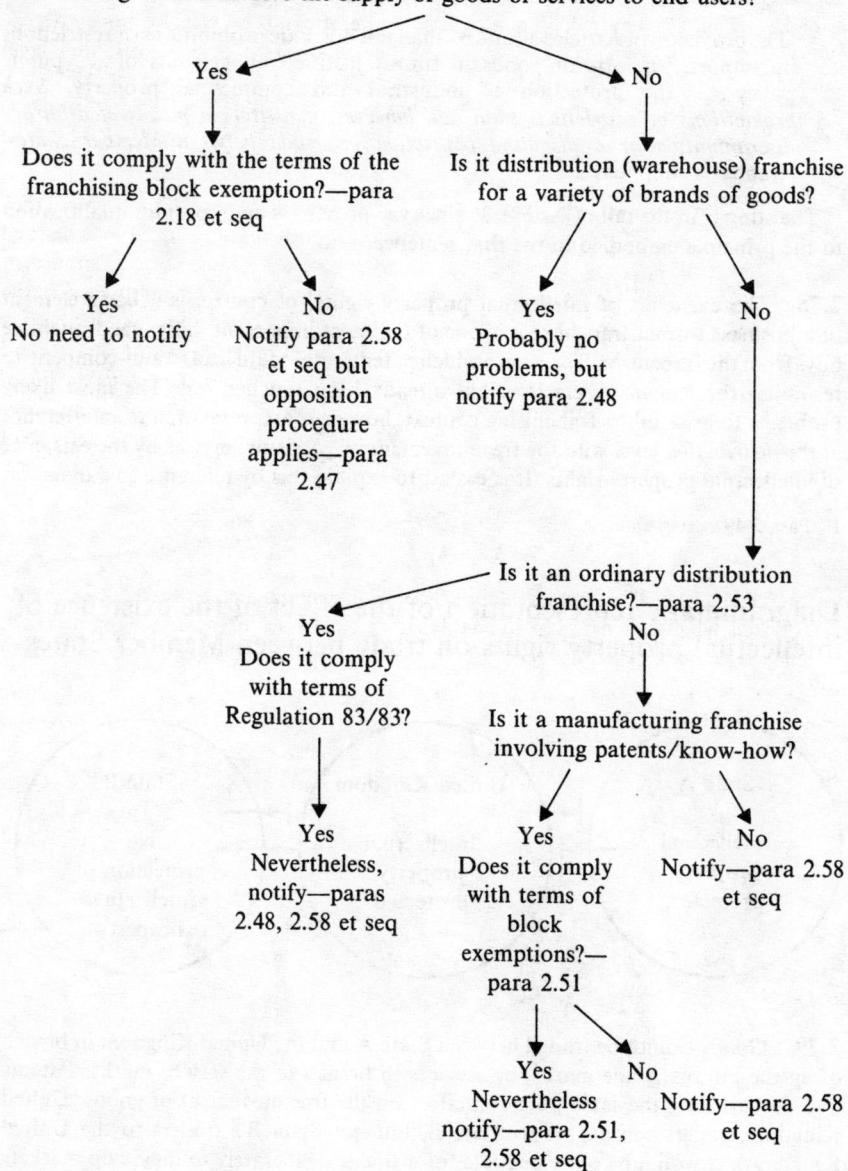

- **Yes** → Does it comply with the terms of the franchising block exemption?—para 2.18 et seq
  - **Yes** — No need to notify
  - **No** — Notify para 2.58 et seq but opposition procedure applies—para 2.47

- **No** → Is it distribution (warehouse) franchise for a variety of brands of goods?
  - **Yes** — Probably no problems, but notify para 2.48
  - **No** → Is it an ordinary distribution franchise?—para 2.53
    - **Yes** — Does it comply with terms of Regulation 83/83?
      - **Yes** — Nevertheless, notify—paras 2.48, 2.58 et seq
    - **No** → Is it a manufacturing franchise involving patents/know-how?
      - **Yes** — Does it comply with terms of block exemptions?—para 2.51
        - **Yes** — Nevertheless notify—para 2.51, 2.58 et seq
        - **No** — Notify—para 2.58 et seq
      - **No** — Notify—para 2.58 et seq

In all cases consider the overall effect of a network of similar agreements.

83

2.77 Competition law

The insulation of markets by the existence of national intellectual property rights

(a) The problem stated

2.77 The existence of national intellectual property rights has a natural tendency to insulate markets. National property rights are recognised by the Treaty. Article 222 provides 'This Treaty shall in no way prejudice the rules in Member States governing the system of property ownership'. In addition, Article 36 provides:

> 'The provision of Articles 30 and 34 shall not preclude prohibitions or restrictions on imports, exports or goods in transit justified on grounds of . . . public policy . . . the protection of industrial and commercial property. *Such prohibitions or restrictions shall not, however, constitute a means of arbitrary discrimination or a disguised restriction on trade between Member States'* [emphasis supplied]

The sting is in the tail of Article 36 since the proviso is an important qualification to the principle embodied in the first sentence.

2.78 The existence of intellectual property rights, of course, is a basic element of a business format franchise: it is one of the most important things the franchisee buys from the franchisor. The way in which patents, etc, could lead to anti-competitive results at the *manufacturing* level has already been touched on[1]. The most likely problems to arise in the franchising context, however, are in relation to interference at the *distribution* level with the free movement of goods or services by the existence of intellectual property rights. It is easiest to explain this by reference to a diagram:

1 Para 2.49 et seq, ante.

Diagrammatic representation of the effect of the existence of intellectual property rights on trade between Member States

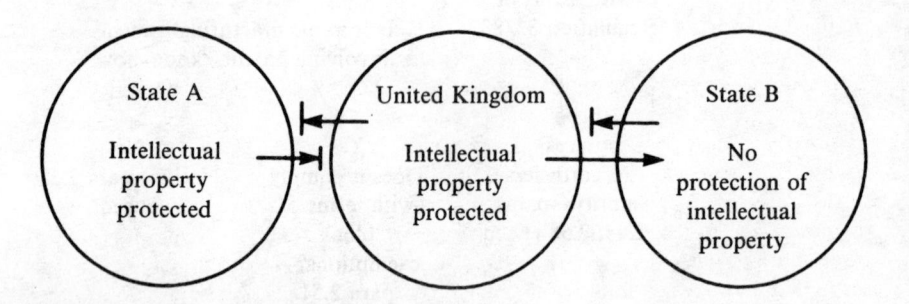

```
    ┌─────────────┐      ┌─────────────┐      ┌─────────────┐
    │   State A   │      │United Kingdom│      │   State B   │
    │             │◄──┤──│             │◄──┤──│             │
    │Intellectual │      │Intellectual │      │     No      │
    │  property   │──┤──►│  property   │──┤──►│ protection of│
    │  protected  │      │  protected  │      │ intellectual │
    │             │      │             │      │  property   │
    └─────────────┘      └─────────────┘      └─────────────┘
```

2.79 Goods cannot be traded between State A and the United Kingdom in breach of eg the internal trade marks, or services in breach of the service marks. Patents and designs have the same potential effect on the free movement of goods. United Kingdom traders can export to State B, but not State B's traders to the United Kingdom[1]. It would be quite possible for a trader deliberately to divide up markets in this way. Suppose for example that X is the manufacturer of 'Golden Widget', brand widgets which are marketed in both France and the United Kingdom. A wishes to stop parallel imports from France to the United Kingdom and vice versa.

All that X would need to do would be to assign the United Kingdom mark to his United Kingdom distributor and his French Mark to his French distributor. Neither they (nor anyone else) could now import and distribute from the other territory without rendering themselves liable for an action for infringement[2]. Provided, however, the right vested in the distributor was not used to create absolute territorial protection, it would be acceptable[3].

1 In the reverse direction it would appear that goods could not be traded unless the doctrine of exhaustion applied. See Case 24/67: *Parke Davis & Co v Probel* [1968] CMLR 47, ECJ; Case 15/74: *Centrafarm v Sterling Drug Co Inc* [1974] ECR 1147, [1974] 2 CMLR 480; Case 434/85 *Allen & Hanburys Ltd v Generics (UK) Ltd* [1988] 2 All ER 454.
2 See eg Cases 56 and 58/64: *Etablissements Consteń SARL and Grundig-Verkaufs GmbH v EEC Commission* [1966] ECR 299, [1966] CMLR 418, CMR 8046.
3 Case 170/83 *Hydrotherm Gerätebau GmbH v Compact de Dott* [1984] ECR 2999, [1985] 3 CMLR 224, ECJ.

(b) Exhaustion and other limitations on rights

2.80 The first limitation to such insulation of markets is the 'exhaustion of rights' doctrine. If goods are put into the market by a person, or by his consent in one Member State, he cannot assert property rights so as to prevent their importation into another Member State. The doctrine applies in the first place to patents[1]. It would be quite wrong if a patentee who had had his turn in one Member State were permitted to prevent import into another. The important consideration is whether or not the goods were put onto the market with the consent of the patentee. In *Pharmon BV c Hoechst AG*[2] the European Court held that a patentee could prevent the marketing of a product manufactured in another Member State by the holder of a compulsory licence under a parallel patent held by the same patentee, but in *Allen & Hanburys v Genericos*[3] it was held that the owner of a UK patent endorsed 'licences of right' could not prevent importation from a territory in which the goods were not patentable, by an importer who had undertaken to take a licence on the terms prescribed by law, and who accordingly could not have been enjoined from manufacturing the product in the relevant Member State: the licensor merely had a right to a fair return. The doctrine of exhaustion also applies to designs[4]. The doctrine is more controversial in relation to trade marked goods, to the extent that goods bearing the same mark may not in fact be the same, or indeed have any connection at all with the proprietor of the mark in the importing country[5]. In some of the early cases the court came near to propounding a *per se* rule that if a trade mark had a common origin, then markets were artificially divided[6]. Indeed, the court and the Commission displayed a general antipathy to trade marks even where the risk of consumer confusion existed[7], and indeed it seems that the mere possibility of consumer confusion is not sufficient for the purposes of Article 36[8]. 'Public policy' cannot be extended to include considerations of consumer protection[9]. The situation reached as a result of these cases must be considered in the light of the *Terrápin*[10] and *Centrafárm* cases[11]. A British company using the trade mark 'Terrapin' began to export to Germany where a company already carried on business under a similar (though not identical) mark. The court ruled that it was consistent with the free movement of goods that the German company might assert its trade mark rights. One of the important points about the *Terrapin* judgment is that it contains an explicit statement of the respective roles of the national courts and the Court of Justice:

'It is for the court at first instance, after considering the similarity of the products, and the risk of confusion, to enquire further in the context of this last provision into whether the exercise in a particular case of industrial and commercial property rights may or may not constitute a means of arbitrary discrimination or a disguised restriction on trade between Member States'[12].

It must be noted however, that the marks in this case did not have a common origin. In *Theodor Kohl KG v Ringelhan and Rennett SA*[13] the Advocate-General contrasted this case with *Van Zuylen Frèses v Hag AG*[14] on the ground that it did not involve the splitting of a common symbol. The mark in the importing state in the *Ringelhan and Rennett* case had belonged to a company which was defunct at the relevant time. The time was therefore a mere memory in the minds of the public. The Advocate-General however suggested that even if the German parent had still existed it could not have prohibited use because the identifying role of the mark is nullified by the splitting.

1 Case 15/74 *Centrafarm BV v Sterling Drug Co Inc* [1974] ECR 1147, [1974] 2 CMLR 480, CMR 8246 ECJ. Article 81 of the Community Patents Convention embodies this principle. It is part of internal United Kingdom law under the Patents Act 1977, s 60(4). See also *Champagne Heidsieck et Cie Monopole SA v Buxton* [1930] 1 Ch 330.
2 Case 19/84 [1985] 3 CMLR 775, ECJ.
3 [1988] 2 All ER 454.
4 Case 144/81 *Keurkoop BV v Nancy Keen Gifts* BV [1982] ECR 2853, [1983] 2 CMLR 47, CMR 8861, ECJ.
5 Apart from this consideration, it clearly applies to trade marked goods: Case 16/74 *Centrafarm BV v Winthrop BV* [1974] ECR 1183, [1974] 2 CMLR 480, CMR 8247.
6 Case 40/70 *Sirena Srl v Eda Srl* [1971] ECR 69, [1971] CMLR 260, CMR 8101; Case 192/73 *Van Zuylen Frères v Hag AG* [1974] ECR 731, [1974] 2 CMLR 127, CMR 8230. But see [1989] 3 CMLR 154.
7 In neither of the above cases was there evidence before the court that the products were the same. In some cases before the Commission there actually was evidence that they were different—*Re Advocaat Zwarte Kip* OJ L237, 29.8.74, p 12; [1974] 2 CMLR D 79; *Re Sirdar Ltd Agreement* [1975] OJ L125, 16.5.75, p.27; [1975] 1 CMLR D 93.
8 Case 177/83 *Theodor Kohl KG v Ringelhan and Rennett SA* [1984] ECR 3651, [1985] 3 CMLR 340, ECJ.
9 Ibid.
10 Case 119/75 [1976] ECR 1039, [1976] 2 CMLR 482, CMR 8362.
11 Case 102/77 *Hoffman-La Roche & Co AG v Centrafarm mbH* [1978] ECR 1139, [1978] 3 CMLR 217, CMR 8466; Case 3/78 *Centrafarm BV v American Home Products Corpn* [1978] ECR 1823, [1979] 1 CMLR 326, CMR 8475.
12 [1976] 2 CMLR 482 at 505. See also Case 24/67 *Parke Davis v Probel* [1968] ECR 55, [1968] CMLR 47, CMR 8054.
13 Case 177/83 [1984] ECR 3651, [1985] 3 CMLR 340.
14 Case 192/73 [1974] ECR 731, [1974] 2 CMLR 127, CMR 8230, ECJ.

2.81 It is for the court at first instance, after considering the similarity of the products, and the risk of confusion, to enquire further in the context of this last provision into whether the exercise in a particular case of industrial and commercial property rights may or may not constitute a means of arbitrary discrimination or a disguised restriction on trade between Member States[1].

1 [1976] 2 CMLR 482 at 505. See also Case 24/67 *Parke Davis v Probel* [1968] ECR 55, [1968] CMLR 47, CMR 8054.

2.82 It must be noted, however, that the marks in this case did not have a common origin. In *Theodor Kohl KG v Ringelhan and Rennett SA*[1] the Advocate-General contrasted this case with *Van Zuylen Frères v Hag AG*[2] on the ground that it did not involve the splitting of a common symbol. The mark in the importing state

Agreements not within the block exemption 2.85

in the *Ringelhan and Rennett* case had belonged to a company which was defunct at the relevant time. The mark was therefore a mere memory in the minds of the public. The Advocate-General, however, suggested that even if the German patent had still existed, it could not have prohibited use because the identifying role of the mark is nullified by the splitting.

1 Case 177/83 [1984] ECR 3651, [1985] 3 CMLR 340.
2 Case 192/73 [1974] ECR 731, [1974] 2 CMLR 127, CMR 8230, ECJ. See, however, opinion of A-G Jacobs OJ C10/89.

2.83 At any rate, in cases where marks do not have a common origin, it is clear from the *Terrapin* case that local conditions are an important consideration. For example the word 'Lowenbrau' is liable to cause confusion in the United Kingdom but not in Germany[1]: consequently the United Kingdom trade mark could prevent the export of other 'Lowenbrau' beers from Germany to the United Kingdom, while the German trade marks might not prevent the export of United Kingdom 'Lowenbrau' to Germany. It may be possible to use the emphasis put on local conditions in this case to support the 'free rider' argument set out below[2].

1 *Löwenbräu München v Grünhalle Lager International Ltd* [1974] 1 CMLR 1, [1974] RPC 492.
2 See paras 2.72 et seq, ante.

2.84 In Case 102/77 *Hoffman-La Roche & Co AG v Centrafarm mbH*[1], La Roche owned the trade mark 'Valium' in the United Kingdom and in Germany. Centrafarm bought United Kingdom Valium (which was cheaper), repacked it and sold it in Germany under the same trade mark. The court's ruling was as follows:

> 1(a) The proprietor of a trade mark right which is protected in two Member States at the same time is justified pursuant to the first sentence of Article 36 of the EEC Treaty in preventing a product to which the trade mark has lawfully been applied in one of those States from being marketed in the other member-State after it has been repacked in new packaging to which the trade mark has been affixed by a third party.
> (b) However, such prevention of marketing constitutes a disguised restriction on trade between member-States within the meaning of the second sentence of Article 36 where:
>> it is established that the use of a trade mark right by the proprietor, having regard to the marketing system which he has adopted, will contribute to the artificial partitioning of the markets between member-States;
>> it is shown that the repackaging cannot adversely affect the original condition of the product;
>> the proprietor of the mark receives prior notice of the marketing or the repackaged product; and
>> it is stated on the new packaging by whom the product has been repackaged.
>
> 2 To the extent to which the exercise of a trade mark right is lawful in accordance with the provisions of Article 36 of the Treaty, such exercise is not contrary to Article 86 of the Treaty on the sole ground that it is the act of an undertaking occupying a dominant position on the market if the trade mark right has not been used as an instrument for the abuse of such a position[2].

1 [1978] ECR 1139, [1978] 3 CMLR 217, CMR 8466, ECJ.
2 [1978] 3 CMLR 217 at 244. See also *Hoffman-La Roche & Co AG v Centrafarm Vertriebsgesellschaft Pharmazeutischer Erzeugnisse mbH* [1984] 2 CMLR 561.

2.85 Case 3/78 *Centrafarm BV v American Home Products Corpn*[1] involved

2.86 Competition law

somewhat similar facts, save that in this case in repacking the goods a different trade mark was affixed—that under which the goods were sold in the Netherlands where Centrafarm proposed to distribute them. The court recognised that differing trade marks applied to similar products in differing Member States could be a method of artificially partitioning markets. It also however recognised that a function of trade marks is the protection of the owner's reputation. Only the proprietor (or his licensees) may confer an identity upon a product by affixing the mark. In *Hoffman-La Roche v Centrafarm* the court had by contrast rather focused on Centrafarm taking advantage of the status and advantage of La Roche's mark.

1 [1978] ECR 1823, [1979] 1 CMLR 326, CMR 8475, ECJ.

2.86 In the Advocate-General's opinion in *Centrafarm v American Home Products Corpn* the view expressed that the doctrine of exhaustion did not apply because a new mark was affixed by the importer—Home Products: Benelux mark. In *Hoffman-La Roche v Centrafarm* the doctrine does not seem to have been thought applicable because the goods were repacked and remarked. It seems simply to have been assumed that if they have not been, parallel imports could not have been prevented, for La Roche stated they would have had no objection in this case. In neither case did the proprietor of the marks succeed in stopping the imports, and it is submitted that the issue must be the same whether or not the goods are remarked or repacked. The question in all cases, whether or not the goods bear the same or a different mark, must surely be: would the markets be divided artificially by the exercise of the right?

Conclusion

2.87 The result of the cases discussed above seem to be as follows:

(1) The proprietor can in principle prevent others from using the same mark, his right to do so being recognised by Article 222 and Article 36.

(2) The protection afforded under Article 222 and Article 36 will be lost if it is established that the owner of the trade marks has pursued a practice (whether deliberately or not) of using them artificially to partition markets and thereby restrict trade between Member States. If the marks have a common origin, the doctrine of exhaustion may nevertheless be applied, even though the goods bearing the mark are different.

2.88 The doctrine of exhaustion is obviously only applicable to the marketing of goods. In relation to services to have two businesses operating under the same mark would inevitably lead to confusion of the public, and damage to the mark in the importing country. In the light of the *Kohl* case discussed above, however, it is by no means clear that if the marks have a common origin, this consideration would carry the day. If the marks do not have a common origin, it is submitted, that in the light of the cases discussed above, the trade mark and service mark rights ought to prevail.

Article 86
2.89

'Any abuse by one or more undertakings of a dominant position within the

Agreements not within the block exemption 2.91

common market or in a substantial part of it shall be prohibited as incompatible with the common market in so far as it may affect trade between Member States. Such abuse may, in particular, consist in:

(a) directly or indirectly imposing unfair purchase or selling prices or other unfair trading conditions;

(b) limiting production, markets or technical development to the prejudice of consumers;

(c) applying dissimilar conditions to equivalent transactions with other trading parties, thereby placing them at a competitive disadvantage;

(d) making the conclusion of contracts subject to acceptance by the other parties of supplementary obligations which, by their nature or according to commercial usage, have no connection with the subject of such contracts.'

2.90 The trigger bringing Article 86 into operation is the requirement that an undertaking occupy a dominant position within the common market or in a substantial part of it[1]. There must be an ability to act independently of the market[2]. First of all, it is clear that the mere possession of intellectual property rights of itself does not confer a dominant position[3] though such rights can be exercised in a way which constitutes an abuse, even under a licensing programme exempted under Article 85(3)[4]. The use by a franchisor of those property rights in order to impose 'tie-ins', etc could in certain circumstances be treated as an abuse of a dominant market position within Article 86 in the same way[5]. The fact that he could not justify the 'tie-in' would tend to suggest that there had been an abuse in that the intellectual property may have been used as a lever to improve the tie. This provision then could be used in addition to Article 85 to break unjustifiable 'tie-ins'. The question as to when 'tie-ins' can be justified, has been discussed already[6].

1 See eg *Re GEMA* OJ L 134, 20.6.71, p.15; [1971] CMLR D 35; *Re European Sugar Cartel* OJ L 140, 26.5.73, p 17; [1973] CMLR D 65.
2 European Economic Community, Serie Concurrence 3 *La probleme de la Concentration dans le Marche Common* (Brussels, 1966). See Case 27/76 *United Brands Co v EC Commission* [1978] ECR 207, [1978] 1 CMLR 429, CMR 8429, ECJ; Case 102/77 *Hoffmann-La Roche & Co AG v Centrafarm mbH* [1978] ECR 1139, [1978] 3 CMLR 217, CMR 8466, ECJ; Case 322/81 *Nederlandsche Banden-Industrie Michelin NV v EC Commission* [1983] ECR 3461, [1985]1 CMLR 282, ECJ; Case 237/87 *Volvo v Veng* [1989] 4 CMLR 122; Case 53/87 *Consorzio Italiana Renault* (5 October 1988, unreported).
3 Case 24/67 *Parke, Davis & Co v Probel* [1968] ECR 55, [1968] CMLR 47, CMR 8054; Case 40/70 *Sirena v Eda Srl* [1971] ECR 69, [1971] CMLR 260, CMR 8101; Case 78/70 *Deutsche Grammophon v Metro-SB-Grossmärkte GmbH & Co KG* [1971] ECR 487, [1971] CMLR 631, CMR 8106; Case 102/77 *Centrafarm*, ante.
4 *Re Tetra Pak BTG* (1C/licence) OJ L 272, 4.10.88, p.27; *Volvo v Veng* [1989] 4 CMLR 1: Case 53/87 *Consorzio Italiana v Renault*. It would appear that so long as the product in question is available on terms that are not abusive; or licences are available on terms that are not abusive (so that a refusal by the rights holder itself to supply is not abusive), then mere refusal of a licence is not in itself abusive—a fortiori if the prospective licensee fails to satisfy the franchisor's objectively justified criteria for franchisees.
5 *Re Hilti AG* [1985] 3 CMLR 619; *Eurofix-Bauco/Hilti* OJ L 65, 11.3.88, p.19 (now before European Court).
6 See para 2.44 ante.

2.91 Article 86 is directly effective, and a party injured in consequence of conduct amounting to an infringement of it may recover damages[1].

1 *Garden Cottage Foods Ltd v Milk Marketing Board* [1984] AC 130, [1983] 2 All ER 770, HL.

2.92 Competition law

Restraint of trade at common law

Introduction

2.92 The principal matters to which regard should be had in the domestic context are the possibility of the common law rendering franchisees covenants not to compete etc, void as being in restraint of trade, and the possibility of voidness of restrictions under the Restrictive Trade Practices Act 1976. This latter is likely to be repealed soon if the charges recommended by the White Paper[1] are implemented and domestic law is assimilated to EEC law.

1 'Opening Markets—New Policy on Restrictive Trade Practices' Cm 737 July 1989.

RESTRAINT OF TRADE AT COMMON LAW

Introduction

2.93 As noted above, franchising lends itself readily only to situations where a business system can readily be 'cloned'. The franchisees 'buy' from the franchisor in return for their payments instruction in this system, as well as the benefits of central marketing and continuing support. For many kinds of franchise, the franchisee may feel at the end of the term that the personal goodwill they have built up is sufficient for them to succeed in providing the goods or services to the public under another name. One of the most common questions is 'what can the franchisor do to stop this?' Obviously, we must assume in the first place that the former franchisee has sufficiently distinguished the new business from the franchisor's to avoid the possibility of an action for passing off or infringement. Secondly, we will assume, as will usually be the case, that no confidential information or trade secrets in the technical sense are involved. If they are, it will usually be possible to obtain an injunction against a former franchisee seeking to exploit them[1]. In the normal situation, however, the franchisor will be seeking protection against the following possibilities after the end of the term:

(1) The former franchisee carrying on the same kind of business from the location of the former franchisee. This problem is avoided if, as is sometimes the case, the franchisor owns the location and simply leases to, or licences, the franchisee for the term of the franchise[2]. Often however, it is only practicable for the franchisee to own or lease the site, in which case the covenants in restraint of trade are the principal source of protection.

(2) The franchisee setting up a competing business from another site within such proximity to the location of the former business that it will damage the surviving goodwill of the former franchise outlet, which the franchisor will commonly want to re-franchise, either from the same or an adjoining site.

(3) The former franchise damaging other franchised outlets by setting up a competing business in close proximity to them.

(4) The former franchisee soliciting customers of the former business, and similarly, employing his former employees, or employees of the franchisor or other franchisees, for the purpose of operating a similar business.

1 See para 3.118 et seq.
2 See para 5.17 et seq, post.

General principles

2.94 An agreement in restraint of trade is one in which 'a party (the covenantor) agrees with any other party (the covenantee) to restrict his liberty in the future to carry on trade with other persons not parties to the contract in such manner as he chooses[1].

1 *Petrofina (Great Britain) Ltd v Martin* [1966] Ch 146 at 180; adopted *Esso Petroleum Co Ltd v Harper's Garage (Stourport) Ltd* [1968] AC 269 at 307, 317, HL.

2.95 One problem with the common law doctrine which must be noted at the outset is that its basis is unclear: it may be based on a view that it is desirable to preserve free competition, on the other hand it may be based simply on the protection of weak parties against oppression[1]. In fact both views may be supported from the cases. There are however straws in the wind suggesting that the latter approach may in future find more favour with the courts. It is proposed to deal with this in the course of the ensuing discussion.

1 *Anson on Contract* ed Guest (1984) (OUP) p 319.

2.96 The modern rules are derived from Lord Macnaughton's speech in *Nordenfelt v Maxim Nordenfelt Guns and Ammunition Co Ltd*[1].

(1) All restraints of trade, in the absence of special justifying circumstances, are contrary to public policy and therefore void.

(2) It is a question of law for the decision of the court whether the special circumstances adduced do or do not justify the restraint; and if a restraint is not justified, the court will, if necessary, take the point, since it relates to a matter of public policy, and the court does not enforce agreements which are contrary to public policy.

(3) A restraint can only be justified if it is reasonable (a) in the interests of the contracting parties, and (b) in the interests of the public.

(4) The onus of showing that the restraint is reasonable between the parties rests upon the party alleging that it is so, that is to say, upon the covenantee. The onus of showing that, notwithstanding that a covenant is reasonable between the parties, it is nevertheless injurious to the public interest and therefore void, rests upon the party alleging it to be so, that is to say, usually upon the covenantor. But once the agreement is before the court it is open to scrutiny in all its surrounding circumstances as a question of law.

1 [1984] AC 535 at 565, HL. The following summary is taken from *Anson on Contract* ed Guest (26th edn, 1984) (OUP) pp 318 et seq.

2.97 A word of caution must be offered about this scheme: although it may seem reasonable to separate the questions[1] 'is there a restraint of trade?' and 'if so, is it reasonable?' the courts have not always done so. Often the problem is posed in the rolled-up form 'does the contract unreasonably restrict?'[1] Nevertheless, although there are merits in the flexibility which results from uncertainty[1], there are also merits in clear thinking about principles.

1 *Esso Petroleum Co Ltd v Harper's Garage (Stourport) Ltd* [1968] AC 269 at 331, per Lord Wilberforce.

2.98 *Esso Petroleum Co Ltd v Harper's Garage (Stourport) Ltd*[1] is a leading authority on the common law doctrine. Since it involved a 'solus' agreement, it is of obvious

2.101 *Competition law*

importance in the context of franchising. Solus agreements were the subject matter of much litigation in the 1960s. The facts of *Esso Petroleum v Harper's Garage* were typical. The garage owners agreed to buy petrol exclusively from Esso for a number of years. In addition they undertook inter alia[2], to keep the garage open at all reasonable hours and in the event of sale of the garage to obtain similar agreements from the purchaser. In return for this, the garage proprietors received a number of benefits including a discount on the normal wholesale price of petrol, and the participation in Esso's dealer co-operation plan. In addition to the 'opening the door' principle[3], two limitations on the common law doctrine of restraint of trade were proposed. Lord Pearce suggested: 'The doctrine does not apply to ordinary commercial contracts for the regulation and promotion of trade during the existence of the contract, provided that any prevention of work outside the contract, viewed as a whole, is directed towards the absorption of the parties' services and not their sterilisation'[4]. Attractive as this view may seem in the context of franchising, it is to be regarded with caution[5]. In the first place it depends on two doctrines which have been rejected by the courts: (1) that restraint of trade does not apply during the continuance of a contract[6]. and (2) that restraint of trade only applies where trade is restricted rather than promoted. As Diplock LJ observed in the *Petrofina* case, this is really an application of the doctrine, not its exclusion[7]. Second, the cases Lord Pearce cited to support the absorption rather than sterilisation proposition arguably in fact involved sterilisation of the covenantor's capacities[8].

1 [1968] AC 269, [1967] 1 All ER 699, HL.
2 There was a resale price clause, but the issues on that were abandoned.
3 See *Ravenseft Properties Ltd's Application* [1978] QB 52.
4 [1968] AC 269 at 328.
5 See Heydon (1969) 85 LQR 229.
6 *Petrofina (Great Britain) Ltd v Martin* [1966] Ch 146, [1966] 1 All ER 126.
7 'I think that it does no more than assert that if on analysis of the effect of the contract as a whole it is likely to promote the expansion of trade, the restrictions will be found to be reasonable' [1966] Ch 146 at 184. See also per Lord Wilberforce in *Esso Petroleum Co Ltd v Harper's Garage (Stourport) Ltd* [1968] AC 269 at 336, HL.
8 See Heydon (1969) 85 LQR 229.

2.99 Lord Wilberforce proposed a 'rule of reason' approach which takes into account amongst other things changing social and economic circumstances:

> 'The doctrine of restraint of trade is one to be applied to factual situations with a broad and flexible rule of reason . . . It is not to be supposed, or encouraged, that a bare allegation that a contract limits a trader's freedom of action exposes a party suing on it to the burden of justification . . . the development of the law does seem to show that judges have been able to dispense from the necessity of justification under a public policy test of reasonableness such contracts or provisions of contracts as, under contemporary conditions, may be found to have passed into the accepted and normal currency of commercial or contractual or conveyancing relations [because] . . . moulded under the pressures of negotiation, competition and public opinion, they have assumed a form which satisfied the test of public policy as understood by the courts at the time, or . . . the trade in question has assumed such a form that for its health or expansion it requires a degree of regulation. Absolute exemption for restrictions or regulation is never obtained. Circumstances, social or economic, may have altered, since they obtained acceptance, in such a way as to call for a fresh examination: there may be some exorbitance or special feature in the individual contract which takes it out of the accepted category:

but the court must be persuaded of this before it calls upon the relevant party to justify a contract of this kind[1].

1   Heydon (1969) 85 LQR 229 at 331–333.

2.100   The rule of reason approach is of course one of the two approaches adopted by American courts in applying their anti-trust legislation[1]. The obvious advantage of the test as formulated by Lord Wilberforce is its flexibility: eg it is capable of explaining why the brewers' tied public-house system in this country should be acceptable[2] when at first sight it would seem to involve restraint of trade. The test's obvious disadvantage is its uncertainty: at what stage can we be sure that a trading practice has become acceptable? Worse still, what becomes acceptable is presumably equally capable of ceasing to be. For example, if in the context of franchising, certain restrictions had become common currency and acceptable, but as happened in the United States the activities of a few unscrupulous operators aroused public concern, would the courts regard those once acceptable restrictions in the same light? It may indeed be reasonable to adopt the guiding principle that an agreement which would satisfy American courts should satisfy the courts of this country[3]. Certainly, this is a principle which may commend itself to the cautious.

1   Lord Wilberforce in fact cited *Standard Oil Co Ltd v United States* 221 US 1 (1910).
2   See ibid at 33.
3   See para 2.02, ante.

2.101   Other points which emerge from *Esso Petroleum Co Ltd v Harper's Garage (Stourport) Ltd* are the following:

(1) The court will look not merely at the particular agreement, but will consider the trading pattern which emerges from a group of similar agreements. Thus in *Esso Petroleum Co Ltd v Harper's Garage (Stourport) Ltd* the House of Lords was prepared to consider the fact that the ties permitted Esso to keep down distribution costs—they needed to distribute between only 7,000 outlets instead of a much greater number: there were in all about 35,000 outlets, 90 per cent of which were tied to one or other of the oil companies. The importance of this in the franchising context is obvious.

(2) The length of the tie which is acceptable will depend upon the facts of the particular trade. In *Esso Petroleum Co Ltd v Harper's Garage (Stourport) Ltd* a period of five years was held not to be longer than was necessary to maintain a stable system of distribution throughout the country, but 21 years was held to stretch beyond any period for which developments were reasonably foreseeable. The shorter periods operated to the garage owners' advantage moreover. In ensuring that some ties ended almost every week, Esso would have to treat the owners reasonably in order to obtain renewals of the ties against intense competition from other oil companies.

(3) The court will consider the benefits received in return for the restraints, such as discounts given on goods which are not given to free outlets, financial assistance, etc, given to the covenantors.

(4) Provided that the agreement is otherwise reasonable, a provision that the covenantor may not dispose of the business except to a person approved by the franchisor will be reasonable on the basis that it is only by such means that the covenantee can ensure that the tie will continue for the full length of the agreement.

(5) It would appear that the courts will be reluctant to interfere with covenants of the kind commonly found in leases[1]. For this reason, where possible, restrictions

2.102 Competition law

of this sort should be contained in the lease and not the franchise agreement. This does not mean however that the franchisor can benefit from this doctrine by such devices as sale and lease-back. The court will consider the transaction as a whole².

(6) The court will consider the relative bargaining strength of the parties. It has indeed been suggested that the basis of the restraint of trade doctrine at common law is not economic theory about the benefits of competition, but rather the protection of those whose bargaining power is weak from those whose bargaining power is strong³. If that is the case, it is possible to regard the matters considered merely as guides to judging the fairness of the bargain struck. Certainly, given the complexities involved in evaluating economic evidence, this is a line that may well commend itself to courts.

1 See discussion in *Ravenseft Properties Ltd's Application* [1978] QB 52.
2 *Amoco Australian Pty Ltd v Rocca Bros Motor Engineering Co Pty Ltd* [1975] AC 561, [1975] 1 All ER 968, PC.
3 *Schroeder Music Publishing Co Ltd v Macaulay* [1974] 1 WLR 1308 at 1315, per Lord Diplock; *Texaco Ltd v Mulberry Filling Station Ltd* [1972] 1 WLR 814 at 826; *Clifford Davis Management Ltd v WEA Records Ltd* [1975] 1 WLR 61 at 65, CA. See also *Shell UK Ltd v Lostock Garage Ltd* [1977] 1 All ER 481, [1976] 1 WLR 1187, CA where an agreement held reasonable at the outset, was held to have become unreasonable because of the hardship inflicted by the oil company's support scheme to other garages.

2.102 When we move beyond the 'solus' cases, the common law of restraint of trade becomes more problematic in its application to franchising. The older cases of restraint of trade fall into two categories: agreements between employer and employee restraining the employee's freedom to work, and covenants entered into on the sale of the goodwill of a business.

Covenants between employer and employee

2.103 Provided that the employer has brought the full time services of the employee¹, restraints which operate *during* the currency of the employment contract are arguably merely an expression of the fact that the general law gives the employer an exclusive right to the services of the employee anyway. In other words, the agreement does not restrain the employee because he is restrained already². At the present time it would seem that this argument would not apply to franchising. Although the reality of the situation is that the franchisee is in many ways simply a manager, even an individual franchisee would not in the strict sense appear to be a servant. The fact that he risks his capital is, as we have already argued, important when considering the relationship of the parties inter se. A provision may well be inserted in the agreement requiring the franchisee to devote himself exclusively to the franchise business, but apart from that term, there appears to be no duty on the franchisee imposed by the general law. However, as we have argued elsewhere³, it may be possible to imply into the relationship similar duties to those implied in partnership agreements⁴. If that argument is accepted, restrictions which simply spell out those duties are not restraints.

1 Ie as opposed simply to limiting the employee's right to work for someone else: *Young v Timmins* (1831) 1 Cr & J 148, 331; *Schroeder Music Publishing Co Ltd v Macaulay* [1974] 3 All ER 616, [1974] 1 WLR 1308, HL; *Clifford Davis Management Ltd v WEA Records Ltd* [1975] 1 All ER 237, [1975] 1 WLR 61, CA.
2 *Lilley v Elwin* (1848) 11 QB 742.
3 Para 1.45, ante.
4 See in particular Partnership Act 1890, s 30 which provides: 'If a partner, without the

consent of the other partners, carries on any business of the same nature as and competing with that of the firm, he must account for and pay over to the firm all profits made by him in that business'.

2.104 Undertakings not to use or disclose the employer's trade secrets and know-how during the course of the agreement except in connection with the running of the franchised business[1] may possibly go no further than an obligation imposed by the general law, and to this extent a covenant will not be a restraint of trade.

1 See eg *Printers and Finishers Ltd v Holloway* [1964] 3 All ER 731, [1965] RPC 239 (which appears to have been misunderstood in *Faccenda Chicken v Fowler* [1986] 1 All ER 617 at 626). See para 3.118 et seq, post.

2.105 Undertakings by an employee not to use the employer's trade secrets and know-how *after* the termination of the contract of employment and non-solicitation covenants[1] will probably be valid at least to the extent that the restraint is coextensive with the area over which, and fields in which, the employer operates[2]. Obviously, however, the nature of the trade secrets and know-how is a relevant consideration[3].

1 See *John Michael Design v Cooke* [1987] 2 All ER 332, CA.
2 *Nordenfelt v Maxim Nordenfelt Guns and Ammunition Ltd* [1894] AC 535, HL. The dangers of drawing such a covenant too widely are illustrated by *Commercial Plastics Ltd v Vincent* [1965] 1 QB 623, [1964] 3 All ER 546, CA.
3 See para 3.118 et seq, post.

Covenants entered into on the sale of a business

2.106 Traditionally these covenants have been dealt with more leniently than those in employer/employee contracts, partly for the obvious reason that they benefit both parties and generally in these cases no important public interest element has been involved. By contrast, anyone employed in a business for a period of time will tend to acquire skill in that business, and it is in the interests of the public that he should be free to employ that skill. He should be restrained from doing so only to the extent necessary to protect his employer's legitimate business interests and in particular his trade secrets and know-how. Arguably, any covenant not to compete during the term of the agreement in the territory granted by the franchisor could fall within this principle, as could covenants given by the franchisee to his purchaser on the sale of the franchise.

Restraint of trade and franchising

2.107 It must be emphasised, that in the absence of confidential information and know-how in the technical sense[1], a franchisee cannot in the absence of a covenant be prevented from using skills and information acquired whilst operating as a franchisee. Thus, in *Faccenda Chicken v Fowler*[2], the plaintiffs devised and operated a delivery system for fresh chilled (as opposed to frozen) chickens. The defendant, who was their manager, naturally learned in the course of his employment the 'van runs' around the area covered, and related customer information. Such information was known generally throughout the firm. When he was dismissed, the defendant set up a rival company using this knowledge. It was held that the defendant could not be restrained: the information he was using was in no sense confidential. In that case there was no express restraint, and it is unclear if there had been whether it would have made any difference. Neill LJ indicated that it would not[3]. It is important to realise, however, that the case was concerned with the 'van runs' as confidential information, which clearly they were in no sense.

1 See para 3.118 et seq—the EEC block exemption uses this term in a wider sense—see para 2.34, ante.
2 [1987] Ch 117, [1986] 1 All ER 617—see para 3.120 post.
3 At 626—see, however, critique of this at para 3.120 post.

2.108 Some guidance of the effectiveness of restraints preventing the former franchisee carrying on the same kind of business from the location of the former franchise, can be gained from the remarks of Whitford J in *Prontaprint plc v Landon Litho Ltd*[1], and of Lord Denning MR in *Office Overload Ltd v Gunn*[2].

1 [1987] FSR 315.
2 [1977] FSR 39.

2.109 In the first case, a former Prontaprint franchisee, having failed to renew its franchise, as it was able to do under the terms of the franchise agreement, continued business in the same premises operating the same type of service, but under the name 'Laserprint'. The franchise agreement with Prontaprint contained a covenant that the defendant company would not:

> 'at any time within three years of the determination of this agreement engage in or be concerned or interested directly or indirectly in the provision of the Service or anything similar thereto within a radius of half a mile of the Premises . . .'.

Whitford J granted interlocutory relief to the plaintiffs. Although the remarks of the judge have to be read in the light of the fact that what was involved was interlocutory relief, nevertheless, they do provide useful guidance on the treatment of these clauses in franchise agreements.

2.110 In the first place, Whitford J considered, in the circumstances of the case[1], the covenants in franchise agreements to be closer to those between employer and employee, than those entered into on the sale of a business[2], and, as noted above, nobody is entitled to protection against the use by a former employee of skills acquired in the course of his employment. But, as Whitford J pointed out, nothing in this covenant was going to stop the defendants from using acquired skills, albeit for three years they were not going to be entitled to do it within half a mile of the present location[3]. It was also suggested by counsel for the defendants that the defendants were in the position of purchasers of know-how and goodwill, and for that reason were entitled to use it. On this point, Whitford J observed that the defendants were not just purchasing know-how and goodwill; they were purchasing a protected interest under this franchise, and nobody had suggested that by enforcement of this particular covenant, they were going to be estopped from using any know-how which they might have acquired[4]. He noted that the plaintiffs wanted to be in a position to enjoy the goodwill attaching to the name 'Prontaprint' and the business associated with it by granting a further franchise for the area in question. If the covenant was unenforceable, as soon as they had managed to get going on the expertise, advice and assistance given by the plaintiffs, franchisees were either going to withdraw, or not renew, their agreements, and franchising would, in effect, become inoperable. The plaintiffs argued, therefore, that this restriction was perfectly reasonable in protecting the interest they legitimately had in running a franchising business, because, without a restriction of this kind, running it would become impossible[5].

[1] Which involved the enforcement of covenants after the end of the term. The situation during the continuance of the agreement could well be different.
[2] *Prontaprint plc v Landon Litho Ltd* [1987] FSR 315 at 324.
[3] Ibid, at 325.
[4] Ibid.
[5] Ibid, at 322.

2.111 It is to be noted that no point had been taken as to whether the period of time was unreasonable[1], and that the covenant by its terms, only bound the defendant, not the person who in fact ran the defendant company, a Dr Landon[2]. It is also to be noted, that no argument was presented on a part of the covenant which sought to prevent the franchisee from carrying on business within three miles of any other franchised premises in the UK in the three year period. Whitford J noted that the plaintiffs had franchises up and down the country and, for that purpose, wanted to ensure that they were in a position to prevent competition against franchisees whom they might appoint, by persons who in fact built up their knowledge and interest as franchisees.

[1] *Prontaprint plc v Landon Litho Ltd* [1987] FSR 315 at 325.
[2] Ibid, at 320.

2.112 On the point at issue, Whitford J referred to an earlier case, *Office Overload Ltd v Gunn*[1] in which the Court of Appeal had held that there was nothing unreasonable in point of time and in point of area in a covenant in the following terms:

> 'For one year after the termination of this agreement the Licensee agrees not to be connected directly or indirectly as employee, proprietor, stockholder, partner or officer in the operation of any business competitive with Overload within the licensed area'.

Whitford J noted that the business in that case was a kind of franchise. Overload were running an employment agency for skilled personnel. Whitford J noted that there were differences between the facts of that case and the situation in *Prontaprint*. However, the observations he made, bearing that in mind, are helpful for the light they shed on the present problem. He noted that anyone who wanted services of the sort provided by Prontaprint would look up printing services in the Yellow Pages, find the name 'Prontaprint' and go to the premises to find a notice 'Same Team, New Name'. Even though that notice had been removed, persons, even going there for the first time, might well assume that it was, in substance, the same business[2]. In the case of many franchises eg of the 'fast-food' restaurant type, perhaps, the Yellow Pages point is less important, because customers generally come in more or less on impulse from off the street. Nevertheless, the substance of what the judge says is that persons going to the premises where they expected to find the franchised business, will often not bother to go elsewhere when they find a business under a different name providing a similar service.

[1] [1977] FSR 39.
[2] *Prontaprint plc v Landon Litho Ltd* [1987] FSR 315 at 326.

2.113 In short, *Prontaprint* gives some encouragement to the view that a covenant in restraint of trade, so far as it relates to the location, is likely to be upheld.

2.114 Competition law

What about the length of the restraint, and the other restraints which it is essential to impose on a franchisee following termination? The franchisor clearly has a legitimate interest to protect, namely, the goodwill attached to the former franchisee's outlet in particular, and the franchise network in general. Although Whitford J was of the opinion that the covenants in a franchise agreement were closer to those between an employer and an employee, than those imposed on the sale of a business, it is apparant from his other remarks that he was prepared to give some weight to this aspect. The truth is that the situation between franchisor and franchisee is *sui generis*, involving considerations which are involved both in relation to the restraints between employer and employee, and between vendor and purchaser on the sale of a business. So far as the latter is concerned, both during the term and after its determination, it is the protection of the franchisor's goodwill which is the relevant consideration. Protection of this is central to the effective operation of the whole system, and it would defeat the intention of both parties when the agreement is entered into, that an individual franchisee would be able to carry on activities calculated to damage that goodwill.

2.114 So far as the situation following termination is concerned, it is clear that goodwill survives a defunct business[1], and that under the normal terms of the franchise agreement, it will have accrued to the franchisor[2]. In the case of many franchises, however, the period of survival will be fairly short, and the practical advice must be to confine the period of restraint to a time sufficient to re-franchise from the same, or a convenient adjacent, site. Although circumstances can be conceived of where a longer restraint might be justified, having regard to Regulation 4087/88[3], the period of restraint should not usually exceed one year[4].

1 In *Ad-Lib Club v Granville* [1972] RPC 673, goodwill sufficient to found an action of passing off was held to survive a well known night club by some years.
2 Usually there will be an express term requiring the franchisee to hold the goodwill as bare trustee for the franchisor, but even in the absence of such a term, it would appear that the goodwill accrues to the franchisor *JH Coles v Need* [1934] AC 82, PC.
3 OJ 1988 L359/82.
4 See para 2.41.

2.115 Similarly, the geographical area of restraint, preventing the former franchisee from carrying on a competing business near the location of the former business, should be based on a reasonable assessment of the territorial extent of the goodwill of the former franchise business[1]. For example, in the case of a high street fast food restaurant, this will be fairly small, probably half a mile at most, but in the case of a similar restaurant situated on an out-of-town shopping mall, it may be much greater. A similar assessment of the territorial extent of the goodwill needs to be made in respect of any restraint preventing the former franchisee from competing with the franchisor's and other franchisees' businesses[2]. Again, the period of restraint should not exceed one year. The legitimate interests of the franchisor in protecting the goodwill of the former business, may well carry greater weight with a court than the less specific claim to protect the other outlets of the network as a whole. Consequently, it is always advisable when drafting these covenants, to make each part severable, so that if one part fails, other parts have a chance of surviving[3].

1 The EC block exemption refers to the territory where [the franchisee] has exploited the franchise, see para 2.41.
2 Such a restraint is outside the EC block exemption—see para 2.41.

3 *Chemidus Wavin Ltd v Société Pour la Transformation et l'Exploitation des Résines Industrielles* [1976] 2 CMLR 387.

2.116 A restraint on the former franchisee soliciting customers and employees has a chance of success, if that is in fact what the franchisee is doing[1]. No restraint can prevent a customer going where he freely chooses[2], however, nor, for the reasons given above, can a person be restrained from freely exercising his trade, except in so far as doing so interferes with the interests of the former employer which the law protects.

1 See *Nicholls v Stretton* (1847) 10 QB 346. See 47 Halsbury's Laws (4th edn) s 38. As noted above, in *Prontaprint* Whitford J considered the covenants in franchise agreements to be analogous to those between employer and employee. Non-solicitation of customers is part of an employee's duty, which, however, subsists only so long as the relationship subsists: *Wessex Dairies v Smith* [1935] 2 KB 80; *Baker v Gibbons* [1972] 2 All ER 759. Thereafter, there has to be a restrictive covenant, but it will be upheld, provided it is reasonably necessary to uphold the employer's business—*Plowman v Ash* [1964] 2 All ER 10. The EC block exemption does not specifically cover such terms.
2 See eg *Oswald Hickson, Collier & Co v Carter-Ruck* [1984] AC 720n, [1984] 2 All ER 15, CA.

2.117 In the common case of corporate franchisees, the above comments apply *mutatis mutandae* to the equivalent covenants which will be required from the active directors of the franchisee. In the latter case, however, there is always to be borne in mind the fact that the effect of the directors entering into such covenants will be to make the agreement technically one particulars of which should be furnished to the Office of Fair Trading under the Restrictive Trade Practices Act 1976.

Will only come into play as incident to litigation

2.118 An obvious, but nevertheless important, point to bear in mind about the common law doctrine, as already noted is that it can only come into play as an incident to litigation between the parties. Usually the matter comes before the court on an interlocutory application, and for practical purposes, the decision to grant or withhold an injunction is often decisive, because of the short time limits involved. The court must accordingly decide if the covenant is prima facie good, and if so, it should in the ordinary course of events restrain an offending defendant[1].

1 *Office Overload Ltd v Gunn* [1977] FSR 39, CA; *John Michael Design v Cooke* [1987] 2 All ER 332, CA.

Effect of an agreement being held to be in restraint of trade

2.119 In the first place, it is clear that it is only the relevant restraining provisions themselves, and not the whole agreement which is void. As Denning LJ pointed out obiter in *Bennett v Bennett*[1]:

'The presence of a void covenant of this kind does not render the deed totally ineffective . . . The party who is entitled to the benefit of the void covenant, or rather who would have been entitled to the benefit of it if it had been valid, can sue upon the other covenants of the deed which are in his favour; and he can sue upon the void covenant, if he can sever the good from the bad . . . even to the extent of getting full liquidation damages for a breach of the good part . . . So also the other party, that is, the party who gave

2.120 Competition law

the void covenant and is not bound by its restraints, can himself sue upon the covenants in his favour, save only when the void covenant forms the whole, or substantially the whole, consideration for the deed.'

1 [1952] 1 KB 249 at 260, CA.

2.120 The courts at the present time appear to be more prepared to sever illegal restraints from legal ones. Thus in *T Lucas & Co Ltd v Mitchell*[1] the defendant, a salesman, had entered into a covenant with his employers not to deal in similar goods, nor to supply or solicit orders for such goods within the allocated districts for one year after termination of his employment. It was held that the restraint on dealing was unreasonable, but that it might be severed from the remainder of the covenant which would be enforced. It is to be noted that this was a master and servant case, where the courts have tended to be unwilling to sever, for the obvious reason that a very wide clause may in practice be effective notwithstanding its notional unenforceability: few employees will question it. Refusal to sever is some sort of sanction against this[2].

1 [1974] Ch 129, [1972] 3 All ER 689, CA.
2 *Mason v Provident Clothing and Supply Co Ltd* [1913] AC 724, HL.

2.121 A limitation on the 'blue pencil' or 'scissors' rule is supposed to be that the severance must not alter the nature of the original contract. This is a principle easier to state than to apply however. The case generally cited for this proposition is *Attwood v Lamont*[1]. The case is virtually indistinguishable from *Goldsoll v Goldman*[2] however. It is perhaps better to explain *Attwood v Lamont* by the former reluctance to sever in master and servant cases which we noted above[3]. If we leave aside *Attwood v Lamont*, the basis of this elusive principle may in reality be no more than a reflection of the principle that the courts are generally reluctant to rewrite a contract for the parties. In *Mason v Provident Clothing and Supply Co Ltd*[4] for example, the court refused to substitute 'in Islington' for 'within 25 miles of London'. The moral is to draft territorial restrictions with the blue pencil in mind: one single provision which is too wide cannot be cut down[5], but an itemised list of territories can be, as in *Goldsoll v Goldman*. The same rule applies to their restrictions[6].

1 [1920] 3 KB 571, CA.
2 [1914] 2 Ch 603.
3 See Treitel—*Law of Contract* (7th edn, 1987) (Stevens) p 390.
4 [1913] AC 724, HL.
5 *Commercial Plastics Ltd v Vincent* [1965] 1 QB 623 at 647, CA.
6 Ibid. Also, eg *T Lucas & Co Ltd v Mitchell* [1974] Ch 129, [1972] 3 All ER 689, CA.

Fair Trading Act 1973 and Competition Act 1980

Introduction

2.122 Part IV of the Fair Trading Act gives the Director General of Fair Trading power to make a reference to the Monopolies and Mergers Commission where it appears that a 'monopoly situation' as defined by the Act may exist. The procedure under the Act is fairly slow, and up to the present time not very many references have been dealt with under it[1]. Of much more potential concern in the franchising context, is the Competition Act 1980. That Act is triggered by the new concept of an 'anti-competitive practice'. The concept is fairly loosely defined, and it would appear that at present most types of conduct considered by the Office of Fair Trading as possible anti-competitive practices could occur in the franchising context. Unlike the Restrictive Trade Practices Act, the Competition Act is not triggered by specific instances. Conduct pursued in accordance with an agreement registrable under the Restrictive Trade Practices Act is exempt from the Competition Act. Conduct pursued under an agreement drafted so as not to be registrable, is not exempt. Subject to this, the actual terms of the agreement between the parties do not directly matter: it is the course of conduct pursued by them and its effects which is at stake.

1 The references made each year under the Act are listed in the Annual Report of the Director General.

Fair Trading Act 1973

2.123 Under Part IV of the Fair Trading Act 1973 the Director General of Fair Trading has powers to make a reference to the Monopolies and Mergers Commission where it appears that a 'monopoly situation' exists in the supply of any goods or service. A 'monopoly situation' is taken to exist where one firm accounts for at least one-quarter of the market in goods or services of that description[1]. Such a 'monopoly situation' may be limited to a part of the United Kingdom[2]. Clearly identifying the relevant market is the problem. A firm could, for example, enjoy a total monopoly of the gas widget market, but be in severe competition with electric widgets of which total market its share is insignificant. Another problem in relation to franchising is whether for these purposes the chain is one firm or many. To the extent that franchisees do not compete against each other, it is possible that it will be treated as one firm.

1 Fair Trading Act 1973, ss 6(1) and 7(1).
2 Section 9.

2.124 In exercising his powers the Director General will consider whether or not there is prima facie evidence that any firm enjoying such a monopoly is operating in any way that might be considered against the public interest. For example, the Director referred credit card operations[1]. These involved franchised[2] dealers and the cause for concern was the clause in the agreement preventing the dealers from charging different prices to credit card and cash customers. The result was a recommendation that franchisees be no longer prevented from discriminating between cash and credit card customers[3].

1 Referred 23 June 1977.
2 'Franchise' is not of course used here in the sense in which it has been defined for the purposes of this book.
3 Annual Report of the Director General 1980, pp 38, 96–98. See Monopolies and Mergers Commission Report on Credit Card Services Cm 718 (1989).

2.125 This legislation is not likely to be used in relation to franchise chains in the present stage of the business. The Competition Act is of much more immediate significance. The problem with the Monopolies and Mergers Commission is that it consists mainly of part-time members and consequently it cannot deal with many references. Its investigations tend to continue for some time therefore, possibly several years. The reference to the Commission under the Fair Trading Act may require it only to report on the facts[1], or it may be required to determine whether

2.126 *Competition law*

the facts found operate against the public interest[2]. The determination as to whether or not any matter operates against the public interest involves an extensive investigation[3].

1 Section 48.
2 Section 49.
3 See section 84.

Competition Act 1980

2.126 The underlying philosophy of this piece of legislation is that the way to fight inflation is not by price controls, but by fostering competition. The Act therefore abolished the Price Commission and conferred on the Director General of Fair Trading powers to control anti-competitive practices. The procedure of investigation under the Act is simpler than under the Fair Trading Act. The introduction of the concept of the 'anti-competitive practice'[1] provides the basis of a more narrowly focused, and therefore swifter, investigation than under the Fair Trading Act. If it appears to the Director that any person has been, or is, pursuing a course of conduct which may amount to an anti-competitive practice, he may on his own initiative carry out an investigation[2]. If the practice is considered to be anti-competitive, and the person concerned refuses to abandon it, reference may be made to the Monopolies and Mergers Commission[3]. The key question, therefore, is, what amounts to an anti-competitive practice?

1 The relevant provisions are based broadly on the Leisner Green Papers Cmds 7198 and 7512.
2 Section 3.
3 Section 5.

2.127 Section 2(1) provides:

'The provisions of sections 3 to 10 below have effect with a view to the control of anti-competitive practices, and for the purposes of this Act a person engages in an anti-competitive practice, if, in the course of business, that person pursues a course of conduct which, of itself or taken together with a course of conduct pursued by persons associated with him, has or is intended to have or is likely to have the effect of restricting, distorting or preventing[1] competition in connection with the production, supply or acquisition of goods in the United Kingdom or any part of it or the supply or securing of services in the United Kingdom or any part of it.'

1 'Palindrome' drafting!—see Article 85(1).

2.128 'Person' means a body of persons corporate or *unincorporated*[1]. In *Davey v Shawcroft*[2] a committee carrying on the business of coal merchants, was held to be a 'person carrying on an undertaking'. It is submitted that for the purposes of the Act a franchise chain as a whole *could* be treated as a person—an interpretation which arguably corresponds to the economic reality[3]. 'Practice' has the same meaning as under the Restrictive Trade Practices Act 1976, ie 'any practice, whether adopted in pursuance of an agreement or otherwise'[4]. The Act gives a fairly narrow definition of 'associated', the effect of which is that the franchisor and franchisees will arguably only be treated as associated if the 'interconnected bodies corporate' strategy has been adopted whether to avoid the need to register under the Restrictive Trade Practices Act 1976 or for other reasons. Section 2(6) provides:

'For the purposes of this section any two persons are to be treated as associated:
(a) if one is a body corporate of which the other directly or indirectly has control either alone or with other members of a group of interconnected bodies corporate of which he is a member, or
(b) if both are bodies corporate of which one and the same person or group of persons directly or indirectly has control;
and for the purposes of this subsection a person or group of persons able directly or indirectly to control or materially to influence the policy of a body corporate, but without having a controlling interest in that body corporate, may be treated as having control of it'[4].

The problem is whether or not for the purposes of subsection (6)(b) the control exercised by the franchisor over the franchisees would be sufficient for them to be associated—clearly the franchisees would have to be corporate, a requirement which would produce a somewhat arbitrary distinction.

1 Interpretation Act 1978, s 5, and Sch 1.
2 [1948] 1 All ER 827.
3 It is believed, however, that at present the Office of Fair Trading takes the view that person means 'legal person'.
4 Section 33(1) and Fair Trading Act 1973, s 137(1).

2.129 During the debates on the Act, Ministers refused even to give a non-exhaustive list of practices which might be treated as anti-competitive[1]. Although it must in part depend on a firm's market position, it is important to note that the firm in question does not have to have a dominant market position. A 'monopoly situation' need not exist[2]. An essential step however must be to identify the market affected. This may be the market in which the firm itself is operating, or it may be other markets. 'Tie-ins', for example, may both affect the franchisees' market and the potential suppliers' market. It does not have to be shown that a practice *does* have an anti-competitive effect, it is sufficient that it is intended to have or is likely to have.

1 Lord Trefgarne did eventually give some examples—HL Debates vol 406, col 64 which correspond quite closely to those listed in the Office of Fair Trading's Guide to the Act, discussed post.
2 The firm must however pass the exemption threshold provided by the Anti-Competitive Practices (Exclusions) Order 1980, discussed post.

2.130 The potential application of the Act is therefore very wide. It is not like the Restrictive Trade Practices Act triggered by a specified list of practices. In the Office of Fair Trading's Guide to the Act, the following possibly anti-competitive practices are mentioned, and any of them might conceivably occur in the franchising context:

'a Pricing policy
Falling into category would be:
*Price discrimination—the practice of selling goods or services, where there are no cost differences, to distinct and separate groups of customers—these groups being charged varying prices according to their degree of sensitivity to price levels. Some variants or price discrimination take the form of differential rates of discount or rebate from list prices—perhaps in return for loyalty or exclusive supply arrangements. An important variant arises where a purchaser's buying power enables him to insist that suppliers grant him advantageous terms, so artificially enhancing his ability to compete on price in the market in which he sells;

2.131 Competition law

*Predatory pricing—which is usually defined as the practice of temporarily selling at prices below cost, with the intention of driving a competitor from the market, so that in the future prices may be raised and enhanced profits extracted;
*Vertical price squeezing—which can arise when a vertically integrated firm controls the total supply of an input which is essential to the production requirements of its subsidiary and also its competitors. The input price can be raised and the downstream output price reduced, so that the profits of competitors are squeezed, possibly with a view to driving them from the market;
b Distribution policy
There are a number of practices which might serve to restrict, distort or prevent competition, either at manufacturing or distribution level. These include:
*Tie-in sales—a stipulation that a buyer must purchase part or all of his requirements of a second (tied) product from the supplier of a first (tying) product;
*Full-line forcing—which requires a buyer to purchase quantities of each item in a product range in order to be able to buy any of them;
*Rental-only contracts—which restrict customers to rental or lease terms only and which can be anti-competitive where there are no alternative methods of acquiring those goods;
*Exclusive supply—whereby a seller supplies only one buyer in a certain geographical area, which limits competition between that buyer and his competitors;
*Selective distribution—which is the practice of choosing as sales outlets only those which satisfy specific qualitative or quantitative criteria;
*Exclusive purchase—which arises when a distributor contracts to stock only the products of one manufacturer, possibly in return for an exclusive supply arrangement.'

2.131 Whilst this list of items is of some assistance, obviously it is not exhaustive nor is it particularly helpful in deciding when particular terms in an agreement are likely to produce anti-competitive effects. In practice, the two problem areas are likely to be 'distributorships' and 'tie-ins' in 'manufacturing' and 'service' franchises. The safe advice for the latter must be again to limit them to items necessary to preserve quality (ie where quality control *cannot* be satisfactorily achieved by specification) and where they are necessary to preserve trade secrets. Business format distributorships lead to the problems already discussed[1]. In principle, the sorts of justifications discussed in relation to Article 85(3) should apply in relation to the Competition Act, particularly the 'free-rider' argument[2]. These arguments *may* be easier to justify to the Director General on the assumption that he will probably not have the overriding concern with inter-Member trade which the Commission has, and is likely to place rather more emphasis on benefits to the consumer.

1 Para 2.71 et seq, ante.
2 Paras 2.72 et seq, ante.

2.132 Under the pricing policy head it is to be noted that minimum advertised price maintenance, which falls outside the Resale Prices Act and Restrictive Trade Practices Act[1] might be included. Certainly Leisner thought this[2] and section 2(1) is widely enough drafted to catch it.

1 See checklist, paras 2.144 and 2.151, post.
2 Leisner II Cmd 7512, paras 5.59 et seq.

(a) Exemptions from the provisions of the Competition Act

2.133 *Agreements registrable under the Restrictive Trade Practices Act 1976.* Section 2(2):

> 'To the extent that a course of conduct is required or envisaged by a material provision of, or a material recommendation in, an agreement which is registered or subject to registration under the Restrictive Trade Practices Act 1976, that course of conduct shall not be regarded as constituting an anti-competitive practice for the purposes of this Act; and for the purposes of this subsection—
> (a) a provision of an agreement is a material provision if, by virtue of the existence of the provision (taken alone or together with other provisions) the agreement is one to which the Act applies.'

2.134 It is quite possible to draft an agreement, conduct under which would have anti-competitive effects, but which is not registrable under the Restrictive Trade Practices Act. For example, an agreement containing only unnecessary 'tie-ins' would not on this account alone be caught because the restrictions would be accepted by only one party, the franchisees. Just as the agreement thus escapes the Restrictive Trade Practices Act net, however, the practices under it are liable to be caught by the Competition Act. It is not the terms of the agreement which matter[1]. Some franchisors impose potentially anti-competitive agreements, but do not operate them in that way. Equally, it is possible that franchisors might enter into quite inoffensive agreements with their franchisees, and then engage in highly anti-competitive practices.

1 See para 2.126, ante.

2.135 *Practices of smaller operations.* The Anti-Competitive Practices (Exclusion) Order 1980[1] excludes practices carried on by a person with an annual turnover of less that £5 million[2] and who enjoys less than 25 per cent share of the relevant market, and who is not a member of a group of inter-connected bodies corporate which has such an aggregate turnover or market share. Identification of the relevant market is likely to be one problem with this provision. For example, an operation engaged in installing solar heating panels might have a greater than 25 per cent share of the solar heating panel market and a qualifying turnover, but an insignificant share of the home heating market. Another problem is identifying the relevant unit.

1 SI 1980 No 979 made under section 2(3)(4) and (5) of the Act.
2 For the method of calculating this see ibid, Sch 2.

2.136 Arguably, if a chain consisted entirely of inter-connected corporate franchisees[1], then the turnover of the chain as a whole would be relevant while if the chain consisted of individuals licensed by a corporate franchisor, the franchisor and each franchisee would have to be considered separately. The distinction does not make much sense, but again it depends on the meaning of 'person' for the purposes of the Act; the term *could* as we argued above, be taken to refer to the chain as a whole[2]. It would appear that otherwise, even if corporate franchisees were deemed to be 'associated' under section 2(6)(b), it would be their individual turnovers and market shares which would matter for the purposes of the exemption.

1 This is one of the devices used amongst other things to avoid the need to furnish

particulars under the Restrictive Trade Practices Act—see s 43(1) and para 1.02, n 1, ante. This problem should be borne in mind when deciding whether or not to adopt this device.
2 Para 2.128, ante.

(b) Practice

2.137 Although there is nothing in the Act to require him to do so, it would appear that for obvious reasons the Director General intends to approach the firm in question informally in the first instance. If he is satisfied that the practice is only trivially anti-competitive or less harmful than the practices of other firms to which higher priority in investigation should be given, the Director General may not proceed to a full investigation. Similarly, if the firm in question is prepared to abandon or ameliorate the practice[1].

1 See Korah 'Competition Act 1980' [1980] JBL 255.

2.138 If an investigation is started, the Director General must proceed with it as expeditiously as possible[1] and publish a report[2]. At this stage further he is not concerned[3] with the public interest. If an anti-competitive practice is identified the matter can be referred to the Monopolies and Mergers Commission for further investigation[4], or the Director General may accept an undertaking from the person concerned[5]. Where the matter is referred to the Commission, the time limit relevant to merger references (six months) applies and the report must be made within that period[6].

1 Section 3(4).
2 Section 3(10).
3 Clearly the public interest comes in to an extent when the Director decides whether or not to institute an investigation since he must decide to allocate resources to it—Korah 'Competition Act 1980' [1980] JBL 255.
4 Section 5.
5 Section 4.
6 Section 7(6).

(c) Anti-competitive practices in relation to patents

2.139 The Act contains specific provisions concerning anti-competitive practices in relation to patents[1]. These amend section 51 of the Patents Act 1977 to allow application to the Comptroller for relief in the event of the Commission concluding on a reference under section 5 that any person is engaged in an anti-competitive practice in relation to goods or services including patented products.

1 Section 14.

Checklist for Competition Act 1980

2.140 (1) Is the agreement registrable under the Restrictive Trade Practices Act 1976?—paras 2.114 et seq, post.
If it does particulars will need to be furnished—paras 2.145 et seq, but there is no need to consider its anti-competitive effects further in relation to this Act (though other provisions, and in particular Article 85(1) must be considered)—paras 2.15 et seq, ante. It would appear that a network of qualifying agreements would be treated in the same way.

(2) Does the business exceed or is it likely to exceed the 'thresholds' of market share and turnover?—para 2.135, ante.

If not there is no need to consider further the application of this Act, and it is *likely* to come within the Notice on Minor Agreements for the purposes of Article 85(1), ie there should be no need to apply for negative clearance—para 2.68, ante.

(3) Subject to the above, consider each element separately for its potential anti-competitive effects (some guidance may be gained from the analysis of EEC competition law at para 2.15 et seq ante).

FORMS LEGISLATION
Restrictive Trade Practices Act 1976

2.141 Although this Act was aimed primarily at horizontal agreements, etc, there is nothing in its wording so to confine it. Consequently, franchise agreements which contain relevant restrictions accepted by *both* parties fall within its provisions. Although both parties accepting relevant restrictions must be carrying on business in the United Kingdom, in practice, this will invariably be the case. Where overseas franchisors are involved, the usual practice is to appoint a master franchisor company within the United Kingdom, which grants franchises, and generally undertakes the management of the network.

The first common way in which both parties come to accept relevant restrictions for the purposes of the Act is where the franchisee is granted an exclusive territory, in which the franchisor undertakes not to compete. Since the franchisee invariably accepts a variety of relevant restrictions, there will be restrictions accepted by more than one party. The validity of such restraints for the purposes of EEC law are considered below, but for the purpose of the Restrictive Trade Practices Act, exclusive territoriality can be achieved very simply without causing the agreement to become subject to the need to furnish particulars: the franchisor undertakes not to use or licence the relevant trade name or mark within the franchisee's territory. This has the effect of giving the franchisee the desired protection, because although the franchisor is free to compete using other names and marks, the market power of the franchised name or mark, backed up as it will be by advertising and promotion obligations on the part of the franchisor, will be unaffected. Since the franchisor is not accepting relevant restrictions as to goods, nor probably as to services, the only restrictions left will be any imposed on the franchisee eg to confine its operations to the territory. The provisions of EEC law must, however, be borne in mind[1].

1 See para 2.12 et seq, ante.

2.142 Similarly, exclusive purchasing requirements can be imposed on the franchisee, and, subject to the argument that these involve an inherent restriction on the franchisor in the requirement to supply the franchisee, there will be relevant restrictions accepted only by one party. Even if the 'hidden restriction' argument is accepted[1], arguably it is a restriction relating exclusively to the goods supplied[2]. In any case, the argument that it indirectly restricts the supply of similar goods to others seems, to say the least, to be stretching it! Again, the provisions of EEC law must be borne in mind.

The principal way in which, in practice, agreements come to fall within the provisions of the Restrictive Trade Practices Act is when the directors of a corporate franchisee execute, as they usually must, non-competition covenants in the same form as those contained in the principal agreement with the franchisee. Such agreements are usually entered into as a result of the arrangement reached between the franchisor and the corporate franchisee when the franchise is negotiated. It would seem, therefore, that such agreements result from an arrangement[3] between two or more persons under which restrictions are accepted by two or more parties: ie because the directors will be parties to that arrangement. Strictly speaking, therefore, particulars should be furnished to the Office of Fair Trading. Provided that other aspects of the agreement are satisfactory, however, it is unlikely that the Office of Fair Trading will take much interest in the matter[4]. Indeed, although EEC law starts from somewhat different premises from domestic law, generally speaking, it would appear likely that an agreement which complies with the guidelines laid down in Regulation 4087/88[5] will be satisfactory to the Office of Fair Trading[6]. It is likely that in the event of legislation being promulgated as proposed in the White Paper, that franchising will be a candidate for a block exemption along similar lines to the Regulation[7].

1 See Lever (1969) 85 LQR 177, 179.
2 See s 9(3). See, however, Lever loc cit.
3 'Agreement' includes an arrangement—see s 43(1).
4 See Restrictive Trade Practices Act 1976, s 21(1) and see Howe 'Franchising and Restrictive Practices Law: the Office of Fair Trading View' [1988] ECLR 439. In general, the OFT takes the view that franchising has enhanced inter-brand competition, and had a pro-competitive effect.
5 OJ 1988 L359/46.
6 It is the normal practice of the DGFT not to refer agreements to the court if they are exempt under Art 85(3)—Howe loc cit p 444.
7 Howe loc cit.

Procedure

2.143 Although the Act envisaged a two-tier procedure; registration of agreements and referral to the Restrictive Practices Court, in practice there is a three-tier procedure. By virtue of section 21(2) if it appears to the Secretary of State on the Director's representation that the restrictions accepted, etc, are not of such significance as to call for investigation by the court, he may give directions discharging the Director from taking proceedings before the court. This could be important for registrable franchise agreements. Referral to the court and arguing the agreement through the 'gateways' is very expensive and it is unlikely that it will be justified in the franchising context. It will almost be better to abandon objectionable restrictions.

Restrictive Trade Practices Act checklist

2.144 It is suggested that in considering the application of the Restrictive Trade Practices Act the following 'checklist' be adopted:

(1) Is it an agreement as to goods?—Part II of the Act applies to agreements relating to goods.

(2) Is it an agreement as to services?—Part III of the Act applies to agreements relating to services. An agreement may relate both to goods and services and therefore come under both Part II and Part III. In this case application of Part II must first be considered, separately from the application of Part III.

(3) Does the agreement contain the restrictions accepted by both parties within the meaning of section 6 (and section 11), or does it contain information provisions which may be covered by the Act?—see para 2.141 et seq.

(4) Does the agreement contain restrictions which may be disregarded under section 9 (or section 18)?.

(5) If there are still restrictions accepted by two or more parties go to Schedule 3 and consider whether or not the agreement qualifies for exemption under any *one* of its heads.

(6) If the agreement does not qualify for exemption, it is possible that particulars must be furnished—for procedure see para 2.143, ante.

Failure to furnish particulars

2.145 The Restrictive Trade Practices Act is a trap for the unwary, and it not infrequently happens that particulars of agreements are not furnished to the OFT which should have been, the most common situation being where an exclusive territory has been granted[1]. The agreement terminates for whatever reason, and the franchisee sets up a competing business in breach of the covenants in restraint of trade. When the franchisor seeks to enforce these, the franchisee alleges that the covenants are void by reason of the Act. Is this so?

1 An exclusive territory can be granted in a way which probably avoids both parties accepting relevant restrictions, however—see para 2.141, ante.

2.146 The relevant provisions are contained in section 35 of the 1976 Act:

'(1) If particulars of an agreement which is subject to registration under this Act are not duly furnished within the time required . . .[1].
    (a) the agreement is void in respect of all restrictions accepted . . . thereunder; and
    (b) it is unlawful for any person party to the agreement who carries on business within the United Kingdom to give effect to, or enforce or purport to enforce the agreement in respect of any such restrictions . . .
(2) No criminal proceedings lie against any person on account of a contravention of subsection (1)(b) above; but the obligation to comply with that paragraph is a duty owed to any person who may be affected by a contravention of it and any breach of that duty is actionable accordingly subject to the defences and other incidents applying to actions for breach of statutory duty.'

1 Generally three months from the date of the agreement—section 25 and Schedule 2, para 5(1).

2.147 The first problem with these provisions is to what extent are the restrictions void? Does 'all restrictions accepted thereunder' mean all restrictions whatsoever contained in the agreement (an interpretation which could be disastrous for a franchise operation), or only those which are 'restrictions' within the meaning of the Act. The natural interpretation would be the latter. Under the 1968 Act[1] this was reasonably clear for the equivalent provision in that Act referred to 'relevant restrictions'. The new subsection however has substituted the word 'all' for 'relevant'. Section 43(1) does not assist, for it merely defines 'restriction' to include a negative obligation. It is at least arguable therefore that in changing the wording, the 1976 Act has increased the sanction for failing to furnish particulars. Such a result is, however, to put it mildly, startling and on normal principles of statutory interpretation it may be avoided. In the first place the 1976 Act was intended to be a consolidating measure, and in the case of a consolidating Act there is a particularly strong presumption that it does not alter the law contained in the

2.148 Competition law

statutes it replaces². Second, again on normal principles of interpretation, it is reasonable to assume that the same expression has the same meaning in all parts of an Act³, so that 'restriction accepted' means 'restriction' as used in the 'trigger' sections in Parts II and III of the Act⁴. Third, it may be an appropriate place to apply the so-called 'golden rule', for to give the subsection its ordinary meaning would, it is submitted, lead to an absurdity⁵. Finally a reason for the change in wording can be advanced. Section 7(1) of the 1968 Act which section 35 essentially reproduces, referred only to agreements within Part I of the 1956 Act (agreements as to goods). That Act however provided that Part I of the 1956 Act might, by order, be applied to 'information agreements'⁶. Section 5(2) expressly provided that references in Part I to restrictions should include references to provisions for the furnishing of information. There is no equivalent provision in the 1976 Act. It is at least arguable however that in using the word 'all' the draftsman intended to indicate that any particular agreement is void in respect *both* of restrictions accepted and information provisions. He did not however intend to include either restrictions or information provisions falling outside the Act.

1 Section 7(1)(a).
2 Maxwell *Interpretation of Statutes* (12th end, 1969) p 116; *Beswick v Beswick* [1968] AC 58 at 73. The presumption is a strong one, because consolidating measures so certified by the draftsman are passed through Parliament under an expedited procedure.
3 Ibid, p 278; *Courtauld v Legh* (1869) LR 4 Exch 126, 187; *R v Poor Law Comrs, Re Whitechapel Union* (1837) 6 Ad & El 34; *Mills v Mills* [1963] 2 All ER 237, CA; *IRC v Henry Ansbacher & Co* [1963] AC 191, [1962] 3 All ER 843, HL.
4 Sections 6, 7, 11 and 12.
5 *Becke v Smith* (1836) 2 M & W 191 at 195.
6 Section 5.

2.148 In conclusion therefore, it is reasonable to assume that failure to furnish particulars will render void only restrictions which contravene the provisions of sections 6 and 11, that it 'relevant restrictions'. One rather tricky point is whether or not this includes disregarded restrictions¹. These are not restrictions by virtue of which the Act applies and under section 1(3) the court would seem to have no jurisdiction to declare them void. It would be somewhat odd if these were made void under section 35 therefore. It might be however that this is intended to be part of the penalty for not furnishing particulars.

1 Under sections 9(3) and 18.

2.149 Although sections 35(1)(b) declares it unlawful to give effect etc to an agreement containing relevant restrictions or information provisions, a party is not therefore rendered liable to criminal proceedings¹. However, a person who has suffered loss as a result of the operation of such restrictions may sue for breach of statutory duty. Bearing in mind the American experience, the most probable plaintiffs in such a suit could be the franchisees themselves².

1 Section 35(2).
2 Eg *Siegel v Chicken Delight Inc* 311 F Supp 847 (ND Cal 1970), para 2.02, ante.

Resale price maintenance

Introduction

2.150 It is possible that a franchisor will wish to impose a common pricing policy—

Resale price maintenance 2.151

in facilities advertising apart from anything else. The extent to which requirements in the franchise agreements that the franchisees follow such a policy is restrictive within EEC Law has already been considered[1]. Although the Resale Prices Act 1976 remains on the statute book, the possibility of an agreement gaining exemption under that Act at the present day is practically non-existent. Accordingly, the position with regard to resale price maintenance may be summarised as follows.

1 Para 2.72 et seq, ante. Because only the franchisee would accept relevant restrictions, such a restriction would not fall within the Restrictive Trade Practices Act —see para 2.141, ante.

Price maintenance check-list

2.151 (1) Minimum resale[1] price terms: not generally permissible under EEC block exemption (Article 5(e)) (para 2.23) or Resale Prices Act 1976 (para 2.150 ante).

(2) Recommended resale prices: permissible under EEC block exemption provided it does not amount to a concerted practice (Article 5(e)) (para 2.23). It is also permissible under s 9(2) of the Resale Prices Act 1976. Consider also application of Competition Act 1980.

(3) Minimum price terms or an advertised prices policy in service and manufacturing franchises will not of themselves require particulars of an agreement to be furnished under the Restrictive Trade Practices Act 1976, because only the franchisee accepts the restriction (para 2.144, ante) unless the policy is pursued through a franchisees' club or the like, but are blacklisted by the EEC block exemption (Article 5(e)).

(4) Maximum price terms are permissible under domestic law, but the EEC block exemption appears to blacklist them (Article 5(e)). On the other hand, regard must be had to the reason for the blacklisting which appears to be concern not to inhibit franchisees in low-price areas selling into higher priced areas (which would not be worthwhile if their maximum prices were controlled). In many franchises, eg fast food, there is a possibility of this, and maximum price terms might be cleared where no other inhibiting factors exist.

1 Though permissible under Restrictive Trade Practices Act 1976 (if restriction on franchisees only—para 2.141), or it is disregardable under s 9(3) as relating exclusively to the goods supplied.

Chapter 3
Setting up the franchise business: intellectual property

INTRODUCTION

3.01 In this chapter we are concerned with two situations: where an entirely new business is being started here, and where a franchisor already operating in another country wishes to franchise in the United Kingdom.

3.02 Although it may seem superfluous to say so, in either case, a necessary precondition to setting up a new franchise business in this country is that the franchisor should actually have something to licence. An idea of itself is not enough. The idea should have been developed into an operating business, and thereby tried, tested and modified as necessary, and, in the case of overseas franchises, tailored to the local market, *before* franchising is commenced. What the franchisee is looking for is a licence to carry on a business under a successful method. Not only must the method be successful, but the trade name and as many aspects of the 'package' as possible must be protected. Undoubtedly one of the most important things licensed by the franchisor is the right to carry on business under a mark or name belonging to the franchisor. Formerly marks were only registerable in relation to goods in this country. However, from 1 October 1986, service marks have been afforded the means of protection by registration. The intellectual property package licensed by the franchisor will also contain, in addition to marks, copyright, and possibly design right, registered designs, and occasionally trade secrets and know-how (in the technical sense). Patented inventions are unlikely to perform an important function in many kinds of franchise business. Patented processes might, though there is the problem that the period of patent protection is short, and by the time the pilot scheme or schemes have been run and the business developed, there may be little time to exploit the patent through franchising. Copyright law and design right can afford some protection to patentable articles but not to processes. Registered designs may also have a part to play. Each of these areas of intellectual property involves an extensive and complex body of law, and it is quite impossible within the compass of this book to give a full account of them. Many of the problems are not peculiar to franchising and are familiar to practitioners in the intellectual property fields anyway. What we attempt to do therefore, is to deal with those things which are of especial importance to franchising, and for the rest to give a general account in order that non-specialist practitioners may be aware of the role the various forms of intellectual property may play, and the procedure for securing protection. We also attempt to alert them to those areas where specialist advice should be sought.

Choice of the name for the franchise business
General considerations

3.03 As observed above, usually the most important right purchased by the franchisees in the 'franchise package', is to carry on business during the period of the franchise under the mark or name belonging to, or associated with, the franchisor.[1] Consequently the choice of, and protection of, that mark or name is one of the most important aspects of setting up a franchise business. Because this is a matter of such importance for the future of the franchise, it may well be that the non-specialist legal adviser should consider engaging the services of a specialist at the outset. A list of members of the Institute of Trade Mark Agents can be obtained by writing to:
> Suit 5,
> Panther House,
> 38 Mount Pleasant,
> London WC1X 0AP.
> (price including postage £5)

Patent agents generally also transact trade mark business. A list of members of the Chartered Institute of Patent Agents can be obtained by writing to:
> Staple Inn Buildings,
> London WC1V 7PZ.

In the following pages we give an outline of the matters to be borne in mind from a legal point of view in choosing the name, and the ways in which it may be protected.

1 See para 1.01, ante.

3.04 The name chosen for the business should be distinctive and should if possible at the outset be *registrable* as a mark, ie without evidence of use. Moreover, the more unusual a name the easier it is by virtue of the name *itself*, ie independently of any particular representation of it, to establish the evidence necessary to succeed in a passing-off action. Proper names are for this reason best avoided. It is quite permissible for other people bearing the same name to carry on business in their name[1], provided they do so without intention to deceive[2]. No doubt use of a name may in certain circumstances be evidence to an intention to pass off goods as those of the plaintiff, but the legal principle that a person is not bound to use extra precautions to avoid confusion arising solely from the similarity of his name to the plaintiffs, is quite clear[3]. Even though a proper name may be represented in a distinctive way, the public may nevertheless tend to confuse the business with other businesses bearing the same name with consequent damage to the goodwill[4]. Purely descriptive names should be avoided because they are of themselves incapable of registration[5]. Misspelled descriptive words may, however, be capable of becoming distinctive[6], if the basic words themselves can also become distinctive but not otherwise[7]. The ideal is an invented or fanciful word which is registrable and which of itself, independently of its representation, will readily enable the evidence necessary for a passing-off action to be established. Unfortunately, there is frequently in practice a tension between what is ideal for legal purposes, and what is thought to be ideal for marketing purposes. It not infrequently happens in practice that the client's legal advisers are advising that a name should not be used, which his marketing advisers have recommended should be used. Where franchisors insist on the use of a word or name which is likely to present difficulties so far as registration is

3.05 *Setting up the franchise business: intellectual property*

concerned, it should nevertheless be possible to present it in a distinctive representation which itself will be registrable as a mark, with a disclaimer of the word or name if required. Another possibility is to combine the word with some sort of symbol which is registrable. In any event, most franchisors will want to adopt a distinctive get-up which in itself may or may not include registrable features, but which will have the capacity of becoming distinctive of the business and be protected through passing off when the franchisor has established his reputation. Some of these features may enjoy copyright protection, or be registrable as designs.

1   *Turton v Turton* (1889) 42 Ch D 128, CA; *Jamieson & Co v Jamieson* (1898) 15 RPC 169. CA.
2   *Sykes v Sykes* (1824) 3 B & C 541; *Croft v Day* (1843) 7 Beav 84; *Holloway v Holloway* (1850) 13 Beav 209.
3   *Jamieson & Co v Jamieson*, ante. See also Trade Marks Act 1938, s 8.
4   The *GEC* case provides a good illustration of the confusion which can arise where names are the same, even though their representations are distinctive—*General Electric Co v General Electric Co Ltd* [1972] 2 All ER 507, [1972] 1 WLR 729, HL.
5   See para 3.28, post.
6   See eg *Re Davis's Trade Mark, Davis v Sussex Rubber Co* [1927] 2 Ch 345, 44 RPC 412, CA and para 3.36, post.
7   Thus 'Orlwoola' was ordered to be expunged, though used for many years—*Re HN Brock & Co Ltd* [1910] 1 Ch 130, 26 RPC 850, CA.

3.05 The best of all possible combinations is a unique word in a unique representation. Needless to say, care should be taken as far as possible to ensure that the name and representation *are* in fact unique. Unfortunately, there is no absolutely certain way of doing this. So far as names are concerned, it is possible of course to search the Companies Register[1], but this will only reveal the names of companies, and these are not necessarily the names under which they trade. The Register of Business Names was abolished by the Companies Act 1981[2], but the most valuable information from this archive can be obtained from the London Chamber of Commerce who operate a business name information and searching service. Searches can be made (for a fee which depends upon whether or not the search is effective) by writing to

LCCI Business Registration Search Dept.,
Greyhound Chambers,
Chepstow,
Gwent NP6 5DB.
Tel: 02912-70138 Telex: 498171

The Trade Marks Register may be searched[3], and trades directories and telephone directories also help. In general however it is necessary to rely on general business knowledge of the particular market to avoid names which may lead to confusion with other businesses. Those businesses do not necessarily have to operate in exactly the same field; it is sufficient if the public might suppose there to exist a connection between them[4].

1   It should be noted that the Companies Register may permit the registration of fairly similar names.
2   Section 119(5).
3   See para 3.41, post.
4   See paras 3.62 et seq, post.

3.06 Taking care to get right the legal, as well as marketing, aspects of the style of the business is of great importance. Nothing is more disastrous for a business which has just begun to take off than to be confronted with an infringement or passing off action. There is a likelihood that the goodwill built up for the original name will not survive an enforced change, and the costs and damages for the action could be considerable, possibly leading to insolvency.

3.07 In the case of an overseas operation thinking of opening in the United Kingdom there are particular difficulties. They will probably want to enjoy the advantage of the spill-over of their reputations in their existing markets, into the United Kingdom market. Accordingly, they will usually not wish to alter their trading style unless absolutely necessary. However, the above remarks about new operations apply equally here, with the difference that an overseas operation may be in a better financial position to fight infringement and passing off actions in the early days of its establishment here. It may also be in a position to buy in any conflicting marks already on the Register.

Business names: requirements of Business Names Act 1985

3.08 In all cases, the franchisor company must ensure that it is complying with the requirements for the disclosure of persons using business names, and an address for service of official documents. These are set out at para 6.24, post.

Personality and character merchandising

Introduction

3.09 Personality and character merchandising are often linked with franchising. Both involve licensing of names, and commonly marks and copyright (though in the case of merchandising the licensing of marks is more problematic since the *Holly Hobbie* case). As explained earlier however, they are very different enterprises, both in their objects and in their legal frameworks[1]. Personality and character merchandising require discussion however to the extent that chains sometimes went to make use of a personality's name in the business, or use a cartoon character or the like as part of the get-up and the question then arises: what has the merchandiser to sell?

1 See para 1.13 et seq.

3.10 Personality marketing or merchandising involves the use of the true identity of a person, or occasionally an animal, in the marketing or advertising of goods or services. Character merchandising is similar, but involves the use of a fictional character or situation often from a cartoon. Between these two clearly distinguishable types there are those cases where the merchandised property is, for example, a well-known actor playing a well-known television role. In these cases it is difficult to decide whether what is involved is a personality or a character. Really it is both, though from a legal point of view, the position is likely to be similar to straightforward personality merchandising. Neither type of merchandising is commonly met with in the franchising context, partly because the life of most properties which form the stock-in-trade of the merchandiser is very short. However, in particular circumstances a merchandiser may have something to offer to a prospective franchisor. Thus, sports shops may benefit from being carried on under the name of a well known sportsman. A cartoon character may occasionally be

3.11 Setting up the franchise business: intellectual property

useful in certain kinds of business, especially if the franchise deals with children as customers. In this case, quite apart from any trade mark protection there is the possibility of the prospective licensor enjoying copyright protection (the basis of the property in the *Holly Hobbie* case itself was paintings of a small girl which formed the basis of the property). The main matter of enquiry for the franchisor seeking a licence should in this case be to establish quite clearly that the proposed licensor actually does own the copyright. Some merchandisers can be somewhat careless in this regard.

3.11 In the absence of good trade or service mark protection, copyright protection or possession of a goodwill capable of supporting a passing off action in respect of the franchisee's proposed activities, the question arises what exactly has the merchandiser got to sell? The answer is, sometimes, very little. Whilst no doubt it may be of advantage to secure his help and co-operation, rather than hostility, it is also important in negotiating a fee to know the strength of his property from a legal point of view. The relevant principles of passing off are to be found elsewhere in this book[1]. Below we consider some of the other branches of law which may have a bearing on the matter.

1 See paras 3.52 et seq and 3.72.

Trade and service marks

3.12 Where marks are involved, both the activities of personality and character merchandising have now to be considered in relation to the *Holly Hobbie Trade Mark* case[1]. A result of that case is that a merchandiser who does not himself trade, and who is unable to bring his activities within the guidelines laid down by the Trade Marks Registry in August 1984[2] in relation to section 29(1)(b) applications, will probably be unable to secure trade mark registration. If by chance he has secured registration, his marks may well be vulnerable on the grounds that his activities amount to trafficking[3]. Moreover, if the merchandiser is a registered user, and is proposing to offer a sub-licence to the franchisor, there is a separate problem created by the Trade Marks Act, section 28(12). It can be argued that this provision has a public interest aspect, and is not merely there for the protection of the mark proprietor[4], though this aspect more obviously is a relevant consideration under section 28(5). The same problem would arise in a situation where franchisees were to be given sub-licences[5].

1 [1984] RPC 329.
2 See Appendix 2, post.
3 Section 28(6); *Holly Hobbie Trade Mark* [1984] RPC 329 at 356–7. See discussion of case at para 1.13.
4 See remarks of Mr Myall in reaching his decision at the Registry stage.
5 See para 1.20 et seq.

3.13 In the rare cases where a merchandiser is agreeable to the franchisor taking an assignment of the mark or marks, there will be no problem. The alternative strategy is for the proprietor to appoint the franchisor agent for the purpose of negotiating licences between the proprietor and the franchisees[1]. In the case of the merchandising operations themselves, however, the possibility of an accusation of trafficking exists unless the proprietor is himself trading in the relevant goods or services. This requirement further weakens the negotiating power of a merchandiser, since it is improbable that a franchisor would be happy about the registered proprietor dealing in competing goods or services under an identical mark though it is conceivable that in some kinds of manufacturing franchise, the franchisor might be agreeable to supplying the goods to the merchandiser under a requirements contract.

1 See para 1.20 et seq.

3.14 There is no copyright protection for a name itself[1]. However, the name of a character or a celebrity may be associated with a particular representation of it in eg a television series. That representation may itself be protected by copyright. A signature is subject to copyright. Generally however the most important category of merchandised property to benefit from copyright protection is the invented character whose likeness is instantly recognisable, such as a cartoon character[2]. In this case it does not matter for the purposes of a copyright infringement action that no particular original sketch is copied, it is sufficient that the copying is done from a reproduction such as a film, or a video[3], derived directly or indirectly from the original work[4]. It is to be remembered also, that copyright protection extends to any substantial part of any image forming part of a film[5]. Copyright can both be used directly to threaten an infringement action, and indirectly for example to block trade mark registration. Thus in the *Oscar*[6] case, the Academy of Motion Picture Arts and Sciences successfully opposed the registration of the word 'Oscar' and an adjacent silhouette for their statuette as a trade mark on the ground that unpublished[7] works of United States origin have continuously been afforded copyright protection in the United Kingdom since 1915[8]. Copyright generally is dealt with below[9]. The duration of copyright protection is reduced to twenty five years from the end of the calendar year in which an artistic work has been exploited by an industrial process. Bearing in mind the extent to which cartoon characters evolve over the years, this reduction should not be too much of a problem in this context[10].

1 See *Exxon Corpn v Exxon Insurance Consultants International Ltd* [1982] Ch 119, [1982] RPC 69, unless it is capable of being recognised as an original literary work.
2 See eg *King Features Syndicate Inc v O & M Kleeman Ltd* [1941] AC 417, 58 RPC 207, HL.
3 Copyright Designs and Patents Act 1988, s 5(1).
4 Ibid, s 16(5)(b).
5 Ibid, s 17(4). *Spelling Goldberg Productions Inc v BPC Publishing Ltd* [1981] RPC 283.
6 [1979] RPC 173.
7 The statuette is awarded only to individual award winners.
8 (SR & O 1915 No 130) made under section 11 of the 1911 Act.
9 Para 3.75 et seq, post.
10 Ie the situation is distinguishable from that in *Interlego AG v Tyco Industries Inc* [1989] AC 217, [1988] 3 All ER 949, PC.

Defamation

3.15 It can be defamatory to state that a person has endorsed a product if he has not. Thus in *Tolley v Fry*[1] an advertisement which caricatured the plaintiff was held to be defamatory because of the innuendo that the plaintiff had allowed his name to be used for gain, thereby prostituting his amateur status. In the absence of facts which make an advertisement defamatory, however, merely to make use

3.16 Setting up the franchise business: intellectual property

of a person's name or portrait for the purposes of promotion would not of itself appear to be defamatory[2].

1   *Tolley v JS Fry & Sons Ltd* [1931] AC 333. Also *Dunlop Rubber Co Ltd v Dunlop* [1921] 1 AC 367, HL.
2   *Corelli v Wall* (1906) 22 TLR 532; *Dockrell v Dougall* (1899) 80 LT 556, CA.

Invasion of privacy/unfair competition

3.16 Consideration of the possibility of a separate tort of invasion of privacy is beyond the scope of this work[1]. It would not be likely to be recognised in English law at the present time. Certainly there is no indication that in England concepts such as violation of a right of publicity[2], or appropriation of the plaintiff's personality[3] are likely to appear, though several European countries do provide protection against the commercial exploitation of a person's name. The Privy Council decision in *Cadbury-Schweppes Pty Ltd v Pub Squash Co Pty Ltd* has effectively put paid to the likelihood of a tort of unfair competition developing in this country in the foreseeable future[4].

1   See *Privacy* ed Young (1979) (Wiley and Sons), Essay 5 by Gerald Dworkin.
2   *Haelon Laboratories Inc v Topps Chewing Gum* 202 F 2d 866 (1953).
3   *Athans v Canadian Adventure Camps Ltd* (1977) 80 DLR (3d) 583.
4   [1981] 1 All ER 213, [1981] 1 WLR 193; *Harrods Ltd v Schwartz-Sackin & Co Ltd* [1986] FSR 490, 494; see also observations of Lord Templeman in *Coca-Cola Trade Marks* [1986] FSR 472, and see paras 3.60 et seq.

Trade Descriptions Act 1968

3.17 If a name is used so as to imply that goods are approved by a person this could amount to a false trade description[1]. A similar argument can be developed in relation to services, from section 14(1)(b)(iv). Furthermore, such a representation would infringe the ASA and IBA codes of practice[2].

1   Trade Descriptions Act 1968, ss 2(1)(g) and 3(4).
2   See paras 7.17 et seq.

Summary

3.18 In the absence of trade marks or service marks or copyrights, a merchandiser has, in legal terms few rights to sell in this country, unless the use of the name, etc, would constitute passing off in the particular context.

Protecting the package

Introduction

3.19 As noted at the beginning of this chapter, a properly protected bundle of intellectual property rights is fundamental to any franchise operation. In the case of trade marks and service marks it is important to secure registrations for the relevant goods or services in which the network will be trading. Copyright is also likely to play a prominent part. There is no requirement of registration to secure copyright protection in the United Kingdom. Some copyright designs can be registered, and the circumstances in which it may be desirable to do so are considered below. Patents will be met with less commonly, for the reasons mentioned above, but may sometimes have a part to play. All of these rights have the advantage of an action for infringement in respect of them. It nevertheless remains the case that passing off is also of considerable importance in protecting the business.

Trade marks and service marks[1]

Introduction

3.20 The protection afforded to the goodwill of a business through the law of passing off is considered below[2]. The principal drawback with passing off is the expense often involved in litigation. Evidence of goodwill has to be assembled, and of the other ingredients of the tort[3]. By contrast, the action for infringement of a mark simply raises the question as to whether the defendant has used the mark in any of the specified ways, in relation to the goods or services for which the mark is registered. The register itself therefore provides the plaintiff's principal weapon. The position was that marks could be registered only in respect of goods in the United Kingdom. From 1 October 1986, however, they have been registrable in respect of services[4]. Both of these matters are considered in this section. The effect of the 1984 Act is to create two 1938 Trade Marks Acts: one for goods and one for services. Because of the importance of service marks in franchising, the plan adopted in this section usually is to give the text of the service marks Act, and to footnote significant variations in the Act relating to goods. In a work of this sort, it is impossible to do more than deal with the more common practical points, and to outline current Registry practice. A detailed description of Registry Practice is given in the Trade Marks Registry Work Manual Ch 9 'Examination of a Trade or Service Mark for Registrability'.

1 At the time of writing it seems likely that a Bill will be introduced in 1991 to update UK law along the lines envisaged in the draft Community Trade Mark Regulation and the Protocol to the Madrid Agreement.
2 See para 3.52 et seq.
3 Ibid.
4 Trade Marks (Amendment) Act 1984.

3.21 It must be remembered that the law of trade marks and service marks registration is national. It is possible for the same mark to be registered in different countries for entirely independent businesses[1]. This can create considerable difficulties for multinational operations. At least in the EEC the position should be somewhat simplified when a European Community trade mark is introduced.

1 This has important implications for freedom of trade between Member States of the European Economic Community—see paras 2.77 et seq, ante.

1 Outline of the registration scheme

3.22 In order to qualify for registration, a mark must fall within the statutory definitions. There are separate definitions for goods and services. So far as goods are concerned:

> '"Trade mark" means ... a mark used or proposed to be used in relation to goods for the purpose of indicating, or so as to indicate, a connection in

3.23 Setting up the franchise business: intellectual property

the course of trade between the goods and some person having the right either as proprietor or as registeed user to use the mark, whether with or without any indication of the identity of that person . . .[1]

The definition in relation to services is slightly different. A possible consequence in relation to licensing has already been alluded to[2].

'"*Service mark*" means a mark . . . used or proposed to be used in relation to services for the purpose of indicating or so as to indicate that a particular person is connected, in the course of business, with the provision of those services whether with or without an indication of the identity of that person[3].

A mark is a means of identification. It must enable members of the public to distinguish the goods with which the owner has a trade connection from those of others. It must therefore be distinctive or be capable of becoming so. As explained below, a mark which is distinctive is registrable in Part A, a mark which is capable of becoming distinctive is registrable in Part B of the register.

1 Trade Marks Act 1938, s 68(1).
2 See para 1.15 et seq.
3 Section 68(1) as amended by the Trade Marks (Amendment) Act 1984, and further amended by the Patents, Designs and Marks Act 1986.

The distinction between trade marks and service marks

3.23 A question which will arise at the outset, in borderline cases, is whether the appropriate classification should be in respect of goods or services. Presumably, on this question, the cases giving guidance on what was registrable as a trade mark, will continue to be referred to. In *Aristoc Ltd v Rysta Ltd*[1] where the respondents carried on a stocking repair service and applied for registration of the word 'Rysta' it was held that a mark used in relation to a repairing system or service was not registrable. Repair of stockings did not constitute a 'connection in the course of a trade' for the purposes of the Act. Lord Maugham observed ' . . . it seems to be beyond doubt that hitherto a registered trade mark has been understood as being used in relation to goods for the purpose of indicating the *origin* of the goods, in other words, for the purpose of indicating either the manufacture or some other dealing with the goods in the process of manufacture or in the course of a business before they are offered for sale to the public[1]'.

1 [1945] AC 68, 62 RPC 65, HL. See also the *Visa Case*, para 3.24 below.

3.24 The lack of service mark registration was a considerable nuisance in the franchising context (and remains so at present in respect of the retailing aspect of businesses, which current practice is not to accept in Class 42)[1]. The difficulties are compounded by some rather curious distinctions drawn by the Registry. Thus 'take away' food obtained registrations in Class 29, whilst food consumed on the premises did not[2]. Since *Visa* (below), however, it is believed that applications have been accepted for food consumed on the premises in Classes 29 and 30 (restaurants are of course a service and registrations may be secured in respect of this service aspect of the business separately). All else failing, the commonest strategy used to attempt to get some sort of protection in service businesses, was to register marks in relation to various goods used in the course of the business. Stationery was common category. The problem was there was often no intention on the part of the proprietor to make trade mark use of the mark in relation to such goods;

the mark accordingly, even if it got on to the register, would be vulnerable[3]. The fact that the goods are 'given away', does not, however, preclude the possibility that a proprietor is making good trade mark use of his mark. It depends on the circumstances. Thus in the *UPDATE* case, a mark used as the title for a free magazine was refused registration for 'printed matter' on the ground that there was no intention to trade in printed matter[4]. The applicant's business was advertising, and the journal being their medium, its free distribution was part of their service.

By contrast, in the *Visa* case[5], where the two registrations applied for were in respect of bank cards and travellers cheques, Whitford J permitted the registrations to go ahead notwithstanding the fact that both types of goods were ancillary to the applicant's banking services, and both were distributed to their customers free. The Registrar had approached the matter from the point of view of the level of interdependence between the applicant's service activities and their dealing in the relevant goods. Whitford J held, however, that the correct approach was simply to ask 'Does this applicant trade in these goods?' The fact that he trades as part of a service, is wholly irrelevant[6]. The Registrar had pointed out that that applicant's 'sold' the travellers cheques and bank cards to their members in the sense that they recouped the cost of production and distribution in their charges. In the view of Whitford J they were both trading in goods and supplying a service. By contrast, in *Aristoc*, the respondent's activities were purely the service of repairing. The implication of the *Visa* case is that items such as book matches, which are distributed freely to the public, could be goods traded in by a franchise. The cost of such items are similarly recouped from the public. It may be that this is a way of distinguishing cases such as *UPDATE Trade Mark*[7]. However, in view of Whitford J's criticism of the *Bank of American National Trust and Savings Association* case[8], and approval of *Golden Pages* (both Irish cases)[9], it could well be that he considered *UPDATE* to be wrongly decided. At all events, even before *Visa*, applications had been accepted by the Registry in respect of 'free' distribution newspapers. This is of importance to the extent that it may well be desirable to obtain registration in respect of 'free' distribution matter.

1 See *Re Dee Corpns Application* [1989] FSR 266.
2 See however *Hong Kong Caterers v Maxim's Ltd* (1983) unreported (Hong Kong).
3 Ie under s 26(1). See *Wells Fargo Trade Mark* [1977] RPC 503, where however at the end of the day the mark was allowed to remain on the register; *Hospital World Trade Mark* [1967] RPC 595; *UPDATE Trade Mark* [1979] RPC 166. Compare *Golden Pages Trade Mark* [1985] FSR 27 (Ireland). See Work Manual para 9.28.
4 *UPDATE*, ante.
5 [1985] RPC 323. Compare *AIRCO Trade Mark* [1977] FSR 485 (Bermuda). See also Work Manual para 9.25 et seq.
6 See, however, *Golden Pages Trade Mark*, ante.
7 Above.
8 [1977] FSR 7.
9 Above.

Part A Registration

3.25 A Part A service mark enjoys the fullest protection under the Act. In order to be registered in Part A, it must satisfy the criteria set out in section 9 (as amended by the Trade Marks (Amendment) Act 1984):

'(1) In order for a service mark . . . to be registrable in Part A of the register, it must contain or consist of at least one of the following essential particulars:

3.26 Setting up the franchise business: intellectual property

(a) the name of a company, individual, or firm represented in a special or particular manner;
(b) the signature of the applicant for registration or some predecessor in his business;
(c) an invented word or invented words;
(d) a word or words having no direct reference to the character or quality of the goods, and not being according to its ordinary signification a geographical name or a surname;
(e) any other distinctive mark, but a name, signature or word or words, other than such as fall within the descriptions in the foregoing paragraphs (a), (b), (c) and (d), shall not be registrable under the provisions of this paragraph except upon evidence of its distinctiveness.
(2) For the purposes of this section 'distinctive' means adapted, in relation to the services in respect of which a service mark is registered or proposed to be registered, to distinguish services with the provision of which the proprietor is or may be connected, in the course of business, from services with the provision of which he is not so connected, either generally, or where the service mark is registered or proposed to be registered subject to limitations, in relation to use within the extent of the registration[1].
(3) In determining whether a service mark is adapted to distinguish as aforesaid the tribunal may have regard to the extent to which:
(a) the service mark is inherently adapted as aforesaid; and
(b) by reason of the use of the service mark or of any other circumstances, the service mark is in fact adapted to distinguish as aforesaid'[2].

It is worth examining some aspects of these provisions further.

1 The equivalent provision for goods reads as follows: '(2) For the purposes of this section 'distinctive' means adapted, in relation to the goods in respect of which a trade mark is registered or proposed to be registered, to distinguish goods with which the proprietor of a trade mark is or may be connected in the course of a trade from goods in the case of which no such connection subsists, either generally or, where the trade mark is registered or proposed to be registered subject to limitations, in relation to use within the extent of the registration.'
2 Text as given effect by the Patents, Designs and Marks Act 1986.

(a) Name marks

3.26 Apart from the requirements that the name be a real name, as opposed to an obviously fictitious or fanciful name[1], and that the whole name is registered (the section refers to *the* name), then the name can either be that of a company, individual or firm, or its trading name. Names not falling within this subsection may in any case be registrable under subsection (e). The requirement that the name be represented in a special or particular manner should be noted. This has the effect of excluding, for example, names represented in ordinary script or type[2]. For the rules on surnames see para 3.33, post.

1 Eg "Trilby" *Holt's Trade Mark* (1896) 13 RPC 16. Compare *Standard Cameras Ltd's Application* (1952) 69 RPC 125 however.
2 *Carroll's Application* (1899) 16 RPC 82; *Gianaclis' Trade Mark* (1889) 6 RPC 467; *Price's Patent Candle Co* (1884) 27 Ch D 681; *Re British Milk Products Co's Application* [1915] 2 Ch 202.

(b) Invented word or invented words

3.27 The *Solio* Case[1] is the leading authority on this provision. Objection was taken to the word 'Solio' for photographic paper, on the ground that it had reference to the character and quality of the goods. The House of Lords however permitted registration. Lord Herschell said:

' . . . if the word be an "invented" one, I do not think the quantum of invention is at all material. An invented word is allowed to be registered as a trade mark, not as a reward of merit, but because its registration deprives no member of the community of the rights which he possesses to use the existing vocabulary as he pleases.

It may, no doubt, sometimes be difficult to determine whether a word is an invented word or not. I do not think the combination of two English words is an invented word, even although the combination may not have been in use before; nor do I think that a mere variation of the orthography or termination of a word would be sufficient to constitute an invented word, if to the eye or ear the same idea would be conveyed as by the word in its ordinary form. Again, I do not think that a foreign word is an invented word simply because it has not been current in our language. At the same time, I am not prepared to go so far as to say that combination of words from foreign languages, so little known in this country that it would suggest no meaning except to a few scholars, might not be regarded as an invented word[2].'

The House of Lords decided that what are now subsections (c) and (d) were separate cases. To qualify as an invented word, a word must not only not already exist in the English language, it must not convey any obvious meaning to an ordinary Englishman[3]. Misspelling does not convert an otherwise ordinary word, or combination of words, into an invented word. The most difficult questions on this subsection are over the standard of invention to be applied[4].

1 [1898] AC 571.
2 At 581.
3 *Philippart v William Whiteley Ltd, Philippart's Trade Mark Diabolo* [1908] 2 Ch 274, 25 RPC 565.
4 For examples see Kerly para 8.20.

(c) A word or words having no direct reference to the character or quality of the goods or services, not being geographical names or surnames

3.28 This is commercially the most important category. From a marketing point of view, it is often desirable to choose a mark suggestive of the product. If however the reference to the product is direct, the capacity of the word to distinguish the applicant's product will be affected. Moreover marks which could interfere with the bona fide trading of other traders will be refused registration. Thus *Tarzan Trade Mark*[1] was refused registration notwithstanding evidence of distinctiveness, because the hearing officer considered it to be a word which other traders were likely, in the ordinary course of their business and without improper motive, to desire to use. A mark must be both inherently adapted to distinguish the applicant's products, and in fact adapted to distinguish them. Examples of words refused registration include *Motor Lodge*[2] for food where the applicant's business was in fact motels, *PIZZA*[3] for pizzas, and *Tastee Freez*[4] for ice cream. Often the question as to whether or not a mark satisfies the requirement of distinctiveness[5], is difficult to answer at the outset. Only when the mark has been used for some time will

3.29 *Setting up the franchise business: intellectual property*

it be possible to know with any certainty. If objections are raised, therefore, it may be possible to reapply at a later date when evidence of distinctiveness is available.

1 [1970] RPC 450.
2 [1965] RPC 35.
3 [1975] RPC 349.
4 [1960] RPC 255.
5 Or, in the case of Part B, possesses the capacity to distinguish—see para 3.36.

(d) Geographical names

3.29 Since the *York Trailers*[1] case, the Registry practice[2] on geographic names for goods has been very strict, and reliable gazetteers must be searched. This said, the rationale for the refusal to register such names must not be forgotten. That is that it might interfere with the legitimate interests of other traders in the particular locality[3]. Thus if evidence can be provided that it would not do so because no other trader could legitimately use the name, then the name should be registrable. Marks have been accepted on evidence that no trader in the locality could legitimately use the mark for the relevant goods[4]. It is expected that service businesses will create some interesting problems in this respect.

1 [1984] RPC 231.
2 For full description of Registry practice see Work Manual 9.84 et seq. Below we give only a summary.
3 The Act thus poses the question as to whether the word is, in its ordinary signification, a surname—s 9(1)(d).
4 Eg Waterford has now been accepted for glass in Ireland.

The Registrar's guidelines on geographical names[1]
Not registrable in Part A or Part B

3.30 Geographical names (that is names with an undisputed geographic connotation, possibly one of several connotations) which cannot fail to have (exclusively or otherwise) a geographical meaning for a substantial number of people in this country for the goods claimed are not registrable in Part A or Part B.

Unless it can be said that the name is so little known as such that it may be regarded as not being, according to its ordinary signification, a geographical name[2], or could not have a geographic meaning for the goods claimed eg *North Pole* for bananas, some evidence of distinctiveness will be required before it can be accepted for Part A of the register. Even with evidence of 100 per cent factual distinctiveness, however, some names will be unregistrable.[3]

1 See Work Manual 9.86 et seq.
2 See eg *Farah Trade Mark* (High Court of Ireland) [1978] FSR 234.
3 See *York Trailers* [1984] RPC 231.

Registrable in Part A

3.31 Geographical names, which cannot on any reasonable basis, have a geographical meaning for the goods concerned.

Registrable in Part B[1]

3.32 (1) Names of places which have another very common and non-objectionable significance with populations below 2000 (in the United Kingdom) and 50,000 (abroad), where the goods are not natural produce, and the place has no reputation for the goods.

(2) Names of places with populations below 5000 (in the United Kingdom) and in the case of industrialised areas such as the USA, Japan and Europe 100,000 population, or in the case of China or South America 250,000 can be considered.

Unless a geographical name falls within one of the categories listed above, it is generally very difficult indeed, if not impossible, to register as a trade mark, even in Part B, regardless of proven factual distinctiveness.

Different considerations apply in the case of service businesses, many of which are necessarily local, eg Hawaii might be accepted for a dry-cleaning business.

1 See Work Manual 11.36–11.37, 11.39–11.40.

(e) Surnames as marks[1]

3.33 Obviously, some restriction has to be placed on permitting the registration of common surnames, because of the inconvenience which could be caused to those bona fide wishing to trade under their own names. A proprietor cannot of course prevent them from using their own names bona fide as trade names or probably as marks[2], but it is not desirable that people should unnecessarily be placed in a position of having to establish their right to use their own names. But what is a surname? The Act refers to 'ordinary signification'. Accordingly, the Trade Mark Registry has laid down guidelines, giving the frequency of the appearance of the name in the London or other relevant telephone directory which they will find acceptable. These are as follows:

(1) Uncommon names with no other meaning—5 times in the London telephone directory for Part A, 15 times in any relevant foreign directory. The frequencies of occurrence for Part B are 15 and 30 times respectively.

(2) For names with another well-known meaning, eg, Cannon (and if that meaning is descriptive of the goods in question it could give rise to separate problems), the frequency of occurrence is 50 times in the London telephone directory for Part A, and 100 times in the London telephone directory (200 times in any relevant foreign directory) for Part B.

1 For detailed practice see Work Manual para 9.123 et seq.
2 Section 8. As to whether or not this section covers use as marks see *Kerly* 15.34.

(f) Device marks[1]

3.34 Distinctive devices, rather than words, may be registered as trade marks[2] and can be very useful.

1 For detailed description of practice, see Work Manual 9.231 et seq.
2 Under s 9(1)(a) or (e).

3.35 Setting up the franchise business: intellectual property

(g) Monograms

3.35 Monograms are a very popular type of mark at the present day. The practice on these is as follows[1]:

(1) *Three letters—monograms* Marks consisting of three or more letters formed into a monogram (by which is meant letters which have been intertwined) are accepted as registrable in Part A of the register. The mere placing of the letters one upon the other, without intertwining, does not necessarily produce a monogram.

(2) *Two letters—monograms* Monograms composed of only two letters are not regarded as sufficiently distinctive for registration (prima facie) under section 9, but are considered to be acceptable for registration in Part B of the register.

(3) *Single letter marks* Single letter marks propounded for registration are notoriously lacking in inherent distinctiveness. Such marks are rarely accepted prima facie in Part A and then only if the overwhelming impression is that of a device. A disclaimer of the letter will normally not be required because the device impression must be well away from the letter. Where the mark gives the impression of a letter but not clearly defined, then such marks may be acceptable in Part B with the letter disclaimed.

1   Work Manual para 9.213 et seq.

(h) Other common types of mark

3.35A Marks consisting simply of numerals or their phonetic equivalent are prima facie unacceptable[1]. Colour can, of course, be a relevant factor in distinctiveness of the mark[2]. Portraits may constitute distinctive devices[3].

Although it was held in the *Coca Cola*[4] case that the shape of a container may not be a mark, that case does not preclude the possibility of three-dimensional devices as marks.

1   *R J Reuter Co Ltd v Mulhens* [1954] Ch 50, 70 RPC 235, CA.
2   And s 16, and *Smith, Kline & French Laboratories TM Application* [1976] RPC 511.
3   *Rowland v Mitchell, Re Rowland's Trade Mark* [1897] 1 Ch 71, 14 RPC 37, CA.
4   [1986] FSR 472. Copying a container can, however, amount to passing off—see *Reckitt & Colman Products v Borden Inc* [1990] 1 All ER 873, [1990] 1 WLR 491, HL.

Part B registration

3.36 The requirements are set out in section 10:

(1) In order for a service to be registrable in Part B of the register it must be capable, in relation to the services in respect of which it is registered or proposed to be registered, of distinguishing services with the provision of which the proprietor of the service mark is or may be connected in the course of business from services with the provision of which he is not so connected, either generally, or, where the service mark is registered or proposed to be registered subject to limitations, in relation to use within the extent of the registration[1].

(2) In determining whether a service mark is capable of distinguishing as aforesaid the tribunal may have regard to the extent to which—

(a) the service mark is inherently capable of distinguishing as aforesaid and;
(b) by reason of the use of the service mark or of any other circumstances, the service mark is in fact capable of distinguishing as aforesaid.

(3) A service mark may be registered in Part B notwithstanding any registration

in Part A in the name of the same proprietor of the same mark or any part or parts thereof[2].

1 The equivalent provision for goods reads as follows: (1) In order for a trade mark to be registrable in Part B of the register it must be capable, in relation to the goods in respect of which it is registered or proposed to be registered, of distinguishing goods with which the proprietor of the trade mark is or may be connected in the course of a trade from goods in the course which no such connection subsists, either generally or, where the trade mark is registered or proposed to be registered subject to limitations, in relation to use within the extent of the registration.
2 Text given effect by the Patents, Designs and Marks Act 1986.

3.37 The rights conferred by Part B registration are the same as those for Part A subject to the following qualification:

> 'In any action for infringement of the right to the use of a service mark given by registration as aforesaid in Part B of the register, no injunction or other relief shall be granted to the plaintiff if the defendant establishes to the satisfaction of the court that the use of which the plaintiff complains is not likely to deceive or cause confusion or to be taken as indicating that a person having the right either as proprietor or as registered user to use the service mark is connected in the course of business with the provision of the services[1].'

A defendant in order to succeed in this defence, however, must prove separately, not only that there is no likelihood of confusion, but also that the use is not likely to indicate a connection between the defendant's goods and the proprietor's, a heavy burden[2]. In fact it is difficult to see why the availability of this defence weakens a Part B registration in any significant way, since these matters if established would equally provide a defence to an action for infringement of a Part A mark. It is conceivable, that in the *Bismag*[3] type of situation, where the plaintiff's goods are compared to the defendant's in such a way as to import a reference[4], that a defendant might establish the defence if words such as 'similar to' were sufficient to distinguish the defendant's goods from the proprietor's[5]. It was suggested by Graham J in *Broad & Co Ltd v Graham Building Supplies Ltd*[6] that the reference in section 5(2) to 'the goods' was to the defendant's goods, so that if another trader's goods were sold as 'similar to' the plaintiff's, the defence would lie. Though, since registration in Part B gives a like right to registration in Part A, it can be argued that Part B marks can be infringed by importing a reference. It must be observed that there is in fact no United Kingdom case in which the defence under section 5(2) has succeeded[7]. The only clear difference between the two parts of the Register is that registration is conclusive as to the validity of Part A marks after seven years[8], but not as to the validity of Part B marks. Apart from this, it is difficult to see how, from a practical point of view, a proprietor is in general going to be worse off with a Part B registration.

1 Section 5(2) as given effect by the Patents, Designs and Marks Act 1986.
2 *Broad & Co v Cast Iron Drainage Co* [1970] FSR 363 at 371-2.
3 [1940] Ch 667, 57 RPC 209.
4 See s 4(1)(b).
5 *Broad & Co v Cast Iron Drainage Co* (above).
6 [1969] RPC 286.
7 There is an Australian decision on an equivalent provision—*Marc A Hammond Pty Ltd v Papa Carmine Pty Ltd* [1978] RPC 697.
8 There is little English authority on the degree of incontestability conferred by this provision. For a useful analysis of the equivalent provisions of the Langham Act see Naresh (1986) 53 Univ Chic LR 953.

3.38 Setting up the franchise business: intellectual property

3.38 It is to be noted that the requirement for Part B is that the mark should be capable of being distinctive[1]. Evidence that a mark has become distinctive between the date of the application and the decision is relevant to the question as to whether or not at the date of the application it was capable of being distinctive. Part B registration is not usually applied for at the outset. Usually registrations arise from rejected Part A registrations. If offered Part B in such circumstances, the best advice is to accept it, rather than to run the risk of pressing on and ending up with nothing.

1 It is sufficient for the application to satisfy the Registrar that it is not incapable of becoming distinctive, a much less strenuous task and one in which the onus lies rather on the opponent than on the applicant—'Ustikon' *Re Davis's Trade Marks, Davis v Sussex Rubber Co* [1927] 2 Ch 345, 44 RPC 412, CA. The goods in 'Ustikon' were stick-on rubber soles, and the word was descriptive therefore, though not purely so. Purely descriptive, albeit misspelled words are not registrable—see eg *Re H N Brock & Co Ltd* [1910] 1 Ch 130, 26 RPC 850, CA.

3.39 When the mark applied for is used by another person in another country, that fact of itself is not sufficient to prevent the applicant from choosing that mark[1]. Registration may however be refused under the discretion conferred by section 17(2), inter alia in circumstances where it would be likely to deceive or cause confusion or otherwise be disentitled to protection in a court of justice[2]. It is not necessary for this purpose therefore that the opponent establish the facts necessary to succeed in a passing off action[3]. Thus one of the grounds for refusing the application in *Re Vitamins Ltd's Application*[4] was that in the case of medicinal products, the public interest may require that articles of different origin should not be advertised and sold here and abroad under the same mark. In *Gaines Animal Foods Ltd's Application for Trade Mark*[5], where the applicants had carried on business under the name and marks of a well-known American company in the same line of business, registration by the applicants of a further mark 'Gro-PUP' used by the American company was refused, although the American company failed to establish a reputation in the United Kingdom sufficient for the purposes of section 11. It was felt that the applicants were engaged in a dishonest system of conduct. It would appear however that mere distaste engendered by the applicants' somewhat sharp business practices, is not enough[6].

1 Re *Cheryl Playthings Ltd's Application* [1962] 2 All ER 86, [1962] RPC 133.
2 Trade Marks Act 1938, s 11.
3 See para 3.52 et seq.
4 [1955] 3 All ER 827, [1956] RPC 1.
5 [1958] RPC 312.
6 See *Re Cheryl Playthings Ltd's Application*, ante.

3.40 It is possible to obtain preliminary advice from the Registrar on the distinctiveness of proposed marks. The fee payable is £32 for a first mark, and £11 for each additional mark. The opinion given by the Registrar is not binding, but if an application to register is lodged on the basis of an opinion, and the Registrar subsequently objects that the mark lacks distinctiveness, the applicant will be entitled to reimbursement of the application fees[1].

1 Section 42(3).

2 Procedure

3.41 Assuming a distinctive work or device has been arrived at, with or without the Registrar's advice, a search can be made. The search will not necessarily ensure complete security against opposition of course. The search procedure is now computerised, and a search can be instigated by calling or writing to the Registry which is at: State House, High Holborn, London WC1, telephone 071-829-6165. No fee is payable at the outset, but when the search is concluded an invoice will be issued for every quarter hour. The search will not necessarily ensure complete security against opposition of course. The law of passing off should also be borne in mind where registrations are found in respect of other goods than those for which registration is sought, and the public might associate both sorts of goods with the same business. It is advisable to consult a trade mark agent or patent agent to carry out the search.

3.42 Application to register[1] in either Part A or Part B is made on Form TM No 2. A representation of the mark should appear in the space provided in Form 2. Three additional representations should be provided, either on Form TM4, or strong paper of the size prescribed in Rule 9.

1 The procedure is governed by section 17 and Rules 21–29 inclusive.

3.43 The Register is divided into 34 'Classes' of goods[1] and there are 8 Classes of services[2]. Every application must specify the Class to which the relevant goods or services belong. These are set out in Schedule 4 to the Trade Marks Rules. One class only must be specified in each application, and usually the applicant will be restricted to certain categories of goods or services within that Class. A guide is published by the Registry containing a fairly comprehensive list of goods and services in alphabetical order, and their classifications. This guide is not a decision of the Registrar however for the purposes of section 3. The advice of the Registry or of a specialist should be sought in cases of doubt. Claims to register the mark in respect of all goods or services in a Class are not usually acceptable and are likely to be queried[3]. This however depends on the Class. From the applicant's point of view, the wider the registration usually the better, but registration will only be allowed in respect of those goods or services the applicant uses or intends to use or provide, or goods or services of the same description, ie roughly all goods or services that would be recognised by business people as belonging to the same trade[4]. The classification may cause problems[5]. Where the applicant wishes to register a series of similar marks (variations on a theme) either in respect of the same, or different goods or services the Registrar can require them to be associated[6]. Use of an associated mark may be accepted as equivalent to the use of any other[7].

1 These follow the internationally agreed scheme of registration adopted in 1938. The classification is revised and updated from time to time. Registrations bearing numbers up to 600,000 are found in the earlier classification, and different searches must be made in respect of them.
2 Trade Marks and Service Marks Rules 1986, Rules 5(2) and (3) and Schedule 4, Part I.
3 Trade Marks and Service Marks Rules 1986 Rule 21(5).
4 *Daiquiri Rum Trade Mark* [1969] RPC 600, HL.
5 For example, if the applicant wishes to protect a range of cosmetics and toiletries, deodorants are in Class 5 while cosmetics, perfumes and soaps are in Class 3.
6 Section 23(2) and (2A).
7 Section 30(1).

3.44 *Setting up the franchise business: intellectual property*

3.44 The specification of the goods or services for the purposes of the application is a matter of considerable importance. This will determine the rights of the applicant conferred by the registration and may affect the validity of the registration. Here again, it may be advisable to seek specialist advice.

3.45 Registration must generally be applied for by the company intending to use the mark but under section 29(1)(a) if the tribunal is satisfied that a body corporate is about to be constituted, and that the mark will be assigned to the corporation with a view to its use by the corporation, registration may be permitted. The assignment must generally take place within twelve months[1]. A more difficult situation exists where a separate mark company is set up, which will trade only through registered users. If the user has been selected and will be registered immediately after registration, registration may be permitted under section 29(1)(b). Reference should be made to the Registry's guidelines of August 1984 for such applications. When a 'franchisor structure' using a separate licence company is adopted, this should provide no problem, as a user company will no doubt be set up for the purposes of the pilot scheme. If no user has been selected section 29(1)(b) cannot help. The applicant may fail to establish sufficient intention to use therefore[2].

1 The power to fix the period is conferred on the Registrar by section 29(4).
2 See *Pussy Galore Trade Mark* [1967] RPC 265 (this decision appears to conflict with dicta in *Bostitch Trade Mark* [1963] RPC 183 at 197, however).

3.46 The form of application should be signed by a director or the secretary or other authorised officer of the company. Alternatively, application may be made through an agent[1]. An agent should sign the application as 'agent'.

The application with accompanying fee of £68 should be sent to the Registrar, State House, High Holborn, London WC1.

1 Trade Mark and Service Mark Rules 1986, Rule 14(1).

3.47 If the Registrar objects to the application and refuses to proceed with its registration, he must make his objections in writing. The applicant has six months to respond[1]. He is then entitled to a hearing before the Registrar, and if the application is then refused, he may appeal to the Board of Trade or the court[2].

1 Rule 33.
2 Section 17(4).

3.48 If the Registrar accepts the application, the intention to register the mark is advertised in The Trade Marks Journal. In some cases, it may be advertised before acceptance (so that objections can be lodged)[1].

1 This applies to marks falling under section 9(1)(e).

3.49 It is beyond the scope of this work to consider the procedure where an objection is made by the Registrar or an opposition is lodged. If there has been no successful opposition to the registration, the mark will be entered on the register on filing Form TM-No 10 (fee £95) which will be increased when the form relates to a series of marks for goods or services not included in one class, or when association of marks is required. A certificate of registration will be issued, and the registration is effective from the date of entry.

3.50 Registration can be maintained indefinitely by payment of the necessary renewal fees. The initial period is seven years and thereafter renewal every fourteen years[1]. The Registrar will notify when renewal is due (and should therefore be told of changes of address on TM-No 18). Renewal applications are made on TM-No 11. The basic fee is £230.

1 Section 20. After the initial seven year period the mark becomes incontestable unless found invalid on the grounds of fraud or infringement of section 11.

3.51 *Forms and Fees*[1]

TM2 Application to Register in Part A or Part B	68
TM4 Additional representations of mark	—
TM7 Notice of opposition	31
TM10 Registration of Trade Mark	95 (but see para 3.49 above)
TM11 Renewal of registration	230
TM18 Change of address	—
Request for preliminary advice	32
Personal searches	£1 per quarter hour

1 These fees are subject to revision. At the time of writing revision is under discussion.

Passing off

Introduction

3.52 Whilst the greatest security for the name of the franchisee business is through a registered mark, against the encroachment on which by other traders an action for infringement is available, it nevertheless remains the case that the common law action for passing off plays a central role. There are many circumstances in which this will provide the franchisor with his *only* protection. Typical problems are:

(1) an overseas company has a name or mark, and seeks to protect it in the United Kingdom prior to starting franchising in the United Kingdom;

(2) the name chosen is not inherently distinctive and requires use to obtain protection;

(3) the name is distinctive, but the mark embodying it is registered for a limited range of goods or services and it is found that another trader has started to use it on other goods or services, in a way which could encroach upon the plaintiff's goodwill.

All of these have to be dealt with by an action for passing off. In the following sections we therefore deal with the general law of passing off, the problem of geography, and the use of names from other fields and protection of the franchisor's name from encroachment.

The general law of passing off[1]

3.53 Lord Diplock in the *Advocaat* case defined the elements of the tort as consisting of[2]: (1) a misrepresentation; (2) made by a trader in the course of a trade; (3) to prospective customers of his or ultimate consumers of goods or services supplied by him; (4) which is calculated to injure the business or goodwill of another trader

3.54 *Setting up the franchise business: intellectual property*

(in the sense that this is a reasonably foreseeable consequence); and (5) which causes actual damage to a business or goodwill of the trader by whom the action is brought or (in a *quia timet* action) will probably do so. Unless a case falls within these five principles, a plaintiff cannot succeed[3]. These essentials were expressed slightly differently by Lord Fraser as follows[4]:

> 'it is essential for the plaintiff in a passing off action to show at least the following facts: (1) that his business consists of, or includes, selling in England a class of goods to which the particular trade name applies; (2) that the class is clearly defined, and that in the minds of the public, or a section of the public, in England, the trade name distinguishes that class from other similar goods; (3) that because of the reputation of the goods, there is goodwill attached to the name; (4) that he, the plaintiff, as a member of the class of those who sell the goods, is the owner of goodwill in England which is of substantial value; (5) that he has suffered, or is really likely to suffer, substantial damage to his property in the goodwill by reason of the defendants selling goods which are falsely described by the trade name to which the goodwill is attached.'

These two statements of principle are said to complement one another[5], Lord Diplock emphasising what has been done by the defendant to give rise to the complaint, and Lord Fraser what the plaintiff has to show as a prerequisite of complaining. Since the remaining members of their Lordships' House agreed with both speeches, the two statements have to be taken as a composite but Lord Fraser's is narrower and would not cover some instances which are undoubtedly passing off[6].

1 See generally Drysdale and Silverleaf *Passing Off Law and Practice* (1986) (Butterworths) para 2.38; Wadlow *Passing Off* (1990) (Sweet & Maxwell) para 1.03.
2 *Erven Warnink v J Townend & Sons (Hull) Ltd* [1979] AC 731 and 742 per Lord Diplock. See also *Cadbury-Schweppes Pty Ltd v Pub Squash Co Ltd* [1981] 1 All ER 213, [1981] RPC 429, PC.
3 *Stringfellow v McCain Foods (GB) Ltd* [1984] RPC 501 at 533 per Slade LJ; *Anheuser-Busch Inc v Budejovicky Budvar Narodni Podnik (Budweiser)* [1984] FSR 413, 462-3 per Oliver LJ, CA.
4 At 755-6.
5 This, at any rate, is the Court of Appeal's view (see below). Others think differently—see Drysdale and Silverleaf, op cit, para 2.38 *Wadlow* para 1.03. In *Reckitt & Colman v Borden Inc* [1990] 1 All ER 873, [1990] 1 WLR 491, HL only L Diplock's definition was relied on.
6 *Anheuser-Busch Inc v Budejovicky Budvar* [1984] FSR 413 at 463 per Oliver LJ, at 472 per O'Connor LJ.

3.54 Passing off may be only a special instance of a more general rule that any misrepresentation calculated to give one trader the benefit of another's goodwill is actionable, or even that any misrepresentation calculated to injure another in his trade or business is to be regarded as passing off (at which point it shades imperceptibly into the tort of injurious falsehood)[1]. 'Goodwill' for these purposes, in connection with any business, is the value of the attraction to customers which the name and reputation possesses[2], or potentially possesses[3]. It survives the termination of a business[4], a point to bear in mind when drafting restraint of trade covenants[5]. It is not necessary for the plaintiff in passing off simpliciter to show malice on the part of the defendant[6], nor need he show that the defendant has gained, or is intending to gain custom, ie is trading on the plaintiff's goodwill[7].

1 Kerly, *Trade Marks* (1986) (Sweet & Maxwell) §1603 citing on latter point Parker J in *Burberry's v JC Cording & Co Ltd* (1909) 26 RPC 693 at 701.
2 *R J Reuter Co Ltd v Mulhens* [1954] Ch 50, 70 RPC 235, CA; *IRC v Muller & Co's*

Margarine Ltd [1901] AC 217 at 223; *Erven Warnink BV v Townend & Sons (Hull) Ltd* [1979] AC 731, [1980] RPC 31, 85. HL (1983). See generally Kerly, *Trade Marks* (Sweet & Maxwell) §1309 et seq.
3   On 'pre-launch' reputation see *WH Allen & Co v Brown Watson Ltd* [1965] RPC 191; *BBC v Talbot Motor Co* [1981] FSR 228; *My Kinda Bones Ltd v Dr Pepper's Store Co Ltd* [1984] FSR 289 and see para 3.59 et seq. A business can build up goodwill after a very short period of trading—see *Stannard v Reay* [1967] RPC 589, compare *Compatibility Research Ltd v Computer Psyche Co* [1967] RPC 210.
4   *Ad Lib Club v Granville* [1971] FSR 1; *Star Industrial v Yap Kwee Kor* [1976] FSR 256 at 270, per Lord Diplock.
5   See Precedent 1, clause 5.
6   *Singer Machine Manufacturers v Wilson* (1877) 3 App Cas 376, HL.
7   *Stringfellows v McCain (GB) Foods Ltd* [1984] RPC 501 at 533 per Slade LJ.

The problem of geography

3.55   It follows from the above that it is the concept of 'goodwill' which lies at the heart of the action of passing off. In *IRC v Muller & Co's Margarine Ltd*[1] Lord Macnaughten observed, 'For my part, I think that if there is one attribute common to all cases of goodwill it is the attribute of locality . . . It must be attached to a business[2].' But what for these purposes is the locality of goodwill? The goodwill attached to an hotel business in Scotland clearly can extend throughout the United Kingdom. The goodwill attached to a fish and chip shop in Perth however is unlikely to extend much beyond its immediate surroundings (though nationally famous fish and chip shops do exist, and in one case, at least, it appears that franchising is being considered). This problem of locality is raised acutely for overseas franchise chains who have no United Kingdom marks (or Convention priority for their marks) and who seek to prevent independent businesses being opened in the United Kingdom under their names. What connection with the United Kingdom must they show? Lord Fraser, in the passage cited above[3], is clear about this. It must be said however, that some of the cases prior to the *Anheuser-Busch* case were by no means easy to reconcile with his views.

1   [1901] AC 217.
2   Ibid, at 223.
3   Para 3.53, ante.

3.56   As Walton J observed in *Athletes Foot Marketing Associates Inc v Cobra Sports Ltd*[1], there appeared, on the cases, to be two schools of thought about this. There was a 'hard line' school of thought, which maintained that it was essential for the plaintiff to have carried on a trade in this country[2], and a much less demanding approach[3]. Part of the problem was that the relevant decisions all involved interlocutory injunctions in the granting or refusing of which special considerations apply, and in which the court does not consider it to be part of its function to decide difficult questions of law[4]. It was therefore very difficult to draw any general conclusions from them. In *Sheraton Corpn of America v Sheraton Motels Ltd*[5] the plaintiffs who operate a well-known hotel chain in the United States were able to obtain an interlocutory injunction to prevent the defendants from opening up an hotel under the same name at Prestwick Airport. Although it is possible to argue that by virtue of the fact that the plaintiffs maintained an office for bookings here, they traded here, Buckley J seems not to have attached any importance to this[6]. In *Baskins-Robbins Ice Cream Co v Gutman*[7] an interlocutory injunction was refused against an established ice-cream business operating in the United Kingdom

3.56 Setting up the franchise business: intellectual property

under a get-up similar to the plaintiff's well-known shops in the United States. In *Maxim's Ltd v Dye*[8] the plaintiffs however obtained an interlocutory injunction, although they produced no evidence of any customers lost to them, or likely to be lost to them in the United Kingdom whatsoever, but merely evidence of a reputation. In the virtually indistinguishable *Crazy Horse* case[9] an injunction was refused. It must be noted however that *Maxim's* was not defended. In *Athletes Foot* Walton J expressly stated that no trader can complain of passing off in territories in which he has neither customers, nor persons in a trade relation with him[10]. He accordingly refused an injunction against a business operating in this country under a name similar to that of the plaintiff's well known franchise chain in the United States. *Athletes Foot* itself was distinguished in *Parnass/Pelly v Hodges*[11] where some evidence of trading had been adduced. Undoubtedly, the growth in international travel has helped to spread the reputations of many local businesses far afield[12]. Such reputations could be damaged by unauthorised businesses trading under their name. For this reason it may be argued that a reputation and goodwill built up by trading in one country, should be protected in another country, even though no trading is carried on there[13]. At all events, for the present, this line of argument would not seem likely to succeed in the English courts. In *Anheuser-Busch v Budejovicky Budvar*[14] the Court of Appeal has, in effect, come down in favour of the 'hard line' school, described by Walton J.

In that case, the plaintiffs, the brewers of the well known American beer 'Budweiser', sought to restrain the brewers of a Czechoslovakian beer, also called 'Budweiser', from marketing their product under that name in the United Kingdom. The defendants had marketed their beer in the United Kingdom since 1973, but their product was certainly less well known than the plaintiffs'. At the time of the action, 1979, the plaintiffs' sales in this country had been sporadic and limited, though they had been large on American bases here, to American service personnel. It was held that the reputation associated with the plaintiffs' beer, which for practical purposes nobody could buy here, did not constitute goodwill in any relevant sense. The sales on the American bases were sales in a separate, artificial and special market, and could not be the foundation for goodwill in a market into which the plaintiffs, for practical purposes, had never ventured. The Court of Appeal helpfully reviewed some of the authorities, including *Athletes Foot, Sheraton, and Crazy Horse*[15]. Oliver LJ, having returned to Lord Macnaughten's definition of goodwill as the attractive force which brings in custom[16], asked the following question[17]:

> 'What custom in this country in 1973 was brought in by the knowledge of members of the indigenous British public of the plaintiffs' Budweiser beer?'

He continued,

> 'The answer must be that there was none, because however attractive they may have found the idea of drinking the plaintiffs' beer, they could not get it. In so far, therefore, as anyone was misled by the defendants' use of the name "Budweiser", the plaintiffs could suffer no damage either by loss of sales, for there were none at that time and none were contemplated, nor by loss of reputation, because if there was any such loss (which seems highly improbable) the reputation was quite unconnected with either an ability or a willingness to supply.'

Both O'Connor and Dillon LJJ expressed similar views.

1 [1980] RPC 343.

2   See *Alain Bernardin et Cie v Pavilion Properties Ltd* [1967] RPC 581 (the *Crazy Horse* case).
3   See *Maxim's Ltd v Dye* [1978] 2 All ER 55, [1977] 1 WLR 1155.
4   *Metric Resources Corpn v Leasmetric Ltd* [1979] FSR 571.
5   [1964] RPC 202.
6   See *Metric Resources Corpn v Leasmetric Ltd* ante, at 578.
7   [1976] FSR 545.
8   [1978] 2 All ER 55, [1977] 1 WLR 1155.
9   See note 2, ante.
10 [1980] RPC 343 at 350.
11 [1982] FSR 329.
12 See *J C Penney Co Inc v Punjabi-Nick* [1979] FSR 26 at 35 citing Leonard J at first instance.
13 Ibid. See *C & A Modes v C & A (Waterford) Ltd* [1978] FSR 126 (Ir).
14 [1984] FSR 413.
15 *Alain Bernardin et Cie v Pavilion Properties Ltd* [1967] RPC 581.
16 See ante.
17 At 469.

3.57 The Court of Appeal did not decide that in order to succeed in passing off it is necessary actually to have a place of business in this country. Neither the *Panhard* case[1], nor the *Poiret* case[2] was criticised, and in fact O'Connor LJ expressed the view that both were rightly decided, and Dillon LJ the view that the *Panhard* case was rightly decided (he did not mention *Poiret*). In the former case, the plaintiffs, car manufacturers, had no business in England nor any agency. Their cars could not be imported into England without a licence from English patentees. There was however an English importer, and individuals bought cars in Paris for import into England. It could be said, therefore, that England was one of their markets. In the *Poiret* case, again, the plaintiff had no place of business here, but he exhibited his goods and sold to customers here either directly or through an agent. Consequently, it could again be said that England was one of the plaintiff's markets. In *Budweiser*, by contrast the plaintiffs had no market, only a reputation.

1   *SA des Anciens Etablissements Panhard et Levassor v Panhard Levassor Motor Co Ltd* (1901) 2 Ch 513, 18 RPC 405.
2   *Poiret v Jules Poiret Ltd and Nash* (1920) 37 RPC 177.

3.58 It would appear therefore that a plaintiff, in order to succeed in passing off, must (subject to the qualification discussed in para 3.59, post) establish significant trading in this country. The *Sheraton* case[1], which was described by Oliver LJ as the 'high-water mark' of the cases in which a plaintiff who had no business in this country, succeeded in obtaining an injunction. He pointed out however that the case involved an interlocutory injunction, and really proceeded on the footing that the plaintiffs might succeed at the trial on establishing a goodwill which was entitled to protection and that the balance of convenience dictated that they should be protected in the meantime. It may be that *Maxim's*, which was not discussed in *Budweiser*, can be explained in the same way.

1   *Sheraton Corpn of American v Sheraton Motels Ltd* [1964] RPC 202.

3.59 Provided that the elements of passing off exist, it does not matter that the plaintiff has not yet begun to trade. Injunctions have been granted in a number of cases where a plaintiff has expended money establishing a reputation which the defendant's activities could damage. Thus in *Elida Gibbs Ltd v Colgate-Palmolive Ltd*[1] the plaintiffs had decided to market a new toothpaste called 'Mentadent'.

3.60 Setting up the franchise business: intellectual property

They launched a marketing campaign based upon a 'tree theme'. The campaign was started in August 1982, and launched to the press in September. The plaintiffs spent a considerable amount of money on it. The defendants deliberately placed advertisements in newspapers in an attempt to pre-empt the plaintiff's campaign. It was held that an injunction should be granted. This decision is consistent with a number of other similar decisions[2]. The question arises however, how do we reconcile these cases with the requirement of a goodwill in this country, as opposed to a reputation which the court held necessary in *Budweiser*? How, also do we reconcile them with the clear decision of the Privy Council in the *Pub Squash*[3] case that there is no tort of unfair competition independent of passing off?

1   [1983] FSR 95. Compare *Maxwell v Hogg* (1867) 2 Ch App 307.
2   *W H Allen & Co v Brown Watson* [1965] RPC 191; *BBC v Talbot Motor Co* [1981] FSR 228; *My Kinda Bones Ltd v Dr Pepper's Store Co Ltd* [1984] FSR 289.
3   *Cadbury-Schweppes Pty Ltd v Pub Squash Co Pty Ltd* [1981] 1 All ER 213, [1981] 1 WLR 193, PC. See also *Harrods Ltd v Schwartz-Sackin & Co Ltd* [1986] FSR 490, 494.

3.60 The answer to the former question is that although the plaintiffs in *Elida Gibbs*, and similar cases had not traded in the relevant goods, they intended to do so, and had spent money establishing a reputation for that purpose. Goodwill is something attached to a business[1] and it can be attached to a proposed business, as in *My Kinda Bones*. In *Budweiser*, the plaintiffs had neither an existing nor a proposed business at the relevant time in this country, merely a reputation. The answer to the latter question is that in the *Pub Squash* case there was no evidence of confusion. The plaintiffs had marketed a soft drink in distinctive cans and bottles, with a distinctive label. The defendants subsequently launched a similar product deliberately adopting an advertising campaign, and trade mark based on the theme and slogan of the plaintiff's advertising. The judge at first instance however found as a fact that the defendants had sufficiently differentiated their product from that of the plaintiffs. The Privy Council held that a deliberate imitation of another's goods, get-up etc did not amount to passing off in the absence of evidence that the defendants had confused or misled the public into thinking that their product was that of the plaintiffs[2]. The possibility that there might be a separate tort in this country of unfair competition, based on the proposition that it is unfair to permit people to reap what others have sown, was not even pursued before the Privy Council. Given that it is difficult to think of a better vehicle for its introduction than this case, the implication must be that such a tort is unlikely to develop in the near future[3].

1   *IRC v Muller & Co's Margarine* [1901] AC 217, HL.
2   Compare *McDonald's Hamburgers Ltd v Burgerking (UK) Ltd* [1986] FSR 45.
3   See also the observations of Lord Templeman in *Coca-Cola Trade Mark* [1986] FSR 472, 473, and *Reckitt & Colman v Borden Inc* [1990] 1 All ER 873, [1990] 1 WLR 491, HL.

3.61 Another aspect of the problem of locality can arise within the United Kingdom itself. It must be borne in mind that a business may already be established in some part of the United Kingdom in a sufficiently related field of activity, itself to be able to restrain the franchisor, at least from franchising within its trading area. Alternatively, the rival business may start up under the same style in another locality before the franchisor has any reputation there. In this case the action of passing off will protect both businesses within their localities. This latter problem provides a very good reason for registering a mark wherever possible at the outset. This is no help in relation to the former problem of course, the answer to which as we have seen[1] is simply careful research, and use of names as distinctive as possible.

1   Para 3.03, ante.

The use of names from other fields, and protecting the franchisor's name from encroachment: the common field of activity problem

3.62 Clearly if you have built up a reputation as say an income tax consultancy business, you cannot complain if someone opens up a garage under the same name. No one is likely to connect the two businesses: the garage does not encroach upon your goodwill, and obviously vice-versa if you choose to start trading as a tax consultant under the garage's name, it cannot complain[1]. The starting point of discussions of this problem is usually the common field of activity test.

1   See eg *Rolls Razor Ltd v Rolls (Lighters) Ltd* (1949) 66 RPC 137.

3.63 In *McCulloch v Lewis A May (Produce Distributors) Ltd*[1] Wynn-Parry J observed 'there is discoverable in all those cases in which the court has intervened the factor that there was a common field of activity in which, however remotely, both the plaintiff and the defendant were engaged and that it was the presence of that factor that grounded the jurisdiction of the court'. The facts of that case were that the plaintiff, 'Uncle Mac,' a well-known children's broadcaster, complained about the defendant's distribution of a breakfast cereal under the name 'Uncle Mac's Puffed Wheat'. The cartons bore the statement: 'Uncle Mac loves children— and children love Uncle Mac; Uncle Mac has a wonderful way of brightening any table to which he has been invited . . . So introduce Uncle Mac to your family, and when you see how popular he is, be neighbourly and recommend him to your friends'. Wynn-Parry J based his refusal of an injunction in favour of the plaintiff on the fact that the parties were not engaged in a common field of activity: 'On the postulate that the plaintiff is not engaged in any degree in producing or marketing puffed wheat, how can the defendant, in using the fancy name used by the plaintiff, be said to be passing off the goods or the business of the plaintiff?'[1] Wynn-Parry J thought that the risk of damage to the professional reputation of the plaintiff as a broadcaster and author and of injury to his means of subsistence and gaining a livelihood was not a real or tangible one.

1   [1947] 2 All ER 845 at 851.

3.64 It is clear that since the *Advocaat* case[1] at any rate it cannot be argued that as a matter of law passing off can never be established when the fields of activity are different[2]. The question is not simply whether the two businesses are as a matter of fact different. The question is in the first place whether or not there is likely to be confusion. As Russell LJ observed in *Annabel's (Berkeley Square) Ltd v Schock*[3] ' . . . Is there an overlap in the fields of activity? But of course, when one gets down to brass tacks this is simply a question which is involved in the ultimate decision whether there is likely to be confusion[4].' Similarly, in the *Lego* case[5], Falconer J[6] observed 'What has to be established by the plaintiff is that there is a real risk that a substantial number of persons among the relevant section of the public will in fact believe that there is a business connection between the plaintiff and the defendant.' The plaintiffs in the latter case were the manufacturers of the well-known children's plastic construction kits. The defendants marketed

3.65 *Setting up the franchise business: intellectual property*

plastic garden sprays and sprinklers under the same name. It was held that the plaintiff's reputation was wide enough to extend to goods of the sort made by the defendant. Evidence was adduced on behalf of the plaintiff of confusion amongst a significant number of people.

1   *Erven Warnink BV v J Townend & Sons (Hull) Ltd* [1979] AC 731, [1980] RPC 31, 85 HL.
2   See *Lego Systems A/S v Lego M Lemelstrich* [1983] FSR 155 at 186–7 per Falconer J; *Stringfellow v McCain Foods (GB) Ltd* [1984] RPC 501 at 531 per Slade LJ. See also earlier dicta in *Lyngstad v Anabas Products* [1977] FSR 62 at 67.
3   [1972] RPC 838.
4   Ibid, at 265. See also *Stringfellow v McCain Foods (GB) Ltd* [1984] RPC 501 at 535 per Slade LJ.
5   *Lego Systems A/S v Lego M Lemelstrich* [1983] FSR 155. See also *Alfred Dunhill Ltd v Sunoptic SA* [1979] FSR 337, CA.
6   At 187.

3.65 Evidence that there is a real possibility of confusion is clearly the heart of the matter. When all is said and done, it simply comes down to the necessity for a plaintiff to adduce evidence sufficient to satisfy the requirements to succeed in passing off[1]. Essentially, once it is proved that A is falsely (though possibly innocently) representing his goods as the goods of B, or his business to be the same as or connected with the business of B, the wrong of passing off has been established[2]. This said, it is by no means always easy to predict what conclusion on the evidence the courts are likely to reach. Thus, in the *Stringfellow* case[3], Stringfellows' nightclub managed at first instance to obtain an injunction against the manufacturers of some extensively and successfully promoted oven chips called 'Stringfellows', on the ground that the association implied could damage the 'up-market' image of the plaintiff's business. The decision was subsequently reversed on appeal, but the differences between the two tribunals (not to mention the differences between the court before which the plaintiffs failed to get an interlocutory injunction and the first instance court which granted one) illustrate some of the uncertainties.

1   See para 3.53 et seq.
2   *Radio Corpn Pty v Henderson* [1960] NSWR 279 at 593 per Evatt CJ and Myers J.
3   *Stringfellow v McCain Foods (GB) Ltd* [1984] RPC 501, CA.

3.66 The plaintiffs in the *Stringfellows* case contended that their goodwill and image had been damaged by the defendants' activities in support of this allegation. They had conducted a survey of public opinion on the question of the image and reputation, and the likelihood of confusion among the public. The plaintiffs also adduced evidence from numerous persons, many of whom frequented the club, of the reputation of the club, and their reaction to the defendants' television advertisement. They also produced expert evidence as to the current status of merchandising rights.

3.67 The plaintiffs succeeded at the trial before Whitford J (having failed to obtain an interlocutory injunction before Walton J). Whitford J was subsequently reversed by the Court of Appeal. There were significant differences between the two tribunals in the way they viewed the same evidence[1]. At the trial, the survey evidence was rejected completely by Whitford J. He said that he could not accept the answers to the questionnaires without some hesitation, because the mere forms and sequence of some of the questions, and the intonation or method by which they were put, might influence the answers and he did not know how careful or otherwise the interviewers might have been in carrying out their duties. In the Court of Appeal, however, Slade LJ whilst expressing some sympathy with the scepticism, felt that because of the specific agreement of the parties as to this evidence, the judge was entitled to treat each of the questionnaire forms as containing true and accurate particulars both of the questions, and of the answers. He felt that the defendant's survey strongly supported the conclusion that very few members of the public on merely seeing a packet of McCain's Stringfellows would be likely to be led to believe that there was any business connection between the persons marketing the chips and the plaintiff's nightclub. Slade LJ agreed that Whitford J had accurately summarised the evidence of the nineteen witnesses. Of these, fifteen described how they had been led to believe that there was an association of some kind between Stringfellows chips and the night club. Again, Slade LJ formed a very different opinion of this evidence from Whitford J, and eventually concluded that only the television advertisement, which twelve of the witnesses said had given rise to the belief that the chips were associated with the plaintiff, involved any degree of misrepresentation. The advertisement showed a 'disco' type setting in a suburban kitchen, which might be thought to be a nightclub. Having narrowly surmounted this hurdle however the plaintiffs failed to satisfy Slade LJ that they had proved the real likelihood of substantial damage to their goodwill. Whitford J by contrast had concluded that the defendant's activities were likely to cause damage to the plaintiffs for two reasons: (a) persons were less likely to choose the club as a venue for special ('up-market') promotions; (b) the expected decline in the plaintiffs' reputation would be likely to prejudice their future chances of exploiting the benefit of the goodwill associated with the name 'Stringfellows', by way of merchandising activities of one form or another. On the first point, the judge attached weight to the evidence of a witness who said that he had in fact taken his custom elsewhere. Slade LJ described this evidence as 'somewhat equivocal'. Slade LJ also did not regard the evidence of experts as establishing that the defendant's activities had foreclosed any merchandising potential the plaintiffs might possess.

1 The Court of Appeal felt entitled to form its own independent judgment as to whether or not there had been a misrepresentation—ibid at 538 per Slade LJ citing *Spalding & Bros v AW Gamage Ltd* (1915) 32 RPC 273, HL.

3.68 Stephenson LJ summed up the Court of Appeal's views when he said:

'When the alleged "passer off" seeks and gets no benefit from using another trader's name and trades in a field far removed from competing with him, there must, in my judgment, be clear and cogent proof of actual or possible confusion or connection, and of actual damage or the real likelihood of damage to the respondents' property in their goodwill, which must, as Lord Fraser of Tullybelton said in the *Advocaat* case[1] be substantial. In this case there was no such proof.'

1 *Erven Warnink BV v J Townend & Sons (Hull) Ltd* [1979] AC 731, [1980] RPC 31, HL.

3.69 A number of useful lessons can be drawn from these recent cases:

(a) If a name is not a household word such as 'Lego', fairly clear evidence that the public do associate the defendant's business with the plaintiff's must be shown. If the evidence can establish that the defendant could expect to derive some real benefit from the plaintiff's reputation, as a result of their choice of name as in

3.70 *Setting up the franchise business: intellectual property*

the *Eastman*[1] or *Harrods*[2] cases (and probably the *Exxon*[3] case), the plaintiff's prospects of success are much enhanced.

(b) If, although the plaintiff's and defendant's businesses are different, they are of such a nature that the public might reasonably suppose them to be connected in some way, it is relatively easier to succeed in passing off. Thus, in *Annabel's (Berkeley Square) Ltd v Schock*[4], Annabel's nightclub succeeded in obtaining an injunction against an escort agency using the name 'Annabels' on the ground that the public would associate the two enterprises to the damage of the plaintiff's reputation.

1 *Eastman Photographic Materials Co Ltd v John Griffiths Cycle Corpn Ltd* (1898) 15 RPC 105.
2 *Harrods Ltd v R Harrod Ltd* (1924) 41 RPC 74, CA. See also *Alfred Dunhill Ltd v Sunoptic* [1979] FSR 337.
3 *Exxon Corpn v Exxon Insurance Consultants International Ltd* [1982] Ch 119, [1982] RPC 69.
4 [1972] RPC 838, CA.

3.70 Survey evidence continues to be treated with scepticism by some judges, though others are much more ready to attach weight to it provided that some basic requisites are fulfilled by it. In particular, the *Raffles*[1] case is helpful in providing guidance when commissioning a survey. The remarks of Whitford J, quoted above, should also be borne in mind.

1 *Imperial Group Ltd v Philip Morris & Co* [1984] RPC 293 at 302. See also *Customglass Boats Ltd v Salthouse Bros Ltd* [1976] RPC 589; *Lego Systems A/S v Lego M Lemelstrich* [1983] FSR 155.

3.71 It is also possible to argue that we have moved to a position where an allegation that the defendant's activities have damaged the plaintiff's goodwill by foreclosing his opportunities for franchising, merchandising, sponsorship or indorsement, has some prospects of success if supported by adequate evidence that that is in fact the probable effect of the defendant's activities[1]. It is now appropriate to return to our adjourned discussion of merchandising[2].

1 See *Lego* (ante) at 194.
2 See paras 3.09, et seq.

3.72 *Passing off in character merchandising* In the *Kojak* case[1], unlicensed manufacturers of 'Kojakpops' succeeded in getting an interlocutory injunction against the *licensed* manufacturers of 'Kojak lollipops', the plaintiffs having established a reputation in their lollipops. Walton J observed, however, that there may come a time when people who see a name such as 'Kojak' attached to a product would say 'This must have been licensed by them and that is a guarantee of its quality'[2] He considered, however, that we are miles from reaching that point. By contrast in the *Judge Dredd* case[3], Goulding said:

> 'That at the present time the public know something about the prevalent practice of character merchandising, though most of them probably do not know that term, and I think therefore that both among people of my own age and among young adults such as my own grandchildren and their friends who buy records and read such magazines as these, a substantial number of people will infer that the record has been authorised and approved by the plaintiff.'

1 *Tavener Rutledge Ltd v Trexapalm Ltd* [1975] FSR 479.

2   At 485. Walton J was presumably putting this forward as an example of evidence which would go towards satisfying the legal requirements for a passing off action, rather than laying down a legal requirement. The legal requirements for passing off are those laid down in the *Advocaat* case—para 3.53.
3   *IPC Magazines Ltd v Black and White Music Corpn* [1983] FSR 348.

3.73   In the *Muppets*[1] case, Helsham CJ held that the defendants and the plaintiffs were operating in a common field of business activity. The business of the plaintiff was to get its character reproductions on to the market in various forms through licensing arrangements. The defendant's goods were deceptively similar to goods produced under those licensing arrangements, and consequently, the public could be misled into believing that the defendant's goods were in some sense the plaintiff's goods. Evidence was given in this case that members of the public did associate the relevant goods with the plaintiff's. Evidence was also adduced that the plaintiffs exercised strict quality control over their licensed products. No such evidence was adduced in *Kojak*. Had it been, the outcome might have been rather different. The same thing applies to the *Wombles*[2] and *Anabas* cases[3].

1   *Children's Television Workshop Inc v Woolworths (NSW) Ltd* [1981] RPC 187. [1981] 1 NSWLR 273.
2   *Wombles Ltd v Wombles Skips Ltd* [1977] RPC 99, [1975] FSR 488.
3   *Lyngstad v Anabas Products Ltd* [1977] FSR 62.

3.74   To summarise:
  (a) a merchandiser who is actually involved in a licensing programme in which adequate quality controls are maintained, and who has accordingly built up goodwill in the relevant products, should be able to succeed in a passing off action no matter that the goods have come on to the market through licensing arrangements;
  (b) where the merchandiser has not embarked on such a programme, it is possible on the basis of dicta in the *Stringfellow* case, if it can in fact be shown that the defendant's activities have foreclosed the plaintiff's opportunities for franchising, merchandising-sponsorship or indorsement, to succeed in passing off. The evidence must show that such activities are part of the goodwill attached to the business carried on by the plaintiff[1]. It would appear therefore that we have moved some way since the days of *Kojak*. Thus in the *Judge Dredd* case[2], the plaintiffs were the publishers of a strip cartoon called 'Judge Dredd'. The defendants marketed a song about the character in the form of a record. It was found that misrepresentation and confusion were likely in that a substantial number of people would assume that the plaintiffs had endorsed the record. In the event however, Goulding J refused an interlocutory injunction because he held that damages calculated on a royalty basis be an adequate remedy[3]. The plaintiffs had not established that in the meanwhile their reputation would suffer damage from the performing artists' lack of fame or the quality of the record, nor were they able to show that the record would encourage others to make unlicensed use of 'Judge Dredd's' reputation.

1   Ie the plaintiff must satisfy the criteria for a passing off action discussed above at para 3.53.
2   *IPC Magazines Ltd v Black and White Music Corpn* [1983] FSR 348.
3   The effect of this of course was to foreclose the possibility of the plaintiffs licensing another song under the name.

3.75 Setting up the franchise business: intellectual property

Copyright: protection of aspects of the 'get up' etc

Introduction

3.75 A distinctive 'get up' will usually form an important part of the operation. It is most important, however, to the extent that this will involve or affect buildings, to remember that planning laws must be complied with. Planning law generally is quite strict but there may be additional local restrictions[1]. Considerations of planning law is beyond the scope of this work, but it is sufficient to observe that it is unlikely that the 'get up' used by some American and other overseas chains, would obtain planning permission *anywhere* in the United Kingdom.

1 Such as in conservation areas.

3.76 To the extent that a 'get up' forms part of the distinctive identity of the business, the goodwill attaching to it is protected in the same way as the trade name, through the law of passing off. Certain aspects of it may also be registrable as marks. This has already been considered. In this section, we consider the role copyright can play in protecting the 'get up'.

3.77 For reasons which are explained in the following pages, the law of copyright assumes considerable importance in most franchises, in protecting the 'get up' and many of the other distinctive features which make up the franchise 'package'. The law of copyright is also capable of fulfilling some of the functions of design registration.[1] Designs will generally only be worth registering in special circumstances, and the possible tax implications need to be carefully considered. Where a new technical concept is involved and patent protection is thought desirable eg because international priority is important the possible tax implications[2] also need to be considered. The 1988 Act has introduced a new right, a design right protecting the functional aspects of products which may be useful in some franchising contexts, though the period of protection is short[3]. Unfortunately, the introduction of this new right, has rendered uncertain the extent of copyright protection[4].

1 The period of protection for designs may now be extended to 25 years. Copyright Designs and Patents Act 1988, s 269 amending Registered Designs Act 1949, s 8.
2 Para 4.02 post.
3 Para 3.102 et seq, post.
4 Para 3.103 et seq, post.

3.78 As well as aspects of the 'get up', the manual, some slogans, publicity materials and the like, and many other similar features of the franchise business are capable of enjoying protection under copyright law. Some things, eg specially designed packaging[1], may also be capable of being protected by registration under the Registration Designs Act 1949. This is dealt with later[2]. In general the law of copyright is often capable of doing much the same job. Formerly it was only worth registering a design if it was suspected at the outset that someone independently was likely to come up with the same design, or innocently import goods bearing the design[3]— which could be a danger in some kinds of franchised distributorship. Once the franchise operation is established, bearing in mind that the design will usually form part of the whole distinctive franchise 'get up', the circumstances in which the design might be used in a potentially damaging way without unauthorised users rendering themselves liable to passing off, must be fairly limited.

1 Ie not mere wrappers—see para 3.91, post.

2 Para 3.89 et seq. The registration procedure is dealt with at paras 3.89 et seq, post.
3 See *Infabrics Ltd v Jaytex Shirt Co Ltd* [1984] RPC 405.

(1) Protection of products under copyright

3.79 Features of articles designed to appeal to the eye can be registered as designs. This is dealt with later. Copyright is, in many cases, capable of doing the same job. Unfortunately the 'division of labour' between design right and copyright under the new Act is, as mentioned above, a major problem.

3.80 An original[1] distinctive *representation* of the franchise name, whether or not it is capable of registration as a mark, is protected[2] as an artistic work under section 1(1) 'irrespective of artistic quality'[3]. Similar protection is afforded to any insignia associated with the 'get up'. Similarly, where a distinctive style of building or facade is to be used, that should qualify for protection under section 1(1)[4].

1 Originality is crucial but for the purposes of the present discussion it is sufficient to say that it must not be copied from elsewhere. Even quite simple designs can be subject to copyright: *British Northrop Ltd v Texteam Blackburn Ltd* [1974] RPC 57 at 68; *Solar Thomson Engineering Co Ltd v Barton* [1977] RPC 537, CA; *British Leyland Motor Corpn v Armstrong Patents Co Ltd* [1986] AC 557, [1986] FSR 221; *Merlet v Mothercare plc* [1986] RPC 115.
2 Not the name itself, nor is the name itself likely to enjoy protection under s 2 as an original literary work—*Exxon Corpn v Exxon Insurance Consultants International Ltd* [1982] Ch 119, [1982] RPC 69. See para 3.14.
3 Section 4(1)(a).
4 See s 4(1)(b) but see para 3.104, post and eg *Re Collier & Co Ltd's Application for Registration of Designs* (1937) 54 RPC 253. The provisions of planning law (including special local laws) must not be forgotten in this respect, however. Some designs used by American operations could not be used in this country.

3.81 The original drawing itself of the design at the outset is protected in the normal way as an artistic work under the 1988 Act, section 1(1), which as noted above protects 'irrespective of artistic quality'[1]. Subject to s 51(1), the acts restricted by the copyright in an artistic work so defined, include 'reproducing the work in any material form'[2], and this includes a version produced by converting the work into a three-dimensional form (or two dimensional if the work is in three dimensions)[3]. There is no longer an equivalent defence to that provided by section 9(8) of the 1956 Act, which provided that the making of an object would not be taken to infringe copyright in a work in two dimensions if the object would not appear to a non-expert to be a reproduction of the artistic work. In *Merlet v Mothercare plc*[4] it was held that a non-expert would not recognise a baby cape with a hood as a reproduction of the pattern drawing showing the panels. The drawing in question was not however a full production drawing showing the finished object, merely being intended to show how the panels were to be cut from a bolt of cloth. It is always more difficult, however, as a matter of evidence to show that a three-dimensional object is a reproduction of a two-dimensional work, than to show that a two-dimensional work is a reproduction of a two-dimensional work[5], and, given the unsatisfactory nature of the drawings, it is doubtful whether the outcome of this case would be different today, when there is no section 9(8) defence.

1 *King Features Syndicate v O & M Kleeman Ltd* [1940] Ch 806 per Clauson LJ. Section

3.82 *Setting up the franchise business: intellectual property*

4(1)(a). But note the restriction on the protection afforded under copyright to drawings other than for artistic works by s 51—see para 3.103 et seq.
2   Section 17(2).
3   Section 17(3).
4   [1986] RPC 115, CA. Compare *LB (Plastics) Ltd v Swish Products Ltd*.
5   *King Features Syndicate v O & M Kleeman Ltd* [1940] Ch 806 at 816.

Infringement of copyright

3.82 One of the principal differences between patent and design protection and copyright is that the former can be infringed quite innocently, but copyright requires evidence of copying[1], or importation or sale *knowing* of the infringement[2]. Of course, once the copyright infringement by importation or sale is discovered and the culprit informed, he becomes liable if he persists. Furthermore, a patent protects the principle or concept and can be infringed by articles which bear no visual resemblance to that manufactured by the patentee.

1   1988 Act, s 16(1) *British Leyland Motor Corpn v Armstrong Patents Co Ltd* [1986] AC 577, [1986] FSR 221, HL.
2   Section 22. See *Infabrics Ltd v Jaytex Ltd* [1984] RPC 405.

Summary

3.83 The protection of designs through artistic copyright is of considerable potential use in franchising. Ordinary literary and artistic copyright is capable of protecting many other respects of the business: the manual, slogans, publicity materials, menus and the like, and even possibly the name provided it can be recognised as an original literary work[1], though the circumstances in which it would be must be very exceptional.

1   *Exxon Corpn v Exxon Insurance Consultants International Ltd* [1982] Ch 119, [1982] RPC 69 per Graham J—see para 3.14, ante.

(2) Duration of copyright protection

3.84 The normal duration of copyright is the life of the 'author' plus 50 years[1], but this is cut down to 25 years where an artistic work has been exploited by making by an industrial process[2]. The period runs from the end of the calendar year in which the articles embodying the work are first marketed[3]. Although it is clear that the copyright in designs on drawings cannot be extended beyond the permitted period, by claiming new periods for every minor alteration[4], in the case of designs usually used in the franchising context, the need constantly to 'refresh' the image, will tend to ensure that designs which may bear a superficial family resemblance, are sufficiently distinct from their predecessors to enjoy new copyright protection. It depends upon the quality rather than the quantity of the addition[5].

1   1988 Acts, s 12(1).
2   Ibid s 52.
3   Ibid s 52(2).
4   *Interlego AG v Tyco Industries* [1989] AC 217, [1988] 3 All ER 949, PC.
5   Ibid.

(3) Steps to be taken to ensure copyright protection

(a) Protection is automatic

3.85 Copyright and design rights comes into existence automatically[1]. They subsist in unpublished works and drawings and in published works and drawings. It cannot be overemphasised that in the case of designs it is the plans and *drawings* to which copyright attaches. It is therefore important to guard against possible infringements by preserving original plans and drawings. The name of the draftsman or designer, the date on which the drawings were prepared, and the fact that they are subject to the franchisor's copyright, should be noted on them. Where outside consultants are used, the ownership of the rights should be stated clearly in the contract employing the architect or designer to be the franchisor's. Otherwise there is a danger that the rights may remain in the architect or designer[2]. The fact that the copyright is the franchisor's should be indicated eg 'Copyright X' or © X'[3]. The date when first marketing of the 'franchise package' incorporating designs took place should also be noted, as that will often be the date from which the terms runs[4].

1 See Part I of the 1988 Act, where the relevant provisions as to literary, artistic etc copyright are to be found.
2 The 1988 Act, s 90(3) sets out the formalities which must be complied with. See *Meikle v Maufe* [1941] 3 All ER 144 at 152. Under the Copyright Designs and Patents Act 1988, s 11(1) the 'author' (ie creator s 9(11)) is the first owner of any copyright, except *inter alia* in relation to works made by an employee in the course of his employment.
3 The © symbol is significant in relation to the Universal Copyright Convention—see para 3.132. It does not signify registration, because there is no copyright registration in the United Kingdom and other Berne union countries.
4 See para 3.84, ante.

(b) The transitional provisions

3.86 Under the transitional provisions of Schedule 1, paragraph 12 the old system of copyright protection for products will continue to subsist for ten years from 1 August 1989. It must be remembered that it is the *drawings* which are copyright, a three-dimensional prototype which is not in itself a work of artistic craftsmanship (highly likely in any commercial context), was not subject to copyright[1]. Where a prototype was made first, and drawings produced thereafter, there could be difficulties. It could be argued that a production drawing of a work which is not itself one of artistic craftsmanship, was simply a reproduction of that object in a two dimensional form, and not subject to artistic copyright. In *LB (Plastics) Ltd v Swish Products Ltd*[2], where the product in question was a knock-down plastic drawer system, Whitford J however said 'even if the situation had been that a three-dimensional model had been made and from those models the drawings had been compiled, I am of the opinion that they would in any event qualify as original works'. This point was not pursued in the House of Lords. If both model and drawings were produced by the same person, it might be possible to argue that both are part and parcel of a single original conception, but the drawing could be viewed in the same light as a copy by an artist, ie it is the original and not the copy which carries copyright.

1 Copyright Act 1956, s 3(1)(c); *Hensher v Restawhile Upholstery Ltd* [1976] AC 64, [1975] RPC 31, HL.
2 [1979] RPC 551. Having regard to s 51 of the 1988 Act, this point is unlikely to arise

3.87 *Setting up the franchise business: intellectual property*

under the new provisions. If the prototypes themselves qualify as artistic works (para 3.104, post) copyright in them will be infringed by reproduction.

Term of protection

3.87 The relevant periods are as follows:

(1) Literary works (notably the Manual)—generally 50 years from the calendar year in which the author died in the case of works whether published or unpublished[1]. The manual is a literary work. The copyright in the typographical arrangement, however, which is separate from the literary copyright, is only 25 years[2].

(2) Artistic works, which are exploited industrially, 25 years from the end of the calendar year in which they are first marketed[3].

1 1988, s 12(1).
2 Section 15.
3 Ibid s 52.

(4) Summary

3.88
(1) What can be protected and for how long?
   (a) As literary works, the manual, some slogans, publicity materials, menus and the like[1] for life plus fifty years—para 3.78, ante;
   (b) As artistic works—subject to section 51(1) designs used in the 'get up' (whether or not registered as marks) for twenty five years from first marketing—paras 3.84 et seq, ante.
   (c) Functional designs may qualify for design right and enjoy up to fifteen years protection—para 3.102 et seq.
(2) How to secure protection:
   (a) ensure as far as possible that drawings *precede* any prototypes, models, etc and that the products are clearly recognisable as reproductions of them;
   (b) ensure original plans or drawings, together with details of their draftsmen and dates, will be preserved;
   (c) have noted on the plan or drawing the name of the draftsman, the date and a statement that the ownership of the copyright is the franchisor's;
   (d) if these are made by independent consultants, ensure the contract with them stipulates copyright to vest in franchisor or take an assignment complying with the provisions of the 1988 Act, section 90(3);
   (e) in order to preserve international protection under the UCC (much less important now the United States has adhered to Berne)[2], ensure items bear the required mark and other particulars—para 3.132, post.

There is a theoretical possibility of protecting trade names, the *Exxon* case leaves the door open, but the practical result of that case is that trade names are not protected by copyright. Their representation in a distinctive lettering or logo can enjoy copyright, however, and is a valuable and important source of protection if the name is not registrable as a mark.

1 Para 3.14, ante. *Exxon Corpn v Exxon Insurance Consultants International Ltd* [1982] Ch 119, [1982] RPC 69.
2 Unless the Soviet Union, which adheres only to the UCC, is a possible market!

Registered designs[1]

Introduction

3.89 For the reasons explained above, the law of copyright is often capable of affording sufficient protection to designs. However, where it is thought there may be a likelihood of someone *independently* coming up with the same design and using it in circumstances where a passing off action could not be brought[2], it may be advisable to register a design. It is also to be borne in mind that designs are relatively cheap to register, and it is easy to restrain infringers. As in the case of patents and marks, registration is the proprietor's principal weapon, and designs thus suffer from none of the difficulties of proving title which frequently attend copyright cases. Licences of registered designs, like patent licences may be excepted agreements for the purposes of the Restrictive Trade Practices Act 1976, Sch 3, para 5, and from the provisions of the Resale Prices Act 1976. Again, the tax problems which are similar to those in patent licences must be considered[3]. The Registered Designs Act 1949 provides for monopoly protection for up to twenty five years[4] for a new design.

1 For more detailed treatment see Morris and Quest *Design Protection* (1987) (Butterworths).
2 This might happen before the chain has built up goodwill.
3 See para 4.02, post.
4 See post. In rare cases where copyright expires earlier, this period is reduced—s 8(5).

3.90 The design must be registered before it has been made available or disclosed to the public in the United Kingdom—otherwise it will not be 'new and original'. However, where the design reproduces a copyright work[1], the work is not to be considered other than 'new and original' by reason only of any previous use of the copyright work other than as an industrial design[2]. Circulars, etc, containing representations of the design may therefore be published without prejudicing subsequent registration.

1 Section 1(2).
2 Registered Designs Act 1949, s 6(4).

What is a registrable design?

Registrable designs

3.91 As noted above the 1988 Act has amended the definition of a registrable design contained in section 1(3). For present purposes, this definition is substantially the same as the definition it replaces, and presumably the old case law on what qualifies as a registrable design will continue to be of relevance[1]. What is meant by a 'design' for the purposes of the Act is features of shape, configuration, pattern or ornament, applied to an article by any industrial process, being features which in the finished article appeal to and are judged by the eye[2]. It must be materially different from other designs. It does not include a method or principle of construction, or features of shape or configuration of an article which are dictated solely by the function it has to perform, or are dependent upon the shape of another article of which it is intended by the author of the design to form an integral part[3]. The Designs Rules 1989 exclude certain articles from registration[4]. These are:

3.92 *Setting up the franchise business: intellectual property*

(1) works of sculpture[5], other than casts or models used or intended to be used as models or patterns to be multiplied by any industrial process;

(2) wall plaques, medals and medallions;

(3) printed matter primarily of a literary or artistic character, including book jackets, calendars, certificates, coupons, dress-making patterns, greetings cards, labels, leaflets, maps, plans, playing cards, postcards, stamps, trade advertisements, trade forms and cards, transfers and similar articles.

Wrapping paper or bags bearing a distinctive insignia other than new and original packaging are also excluded[6]. Some of these things can enjoy copyright protection, of course.

1 Copyright Act 1988, s 265(3) prohibits the registration of designs in respect of which aesthetic considerations would not normally be taken into consideration. Apart from emphasising the importance of aesthetic criteria, this would not appear materially to affect previous interpretations.
2 Registered Designs Act 1949, s 1(3) (as amended by Copyright Designs and Patents Act 1988, s 265(1)).
3 Ibid.
4 SI 1989 No 1105. Rule 26 made under s 1(4) of the Act.
5 As to the meaning of this see *Wham-O Manufacturing Co v Lincoln Industries* [1985] RPC 127; *J & S Davis v Wright Health Group Ltd* [1988] RPC 403 discussed at para 3.104, post.
6 *H Klarmann Ltd v Henshaw Linen Supplies* (ante). On the question of what amounts to 'new and original'; see *Aspro-Nicholas Ltd's Design Application* [1974] RPC 645 at 654.

3.92 The most obvious sorts of things which are likely to qualify for registration are articles such as specially designed packaging[1], small advertising articles such as trays and ashtrays, so long as they are not purely functional[2]. Similarly, functional items may bear articles of registrable design such as key-ring pendants. Cardboard cut-outs may be industrial designs[3]. Trade marks may also be registered as designs[4].

1 Ie not mere wrappings, *H Klarmann Ltd v Henshaw Linen Supplies* [1960] RPC 150.
2 *Dorling v Honnor Marine Ltd* [1965] Ch 1, [1964] RPC 160, CA; *Amp Inc v Utilux Pty Ltd* [1972] RPC 103, HL.
3 *Gunston v Winox Ltd* [1921] 1 Ch 664, 38 RPC 40, CA; *Con Planck Ltd v Kolynos Inc* [1925] 2 KB 804.
4 *Sobrefina SA's Trade Mark Application* [1974] RPC 672.

3.93 If it is thought that a similar design may have been registered already, a search may be made in the Designs Register[1].

1 Designs Form 22. Two representations should accompany the form. The address of the Registry is Room 1124, Patent Office, 11th Floor, State House, High Holborn, London WC1R 4TP.

3.94 Application to register a design should be made in the name of the franchisor company whether or not it is resident in the United Kingdom[1]. As with patents, if the design represents an important aspect of the franchise 'package' it may be advisable to employ a patent agent who deals in designs. A list of these may be found in the Science Reference Library (Holborn) in the Patent Office, 25 Southampton Buildings, London WC2A 1AW or obtained from the Chartered Institute of Patent Agents, Staple Inn Buildings, London WC1V 7PZ (price 50p including postage).

1 Overseas companies must have an address in the United Kingdom for service of letters. This will usually be that of their solicitors or patent agent—Rules 8 and 10.

3.95 Form No 2A is the prescribed application form[1]. The form should be signed by a director or secretary of the franchisor company, or the agent acting on their behalf (the patent agent or solicitor)[2]. Separate forms must be submitted for each different design and article[3]. Four identical representations or specimens of the design are required[4].

1 Registered Designs Rules 1989, Rule 12.
2 Rule 10.
3 Rule 13.
4 Rule 17.

3.96 Photographs may suffice, and should be taken against a plain contrasting background so as to show off detail. The representation/s should be mounted on one side of approximately 330 × 200 mm paper (A4) with the narrower edge at the top[1]. Views for mounting should not be trimmed closer than 6mm from the outline of the article. Specimens may be lodged in lieu provided they are not fragile and are suitable for storing with documents without causing damage[2]. Specimens larger than A4 paper size must be capable of being folded. Words, letters and numerals which are not of the essence of the designs should be omitted[3]. If they cannot be so removed, the Registrar will require a disclaimer of this aspect of the design[3], since it is the purpose of the legislation to confer a monopoly in designs, not names, etc.

1 Rule 5.
2 Rule 21.
3 Rule 22.

3.97 Each application should be accompanied by a statement identifying the design feature for which novelty is claimed, ie in shape, configuration, pattern or ornament[1]. A statement such as 'The features of the design for which novelty is claimed are the shape and configuration of the article as shown in representations' suffices.

1 Rule 15.

3.98 Where the design incorporates portraits of living persons, armorial bearings or flags of any country or the like the Registrar may require a written form of consent to be lodged[1].

1 Rules 24 and 25.

3.99 An application should normally be completed and official requirements met within twelve months, but extension of time may be applied for on Form 8[1].

1 Rule 51.

3.100 The initial period of protection is five years[1] but application for extension for four further five year periods can be made on Form 9A in respect of further periods[2].

1 Registered Designs Act 1949, s 8(1).
2 Ibid, s 8(2) (as amended Copyright Designs and Patents Act 1988, s 269) and Rule 38.

3.101 *Forms and fees*

Designs Form 21 (search when registration number is not supplied)	20
Designs Form No 2A (application) [*excluding certain textile articles*]	45

3.102 *Setting up the franchise business: intellectual property*

Designs Form No 8 (extension of time for application):
one month   13
two months   26
three months   39
Designs Form No 9A (extension of period of protection) second period   107
Designs Form No 9A (extension of period of protection) third period   158

Design right

3.102 This is an innovation of the 1988 Act By section 213 of the 1988 Act 'design' in which design right subsists means any aspect of the shape or configuration (external or internal) of the whole or part of an article. It does not, however, subsist in:
  (a) a method or principle of construction;
  (b) feature of shape or configuration of an article which:
      (i) enable the article to be connected to, or placed in, around or against another article so that either article may perform its function, or
      (ii) are dependent upon the appearance of another article of which the article is intended by the designer to form an integral part;
  (c) surface decoration[1].

A design is not 'original' for the purposes of the Act if it is commonplace in the design field in question at the time of its creation[2].

The scope of (b)(i) and (ii), the so-called 'must fit' 'must match' exclusions, is unclear. Arguably the shape of a car exhaust is almost entirely dictated by the shape of the car and the body features by which it is attached, and so is excluded from design right. If this is so, the law has been changed in a major way[3]. Is the 'must match' exclusion limited to parts in physical contact with each other, such as car body panels, or does it extent to a range of physically quite distinct articles of which it is a part, such as a set of food trays?

1 Section 213(3).
2 Section 213(4).
3 See *British Leyland v Armstrong Patents* [1984] FSR 591.

3.103 The overlap between design right and copyright is dealt with in sections 51(1) and 236.

Section 51 does not eliminate copyright protection for designs for functional items altogether. It is not an *infringement* of copyright in a design document or model recording or embodying a design for anything *other than an artistic work* to make an article to the design or to copy it. It does not exempt reproduction of a design or document, other than by copying an article made to the design. Consequently, any reproduction by a franchisor by photocopying any design document forming part of the manual would infringe ordinary artistic copyright in that document.

3.104 But what is a design document for an artistic work? In *Wham-O Manufacturing Co v Lincoln Industries*[1] the New Zealand Court of Appeal held that the mould used to make 'Frisbees' was an engraving. An engraving included a print and each moulded plastic disc was an engraving in that it was an image produced from an engraved plate. The wooden models were held to be sculptures. Since the New Zealand Copyright Act is worded in essentially the same way as the new UK Act, it would be open to a court to reach a similar decision though in the light of present House of Lords feelings about expanding intellectual property[2], it might be that an English court would reach a less startling result[3]. Designs for buildings (*quaere* 'irrespective of artistic quality'?), could be for artistic works, and so also could designs for works of 'artistic craftsmanship', though the meaning of the latter term is hardly much clarified by *Hensher v Restawhile*[4]. Nevertheless, Lord Kilbrandon's view in that case that in deciding whether a work is a work of 'artistic craftsmanship', the intention of the creator is relevant, is probably of relevance in deciding whether a design document is *for* an artistic works[5]. Thus, a modern plastic foam hockey shin pad has attractive indentations apparently there only as design features. Indeed the whole, in its initial flat state looks as though it might be an architectural feature designed to be stuck on a wall and painted over. It is only by taking account of the designer's intentions that we know that he set out to design a shin pad, and that the indentations are to enable parts of the pad to be torn off to configure it to an individual leg.

1 [1985] RPC 127.
2 See *Reckitt & Colman Products v Borden Inc* [1990] 1 All ER 873, [1990] 1 WLR 491, HL.
3 See *J & S Davis v Wright Health Group Ltd* [1988] RPC 403.
4 [1976] AC 64.
5 See Dworkin and Taylor [1990] 1 EIPR 33. For a contrary view see Christie [1989] EIPR 253.

3.105 As noted above, design right does not apply to 'must fit' or 'must match' designs, but the copyright does apply to those. However such copyright is subject to the restriction in section 51 mentioned above. Where copyright subsists in anything which is the spare part for a larger unit, and infringement is not restricted by section 51, it will in any event be subject to the spare parts exception laid down in *British Leyland v Armstrong*[1], whereby a copyright owner will not be permitted to enforce its right where that would amount to a derogation of the rights granted to the purchaser of the object for which the spares are needed. Thus, for example a franchisor which had supplied a specially developed light fitting[2] could not enforce its copyright in the drawings for the spares (even assuming they were drawings for artistic works) to prevent these being supplied by third parties. On the other hand, items of matched non-fixed shop fittings such as tables and chairs are clearly not spare parts within this exception, but unless they are 'artistic works', they may be unprotected because they might be excluded from design right by the 'must match' exclusion. Buildings can be artistic works (*quaere* irrespective of artistic quality)[3], and parts of buildings can be works of architecture, and thus artistic works. But what about specially designed fittings? Are these 'part of a building'[4] and thus subject to copyright?

1 [1986] RPC 279.
2 The extent of the 'spare parts' exception is unclear after the *British Leyland* case. It is not clear what amounts to 'spare parts', nor whether the object whose supply is subject to the non-derogation principle has to be a mass produced article such as a motor car.
3 Section 4(1)(b).
4 Section 4(2).

3.105A *Setting up the franchise business: intellectual property*

Illustration

3.105A Pieces of handmade dining room furniture might well be artistic works, therefore to reproduce the chairs (even by photographing them), for example, would infringe copyright in the design drawings for them. However, would a matched set of plastic cutlery trays be protected by either copyright or design right? Arguably, the individual items could be excluded from design right by the 'must match' exception (it depends upon whether 'the article' referred to in section 213(3)(ii) of which each tray is an *integral* part is the set—but see suggestion below). They appear to fall within section 51(3) ('any aspect of shape or configuration'), and to be excluded from copyright infringement because they are not artistic works. They are unprotected, unless we can give a narrow reading to section 213(3)(b)(ii) and read 'integral' to require physical contact.

The definition of 'design' for the purposes of design right clearly excludes registrable designs. A new section 1 to the Registered Designs Act 1949 defines 'design' as features which in the finished article appeal to and are judged by the eye[1]. The period of registered design protection can now be extended for up to 25 years[2]. Artistic copyright in industrial products is cut down as provided by section 52, to twenty five years from the end of the calendar year in which articles protected by copyright are first marketed. A licence from the owner of a registered design precludes infringement by the licensee of artistic copyright[3].

At present, the only countries to afford similar protection to design right, ie protection without registration of any kind, are New Zealand and South Africa.

1 Section 265(1).
2 New s 8, Designs Act 1949—1988 Act, s 269.
3 Section 53(1)(a).

Patents[1]

Introduction

3.106 Although patents may feature incidentally in cases where manufacturing enterprises are restructured as franchises, they are not likely to be an important type of property right in many franchise operations. It is difficult to envisage many situations in which patentable inventions or processes of manufacture are likely to fulfil a sufficiently important role to justify secural at the time franchising is undertaken, although they may have underpinned the business on which the franchising operation is based. Patents take a very long time to obtain, are expensive to maintain and have a relatively short life. The maximum term of a patent is twenty years from the date of filing the application[2]. There is an annual fee, and if they are attacked, actions for infringement of patents are in a class by themselves in complexity, in cost and in the time needed to bring them to trial. Few patent disputes are settled within three years. Furthermore, the law of copyright or design right may afford adequate protection in some cases[3]. There are also possible tax problems to consider[4].

1 See *Terrell on Patents* (13th edn, 1982); *Blanco White on Patents* (5th edn, 1983) CIPA *Guide to the Patents Act 1977* (the 'Black Book'); Walton and Laddie *Patent Law of Europe and the United Kingdom* (Butterworths).
2 Patents Act 1977, s 25.
3 See para 3.79 et seq.
4 See para 4.02, post.

3.107 Circumstances do exist however where the monopoly provided by a patent may offer more security than can be achieved for example through design right even where design right protection is available. The principal limitation of design right is that it protects the owner only against unauthorised reproduction[1] and protects only shape or configuration (external or internal)[2]. If for example there is a real danger of the invention being independently arrived at therefore[3] or of innocent importation of goods of the design[3], it may be advisable to apply for a patent. There may be circumstances too where an overseas manufacturer proposing to franchise in this country goods available on the market overseas, might be advised to apply for a United Kingdom patent to prevent parallel imports—though this *cannot* be done to prevent parallel imports from other European Economic Community countries[4]. Moreover, in the case of patent rights owned by the same person in different countries, the doctrine of 'exhaustion of rights'[5] could be applied and might prevent the patentee from stopping parallel imports. If patented goods have been marketed by the patentee in the United States for example, and lawfully acquired by a United Kingdom importer, the patentee may be unable to prevent the importation into the United Kingdom[6]. His rights are exhausted by the marketing in the United States. This may not, however, apply if the goods are manufactured and sold in the United States by a licensee or franchisee[7]. Manufacturing licences under patents can be exempted agreements under the Restrictive Trade Practices Act 1976[8] and are exempted from the provisions of the Resale Prices Act 1976[9], though probably even without exemption, the Act is not apt to apply to manufacturing licences, whether under a patent or not, anyway[10].

1 Copyright Designs and Patents Act 1988, s 226.
2 Ibid, s 213(2).
3 See eg *LB (Plastics) Ltd v Swish Products Ltd* [1979] RPC 611, HL.
4 Copyright Designs and Patents Act 1988, s 213(2), see para 2.77, ante.
5 See paras 2.80 et seq, ante.
6 See *Champagne Heidsieck et Cie Monopole SA v Buxton* [1930] 1 Ch 330, 47 RPC 28. The inadequacy of copyright law to provide protection in such cases is illustrated by *CBS United Kingdom Ltd v Charmdale Record Distributors Ltd* [1981] Ch 91, [1980] 2 All ER 807.
7 Para 2.80 et seq, ante.
8 Schedule 3, para 5.
9 Section 10.
10 Ie because there is no resale of goods—see s 9.

3.108 The most likely type of operations where patents may be involved are those where a person invents a product such as a chemical formula or process which could not therefore enjoy design right protection, eg a new type of carpet cleaning fluid or process, or a combination of chemical treatments for carpet cleaning, which he decides to exploit by franchising. In such cases, however, it must be decided whether or not simply keeping the formula secret does not offer better protection: a patent is available to all the world on its expiry.

3.109 Because it is not felt likely that patents will often be of much importance, only a very brief sketch of the law and procedure is given on the following pages. If an invention is thought to be worth patenting in connection with a franchise business, a patent agent should be employed who will provide the necessary expert advice on specifications and conduct the negotiations with the examiner[1].

1 A list of patent agents may be found in the Science Reference Library (Holborn) in the Patent Office, 25 Southampton Buildings, London WC2A 1AW, or obtained from the

3.110 *Setting up the franchise business: intellectual property*

Chartered Institute of Patent Agents, Staple Inn Buildings, London WC1V 7PZ (price 50p including postage).

3.110 New patents can be either United Kingdom or European. European patents are given effect to in the United Kingdom by the Patents Act 1977. European patents are applied for through the European Patent Office at Munich. Such a patent will designate in which of the Contracting States it is effective, and will there have 'the effect of and be subject to the same conditions as are national patents granted by that State[1]'. They are expensive, and since patents are unlikely often to be of importance to franchise operations, they are not considered further. If an invention is important enough to justify such protection, the services of a patent agent a fortiori should be sought. In general a European patent must meet the same standards as are now required for a United Kingdom patent.

1 European Patent Convention, Art 2; Patents Act 1977, s 77(1).

United Kingdom patents

3.111 Patentable inventions or processes must (1) be new, (2) involve an inventive step, and (3) be capable of industrial exploitation[1]. The Patents Act 1977, s 1(2) provides that certain things are not inventions for the purposes of the Act. In particular it is to be noted that the following are excluded: (1) aesthetic creations; (2) methods of doing business; and (3) presentation of information. Section 1(2)(c) provides that 'a scheme, rule or method for performing a mental act, playing a game or doing business' is not an invention. A scheme for doing a physical act however is patentable and the contrast with a mental act can be seen from *Pitman's Applications*[2]. That case involved a system for teaching the pronunciation of language by a printed notation. In the earlier case of *Re C's Application*[3] a new musical notation had been held not to be patentable. In distinguishing that case, Lloyd-Jacob J said ' . . . there was no indication that the method of notation which constituted the alleged invention was indicated as associated with or ancillary to some particular instrument for operation. If the applicant's alleged invention is considered in relation to its recommended use in a speaking machine a definite mechanical purpose is plainly apparent. In its broader aspect of association with the organs of human speech, a functional purpose is not less apparent and it cannot with confidence be asserted that the mechanism of voice production would be assuredly excluded from consideration as adding nothing to the mere arrangement of letters upon a sheet'. It is possible that this decision could be of relevance for example to skill teaching franchises such as the playing of musical instruments or dancing. It is often possible by careful wording to avoid the excluded categories, even if the novelty of the invention lies principally in the excluded field. This is a matter for the advice of a patent agent.

1 Patents Act 1977, s 1(1).
2 [1969] RPC 646.
3 (1919) 37 RPC 247.

Applications for patents

3.112 The patent law of the United Kingdom was substantially revised by the Patents Act 1977. The old British system will carry on for up to twenty years[1].

Since however the focus of this section is new franchises, it is not proposed to deal with this. In the case of franchises involving the use of old existing patents, reference should be made to the standard works[2]. For new patents the choice as we have noted is between United Kingdom domestic and European patents. European patents in general have the effect of and are subject to the same conditions as a national patent[3]. United Kingdom residents must in the first place apply for a United Kingdom patent or obtain appropriate clearance from the Patent Office[4]. National patent laws inevitably tend to operate against the free movement of goods between Member States which is one of the objects of the Treaty of Rome, and this needs to be watched carefully[5].

If it does appear to be necessary to apply for a patent through the European Patents Office as we have already suggested, the services of a patent agent should be sought[6].

1 Patents Act 1977, Schs 1, 3 and 4.
2 See Walton & Laddie *Patent Law of Europe and the United Kingdom* (Butterworths) (last service January 1978).
3 European Patent Convention, Art 2(2); and Patents Act 1977, s 77(1).
4 Patents Act 1977, s 23.
5 See paras 2.77 et seq, ante.
6 The address of the Chartered Institute of Patent Agents is given at para 3.109 n 1, ante.

3.113 The right to apply for a patent belongs in general to the inventor, or to anyone entitled to the property in it by virtue of any agreement or rule of law[1] (the most important of which is of course that an employer owns the inventions made by employees).

1 Patents Act 1977, s 7.

3.114 Applications should be made on Form 1/77 'Request for the Grant of a Patent'. A description of the invention typed on one side of A4 paper with 1½ spacing, reasonable margins and consecutive page numbering, should accompany the form. A duplicate copy should be supplied. The description should commence with the title of the invention stated on the Request Form. The description should be as full as possible. It is not permitted to add new descriptions later. It should be possible from the description for a person to make an example of the invention. Drawings may be submitted on A4 paper. The application should be submitted to The Patent Office, 25 Southampton Buildings, London WC2A 1AW.

3.115 Within twelve months of the application, a request for preliminary examination and search must be filed on Form 9/77 together with the specified fee. An abstract containing a concise summary of the invention not exceeding 150 words should also be filed. Before the search can be acted on, the Patent Office must be provided with one or more 'claims'. These specify or define the scope of the protection of the invention. The drafting of claims is a difficult and skilled job, and at this stage at least it is advisable to consult a specialist.

3.116 The Examiner will search and issue a report, together with further instructions. The next stage, all being well, is to file a 'Request for Substantive Examination'—Form 10/77 with the appropriate fee. The Examiner will then write further, explaining what is required and the application continues until the patent is granted. The patent has to be maintained by annual payments.

3.117 *Setting up the franchise business: intellectual property*

3.117 *Forms and fees*

1/77	'Request for the Grant of a Patent'	£15
9/77	'Request for Preliminary Examination and Search'	£95
10/77	'Request for Substantive Examination'	£110.

Trade secrets, know-how, etc[1]

3.118 The operation of any franchise business is likely to involve the imparting of confidential information to the franchisees. Much of this information is not of a sort that would be patentable[2]. However, the accumulation of such information in the franchisor's business system is an important element in the package which the franchisor has to offer to the franchisee. In general, the preservation of this confidentiality is a function of the franchise agreement itself. The extent to which the franchisee may be restrained from using that information outside the terms of the franchise depends on the doctrine of restraint of trade[3]. Subject to the validity of the restraint, third parties who knowingly procure the franchisee to disclose it to them and thereby commit the tort of inducing a breach of contract, may also be restrained from using the information[4] (or be liable to pay damages). The position with regard to innocent recipients is more difficult[5], but it seems that once they get to know that the information was originally given in confidence, they can be restrained[6].

1 See Copinger and Skone-Jones *Copyright* (12th edn, 1980) (Sweet & Maxwell), para 711 et seq.
2 Because it satisfies neither the requirements of novelty nor inventiveness.
3 See paras 2.93, et seq, ante.
4 See, eg *Exchange Telegraph Co v Gregory & Co* [1896] 1 QB 147, CA; *Printers and Finishers Ltd v Holloway* [1964] 3 All ER 731, [1965] RPC 239; *Cranleigh Precision Engineering Ltd v Bryant* [1966] RPC 81 at 90; *Fraser v Thames Television* [1984] QB 44, [1983] 2 All ER 101.
5 See Turner *Law of Trade Secrets* (1962) (Sweet and Maxwell) pp 401 et seq.
6 *Fraser v Evans* [1969] 1 QB 349, [1969] 1 All ER 8, CA; *Butler v Board of Trade* [1971] Ch 680 at 690 and see para 3.123, post.

3.119 The types of confidential information which will in general be subject to valid restraints on trade are:

(1) patentable inventions or processes[1];

(2) other novel ideas reduced to practical technical procedures;

(3) 'know-how'—ie the fund of technical knowledge and experience acquired by a highly specialised production organisation. It may be and usually is, noted down in documents, drawings, etc[2];

(4) ideas such as advertising schemes.

1 And the written or drawn representation of it may itself enjoy copyright or design right. See para 3.75 et seq, ante.
2 See *Stevenson (or Stephenson) Jordan and Harrison Ltd v MacDonald and Evans* [1952] 1 TLR 101, 69 RPC 10, CA; *Rolls Royce Ltd v Jeffrey* [1962] 1 All ER 801, [1962] 1 WLR 425, HL.

3.120 In *Faccenda Chicken v Fowler*, at first instance[1], Goulding J distinguished three categories of confidential information[2]:

(1) information which because of its trivial character or its easy accessibility from public sources of information, cannot be regarded as confidential at all;

(2) information which a servant must treat as confidential, either because he

has been told it is, or because from its character it obviously is, but which once learned, becomes part of the servant's general skill applied in the course of the master's business. Use of such information can only be restrained by a covenant in restraint of trade (which will be subject to the requirement that it is reasonable)[3];

(3) trade secrets proper[4].

Neil LJ in the Court of Appeal expressed the view that use of the second category of information could not be restrained even by a restrictive covenant[5]. In reaching this conclusion he appears to have misread a passage in Cross J's judgment in *Printers and Finishers v Holloway*[6], in which Cross J said that if there were features of a process which could fairly be regarded as trade secrets, the proper way for the employer to protect himself would be by a restrictive covenant. But, given that use of a trade secret can be restrained without a restrictive covenant[7], what could be the point of Cross J's remarks unless he was referring to information less than a trade secret proper?

1 [1985] 1 All ER 724.
2 At 731.
3 See para 2.93, ante.
4 See *Sager v Copydex* [1967] 2 All ER 415; *Coco v A N Clark (Engineers) Ltd* [1969] RPC 41.
5 [1986] 1 All ER 617 at 626.
6 [1964] 3 All ER 731 at 732.
7 *Coco v A N Clark (Engineers) Ltd* [1969] RPC 41.

3.121 To the extent that the information is of a trivial character, or generally known or readily knowable or simply depends on the skill of the person using it for its utility, its disclosure or use elsewhere may not be restrained. This applied even though the person using it was given the opportunity to acquire the skill through the contract which purports to restrain him. In the case of *Stevenson Jordan and Harrison Ltd v MacDonald and Evans*[1] the plaintiff company's business consisted of known principles of business management applied to the problems involved in certain functions of commercial activity, with a view to isolating details of production and expenditure and fixing responsibility for their control. The plaintiffs failed to restrain publication of a book containing a complete disclosure of their system of working. The reason was that the principles of cost accounting on which the system was based were generally known, and simply depended on the skill of their application by the plaintiff's employees for their success in any given case. Much information imparted in the usual type of franchise will be of this character.

1 (1951) 68 RPC 190.

3.122 The use of the names of customers learned bona fide by an employee in the course of his employment cannot be restrained[1]. This must apply a fortiori to franchisees. It is likely that they cannot be restrained from using their own customer lists (as opposed to the franchisor's) anyway—the business *is* their own.

1 *Helmore v Smith* (No 2) (1886) 35 Ch D 449, CA; *Re Irish, Irish v Irish* (1888) 40 Ch D 49. Cf *Robb v Green* [1895] 2 QB 1; *Faccenda Chicken Ltd v Fowler* [1987] Ch 117, [1986] 1 All ER 617, CA; see Hull [1986] 10 EIPR 319.

3.123 One useful application of the doctrine in the franchising context is illustrated by the Australian case of *Wheatley v Bell*[1]. The plaintiffs had developed a 'Teleguide' system which consisted of information about local businesses. They exploited this system by selling exclusive franchises for particular areas. The first defendant attended

3.124 *Setting up the franchise business: intellectual property*

a meeting for prospective franchises. He did not enter into a franchise agreement, but used the information he had obtained at the meeting to set up his own system in another area in advance of the plaintiffs' launch in that area. An interlocutory injunction was granted against the first defendant, and also against his franchisees, notwithstanding the fact that at the time they entered into their franchise agreements they had acted innocently[2].

1 [1984] FSR 16.
2 See para 3.118 at n 6, ante.

Protection of intellectual properties abroad

Introduction

3.124 If patents or designs are involved, the services of a patent agent should be sought. In the case of trade marks, the six months priority protection given in Convention countries is unlikely to be important, because usually it will only be worthwhile seeking international protection when a concept has become an established success. International protection will therefore have to be secured by registering marks—an expensive procedure and one on which specialist advice should be sought. Copyright protection endures automatically in Convention countries, but its extent depends upon the law of those countries, and the possibility of protecting designs is usually much more limited than under United Kingdom law[1]. The advice must be, if a business looks as though it is going to be worthwhile marketing abroad under the *same* name and marks, consult a specialist as soon as possible. However, whilst the question of international protection per se is a matter for the specialist, it is useful at least to understand the outlines of the rules, especially as tax problems can arise. In the following pages we attempt only to provide a sufficient account to alert the reader to the difficulties, and to make comprehensible the discussion of the tax position[2].

1 See para 3.75 et seq, ante.
2 Paras 4.77 et seq, post.

Patents

3.125 An application for a United Kingdom patent will provide the applicant with priority over subsequent applicants claiming in respect of the same invention. If the application is successful and the patent is granted it will be effective in the whole of the United Kingdom (subject to challenge by third parties in the Patent Office or the courts). In addition, because the United Kingdom is a party to the Paris Industrial Property Convention 1883[1], the applicant has priority in filing a patent application (within one year of his United Kingdom application)[2] in the other member nations of the Convention. These comprise most of the major industrial nations and many 'third world' countries. The list of members occasionally alters due to political changes amongst the smaller members. It is possible that the People's Republic of China will become a Convention country in the near future.

1 The 'International Convention for the Protection of Industrial Property' or the 'Paris Union', subsequently revised on several occasions. The last revision was in 1967. The United Kingdom ratified the revised Convention in 1969.
2 Article 4C.

Protection of intellectual properties abroad 3.128

3.126 The United Kingdom adheres to the European Patent Convention, and domestic law accordingly has been brought into conformity with it[1]. If a successful patent application is made to the European Patent Office in Munich, the applicant will be granted a bundle of national patents, all offering virtually identical protection. This system of application is complementary to existing national registration systems. The Patents Act 1977 incorporates the procedure for dealing with European Convention patents in the British Patent Office[2]. It is still possible to apply in both the European Patent Office and the Patent Office of a nation which is a member of the Convention at the same time, although to the extent that the national patent provides the same protection it is pre-empted by the European patent in that country. Indeed, such application may be necessary if it is intended to obtain a United Kingdom patent in those countries which are former British Colonies and in which the United Kingdom patent can be obtained—for example Singapore. Certain of these countries do not accept European (UK) patents, but only patents issued by the United Kingdom national procedures. Although it is not in these cases customary to file a patent initially in the European Patent Office, such application serves to generate priority for foreign applications in the same manner as United Kingdom national applications[3].

1 Patents Act 1977, s 77.
2 Ibid, ss 78–85.
3 Patents Act 1977, s 5 and s 78; European Patent Convention, Art 87: Paris Convention (as revised at Lisbon), Art 4A2 (not all countries have ratified this revision, so that not all countries accept a European Patent Office generated date).

3.127 An application under the Patent Co-operation Treaty[1] provides another method of simplifying certain application procedures. An application can be filed within twelve months of a national or regional application[2], and the countries of interest (participating countries include the United States of America, the Soviet Union and many other European countries), together with the European Patent Office, must be designated on filing. The application will be subjected to an international search by a number of international search authorities. Within twenty months (or 25 months if the applicant submits to a preliminary examination) the applicant must decide in which countries he will complete the application and start the national procedure, ie pay the national fees, submit translations, etc. The Treaty does not provide an international patent, but each national or regional patent office will decide if any patent is to be granted. The United Kingdom is a party to the Treaty and there is a procedure for developing an application under the Treaty into an application to the British Patent Office[3].

1 Effective 1 June 1978.
2 Such as an application to the British Office of the European Patent Office respectively.
3 Patents Act 1977, s 89.

3.128 At some time in the future, it may be possible to apply for a European Economic Community Patent under the Community Patent Convention of 1975. This will be granted at the same time as other national patents granted by members of the European Patent Convention, which are not members of the European Economic Community[1]. A community patent will not become a patent under the Patents Act 1977 but will have an independent existence subject to the provisions of the European Patent Convention. It is intended to cover all the member states of the European Economic Community and not be divisible in any absolute alienation of the patent. Domestic law was brought into conformity with the Convention

3.129 *Setting up the franchise business: intellectual property*

by the 1977 Act. It will remain possible to have a UK patent after the Convention comes into effect but this will not often be an alternative option.

1 Part II of the Patents Act 1977 already makes provision for a community patent procedure.

3.129 The applicant for a patent is presumed to be entitled to it until challenged[1]. In the rare event of a challenge as to the ownership of an invention, the Comptroller-General of Patents of the British Patents Office has the power to determine entitlement before or during an application[2]. The Comptroller may also determine questions of rights to apply in other countries[3]. This is important because of the European Patent Convention and the Paris Union implications. Unless there is a contract splitting ownership of the 'invention' in respect of different countries, the Comptroller (or the court) will find one owner worldwide. In general, only the following are entitled to apply for a patent in the United Kingdom:

(1) the inventor or co-inventors[4];
(2) the employer of the inventors when the invention is made during the course of employment[5];
(3) persons entitled under foreign law; or
(4) a successor of any of these by agreement or operation of law.

It is possible for different persons to own the patent in different countries[6]. Also, depending on the first party to apply in a given country (or the applicant with the first priority right) different parties might secure patents on what is essentially the same invention. This is particularly true of the United States where it is the first person to have rights to the invention in the United States (by making the invention) who prevails. The possibility of different parties owning different rights in different countries can have important tax consequences in international franchising, if differences in ownership arise from assignments by the original owner[7].

1 Patents Act 1977, s 7(4).
2 Ibid, s 8(1).
3 Ibid, s 12.
4 Ibid, s 7(2); European Patent Convention, Arts 58 and 60(1).
5 Patents Act 1977, s 7(1).
6 European Patents Convention, Art 50; Patents Act 1977, s 12.
7 See para 4.77, et seq, post.

3.130 In most countries (including the United Kingdom) it is not possible to sue for infringement until the patent is granted. However, certain rights to damages may run from the date a pending application is published. This takes place in the United Kingdom, other European countries and Japan (but not the United States) eighteen months from the priority date asserted. Changes in the statement of invention as expressed in the claims between this publication date and grant may affect these rights[1]. Naturally, infringement in other countries can only be claimed if patent protection is sought in those countries.

1 Patents Act 1977, s 69(1) and (2).

Designs

3.131 The Paris Industrial Property Convention 1883 covers designs in a similar way to patents but the priority period is six months[1].

1 See para 3.125 et seq, ante—see Registered Designs Act 1949, s 14(1).

Copyright

3.132 The United Kingdom is a member of the Berne Union and the Universal Copyright Convention. Most of the countries of the world are members of either or both Conventions. By Order in Council, the provisions of the Act have been extended or is deemed to extend to certain of the former colonies and has been applied to Convention countries[1]. The works of authors connected with any one Member State, either by personal status or place of publication, enjoy the same protection in other Member States as the works of authors connected with those states. Such protection only applies from certain dates in some cases[2]. Similarly, the works of British nationals are afforded the same protection as those of the nationals of other Convention countries in those countries. Very few countries however afford the same protection to products as does British law[3]. Both the Berne Union and the Universal Copyright Convention have been revised by Protocol[4]. Changes were made to UK copyright law to permit adherence to the latest version of the Berne Convention, by the 1988 Act[5]. Work first published in the United Kingdom or created by British nationals is protected (in different ways) in the member countries of the Union and the Convention. Proposals have been made for a European Economic Community copyright[6]. No formalities are required to preserve copyright under the BCU, but under the UCC the use of the symbol © on all published copies of the work, accompanied by the name of the copyright proprietor and year of first publication, may be required. These details must be sufficiently prominent to give reasonable notice of the claim to protection. The United States is now a party to the Berne Convention, consequently the legal value of this marking is much diminished, but it does serve a practical purpose, however, in warning off third parties.

1 See The Copyright (Application to Other Countries) (No 2) Order 1989, SI 1989 No 1293.
2 See ibid Sch 1.
3 See para 3.75, et seq.
4 Berne Union—Stockholm 1967 and Paris 1971 and the UCC—Paris 1971.
5 For current texts adhered to by the UK see Cmnd 5002 and Cmnd 4905.
6 *Copyright in the European Community* (1975) (Dietz).

Trade marks

3.133 The United Kingdom is not a party to the Madrid Agreement on the International Registration of Trade Marks[1] which was intended to create a form of international registration which automatically applied to member countries unless objection to the registration of a particular mark was raised by any nation under its national law within twelve months. In 1973 the United Kingdom and other countries and members of the Madrid Agreement signed the Trade Mark Registration Treaty. This is another attempt at a form of international registration by simultaneous application in a number of the member countries. It has not yet been implemented. The United Kingdom is a party to the Paris Industrial Property Convention 1883[2]. The Convention covers (inter alia) trade marks, trade names, service marks[3] and indications of source or origin. If a United Kingdom franchisor applies for registration of a trade mark in the United Kingdom, it will have a right of priority to make an application in other member nations of the Convention during the subsequent six months[4]. The position with regard to service marks is the same in those Convention Countries in which protection is afforded to service marks[5].

3.133 *Setting up the franchise business: intellectual property*

1   1891. Now administered by WIPO.
2   See para 3.125, note 1, ante.
3   Included by the Lisbon Convention.
4   Article 4C, Paris Convention.
5   It was not possible to anticipate 1 October 1986 by making a Convention application—Patents, Designs and Marks Act 1986, s 2(3), and Schedule 2, Part III, paras 3, 5 and 11.

3.134   A European Community trade mark is proposed[1]. Problems of language may ensure however that trade marks are still chosen and registered on a national basis.

1   Doct IIID 73578—translation (1979) 10 IIC 176, IIID 5579.

Procedural aspects of licensing of intellectual property
Introduction

3.135   In the preceding sections we considered the intellectual property which protect the name, 'get up' and other aspects of the franchise package. In this section we consider the procedural aspects of licensing those rights.

Trade marks: need franchisees be registered as users of registered trade marks and service marks?
Introduction

3.136   Whilst there is nothing especially difficult about the registration of users, in the case of small scale franchise businesses it may be felt unnecessarily cumbersome and franchisees may object to the expense. For the reasons explained below, it is not *necessary* to register a user. However the dangers of failing to do so should be weighed up. These are briefly (1) that paragraph 4(2) of Schedule 3 to the Restrictive Trade Practices Act 1976 exempts only registered user agreements from the provisions of the Act; (2) more importantly, in the case of franchises where the franchisee applies the mark to the goods, there may be a danger to the mark if the franchisor himself does not also trade in the marked goods. This is discussed below[1]. The fact that under section 28(3) (as amended) of the Trade Marks Act 1938 the registered user of a mark can acquire the right to sue for infringement would appear to be of academic interest only, since in practice the action for infringement is likely to be coupled with a complaint of passing off, and only the franchisor can bring a passing off action because it is to him that the goodwill accrued. Furthermore, in practice, the franchisees will want the franchisor to take the steps necessary to protect the mark anyway.

1   See para 3.138, post.

Registration is permissive

3.137   It is clear that the registered user provisions of the Trade Marks Act 1938 (as amended) are permissive. Section 28 provides that subject to the provisions thereof, a person other than the proprietor of a trade mark may be registered as a user thereof in respect of all or any of the goods in respect of which it is registered[1]. This provision is permissive, not mandatory however. In the well known

Bostitch case[2] the plaintiffs and defendants had entered into an agreement which permitted the defendants to manufacture some of the plaintiffs' products and apply the trade mark 'Bostitch' to them. The plaintiffs were an American company and one of the reasons for the arrangement was the problem of importing during the war. The agreement was never registered under the provisions of section 28. A dispute arose between the parties and the plaintiffs withdrew their consent to the defendant's further use of the mark. The dispute culminated in infringement proceedings by the plaintiff and an application by the defendant to have the plaintiff removed as registered proprietor of the mark in this country. It was held that the goods sold by the defendants bore a sufficient indication of American origin. The defendants had advertised themselves as distributors of the plaintiffs' goods. Consequently the connection in the course of a trade between the goods and the plaintiffs was maintained. The mark had never been used in such a way as to suggest that the defendants were proprietors of the mark. Lloyd-Jacob J observed that there was nothing anywhere in section 28 to justify the view that an arrangement between the registered proprietor of a trade mark and party concerned to use such mark, requires to be registered. This decision was approved (though distinguished) in *Re Weston Trade Mark*[3]. It was also approved in *Re G E Trade Mark*[4] and *Re Molyslip Trade Mark*[5]. This aspect of the case was not discussed by the House of Lords in the *Holly Hobbie*[6].

1 Section 28(1).
2 [1963] RPC 183.
3 [1968] RPC 167.
4 [1970] RPC 339 at 394.
5 [1978] RPC 211.
6 [1984] 1 All ER 426, [1984] FSR 199.

3.138 In the *Bostitch* case the licensor was also engaged in manufacturing the trade marked goods. It could not be argued therefore that there was no bona fide use of the mark by the proprietor which would permit its removal[1]. Where the licensor has *never* actually manufactured or traded in the goods there may also be a danger to the mark under section 26(1)(a) on the ground that it was registered without any bona fide intention to use it. In the *Manus* case[2], the impact of war conditions was held to amount to special circumstances in the trade and section 26(3) provides that an applicant shall not be entitled to rely on any non-use that is shown to have been due to special circumstances in the trade[3]. These difficulties are coped with in relation to *registered* users by section 28(2) which provides that the permitted use[4] of the trade mark (by the registered user) shall be deemed to be use by the proprietor of the mark. If the user is not registered this subsection cannot help.

1 Under sections 26(1)(b) and 32.
2 *Manus Akt v R J Fullwood and Bland Ltd* (1948) 65 RPC 329—see para 1.10, ante.
3 See also *Mouson & Co v Boehm* (1884) 26 Ch D 398.
4 Section 28(1).

3.139 The lesson of the foregoing is that in the rare case of franchising systems where the franchisor is proposing entirely to leave the manufacturing and marketing of goods to his franchisees, and for safety's sake in other cases too, *at least some franchisees* should be registered as users.

3.140 *Setting up the franchise business: intellectual property*

Registration of users

3.140 Registration of users is permitted by section 28(1). The proprietor and the proposed registered user must apply in writing to the Registrar in the prescribed manner and must furnish him with a statutory declaration:

(a) giving particulars of the relationship between the parties, including particulars showing the degree of control by the proprietor over the permitted use which their relationship will confer. The fact that it is not contemplated that the registered user should be the sole registered user should also be stated;

(b) stating the goods in respect of which registration is proposed;

(c) stating any conditions or restrictions proposed with respect to the characteristics of the goods, to the mode or place of permitted use, or to any other matter; and

(d) stating whether the permitted use is to be for a period or without limit of period, and if for a period, the duration thereof[1].

1 Section 28(4).

3.141 The control to be exercised by the proprietor over the use of the mark by the user is an important consideration in deciding whether or not to allow an application to register a user. The Registrar will allow registration inter alia: (1) where marked goods will be made under licence under the proprietor's patents[1]; (2) where an agreement between the parties entitled the proprietor to prescribe standards of quality for the marked goods[2] (these situations are not exhaustive). In the case of franchising agreements, given that control to ensure uniformity lies at the very heart of the system, there should be little difficulty. It is to be noted that only breach of the terms and conditions *on the Register*, will lay the licensed user open to an action for infringement. Otherwise, activities which may be in breach of the franchising agreement, but not of the terms and conditions on the Register, will nevertheless be a permitted use. The appropriate form of action in such cases is for breach of contract.

1 This corresponds to the position in the case of unregistered users—see *Manus Akt v R J Fullwood and Bland Ltd* [1949] 1 All ER 205, 66 RPC 71, and *Bostitch Inc v McGarry and Cole Ltd* [1964] RPC 173 discussed in paras 1.10 et seq ante.
2 See *Stringfellow* [1984] FSR 199.

3.142 *Forms and fees*
TM 50 Application to Register a User   50
TM 33 Request to enter address for service in Register   —

Copyright

3.143 With trade marks, copyright is the most important branch of intellectual property law in the context of franchising. The right to grant licences is recognised by the Copyright Designs and Patents Act 1988, s 90. A licence of itself confers no proprietary right on the licensee, who must join the licensor for any action for infringement[1]. In practice the franchisees are likely to be quite happy to leave the franchisor to take action in respect of breach of copyright, and under the terms of the agreement they should be able to compel him to do so.

No particular form is required for copyright licences.

1 *Neilson v Horniman* (1909) 26 TLR 188, CA on Copyright Act 1956, s 19(3); *CBS United Kingdom Ltd v Charmdale Record Distributors Ltd* [1981] Ch 91, [1980] 2 All ER 807.

Patents

3.144 The licensing of patents is recognised by the Patents Act 1977, s 30(4). There is no requirement that licences be registered, but registration affords protection against, eg subsequent assignees who might take without notice of the licence[1]. Furthermore, exclusive licensees[2] may not recover damages for infringement unless the transaction is registered within six months of its date or the court is satisfied that it was not practicable to register it[3]. Otherwise, the exclusive licensee has the same rights as the proprietor to bring proceedings for infringement[4], though he must join the proprietor[4]. In practice, however, as with infringement of the other property rights in the package, the franchisees are likely to be quite happy to leave the franchisor to take any necessary action, and these provisions would seem probably therefore to be of academic interest.

1 Section 33(1).
2 Ie licences conferring on the licensee to the exclusion of all other persons including the patentee rights in respect of the invention—section 130(1).
3 Section 68.
4 Section 67(1).

3.145 If a case should occur where it is thought desirable to register the licensee the procedure is set out in the Patents Rules 1978[1]. Application is made on Form 21/77. A certified copy of the licence must be produced[2].

Forms and fees   Form 21/77   £22 + £3 for each patent after the first

1 The Patents (Fees) Rules 1989 (SI 1989 No 899).
2 Rule 46(2).

Registered designs

3.146 The licensing of the use of registered designs is permitted by section 19(4) of the Registered Designs Act 1949. Licensees may be registered[1], but as with patents, circumstances in which it would be worthwhile doing so in the context of franchising are difficult to envisage.

1 Section 19.

3.147 The principal advantage of registration, as with patents, is the preservation of priority against assignees etc. If it is desired to register a licence, the relevant forms are Designs No 12 on application by the licensee, and Designs No 13 on application by the licensor.

3.148 *Forms and fees*

Designs No 12A application by licensee for registration in respect of one design—£13.

Chapter 4
Tax problems

Introduction

4.01 It is the object of this chapter to review some of the special tax problems, which may confront both franchisors and franchisees in the franchise business. It must be remembered that most franchisees will be small businessmen, who are trading as individuals, in partnership, or as private companies. Each type of organisation will have its own tax status and peculiarities and any potential franchisee must consider, carefully, which type is best suited to his own particular financial circumstances. However that choice will face all small businessmen and will not be the subject of discussion in this book. Most franchisors are corporations. We will not, therefore, consider the problems of an individual franchisor. The relationship between the franchisor and its franchisees is distinguished by the payment by those franchisees of franchise fees. Those fees will be the consideration, or part of it, for the use by the franchisee of the intellectual property[1] of the franchisor and the provision of continuing services[2] by the franchisor to the franchisee. The mixed nature of those fees may obscure the original reason why they are paid by the franchisee. That part of the fees, which is attributable to the use of intellectual property, will be in the nature of a royalty.

1 Intellectual property is a generic term for patents, trade marks copyright and know-how. An alternative description is 'industrial property'. See generally Ch 3, ante.
2 For example: promotional and advertising services, accounts supervision, stock control, and other general business advice (occasionally known as 'show how' and other services).

Royalties

4.02 The payment of royalties or franchise fees by a franchisee to his franchisor, both of whom are resident in the United Kingdom, may be subject to deduction of tax at source by the franchisee. Generally, remarks made in this chapter should be read in the light of the following:

(1) An individual franchisee who pays royalties wholly out of profits or gains charged to tax is entitled to deduct tax at source from relevant payments, but is not obliged to do so.

(2) An individual franchisee who pays royalties not out of profits or gains charged to tax must deduct tax at source from such payments.

(3) A corporate franchisee is obliged to deduct tax at source from such payments.

If part of those payments is in respect of the use of a patent, then the franchisee should make a deduction before payment to the franchisor[1]. If part of those payments is in respect of the use of a trade mark, the obligation to make a deduction is less clear. If the franchisor is the proprietor of or is licensed to use that trade

Royalties 4.02

mark in the franchised business, exercises control functions usually associated with a business format franchise and provides other services on a recurring basis for the benefit of the franchisee (such as the administration and implementation of an advertising and promotional programme for the franchise business), then the franchise fees payable to that franchisor may be deemed to be income derived from a trade carried on by the franchisor in the United Kingdom[2]. In that case, it is unlikely that the franchisee will be obliged by the Inland Revenue to deduct tax at source from his payments to the franchisor. However, if the proprietor of the trade mark to whom payments are made is not the entity which exercises those control functions or provides those additional services, and the payments are in the nature of 'pure income profit'[3] in the hands of the franchisor, then the fees payable to it in respect of the use of the trade mark may be deemed to be annual payments.[4] If that is the case, those payments will be subject to deduction of tax at source by the franchisee[5]. The franchisor should strive to avoid such a situation because the tax so deducted is calculated at the basic rate of income tax in force at the relevant time[6]. Any such deduction will cause serious cash flow problems for the franchisor and limit the extent of its financial supervision of the franchisee. Since the question whether the franchisee is liable to deduct tax at source appears to depend upon the source of the franchise payments in the hands of the franchisee and the status of the franchise payments in the hands of the franchisor (income from a trade or annual payments), the franchisee must investigate the nature and method of the payments he is obliged to make to the franchisor, because he may be liable to account to the Inland Revenue for the amount of tax which should have been deducted by him[7]. In practice the Inland Revenue may collect the amount of tax which a franchisee is obliged to deduct from the franchisor, where it is practicable to do so. If not, it will be of no consolation to him to be able to deduct the amount of any tax payable by him to the Inland Revenue, because of his failure to make such a deduction in the past, from future payments due to his franchisor[8], especially if he wishes to terminate the agreement because his relationship with the franchisor is otherwise unprofitable or unsatisfactory, or because the franchisor is insolvent[9]. In addition, if he is obliged by the terms of his franchise agreement to make payments to the franchisor 'without deduction', then he may have to pay tax to the Inland Revenue in respect of the amount of his franchise fees on the grossed up amount of the payments.

1 Income and Corporation Tax (ICTA) 1988, ss 348, 349 and 350, *International Combustion Ltd v IRC* (1932) 16 TC 532.
2 Schedule D, ICTA 1988, ss 18(1)(a) and 19(1) and (2). Case I. Otherwise the income of the franchisor may be treated as investment income taxable under Schedule D Case III.
3 *IRC v National Book League* [1957] Ch 488, 36 TC 455, ICTA 1970, Schedule D, ICTA 1988, s 19(2), Case III.
4 ICTA 1988, ss 348 and 349(1)(a).
5 See note 1, ante.
6 ICTA 1988, s 4 (1986/87—29%).
7 In the case of an individual franchisee ICTA 1988, ss 348, 349, 350 and 352. In the case of a corporate franchisee ICTA 1988, s 350(4) and Sch 16. See also ICTA 1988, s 276.
8 The franchisee is not entitled to deduct tax which should have been deducted from past payments due to the franchisor in the future (*Countess Shrewsbury v Earl of Shrewsbury* (1907) 23 TLR 224) unless this failure to do so arose because of a genuine error of fact (*Turvey v Dentons (1923) Ltd* [1953] 1 QB 218, [1952] 2 All ER 1025). It may be open to a franchisee to argue that he thought his franchise fees were not 'royalty' payments but merely payments for services rendered by the franchisor.
9 Although in practice the Inland Revenue may endeavour and are entitled to collect from the recipient *Glamorgan County Quarter Sessions v Wilson* [1910] KB 725, 5 TC 1, there

4.03 *Tax problems*

have been occasions when they have declined to endeavour to collect from the recipient and assessed the payer. *Grosvenor Place Estates Ltd v Roberts* [1961] Ch 148, 39 TC 433.

4.03 For example, if he is permitted by his agreement to make deductions then his payments to his franchisor will be:

	£
Franchise fee	100
Deduction (current rate of income tax 1989–90)	25
Net payment to franchisor	75

However, if his agreement does not permit him to make deductions, then his payments to his franchisor will be:

	£
Franchise fee	100
Plus grossed up amount of fee (same rate of income tax)	33
	133
Less deduction of tax	33
Net Payment	100

It will be noted that in the first example the total of payments to the franchisor and the Inland Revenue by the franchisee is:

Fee £75 + Tax £25 = £100

Whereas in the second example the total of such payment is:

Fee £100 + Tax £33 = £133

4.04 The franchisee will account to the Inland Revenue for the full amount of tax so deducted or liable to be deducted, in the case of an individual franchisee usually at the end of his accounting year and, in the case of a corporate franchisee, within fourteen days of the expiry of each quarter or the end of an accounting period which does not fall within the specified quarter days[1]. Accordingly, a franchisee should not make any franchise payments (including any initial fees or other pre-commencement liabilities) to the franchisor until he has received proof of the advance written clearance by the Inland Revenue that the whole of such payments are not subject to deduction of tax at source. In addition, he should be reluctant to accept an unqualified obligation to make payments in the future without deduction, because regulations may alter and he may become obliged by law to deduct tax at source whilst being liable to make a gross payment. In that event, the situation in the second example will apply. If the basic rate of income tax is increased beyond its current level, the burden upon the franchisee will correspondingly increase. It should be noted that in the event that a corporate franchisee fails to make a deduction of tax in respect of a payment to a non-resident franchisor in circumstances where the deduction should have been made, it may be that the whole of the payment due to the franchisor will not be allowed as a charge against the income of the franchisee[2], unless the income of the franchisee which is used to frank the payment arises from Schedule D, Case IV or Case V sources[3]. The Inland Revenue may permit deduction of tax at a lower rate than the standard rate of tax if a double taxation agreement applies[4].

1   ICTA 1988, s 350(4), Sch 16, paras 2(2) and 4(1). Returns should be made on Form CT 61.
2   ICTA 1988, ss 338(3)(a), (4) and 337(2). See also ICTA 1988, s 349(1)(a).
3   ICTA 1988, s 338(4)(a).
4   If, for example, the licensor is resident in the Netherlands (see post). Double Taxation Relief (Taxes on Income) (General) Regulations 1970 (SI 1970 No 488).

4.05 In the event that any part of the franchise fees payable by the franchisee to a non-resident franchisor relates to the use of copyright, then tax should be deducted at source by the franchisee from that part of those payments[1]. Any agreement which requires payment of copyright royalties gross to a non-resident in circumstances when a deduction should be made is void[2]. In that event, any franchisee of a non-resident franchisor who wishes to avoid his obligations under his franchise agreement may find this provision useful because it may be difficult for any franchisor supplying an Operations Manual and 'house-style' designs, not protected by a trade mark registration, to demonstrate that no part of the franchise fees payable to it represent a copyright royalty. Most franchise agreements contain a clause requiring payment of fees gross[3]. A severance clause may be useful to a franchisor in this context[4].

1   ICTA 1988, s 536.
2   ICTA 1988, s 536.
3   See Ch 8, precedent 1, clause 7.13, post.
4   See Ch 8, precedent 1, clause 10.14, post.

4.06 A franchisee will be liable to deduct withholding tax at the current income tax rate from patent trade mark (in the case of 'pure profit income') or copyright royalties payable to his non-resident franchisor[1], except where that franchisor has the benefit of a double taxation agreement between the country of its residence and the United Kingdom, whereby the rate of such withholding tax is reduced, or the obligation to deduct is removed altogether[2]. If a franchisee is liable to make payments to a non-resident franchisor, proof should be obtained of the written clearance of the Inland Revenue that no, or a reduced rate of, tax should be deducted from payments to that franchisor. A franchisee must always ascertain where a franchisor is resident for tax purposes because it may be outside the country of its ostensible residence, or it may be unfortunate enough to be resident for tax purposes in several countries. The franchisee must be wary when a non-resident franchisor is providing services in the United Kingdom in consideration for franchise payments. It may be, in that case, that the franchisor is trading in the United Kingdom from a 'permanent establishment' or through a 'branch or agency'[3] in the United Kingdom. The articles of the double taxation agreements, to which the United Kingdom is a party, provide that a corporation, which is trading through a permanent establishment in the United Kingdom, will be taxable there on the income or profits arising from that trade and the relevant provisions of the particular double taxation agreement may not apply[4]. It could be the case that such a non-resident franchisor is trading through a permanent establishment in the United Kingdom, but is trading in a separate trade[5] or is providing insufficient services to its franchisees to fall outside ICTA 1988, s 348(1) or s 349(1)(a), whereupon the franchisee may be liable to deduct tax at source from its franchise fees, notwithstanding the existence of the relevant Double Taxation Agreement (unless clearance has been received by the franchisor). Indeed, it is difficult to conceive how any overseas franchisor can provide for its franchisees any of the usual services

4.07 *Tax problems*

associated with a business format franchise in the United Kingdom without serious danger of engaging in a trade in the United Kingdom and creating a permanent establishment or establishing a branch or agency[6]. If any franchisee is obliged to pay composite franchise fees (comprising a mixture of royalties and service charges) to an overseas franchisor, that franchisee must investigate the tax and residence status of the franchisor before making any payments and obtain advance clearance from the Inland Revenue in the United Kingdom to make the relevant payments[7]. In relation to interest, the provisions of ICTA 1988, s 818 must be noted.

1 ICTA 1988, ss 349(1), 338(3)(a) and (4)(a) and 536—see opening remarks in this chapter.
2 For example: US/UK Double Taxation Convention 1975, Art 12(2) (as amended by protocols); The Double Taxation Relief (Taxes on Income) (Netherlands) Order 1980, Art 12(1); and The Double Taxation Relief (Taxes on Income) (Switzerland) Order 1978, Art 12(1).
3 ICTA 1988, s 11.
4 For example: US/UK Double Taxation Convention 1975, Arts 12(4), 14 and 7; Double Taxation Relief (Taxes on Income) (Netherlands) Order 1980 (SI 1980 No 1961), Art 5.
5 However, for example US/UK Double Taxation Convention 1975, Art 12(4) stipulates that the permanent establishment must be effectively connected with the intellectual property rights for which royalties are being paid.
6 See post.
7 ICTA 1988, s 11.

Checklist

4.07 A practitioner acting for the franchisee should check the following:
 (1) where is the franchisor resident? (See PE1)[1]
 (2) has the franchisor a permanent establishment in the United Kingdom? (PE1)
 (3) has the franchisor written clearance from the Inland Revenue permitting payment of franchise fees gross? (PE78)
 (4) is there a requirement in the franchise agreement for payment of fees gross in all circumstances?[2]
 (5) is there a severance clause in the agreement?[3]
 (6) if no Inland Revenue clearance is available the franchisor must specify what proportion of the franchise fees relates to royalties:
  (a) for a patent (if any)
  (b) for a trade mark
  (c) for know-how
  (d) for copyright
and what proportion relates to the supply of services.

1 PE means preliminary enquiry. These are set out in paras 6.03 et seq, post.
2 See Ch 8, precedent 1, clause 7.13, post.
3 See Ch 8, precedent 1, clause 10.14, post.

Value Added Tax

4.08 If a franchisor resident in the United Kingdom supplies goods or services to its franchisees who are resident in the United Kingdom and the annual turnover in the supply of such services of the franchisor is likely to or does exceed the minimum turnover limits stipulated from time to time[1], then that franchisor is obliged[2] to register[3] as a trader for Value Added Tax[4] purposes with its local VAT office. It is, then, required to charge VAT on the price of all its supplies and

services at the rate stipulated from time to time[5]. Certain supplies are not subject to a VAT charge. There are two categories of such supplies:
(1) Those supplies which are exempt[6]; and
(2) Those supplies which are zero-rated[7].

Examples of the two categories are as follows:
(1) *Exempt supplies:* Sales of land; provision of insurance; finance; education; air transport.
(2) *Zero-rated supplies:* Supply of food of a kind used for human consumption (other than a supply in the course of catering)[8] (and except for excepted items[9]) exports[10].

1   1990 budget figure £25,400 p.a. (VATA 1983 s 2(5), Sch 1, para 1 (as amended)). With effect from 21 March 1990 a business is required to register for VAT at the end of any month during which its taxable supplies in the last 12 months exceeded the annual threshold or at any time if those supplies are liable to exceed that threshold within the next 30 days or, if it is a large business, immediately if supplies are likely to exceed the threshold within 30 days.
2   VATA 1983, s 2(5), Sch 1, para 1 (as amended by FA 1987, s 13 and FA 1988, s 14).
3   VATA 1983, s 2(5) and Sch 1 (as amended by FA 1987, s 13 and FA 1988, s 14).
4   Referred to elsewhere in this book as 'VAT'.
5   15% at the date of going to press.
6   See VATA 1983, Sch 6.
7   VATA 1983, s 16 and Sch 5—zero-rated supplies are still treated as taxable supplies but the rate of tax is nil.
8   VATA 1983, Sch 5, Group 1 and Notes 4 to 6 thereto. Catering includes take-away sales.
9   For example: ice cream; crisps; confectionery.
10 Section 44. Value Added Tax (General) Regulations 1985 (SI 1985 No 1886).

4.09 If the franchisor licences its United Kingdom franchisees to use its trade mark and supplies services (such as administering the common advertising fund and providing training and systems)[1] then the franchisor must charge VAT on all its franchise fees, including that proportion which is attributable to the use of the trade mark. If the franchisor provides electricity to the site, VAT will also be payable on that.

If the franchisor merely licenses its franchisees to use its trade mark and does not, itself, supply any services to them, so that the franchise fees are in the nature of 'pure income profit', then it is arguable that those payments are outside the scope of the tax because no services are supplied and the royalties are in the nature of rent. If this is correct, then franchise fees which include elements for the supply of services will be subject to VAT but if no such supply is involved, VAT may not be charged. However 'pure income profit' franchise fees will normally be subject to deduction of tax at source[2].

If the franchisor issues franchises to overseas franchisees any licence fees for the use of intellectual property rights will not be subject to VAT as the supply of services will be treated as being made where it is received[3].

However, if the franchisor supplies services to those foreign franchisees, which are performed in the United Kingdom (for example, the control of advertising programmes, franchisee training in the United Kingdom, supervision of accountancy systems) then those services will be subject to VAT. Overseas franchisees may not be able to reclaim this VAT, unless they are registered for VAT in the United Kingdom (which is unlikely) or EEC regulations apply. The VAT system relies upon a registered trader accounting for and paying to HM Customs and Excise the difference between VAT charged by that trader upon the supplies of goods

4.10 *Tax problems*

or services made by it and the VAT charged upon the supplies of goods or services supplied to it[4]. VAT on supplies made by it are described as 'output tax' and VAT on supplies to it as 'input tax'. The trader is responsible for payment of that balance within one month of the end of each 'prescribed accounting period'. Accounting periods are a matter for agreement with HM Customs and Excise but are usually quarterly. The first accounting period may be longer.

1 See para 4.02, ante. ICTA 1988, Schedule D, Section 18(3), Case I.
2 ICTA 1988, ss 348 and 349(1)(a).
3 VATA 1983, s 7, (as amended by FA 1987, s 19 and Sch 2).
4 VATA 1983, s 14(2) (as amended by FA 1987, s 19 and Sch 2 and FA 1988, s 11 and Sch 14).

Cash flow

4.10 In any business in which the service proportion of supplies by the trader is much greater than any material content which is supplied to the trader by other registered suppliers, a substantial difference between input tax and output tax can be accumulated. This may create significant cash flow advantages for the trader which is in the position to accumulate that difference, between its due payment dates. Indeed, the interest costs of many businesses may be reduced or removed completely by the accumulation of VAT during each prescribed accounting period. For example, the quarterly accounts of a restaurant business may be as shown below.[1]

Value added tax account

Extract from ledger[1]

	(A)[2] Input Tax (On purchases) £	(B)[3] Output Tax (On sales) £	(C)[4] Balance available to bank £
Month 1	898.21	5,191.57	4,293.36
Month 2	1,312.60	5,273.61	3,961.01
Month 3	1,281.30	6,033.26	4,751.96
	£3,492,11	£16,498.44	£13,006.33

The extent of the benefits will vary on a day to day basis and to achieve the optimum trading advantage, it is suggested that part of any formal bank financing undertaken by the company be on a floating overdraft basis.

1 This is an actual VAT account of the trade of a 'My Old Dutch' restaurant in the United Kingdom for a three month period ending 31 March 1981.
2 Column (A) represents the amount of value added tax charged and paid for each month.
3 Column (B) represents the amount of value added tax collected each month.
4 Column (C) represents the cash flow benefit accruing from the collection of value added tax.

4.11 If franchise fees are paid by the restaurateur/franchisee to its franchisor monthly during the quarter on fees of 10 per cent of gross turnover (say 7 per cent franchise fee and 3 per cent advertising contribution) the restaurant business would be obliged to pay to the franchisor an additional 15 per cent calculated upon those fees in respect of VAT. This input tax is deducted from the total output tax in the quarter leaving a balance to be paid to HM Customs and Excise, in this example of £2,925. That balance will have accumulated throughout the quarter.

The franchisor will charge VAT on all its franchise fees[1] and, probably, will not incur large amounts of input tax against the output tax. For example, quarterly accounts of a franchise business may be as shown opposite[2].

1 See paras 4.02 and 4.09, ante.
2 It is assumed that the franchisor company has ten franchised units each year with a revenue of £3,000 per week. The royalty fee is 10 per cent to include 3 per cent advertising fund.

	Fees	VAT	Advertising contribution	VAT
Income				
Franchise Fees	25,200	3,780	10,800	1,620
Rent	750	—		
Rates	152	—		
Insurance	120	—		
Energy costs	100	—		
Telephone	750	112.50		
Salaries	11,250	—		
National insurance	1,541	—		
Equipment lease rentals	100	15.00		
Interest	—	—		
Motoring rental and expenses	1,850	277.50		
Hotel and travelling	2,000	300.00		
Post and stationery	2,000	150.00		
	20,613	855.00		
Net profit	4,587			
Balance of output		2,925.00		
Advertising costs			5,000	750
Designer fees			2,000	300
Agency fees			2,000	300
Printing			1,800	270
Expenditure on advertising			10,800	
Output tax			1,620	

4.12 Any registered trader (franchisor or franchisee) must guard against delay in making payment of VAT at the end of each prescribed accounting period. A daily penalty of £10[1] or one half of one per cent (0.5 per cent) per day, whichever is the greater[2] applies in the event of late payment. The Value Added Tax (Accounting and Records) Regulations 1989 (SI 1989 No 2248) came into force on 1 April 1990 (deferred after public consultation from 1 January 1990). As a result of that consultation, the aggregate net value of errors under which no interest or penalty will be incurred is £1,000 (raised from £500). The regulations impose a duty upon a taxpayer to maintain 'normal business and accounting records'.

In the case of a corporate trader, HM Customs and Excise are preferential creditors[3], in the event of the winding-up or appointment of a receiver to that trader, for outstanding VAT in the preceding twelve months[4]. Floating charges

4.13 *Tax problems*

rank after preferential creditors, of which HM Customs and Excise are one[5]. Fixed charges rank in priority to them. Accordingly, any investors in a corporate trader who have, themselves, advanced monies to, or have personally guaranteed the borrowings of that trader, from third party financial sources, must ensure that those borrowings are secured by fixed charges on all the available assets of the company. If that is the case, any accumulated VAT, if not the subject of a trust in favour of HM Customs and Excise (which may arise if a separate bank account is used to accumulate output tax due) will be available to reduce or discharge the outstanding secured borrowings of the trader. Such an arrangement may significantly reduce the total financial risk to investors in the trading company, especially in the early months of the business of the company. A decision concerning the solvency of the corporate trader may be made at or near the end of the first prescribed accounting period.

1 VATA 1983, s 39(7).
2 FA 1980, s 14(1) (as amended by FA 1987, s 11 and FA 1988, Sch 14).
3 VATA 1983, Sch 7, para 12 (repealed as from a day to be appointed).
4 VATA 1983, Sch 7, para 12(1), (2)(c) (as amended by FA 1987 and FA 1988).
5 VATA 1983, Sch 7, para 12(1)(c) (as amended by FA 1987 and FA 1988).

4.13 The practitioner acting for the franchise must enquire whether the franchisor is registered for VAT and, if so, its VAT number[1].

1 See para 6.03, post, Preliminary enquiry 79.

Know-how

4.14 A United Kingdom resident franchisee who pays an initial fee to its United Kingdom resident franchisor for the disclosure to him of the know-how contained in the operations manual, and any other business information or secrets of the franchisor and for pre-commencement training may be making a payment for the acquisition of know-how. If that know-how falls within the definition contained in ICTA 1988, s 533(7)[1], such a payment will not be treated as a normal trading expense on the part of the franchisee, although it may be taxed as a trading receipt in the hands of the franchisor. The payment will be permitted to be written-off by the franchisee at the rate of 25% per year beginning with the chargeable period in which the expenditure is incurred[2]. At first sight, the definition of know-how contained in ICTA 1988, s 533(7), may not appear relevant to a franchise business. However, an alternative (and more common) definition of 'intellectual property' is 'industrial property' and it would be unwise to construe the word 'industrial' too narrowly. The words 'information' and 'techniques' are general and would encompass any form of know-how. Most franchises will involve some form of processing of goods or materials, however small. It is, therefore, arguable that the statutory definition will apply to most franchise businesses. If the franchisor grants to the franchisee an exclusive territory[3] it may be that the payment is in respect of the transfer of know-how, together with part of a trade[4] in which case that payment will be treated as a payment for goodwill by the franchisee to the franchisor[5]. In that event, the payment will not be a deductible expense for, or be eligible to be written-off by, the franchisee and will be subject to corporation tax at the capital gains tax rate in the hands of the franchisor. Where an exclusive territory is granted by the franchisor, the Inland Revenue have considered that the initial fee is a payment for goodwill, even if the franchisor has not, itself, traded from a location within the territory. Presumably, that view is founded on the belief that the franchise business has some form of national goodwill, part of which is being transferred to the franchisee.

1 'In this section "know-how" means any industrial information and techniques likely to assist in the manufacture or processing of goods or materials, or in the working of a mine, oil-well or other source of mineral deposits (including the searching for, discovery, or testing of deposits or the winning of access thereto), or in the carrying out of any agricultural, forestry or fishing operations.'
2 ICTA 1988, s 530(1), (6) and (7).
3 See Ch 8, post.
4 *Evans Medical Supplies Ltd v Moriarty* [1957] 3 All ER 718, 37 TC 540, HL.
5 ICTA 1988, s 531(2).

Outlets

4.15 One of the major problems which any franchisor will face, when franchising in the United Kingdom, will be the lack of suitable trading locations for its franchisees, if the franchise business depends upon retail outlets. With the growth of multiple stores and retail chains, high public exposure locations are becoming increasingly scarce. To obtain suitable locations, the franchise business may have to compete with a number of substantial retailers. It may be necessary for the franchisor to purchase the freehold interest in the proposed outlet, or in a larger building of which the outlet forms part, and, then, let the outlet to its franchisee. Alternatively, because the freeholders of a potential outlet will only wish to let the property to a tenant with a satisfactory covenant, it may be necessary for the franchisor, itself, to take a lease of the outlet and to sub-let it to its franchisee, or to guarantee a lease to its franchisee[1].

If the franchisor has sufficient access to funds to enable it to acquire freeholds or long leaseholds and to let or sub-let them to its franchisees, it will have the chance of establishing an appreciating asset base which may, eventually, outweigh the value of the franchise business itself.

Any franchisor which requires retail outlets for its franchise business must endeavour to arrange long-term finance to enable it to purchase those outlets, both for the purposes of achieving steady growth in its franchise chain and of investment[2].

However, before embarking on this course it must consider certain tax problems.

1 See para 5.18 et seq, post for discussion on leasing or licensing.
2 See para 4.22 post, for discussion on investment aspects.

4.16 If the franchisor has acquired the freehold interest in premises for a capital payment, it may wish to pass to the franchisee part of the responsibility for that payment when the franchisor grants a lease of the premises to the franchisee. If the franchisee pays such a premium[1] for a 'short' lease[2], the premium will be assessable in the hands of the franchisor as rent under Schedule A[3], less a deduction of 2 per cent for each complete year of the term[4] of the lease (other than the first)[5]. Similar provisions apply to payments in lieu of the whole or part of the rent for any period[6] or for the waiver of any terms of the lease[7].

If the franchisor is an intermediate landlord and pays a premium to its head landlord, it may deduct the chargeable amount of that premium, over the term of the lease, as if it was a deductible expense of the property[8]. If a premium is paid by the franchisee to the franchisor on the grant of a sub-lease to the franchisee, the franchisor may deduct for tax purposes from a proportion of the premium

4.17 Tax problems

paid to it on the grant of the sub-lease, a proportion of the premium paid by it, on the grant to it of the superior lease[9].

1 ICTA 1988, s 24(1), definition of 'premium'.
2 ICTA 1988, s 34(1); a short lease in this context is a lease which does not exceed 50 years.
3 ICTA 1988, s 15(1)(i)(a).
4 Rules for ascertaining duration of lease. ICTA 1988, s 38.
5 ICTA 1988, s 34(1).
6 ICTA 1988, s 34(4).
7 ICTA 1988, s 34(5).
8 ICTA 1988, s 37.
9 ICTA 1988, s 37(5) and (6). The proportions are calculated in accordance with ICTA 1988, s 52.

4.17 If the franchisor, on the grant of a 'short' lease, imposes an obligation on its franchisee/lessee to undertake work on the leased premises, the amount by which the value of the franchisor's interest in the property is increased by those works, will be treated as a disguised premium and assessed under Schedule A accordingly[1]. This does not apply to work which, if the franchisor had undertaken the same, would have been deductible from the rent of the property[2]. Disguised premium work will be in the nature of improvements, but the restrictive nature of ICTA 1988, s 25, means that repairs in respect of dilapidations occurring before the franchisor acquired the property will not be deductible. In usual circumstances, where the landlord has no other business relationship with the tenant, it is arguable that the installation of special equipment and the alteration of premises to suit the requirements of the tenant may not increase the value of the landlord's interest in the property. However, where the landlord is the franchisor and the property is being adapted by the franchisee to suit the requirements of the franchise business, it is arguable that a substantial proportion of that work may increase the value of the franchisor's interest in the property, in view of the use to which the franchisor, itself, could put the property after that work. It should be noted that ICTA 1988, s 34(2) and (3), does not apply any open market value test of the increase of the landlord's interest in the property and the Inland Revenue may argue that a test taking into account the particular circumstances of the franchisor should apply.

1 ICTA 1988, s 34(2) and (3).
2 Proviso to ICTA 1988, s 34(2) and (3) and ss 25, 26, 28, 29 and 30.

4.18 The franchisee must be careful that the franchisor does not grant or make an assignment of a 'short' lease, without, or at a lower premium, in circumstances where a premium, or greater premium, could have been charged[1]. In either event, on any subsequent assignment of the lease at a, or at a greater, premium, the amount foregone on the original grant of the lease, or assignment, may be assessed upon the assignor (who took the grant of the lease or made the assignment of it at an undervalue) or any subsequent assignee[2] when that assignee assigns the lease.

This is an anti-avoidance measure, designed to overcome transactions between related persons, who intend to convert income into capital gains. However, the effect of the section is not confined to related persons and even where the landlord and tenant are not related and it is demonstrated that the lease was granted or assigned for no, or an undervalued, premium, the franchisee and/or its subsequent assignees may be faced with an assessment under Schedule A, under the provisions of this section.

1   ICTA 1988, s 35.
2   ICTA 1988, s 35(2)(a) and (b).

4.19 A franchisee, who pays a premium on the grant of a 'short' lease (not on an assignment), which is chargeable in the hands of the franchisor/landlord under sections 34 or 35 of ICTA 1988, may be entitled to treat the amount of the premium as additional rent which is deductible over the 'relevant period'[1]. If the franchisee (which will almost certainly be the case) is trading at the leased premises[2], the franchisee will be entitled to deduct the amount of the premium as a rent on a day by day basis throughout the whole of the term of the lease. If part only of the leased premises are used for trading purposes by the franchisee (for example, if part of the premises are used as living accommodation by the family of the franchisee) the amount of the premium shall be reduced, for the purposes of relief, by a just apportionment relating to the proportion of the total of the premises not occupied for trade purposes.[4]

1   ICTA 1988, s 87(1)(a).
2   ICTA 1988, s 87(2).
3   ICTA 1988, s 87(9)(a).
4   ICTA 1988, s 87(3).

4.20 If a lease exceeding 50 years is granted by a franchisor to its franchisee, any premium received will be chargeable to capital gains tax.

4.21 It is essential that the franchisor distinguish between any premium value in the actual property, which is leased to the franchisee, and the value of any goodwill, which is being transferred with it, or the value of any know-how, which is being disclosed to the franchisee at the same time[1]. The consideration for the transfer of goodwill or the disposal of know-how will be treated as a capital gain arising from the disposal of an asset[2] provided that in the case of a disposal of know-how the grant of the lease is deemed to be a disposal of part of a trade. This will occur if the franchisor has been trading in the franchise business from the premises to be leased or, possibly, if an exclusive territorial restriction is entered into by the franchisor. Corporation tax at the capital gains tax rate may not be more favourable than taxation under ICTA 1988, s 34(1).

1   See para 4.14, ante.
2   ICTA 1988, s 531(2).

4.22 If the franchisor lets premises to its franchisee, the rent paid by the franchisee will be charged to tax under Schedule A[1]. Certain deductions are permitted when computing the amount of tax to be charged[2]. These are mainly revenue expenses and costs arising from the management of the property[3]. A company is charged to tax under Schedule A by virtue of the general corporation tax provisions[4]. Rental payments should not be mixed with franchise fees, because the franchisor will not be able to deduct, for tax calculation purposes, its general business and trading expenditure from that rental income in the first instance, but will be able to do so if it makes a surplus trading loss[5]. A clear distinction should be made between rent for the premises and any consideration for the use of the intellectual property of the franchisor or the provision of services by it[6].

1   ICTA 1988, s 15. Certain receipts may not be rent. *Martin v Routh* (1964) 42 TC 106. A

4.23 *Tax problems*

licence fee may be charged under Schedule D, Case I, where other services are provided by the franchisor.
2   ICTA 1988, ss 25, 28(1), 29(1) and 31(1).
3   ICTA 1988, s 25.
4   ICTA 1988, s 6(1) to (4).
5   ICTA 1988, s 393(2).
6   *Whelan v Alfred Leney & Co Ltd* [1936] AC 393, 20 TC 321, HL.

4.23 If a tenant pays rent (or a premium on the grant of a lease) directly to a non-resident franchisor/landlord, the tenant must deduct tax at source at the basic rate of income tax from the amount of the payment[1]. In the event that such deduction exceeds the total tax liabilities of the non-resident franchisor in the United Kingdom, the franchisor may make a claim for repayment of that excess[2]. If the rent or premium is paid to an agent of the franchisor, then that agent may withhold[3] from its principal tax at the basic rate and any higher rate[4] for which the agent was assessed in respect of the rental or premium income of the franchisor. If the tenant fails to make the appropriate deduction, he will be liable to account to the revenue for an amount calculated as if the rent actually paid was the net rental after the proper deductions[5]. The authors are not aware of any double taxation agreements, to which the United Kingdom is a party, which still contain provisions whereby such deductions may be reclaimed by the non-resident franchisor/landlord.

1   ICTA 1988, ss 349(1), 350(1), (3) and (4)(a) and 43(1).
2   ICTA 1988, s 43(3).
3   Taxes Management Act (TMA) 1970, s 83.
4   TMA 1970, s 78, as amended by FA 1985, s 50(1), (3).
5   See para 4.02 et seq, ante.

4.24 If a potential United Kingdom resident franchisee decides to purchase a 'company owned store'[1] from his franchisor, with the object of trading under the franchise business from the outlet, part of the consideration for the acquisition will be treated as being in respect of the goodwill of the business which accumulated whilst the franchisor was trading there. That payment will not be eligible as a deduction or be capable of being written-off in the hands of the franchisee. It will, merely, be the base value for calculating any capital gains or loss in the event that the franchisee disposes of the business. In addition, the franchisee should take care that no part of the payment for that purchase or any subsequent instalment payments or any part of his future franchise fees are treated as payments for know-how[2]. Otherwise, that part of any of those payments attributable to the disposal of know-how will be treated as the acquisition of goodwill and will not be available to him as a deduction or eligible to be written off[3], because the sale of the store will be treated as a disposal of part of a trade, unless both the franchisor and himself elect to treat such payments in another manner[4]. This may be important in the light of the relief otherwise available to the franchisee under section 87 of the ICTA 1988 in respect of a premium paid on the grant of a lease[5] and may be important in relation to the proportion of his future franchise fees in respect of know-how which may be treated as instalments attributable to a 'disposal' of know-how. It is essential that the franchisee obtain the agreement of his franchisor to serve the notice upon the Inland Revenue stipulated in ICTA 1988, s 531, in respect of future franchise fees as a condition of the transaction or it is made clear that the sale does not relate to a 'disposal' of know-how and that future franchise fees relate to the disclosure of know-how under 'licence' made available to the franchisee after the date of the sale and independently of it. Generally, a considerable proportion of franchise fees is attributable to know-how supplied by the franchisor. In addition, if the franchisor enters into restrictive covenants or other restrictions in favour of the franchisee, as part of the sale, or as part of its standard franchise agreement (such as a territorial restriction), which is executed at the same time and as part of the total sale transaction, any consideration passing to the franchisor for the restriction, may be treated as a receipt for the sale of know-how[6]. Accordingly, any part of the payments to the franchisee by the franchisor, attributable to such a restriction, will be taxed in the manner stipulated in section 530(1), (6) and (7) of ICTA 1988, depending on the circumstances. If there is a disposal of a trade (such as the sale of a company owned store) at the same time as the covenant, then the consideration will be treated as a sale of goodwill[7], with the same results as mentioned above.

It should be noted that it may not be in the interests of a franchisor to agree to the taxation of a disposal of know-how in any other manner than a sale of goodwill. However, in this case, the possible fiscal benefits to the franchisor may be outweighed by intellectual property ownership considerations. The current rate of capital gains tax is relatively high for short-term gains especially and the franchisor may welcome an attempt to treat the consideration for the disclosure of know-how as trading income.

1 An outlet owned by the franchisor and from which it trades in the franchise business.
2 For definition see para 4.14, ante, and ICTA 1988, s 533(7).
3 ICTA 1988, s 531.
4 ICTA 1988, s 530(1), (6) and (7) and 531.
5 See para 4.19 ante.
6 ICTA 1988, s 531(8).
7 Ibid.

4.25 A landlord is now entitled to charge VAT on rent for commercial property. If the landlord is already VAT registered because of its general business (such as a franchisor) then it is likely that commercial buildings which it owns will become subject to VAT on rent. This could have serious cash-flow consequences for a franchisee/tenant. For businesses which are not within the VAT system, such as banks, the VAT on rent will be an additional expense.

4.26 The Uniform Business Rate ('UBR'), which applies from April 1990, has substantially increased business rates in some areas of Britain, although reductions have been welcomed in other areas. UBR increases are phased over five years but upon assignment of a lease or the grant of a new lease to a new tenant, the full rate of UBR becomes payable immediately.

Checklist

4.27 The practitioner should check the following:
 (1) If a 'short' lease is being assigned, is the consideration at market value?
 (2) If a 'short' lease is being granted, is the premium chargeable under Schedule A?
 (3) What is the value of the goodwill being assigned, if goodwill is being assigned?
 (4) Is there any disposal of know-how? If so, is this together with part of a trade?
 (5) Will the landlord charge VAT on the rent?

4.28 *Tax problems*

Finance

4.28 One of the major problems for a franchisor, which is in the process of establishing a franchise chain in the United Kingdom, is arranging finance for its most suitable potential franchisees. Often the most suitable franchisees are those with the least capital. They are willing to work harder and will accept the controls imposed by the franchisor more readily than their more secure fellows. The growth of a successful franchise business will be limited by any lack of availability of funds for franchisees. A responsible franchisor will expend great efforts to locate such funds, rather than accept less suitable persons, with capital, as its franchisees.

A franchisor should consider, carefully, any tax-effective investment incentive arrangements, which may assist its franchisees in this respect and which may either reduce its own tax burden or assist others to do so. The methods of arranging such finance will be reviewed in this chapter under the following headings:

(1) Business expansion scheme;
(2) Relief in the event of failure of a corporate franchisee;
(3) Interest relief for investment in close companies;

It is not the purpose of this book to discuss the relative merits (taking into account commercial risk and taxation) of the operation of a franchised outlet by a corporation, limited partnership[1], general partnership or an individual. Such a discussion would be relevant to any small business venture. It is the object of this section of this book to review the methods by which a franchisor may materially assist its potential franchisees to raise capital. If the franchisor advises its potential franchisees concerning, or procures for them, credit then it must be registered under the Consumer Credit Act 1974[2]. The three methods are of particular interest to individuals who have access to funds and have substantial income subject to United Kingdom income tax. If the most suitable franchisees have insufficient funds to finance the franchised business, they are unlikely to fall within this category of persons. The potential franchisee must, therefore, make arrangements with other individuals, so that they provide equity or other risk finance to assist the franchisee to take up the franchise. They will be 'sleeping partners', whilst the potential franchisee will work in the franchised business.

The franchise industry is, perhaps, uniquely placed to take advantage of such methods of financing a business. It is unlikely that any individual would risk substantial sums in investing in any business which has no proven record and is conducted by an individual with no experience of it, whatever the tax advantages for the investor of such an investment. However, the franchise business will:

(1) have a proven record, although, probably, not at the outlet from which the franchisee wishes to operate. However, the franchisor will have approved the location of the outlet in the light of its experience in the business elsewhere;
(2) be conducted by a franchisee who has been fully trained by the franchisor[3];
(3) be continually supervised by the franchisor[4];
(4) in the case of difficulty, be assisted by the management personnel of the franchisor[5];
(5) be promoted by the general advertising and promotional programme of the franchisor[6].

An investor in a small business is not only concerned about the risk of failure of that business but is, also, concerned that he will not receive the proportion of the real profits of the business, to which he is entitled, because of financial manipulation by the franchisee. The financial supervision and controls imposed and maintained by the franchisor will reduce the opportunities available to the franchisee to obscure the real profit performance of the business.

The involvement of the franchisor in the business and the desire of the franchisor, in its own interest, that every franchisee will succeed, must make investment in a franchised business an attractive proposition for 'sleeping partners', who wish to take advantage of the tax reliefs available to them and arising from such an investment.

However, a franchisor may decide that it does not wish to permit 'sleeping partner' investors in its corporate franchises. There are potential problems for any franchisor, if the franchisor is forced to deal with aggrieved investors, in the event that the franchised business experiences difficulties or the working shareholder in the franchisee company engages in a dispute with them. The franchisor must satisfy itself that the relationship between the working shareholder and his outside investors will not interfere with the supervisory functions and powers of the franchisor.

The franchisor must be an 'authorised person' carrying on an investment business if it engages in the sale or placing of shares in its franchisee companies[7].

1 Registered under the Limited Partnerships Act 1907. Limited partnerships have become the 'Cinderella' of tax-based investment opportunities, overshadowed by the business expansion scheme. However, where there are high start-up costs and a high risk of failure, a limited partnership may be more effective in generating reliefs for an investor than a BES company.
2 See para 6.21, post.
3 Ch 8, precedent 1, clause 7.1, post.
4 Ch 8, precedent 1, clause 7.31, et seq, post.
5 Ch 8, precedent 1, clauses 10.3 and 10.32, post.
6 Ch 8, precedent 1, clause 6.4, post.
7 Financial Services Act 1986, s 3.

Business Expansion Scheme ('BES')

4.29 The BES was introduced in the Finance Act 1983. The aim of the scheme was to encourage investment by private individuals in companies run by other persons. The Treasury appear to have assumed that the BES would generate capital for high-risk technology industries. It is true that some new technology businesses have been started or expanded by the injection of BES-based finance. However, from the commencement of the BES, it became apparent that potential investors could be divided into two categories. First, those who were interested in high-risk but potentially very rewarding gambles and second, those who were only really interested in finding a secure haven for their money. The second category is much more populous than the first.

4.30 As a result of the cautious attitude of investors, BES funds were set up, mainly by financial institutions, which spread their investors' money through a number of BES companies[1]. In this way, investors were not confined to making one or a very few share subscriptions and could rely upon the specialist skills of the investment managers of the BES funds. The caution of the investors was reflected by the conservative attitudes of some of the funds. With some notable exceptions, the funds concentrated their attention upon asset-rich low-risk businesses. Potential growth was not as important as security. Individual investors, who invested directly in BES companies, were mainly interested in similar opportunities.

1 ICTA 1988, s 289, and Inland Revenue Press Release 26 May 1983.

4.31 Tax problems

4.31 The government were not pleased with this result. Perhaps the most notorious examples of these breaches of the spirit rather than the letter of the regulations of the BES were farming (several millions of pounds were raised for investment in prime agricultural land and for farming on it, although as a result of EEC policy, the fall in the value of farmland may, ironically, have caused huge potential capital losses for the BES farming companies), fine wine investment, antiques and works of art, land development (as distinguished from dealing in land) and nursing and rest homes for the elderly.

4.32 From the commencement of the BES, the government had excluded certain businesses from the scope of the scheme. Those were[1]:

(a) dealing in commodities, shares, securities, land or futures;

(b) dealing in goods otherwise than in the course of an ordinary trade of wholesale or retail distribution, (see ICTA 1988, s 297 (3)(a) and (b));

(c) banking, insurance, money-lending, debt-factoring, hire-purchase financing or other financial activities;

(d) leasing (including letting ships on charter or other assets on hire) or receiving royalties or licence fees;

(e) providing legal or accountancy services; or

(f) providing services or facilities for any trade carried on by another person which consists to any substantial extent of activities within any of the foregoing paragraphs and in which a controlling interest is held by a person who also has a controlling interest in the trade carried on by the company.

As a result of the BES schemes which concentrated upon low-risk high asset companies, farming[2] and 'property development'[3] were added to the excluded businesses in 1984.

1 ICTA 1988, s 297(2)(a)–(c) and (e)–(g) (but see para 4.42 post).
2 ICTA 1988, ss 297(2)(j) and 298(6)(b) (in relation to shares issued after 13 March 1984).
3 ICTA 1988, ss 279(2)(g) and 298(6)(a) (in relation to shares issued after 19 March 1985).

4.33 After 31 March 1988, a general maximum limit of £500,000 raised in any tax year by a BES company was imposed[1]. This does not apply to residential letting companies (£5,000,000 limit).

1 ICTA 1988, s 290(A) inserted by FA 1988, s 51(1)(b).

4.34 However, with their usual ingenuity, financial institutions managed to discover fresh low-risk high-asset companies for BES investors. As a result, the BES was revised again in 1986 in an attempt to limit investment in companies which have substantial interests in land[1] or deal in assets which are slow-moving and are more in the nature of investments.[2] Broadly, a company whose interests in land[3] exceed 50% of its total assets (see ICTA 1988, s 294(3)) will not qualify. A lease acquired for a premium or otherwise at a below market rent will form an interest in land for these purposes. A company which has issued not more than £50,000 worth of BES shares within a 12 month period will not be affected by the valuation limit[4]. The restriction does not apply to specialist residential letting companies[5] (see para 4.40 et seq below for more details). A company may undertake some non-qualifying activities provided they do not exceed about 20% of the total trade[6].

1 ICTA 1988, s 289 (in relation to shares issued after 18 March 1986).
2 ICTA 1988, s 289 (in relation to shares issued after 18 March 1986).

3   ICTA 1988, s 294(5).
4   ICTA 1988, s 296(1).
5   FA 1988, s 50.
6   HC Standing Committee 17 July 1986 (Col 1268).

4.35 The authors do not understand why the BES funds were not more attracted in the past to franchise businesses for the reasons set out in para 4.45, post. However, the changes in the BES may be to the advantage of potential franchisees who have insufficient capital themselves to set up franchised businesses. Franchisors must study the effect of the restrictions and tailor their franchise start-up costs to suit the resulting requirements of the BES funds[1]. Many franchise businesses require high profile leasehold premises from which to trade. They generally command high premiums and appreciate in value, although the recent retail slump in the south (1989/90) is significantly reducing premiums. Most franchise businesses would not require more than £50,000 of outside equity capital. The 50% limit on interests in land would not apply to such a small franchisee BES company. With the advantages outlined earlier (para 4.28) and the attraction of a secure property foundation, BES franchise investments may prove more attractive[2].

1   ICTA 1988, ss 289 and 296.
2   See para 4.43 et seq below.

4.36 Relief for investment in corporate trades (BES relief) may be available:
(a) to an individual[1] who is resident and ordinarily resident in the UK (including Crown employees serving overseas[2]); and
(b) who subscribes[3] (not purchases) for new ordinary[4] shares (which carry no special rights throughout a period of 5 years from the date of issue[5]);
(c) in a qualifying company[6] (an unquoted company, resident in the UK and not resident elsewhere); and
(d) which exists wholly or substantially for the purpose of undertaking one or more qualifying trades[7] wholly or mainly in the UK (or is a holding company whose subsidiaries carry on such trades);
(e) if the individual subscriber is not connected with the company[8];
(f) subscribes not less than £500 nor more than £40,000[9] (£40,000 is the total qualifying subscription in any year for an individual); . . .
(g) the company is not controlled[10] by another company (or is in control of another company other than a subsidiary permitted by the scheme[11]); and
(h) the company must have carried on the qualifying trade for four months (and commence the trade within two years of the issue of the qualifying shares); and
(i) all shares of the company must be fully paid[12]; and
(j) no person who carries on a similar trade to the company (parallel trading) can have 30 per cent or more of the shares of the company[13]; and
(k) the trade of the company must be carried on with the intention of realising a profit[14]; and
(l) the conditions of the relief must be observed for five years (and for two years before the issue of the shares if the company was then incorporated[15] ('the relevant period')); and
(m) the amount raised in eligible shares shall not exceed £500,000 in the relevant financial year or the previous six months whichever is applicable[16]; and
(n) the interests in land of the company must not exceed 50% of its total assets[17]; and
(o) the subscriber holds the shares for 5 years[18].

4.37 *Tax problems*

1   ICTA 1988, s 289.
2   ICTA 1988, s 289.
3   ICTA 1988, s 289.
4   ICTA 1988, s 289.
5   ICTA 1988, s 289.
6   ICTA 1988, ss 289, 293(1) and (2).
'Unquoted' means a company not dealt in on the official list of the Stock Exchange or the Unlisted Securities Market.
7   ICTA 1988, ss 289 and 293(2)(a).
8   ICTA 1988, ss 289 and 293(5).
9   ICTA 1988, ss 289 and 293(3).
10 ICTA 1988, ss 289 and 293(8).
11 ICTA 1988, ss 289 and 293(8) and 264 (UK subsidiaries only).
12 ICTA 1988, ss 289 and 293(7).
13 ICTA 1988, ss 289 and 298(1)(a)(i).
14 ICTA 1988, ss 289 and 297(8).
15 ICTA 1988, ss 289 and 297(12).
16 TA 1988, s 290 as inserted by FA 1988, s 51(1)(A). This does not apply to BES companies engaged in private housing rentals.
17 ICTA 1988, s 294.
18 ICTA 1988, s 299(1).

4.37 The relief will take the form of a deduction in the amount of the qualifying individual's subscription for eligible shares in a qualifying company carrying on a qualifying trade from his total income in the year of assessment in which the shares are issued.[1] Accordingly, if the individual has substantial income, part of which would otherwise have been subject to tax at the maximum rate[2] and he subscribes for shares up to the full amount of his income subject to that rate (up to the maximum subscription of £40,000)[3], the relief will amount to 40% of the total subscription. In 1987–88 the cost to the Exchequer or the BES was £110 million. The cost for 1988–89, according to estimates in February 1990 was likely to be £130 million. In 1988–89 about £350 million was invested in total in residential letting properties owned by BES companies[4].

1   ICTA 1988, s 289.
2   60% 1986–87, for income in excess of £41,200. FA 1986, s 15.
3   ICTA 1988, ss 289 and 290(2).
4   Hansard. 20 February 1990 col 679–680.

4.38 If the company is wound up or otherwise dissolved without winding up before the expiry of the relevant period[1], the relief will continue to apply provided it is shown that the winding up or dissolution was done for genuine commercial reasons and is not part of a tax avoidance scheme[2]. The same will apply if the company is wound up or dissolved within four months of the issue of the shares.

1   ICTA 1988, s 289.
2   ICTA 1988, ss 289 and 293(6).

4.39 If the shares are disposed of within the relevant period by bargain not at arm's length, the relief will be lost[1]. In the case of an arm's length bargain, the relief will be reduced by any consideration received on such disposal[2]. The grant of an option to sell the shares shall be treated as a disposal[3]. On disposal after the expiry of the relevant period no capital gains tax will apply to any capital gain made on the shares by the subscriber[4].

1   ICTA 1988, ss 289 and 299(1)(a).
2   ICTA 1988, ss 289 and 299(1)(a).

3 ICTA 1988, ss 289 and 299(5).
4 ICTA 1988, s 289 and Sch 29.

4.40 In the 1986 Budget, the government radically revised the qualifications of the company and its trade. A company is not a qualifying company if at any time during the relevant period its interests in land exceed one half of its total assets[1]. The value of those interests is calculated by aggregating the market value of its land assets and deducting its relevant debts. Those debts comprise:

(a) debts secured on the land (including floating charges in the property)[2];

(b) unsecured debts falling due within 12 months[3];

(c) the total paid up on the preference shares[4].

1 ICTA 1988, ss 289, 294, 307(8) and 828. The calculation is based on the lower of the valuation at any time during the relevant period or immediately after the eligible shares were issued. The procedure is set out in ICTA 1988, ss 289 and 295.
2 ICTA 1988, ss 289 and 294(2)(a).
3 ICTA 1988, ss 289 and 294(2)(b).
4 ICTA 1988, ss 289 and 294(2)(c).

4.41 The one-half fraction relating to interests in land as a proportion of total assets may be amended by statutory instrument[1]. An interest in land is widely defined[2] but does not include the interests of a creditor. The assets and liabilities of a company which has one or more subsidiaries shall be aggregated with those of its subsidiaries for this purpose[3].

1 ICTA 1988, ss 289 and 828.
2 ICTA 1988, ss 289 and 294(5).
3 ICTA 1988, ss 289 and 294(8).

4.42 The excluded trades now comprise the following[1]:

The trade must not at any time in the relevant period consist to any substantial extent of:

(a) dealing in commodities, shares, securities, land or futures;

(b) dealing in goods otherwise than in the course of an ordinary trade or wholesale or retail distribution;

(c) banking, insurance, money-lending, debt-factoring, hire-purchase financing or other financial activities;

(d) oil extraction;

(e) leasing (including letting ships on charter or other assets on hire) or receiving royalties or licence fees;

(f) providing legal or accountancy services; or

(g) providing services or facilities for any trade carried on by another person which consists to any substantial extent of activities within any of paras (a) to (e) above and in which a controlling interest is held by a person who also has a controlling interest in the trade carried on by the company;

(h) property development;

(i) farming.

However, the second radical alteration of the BES was a restriction upon the nature of retail or wholesale distribution[2]. The trade will not be treated as an 'ordinary trade' and therefore not a 'qualifying trade' if the company deals to a substantial extent in goods of a kind which are collected or held as an investment and a substantial proportion of those goods are held by the company for a longer period than a

4.43 *Tax problems*

willing vendor would reasonably expect to do so. This is an attempt to exclude such as wine investment and antique collecting as qualifying trades.

1 ICTA 1988, ss 289 and 297(2)(a)–(h).
2 ICTA 1988, ss 289, 297(3) and 298(3).

4.43 The condition relating to property-based assets does not apply to a company if during any twelve month period the total sums raised through the issue of eligible shares does not exceed £50,000[1]. Where the total exceeds £50,000, and the company is in breach of the condition, relief will only be denied in respect of the excess[2].

1 ICTA 1988, ss 289 and 296(1)(a).
2 ICTA 1988, ss 289 and 296(1)(g).

4.44 The £50,000 de minimis exemption is reduced if the company trades in partnership or as a party to a joint venture with another company[1]. This is intended to prevent two or more small BES companies collaborating on some land-based project which would cause the relief to be denied if only one of them undertook the scheme. Relief will also be denied where companies under common control engage in parallel trading[2].

1 ICTA 1988, ss 289 and 296(2).
2 ICTA 1988, ss 289 and 292.

4.45 This de minimis exemption may be particularly useful for franchisees who do not themselves have sufficient capital to start a franchised business. Many franchised businesses will not require more than £50,000 in outside equity. The advantages of franchising for outside investors[1] may tempt financial institutions to form a BES fund which specialises in investment in franchised businesses which are below the £50,000 limit. This may provide secure investment prospects without the usual disadvantages of investment in small businesses (management time in proportion to potential rewards, supervision problems, availability of crisis management in the event of illness of the principal director and many others) because most of the potential problems and inconveniences will be the responsibility of the franchisor[2].

1 Para 4.28, ante.
2 See Ch 8, precedent 1, clause 10.3 for example.

4.46 For the financial year 1990–91 onwards a husband and wife living together shall be taxed separately on their respective incomes[1]. Accordingly, BES relief may be claimed by each of them.

1 FA 1988, s 32.

4.47 Eligible shares in a BES company subscribed for at any time after 18 March 1986 on which relief has been given and not withdrawn for any reason will be exempt from capital gains[1] tax on their subsequent disposal on or after expiry of the five year period[2]. If there is a transfer of the shares between spouses they will still be exempt on a subsequent disposal.[3]

1 CGTA 1979, s 149C(1) and (2).
2 ICTA 1988, s 299.
3 CGTA 1979, s 149C(1) and (6).

4.48 The 1990 budget contains proposals to allow subscribers who subscribed for shares prior to 18 March 1986 to choose to exchange those shares for shares in another company exempt from capital gains tax or within the capital gains tax regime.

4.49 Although beyond the scope of this book, a precedent for a prospectus for a limited liability public unquoted company is set out later in this book[1]. Practitioners should be aware of the changes which occur from time to time in company law and in the law relating to the sale of securities and investments before proceeding to draft a prospectus for a corporate franchisee. However, it is useful for a draft prospectus to be available for the use of franchisees and a responsible franchisor will prepare a standard form in advance which will only require the inclusion of the corporate franchisee's particular details and material from its business plan for completion.

1 Ch 8, precedent 5.

Relief in the event of the failure of a corporate franchise

4.50 Under the provisions of section 37 of the Finance Act 1980 an individual who subscribed[1] on or after 6 April 1980 for ordinary shares in an unquoted[2] United Kingdom resident[3] trading company[4] and who incurs an allowable loss on disposal of those shares, may make a claim for relief from income tax for an amount equal to the loss within two years of the year of assessment in which the disposal occurs[5]. If such a claim is made no relief will be available for capital gains tax purposes. A subscriber has to be resident in the United Kingdom throughout the year of assessment in which the shares were issued[6].

1 ICTA 1988, s 574(3).
2 ICTA 1988, ss 576(4), 349(1), 350(1), 350(3) and 350(4)(a). Companies whose shares are dealt in under Rule 163 of the Stock Exchange or on the Unlisted Securities Market were not regarded as quoted for the purposes of sections 574, 575 and 576(1)–(5) of the ICTA 1988.
3 ICTA 1988, s 576(4)(c).
4 ICTA 1988, s 576(5) and Sch 19, para 7. Unlike the BES the trade is not confined to the UK.
5 ICTA 1988, s 574(1).
6 FA 1981, s 54(1).

4.51 Originally, the relief was only available on 50% of the issued share capital of the company. This restriction was abolished for events occurring after 6 April 1983[1]. The minimum subscription was £500 and the maximum was raised to £20,000[2] in 1982–83. Restrictions on the type of shares eligible for relief were also modified from 6 April 1983[3]. The trade undertaken by the company had to be a new qualifying trade[4]. This means new to the company which could acquire an existing business provided the previous proprietor of the business did not acquire a controlling interest in the company[5].

1 FA 1983, Sch 5, para 22.
2 FA 1981, s 53(1) and (2).
3 FA 1983, Sch 5, para 23.
4 FA 1981, s 56(2)–(4).
5 FA 1981, s 56(6) and (7).

4.52 These provisions meant that if any individual, who has reasonable levels of income, from any source, which is taxable in the United Kingdom, incurs such a loss, then that loss will be set off against that income for income tax purposes. In this way, the Inland Revenue are taking responsibility for a varying degree of risk in the investment in the manner envisaged by section 37. The higher level of income of the individual, the greater the advantage he will derive from these provisions, if any of his appropriate investments fail to prosper. This was a most important allowance and was an incentive to individuals to make more adventurous investment decisions. However, it was clear that the allowances did not apply to investment in non-resident companies. This restricts the scope of the relief available. It is unlikely that a franchisee which has shareholders who wish to take advantage of this relief will be quoted on a recognised stock exchange. Indeed, in any business which is subject to a significant continuing risk factor, the directors must carefully consider the disadvantage which may be suffered by its shareholders, in the event of insolvency, if the company arranges to be floated or raises finance in such a way that it becomes a quoted company.

Interest relief for investment in close companies

4.53 An individual[1] shareholder who has a material interest[2] in a close company who borrows money to:

(1) acquire any part of the ordinary share capital of a close company[3] which satisfies certain conditions[4];

(2) lend to that company for its business purposes[5]; or

(3) replace an existing qualifying loan to that company[6],

will be entitled to relief[7] upon the interest paid by him upon that loan, provided the loan satisfies the conditions of ICTA 1988, ss 360 or 424, as amended by FA 1989, Sch 12, para 12. Generally, the close company must be a trading company (in respect of interest paid before 27 July 1989) or a trading or holding company (in respect of interest paid after 27 July 1989) and the individual shareholder must have a material interest in the company and must not have received a capital repayment from it. The interest paid on the loan will only attract relief to the extent that it represents a reasonable commercial rate[8]. The interest must be interest which is chargeable to tax under Case III of Schedule D[9] or is payable in the United Kingdom to a bank carrying on a bona fide banking business in the United Kingdom or certain other restricted persons or entities[10].

The borrower is no longer required to work in the company[11], unless the company owns a house which he occupies[12].

It is clear that this relief only applies to individuals, not corporations. Provided the company was a close company when the loan was made it need not still be a close company when the interest is paid[13] provided all other conditions for this relief are satisfied.

The relief is unavailable if the claimant or his spouse claims relief under the BES in respect of shares in the company acquired after 13 March 1989[14].

1 ICTA 1988, s 360(1).
2 FA 1989, Sch 12, para 13.
3 ICTA 1988, Sch 1, para 9(1)(a).
4 ICTA 1988, s 424(4)(a).

5   ICTA 1988, s 360(1)(b).
6   ICTA 1988, s 360(1)(c).
7   ICTA 1988, s 353.
8   ICTA 1988, s 353(3)(b).
9   FA 1972, s 74(1)(a).
10 ICTA 1988, s 353(1)(b).
11 FA 1980, s 28(1)(a).
12 ICTA 1988, ss 353 and 360(3).
13 Inland Revenue SP3/78 19 October 1978.
14 FA 1989, s 47.

4.54 It should be noted that shareholders in a close company[1] may suffer tax disadvantages, such as apportionment of some undistributed profits. It is beyond the scope of this book to discuss the increasingly complex tax affairs of close companies. However, the practitioner must be aware of possible future problems for a corporate franchisor or franchisee in this context[2].

1   ICTA 1988, s 417 et seq.
2   See also para 4.97, post.

Corporation tax and advanced corporation tax

4.55 To appreciate certain of the remarks made later in this book, it may be appropriate to discuss briefly the present system of corporate and dividend taxation in the United Kingdom. It will be assumed that any franchisor is a corporation and not an individual.

Corporations resident in the United Kingdom are chargeable to corporation tax on all their profits wherever arising[1]. Such corporations are not chargeable to income tax[2]. However, corporation tax is assessed and calculated in accordance with income tax principles[3]. Chargeable capital gains made by companies are taxed at the capital gains tax rate. In the event that a corporate franchisor receives United Kingdom source royalty payments, from which income tax has been deducted[4], the amount of that deduction will be relieved in full[5]. When a corporation pays a dividend or other qualifying distribution[6] it must, in addition, account for Advanced Corporation Tax ('ACT')[7]. The franchisor must make returns and account for ACT in accordance with the approved timetable[8]. There are a number of technicalities which will not be discussed in this book.

Accounting for ACT will also satisfy a United Kingdom resident individual shareholder's liability to income tax at the basic rate and is therefore classified as a tax credit. Non-United Kingdom resident shareholders may be entitled to a (part) repayment of this tax credit according to the terms of the relevant Double Taxation Agreement (even in the case of an apportionment assessment arising from a shareholding in a UK resident close company).

Example 1

	£
Corporate profit assessable to corporation tax	1,000
Less: Corporation tax at maximum rate of 35 per cent[9]	350
	£ 650

4.56 *Tax problems*

Cash dividend (all post-tax profits)	£650
Add ACT 25/75 × dividend[10])	216
Franked payment	£866

Total amounts for which company is accountable to Inland Revenue

1	ACT	£216
2	Mainstream corporation tax (MCT)	134
		£350

1 ICTA 1988, s 8(1). This takes no account of whether revenue is actually received and remitted to the United Kingdom.
2 Ibid, s 6(2).
3 Ibid, s 9(1).
4 See paras 0.00 et seq, ante.
5 ICTA 1988, s 7(2).
6 Ibid, ss 209–211 and 254.
7 ICTA 1988, Sch 29. Referred to as ACT throughout the rest of this book.
8 ICTA 1988, ss 14(1)–(3) and 238(1) and (5).
9 Corporation tax rates vary according to the amount of the taxable profit from 25 to 35 per cent for the financial year 1990. Profits less than £1,000,000 may not suffer tax at 35 per cent. Profits below £200,000 should suffer tax at 25 per cent. Between £200,000 and £1,000,000 effectively a sliding scale applies.
10 The rate of ACT is now calculated in accordance with the formula 1/100-1 (income tax rate) (ICTA 1988, ss 14(3) and 246(1)–(4)). The rate for 1990/91 is therefore 25/100-25 = 25/75.

4.56 ACT must be paid on submission of the relevant return[1] which is normally fourteen days after the return period. MCT is usually payable nine months after the end of the company's accounting period[2]. Ignoring certain 'carry-back' provisions[3], ACT may only be off-set against a company's corporation tax liability for an accounting period to the extent that ACT is actually paid in respect of a distribution made by it in that accounting period.

For tax planning purposes, a dividend should therefore generally be paid on the last day of a company's accounting period. If interim dividends are to be paid, they should be paid on the first day of a 'new' return period rather than the last day of an 'old' return period.

It should be noted that the Inland Revenue have declared that from 1993 a new system of paying at the same time as tax returns are filed will come into operation.

1 ICTA 1988, Sch 13, para 1(3).
2 ICTA 1988, ss 8(1)–(6) and 10(1).
3 ICTA 1988, s 239(3).

Example 2

4.57 A United Kingdom company prepares its accounts for the year to 31 December 1990—using facts as shown in Example 1, ante:
   (1) If no dividend paid, corporation tax of £350 payable on 1 October 1991.
   (2) If cash dividend is paid £650 paid on 1 October 1990.
      (i) ACT of £216 payable 14 January 1991
      (ii) MCT of £134 payable 1 October 1991

(3) If cash dividend of £650 paid on 31 December 1990
 (i) ACT of £216 payable 14 January 1991
 (ii) MCT of £134 payable 1 October 1991

It will therefore be noted from (2) and (3) above that, by accelerating the dividend payment from 31 December 1990 to 1 October 1990, the shareholder will receive funds earlier but the tax payable (ACT and MCT) dates will not change. However, from an as yet unspecified date in the future (not earlier than 1993 according to the Treasury), a 'pay and file' system will be introduced[1]. There are penalties for failure to make returns within certain time limits and to pay the tax due under the returns[2].

1 F(No 2)A 1987, s 95.
2 F(No 2)A 1987, s 83.

4.58 United Kingdom resident shareholders of a corporate franchisor will be taxed upon all dividend income received by them from that company. Cash dividends received together with the appropriate tax credit are called 'franked payments'[1] or 'franked investment income'[2]. Both United Kingdom resident individual and corporate recipients of such dividends are entitled to a tax credit in respect of the ACT[3]. An individual is entitled to utilise the tax credit against income tax payable by him upon his total income in the year of assessment on which the dividend is paid[4], or may be recovered, if no tax is payable by him. Corporate recipients are entitled to treat the tax credit available to them in various ways, each of which would require detailed analysis depending on the circumstances.

1 ICTA 1988, s 238(1).
2 Ibid, s 238(1).
3 Ibid, s 231(1).
4 Ibid, s 231(3).

Investment risk

4.59 The ratio between risk and reward in any business venture will be materially affected by the impact of taxation. In certain cases, taxation concessions may reduce the gross effect of capital investment or losses but conversely taxation of profits or gains will limit the amount of new capital being generated by a business for further investment or expansion. Ideally, each business will organise its affairs in such a manner that it takes advantage of the tax concessions available to it and to reduce or defer the tax payable by it in respect of its profits or gains. If the proprietors of a business wish it to expand, they must recognise that the rate of that expansion will be greater or lesser depending upon their ability to maximise the amount of funds actually retained by the business from its profits. The following remarks are made upon the assumption that the franchisor is a United Kingdom resident company, not an individual.

Let us consider:

(1) some of the tax problems which may be faced by the United Kingdom resident franchisor if it trades directly overseas;

(2) methods of reducing United Kingdom taxation on those profits;

(3) methods of reducing overseas investment risks;

(4) methods of reducing foreign taxation of overseas profits.

4.60 *Tax problems*

The franchisor trading overseas itself

4.60 First, let us briefly consider the position of the franchisor if it proceeds to conduct its franchise business overseas in a direct relationship with its foreign franchisees. The franchisees will be responsible for paying to the franchisor their franchise fees which will be a mixture of licence fees for the use of any intellectual property rights (patents, copyright, designs, trade marks and know-how) contained in the franchise package and, in certain cases, payments for the supply of services required in the franchise business. The franchisor will be liable to corporation tax on that income but the basis of assessment will be calculated by reference to income tax criteria[1].

That part of the franchise fees which is attributable to the use of intellectual property rights will be taxed as income under Case V of Schedule D[2]. Such income is taxable on an arising basis whether or not it is remitted to the United Kingdom[3]. Certain deductions are allowed[4]. In addition, the income is treated as foreign source income, so that foreign tax credits may be claimed except for those services (not being incidental) which are supplied in the United Kingdom[5]. That part which is attributable to the supply of services will be taxed according to the location of the control of that trade. If that trade is controlled in the United Kingdom, then the profits of the trade will be taxed under Case I of Schedule D[6]. If the trade is controlled overseas, then the profits will be taxed under Case V of Schedule D[7]. In the former case, profits will be taxed on an arising basis also[8].

There are some potential problems for the franchisor. In the absence of any double taxation agreement, unilateral relief will be available to the franchisor in respect of foreign taxes charged on the income arising in the country which has levied the tax[9]. However, this means, for example, that the franchisor must exercise great care when entering into arrangements with residents of one country for the grant of an area franchise which may extend to other countries. Any franchise fees collected by the area franchisee on behalf of the franchisor from sub-franchisees who are resident outside the country of residence of the area franchisee will not be eligible for unilateral relief. This restriction does not apply to the Isle of Man or any of the Channel Islands[10].

1 ICTA 1988, s 9 and see para 4.55, ante.
2 Ibid, s 18(3).
3 Ibid, s 65(1).
4 Ibid, s 65(1)(a)–(b).
5 Inland Revenue concession B.8 and in the absence of any double taxation agreement; ICTA 1988, s 790.
6 ICTA 1988, s 18(3). *Ogilvie v Kitton (Surveyor of Taxes)* (1908) 5 TC 338; *Spiers v Mackinnon* (1929) 14 TC 386.
7 ICTA 1988, s 18(3) (as amended). *Colquhoun v Brooks* (1889) 14 App Cas 493, 2 TC 490, HL; *Ferguson v Donovan* [1929] IR 489; *Newstead (Inspector of Taxes) v Frost* [1980] 1 All ER 363, [1980] STC 123, HL.
8 ICTA 1988, s 8(1).
9 Ibid, s 790(4).
10 Ibid, s 790(5)(a).

4.61 Unilateral relief only applies to tax which is charged on income and corresponds to United Kingdom income or corporation tax[1]. This includes any state, provincial or local income tax. However, any other form of tax will not be eligible for unilateral relief.

If the services supplied by the franchisor are substantially supplied in the United Kingdom, then any income arising from that supply will not be treated as foreign-source income[2] and no tax credit will be available for any foreign tax charged on that income.

Inland Revenue concession B.8 is as follows:

> 'Payments made by a person resident in an overseas country to a person carrying on a trade in the United Kingdom as consideration for the use of, or for the privilege of using, in the overseas country any copyright, patent, design, secret process or formula, trade-mark or other like property may in law be payments the source of which is in the United Kingdom, but nevertheless treated for the purpose of credit (whether under double-taxation agreements or by way of unilateral relief) as income arising outside the United Kingdom except to the extent that they represent consideration for services (other than merely incidental services) rendered in this country by the recipient to the payer.'

In all these cases, the franchisor will be liable to United Kingdom corporation tax on the full amount of the income that arises without any deduction for foreign tax being allowed. Accordingly, it will be taxed twice on the full amount of that income[3] unless the franchisor is permitted to treat the foreign tax payments as a trading expense[4].

Income tax in the United Kingdom has habitually been charged upon the various types of income classified under the case system. Corporation tax is founded on the same principles. Accordingly where a company makes profits in its overseas branch from its trade, makes losses in that trade in the United Kingdom but receives other non-trading income here, then the tax paid in the foreign jurisdiction on its trading profits cannot be taken into account when calculating the tax payable on its domestic non-trading income[5].

1 ICTA 1988, s 790(12).
2 Inland Revenue concession B.8.
3 ICTA 1988, ss 338 and 339.
4 Ibid, s 811.
5 *George Wimpey International Ltd v Rolfe (Inspector of Taxes)* [1989] STC 609.

4.62 If the franchisor decides to finance its overseas franchise business or invests in company-owned stores, from borrowings, then it must take care how the interest payable upon those borrowings is paid. The franchisor will not be permitted to treat that interest as a trading expense or a charge on income for corporation tax purposes unless the stipulations of ICTA ss 337–340 are observed.

4.63 In summary, if the franchisor borrows funds to finance its overseas franchise business, it must:

(1) pay short interest; or
(2) borrow from a United Kingdom bank[1]; or
(3) pay annual interest; and[2]
(4) deduct tax at source[3]; or
(5) be obliged to pay and actually pay the interest outside the United Kingdom[4];

and either

(6) incur the interest wholly or mainly for the purposes of the trade of the company outside the United Kingdom[5]; or
(7) pay in a foreign currency[6]; or
(8) pay it out of income under Case IV or V of Schedule D[7].

In addition any interest paid to a person not resident in the United Kingdom must be at a reasonable commercial rate, if it is to be deducted from profits or gains

4.64 *Tax problems*

charged to tax under Case I of Schedule D[8]. If the franchisor desires to commence and maintain an overseas franchise business, especially if it decides to open and operate company-owned stores overseas, it is unlikely to wish to arrange such short term loans to enable it to undertake the business that short as opposed to annual interest is payable by it. If the franchisor borrows from overseas sources to finance its overseas franchise business, it is unlikely that the lender will permit deductions of tax from the interest payments due to it. Most international loan documents impose obligations upon the borrower to pay interest gross, irrespective of any regulations to the contrary in the country where the borrower is resident. Therefore, the franchisor must ensure that the interest is payable and is actually paid overseas for overseas trade purposes or in foreign currency, to permit it to pay interest gross without suffering tax penalties in the United Kingdom. Alternatively, the interest may be paid gross out of income subject to Case V of Schedule D because fees payable by overseas franchisees of the franchisor in respect of the use of intellectual property or arising from a trade controlled overseas are assessed under Case V of Schedule D, the franchisor may have sufficient income of this class available to discharge its interest obligations. In addition, a means of generating this type of income is to arrange a loan to the United Kingdom franchisor by a United Kingdom bank. That loan will be deposited by the franchisor with a foreign bank, which is able to pay interest to a foreign depositor without any withholding tax. Interest arising from overseas deposits income are subject to Case V of Schedule D[9]. This arrangement is only feasible commercially, if the interest rates of the United Kingdom bank and the foreign bank are similar, so that the franchisor suffers a small margin between the loan rate and the deposit rate. Exchange risk exposure should be avoided. In the event that the franchisor is, itself, a 75 per cent or more subsidiary of a non-resident and borrows from its parent or from another source with which the parent is connected, any interest payable to either of those lenders will be treated as a distribution by the franchisor[10] unless overriding provisions of any double taxation agreement apply[11].

1 ICTA 1988, s 338(3). See also sections 337(3), 349(2) and (3)(a)(b) and 350(1), (3) and (4).
2 Ibid, s 338(3)(a).
3 Ibid, ss 338(3)(b), 349(2), (3)(a)–(b) and 350(1), (3) and (4).
4 Ibid, s 340(1)(a) and (b).
5 Ibid, s 340(1)(c)(i).
6 Ibid, s 340(1)(c)(ii).
7 Ibid, s 338(4)(a).
8 Ibid, s 74(n).
9 Ibid, s 18(3).
10 Ibid, s 209.
11 For example Article 11(7) of the US/UK Convention 1975; Article 11 of the Double Taxation Relief (Taxes on Income) (Switzerland) Order 1978.

4.64 Where a United Kingdom franchisor is conducting a trade or business overseas through a branch or agency, and transfers the trade together with all the assets of that trade to a company not resident in the United Kingdom[1] the franchisor will be entitled to a form of roll-over relief in respect of any chargeable gains arising from the transfer[2] provided:

(1) The trade is transferred wholly or partly in exchange for shares or for shares and loan stock in the transferee company[3]; and

(2) the transferor then owns a total of not less than 25 per cent of the ordinary share capital of the transferee company[4].

Investment risk 4.66

This relief is a deferral only of capital gains tax[5]. The procedure does not apply if there are net capital losses. The deferred gain may become payable if the transferee company disposes of the relevant assets within 6 years of the transfer.

1   ICTA 1970, s 268A(1)(a) as substituted by FA 1977, s 42.
2   Ibid, s 268A(2) as substituted by FA 1977, s 42 and amended by CGTA 1979, s 157(2), Sch 7, para 8(a) (as amended by ICTA 1988, Sch 29).
3   Ibid, s 268A(1)(g) as substituted by FA 1977, s 42.
4   Ibid, s 268A(1)(c) as substituted by FA 1977, s 42.
5   ICTA 1970, s 268A(4) as substituted by FA 1977, s 42.

Methods of reducing tax on overseas profits

4.65 Let us now consider the reduction or deferral of taxation on the future overseas profits of the franchisor. Upon the assumption that the franchisee has traded successfully in the United Kingdom, it will not wish to pay corporation tax in the United Kingdom on its future overseas profits. Is it possible to achieve the creation of a profitable overseas business without immediate liability to United Kingdom tax? If the franchisor is to succeed in this aim, the profits arising from that overseas business must not be deemed to be received by it as they arise[1] and must, therefore, be received by another entity outside the scope of United Kingdom tax. In addition, the profits of that other entity must not be apportioned or attributed to the franchisor. The franchisor will, therefore, wish to cause the incorporation of a company or series of companies as its subsidiaries[2] or which are associated with it, located[3] outside the United Kingdom for the purpose of minimising the total effect of foreign taxes, and withholding taxes on royalty income and dividends in particular, and to provide an effective haven for the accumulation of profits in a low tax jurisdiction which will not suffer United Kingdom corporation tax until they are remitted to the United Kingdom for the benefit and by the choice of the franchisor. Upon the abolition of exchange controls[4] there was no obligation upon a United Kingdom corporation to remit the profits or part of the profits of its overseas subsidiaries to the United Kingdom, nor was that corporation taxed upon those profits, or a proportion of them, as they arose[5]. However, this means of tax deferral or even avoidance was recognised by the Inland Revenue and appropriate steps taken to minimise its scope[6]. In the light of those steps, the remarks made later in this book[7] concerning avoidance arrangements must be considered carefully. There is an informal Inland Revenue clearance procedure.

1   The Exchange Control (General Exemption) Order 1979 (SI 1979 No 1660) which replaced various piecemeal exemptions. Abolition effective from 24 October 1979. This abolition removed many effective fiscal controls over the profits of overseas subsidiaries of UK companies.
2   ICTA 1988, ss 416, 838 and 840.
3   See paras 4.99 et seq, post.
4   See note 1, ante.
5   This position may be contrasted with para 861 of the Internal Revenue Code of the United States of America. See post.
6   ICTA 1988, s 747, and see Inland Revenue press releases 16 July 1984 and 25 July 1985.
7   See paras 4.99 et seq, post.

4.66 When considering possible methods by which the franchisor may accelerate its rate of growth overseas, by the reduction or deferral of United Kingdom taxation on its overseas profits, it is necessary to acknowledge the following distinct questions:
   (1) Whether any arrangements, by which any overseas entity, which is a subsidiary

4.67 *Tax problems*

of, or associated with the franchisor is enabled to undertake the franchise business overseas, will infringe any of the anti-avoidance legislation which exists.

(2) Whether any of the usual intellectual property assets of a franchise business has an international value even if that business has been conducted solely in the United Kingdom[1].

(3) If the franchisor has unsuccessfully attempted to avoid tax or accepts that it has transferred property to an associated entity, how will that deemed or actual transfer be taxed?

(4) Whether the profits or gains of that entity will be attributed to the franchisor and taxed in its hands in the United Kingdom[2] in any circumstances.

(5) Whether the subsequent conduct of the franchisor and its relationship with that entity will cause that entity, itself, to be treated as a resident of the United Kingdom for tax purposes[3].

1 See paras 4.77 et seq, post.
2 See paras 4.87 et seq, post.
3 See paras 4.98 et seq, post.

Anti-avoidance

4.67 We must consider the application of anti-avoidance measures by the Inland Revenue and the attitude of the courts to avoidance arrangements.

It should be understood by anyone interested in reducing or deferring United Kingdom taxation that legislative changes introduced at the request of the Inland Revenue may nullify any advantages previously gained from a planned group structure or other arrangements. In addition, decisions in the House of Lords[1] indicate that the courts have developed a different approach to tax avoidance arrangements, in response to the increasing sophistication of tax planners. In the first two of those cases[2] Lord Wilberforce said:

> 'While the techniques of tax avoidance progress and are technically improved, the courts are not obliged to stand still. Such immobility must result either in loss of tax, to the prejudice of other taxpayers or to Parliamentary congestion or (most likely) to both.'

Until those cases, it appeared that the courts were restricted to reviewing the documents which formed part of any arrangement and would not investigate its substance[3]. This is not to say that 'sham' transactions, which were not intended to be what they appeared, were protected merely by their apparent structure or description[4]. However, there may be a fine line between 'sham' transactions and arrangements which may appear artificial. The approach adopted by the House of Lords in the *Ramsey* and *Rawling* cases was to prevent the intended effect of the transactions, the subject of the cases, because their only motive was to avoid tax and they did not have any commercial reality. Lord Wilberforce stated the principles which governed this new approach in those cases as follows:

(1) the only purpose of the transaction was to avoid tax;

(2) the series of transactions was planned and arranged in advance and there was no intention of halting the intended process at any stage; and

(3) the taxpayer was not expected to use his own funds to finance each stage of the series of transactions.

Those principles may not appear to diverge from previous approaches in tax cases but Lord Wilberforce went on as follows:

'To force the courts to adopt in relation to closely integrated situations a step by step dissecting approach which the parties themselves may have negated would be a denial rather than an affirmation of the true judicial process. In each case the facts must be established and a legal analysis made, legislation cannot be required or even be desirable to enable the courts to arrive at a conclusion which corresponds to the parties' own intentions.'

It appears from this statement that the courts may now review the intentions of the parties to the transaction as a whole and will not restrict themselves to considering those intentions separately at each stage of the arrangements. It is arguable that this approach is a review of the substance rather than the form of an arrangement. This view may be reinforced by the favourable references made by Lord Wilberforce to United States of America practice in this field.

In another case[5], Lord Wilberforce again considered a tax avoidance scheme. That case involved interpretation of sections 703 and 704 of ICTA 1988 and the nature of the transactions comprising and arising from the scheme in the light of that interpretation. At each level[6], the courts placed a strict and perhaps narrow construction on the relevant words of those sections and Lord Wilberforce in his judgment appeared to consider that, because the final step in the arrangements was not certain at the time the remainder of the scheme was effected and only occurred approximately one year later[7], there was insufficient causal connection between each of those steps for the arrangements to be a 'transaction' which was caught by paragraph (c) of section 704 of ICTA 1988. It is arguable that the decision in the *Garvin* case reaffirmed the principle that the intention of tax legislation may only be established by examination of the words used[8]. However, on his way to reaching a decision favourable to the tax payer, Lord Wilberforce reviewed the entire sequence of steps which were alleged to form part of the transaction. It is possible to contrast the preconceived circular arrangements in the *Ramsey* and *Rawling* cases with the arrangements in the *Garvin* case in which one step was not in place at the time that the other steps were completed and which, apparently, was not certain to be completed at any time. In the *Garvin* case, it would be difficult to perceive the commercial reality behind many of the earlier steps, indeed, it is arguable that each would have been an act of folly if the arrangements had been implemented for mere commercial reason. It may be that the break in the sequence of steps was more important in the particular circumstances of that case, than any test of commercial reality.

Guidance note TR 588 was issued by the Institute of Chartered Accountants and the text of a letter of 8 July 1985 was issued by the Institute following a meeting between the Inland Revenue and representatives of the Institute and the Law Society and the reply of the Board of the Inland Revenue dated 20 September 1985.

In more recent related cases, (*Shepherd (Inspector of Taxes)* v *Lyntress Ltd*; *News International plc v Shepherd* [1989] STC 617 the principles in *Ramsay* and *Dawson* were not followed, mainly, it seems, because shares in companies quoted on The Stock Exchange can be sold instantly and, therefore, the speed of a transaction or series of transactions does not necessarily indicate a pre-ordained avoidance scheme. The Revenue failed to establish such a scheme in the case of *Baylis v Gregory* [1986] STC 22 although the arrangements made by the taxpayers were very similar to those in the *Dawson* case. In both cases, shares in an Isle of Man holding company had been exchanged for shares in the United Kingdom resident company intended to be sold. In the *Gregory* case, the original sale fell through

4.68 *Tax problems*

and two years passed before another purchaser was found. This was held by the House of Lords to break the chain. However, the anti-avoidance principles laid down in the *Ramsey* case were confirmed in two related cases before Hoffman J (*Moodie v IRC* and *Sotnick v IRC* (1990) Times, 9 May), when the judge stated that the decision favourable to the taxpayer of the House of Lords in *IRC v Plummer* [1980] AC 896 which concerned the same scheme as the *Moodie* and *Sotnick* cases had been struck down by the *Ramsey* case.

1   *W T Ramsay Ltd v IRC; Eilbeck (Inspector of Taxes) v Rawling* [1982] AC 300, [1981] STC 174, HL and *Furniss v Dawson* [1984] AC 474, [1984] STC 153, HL.
2   Which were decided together and concerned capital gains tax avoidance.
3   *IRC v Duke of Westminster* [1936] AC 1, 19 TC 490, HL.
4   *Newstead (Inspector of Taxes) v Frost* [1978] 2 All ER 241, [1978] STC 239. For a definition of a 'sham' see *Snook v London and West Riding Investments Ltd* [1967] 2 QB 786 at 802.
5   *IRC v Garvin* [1981] 1 WLR 793, [1981] STC 344, HL.
6   Templeman J dissenting in the Court of Appeal.
7   The payment of an abnormal dividend.
8   *Russell v Scott* [1948] AC 422, 30 TC 375, HL.

Transfer of a business

4.68 Up to 14 March 1988, a company could not transfer overseas a trade or business or part of it from the United Kingdom without being granted consent to do so by the Treasury. The original regulations were introduced in 1951 but were deemed inappropriate in the late 1980s[1]. Accordingly, it is now lawful to transfer a trade or business (or part of it) overseas but there may be significant taxation consequences. Therefore the transfer to a new overseas company of an actual trade or business would probably not be sensible[2] because it may accelerate rather than defer any tax charge.

1   See ICTA 1970 s 482 for position pre 15 March 1988.
2   But see paras 4.87 et seq, post.

4.69 The tax consequences of such a transfer would depend upon individual circumstances but could include the following:

(1) capital gains tax upon the actual or deemed value of the assets involved (see paras 4.87 et seq, post);

(2) balancing charges on the transfer of the trade which is the subject of capital allowances[1];

(3) acceleration of or an increase in corporation tax because of cessation of trade;

1   ICTA 1988, s 343 (and see ICAEW Technical Release TR500).

4.70 If the United Kingdom franchisor incorporates a company or companies[1] overseas and transfers[2] to them any property[3] then section 770 of ICTA 1988 may apply to that transfer, if the nature of the transaction is such that the proceeds are taxable as income and both companies are under common control. If that is the case and that property is so transferred at an undervalue then section 770(1) may apply.

Section 773 is widely drawn: subsection (4) states:

'(4) The preceding provisions of this section shall, with the necessary adaptations, have effect in relation to lettings and hirings of property, grants

Investment risk 4.72

and transfers of rights, interests or licences and the giving of business facilities of whatever kind as they have effect in relation to sales, and the references in the said preceding provisions to sales, sellers, buyers and prices shall be deemed to be extended accordingly.'

Accordingly, in cases where section 770 applies, a transfer of the assets or right of the franchisor to an overseas company may be subject to treatment by the Inland Revenue, as if that transfer had been at arm's length. The franchisor may, therefore, be assessed on any additional profits arising from a deemed transfer at an arm's length price. The powers of investigation of the Inland Revenue in relation to suspected infringements of section 770 are set out in section 772.

The transferor only is charged tax on the basis of the revised price. The transferee, if it is a foreign entity, is not able to off-set the revised price against its own tax liabilities (if any). This could cause difficulties if the transferee is a controlled foreign corporation which is a subsidiary of the transferor. The profits of that CFC may be apportioned to its parent[4]. Thus the transferor could be taxed twice on the same disposal, when the CFC subsidiary disposes of the asset transferred to it. At present, this problem is only covered by discretion on the part of the Inland Revenue.

1   ICTA 1988, ss 773(2) and 840.
2   Ibid, s 773(4).
3   Ibid, s 770(1) and (2)(a).
4   FA 1984, s 82 et seq.

4.71 Sections 19, 20(1)(c) or (d) and 25(1) of Capital Gains Taxes Act 1979[1] may apply to any transfer of the assets of the franchisee, depending on the manner in which each asset is treated for tax purposes[2]. The Capital Gains Taxes Act 1979 (CGTA 1979)[3] was stated to be a consolidating statute incorporating (amongst others) the provisions of section 22(3) of FA 1965. In general, property which is created by a person disposing of it, such as patents, designs, copyrights and, even, goodwill are deemed to be chargeable assets[4].

1   Capital Gains Taxes Act 1979, s 26 (as amended by ICTA 1988, Sch 29) may apply in certain circumstances (where there is an actual rather than a deemed disposal) but not where there is a transfer between members of a group of companies because of the operation of ICTA 1988.
2   See paras 4.72 et seq, post. These provisions apply only to the disposal of an asset which is subject to capital gains tax and not income tax treatment. However, the manner of disposal or deemed disposal may make the disposal subject to these provisions rather than ICTA 1988, ss 770 and 773.
3   Indexation of capital gains is permitted from March 1982 where expenditure was incurred before that month and from the time of acquisition where the asset was acquired after 5 April 1985. The index for February 1990 is 120.2 (January 1987 = 100).
4   CGTA 1979, s 19(1).

4.72 If the provisos of sections 19, 20(1)(c) and or 25 do so apply, then any surrender of rights in or over an asset by the franchisor will be deemed to be a disposal and subject to valuation by the Inland Revenue on an arm's length basis. Part of CGTA 1979, s 19 is as follows:

'(1) All forms of property shall be assets for the purposes of this Act, whether situated in the United Kingdom or not, including:
   (a) options, debts and incorporeal property generally, and
   (c) any form of property created by the person disposing of it, or otherwise coming to be owned without being acquired'.

4.73 *Tax problems*

(2) For the purposes of this Act:
(a) references to a disposal of an asset include, except where the context otherwise requires, references to a part disposal of an asset, and
(b) there is a part disposal of an asset where an interest or right in or over the asset is created by the disposal, as well as where it subsists before the disposal, and generally, there is a part disposal of an asset where, on a person making a disposal, any description of property derived from the asset remains undisposed of.'

4.73 Part of CGTA 1979, s 20 is as follows:

'(c) Capital sums received in return for forfeiture or surrender of rights, or for refraining from exercising rights, and
(d) Capital sums received as consideration for use or exploitation of assets.'

4.74 Part of CGTA 1979, s 25 is as follows:

'(1) Without prejudice to the generality of the provisions of this Act as to the transactions which are disposals of assets, any transaction which under the following sub-sections is to be treated as a disposal of an asset shall be so treated (with a corresponding acquisition of an interest in the asset) notwithstanding that there is no consideration and so far as, on the assumption that the parties to the transaction were at arm's length, the party making the disposal could have obtained consideration, or additional consideration, for the disposal the transaction shall be treated as not being at arm's length and the consideration so obtainable, or the additional consideration so obtainable added to the consideration actually passing, shall be treated as the market value of what is acquired . . .
(5) If an asset is subject to any description of right or restriction the extinction or abrogation, in whole or in part, of the right or restriction by the person entitled to enforce it shall be a disposal by him of the right or restriction.'

4.75 If the franchisor is trading and franchising in the United Kingdom, it is clear that it has a trade or business in the United Kingdom, but does it have any trade or business or any assets or rights elsewhere? If it is not to be caught by anti-avoidance measures, it must ensure that any foreign business, if undertaken by the overseas company which is intended to receive the profits of that business[1], does not arise from the transfer[2] or surrender[3] of any material business, assets or rights to that company by the franchisor (see paras 4.87 et seq, post if an actual transfer must take place).

1 But see ss 747–753, 754(1)–(9), 755, 756 and Sch 29 of ICTA 1988 and paras 0.00 et seq, post.
2 ICTA 1988, s 770(1) and (2)(a).
3 CGTA 1979, ss 19, 20(1)(c) or (d) and 25.

4.76 What comprises the business, rights or assets of a franchisor franchising in the United Kingdom? In general they will consist of any registered patents, copyright, registered or unregistered trade marks, any know-how used in the business and any goodwill arising from that use. Is that business and those rights or assets exclusively attributable to the United Kingdom or do they have some international dimension which would render them subject to current anti-avoidance measures? They may form part of the trade or business of the franchisor in which case unfortunate tax consequences may arise[1] or they may merely be 'property' owned by the franchisor in which case only section 770 of ICTA 1988 or sections 19, or 20(1)(c) or (d), or 25 of CGTA 1979 will be relevant at this stage.

1 See paras 4.69 et seq, ante.

Intellectual property assets

4.77 Let us consider the nature of each type of right or asset of the franchise business. When reading the following sections, it may be useful to remember that there are several types of asset used in a franchise business which include:

(1) those assets which are personal to the franchisor but are strictly local in nature (such as the local goodwill generated by company owned stores and not supported by any advertising or promotion outside the locality or a local trade mark registered with a territorial restriction);

(2) those assets which are local or national, but which may have attendant rights in certain circumstances which may enable the franchisor to commence its business overseas (for example, patents or trade marks which are the subject of the provisions of international conventions and whose priority periods have not expired);

(3) those assets which are clearly international by virtue of the protection afforded to them by international agreement (such as copyright); and

(4) those assets which are the exclusive and secret property of the franchisor and which are crucial to the franchise business wherever it is conducted (for example any secret recipe or process not protected by a patent).

4.78 *Patents.* Most franchise businesses do not involve patents[1]. Patents may be secured in the patent offices of each country in the world which has some form of inventor protection law. In general, a patent in one country does not confer protection in another. A patent is, therefore, an asset which is of value only within the boundaries of the country in which it is granted. In the chapter of ICTA 1988 dealing with the taxation of receipts from the exploitation or disposal of patents, 'patent rights' are defined as 'the right to do or authorise the doing of anything which would, but for that right, be an infringement of a patent'[2]. At first sight, therefore, it would not appear that a United Kingdom patent creates an asset which is transferred or a right which is surrendered, if the patentable item or process is patented outside the United Kingdom by a person other than the proprietor of the United Kingdom patent. However, the application for a patent in one country may confer upon the proprietor of that patent certain rights in other countries[3]. If the franchisor acquires sole rights to apply for the grant of a patent in the member countries of the European Patent Office, or to apply for a patent search under the provisions of the Patent Co-operation Treaty, because of its own British patent, then failure to proceed with patent applications in those member countries whilst its overseas subsidiary or another related party proceeds to register a similar patent in those countries on a piecemeal basis, may cause the Inland Revenue to allege that such failure is a deliberate surrender of rights[4]. However, it should be stressed that mere failure to take advantage of the various priority rights to apply for a patent overseas will not be a surrender of rights, unless that failure is part of an arrangement between parties to pass the benefit of the patentable process out of the scope of United Kingdom taxation. Failure to apply for a patent followed by an application by a 'pirate' may not be a surrender of rights. If there is any arrangement between the franchisor and its overseas subsidiary or other related party permitting the overseas subsidiary or the related party to apply for any patents

4.79 *Tax problems*

overseas, then a transfer of rights may occur. For sales between connected persons where the purchaser is claiming capital allowances there are restrictions preventing the minimisation of balancing charges[5].

1 See paras 3.106 et seq, ante.
2 ICTA 1988, s 533(1).
3 See paras 3.125 et seq, ante.
4 See paras 3.125 et seq, ante.
5 Capital Allowances Act 1990.

4.79 *Design.* The United Kingdom has design registration only, but subject to this, the above paragraph, *mutatis mutandae* applies to designs and utility models.

4.80 *Copyright.* In many businesses which directly serve the consumer, the creation and protection of a 'house style' or 'get up' depends more on copyright than on trade marks. Copyright in this context, includes all original written material, designs, as well as design right. International copyright protection is afforded by the provisions of the Copyright Designs and Patents Act 1988 and the terms of the Berne Convention and the Universal Copyright Convention[1]. If the owner of copyright in the designs of a franchise business house style and the literary work contained in the Operations Manual of that business in the United Kingdom, allows a third party to reproduce those designs and work outside the United Kingdom, then some form of transfer or surrender of rights must have occurred, unless such reproduction is an act of piracy. The franchisor, must, therefore, arrange that its overseas subsidiary makes new designs and writes a fresh Operations Manual that are sufficiently different not to infringe the existing copyright of the franchisor. This is not as difficult as may first appear, since the protection afforded by copyright is generally restricted to the form of the work, not the idea[2]. However, if the franchisor, as is usual, protects the contents of its Operations Manual by non-disclosure and non-competing use covenants on the part of the franchisee and its directors, officers, and employees, the use by the overseas company of the ideas contained in the Operations Manual may be open to challenge[3]. One potential copyright problem, the incorporation of an overseas company with a name similar to that used by the franchisor in the franchise business, appears to have been removed by the decision in the *Exxon* case, if the name consists of one word only[4]. It was noted in that case that a single word did not qualify as an 'original literary work' within the then Copyright Act 1956.

1 See paras 3.132 et seq, ante.
2 *Gleeson and Gleeson Shirt Co Ltd v H R Denne Ltd* [1975] RPC 471, CA. But see para 4.83, post.
3 See para 4.83, post.
4 *Exxon Corpn v Exxon Insurance Consultants International Ltd* [1982] Ch 119, [1982] RPC 69, CA.

4.81 *Trade marks.* In most franchise businesses, the major apparent rights or assets are the trade name or trade mark or service mark under which the franchise operates. The trade marks and service marks used in a franchise business may be of two types. Unregistered marks generally may only be of value in the country in which they are used, although they will form part of the goodwill of the franchise business. The user of such marks may acquire no exclusive right to use them elsewhere[1]. Registration of a mark in one country does not provide protection in another, but like patents, the registration of a mark in one country may confer upon the proprietor of that registered mark certain rights in other countries[2]. In particular, if the franchisor fails to take advantage of the priority period available to it under the Paris Convention, and its overseas subsidiary or another related party registers the mark in a member country of the Convention, has some form of surrender of rights occurred? This question is complicated by the past absence of service marks in the United Kingdom[3]. If only trade marks relating to goods are registered by the franchisor in the United Kingdom, can any surrender of rights occur if the overseas company only registers a service mark overseas in respect of the franchise business and not its products? This problem persists since the introduction of service mark registrations, as service marks do not enjoy priority under Article 4 of the Paris Convention. The Vienna Trademark Registration Treaty[4] and any Community Trade Mark may complicate this matter, in a similar manner to the situation with regard to patents mentioned earlier[5]. The effect of sections 17(2) and 11 of the Trade Marks Act 1938 (as amended) should be considered carefully in this regard.

1 See paras 3.21 et seq, ante.
2 See paras 3.133 et seq, ante.
3 If an overseas subsidiary of a United Kingdom restaurant business registered in overseas countries the Trade Name and logo in Class 42, Miscellaneous Services (Restaurants), but did not register any goods under Classes 29 and 30 respectively which are registered in the United Kingdom can any surrender of rights have occurred in favour of the overseas subsidiary? See paras 3.20 et seq, ante. However, as service marks are now registered in the UK this loophole may be closed.
4 1973.
5 See para 4.76, ante.

4.82 A franchisor, which has registered a trade mark in the United Kingdom, must exercise care in the choice of the country where he proposes to incorporate the overseas company. For example, the Isle of Man is part of the United Kingdom for trade mark purposes and only the registered proprietor of a United Kingdom trade mark may register a trade mark in Jersey[1] or Guernsey[2]. Similar restrictions apply in former British territory tax havens[3]. Other former British territories allow special rights to register to a proprietor of a United Kingdom registered trade mark[4]. Even if the new overseas company does not register a trade mark in say Jersey or Guernsey, the existence of the restrictions upon registration to the effect that only the franchisor may register the trade mark there (if it has already registered a United Kingdom trade mark) may justify an allegation by the Inland Revenue that the franchisor is transferring or surrendering its rights in some manner. Because the trade mark registration of the franchisor in the United Kingdom will already extend to the Isle of Man, the incorporation of a subsidiary or associated company on the island, which uses the same trade mark, even if that use is limited to grant of licences to foreign franchisees and does not extend to any actual use of the trade mark in the eyes of the general public in the island, must involve the transfer or surrender of rights by the franchisor. Therefore, the Isle of Man should not be used in this context. Any United Kingdom franchisor which proposes to incorporate an overseas company in a tax haven to own and license overseas trade mark rights must investigate with care the relationship between the haven trade mark registry and the United Kingdom registry. This also applies to foreign franchisors who have already registered their trade marks at the United Kingdom registry and are trading through a permanent establishment in the United Kingdom.

1 Trade Marks (Jersey) Law 1958.

4.83 *Tax problems*

2 Patents Designs and Trade Marks Law 4/11/1922 (as amended).
3 Eg Gibraltar.
4 Eg Barbados, Bermuda, Cayman Islands.

4.83 *Know-how.* The nature of know-how in the franchise business is discussed elsewhere[1]. In our present context, we must consider the extent to which the know-how of a franchise business is the exclusive asset of the franchisor. Much of the know-how in franchising is merely the codification of sound and successful general business principles. For example, the franchisee will be taught how to implement and maintain proper financial controls for the mutual benefit of himself and his franchisor. Standard methods of obtaining and maintaining custom and customer loyalty will be set down by the franchisor. In these business areas, there will be little real difference between the know-how supplied by franchisors in several different businesses, or the know-how acquired through experience and advice by a successful independent small businessman[2]. This type of general know-how cannot be an exclusive asset of the franchisor although the manner in which it is expressed in the operations manual may be the copyright of the franchisor[3]. However, if the franchisor devises and allows its franchisees to use specialist know-how which relates to any produce, process or services, and which forms part of the franchise business, that type of know-how may be an exclusive asset of the franchisor and an essential ingredient in the goodwill, which is being generated by the franchise business. It may not be possible for a franchisee to conduct his own business without that specialised know-how. Is that asset of the franchisor only of value within the boundaries of the United Kingdom? Does the revelation of the contents of that know-how to the overseas company for use by that company constitute the transfer or surrender of a business' asset, right or property or a transfer of an asset or surrender of rights?

1 See paras 3.118 et seq, ante.
2 *Stevenson Jordan and Harrison Ltd v MacDonald and Evans* (1951) 68 RPC 190.
3 See paras 3.78 et seq, ante.

4.84 Rights comprising know-how are the right to use that knowledge in the relevant business, and the right to protect and keep secret all specialist aspects of that knowledge and, possibly, the right to prevent others using that know-how, where it has been obtained by those others, otherwise than as a result of their own separate research and development or as a result of the know-how becoming common knowledge in some manner[1]. Any license granting the licensee the right to use know-how in his business will contain restrictions on the uses to which the know-how may be put and on disclosures of it. It should be remembered that the definition of know-how contained in ICTA 1988, s 533(7) only applies to the provisions of that section. If that definition is restricted and, possibly, not applicable to business format franchising, it should not be taken as a definition of know-how in the context of tax avoidance.

It is possible that the overseas company will develop its own know-how. This will be know-how which is particularly suited to the circumstances in each overseas country where the franchise business is conducted. In addition, exposure of the processes comprising the business to new problems, may cause the invention and development of fresh know-how, which is relevant to the business operated by the franchisor in the United Kingdom. It may be advantageous if the overseas company arranges for the franchisor to receive a direct or indirect licence to use that know-how in the United Kingdom[2]. If any consideration is to pass between the franchisor and the overseas company, it is essential that any original actual transfer or licence of know-how between the franchisor and its overseas subsidiary does not contain a 'feedback' clause[3], otherwise the franchisor will have the automatic free right to use the new know-how. Failure to include such a 'grant back' clause may be defended, if necessary, upon the grounds that it may be similar to 'black' clauses in agreements relating to the use of patents as set out in the Group Exemption[4] and that a non-exclusive reciprocal agreement for the disclosure and use of improvements by both parties and their respective franchisees will be commercially unacceptable in the circumstances. Any actual transfer of know-how between the franchisor and the overseas company should include a covenant on the part of the franchisor to disclose to and permit the overseas company to use and sub-license the right to use any improvements and developments in the franchise business at no additional charge. However, in the event that a significant improvement in any process or other matter involved in the franchise business is made by the franchisor, any disclosure of the same to the overseas company may be subject to the anti-avoidance measures mentioned earlier[5].

1 Breach of confidence action—*Seager v Copydex Ltd* [1967] 2 All ER 415, [1967] RPC 349, CA, and *Coco v A N Clarke (Engineers) Ltd* [1969] RPC 41. See paras 3.118 et seq, ante.
2 See para 4.129, post.
3 See Ch 8, precedent 1, clause 7.43.
4 Reg 2349/84.
5 See paras 4.67 et seq, ante.

4.85 *Goodwill.* The goodwill of a franchise business arises from the recognition by the public of the name of the business and the recurring nature of their custom or their personal recommendation of the business to other potential customers. Goodwill is an intangible asset which is directly related to the quality of produce or service provided by the business and the extent of exposure of the name of the business. If the business is local, is it possible for the asset of goodwill to have a more than local application? Goodwill has been described as:

> 'Goodwill regarded as property has no meaning except in connection with some trade, business or calling. In that connection I understand the word to include whatever adds value to a business by reason of situation, name and reputation, connection, introduction to old customers, and agreed absence from competition, or any of these things, and there may be others which do not occur to me. In this wide sense, goodwill is inseparable from the business to which it adds value, and, in my opinion, exists where the business is carried on. Such business may be carried on in one place or country or in several, and if in several there may be several businesses, each having a goodwill of its own[1].'

The question of the location of goodwill has already been discussed[2].

Perhaps the lesson of all three cases, for a franchisor which wishes to overcome any allegation that it transferred or surrendered any goodwill to the overseas company is as follows:

(1) Do not open any representative office overseas.

(2) Do not endeavour to create overseas custom for the business in the United Kingdom by making special arrangements with foreign tour operators or travel agents.

(3) Do not advertise in publications distributed abroad or in 'in-flight' magazines.

(4) Do not otherwise solicit overseas custom or publicity.

4.86 *Tax problems*

1 Per Lord Linley in *IRC v Muller & Co's Margarine Ltd* [1901] AC 217, HL. See para 3.55, ante.
2 Paras 3.55 et seq, ante.

4.86 The directors of a United Kingdom resident franchisor must carefully consider the nature and extent of the intellectual property rights which form part of the business of their company in the United Kingdom. If the franchisor has not traded abroad and has not registered any patent or trade mark in respect of its business outside the United Kingdom, and the relevant priority periods under the applicable international conventions have expired, then they may reasonably consider that no such international rights are retained by the franchisor. If this is the case, they must examine the scope of the international copyright which applies to the designs, 'house style', operations manual and other literature of the franchisor, to establish whether or not any part of those designs and literature are crucial to the franchise business, and are incapable of sufficient variation not to infringe the copyright of the franchisor so that copyright in them would have to be transferred to the overseas company. If they are able to satisfy themselves on that point, then they must review the processes and ingredients used in the franchise business and decide whether any of those processes or ingredients are essential trade secrets or specialised know-how, which are the exclusive property of the franchisor. If there are no such secrets or know-how, then they should decide whether the franchisor has any international goodwill which would be transferred, if the overseas company commenced the franchise business overseas. If they are unable to satisfy themselves on any of the previous points, then they must consider whether the rights of the franchisor, which have an international dimension, form part of the trade or business of the franchisor. If they do, then significant tax liabilities may arise[1].

The directors must consider whether there is an actual transfer or a surrender of rights by the franchisor to the overseas company. In the case of an actual transfer, the nature of the asset and the method of disposal will determine whether any proceeds or deemed proceeds are taxable as income, in which event ICTA 1988, s 770 will apply[2]. If the proceeds of the transfer are chargeable gains or if there is a surrender of rights, CGTA, s 20 or s 26 will apply.

1 See para 4.68 et seq, ante.
2 ICTA 1988, ss 770(1), (2)(a), (b) and (d) (3) and 773(1)–(4) but see later comments concerning disposal of copyright and ICTA 1988, s 536 and earlier comments concerning CGTA 1979, ss 19 and 25.

Taxation of actual or deemed transfers

4.87 Even if the United Kingdom franchisor is shown to have transferred an asset to its overseas subsidiary in circumstances where ICTA 1988, s 770 will apply, or surrendered a right in such a way that CGTA 1979, ss 19, 20 and 25 will apply, it may be that the value of that asset or right is technically negligible. For example, the mere right to apply for registration of a trade mark in a foreign country arising from the relevant international convention[1] may be of no value if the trade mark has no reputation whatsoever in that country. The expense of application and consequent prosecution and registration fees may outweigh any potential commercial benefit to the entity which applies to register the mark. It is, therefore, difficult to assess the value of a bare right to apply for registration of a trade mark, especially

Investment risk 4.91

if the franchisor has made no use of the mark in the relevant country and there is a requirement of use prior to registration in that country[1].

1 See paras 3.133 et seq, ante.

4.88 In the event that intellectual property is sold, transferred or otherwise dealt with by its proprietor in the United Kingdom, that disposal is treated for tax purposes in different ways depending upon the nature of the rights and the manner of disposal.

4.89 If a United Kingdom resident franchisor disposes of a patent or patent rights for a capital sum then it may be taxed upon that disposal as if the proceeds were income, wherever the patents are registered. However, that income will be charged to tax under Schedule D, Case VI on the net proceeds and, unless there is a contrary election by the franchisor, will be treated as if it arose in six equal instalments commencing in the chargeable period in which the capital sum is received by it[1]. In the case of a corporation the income received from the disposal of a patent will be charged to corporation tax. It is important to note that the liability to tax arises on receipt, not when the payment is receivable. If a United Kingdom resident purchases all or part of a patent for a capital sum from a non-resident, the purchaser must deduct income tax at the standard rate from the payment and account to the Inland Revenue[2]. Some exceptions apply. A part disposal of patent rights for a lump sum (such as the grant of an exclusive licence within a limited geographical area or the grant of a non-exclusive licence or a restricted right to use) may be treated by the Inland Revenue as a royalty and not a capital sum. In that event, the whole of the consideration for the transfer will be taxable as income in the chargeable period in which it is received. There are no similar provisions relating to the disposal of a trade mark. In general, however, where a lump sum payment is made in respect of the outright sale, or exclusive use of a trade mark, in a particular territory, that payment will be treated as a capital payment and taxed as a capital gain. Where no such sale or grant of exclusive rights is made, then the payment will be treated as a trading receipt.

1 ICTA 1988, s 349(1).
2 Ibid, s 524(1).

4.90 The franchisor will be permitting the overseas company to use the trade mark in territories outside the United Kingdom. That use may be deemed to be exclusive, because the franchisor has no desire to become involved in the franchise business or otherwise use the trade mark overseas. Consent to the right to register and use the trade mark overseas may be in the nature of an exclusive grant by the franchisor to the overseas subsidiary, or may be a surrender of its rights to register and use the trade mark overseas, so that in either case any assessed value of the right transferred or surrendered will be subject to capital gains tax (or in the case of the corporate franchisor, corporation tax at the capital gains tax rate).

4.91 If a trader acquires know-how after 5 April 1986, then the acquisition cost will form part of a pool. In each year, the amount of expenditure on, and the proceeds of any disposal of, know-how are calculated and any excess of expenditure attracts capital allowances in the same manner as plant and machinery. Similarly, any excess of the net proceeds of disposal over expenditure, suffers a balancing charge.

4.92 *Tax problems*

4.92 In the context of studying the effect of the various assessment measures available to the Inland Revenue[1], in relation to the transfer of know-how[2], ICTA 1988, s 531 is important. The relevant subsections of section 531 are as follows:

'(2) Subject to the said sub-section (7), where after 19 March 1968 a person disposes of know-how which has been used in a trade carried on by him, and continues to carry on the trade after the disposal, the amount or value of any consideration received by him for the disposal shall, so far as it is[3] not chargeable to tax as a revenue or income receipt, be treated for all purposes as a trading receipt.
(3) Where after the said 19 March a person disposes of a trade or part of a trade and, together therewith, of know-how used therein, any consideration received by him for the know-how shall be dealt within relation both to him and to the person acquiring the know-how, if that person provided the consideration, and for the purposes of corporation tax, income tax and capital gains tax, as a payment for goodwill[4] . . .
(6) The preceding provisions of this section, except sub-section (2), shall not apply on any sale of know-how where the buyer is a body of persons over whom the seller has control, or the seller is a body of persons over whom the buyer has control, or both the seller and the buyer are bodies of persons and some other person has control over both of them; and the said sub-section (2) shall apply on any such sale with the omission of the proviso. In this sub-section, references to a body of persons include references to a partnership . . .
(8) Where, in connection with any disposal of know-how a person gives an undertaking (whether absolute or qualified, and whether legally valid or not) the tenor or effect of which is to restrict his or another's activities in any way, any consideration received in respect of the giving of the undertaking or its total or partial fulfilment shall be treated for the purposes of this section as consideration received for the disposal of the know-how.'

1 See paras 4.70 et seq, ante.
2 ICTA 1988, s 533(7). See para 4.84, ante.
3 Words inserted by FA 1985, s 65(3)(a), in respect of disposals after 31 March 1986 omitted.
4 Proviso to section 386(3) omitted.

4.93 There is, therefore, a difference in the tax treatment of any consideration received by the proprietor for the disposal of know-how depending upon whether the trade or part of the trade which uses that know-how is transferred at the same time. If there is a bare transfer of know-how, and the proprietor continues to use that know-how, then the consideration will be treated as income[1]. If the transfer is part of the general transfer of the trade or part of the trade undertaken by the proprietor it will be treated as the disposal of a capital asset, subject to capital gains tax[2]. However, a transfer of know-how together with the business of the proprietor in a restricted territory may be deemed to be the transfer of know-how together with a trade, notwithstanding that the proprietor continues to use the know-how elsewhere[3]. If know-how alone is transferred between connected persons, (for example, the franchisor and the overseas subsidiary) then subsection (2) of section 531 is stated not to apply[4]. No election by either of the parties to treat the proceeds of a disposal as income receipts[5] is available to connected persons[6]. Where such an election can be made, the net proceeds will be treated under Case VI[7]. Accordingly, any transfer of know-how alone between connected persons will be treated as a transfer of goodwill. If the disposal of know-how includes a restrictive covenant for which consideration is given, then that consideration is taxed as a disposal of know-how. The difference in tax treatment mentioned above will apply to that consideration.

1   ICTA 1988, s 531(2). See *Jeffrey v Rolls Royce Ltd* [1962] 40 TC 443 and *Musker v English Electric Co Ltd*(1964) 41 TC 556.
2   Ibid, s 531(2) or in the case of a company—corporation tax at the capital gains tax rate.
3   *Evans Medical Supplies Ltd v Moriarty (Inspector of Taxes)* [1957] 3 All ER 718, 37 TC 540.
4   ICTA 1988, s 531(3).
5   ICTA 1988, s 531(2).
6   ICTA 1988, s 531(7).
7   ICTA 1988, s 531(4).

4.94 The proceeds of the disposal of copyright by a United Kingdom resident seller, whether for a lump sum or royalties are subject to tax as income. If the seller is the author of the work, then he is entitled, on making a claim, to reliefs which spread the tax charge over two or three chargeable periods[1]. This relief does not apply to a seller who is not the author of the work. It is unlikely that the franchisor, itself, will be the author of the literary or artistic work comprised in the operations manual or promotional material in the franchise business. Although the 'author' of any literary work which is computer-generated is deemed to be the person by whom the arrangements necessary for creation of the relevant literary work are undertaken[2]. Any transfer of copyright material in the franchise business will, in the case of most franchisors, be subject to tax at the standard corporation tax rate applicable to income rather than gains[3]. This applies to any assessed value of the copyright material[4].

1   ICTA 1988, s 534. See also s 535.
2   Copyright Designs and Patents Act 1988, s 3(1).
3   See para 4.55, ante and 4.95, post.
4   ICTA 1988, ss 770(1), (2)(a), (b) and (d), (3) and 773(1)–(4).

4.95 On disposal of a design or registered design by the designer or joint designers, similar reliefs to those available to the author of a work the subject of copyright[1] will apply[2].

1   See para 4.94 ante.
2   ICTA 1988, s 537A(1)–(6); SI 1989 No 816.

4.96 A sale of goodwill is treated as the sale of a capital asset subject to capital gains tax (or corporation tax at the capital gains tax rate applicable to companies). Therefore, any transfer of goodwill by the franchisor to the overseas company will be subject to CGTA 1979, ss 19 and 20(1)(d).

4.97 If the United Kingdom franchisor is a close company[1] and it makes a transfer of value[2], inheritance tax will be charged as if each participator (other than a loan creditor) had made an apportioned amount of that transfer[3] after deduction of tax. Inheritance tax will be charged on the company, unless it is not paid by the company, whereupon those persons to whom amounts have been apportioned will be liable, subject to certain conditions[4].

The franchisor, when arranging the structure of its overseas business must be careful not to fall within the scope of the Inheritance Tax Act 1984, ss 94-102, otherwise it may be charged amounts of inheritance tax, especially if its participators have, previously, used up the exempt amounts of their lifetime gifts. However,

4.98 Tax problems

where a transfer of value falls to be taken into account in computing the transferee's profits or gains or losses for income or corporation tax purposes, then the apportionment for inheritance tax purposes does not apply[5]. If a transfer from one close company increases the value of another company in which a participator or participators in the first company have an interest, then the increase in value in the second company may be apportioned and the appropriate part offset against the apportionment made upon those participators in the first company arising from the transfer[6].

1 Definition of close company, ICTA 1988, s 414(1) and (2).
2 CTTA 1984, s 160.
3 Ibid, s 94(1).
4 Ibid, s 94(4).
5 Ibid, s 94(2)(a).
6 Ibid, s 95.

Will the shareholders of the overseas company be taxed on their proportion of its profits or gains?

4.98 Every person who is resident or ordinarily resident[1] in the United Kingdom and who holds shares[2] in a non-resident company[3], which would be a close company, if it was resident in the United Kingdom[4] and which makes a chargeable gain[5] shall be treated as if that part of the gain, which is equal to the proportion of the assets of the company to which the shareholder would be entitled on liquidation of the company[6], had accrued to the shareholder, provided the shareholder is entitled to not less than 5 per cent of those assets[7]. The provisions of the section apply to both individuals (provided that they are domiciled in the United Kingdom)[8] and to companies. The gain may be traced through a chain of non-resident companies[9]. Capital losses of the company arising in the same year of assessment as the gain may be used to reduce or extinguish that gain[10]. The provisions apply to 'income gains'[11]. Certain exemptions apply[12]. Tax paid by the company itself shall not be treated as a payment to the tax payer shareholder[13].

1 See paras 4.105 et seq, post for discussion about residence.
2 CGTA 1979, s 15(2) (as amended by ICTA 1988, Sch 29).
3 Ibid, s 15(1)(a).
4 Ibid, s 15(1)(b).
5 Ibid, s 15(1).
6 Ibid, s 15(3).
7 Ibid, s 15(4).
8 Ibid, s 15(2).
9 Ibid, s 15(9).
10 Ibid, s 15(8).
11 ICTA 1988, ss 431, 441(8), 473(2)(a), 663(2), 687(3), 757(1)–(7), 758–764.
12 CGTA 1979, s 15(5).
13 Ibid, s 15(10).

4.99 If the Inland Revenue have reason to believe that a non-resident company which is subject to a lower level of taxation in the territory (or none)[1] in which it is resident than would apply in the UK and is controlled by UK residents, the Board may direct[2] that the company shall be deemed a 'controlled foreign company' ('CFC')[3]. The chargeable profits of a CFC will be apportioned amongst its UK shareholders[4]. The CFC will be subjected to tax calculations as if it were resident in the UK[5]. These provisions do not affect the liability to tax of a CFC trading through a permanent branch or agency in the UK[6]. Chargeable profits do not include chargeable gains[7]. Chargeable profits will suffer the equivalent of corporation tax less any allowable tax credits[8] and may then be apportioned amongst the shareholders of the CFC. No direction will be made if the chargeable profits of the CFC do not exceed £20,000[9] in the relevant accounting period (or less pro rata if that period is less than 12 months). Further if the CFC pursues an 'acceptable' distribution policy,[10] is engaged in 'exempt activities'[11] or is a publicly quoted company[12], no direction may be made by the Board of Inland Revenue. If it appears to the Board that the motive for incorporating the CFC was not tax avoidance or the tax avoided was minimal then no direction may be given[13]. The Inland Revenue publishes a list of countries which are excluded or partially excluded for the purposes of apportioning chargeable profits of a CFC[14]. There are provisions for postponement of tax and reliefs may be claimed[15]. There are powers to obtain information[16]. Control is widely defined and includes some loan creditors[17].

1 ICTA 1988, s 749(3).
2 ICTA 1988, s 747(1).
3 ICTA 1988, s 747(2).
4 ICTA 1988, ss 747(3) and 752.
5 ICTA 1988, ss 747(6), 750(2), 751(6) and Sch 24, para 1(1).
6 ICTA 1988, ss 747(6), 750(2), 751(6) and Sch 24, para 1(5).
7 ICTA 1988, Sch 24.
8 ICTA 1988, s 751(6).
9 ICTA 1988, s 748(1)(d).
10 ICTA 1988, s 748(1)(a) and Sch 25.
11 ICTA 1988, s 748(1)(a) and Sch 25, Part II.
12 ICTA 1988, s 748(1)(c) and Sch 25, Part III.
13 ICTA 1988, s 748(7) and Sch 25, Part IV.
14 Inland Revenue Press Release 25 July 1985.
15 ICTA 1988, Sch 26.
16 ICTA 1988, s 755 and Sch 29.
17 ICTA 1988, s 749(5).

4.100 If the CFC is a subsidiary of the franchisor then the following will apply:

(1) The CFC is presumed not to be a member of a group. Therefore, group relief is not available and losses made by other members of the group cannot be surrendered to the CFC[1].

(2) No ACT may be surrendered to the CFC[2].

1 ICTA 1988, Sch 24, para 5.
2 Ibid, Sch 24, para 7.

4.101 Accordingly, if a corporate UK franchisor incorporates a foreign subsidiary in a tax haven with the intention of that subsidiary undertaking overseas franchising, it may be that the subsidiary will be a CFC. However, there are several points to note which may be of assistance to the franchisor.

4.102 The CFC may be engaged in 'exempt' activities. To do so, it must comply with strict criteria set out in Schedule 25 of ICTA 1988. Briefly, a CFC which hopes to demonstrate that it is engaged in 'exempt' activities must:

(a) be effectively managed in a territory outside the UK (this means business management rather than mere residence through registration or similar means)[1];

(b) maintain a 'business establishment' in the territory in which it is resident throughout the relevant accounting period[2];

(c) not be engaged in 'investment business' or dealing in goods for delivery to

4.103 *Tax problems*

or from the UK or connected or associated persons (or is a holding company whose subsidiaries are themselves engaged in exempt activities or are holding companies whose own subsidiaries are engaged in exempt activities)[3].

'Business establishment' is defined[4]. 'Investment business' is also defined[5] and includes the holding of any securities, patents or copyrights or the leasing of any description of any property or rights. It is necessary to demonstrate that the CFC or a local associate employs sufficient people in the territory to deal with its business and that no services which are performed by the company for persons resident outside the territory are provided in the UK. A UK branch or agency which merely supplies incidental services may be ignored.

1 ICTA 1988, s 748 and Sch 25, para 5(8).
2 ICTA 1988, s 748 and Sch 25, para 6(1)(a).
3 ICTA 1988, s 748 and Sch 25, para 6(2)–(4).
4 ICTA 1988, s 748 and Sch 25, para 7.
5 ICTA 1988, s 748 and Sch 25, para 9.

4.103 The object of ICTA 1988, Sch 25, para 4 is to prevent the creation of chains of companies through which income may be channelled, taking advantage of favourable double taxation agreements, and accumulated in a tax haven. However, this does not prevent the CFC having subsidiaries outside the tax haven territory provided they are trading in an exempt manner[1] and provided 90% of its gross income is derived from companies which it controls. Since most tax havens do not have favourable double taxation agreements with most developed countries, the passage of dividend income from subsidiaries located in high tax jurisdictions to a CFC in a tax haven may be difficult. In addition, if the main activity of the CFC and its subsidiaries is the receipt of royalty income from intellectual property, the CFC may be engaged in 'investment business' rather than 'exempt' activities.

1 ICTA 1988, s 748 and Sch 25, para 6(4).

4.104 This may cause problems for a UK franchisor which wishes to trade abroad and which wishes to use the profits generated by that overseas trade for more investment abroad without suffering UK corporation tax upon them. However, in view of the relatively low rates of corporation tax now payable in the UK[1], and because the losses incurred in the early trading period of the overseas trade may be deducted from the profits earned by the franchisor in the UK, the franchisor may consider that the difficulties created originally by the 1984 Finance Act (now ICTA 1988) outweigh the advantages[2].

However, there are many reasons why a franchisor may wish to set up an overseas business which is operated by a foreign subsidiary. Those reasons may have little to do with avoidance of UK tax.

1 See para 4.55, ante.
2 See para 4.107, post.

Is the overseas company resident in the United Kingdom?

4.105 If the franchisor wishes to incorporate an overseas company, it is sensible to plan to avoid the complications of deemed UK residence or even dual residence which may arise. Therefore a review of the basis of UK residence is relevant. For many years under United Kingdom tax law, the residence of a company has depended upon the location of its 'actual management and control'[2]. The management and control of a company is vested in its directors and executives. This has been described as:

> 'A company may in many ways be likened to a human body. It has a brain and nerve centre which controls what it does. It does have hands which hold the tools and act in accordance with directions from the centre. Some of the people in the company are mere servants and agents who are nothing more than hands to do the work and cannot be said to represent the mind or will. Others are directors and managers who represent the directing mind and will of the company, and control what it does. The state of mind of these managers is the state of mind of the company and is treated by the law as such[3].'

The apparent anomaly that ultimate control of the company was vested in the shareholders who may be resident in the United Kingdom, has been the subject of review[4]. If the franchisor is to avoid the consequences of its overseas companies being deemed to be resident in the UK[5], the following guidelines should be noted in connection with the conduct of the business of the foreign company:

(1) that the majority of directors are not resident in the United Kingdom; and

(2) that the meetings and all decisions of the directors are held and made outside the United Kingdom; and

(3) that all decisions are made by the board or by executives who have delegated authority and are, themselves, not resident in the United Kingdom; and

(4) the franchisor does not become involved or interfere in any way in the conduct of the business; and

(5) that the facilities of the overseas company are adequate to undertake its business without assistance from the franchisor.

In addition, the franchisor should consult Inland Revenue Statement of Practice (SP1/90) published on 9 January 1990[6].

1 *Swedish Central Rly Co Ltd v Thompson* [1924] 2 KB 255.
2 *De Beers Consolidated Mines Ltd v Howe* [1905] 2 KB 612, 5 TC 198.
3 Per Denning LJ in *H L Bolton (Engineering) Co Ltd v T J Graham & Sons Ltd* [1957] 1 QB 159, [1956] 3 All ER 624, CA.
4 Eg 1955 Royal Commission on taxation of profits and income; 'Company Residence: A Consultative Document' 26 January 1981.
5 Residence will be determined by the facts as they exist. In the *De Beers* case (see note 2 above) it was stated by Lord Loreburn:
> 'This [the question of residence] is a pure question of fact, to be determined, not according to the construction of this or that regulation or byelaw, but by a scrutiny of the course of business and trading.'
6 This is reproduced in Appendix 6, post.

4.106 Whereas points (1) to (3) (inclusive) are clear, points (4) and (5) may cause problems for the franchisor. The franchisor must resist any temptation to interfere directly in the operation of the business of the overseas company, and must allow it to conduct and be seen to conduct its own affairs in its own manner. In this context, it is essential that the United Kingdom franchisor does not involve itself in the process of the creation or acquisition of the necessary intellectual property rights for use in the franchise business by the overseas company. For example, it must not itself instruct foreign patent or trade mark agents, or licensing lawyers, or pay any of their costs, or the filing fees payable on application for, or registration of any such patent or trade mark. All such instructions and all these costs and expenses must be given and be met out of the resources available to the overseas company. Other useful precautions are the engagement of separate accountants,

4.107 *Tax problems*

lawyers and bankers who are not in partnership or closely associated with those instructed by the franchisor.

If the overseas company is a trading company, then its 'presence' in the place of its incorporation or intended residence, and its levels of administrative and management facilities must be clearly adequate to deal with its trade on a proper commercial basis. If the overseas trader is resident or incorporated in a tax haven[1], that may be difficult to achieve due to restrictions on the immigration of qualified employees and poor communications. The establishment and maintenance of adequate facilities will be necessary if the overseas company is not to be held to be a 'sham'[2]. If the overseas company is a holding company, which receives, directly or indirectly, royalty or other income from overseas franchisees or its own subsidiaries, the extent of its 'presence' need not be substantial[3]. In both cases, it is essential that none of the business activities of the overseas company depends upon the intervention or capabilities of the franchisor.

1 If the overseas company is registered in a tax haven then it may be a CFC—see paras 4.99 to 4.104 (inclusive) ante.
2 See Canadian case, *Spur Oil Ltd v R* (1980) 22 February, doc 80–5948. See also note 4 para 4.68 ante.
3 But see ICTA 1988, Sch 25.

4.107 The incorporation of an overseas company, which is merely a holding company may appear to be the safest solution in this context[1]. However, a number of difficulties may arise because of the passive nature of the overseas company. These include:

(1) If the overseas company is intended to own trade marks, then it must apply to register them. Certain jurisdictions require proof of use prior to registration[2] and others require use prior to the expiry of a term of years from registration, if the mark is to remain valid[3]. In either case, it would be simple for the franchisor, itself, to comply with the requirements on behalf of the overseas company. That would be dangerous both in terms of the validity of the mark and the non-residence status of the overseas subsidiary.

(2) It is probable that potential foreign franchisees of the overseas company will require information concerning the status and success of the business of the franchisor in the United Kingdom, unless the overseas company or its own subsidiaries establish successful company owned stores in each country where they wish to conduct the franchise business. Those franchisees may require some form of guarantee from the franchisor of the performance of the overseas company, especially if the business depends on the continual supply of a special product or raw material or if a substantial initial franchise fee is payable by them. If the franchisor becomes involved in the submission of information, based upon the performance of the franchise business in the United Kingdom, as part of the inducements to foreign potential franchisees to take up franchises, it will be using its business or assets in the United Kingdom to assist the growth of the business of its overseas subsidiary. However, it is unlikely that mere disclosure of financial information is sufficient interference in the activities of the overseas company to justify a claim by the Inland Revenue that the overseas company is only a 'sham'. If the franchisor uses its financial status or assets to guarantee the performance of its overseas subsidiaries, then it is arguable that it is dealing with the assets in such a way that the transfer of those assets is liable to occur.

1 But it may cause more tax problems; see paras 4.99 to 4.104 (inclusive), ante.

2 For example the United States of America.
3 For example France.

4.108 In addition, the provision of guarantees by the franchisor to assist the business activities of its overseas subsidiary may be questionable without adequate consideration passing to the franchisor. However, this aspect of the establishment of the credibility of the overseas business will become a serious matter only if the guarantee is called. In any event, any such guarantee will be a contingent liability of the franchisor and, at the least, a note of the same must be endorsed upon its audited accounts. If the guarantee is called, then, unless the exposure of the franchisor is large, the resulting fulfilment of the terms of the guarantee will be a transfer of an asset only and not the transfer of a trade or part of a trade[1]. Presumably, the guarantee will be issued in favour of the foreign franchisee, so that the franchisor and the franchisee are not connected persons. If this is the case, then the present anti-avoidance measures may not apply[2], unless the effect of the fulfilment of the obligations of the franchisor under the guarantee is in the nature of the transfer of its trade overseas[3] or unless the fulfilment of the guarantee is in the nature of the transfer of assets through the overseas subsidiary of the franchisor. Care must be taken to ensure that this does not happen. If the guarantee is called, presumably any assets transferred to satisfy it will be so transferred at market value. The above comments apply to other forms of guarantee by the franchisor of the obligations of its overseas subsidiary (such as bank guarantees, guarantees to suppliers and landlords). No relief may be available to the franchisor in respect of any payments made by it under any such guarantee[4]. However, we must distinguish between anti-avoidance measures relating to transfers of a trade or between connected persons, or the surrender of rights, and the extent of interference by the franchisor in the activities of its overseas subsidiary, so that it may be deemed to manage and control it or be effectively managing it[5]. Large scale provision of guarantees by the franchisor for its overseas subsidiaries, without adequate consideration, will probably cause the Inland Revenue to challenge the non-resident independent status of any such overseas subsidiary.

1 See para 4.87 et seq, post.
2 CGTA 1979, ss 19 (as amended), 20 or 25.
3 ICTA 1988, ss 765, 766(1)–(4) and 767(1)–(6).
4 CGTA 1979, s 136 (as amended by ICTA 1988, Sch 29).
5 See para 4.105 et seq, ante.

Methods of reducing overseas investment risks

4.109 How can the franchisor, especially if it is conducting its business profitably in the United Kingdom, take advantage of the tax concessions or allowances available to resident tax payers to reduce its tax liability and to minimise the risk of its overseas investment?

4.110 Group relief (the passage of losses from one member[1] of a group of companies to fellow members to offset their profits for tax purposes) is not available except between United Kingdom resident[2] corporations which does not include a 'controlled foreign company'[2]. Accordingly, the benefit of any losses sustained by the overseas company or its own subsidiaries, will not be available to the franchisor for this purpose. It cannot, therefore, take advantage of the usual reliefs available

4.111 *Tax problems*

to a holding company, if one or more of its subsidiaries trades unsatisfactorily or, otherwise, sustains losses, except in respect of United Kingdom resident members of its group. Briefly, group relief is available between resident members of a 75 per cent group in the corresponding accounting period[3]. Group relief cannot be carried forward or back. Group relief is not available between subsidiaries of a non-resident holding company. Consortium relief is now available both upwards and downwards so that surrenders for group relief purposes among members of a consortium may take place between subsidiary and holding companies and vice versa[4].

1 ICTA 1988, s 402(3) and (4).
2 Ibid, s 413(5).
3 ICTA 1988, ss 403 and 408.
4 ICTA 1988, ss 403(10), (11), 405(1)–(6), 406(1)–(8), 409(5)–(8), 411(3)–(9) and 413(2).

4.111 In the absence of group relief in respect of the losses of foreign resident subsidiaries of a United Kingdom resident franchisor, where there is a substantial degree of risk anticipated in the overseas business and a considerable chance of suffering loss, it is essential that the franchisor or its shareholders minimise the risk. This will be the case when 'pilot' operations are commenced in a new country. Accordingly, it may be useful to review the following possible structures:

(1) The franchisor incorporates a United Kingdom resident subsidiary or subsidiaries which trade overseas. The losses of any such subsidiary may be available to the franchisor for group relief purposes.

(2) The incorporation of a finance and moneylending subsidiary of the franchisor which engages in the business of making loans. Those loans would be made to overseas companies undertaking the franchise business.

We shall consider point (2) in more detail.

Finance company

4.112 If the finance company is funded by the franchisor either by way of loan or equity capital and does not take deposits from unrelated parties, the restrictions upon deposit-taking contained in the Banking Act 1979 may not apply to that company. If the finance company desires to engage in the trade of moneylending, it must obtain a licence under the Consumer Credit Act 1974. If it lends money to United Kingdom resident borrowers, those borrowers must deduct tax at source[1] unless the finance company is a bank carrying on a bona fide banking business in the United Kingdom[2].

If the finance company suffers losses, as a result of its loans, it may be entitled to treat those losses as losses in the course of its trade.

However, where the franchisor is related to the borrowers from its finance subsidiary, the so-called 'thin capitalisation' rules may apply[3]. If the finance company is a member of a United Kingdom resident group, then it may surrender its losses to other resident members of that group[4].

1 ICTA 1988, s 349(2).
2 Ibid, s 349(1)(a).
3 See para 4.155, post.
4 See para 4.110, ante.

4.113 A combination of all or any of the arrangements discussed in this chapter whereby any of the companies trade overseas in partnership with each other and/ or in partnership with a resident of the country where the franchise business is being conducted and/or in partnership with a company located in a low tax jurisdiction to commence the 'pilot' operations in each foreign country may reduce overseas investment risk. The partnership agreement between the various companies may be as follows:

(1) One or more United Kingdom resident trading companies whose shareholders are able to take advantage of BES investment incentive reliefs available may provide risk capital for the business, by providing services in the UK to overseas subsidiaries of the franchisor or its franchisees.

(2) A tax haven located company (subject to the effect of local tax laws) undertakes the management of the partnership business and takes the major share of the profits. It is not required to provide capital but management skills. By judicious allocation of the profits of the business between the partners the profits of the United Kingdom resident companies may be minimised.

(3) The balance of funds required is provided by the finance subsidiary of the franchisor subject to the existence of a double taxation agreement between the relevant country and the United Kingdom which permits the payment of interest gross to lenders resident in the United Kingdom.

(4) A further partner may be a local resident.

(5) The partnership will pay royalties or franchise fees directly or indirectly[1] to the overseas company which owns all the intellectual property required in the franchise business.

1 See paras 4.120 and 4.142, post.

4.114 The object of these arrangements is to achieve relief against the income of the investors, when a 'pilot' operation fails and losses are suffered. It may also be advantageous if the shareholders or other individuals shoulder the risk of those losses, rather than the franchisor or members of its group, so that the balance sheet of the franchisor is not adversely affected, if the intention of its directors is to arrange a public quotation for the franchisor on a recognised stock exchange in the future. By this means, those shareholders may obtain the benefit of income relief, if losses are suffered, whilst the losses will not reduce the growth in the value of their shares in the franchisor.

4.115 It must be remembered that the arrangements for the incorporation of the resident companies in this section of this book and their subsequent conduct should not infringe (in the case of an individual investor) ICTA 1988 ss 739 et seq (transfer of assets abroad to avoid income tax)[1].

1 See paras 4.68 et seq, ante.

4.116 It should be noted that the profits and gains of the partnership will be charged to tax in the country where the business is undertaken by the partnership. It is essential that those foreign taxes are available as tax credits in the United Kingdom in the hands of the United Kingdom resident corporate partners, either by way of the provision of the relevant double taxation agreement or because of unilateral relief[1]. Those companies should endeavour to arrange their affairs accordingly.

1 ICTA 1988, s 790.

4.117 *Tax problems*

4.117 The franchisor may consider that it does not wish to contemplate the conduct of the franchise business overseas by companies which are not controlled by it or by its current shareholders. In these circumstances, its directors may decide that shareholders in the trading companies should be shareholders in the franchisor and that independent ownership of the franchisor and those companies will not be permitted. The technical requirements of the appropriate reliefs must be observed, but it may be possible to 'staple' the shares of the trading companies to those of the franchisor. This will mean that neither the shares of the franchisor nor the trading companies, may be dealt in independently by shareholders common to both, and that those shares must be disposed of together.

4.118 It must be stressed that before embarking on any tax saving or deferred arrangements, the franchisor or its shareholders must take advice in each country where the franchise business is intended to be conducted.

4.119 Careful consideration must be given to the possibly conflicting requirements of commerce and tax avoidance. It may be necessary for commercial reasons to form a relationship with a resident of each country, where the franchise business is conducted, so that such resident is a participator in that business. Indeed, because of local law it may be obligatory[1]. It may be commercially or financially disadvantageous for him if the business of operating the 'company owned' stores is structured as a partnership, rather than a limited liability local corporation, of which the partners are members. There may be tax penalties in operating as a partnership rather than a corporation. In addition, a distinction must be made between the risk involved in the formation of 'company owned' stores and the conduct of the franchise business, the main purpose of which is to collect franchise fees or royalties. Generally, much larger investment will be required to form and operate 'company owned' stores, than to set up the administration required to conduct the franchise business. It is, therefore, essential that the capital actually at risk in the formation of the stores is as low as possible. The arrangement of reliefs and allowances for the providers of that capital will be of prime importance. There will be more flexibility in the formation of the franchise business, when the capital required is relatively low, subject to the limits imposed by the necessity of maintaining a low-tax or tax free royalty flow from the franchisees in each country to the overseas subsidiary. If there is little commercial risk in opening 'company stores', then the arrangements described in this part of this book may be inappropriate, especially if the expected returns from the business are high. In such a case, it will be advantageous for the franchisor to concentrate on minimising the tax charge of its group in each country where it proposes to conduct the franchise business.

1 For example: Saudi Arabia and now some businesses in former Eastern Bloc countries.

Methods of reducing foreign taxation of overseas profits

4.120 One of the objects of any international group structure, which is based upon the exploitation of intellectual property rights, is the receipt of royalty or fee income after the deduction of the minimum or no withholding tax. Many countries impose some form of withholding tax on royalty payments, especially those which are payable to non-resident licensors. In addition, many countries still impose exchange controls of varying degrees of severity, limiting or preventing the payment of royalties, except in their own currency and, occasionally, without the right on the part of the licensor to convert that currency into foreign currencies and export it. The same restrictions may apply to interest on loans made by the franchisor and to dividend income paid by its overseas subsidiaries. It will be the object of this section of this book to explore means by which royalties and dividend income may be paid by franchisees or subsidiaries to the overseas company with the minimum of withholding tax deducted from the gross amounts of the payments. However, because in the majority of cases, the subsidiary of the franchisor will be a 'controlled foreign company'[1], it may be necessary for the individual shareholders of the franchisor company to make arrangements which will be of long-term benefit.

1 See para 4.99 et seq, ante.

4.121 To avoid the consequences of legislation taxing deemed remittances from overseas subsidiaries or requiring funds to be remitted to the United Kingdom resident parent[1] it may be wise for the United Kingdom shareholders of the franchisor to consider the incorporation of any overseas companies in such a way that they or the franchisor are unable to control or require the remittance of dividends or other distributions or gains from those companies to be deemed to be entitled to them so that no charge may be made by the Inland Revenue. This may be achieved by the use of so-called 'limbo' trusts. Such a trust is created so that it falls outside the scope of FA 1981, s 80 in respect of capital gains and the similar provisions of ICTA 1988, ss 739 et seq in respect of income and so that the companies which form part of its assets are not managed and controlled or the place of effective management is not in the United Kingdom. Section 80(1) of the FA 1981 reads as follows:

> '(1) This section applies to a settlement for any year of assessment (beginning on or after 6 April 1981) during which the trustees are at no time resident or ordinarily resident in the United Kingdom if the settlor or one of the settlors is at any time during that year, or was when he made his settlement, domiciled and either resident or ordinarily resident in the United Kingdom.'

It is clear from that subsection that the provisions of the whole of FA 1981, s 80 are intended to catch foreign trusts which have been settled by persons domiciled and resident or ordinarily resident in the United Kingdom when the settlement was made (or made a domicile of choice in the United Kingdom and was also resident or ordinarily resident there in the tax year when a gain was realised). In that case, the United Kingdom domiciled beneficiaries under the trust will be assessed for a due proportion of the chargeable gains for which the trustees would have been charged, as if they had been subject to United Kingdom capital gains tax, in any year of assessment[2], if he receives a capital payment[3] from the trust with the maximum amount of the assessment being the total of the payments made to him in each year of assessment[4].

The provisions of section 15(5) and 17 of the CGTA 1979 were separate and could not be used together. However, the gains of a non-resident company in which non-resident trustees have a shareholding (not less than 5 per cent)[5] and which are accumulated by the company are subject to apportionment as a result of a combination of sections 80 and 81 of the FA 1981.

Where the settlor of a trust is not domiciled, resident or ordinarily resident in the United Kingdom in any year of assessment then income arising under the

4.122 *Tax problems*

settlement in that year shall not be subject to tax except to the extent that it would be chargeable on him if he received it.

1 ICTA 1988, ss 747–753, 754(1)–(9), 755, 756 and Sch 29.
2 FA 1980, s 80. In the case of gains arising before 6 April 1981, CGTA 1979, s 17(2).
3 FA 1980, s 80 for definition. Section 762 of ICTA 1988 extended s 80 FA 1981 (with modifications) to offshore income gains.
4 Section 762 of ICTA 1988.
5 CGTA 1979, s 15(4) (as amended by ICTA 1988, Sch 29).

Trusts

4.122 If the trust is settled by a settlor who is not and, at the time that the trust was settled, was not domiciled and resident or ordinarily resident in the United Kingdom, no such assessment on the beneficiaries may be made, provided the trustees are, also, not resident or ordinarily resident in the United Kingdom. In those circumstances, the trustees may deal with the assets of the trust in an unfettered manner. There will be no necessity to remit funds to the United Kingdom to cover assessments upon the beneficiaries of the trust.

4.123 Non-resident trustees should beware of investing funds in the United Kingdom. Notwithstanding the effect of Inland Revenue Concession B.13 (untaxed interest paid to non-residents), non-resident trustees may be subject to investment income surcharges on the income from the investments[1], although the manner in which the trust was settled and the existence of a double taxation agreement which contains provisions relating to interest may affect this situation.

1 ICTA 1988, ss 677(2)(b) and (6), 686 and Sch 29 and *IRC v Regent Trust Co Ltd* [1980] 1 WLR 688, [1980] STC 140.

4.124 The companies which form part of the assets of the trust must be:
 (1) registered outside the United Kingdom and
 (2) managed and controlled or effectively managed outside the United Kingdom[1].

1 See paras 4.105 et seq, ante.

4.125 The companies must be controlled by trustees:
 (1) who are not resident, ordinarily resident or domiciled in the United Kingdom; and
 (2) upon whom shares carrying voting control over the companies are vested together with sole rights to receive income and capital distributions from the companies;
 (3) who are trustees of a trust of which the franchisor or its shareholders are only discretionary[1] beneficiaries and the objects of which trust are primarily to accumulate funds for overseas investment and which prohibit any remittances to beneficiaries in the United Kingdom except at the unconditional discretion of the trustees[2];
 (4) who appoint directors and managers who are not resident in the United Kingdom.

1 If the beneficiaries are not discretionary then income accumulated overseas may be deemed to be a transfer within the provisions of ICTA 1988, s 739 (as amended).
2 In the case of individual beneficiaries, the provisions of ICTA 1988, s 740(1) must be considered if a transfer of assets abroad has occurred in any way.

4.126 It may be prudent if all share capital is expressed and subscribed for in foreign currency. It is impossible to predict the scope of possible future tax legislation, but any United Kingdom franchisor should arrange its overseas affairs in such a way that the impact of future compulsory repatriation of overseas profits is minimised.

4.127 However, it must face one major problem in this context. Who is the foreign settlor, who will settle sufficient funds to enable the overseas company to commence, and maintain the franchise business? In addition, for the purpose of ICTA 1988, Chapter III, Part XV (the chapter dealing with settlements) the definition of settlement is as follows:

> 'In this Chapter, "settlement" includes any disposition, trust, covenant, agreement or arrangement, and "settlor", in relation to a settlement, means any person by whom the settlement was made; and a person shall be deemed for the purposes of this Chapter to have made a settlement if he has made or entered into the settlement directly or indirectly, and in particular (but without prejudice to the generality of the preceding words) if he has provided or undertaken to provide funds directly or indirectly for the purpose of the settlement, or has made with any other person reciprocal arrangement for that other person to make or enter into the settlement.'

In view of the apparent present attitude of the courts to avoidance arrangements it would be unwise to assume that when reviewing settlement arrangements they would not apply this type of definition to the 'substance' of those arrangements.

4.128 Many double taxation agreements between major trading nations contain provisions, whereby royalties or dividends payable by a resident of one of the parties to the treaty to a resident of the other party do not suffer withholding tax or, at least, suffer a substantially reduced withholding tax upon them. It is, therefore, possible to choose a country which has a number of favourable double taxation agreements with other major nations which can receive royalties, dividends or franchise fees from franchisees or subsidiaries in various countries. However, those countries which benefit from the most favourable double taxation agreements in this respect, often subject income of their own resident companies (from whatever source) to high corporate income tax rates.

4.129 If a United Kingdom resident company is used as a royalty receiver, it will suffer corporation tax in the United Kingdom on that income. It is necessary, therefore, to incorporate a company, which will receive royalties in a country which has a number of favourable double taxation agreements, and which does not charge high rates of tax on that income, or has a special arrangement for this type of income. Such a country is the Kingdom of the Netherlands.

4.130 It is possible to arrange the incorporation of a Netherlands private resident company (Besloten Vennootschap met beperkte aansprakelijkheid or BV) which is a wholly-owned subsidiary of the haven company. The Dutch company may have to apply to the Netherlands Tax Administration for a favourable tax ruling on royalties and for 'participation exemption' (Deelnemingvrijstelling) status in respect of dividends receivable by it. These are some of the most important aspects of the Netherlands tax legislation, particularly for international corporate groups which are seeking to minimise or defer their total tax liabilities.

4.131 *Tax problems*

4.131 The Netherlands Tax Administration may issue advance rulings in respect of the tax treatment of royalty receipts and payments by a resident Netherlands company to a licensor. The tax authorities were obliged to issue rulings in response to applications by resident companies. Due to pressure of business that obligation was suspended. A resident company need not be related to its licensor, although this is generally the case. The rulings are, usually, for a period of three years, but may be renewed on further application. The rulings are discretionary and may be issued after negotiations between the professional advisers of the Dutch company and the local tax inspector (inspecteur). There are nine inspectorates of corporation taxation in the Netherlands.

4.132 Rulings may vary from local area to local area, depending on the attitude of individual inspectors. The object of each ruling is to determine the taxable spread between royalties which are received by the Dutch company and the royalties paid by it to its licensor. The taxable spread is the basis of the minimum taxable amount payable and the Dutch company must waive any claim to reduce the taxable amount by any expenses or losses incurred by it. Corporate income tax at the rate applicable from time to time is calculated on the taxable spread. The present applicable rate lies around 42 per cent. The taxable spread, from which no deductions will be allowed, will probably be in the region of the following:

Amount of royalties received by Netherlands company		Net taxable spread
Dfl	up to 1,999,999	7%
Dfl 2,000,000	to 3,999,999	6%
Dfl 4,000,000	to 5,999,999	5%
Dfl 6,000,000	to 7,999,999	4%
Dfl 8,000,000	to 9,999,999	3%
Dfl 10,000,000	upwards	2%

An example of the effect of the ruling is as follows (using the 7 per cent spread):

Royalty receipts		100.00
Taxable spread	7% × tax rate 42%	
Tax payable		2.94
Payment to licensor		97.06

The Netherlands do not impose any withholding tax on the payment of royalties to non-residents. To obtain a ruling it will be necessary to produce to the inspector all licences and ancillary contracts between the Dutch company and its licensor. It must be stressed that a ruling is not automatic and the attitude of the Dutch tax authorities has become less accommodating in recent years, possibly because of pressure from other nations.

4.133 The advantages of an arrangement using a Dutch company as an intermediary for the collection of royalties quickly becomes apparent. For example, the normal withholding tax imposed by the United Kingdom on royalty payments to non-residents is now 25 per cent (based on the standard rate of income tax)[1]. By virtue of the convention between the Kingdom of the Netherlands and the United Kingdom, this is reduced to nil[2]. If the royalty received from the United Kingdom is (or any of the other countries with which the Netherlands has a Double Taxation Agreement) passed through the Dutch company to the licensor, the amount of tax suffered will be small. Because no withholding tax is imposed by the Netherlands upon royalty payments, the licensor which receives royalties from the Dutch company may be located in the most advantageous low tax jurisdiction without any need to compromise because of tax treaties.

1 See paras 4.55 et seq, ante.
2 Article 12(1) of the Double Taxation Relief (Taxes on Income) (Netherlands) Order 1980 which replaced the treaty of 31 October 1967 on 6 April 1981.

4.134 The 'participation exemption' in respect of dividend income received by a Dutch company exempts that income from corporate income tax provided that:

(1) the shares in the paying company have been owned by the Dutch company since the commencement of the financial year in which the exemption is claimed, and

(2) the holding of the Dutch company in the paying company amounts to at least 5 per cent of the issued share capital, and

(3) if the holding is in a foreign company, the profits of that company must be subject to a tax similar to Netherlands corporate income tax and

(4) the holding is not merely a passive investment, but the Dutch company is involved in the business operations of the paying company or acts as an intermediate holding company of a group of companies.

Where a company with 'participation exemption' status disposes of its qualifying participation (its shareholding in the relevant subsidiary company) gains made on that disposal are free of income tax. Any losses incurred are not deductible. 'Participation exemption' status may be achieved by obtaining a favourable ruling from the Dutch Tax Administration. However, our earlier comments concerning royalty rulings apply to applications for participation exemptions[1].

1 See para 4.132 et seq, ante.

4.135 Unlike royalties, the Netherlands Tax Administration imposes a withholding tax (Dividendbelasting) at the rate of 25 per cent upon dividends paid by a Dutch company, except to shareholders in jurisdictions with which the Netherlands has favourable double taxation agreements.

4.136 If the Dutch company is merely acting as an intermediary for the collection of dividends, it is essential that its parent to which it pays dividends is located in a low tax jurisdiction with which the Netherlands has favourable tax treaties. Some treaties only impose a withholding tax of five per cent on dividend payments from Netherlands companies. In some cases no withholding tax is imposed. Because of the special relationship between the Netherlands and the Netherlands Antilles, the latter is the most common jurisdiction for the location of parent companies of Netherlands intermediate royalty, holding and finance companies. However, because of the terms of Article 10(3)(d) of the agreement with the United Kingdom, the Netherlands Antilles is no longer an appropriate location for a holding company, if the object of any arrangements is to avoid or defer tax on dividends arising in the United Kingdom.

4.137 The majority of double taxation agreements to which the Netherlands is a party contain provisions for the payment of interest without suffering taxation

4.138 *Tax problems*

by a borrower in one country, which is a party to the agreement to a resident of the Netherlands. For example Article 11(1) of the agreement between the United Kingdom and the Netherlands[1] states as follows:

'(1) Interest arising in one of the States which is derived and beneficially owned by a resident of the other State shall be taxable only in that other State'.

'Interest' is defined[2]. Interest is not treated as a dividend or distribution[3]. If the debt on which interest arises is effectively connected with a permanent establishment or fixed base from which independent personal services are performed by the creditor, then Article 11(1) will not apply[4] and Articles 7 or 14 will apply.

Where there is a special relationship between the debtor and creditor any excessive amount of interest shall be taxed in the debtor's country[5]. The relief will not apply if the loan was made mainly to take advantage of the provisions of the Article and not for bona fide commercial reasons[6]. The above provisions are similar to those contained in the 1967 United Kingdom/Netherlands Convention as amended by the Protocol of 1977. No withholding tax is deductible from payments of interest paid by Dutch debtors to creditors.

1   The Double Taxation Relief (Taxes on Income) (Netherlands) Order 1980.
2   Ibid, Art 11(2).
3   Ibid, Art 11(2), referring to Article 10.
4   Ibid, Art 11(3).
5   Ibid, Art 11(5).
6   Ibid, Art 11(6).

4.138 It should be noted that the present favoured position of the Netherlands which has been achieved because of its double taxation agreements with other nations and its favourable treatment of royalty and dividend income is under attack. For example, in relation to dividends, the double taxation agreement between the United Kingdom and the Kingdom of the Netherlands issued on 17 December 1980 (SI 1980/1961)[1] is intended to reduce significant benefits previously available to Dutch holding companies which own more than 10 per cent of the voting power of a United Kingdom resident company. Under the previous agreement, if the Dutch company made an investment in a United Kingdom resident corporate franchisee and controlled at least 25 per cent of the voting of the franchisee[2] then United Kingdom tax would be charged on the gross amount of the dividends at the rate of 5 per cent. If the holding of the Dutch company provided less than 25 per cent voting power, the rate of tax would have been 15 per cent[3]. The final sentence of Article 11(2) of the amended Convention of 1967 between the United Kingdom and the Netherlands reads as follows: 'This paragraph shall not affect the taxation of the company in respect of the profits out of which the dividends are paid.'

Accordingly, the United Kingdom corporate franchisee in this example will continue to be taxed in the usual manner applicable to corporations in the United Kingdom, and in a similar manner to Dutch corporate taxation. The Dutch company must not have a permanent establishment in the United Kingdom which is effectively connected with the business undertaken by the United Kingdom company[4]. As further evidence of the international challenge to the favourable nature of some Netherlands case law, certain companies (other than trading companies under ICTA 1988, s 756(1)), which obtain deductions under Article 14a of the Netherlands Income Tax Law (usual equity deductions) are not within the excluded countries lists issued by the Inland Revenue in respect of 'controlled foreign companies' under ICTA 1988, ss 747–753, 754(1)–(9) and Sch 29.

1 The Double Taxation Relief (Taxes on Income) (Netherlands) Order 1980.
2 Article 11(2) of the Netherlands/UK Convention, 31 October 1967, as amended by Protocol of 22 March 1977.
3 Ibid, Art 11(2)(b).
4 Ibid, Art 11(6).

4.139 An approximate example of the operation of these arrangements is as follows:

UK co is wholly-owned subsidiary of Dutch co. On 1 September 1980 UK co pays a dividend of £75.00.

To Dutch co

	£	
Dividend	75.00	} 100.00
ACT = 25/75 × £75	25.00	

Dutch co *receives*	75.00
Dutch co claims	
From Inland Revenue:	
Tax credit = 0.5 × (ACT) 25 = 12.50	
LESS withholding tax	
(at rate relevant to holdings of	
more than 10% of UK company)	
= 5% × (dividend) 75	
+ (credit) 12.50 = 4.37	8.13
	83.13

The agreement with the Netherlands is similar to only eight such agreements which allow a partial tax credit to residents of the other party to the treaty owning 10 per cent or more of the voting power in a United Kingdom resident company. These countries are: Denmark, Finland, Luxembourg, Netherlands, Norway, Sweden, Switzerland and the USA.

Because United Kingdom corporation tax is similar to Netherlands corporate income tax, the 'participation exemption' may apply to the dividend received by the Dutch company, provided it fulfils all the conditions mentioned above. One of the objects of the present agreement is to reduce the amount of the tax credit to the Netherlands parent company arising from the payment by the United Kingdom company of ACT when issuing its dividends[1]. The measures are generally similar to the United States/United Kingdom Convention of 1975[2] with the significant exception that no tax credit will be allowed to a Netherlands parent company, which is controlled by persons who would not have been entitled to a tax credit if they had been the beneficial owners of the dividends[3]. This appears to be an attempt to reduce so-called 'treaty-shopping', using the Netherlands as a conduit for dividends.

1 Article 10(3)(c). See para 4.55 et seq, ante for discussion on ACT.
2 See paras 4.145 et seq, post.
3 Article 10(3)(d).

4.140 *Tax problems*

4.140 The following matters should be noted:

(1) If the Netherlands company 'controls directly or indirectly 10 per cent or more of the voting power in the company paying the dividend'[1] the tax repayment to that Netherlands company amounts to one half of the tax credit (one half of the ACT accounted to the Inland Revenue by the paying company)[2] less not more than 5 per cent of the aggregate of the net dividend plus that half of the tax credit[3].

(2) That arrangement only applies if the Netherlands company is quoted on a Netherlands stock exchange or is not controlled by persons who would not have been entitled to any tax credit if they had beneficially owned the dividend[4]. The latter stipulation may cause problems in its interpretation. A Netherlands Antilles resident company is not entitled to any tax credit arising from the ACT paid by a United Kingdom resident company on payment of a dividend, by that company to the Antillean company[5]. Accordingly, Article 10(3)(d)(ii) will apply and no tax credit will be allowed to the Netherlands company.

(3) Article 10(3)(d)(i) and (ii) are not similar to any provision of the US/UK Convention. Presumably, the stipulations contained in those sections were inserted to reduce the benefits of the 'participation exemption' available to Netherlands companies controlled by tax haven resident shareholders. The definition of 'control' in Article 10(3)(d)(ii) is more extensive than in other treaties. Interpretation of 'control' is under 'the laws of the United Kingdom'. There are several definitions of control under United Kingdom tax law[6]. Perhaps the two most important are set out in section 416 of ICTA 1988 (which relates to control of close companies and extends beyond mere voting) and s 840 of ICTA 1988 (which is limited to voting control, either through the number of shares or any special provisions of the Articles of Association of the company). It is the Inland Revenue view that both definitions apply.

1 Article 10(3)(c). See para 4.139, ante.
2 At present ACT is around one-third.
3 See para 4.55, ante.
4 This is limited by Article 10(3)(d)(ii).
5 The Double Taxation (Netherlands Antilles) Order.
6 ICTA 1988, ss 416 and 840.

4.141 The Netherlands Antilles is, probably, the most suitable location for a parent company which has a Netherlands subsidiary, because of the special relationship between the Netherlands and the Netherlands Antilles, provided that United Kingdom sourced dividends are not intended to be received. The UK/Netherlands Antilles Convention (SI 1968 No 577) ceased to have effect from 5 April 1989. However, Eurobond interest gross payments routed through the Netherlands Antilles may still be paid gross[1].

1 ICTA 1988, s 116.

4.142 If a Netherlands Antilles company is proposed to be used because the income which will flow through its Netherlands subsidiary is not from the United Kingdom and provided the Antilles company is owned by shareholders who are not residents of the Netherlands Antilles, derives its income outside the Antilles and is deemed to be a 'portfolio investment company' with a foreign exchange licence[1] any dividend income or interest will be subject to Antilles corporate income tax at the rate of 3 per cent. In addition, no local island surcharges (15 per cent) are levied on patent holding or portfolio investment companies. Capital gains are tax free and capital losses are not deductible. By virtue of the agreements between the Netherlands and the Netherlands Antilles, a Dutch company is not obliged to deduct any withholding tax from dividends paid by it to its Antilles parent company (Namloze Venwootschap or NV)[2]. The objects of a portfolio investment company must be investment in securities such as stock and shares, bonds, debentures and other interest bearing deposits of all types.

1 The Profits Tax (Corporate Income Tax) Ordinance 1940, paras 8, 14 and 14(a) (as amended).
2 Aruba is no longer part of the Netherlands Antilles.

4.143 If the Antilles company is a patent holding company[1] then similar tax rates will apply to royalty income received by it from sources outside the Antilles. The term 'patent holding' applies to most forms of intellectual property including patents, copyright, designs, trade marks and secret processes. Any royalties received by such an Antilles company would be subject to tax varying between 2.4 and 3.00 per cent. Because of the different nature of dividend and royalty income it may be necessary to incorporate two separate Antillean companies to obtain these low tax rates. It may be more suitable for the overseas company which is intended to receive and accumulate royalty income to be located in a different low tax jurisdiction.

If we refer to Diagram 1, post, it may be appropriate for the international corporate group structure to be as follows:

(1) A 'limbo' trust is settled by a non-resident non-domiciled settlor which holds all the shares in a tax haven resident company.

(2) The tax haven company owns all the issued share capital of the overseas company and the Netherlands Antilles company.

(3) The overseas company issues a licence to the Dutch intermediary company to use the patents (if any), trade marks, copyright, designs and know-how associated with the franchise business and, either owned by it or used by it with the consent of the United Kingdom franchisor, depending upon the anti-avoidance problems experienced by the United Kingdom franchisor[2]. The licence conforms to the requirements of the inspecteur in the Netherlands, who is responsible for the Dutch intermediary company and the taxable spread is agreed with him[3].

(4) The Dutch intermediary company grants franchises to its overseas franchisees and to the companies or partnerships arranged to minimise investment risk[4] or its own partly or wholly-owned subsidiary companies which own and operate company stores, subject to the tax treatment of royalties payable to Dutch residents by the tax authorities in each country in which the franchise business is conducted.

(5) The Netherlands Antilles company owns all the issued share capital of the Dutch intermediary company. The Netherlands Antilles company is a portfolio investment and holding company[5].

(6) The Dutch intermediary company applies for and obtains a 'participation exemption' in respect of its dividend income.

(7) Loans are made by the overseas company to the Dutch intermediary company, which then makes loans to overseas franchisees or its own subsidiaries.

(8) The income of both the overseas company and the Netherlands Antilles company is accumulated and not remitted to the United Kingdom so far as is possible.

4.144 *Tax problems*

1   The Profits Tax (Corporate Income Tax) Ordinance 1940, s 14a.
2   See paras 4.67 et seq, ante.
3   See para 4.132, ante.
4   See paras 4.109 et seq, ante.
5   The Profits Tax (Corporate Income Tax) Ordinance 1940, paras 8 and 14.

4.144 The level of interest or franchise fees charged by the Dutch intermediary company to its partly or wholly-owned subsidiaries must be reasonable in the prevailing commercial circumstances. Tax authorities, even in developed industrial countries, which do not impose general restrictions upon the payment of royalties or interest to non-residents, may tax or disallow that part of royalty or interest payments between related parties which they consider excessive. This may have a seriously adverse effect upon the net after-tax profits of the payer, because the amount disallowed may be treated as a distribution. It may be advantageous in these circumstances to interpose a separate Dutch royalty receiving company between the overseas company and the overseas franchisees to receive franchise fees on that part of those fees as is attributable to the use of intellectual property.

The United States franchisor

4.145 If a corporate franchisor resident in the United States of America decides to commence its franchise business in the United Kingdom in what manner will the income received or receivable by it from its United Kingdom franchisees be taxed (if at all) in the United Kingdom?

4.146 Article 12(2) of the US/UK Convention of 1975 states:

'(2) Royalties derived and beneficially owned by a resident of the United States shall be exempt from tax by the United Kingdom'.
'Royalties' are defined in Article 12(3) as follows:'(3) The term "royalties" as used in this Article (a) means payments of any kind received as a consideration for the use of, or the right to use, any copyright of literary, artistic or scientific work (but not including cinematographic films or films or tapes used for radio or television broadcasting); any patent, trade mark, design or model, plan, secret formula or process, or other like right or property, or for information concerning industrial, commercial or scientific experience; and (b) shall include gains derived from the alienation of any such right or property which are contingent on the productivity, use, or disposition thereof; including the supply of assistance of an ancillary and subsidiary nature furnished as a means of enabling the application or enjoyment of any such right or property.'

4.147 The term 'royalties' also includes payments for the supply of ancillary services as a means of enjoyment of the intellectual property right for the use of which the royalty payments are made. Accordingly, when a franchisor resident in the United States issues franchises to franchisees resident in the United Kingdom, the franchise fees (comprising a mixture of pure royalties and payments for ancillary services) will not be taxed nor be subject to withholding tax in the United Kingdom. Inland Revenue written clearance should be obtained, so that franchisees are not obliged to deduct tax at source from franchise fees[1]. However, when the franchisor is related to any of the franchisees, and a proportion of the franchise fees which are payable by those franchisees is excessive, the amount of that excess shall be taxable in the United Kingdom[2]. In the absence of a convention between the United

Investment risk 4.147

Diagram 1

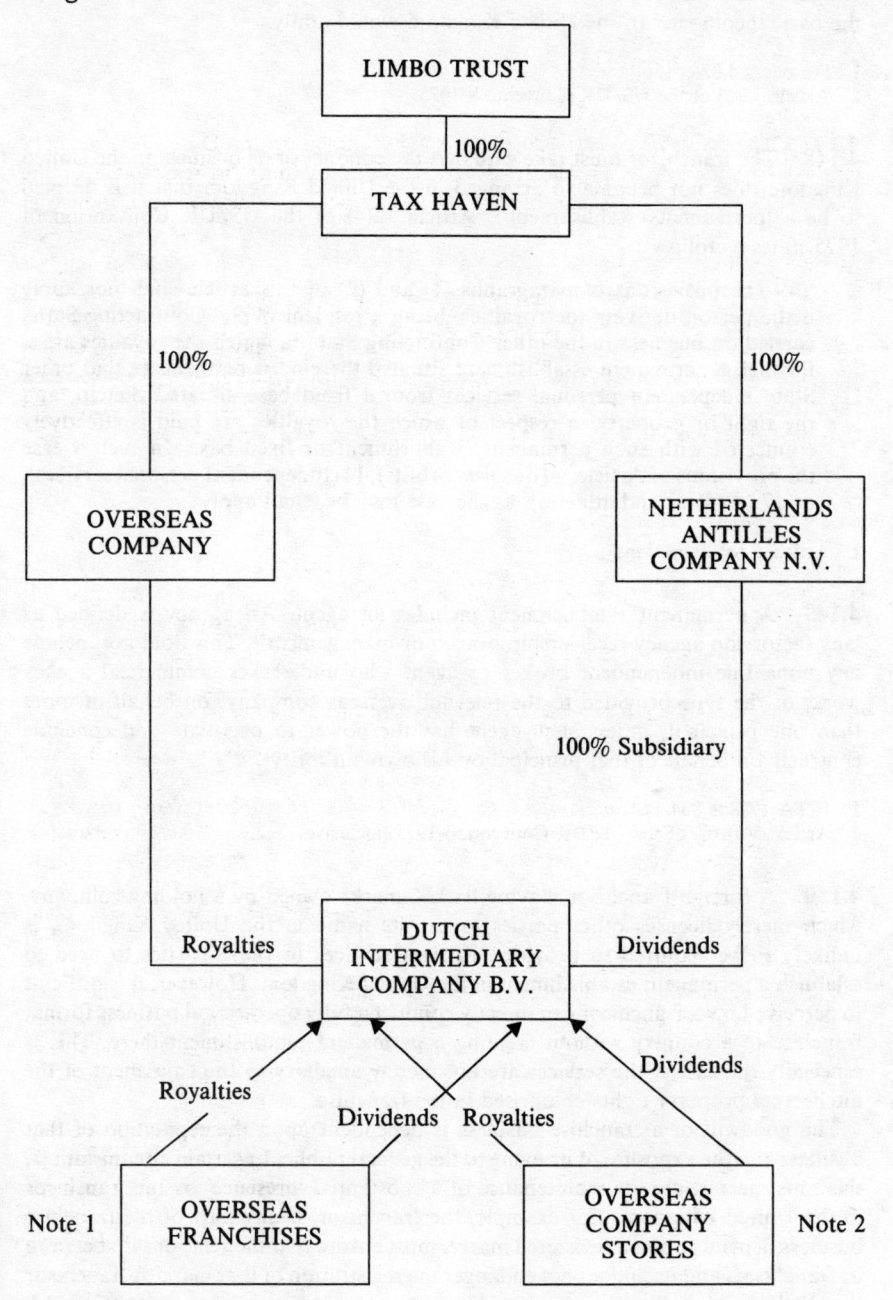

```
                    ┌─────────────────┐
                    │   LIMBO TRUST   │
                    └────────┬────────┘
                           100%
                    ┌────────┴────────┐
                    │    TAX HAVEN    │
                    └────────┬────────┘
            ┌────────────────┴────────────────┐
          100%                               100%
    ┌───────────────┐                 ┌─────────────────┐
    │   OVERSEAS    │                 │   NETHERLANDS   │
    │   COMPANY     │                 │    ANTILLES     │
    │               │                 │ COMPANY N.V.    │
    └───────┬───────┘                 └────────┬────────┘
            │                                  │
            │         100% Subsidiary          │
            │                                  │
            │      ┌─────────────────┐         │
            └──────┤     DUTCH       ├─────────┘
         Royalties │  INTERMEDIARY   │ Dividends
                   │   COMPANY B.V.  │
                   └────────┬────────┘
               ↑       ↑        ↑        ↑
          Royalties  Dividends Royalties  Dividends
       ┌──────────────┐              ┌──────────────┐
       │   OVERSEAS   │              │   OVERSEAS   │
Note 1 │  FRANCHISES  │              │   COMPANY    │ Note 2
       │              │              │    STORES    │
       └──────────────┘              └──────────────┘
```

Notes:
1 If any of the overseas franchisees is partly owned by the Dutch intermediary company, dividends will be payable by it to that company in addition to royalties.
2 Wholly or partly-owned subsidiaries of the Dutch intermediary company will pay both royalties and dividends.

4.148 *Tax problems*

Kingdom and the United States of America, withholding tax at the same rate as the basic income tax in the United Kingdom would apply.

1 See paras 4.02 et seq, ante.
2 Article 12(5) of the US/UK Convention 1975.

4.148 The franchisor must take care that the conduct of its business in the United Kingdom does not become so arranged in the United Kingdom that it is deemed to be a 'permanent establishment'[1]. Article 12(4) of the US/UK Convention of 1975 states as follows:

'(4) The provisions of paragraphs (1) and (2) of this article shall not apply if the person deriving the royalties, being a resident of the Contracting State, carried on business in the other Contracting State in which the royalties arise, through a permanent establishment situated therein, or performs in that other State independent personal services from a fixed base situated therein, and the right or property in respect of which the royalties are paid is effectively connected with such permanent establishment or fixed base. In such a case the provisions of Articles 7 (Business profits), 14 (Independent personal services), or 17 (Artistes and athletes), as the case may be, shall apply.'

1 Article 5 for definitions.

4.149 A permanent establishment includes an agent. An agency is defined as 'any factorship agency receivership branch or management'[1]. This does not include any bona fide independent broker or agent who undertakes commercial agency work, of the type provided to the relevant overseas company, on behalf of more than one principal, unless such agent has the power to negotiate and conclude contracts on behalf of that principal on his own authority[2].

1 ICTA 1988, s 834(1).
2 Article 5(3)–(6) of the US/UK Convention 1975 (inclusive).

4.150 A foreign franchisor, having its UK marks owned by a holding company, which merely licenses other parties to use its name in the United Kingdom, is unlikely to be required to provide sufficient services to those parties to need to establish a permanent establishment in the United Kingdom. However, it is difficult to perceive how a franchisor can directly conduct a fully operational business format franchise in a country without creating a permanent establishment there. This is especially the case if the services are not merely ancillary to the enjoyment of the intellectual property rights comprised in the franchise.

The goodwill of a franchise business is dependent upon the reputation of that business and the exposure of its name to the general public. In certain circumstances, this must necessitate the maintenance of a substantial 'presence' by the franchisor in the United Kingdom. For example, the franchisor, if any part of the franchise business depends upon a registered mark[1], must ensure that the relationship between its franchisees and itself does not endanger the registration of that mark. A franchisor should insist that some of its franchisees become registered users of its mark[2]. Registration is permissive. Use by registered users complying with the conditions of registration 'shall be deemed to be used by the proprietor thereof, and shall not be deemed to be used by a person other than the proprietor'[3] This applies to the provisions of the Trade Marks Act 1938 (as amended). Provided that a 'connection in the course of trade subsists' between the franchisor and the franchisee, such use of the mark by the franchisee shall not be deemed to be deceptive or likely to cause confusion[4]. Users of a mark are only to be registered if the Registrar is satisfied that the proprietor is entitled to exercise control over the use of the mark by the user[5]. There is no method available to the Registrar to enforce this requirement. In general, the control intended to be exercised is in the nature of quality control over the goods and services supplied by the user of the mark. It may be, that if such control is not exercised by the franchisor, the registration of its mark in the United Kingdom may be endangered. Accordingly, the franchisor should be in a position to demonstrate to the Registrar that it is able properly to control the use of the mark and actually exercise that control over its franchisees. This will be difficult if the franchisor merely intends to permit its franchisees to use its mark and does not intend to supervise and control the activities of its franchisees in any way. If it does supervise and control those activities directly, it is likely to be deemed to have established a permanent establishment or a branch in the United Kingdom. If it appoints an agent to undertake the supervision and control, the agent must be a bona fide independent commercial agent acting for other principals in the same business unless the agent is to become the 'permanent agent' of the franchisor in which case the profits accruing to the franchisor as a result of the activities of the agent will be charged to tax in the United Kingdom. If it does not exercise any such control, then the validity of the registration of the trade mark may be open to challenge by disgruntled franchisees or competitors and the goodwill being generated by the franchise business seriously damaged. It is arguable that any activity in the United Kingdom to encourage the exploitation of intellectual property protected in the United Kingdom may be carrying on a trade in the United Kingdom[6]. If that activity is undertaken by employees or authorised exclusive agents of the franchisor then a permanent establishment or branch or agency may be deemed to arise. In these circumstances, the franchisor may be prudent if it incorporates a United Kingdom resident subsidiary to undertake its supervision and control activities[7]. If the United States franchisor makes investments in the United Kingdom which are subject to a considerable degree of commercial risk, then, because group relief is not available between United Kingdom resident subsidiaries of a non-resident parent company, the United States franchisor should incorporate a United Kingdom resident holding company, so that such relief may be passed between the resident members of the group[8].

1 See paras 3.20 and 4.77 et seq, ante.
2 Trade Marks Act 1938, s 28. See paras 3.137 and 4.81 et seq, ante.
3 Trade Marks Act 1938, s 28(2).
4 Ibid, s 62.
5 Ibid, s 28. See para 3.140 and 4.81, ante.
6 *Noddy Subsidiary Rights Co Ltd v IRC* [1966] 3 All ER 459, 43 TC 458.
7 See para 4.151, post.
8 See para 4.110, ante.

4.151 If the franchisor does set up a permanent establishment in the United Kingdom, then Article 7 of the Convention will apply:

'(1) The business profits of an enterprise of a Contracting State shall be taxable only in that State unless the enterprise carries on business in the other Contracting State through a permanent establishment situated therein. If the enterprise carried on business as aforesaid, the business profits of the enterprise may be taxed in that other State but only so much of them as is attributable to that permanent establishment.'

4.152 *Tax problems*

'Business profits' are defined in Article 7(7) and include 'the furnishing of services'. A potentially ambiguous situation could arise, if the permanent establishment of a United States resident company is not engaged in the franchise business, but in some other business of the company so that the fees paid by franchisees are not income of that establishment[1]. In that case Article 7(6) would apply:

'(6) Where profits include items of income which are dealt with separately in other Articles of this Convention, then the provisions of those Articles shall not be affected by the provisions of this Article.'

Royalties are treated separately under Article 12 and Article 12(2) therefore, would be relevant. If the United States corporate franchisor conducts its business in the United Kingdom through a permanent establishment, it will be taxed on the profits attributable to the permanent establishment at the highest rate of United Kingdom corporation tax[2]. Those profits are calculated after assessing the level of income which an independent organisation undertaking the same business would be expected to achieve[3] and deducting from that amount expenses incurred including reasonable allocations of general administrative expenses (whether or not incurred in the United Kingdom)[4].

1 See paras 4.105, ante and 4.154 et seq, post.
2 See para 4.152, post.
3 Article 7(2) of the US/UK Convention 1975.
4 Article 7(3) of the US/UK Convention 1975.

4.152 The franchisor will wish to use all taxes paid by it in the United Kingdom as a foreign tax credit against its United States tax liabilities, by virtue of Article 23(1) of the US/UK Convention, in respect of business profits[1] earned through a permanent establishment located in the United Kingdom. Those business profits include not only income arising from 'the furnishing of services', but, also 'any other income effectively connected with a permanent establishment which the recipient being a resident of one of the Contracting States, has in the other Contracting State'[2].

Royalties which are the subject of Article 12(2), but, which are caught by the operation of Article 12(4) (permanent Establishment rules) will be eligible for treatment as business profits for the purposes of Article 23(1). The franchisor may not receive tax credits in the United States for the full amount of United Kingdom corporation tax suffered by it. Calculation of the foreign tax credit allowable is based on detailed regulations concerning the apportionment of expenses and deductions between foreign and domestic income and the following formula:

$$\frac{\text{Net foreign income from all Sources and countries}}{\text{Total taxable income}} \times \text{US Tax rate} = \text{Foreign tax credit allowable}$$

1 Article 7 of the US/UK Convention 1975.
2 Article 7(7) of the US/UK Convention 1975.

4.153 If the United States resident franchisor commences and undertakes its franchise business in the United Kingdom, through a branch or permanent establishment, it will face some disadvantages as follows:
(1) a permanent establishment located in the United Kingdom of a company

resident overseas will be taxed on the profits of the permanent establishment arising in the United Kingdom at the maximum rate of corporation tax irrespective of the amount of profit[1];

(2) any interest (other than short interest)[2] payable by the franchisor in respect of funds borrowed by it to finance the trade of its branch in the United Kingdom will not be treated as a deduction or a charge on income, unless:

    (a) that interest is paid to a bank conducting business in the United Kingdom or a member of the Stock Exchange or a discount house, or

    (b) is interest to which ICTA 1988, s 340 applies unless any relevant Article of a double taxation agreement applies[3]. If such a provision applies it will be allowed as a charge on income;

(3) any royalties payable by the franchisor to a third party who is not resident in the United Kingdom will suffer the same fate unless the franchisor deducts income tax at source[4] and the payment of that royalty was incurred for valuable and sufficient consideration and wholly and exclusively for the purposes of the trade of the branch in the United Kingdom[5]. This restriction may appear irrelevant, but if the franchisor is paying to a third party a royalty for the use of a patent for equipment used in the franchise or in respect of a licence for the use of characters in a promotional programme, these provisions may have serious consequences. If the third party is resident in the United Kingdom and the royalty is in respect of a patent[6] or if the payment is in the nature of 'pure income profit' in respect of the use of a trade mark[7] then tax must be deducted at source from those payments[8]. The same comments concerning the provisions of a double taxation agreement made in paragraph (2) above will apply to payments to a non-resident.

If the taxable income of the branch is expected to be low and the franchisor intends to repatriate the earnings of the branch, mainstream corporation tax only will be payable and the cash flow of the franchisor may be more satisfactory than that derived from a similarly performing United Kingdom subsidiary which must account to the Inland Revenue for ACT when it makes distributions. These may be earlier than the date when mainstream corporation tax must be paid[9].

1   ICTA 1988, s 13. Current maximum corporation tax rate is 35 per cent.
2   ICTA 1988, s 338(3)(a) and (4)(a). See paras 4.62 et seq, ante.
3   For example Article 11(2) of the US/UK DTC 1975.
4   ICTA 1988, s 338(4)(a).
5   Ibid, s 338(5)(b).
6   Ibid, s 348(2)(a).
7   *IRC v National Book League* [1957] Ch 488, 37 TC 455. See paras 4.01 et seq, ante.
8   See paras 4.01 et seq, ante.
9   Usually 1 January in each year after the expiry of the financial year of the company.

4.154 As an alternative to direct franchising the United States franchisor may wish to incorporate a subsidiary in the United Kingdom which undertakes the franchise business for the franchisor. In this case, the subsidiary/head franchisee may take an area franchise agreement for the territory of the United Kingdom. It will pay royalties to its United States parent which will not be subject to tax in the United Kingdom[1] provided that the amount of the royalties is not excessive[2]. Any further profits made by the subsidiary/head franchisee will be subject to United Kingdom corporation tax in the usual manner[3]. The United States franchisor may make loans to the subsidiary. Interest paid by a United Kingdom resident corporation is allowable as a charge on income for corporation tax purposes in certain circumstances.[4] Interest derived and beneficially owned by a resident of the United

4.155 *Tax problems*

States is exempt from tax in the United Kingdom[5]. Interest is defined by Article 11(3) of the US/UK Convention as:

'(3) The term "interest" as used in this article means income from Government securities, bonds or debentures, whether or not secured by mortgage and whether or not carrying a right to participate in profits, and other debt claims of every kind as well as all other income assimilated to income from money lent by the taxation law of the State in which the income arises but, subject to the provisions of paragraph (7) of this Article, shall not include any income which is treated as a distribution under the provisions of Article 10 (Dividends). Penalty charges for later payment shall not be regarded as interest for the purposes of this article.'

If the recipient of the interest has a permanent establishment in the United Kingdom, with which the debt, from which the interest arises, is effectively connected, the interest is taxable in the United Kingdom[6]. If the franchisor is trading in the United Kingdom in a different field of business through a permanent establishment, it must ensure that there is a clear distinction between its own activities and those of its subsidiary.

1 Article 12(2) of the US/UK Convention 1975.
2 Ibid, Art 12(5).
3 See para 4.55, ante.
4 See paras 4.55 and 4.62 et seq, ante.
5 Article 11(2) of the US/UK Convention 1975.
6 Article 11(4) of the US/UK Convention 1975.

4.155 If the franchisor incorporates a subsidiary/head franchisee and lends funds to that company, Articles 11(5) and 11(7) will apply:

'(5) Where, owing to a special relationship between the payer and the person deriving the interest or between both of them and some other person, the amount of the interest paid exceeds for whatever reason the amount which would have been paid in the absence of such relationship, the provisions of the article shall apply only to the last-mentioned amount. In that case, the excess part of the payments shall remain taxable according to the law of each Contracting State, due regard being had to the other provisions of this Convention.'
'(7) Any provision in the law of either Contracting State relating only to interest paid to a non-resident corporation shall not operate so as to require such interest paid to a resident of the other Contracting State to be treated as a distribution by the corporation paying such interest. The preceding sentence shall not apply to interest paid to a corporation of one Contracting State in which more than 50 per cent of the voting power is controlled, directly or indirectly, by a person or persons who are residents of the other Contracting State.'

If the interest payable by the subsidiary/head franchisee to its parent is excessive, then the excess amount will be treated as a distribution[1] by the Inland Revenue. In that event, the provisions of the Double Taxation Agreement relating to dividends[2] will come into effect[3]. Any rate of interest which exceeds a commercial rate, which would have been negotiated by independent parties in the same financial and security circumstances, will be deemed to be excessive. In addition, the Inland Revenue may insist upon disallowance of all interest payable on that proportion of the loan finance which they consider should have been contributed by the parent as capital

Investment risk 4.156

rather than debt. This is the so-called 'thinly capitalised' rule and is based upon the words 'for whatever reason' in Article 11(5).

It is arguable that whilst Article 11(7) overcomes the problems posed by ICTA 1988, s 209, it does not overcome the difficulties caused by sections 338–340 of that Act. A combination of Article 11(2) (exemption of interest from tax in the United Kingdom) and Article 11(7) (which prevents the payment of interest being treated as a distribution) may not prevent the interest paid by the subsidiary/ franchisee being disallowed as a charge on its income[4] unless in the case of yearly interest, the subsidiary/franchisee is deemed to have deducted tax at source from the interest payment[5] and added back the deduction by virtue of the provisions of the Convention[6]. Clearance on this point should be obtained from the Inland Revenue. Accordingly, if the franchisor lends money to its subsidiary/head franchisee, it must ensure that its subsidiary is sufficiently capitalised by it, so that any loans made by it to the subsidiary are not treated as being part of 'thin capitalisation'. In addition, any interest payable by the subsidiary to the franchisor must be at a reasonable commercial rate in all the circumstances.

1 ICTA 1988,s 209(2)(e)(iv) and (a).
2 Article 10 of the US/UK Convention 1975.
3 See para 4.156, post.
4 ICTA 1988, s 340(2).
5 Ibid, s 338(4)(a).
6 Article 11(2) of the US/UK Convention 1975.

4.156 If the subsidiary/franchisee makes profits after payment of royalties and interest to the United States franchisor, those profits will be subject to United Kingdom corporation tax[1]. Upon the assumption that the franchisor owns more than 10 per cent of the shares of its subsidiary/head franchisee, then Article 10(2)(a)(i) of the US/UK Convention 1975 will apply:

'(2)(a) In the case of dividends paid by a corporation which is a resident of the United Kingdom: (i) to a United States corporation which either alone or together with one or more associated corporations controls, directly or indirectly, at least 10 per cent of the voting stock of the corporation which is a resident of the United Kingdom paying the dividend, the United States corporation shall be entitled to a payment from the United Kingdom of a tax credit to which an individual resident in the United Kingdom would have been entitled had he received the dividend, subject to the deduction withheld from such payment and according to the laws of the United Kingdom of an amount not exceeding 5 per cent of the aggregate of the amount or value of the dividend and the amount of the tax credit paid to such corporation.'

There are a number of points in Article 10 which must be considered:

(1) The words 'controls, directly or indirectly' means that where a franchisor holds less than 10 per cent directly in the franchisee, but owns shares in another company, which, itself, owns shares in the franchisee, the franchisor will be deemed to own both the shares held in its own name and a proportion of the shares of the franchisee held by the other company. For example:

Issue share capital of franchisee = 100

Direct shareholding of franchisee = 5

Shareholding of franchisor in other company $\frac{50}{100}$

4.157 *Tax problems*

Shareholding of other company in franchisee = $\underline{40}$

Indirect shareholding of franchisor in franchisee $\frac{50}{100} \times 40 = \underline{20}$

Total shareholding of franchisor in franchisee = $\underline{20}$

% of total shares of franchisee held by franchisor $\frac{25}{100} \times \frac{100}{1} = \underline{25\%}$

Indeed, the Article does not mention 'ownership' but merely 'control'. The franchisor need not, therefore, hold any shares of its subsidiary/franchisee provided that it is able to control them.

(2) The Article refers to 'voting stock'. It is possible to incorporate a company in the United Kingdom with different classes of shares to which different rights are attached. If the franchisor is willing to relinquish voting control of the company, then it may take shares in the company, to which all rights as to dividends and distributions are attached, but, which command no votes within the franchise company. Any voting shares, of which very few would be issued, would be held by independent third parties. If the franchisor controls less than 10 per cent of the voting stock of the franchisee, Article 10(2)(a)(ii) of the Convention may apply and the additional withholding tax (or non-allowance of the full tax credit) of not more than 5 per cent may not be levied. The text of Article 10(a)(a)(i) of the US/UK Convention must be contrasted with Articles 10(3)(c) and 10(3)(d)(ii) of the UK/Netherlands treaty[2].

(3) The effect of Article 10(2)(a)(i) is to provide the United States franchisor, which controls more than 10 per cent of the voting stock of its franchisee with a repayment of one half of the tax credit, which would have been available to a United Kingdom resident[3], as a result of the payment of ACT by the company on payment of its dividend to its shareholders, less the additional withholding tax of 5 per cent. A United Kingdom resident is assessed for tax on the gross amount of the dividend paid to him, but the amount paid by the company to the Inland Revenue in the form of ACT is allowed as a credit against his total tax liabilities[4]. The additional withholding tax is calculated as a proportion of the cash dividend paid by the United Kingdom resident company plus one half of the deduction made by it. The net amount receivable by the United States franchisor parent would be calculated as set out in para 4.139 ante. That arrangement was successfully challenged by a parent company resident in the United States of America[5]. However, the Treasury restored the original interpretation by FA 1989, s 115(2).

(4) In the event that the United States franchisor 'controls' less than ten per cent of the "voting stock" of the United Kingdom resident company, then it will be entitled to receive a cash refund of the whole of the ACT, less a deduction from the tax credit payment of 15per cent of the aggregate of the net dividend and the tax credit (in this case the full amount of ACT).

1 See para 4.55, ante.
2 See para 4.140, ante.
3 See para 4.55, ante.
4 For cash dividend and ACT example see para 4.55, ante.
5 *Union Texas International Corpn v Critchley (Inspector of Taxes)* [1990] STC 305, CA.

4.157 The United States franchisor must file form US7/Credit with the Internal Revenue Service. If the franchisor files United States tax returns, then the Internal

Investment risk 4.158

Revenue Service will certify that fact and forward the form to the Inland Revenue (Inspector of Foreign Dividends).

The inspector will authorise the United Kingdom subsidiary/franchisee to pay to its parent one half of the applicable ACT (less the additional tax where relevant)[1]. The United Kingdom subsidiary/franchisee must account to the Inland Revenue for the other half of the ACT (and the additional tax where relevant)[2].

1 The Double Tax Relief (Taxes of Income) (General) (Dividend) Regulations 1973.
2 ICTA 1988, s 350(4), Sch 16, paras 2–4.

4.158 If a United States resident franchisor desires to commence franchising in Europe or elsewhere outside the United States of America, it may wish to consider the accumulation of the profits of its overseas franchise business outside the scope of United States tax. Similar arrangements to those discussed in connection with a United Kingdom resident franchisor and the incorporation of a Netherlands intermediary company may be suitable.

However, in view of the restrictive nature of the sub-part F rules of the Internal Revenue Code, such arrangements may be more difficult than for United Kingdom residents.

Chapter 5
Setting up the franchise business: some other considerations

Introduction

5.01 Because of the wide variety of franchise operations which it is possible to envisage, it is impossible to deal with every point which may arise in practice. In this section we consider some of the matters which *commonly* need to be borne in mind when setting up a franchise business. A commentary on individual clauses is provided alongside the precedents in Chapter 8. In this section we set out some general considerations, drawing as appropriate on the detailed exposition of the key areas of law, set out earlier. Franchisors may of course be unwilling to accept some of the suggestions we make. Draftsmen thus forced to live dangerously will simply have to do the best they can.

5.02 It is particularly important in the case of franchise agreements to attempt to anticipate all possible difficulties which may be raised by a franchisee's solicitor. The bedrock of the operation is the preservation of strict uniformity between outlets. It is essential therefore that the terms of individual agreements should not be negotiable. Indeed a franchisee's solicitor who raises objections and who in return receives an offer to change terms ought to be suspicious, since it suggests that the franchisor may be prepared to enter into different agreements with different franchisees. Apart from the possible danger of this to the success of the operation, it suggests market weakness on the part of the franchisor. Indeed franchising is an area where the *proferens* should look upon an adhesion contract[1] as a favourable sign. However, the franchisor must clearly distinguish between his role as controller of the franchise chain and his role in negotiating with individual franchisees[2].

1 Ie preformulated stipulations in which the proferor's will is predominant: Saleilles, *Declaration de Volonté*.
2 See para 6.03 et seq, post.

5.03 Subject to this, the principal difficulty in drafting agreements is to impose as much control over the franchisees as possible in order to ensure uniformity and quality of service, while at the same time avoiding possible collision with competition law, and avoiding creating a relationship which could result in the franchisor being held liable to third parties[1]. Whilst so far as competition law is concerned it may be considered that because of the *de minimis* policy there is no need to bother about EEC or United Kingdom 'effects' legislation either (though circumstances when it will be possible to be sure about this will not often arise[2]), competition law[3] must not be ignored. In particular, the Restrictive Trade Practices Act is a trap for the unwary, so long as it remains in force, since it has the potential to render void covenants in restraint of trade.[4] Moreover, if the chain prospers, difficulties could arise, especially if there are disgruntled franchisees[5]. The practitioner should be aware of the problems all of these measures potentially present from the outset.

1 See paras 5.44 et seq, post.
2 See para 2.68 ante.
3 Including the common law doctrine of restraint of trade.
4 See para 2.141 et seq.
5 See eg *Pronuptia*, para 2.16 ante.

The operating manual

5.04 This is a crucial part of the whole package. It should contain details of the intellectual property, equipment, and various procedures covered in the training programme which are needed to operate the business[1]. These will include accounting systems, sales and service report forms, VAT returns, equipment maintenance, preparation of product, dealing with staff, customer complaints procedures, advertising and promotion at a local level. A provision should be inserted requiring the franchisee not to disclose the contents of the manual other than as necessary to persons actually engaged in the running of the business[2], and requiring the manual to be returned in the event of the franchise agreement terminating or not proceeding[3]. A provision for updating the manual should also be inserted[4]. The strategy adopted in precedent 1 is to make the manual the linchpin of the whole agreement by incorporating it into the agreement[5]. This allows the same form to be used for different kinds of franchise business. The manual should always remain the property of the franchisor. A serial number for each manual issued should be given and, if practicable, printed across each page. If the manual is then copied for use by unauthorised persons, at least the source of the 'leak' may be ascertained if the copies are discovered by the franchisor. The franchisee should be obliged by the express terms of the agreement not to copy any part of the manual. The device of incorporating the manual has the effect that throughout the duration of the franchise agreement, the franchisor will be able to make detailed or substantial changes to the administration of the franchised business by altering the relevant instructions in the manual. This means that the business will be flexible enough to absorb and respond to changes in legislation, taxation, competition, new technology, fashions in 'house-styles', banking and accountancy procedures, and any other matters which a prudent but innovative franchisor considers may affect the franchised business.

1 See Ch 8, precedent 1, clause 6.7, post.
2 See Ch 8, precedent 1, clause 7.26, post.
3 See Ch 8, precedent 1, clause 9.1:6, post.
4 See Ch 8, precedent 1, clause 6.3, post.
5 See Ch 8, precedent 1, clause 10.7, post.

Safeguard trade secrets and know-how if possible by non-legal strategies

5.05 Legal restrictions may in practice provide a poor safeguard for the franchisor. Trade secrets are best preserved by not being revealed to franchisees. Essential material made to a secret formula, or by a secret process, can be supplied to franchisees ready made. This strategy is well known in manufacturing licences,

5.06 Setting up the franchise business: some other considerations

and may well be applicable to some franchise operations. Even American courts have accepted that such ties might be justified, as also has the European Commission[1]. Another strategy sometimes used in manufacturing licences is to have an essential part of the process carried out by an employee of the licensor at the premises of the licensee. The employee has no contact with the licensee save through his employers, and may be able to cover a number of outlets. This plan might be applicable to some kinds of franchise operations.

1 See Reg 4087/88 Art 3 1.(b) and 5(e)—see para 2.20 and 2.23 ante. For American examples see eg *Coca-Cola Bottling Co v Coca-Cola Co* 269 F 796 (1920); *Susser v Carvel Corpn* 206 F Supp 636 (1962); on appeal 332 F 2d 505 (1964).

Supply of the initial equipment, etc

5.06 Probably the requirement that the franchisee acquire the initial equipment and items needed to start the business from the franchisor does not of itself involve restrictions accepted by two parties, so as to make the agreement registrable under the Restrictive Trade Practices Act[1]. However, it may in effect in certain circumstances amount to a type of full line forcing which could be held objectionable under the Competition Act 1980. It could also lead to difficulties with regard to Article 85.1 of the Treaty of Rome. It is clearly outside the block exemption, unless it is impractical owing to the nature of the goods, to apply objective quality specifications. Protection of the franchisor's intellectual property, such as trade marks, is also a permissible reason for specifying the supplies of the initial equipment[2] provided that this is genuinely necessary and that it is not disguised full line forcing. Ideally, as far as possible, the franchisee should be provided with specifications and left to purchase items where he likes. He may well in fact prefer not to have the bother of shopping around. However, it is the fact that he has the freedom to do so, should he so choose, which matters.

1 See paras 2.141 et seq ante. Certainly a requirement that the franchisee acquire equipment from approved suppliers, would seem not to involve such restrictions.
2 Reg 4087/88 Art 5(c)—para 2.23, ante.

Ties

5.07 It is certainly in general true that there may be merit from a business point of view in allowing the franchisee to purchase as many of the goods needed by him in the course of the business from whatever sources he chooses. If he is thereby able to purchase equivalent quality goods more cheaply than from the franchisor, he may be able to lower prices and be more competitive—and after all one of the bases of the system is individual initiative though within limits acceptable to the franchisor for the good of the network as a whole. A franchisee who can do this is less likely to become frustrated with the restrictions which have been imposed on him in the interests of preserving the public image of the business as a whole. This is in the interests of the franchisor as well, whose success depends on the success of the individual franchisees. The trouble with franchising in this respect, however, is that what benefits an individual franchisee does not necessarily benefit the network. An obvious example of this is the problems created by transport costs. Let us assume that the franchisor has placed his outlets in a town strategically so that one delivery van can service them quickly and economically. Two franchisees drop out because they can obtain some of the particular goods more cheaply elsewhere. The increased costs of delivery now have to be borne by the others, who thereby suffer. Worse still, their increased costs may cause the network as a whole to suffer because the public do not distinguish between outlets. If ten outlets are expensive and two cheap they may well not realise this, and the two franchisees who 'dropped out' will suffer also. Whether or not in an individual business, ties are beneficial to the welfare of all parties, must depend on the particular circumstances of the business concerned. Obviously, if the benefits of bulk purchasing can be passed on, and distribution costs lowered overall, the fact that one individual franchisee can do better for himself may not be an argument for allowing him to do so[1]. Franchisees often argue that the lower costs afforded by bulk discounts available to the 'network' should at least compensate for the amount of the fees payable to the franchisor. That argument has some validity, especially in the early years of a franchise, before a nationally recognised image for the franchise has been created. However, especially in later years, when the franchise is clearly successful, it ignores the value of trading under a group image.

1 This possibility is not, however, covered by Reg 4087/88—see para 2.18 et seq and 2.44 ante.

5.08 In the case of 'manufacturing' franchises[1], as explained above[2], 'tie-ins' may be a useful device for preserving trade secrets and know-how, and they may be justified as a means of quality control necessary to preserve goodwill. In this last regard, however, the best course wherever possible is to provide the franchisees with detailed specifications and leave them to purchase where they like. This strategy may also be appropriate for the 'tie-ins' in other franchises. There can be sound business reasons for this, quite apart from avoiding the legal problems to which ties potentially give rise, even where a franchisor has chosen franchising as a way of distributing goods made by him. If the cost at which the franchisor's manufacturing business is able to supply the goods to the outlets becomes uncompetitive, both the manufacturing enterprise and the franchise chain will go under. If on the other hand the franchisor provides the franchisees with specifications and requires only that they sell goods corresponding to those specifications under, where appropriate, the franchisor's marks and monitors the quality, then if the franchisees are able to get the same goods made more cheaply elsewhere, the franchise chain may flourish while only the franchisor's original manufacturing enterprise sinks. These considerations need to be balanced against those set out in the previous paragraph.

1 Para 2.49, ante.
2 Para 5.05, ante.

5.09 If possible, franchisors should be steered away from the superficially attractive policy of charging a low fee and recouping most of their profits from tied items. Although this strategy is general in the brewing industry through the tied public-house system, where a small 'dry-rent' is charged, and most of the brewery's profits recouped on the 'wet rent' charged on the products delivered to the licensee, it cannot be too strongly emphasised that what is hallowed by tradition in one trade will not necessarily be thought acceptable in another. It is, after all, to some extent a rational strategy because of the experiences of distributing draft beer. The arguments in favour of this payment strategy in franchising are both reputable and disreputable. The reputable argument is that it is a very simple way of accounting. The disreputable argument is that it is a means of disguising a high royalty fee. The American

5.10 *Setting up the franchise business: some other considerations*

experience, and indeed the experience with 'solus' agreements in this country, should offer a warning in this respect[1]. There is a very real possibility that disgruntled franchisees might attempt by one means or another to break the ties. If a franchisor insists upon a 'mark-up' on goods or services supplied by it or by its direction, the agreement must contain a clause[2] which permits him to charge a royalty based upon turnover if tied-sales become impossible to enforce because of competition laws.

1 See generally paras 2.02 et seq and 2.98 et seq, ante. The leading 'solus' cases are *Petrofina (GB) Ltd v Martin* [1966] Ch 146, [1966] 1 All ER 126; *Esso Petroleum Co Ltd v Harper's Garage (Stourport) Ltd* [1968] AC 269, [1967] 1 All ER 699, HL.
2 See for example precedent 1, clause 7.14, post.

Checklist

5.10 (1) Where ties are imposed in relation to any type of franchise agreement, the checklists in chapter 2, ante, should be referred to.

(2) Consider inserting a contingent provision for the charging of royalties on turnover should the tie be struck down (precedent 1, clause 7.14).

'Tie-ins' in patent licence

5.11 Under the Patents Act 1977 (s 44, relating to contracts to supply patented products) terms requiring the franchisee to acquire other than the patented product from the franchisor or other specified supplier, or which prohibit him from acquiring elsewhere are void. In the case of licences to work patented inventions, terms requiring the franchisees to acquire from the franchisor or specified suppliers, or which prohibit him from acquiring from elsewhere, anything other than the invention (or product produced by a patented process) are void. Similarly prohibitions on the franchisees using other articles. The existence of such a tie can nullify the patent[1]. Exclusive distributorships prohibiting the distributor from selling goods other than those obtained from a specified person are an exception to this rule, as also are ties requiring spare parts to be purchased from the franchisor or his nominees[2].

1 Section 44(3).
2 Section 44(6).

5.12 There is a loophole to these provisions under section 44(4). Provided the licensor was willing to grant a licence on reasonable terms without such a tie and the licensee can relieve himself of it by three months' written notice (and payment of suitable compensation), the condition of the licence imposing the tie is not void. Where advantage is sought to be taken of this provision, a recital should be included in the agreement. It is possible to use this provision to tie the franchisee also to approved suppliers, and even in cases where it is difficult to compute royalties on sales (surely rare in franchising), to provide by an arrangement with the supplier that the supplier will charge an additional sum to the franchisee on each sale which will be paid over to the franchisor. If any ties of any sort are contemplated however, antitrust law must be considered quite independently of the validity of the tie under patent law[1].

1 See generally Ch 2 and especially at para 2.44, ante.

Patent 'tie-in' checklist

5.13 (1) Recite fact that franchisor was willing to grant licence without 'tie-in'.

(2) Include term under which tie may be terminated by three months' written notice.

(3) Consider application of competition laws.

Consumer Credit Act 1974

5.14 Where an *individual* franchisee is raising a sum of under £15 000 in order to purchase the franchise, attention needs to be paid to the possibility of the franchise agreement being a 'linked transaction' in relation to the loan. The two main consequences of it being a linked transaction are that it may fall with the credit transaction if that is cancellable and the franchisee cancels within the cooling off period; moreover termination of the credit transaction under Part III will terminate the franchise agreement. 'Linked transaction' is defined in section 19.

Section 19 provides as follows:

'(1) A transaction entered into by the debtor or hirer, or a relative of his, with any other person ("the other party"), except one for the provision of security, is a linked transaction in relation to an actual or prospective regulated agreement (the "principal agreement") of which it does not form part if—

(a) the transaction is entered into in compliance with a term of the principal agreement; or

(b) the principal agreement is a debtor-creditor-supplier agreement and the transaction is financed, or to be financed, by the principal agreement; or

(c) the other party is a person mentioned in subsection (2), and a person so mentioned initiated the transaction by suggesting it to the debtor or hirer, or his relative, who enters into it—

(i) to induce the creditor or owner to enter into the principal agreement, or

(ii) for another purpose related to the principal agreement, or

(iii) where the principal agreement is a restricted-use credit agreement, for a purpose related to a transaction financed, or to be financed, by the principal agreement.

(2) The person referred to in subsection (1)(c) is—

(a) the creditor or owner, or his associate;

(b) a person who, in the negotiation of the transaction, is represented by a credit-broker who is also a negotiator in antecedent negotiations for the principal agreement;

(c) a person who, at the time the transaction is initiated, knows that the principal agreement has been made or contemplates that it might be made.

(3) A linked transaction entered into before the making of the principal agreement has no effect until such time (if any) as that agreement is made.

(4) Regulations may exclude linked transactions of the prescribed description from the operation of subsection (3).'

If circumstances exist where the franchise agreement could be a linked transaction, it may be advisable to require the franchisee to incorporate. The main reason for requiring this is of course the termination problem if that is likely to be a problem in the particular case.

5.15 *Setting up the franchise business: some other considerations*

The franchise premises

Finding sites

5.15 One of the reasons why a franchise may be a safer investment than starting up a business independently, is that the franchisee can obtain the benefit of skilled advice on site selection. Successful franchise companies are national organisations, operating with a more or less standard set of criteria for evaluating sites, which they have built up from experience gained in their pilot schemes and previous franchise operations. It is always possible, however, that the potential franchisee may have knowledge of local conditions which makes his own evaluation of a site more reliable. This is one of the advantages franchising offers to a franchisor as against marketing through company owned outlets. In site selection, the franchisor should always give considered attention to the franchisee's observations. Although in theory the franchisee can always simply refuse to go ahead, in practice it may well be that he may allow himself to be pushed into a site which he knows intuitively is inferior.

5.16 Where the agreement is signed before a site has been found, it should be stipulated that its coming into operation is conditional on a suitable site being found, and obtaining the necessary planning and other consents[1]. The agreement should also stipulate who is to obtain those consents[2]. Where the franchisor is to license or lease the premises to the franchisee this will presumably be the franchisor[3]. In the event of the franchisee being expected to acquire the site and obtain the necessary consents, the franchisor should of course offer assistance and advice on this[4]. The introduction to the precedents[5] sets out the sequence of agreements and commitments in the grant and acceptance of a franchise.

1 See Purchase Agreement precedent 9, clause 5, post, chapter 8.
2 Ch 8, Purchase Agreement, precedent 9, clause 4.7, post.
3 See paras 4.18 et seq, ante for potential tax problems.
4 The question of which strategy to adopt is considered in the next paragraphs.
5 See p 308.

Who should own the premises?

5.17 An initial problem which will have to be confronted in most cases is the acquisition of the franchised business premises. In general the advice should be that if capital is available, and the franchisee is prepared to agree to this, these should be acquired by the franchisor and the franchisee granted a lease or a licence to use them[1]. The possession of a large number of prime sites has proved a considerable asset in raising capital for further expansion and diversification for some successful American networks, and the same thing should apply a fortiori in the United Kingdom. A further advantage of site ownership is that it makes the situation on termination more straightforward, without the franchisor having to sacrifice a good site. Assuming that the franchisor is able to buy the premises for the franchised business, and the franchisee is willing to proceed on the basis that he is to be granted a lease or a licence of them, the question arises under which form should he be let into occupation?

1 Full precedents have not been provided for these, because so long as the problems discussed in the following pages are borne in mind, the precedents generally used for

commercial leases or licenses suffice. We have however included some individual clauses which may be of use.

Lease or licence?

5.18 At present, under the Landlord and Tenant Act 1954, a tenant has both security of tenure and the right to compensation for improvements. Bearing this in mind, it would seem if possible preferable to grant the franchisee a licence rather than a tenancy. So far as the Restrictive Trade Practices Act 1976 is concerned, there would appear to be little to choose between the two forms. The court in the *Ravenseft* case[1] rejected the argument that the Act had no application to covenants in leases, and based its decision on the 'opening the door' principle[2] which is equally applicable to licences. Tax treatment of licence fees is the same as that of rents.[3]

1 *Ravenseft Properties Ltd's Application* [1978] QB 52, [1977] 1 All ER 47.
2 *Re Automatic Telephone and Electric Co Ltd's Application* [1963] 2 All ER 302, LR 3 RP 462; *Esso Petroleum Co Ltd v Harper's Garage* [1968] AC 269, [1967] 1 All ER 699, HL.
3 Income and Corporation Taxes Act 1988, s 15(1) Schedule A 1.(c). Because of the definition of 'lease' in s 24, however, the special provisions on the treatment of premiums (s 34) do not appear to apply to licences.

5.19 The test of whether or not the transaction has created a lease or a licence is not how the parties choose to describe it, but whether or not it is personal in character. Certainly, it could be argued that the relationship between franchisor and franchisee is personal. Thus in *Shell-Mex and BP Ltd v Manchester Garages Ltd*[1] it was held the transaction between the plaintiffs and defendants, under which the defendants operated a filling station, was a licence. The court had regard to the fact that the agreement required the defendants to do all they could to foster the sale of the plaintiff's products and not to impede the plaintiff's right of possession and control of the premises. Indeed, the usual form of franchise agreement is at least arguably inconsistent with a lease, where it contains all or any of the following rights on the part of the franchisor:

(1) to enter and inspect the premises and the conduct of the business at any time;

(2) to exercise supervision and control over the conduct of the business and to impose regulations concerning opening times, delivery schedules, cleaning arrangements and repair and decoration timetables;

(3) to enter the premises and to take over the management of the business;

(4) to require alterations to the premises from time to time to accommodate changes in the 'get up' of the franchise;

(5) to take over the business telephone number.

The question of assignability is also relevant, for a tenancy normally is assignable. Sachs LJ in the *Shell-Mex* case also noted that the agreement involved mutual obligations which must to some extent depend on the personal capabilities of the defendants. He observed: 'Remembering that the plaintiffs are entitled to select who shall be entrusted with the promotion of their product, it seems to me at least very doubtful whether the contract embodied in the relevant document could as a whole be assignable'. A landlord's objection to an assignee, where his consent to an assignment is required, must have reference to the relationship of landlord and tenant[2], whereas objections to prospective franchisees can be based on much wider considerations such as motivation. Consequently the restrictions on assignment contained in franchise agreements are also likely to be more characteristic of a

5.20 *Setting up the franchise business: some other considerations*

licence. In short, if the transaction is described as a licence, there is a likelihood that the court will hold that it is a licence[3].

1 [1971] 1 All ER 841, [1971] 1 WLR 612, CA.
2 *Re Gibbs and Houlder Bros & Co Ltd's Lease, Houlder Bros & Co Ltd v Gibbs* [1925] Ch 575, CA.
3 There is probably no difference for tax purposes between a lease or a licence if a premium is charged on the grant of either. See paras 4.15 et seq, ante.

Leasing

5.20 Where a lease is granted, and the franchise agreement contains all or any of the rights of entry etc set out in para 5.19 above, it could be argued that the exercise of those rights by the franchisor is a breach of his covenant for quiet enjoyment, and a derogation from grant. Accordingly, the quiet enjoyment covenant should be modified as suggested in precedent 12.

5.21 One of the objects of a franchisee is to create a capital asset which is a combination of the increase in value of the leasehold premises (if any) and the goodwill of the franchise business operated there. The stronger and more profitable the franchise business itself, the less important will be the premium value in the lease of the business. However, even well-known, nationally, successful, franchise businesses may make only a marginal difference to the value of leasehold premises, when an assignment of the franchise business and of the lease are made at the same time, such is the demand in parts of the United Kingdom for suitable trading outlets from many sources. A franchisee will be reluctant to incur substantial expenditure on the premises, unless he knows that any future premium value in his lease will be generated for his own account. In an ideal world, therefore, the franchisor should devise arrangements, whereby it has the power to terminate the tenure of the premises by the franchisee on termination (for whatever reason) of the franchise agreement, but will compensate the franchisee for his loss of any premium attributable to the premises as if the tenure of the franchisee had been a normal commercial lease, if the franchisor wishes to retain the premises for the franchise network. This may prove to be extremely expensive, but achieves a balance between the long-term aims of the franchisee and the necessity of the franchisor to retain established sites within its control[1]. The term of the lease should not exceed the term of the franchise agreement.

1 As to insurance, see para 5.52.

5.22 One way of compensating the franchisee for the increase in premium value, yet protecting the franchisor's interest in keeping the site if it chooses would be to include in the lease a surrender option in favour of the franchisor. If the franchisor wishes to keep the site, it therefore has to purchase the residue of the term from the franchisee at market value. If it does not, the franchisee simply assigns to a third party who becomes the franchisor's tenant. The question which must be asked, is whether such an option conflicts with the Landlord and Tenant Act 1927, section 19(1). This provides that 'In all leases . . . containing a covenant condition or agreement against assigning, underletting, charging or parting with the possession of demised premises . . . without licence or consent, such covenant or agreement shall . . . be deemed to be subject—(a) to a proviso to the effect that such licence or consent is not to be unreasonably withheld'. In *Adler v Upper Grosvenor Street*

Investment Ltd[1] it was held that a requirement that before assignment, a tenant should offer to surrender the property to his lessor, did not conflict with this provision. In *Greene v Church Comrs*[2], both Lord Denning MR and Sir Eric Sachs[3] expressed doubts about this decision[3]. However, given that the section has no application to a lease containing an absolute prohibition[4], it would appear that provided that an absolute covenant against assignment is included in the lease, these difficulties should be avoided.

1 [1957] 1 All ER 229, [1957] 1 WLR 227
2 [1974] Ch 467, [1974] 3 All ER 609, CA.
3 Ibid at 477 and 479.
4 *Pearl Assurance v Shaw* [1985] 1 EGLR 92; *Bocardo SA v S & M Hotels* [1980] 1 WLR 17 at 20 per Megaw LJ.

5.23 Any lease or licence between the franchisor and the franchisee should contain a user covenant on the part of the lessee restricting the use of the property to the franchise business.

5.24 If the franchisor is the owner of the freehold or long leasehold interests in the property, he will be concerned to ensure that its rental yield from the property is maintained at a level commensurate with properties of a similar type in the locality. If the lease or licence to the franchisor is of sufficient length to warrant a rent review during the course of it, a restriction upon the use of the property to the franchise business may reduce the amount of any increase in rent upon that rent review. It is essential therefore that any rent review clause excludes the effect of the user restriction.

If the franchisor is the head lessee of the property and sub-lets it to the franchisee, he will wish to incorporate in the lease or licence the same restrictions, as would be included in the lease or licence in which the franchisor is the head landlord. The franchisor must take care to ensure that the contents of the sub-lease do not conflict with those of the head lease.

Landlord and Tenant Act 1954

5.25 The two principal problems which need to be considered where it is proposed to lease[1] the premises on which the franchised business will be operated to the franchisee, are security of tenure and tenant's right to compensation for improvements under the Landlord and Tenant Acts 1927 and 1954. This legislation applies only to England and Wales. The lease should contain a clause excluding sections 24–28 of the 1954 Act. This clause must be approved by the court on the joint application of both parties[2], otherwise the following provisions will apply.

1 The alternative of a licence is considered at para 5.19, ante.
2 Landlord and Tenant Act 1954, s 38(4)—see precedent 13, clause 7.

Security of tenure

5.26 Part II of the Landlord and Tenant Act 1954 provides that a tenancy of business premises[1] shall not come to an end unless terminated in accordance with

5.27 Setting up the franchise business: some other considerations

the provisions of the Act[2]. This is the case whether the tenancy is determined by notice, or by expiration of time. There is an exception for tenancies granted by reason that the tenant was holder of an office, appointment or employment from the grantor[3]. It is unclear what constitutes an appointment for these purposes. The current editor of Woodfall on *Landlord and Tenant*[4] takes the view that a mere agency to sell the landlord's products in the course of a tenant's business carried on upon the demised premises would not qualify. It should be borne in mind however that the purpose of giving the tenant of business premises security of tenure was to protect him against unconscionable increases in rent and loss of business goodwill consequent on having to move to other accommodation[5]. Once a franchise expires, the franchisee's right to use the trade name, and other means of identification, ceases. He could not, therefore, even if his lease continued, go on operating the franchised business. Furthermore, it is possible that a limited covenant in restraint of trade will be effective to prevent him from carrying on a similar business from the premises.[6] The effect of holding therefore that a franchisee is not within the exception to Part II and that his lease is continued would be not to protect his goodwill, but rather to enable him to start up a new business. Whilst it is no doubt true that most tenants at the end of their franchise will also wish to end their tenancy rather than start up a new business, there may be some tenants who might see that a valuable site could be profitably used for other purposes. This could lead to the unfair result that a franchisor who has a queue of potential franchisees prepared to operate a franchised business on the site, has to sit back and watch the site converted to other purposes from which he will derive no benefit. In short, it is at least arguable that franchisees should fall within the exception to Part II. In order to gain the benefit of this exception, the purpose for which the tenancy was granted must be stated[7]. It is possible to apply to the Court for approval of a term excluding sections 24 to 28 of the Act[8] and for the reasons stated in this paragraph, such approval ought to be forthcoming.

1 Section 23(1).
2 Section 24(1). There is no contracting out of these provisions—section 38(1).
3 Section 43(2) as amended by the Law of Property Act 1969.
4 (Sweet and Maxwell) s 2-0654.
5 Report of the Select Committee on Business Premises 1920.
6 See para 2.108 et seq.
7 Section 43(2).
8 Section 38(4)(a).

5.27 If the tenancy falls within Part II and sections 24 to 28 have not been excluded, determination can only be effected under the provisions of the Act[1]. The court is bound to grant a new tenancy unless the landlord establishes one or more of the seven statutory grounds of opposition. These are[2]: (1) disrepair; (2) arrears of rent; (3) breach of the agreement; (4) offer of alternative accommodation by the landlord; (5) that the premises are part of larger premises which will be more valuable as a whole; (6) demolition or reconstruction[3]; and (7) that the landlord intends to occupy the premises for the purpose of a business carried on by him. Obviously, this last ground is likely to be important in franchising where not infrequently the franchisor may wish to carry on the business itself at the termination of the franchise. The landlord however must establish a settled intention of carrying on the business[4]. A mere intention to carry on the business until another franchisee can be found will not suffice. This head is not available to a landlord whose interest was created or terminated less than five years before the termination of the current tenancy[5]. Where the tenancy is terminated under any of the last three heads, the tenant may claim compensation for improvements.

1 For the procedure see Woodfall on *Landlord and Tenant* (Sweet and Maxwell) §§2.0669 et seq.
2 See section 30.
3 See *Price v Esso Petroleum Co Ltd* (1980) 255 Estates Gazette 243, CA.
4 *Reohorn v Barry Corpn* [1956] 2 All ER 742, [1956] 1 WLR 845, CA; *Gregson v Cyril Lord Ltd* [1962] 3 All ER 907, [1963] 1 WLR 41, CA.
5 Section 30(2).

5.28 A tenant whose new tenancy is successfully opposed under one of the last three heads mentioned in the previous paragraph is entitled to compensation equal to the rateable value of the premises, or twice that sum if the tenant or his predecessor in the business have occupied the premises for business purposes for the preceding fourteen years[1]. If the lease is renewed by the court, the rent will be set in the light of all circumstances including user of the property.

1 Landlord and Tenant Act 1954, s 37 as amended by Law of Property Act 1969, s 11.

Compensation for improvements

5.29 The tenant at the termination of the tenancy is entitled to compensation for improvements (including the erection of a building) made with his landlord's consent. The improvements must add to the letting value of the property and not be such that the tenant is entitled by law to remove them[1], ie they must *not* be trade fixtures. 'Trade fixtures' includes display cabinets, machinery, boilers, pipework, shop and office fittings, partitions, etc[2]; it is advisable to include a term in the lease providing that at the termination of the lease the tenant shall deliver up trade fixtures to the franchisor. This may be especially important if a comprehensive 'house-style' forms part of the franchise package and special fixtures installed by the franchisee.

1 See Woodfall on *Landlord and Tenant*, §§1-1554 et seq.
2 Landlord and Tenant Act 1927, s 1.

5.30 Section 2(1)(b) of the 1927 Act excludes improvements which the tenant or his predecessor in title were under an obligation to make in pursuance of a contract entered into for valuable consideration, including a building lease[1]. This exclusion is very important because, in franchising, virtually all the relevant improvements are likely to have been made in consequence of the requirements of the franchise agreement. The benefit conferred upon the franchisee in consideration of those improvements is the ability to carry on a business for the specified term under the licensed 'house-style'. It may, also, be worthwhile to consider, however, whether or not to insert a clause under which improvements are written down year by year in order to try to forestall arguments about compensation. Such a clause in any event is desirable where the policy of the network requires regular refurbishment[2].

1 See paras 4.15 et seq, ante for potential tax problems.
2 This is essential in most kinds of retail franchise. Franchisees themselves are usually anxious that all outlets present a good appearance to the public, and should usually view

5.31 *Setting up the franchise business: some other considerations*

such a clause as a useful insurance that regular refurbishment and renewal is likely to be carried out throughout the chain. See Ch 8, precedent 1, clause 7.42, post.

Rates

5.31 The liability for payment of rates under a licence is the licensor's[1]. In the case of a lease, it is the tenant who is liable. For as long as the rating system subsists, this should be borne in mind when fixing the franchisee's payments to the franchisor. The rent payable by the franchisee under the lease may not, necessarily, be at full commercial rates, but can fulfil the same function as the 'dry rent' in a public-house lease, the main part of the franchisor's income being derived from fees, ie the rental is functionally the same as a minimum royalty payment. The franchisor should consider carefully taxation and VAT implications of this method.

1 *Morrish v Hall* (1863) 2 New Rep 448.

Note: It is not within the scope of this book to review the relationship between a landlord and tenant of residential premises. However, many retail premises combine the retail outlet with living accommodation over. Indeed, where the franchise business is a 'Momma and Poppa'[1] operation, such accommodation may be essential, especially if the business requires unsocial hours to be worked. Practitioners must be aware of the potential problems associated with residential tenancies. If the franchisor is a head lessee, it may find itself caught between the rights of its own landlord under the head lease to it and the security of tenure of its individual franchisee, to whom it has sub-let the property. Perhaps the safest method of diminishing this problem is to insist that all franchisees who wish to trade from and live in mixed premises should incorporate a private company as the franchisee/lessee (whose obligations are guaranteed by the individuals involved)[2], which issues a service tenancy to those directors/employees, who occupy the residential part of the property. It must be a requirement of the lease or licence to that corporate franchisee, that it does not permit any persons to occupy the residential part of the premises without a service tenancy. A practical point to bear in mind if a franchisee refuses to leave residential accommodation is that, so long as the franchise subsists, the franchisee can be required to pay for the franchisor's personnel running the business. This may be a substantial disincentive for the franchisee remaining.

1 An American expression current in the franchise industry meaning a family-run business.
2 See deed of guarantee, precedent 11, post.

Checklist

5.32 (1) Include in leases a recital of the purposes for which the lease is being granted, ie to enable the franchisee to carry on the franchised business on the site. There is no harm in including a similar recital in a licence agreement, to provide a fall back, in case it is held to be a lease. Modify the covenant for quiet enjoyment to permit necessary rights of entry.

(2) Whether a lease or a licence consider including a 'write down' clause on equipment.

(3) If a lease, include a covenant to deliver up trade fixtures on termination. There may be a danger in including such a clause in the usual form in a licence where it might tend to suggest the existence of a lease. There would seem to be

The franchise premises 5.32

The franchise premises
Flowchart

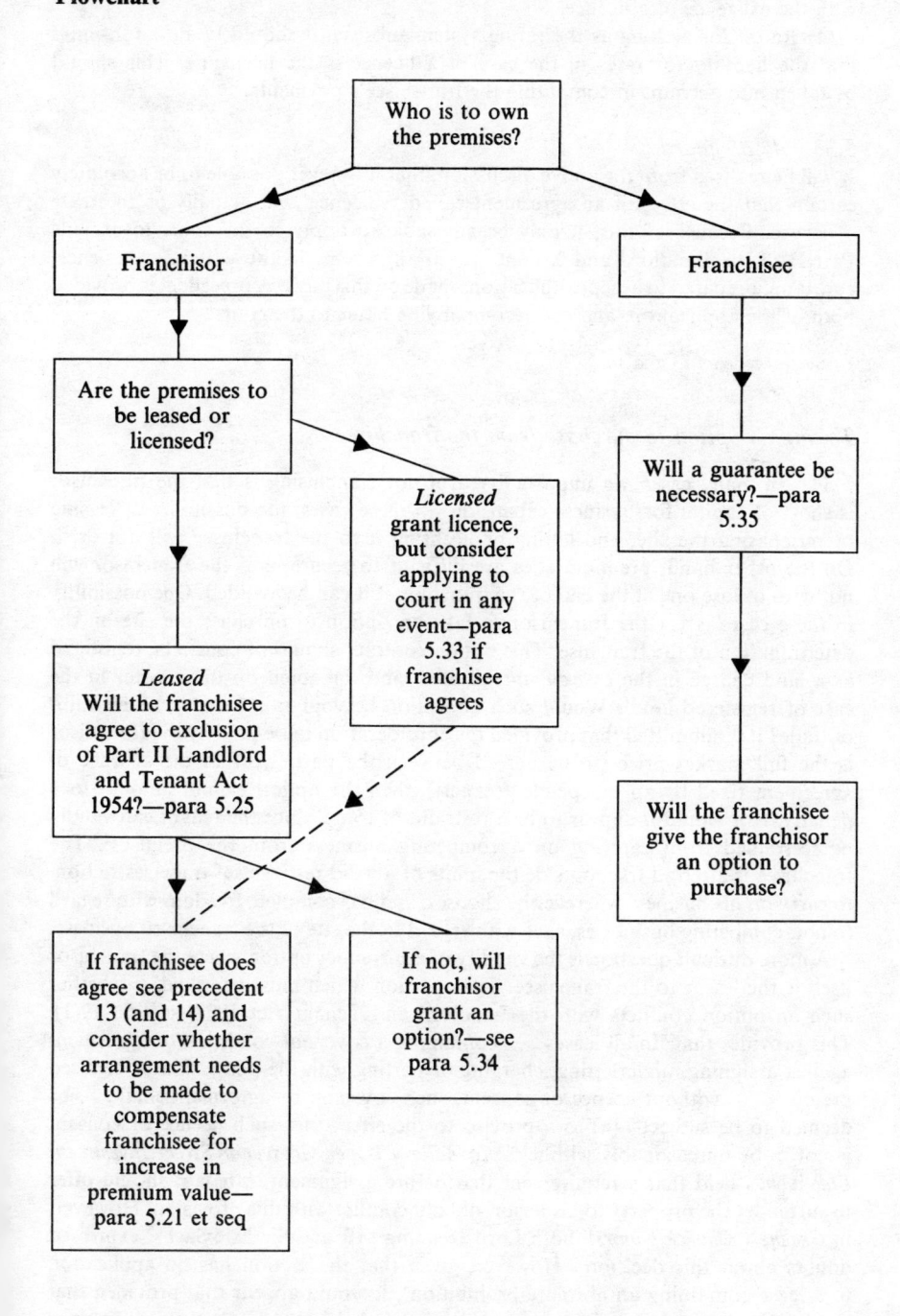

```
                    ┌──────────────────┐
                    │  Who is to own   │
                    │  the premises?   │
                    └──────────────────┘
                     ↙                ↘
         ┌──────────────┐        ┌──────────────┐
         │  Franchisor  │        │  Franchisee  │
         └──────────────┘        └──────────────┘
                ↓                        ↓
    ┌──────────────────┐      ┌──────────────────┐
    │ Are the premises │      │ Will a guarantee │
    │    to be leased  │      │ be necessary?—   │
    │   or licensed?   │      │      para 5.35   │
    └──────────────────┘      └──────────────────┘
         ↓         ↘                   ↓
         │    ┌──────────────┐
         │    │  *Licensed*  │
         │    │ grant licence│
         │    │ but consider │
         │    │ applying to  │
         │    │ court in any │
         │    │ event—para   │
         │    │ 5.33 if      │
         │    │ franchisee   │
         │    │ agrees       │
         │    └──────────────┘
         ↓                         ┌──────────────────┐
  ┌──────────────┐                 │ Will the         │
  │  *Leased*    │                 │ franchisee give  │
  │ Will the     │                 │ the franchisor   │
  │ franchisee   │                 │ an option to     │
  │ agree to     │                 │ purchase?        │
  │ exclusion    │                 └──────────────────┘
  │ of Part II   │
  │ Landlord     │
  │ and Tenant   │
  │ Act 1954?—   │
  │ para 5.25    │
  └──────────────┘
         ↓            ↘
  ┌──────────────┐   ┌──────────────┐
  │ If franchisee│   │ If not, will │
  │ does agree   │   │ franchisor   │
  │ see precedent│   │ grant an     │
  │ 13 (and 14)  │   │ option?—see  │
  │ and consider │   │ para 5.34    │
  │ whether      │   └──────────────┘
  │ arrangement  │
  │ needs to be  │
  │ made to      │
  │ compensate   │
  │ franchisee   │
  │ for increase │
  │ in premium   │
  │ value—       │
  │ para 5.21    │
  │ et seq       │
  └──────────────┘
```

Consider points (1)–(4) in para 5.32 in addition.

5.33 Setting up the franchise business: some other considerations

no harm however in providing that all items which constitute the 'get up' of the premises shall be the property of the licensor—that certainly would not be inconsistent with the existence of a licence.

(4) Rates: for as long as the rating system subsists, it should be borne in mind that the liability for rates in the case of a licence is the licensor's. This should be taken into account in computing the franchisee's payments.

5.33 A safeguard

It will be realised from the above discussion, that it is never possible to be absolutely certain that the effect of an agreement called 'a licence' will actually be to create a licence. Because of this, it may be advisable to apply to the court to exclude Part II of the Landlord and Tenant Act in any event. In the writers' experience, courts are prepared to accept applications made on this basis. A precedent is provided both of the application, and the accompanying letter to the court[1].

1 See precedents 13 and 14.

Taking an option to purchase from the franchisee

5.34 In many cases, an important reason for franchising is that the franchisor is short of capital for business expansion. In these cases, the possibility of leasing or purchasing the site, and letting or licensing it to the franchisee will not exist. On the other hand, premium sites are difficult to secure, and the franchisor will not wish to lose one at the end of the franchise, if it can be avoided. One possibility in these cases is for the franchisor to take an option to purchase the site on the determination of the franchise. This option contract should of course be registered as a land charge in the case of unregistered land, or noted on the register in the case of registered land[1]. Would such an option be void as a penalty, or restraint of trade? It is submitted that provided the consideration to be paid by the franchisor is the full market price (to be agreed between the parties, or in the absence of agreement fixed by an independent expert), then the option cannot amount to a penalty. Nor would it appear to be a restraint of trade, since the tenant can validly be restrained from carrying on a competing business from the premises[2]. The franchisee is after all free, outside the limits of a valid restraint of trade restriction, to carry on his business wherever he chooses, and has complete freedom with regard to non-competing businesses, save with regard to the site of the franchised business.

A more difficult question is the validity of a surrender option where the franchisor itself is the lessor to the franchisee. The question which must be asked, is whether such an option conflicts with the Landlord and Tenant Act 1927, section 19(1). This provides that 'In all leases . . . containing a covenant condition or agreement against assigning, underletting, charging or parting with the possession of demised premises . . . without licence or consent, such covenant or agreement shall . . . be deemed to be subject—(a) to a proviso to the effect that such licence or consent is not to be unreasonably withheld.' In *Adler v Upper Grosvenor Street Investment Ltd*[3] it was held that a requirement that before assignment, a tenant should offer to surrender the property to his lessor, did not conflict with this provision. However, in *Greene v Church Comrs*[4], both Lord Denning MR and Sir Eric Sachs[5] expressed doubts about this decision[5]. However, given that the section has no application to a lease containing an absolute prohibition[6], it would appear that provided that an absolute covenant against assignment is included in the lease, these difficulties should be avoided.

1 Although the Court of Appeal has held that a right of pre-emption does not initially give a grantee an interest in land—*Pritchard v Briggs* [1980] Ch 338, as the editors of *Ruoff & Roper* (5th edn, 1986) p 798 points out, it would seem most imprudent for anyone entitled to first offer or first refusal not to protect their interest.
2 See para 2.109 et seq.
3 [1957] 1 All ER 229, [1957] 1 WLR 227.
4 [1974] Ch 467, [1974] 3 All ER 609, CA.
5 Ibid at 477 and 479.
6 *Pearl Assurance v Shaw* [1985] 1 EGLR 92. *Bocardo SA v S & M Hotels* [1980] 1 WLR 17 at 20 per Megaw LJ.

Guarantees

5.35 It may be that in order to raise the capital necessary to acquire the site and start up the business, the franchisee will have to find a guarantor. Possibly the franchisor may be prepared to do this, since excellent prospective franchisees can be young and impecunious. At all events, such guarantor should bear in mind the following points. The sum of money borrowed should not, if possible, itself be guaranteed. The amount guaranteed should be limited to the amount lent against the premises and the interest on that loan. It should therefore not exceed the value of the premises on the open market. The sum lent against the property should reduce over the period of the franchise on a straight line basis. The interest on such loan should be payable quarterly in arrears, and should not be out of line with market rates at the relevant time. Where banks act as guarantors, they will usually have their own standard form of guarantee.

Preliminary contract?

5.36 Many franchises are granted by a single contractual document. It is worth considering, however, whether or not it may be better to separate the agreement to take up the franchise, from the actual grant of the franchise agreement itself. There may be a number of advantages in this arrangement. If a prospective franchisee is found before a suitable site has been acquired, it helps to ensure that the franchisor will not expend time and money finding a suitable site, only to find that the prospective franchisee has changed his mind and decided not to go ahead. The franchisee will be contractually bound to go ahead provided the site is suitable or alternatively to forfeit a part of the deposit. In the case of successful franchises prospective franchisees will, no doubt, be queuing up so that the cost to the franchisor of the prospective franchisee pulling out will be minimal. This arrangement also benefits the prospective franchisee by securing his place ahead of the queue if there is one[1]. As the cost of setting up most franchised businesses escalate, especially those that involve the acquisition of a property, a prospective franchisee will need to secure his funding before committing himself to proceed to an agreement with the franchisor. He will need much financial information which is, probably, valuable and confidential. That information, probably, comprises projected turnover, margins, costs, projected net profits and cash flows. Any competitor or prospective competitor of the franchisor will find it interesting and useful. The franchisee cannot make an informed judgment about the potential success of the proposed business or the finance that he will require without all that information. The franchisor may be prejudiced by its disclosure. Accordingly, the preliminary contract must include a confidentiality agreement[2] by the franchisee which must be signed before he receives

5.37 Setting up the franchise business: some other considerations

that information. This will bind him only to disclose the information to certain categories of professional adviser or financial sources and will contain non-competition restrictions[3]. The franchisor is bound not to grant a franchise to a third party in the area preferred by the franchisee for a limited period. In this way, the franchisee will have sufficient time and information to enable him to research comprehensively the business and funding availability[4]. At the same time the franchisor has a measure of protection from potential industrial espionage.

1 See Purchase Agreement precedent, chapter 8, post.
2 See Confidentiality Agreement, precedent 4, chapter 8, post.
3 See paras 2.107 et seq.
4 See precedent 4, clause 4.4.

Territorial rights

5.37 Many franchises grant to the franchisee an exclusive territory. In such cases, the application of competition laws need to be considered carefully[1]. Apart from this, the important thing is to try to avoid granting away too large a territory. This is especially a problem for new networks. If they become successful they may find expansion in particular areas hampered because they granted away exclusive territorial rights to franchisees who are not interested in exploiting the full market potential. There is no real answer to this problem, except to try in the early days to negotiate the best deal possible or to include in the franchise agreement clauses[2] reserving the right on the part of the franchisor to reduce the territory in the case of poor performance by the franchisee, or if the franchisor considers that the territory is too large for one operation. Once established, the market power of the franchisor may be such that he can refuse to grant any territorial exclusivity at all. Certainly some of the larger American networks have reached this position, and it is becoming increasingly common in this country.

1 See para 2.38.
2 See Master Franchise Form, precedent 1, clauses 10.32 and 10.33.

5.38 If the franchisor has to grant an exclusive territory, the form of the clause should if possible simply be that he will not operate, or licence other persons to operate within the territory, under the same trade name[1]. It should take this form if it is desired not to have the agreement fall within the Restrictive Trade Practices Act 1976 on this account[2]. It will be necessary to link any such agreement on the part of the franchisor to the definition of the business in the franchise agreement. That definition should itself specifically refer to the name under which the franchise business trades. In this way, the restriction accepted by the franchisor is merely the use of the name and he is free to trade within the exclusive territory of the franchisee, in competition with the franchisee, in the same business as the franchised business provided he uses a different name. That aspect of the limited restriction should be supported by board resolutions if the franchisor is a company[3]. This strategy is not suitable in the case of franchises to operate inventions or appliances which in themselves are as important as the name or get-up. In this case it may be considered advisable to make the franchisee a subsidiary company of the franchisor[4]. The danger of this strategy is that it will clearly result in the network being considered as a whole for the purposes of the de minimis exemption to the Competition Act 1980[5]. If neither strategy is suitable, the application of the Restrictive Trade Practices Act needs to be considered with care. The Restrictive Trade Practices

Act is not the only legislation having bearing on area grants. Even if that Act does not apply, because restrictions are imposed only on the franchisees, who are granted territories and forbidden to operate outside of them, the application of the provisions of EEC competition law[6] and the implications of the Competition Act 1980[7] need to be considered carefully (agreements registrable under the Restrictive Trade Practices Act are exempted from the latter[8]). To the extent that restrictions are also imposed upon the franchisees, the common law doctrine of restraint of trade will also have to be considered[9].

1 See paras 2.141 et seq, ante. Grant of a non-exclusive territory may avoid possible tax complications.
2 See Ch 8, precedent 1, clause 3.28, post.
3 See Franchise Agreement precedent, precedent 1, clause 6.2 for restrictive agreement by franchisor, clause 3.3 for definition of the franchised business and precedents 7 and 8 for board minutes and consequential letter to the Office of Fair Trading.
4 Such arrangements do not fall within the British Franchise Association's definition of a 'franchise'—para 1.103, ante.
5 See para 2.135 et seq, ante, the position otherwise is not entirely clear at present.
6 See para 2.39.
7 See Checklists at para 2.140, ante.
8 See para 2.133, ante.
9 See paras 2.107 et seq.

Checklists

5.39 Possible anti-competitive *effects* of exclusive territorial grants are considered in Chapter 2, ante. Reference should be made to that chapter, and the checklists therein.

The initial fee

5.40 The sum to be paid by the franchisee to the franchisor on signing the agreement will be stated. This may be the full franchise fee, or a deposit. The matters covered by the initial fee will no doubt be expressly stated[1], however any items *not* included ought also to be expressly stated, even though by implication it might be reasonably clear that they are not[1]. Unexpected charges are likely to be an early cause of friction, and friction at any stage, but especially at an early stage is to be avoided at all costs. Obvious matters which may not be included in the fee are delivery charges, installation and shopfitting, and VAT[1]. However, in practice it is sensible to separate the provisions governing the continuing relationship between the franchisor and the franchisee (best confined to the franchise agreement itself) from the short term mutual obligations of the parties (best confined to the Franchise Purchase Agreement).

1 See Ch 8, Purchase Agreement precedent, Form 9, clauses 4 and 5, and Form 1, clause 7.13, post.

Continuing fees or royalties

5.41 There appear to be three strategies commonly employed:
(1) the franchisor is paid a royalty based on the franchisor's gross[1] takings;
(2) the franchisor is paid a straight annual fee;

5.42 Setting up the franchise business: some other considerations

(3) the franchisor recovers his income from profits on sales of tied items to the franchisee.

The last can give rise to problems and careful thought must be given to these when it is adopted. It is of course in general use in the brewing industry where it is usual to pay a low fixed 'dry rent', the brewer recovering the balance on a 'wet rent' on beer, and other consumables, supplied to the licensee. The problem is that in franchising this policy can lead to disgruntled franchisees who resent paying a high price for items which they could quite easily buy more cheaply elsewhere, and could give rise to competition law problems[2]. The American experience should be a warning in this respect. The advice must be to use this strategy only in relation to tied items which are necessary for quality control or to preserve trade secrets or the franchisor's intellectual property such as its trade marks. In these cases, it can be a simple and convenient method of accounting for both parties. It may also be felt that the dangers are counterbalanced by the fact that this method of taking a royalty is easier to police. One inevitable problem of either taking a royalty, as a percentage of gross takings or as a profit on tied items, is guarding against fraud. In the case of tied items, this is relatively easy if the franchisee is required to produce his VAT return or assessment, for the return will show the amount of VAT invoices in respect of which he is claiming credit and therefore the items acquired from third parties and an assessment will alert the franchisor to possible financial problems faced by the franchisee or possible manipulation of the books. This can be a useful device in the case of percentage royalties also, to the extent that the level of VAT indicates the turnover of the business[3].

1 Never net takings—a royalty based on net takings could indicate a partnership—see para 1.45 et seq. See Ch 8, precedent 1, clause 3.11, post. Net takings are much more difficult to calculate accurately than gross turnover in any case.
2 See para 2.44.
3 See Franchise Agreement precedent 1, clause 7.28:5, Ch 8, post.

5.42 Where a royalty is to be taken as a profit on tied items it may be advisable to recite the fact that this is the method of accounting between the parties, certainly where a straight royalty is paid in addition. It may also be possible in some cases to state specifically that the profit will be a percentage mark up on cost. The object of this is to forestall complaints from the franchisees that the franchisor is making excessive covert profits. The franchisor should have the option to convert from a tied supply profit basis to a royalty basis[1].

1 See Franchise Agreement, precedent 1, clause 7.14, post.

Liability of the franchisor to his franchisees

5.43 If it is desired to exempt possible liability of the franchisor to his franchisees, whether in contract or in tort, the possible application of the Unfair Contract Terms Act 1977 will have to be considered. The application of this Act to franchise agreements is not entirely clear. Sections 2 and 3 of this Act regulate the exclusion of liability for negligence and breach of contract. For our purposes the effect briefly is that liability for death or personal injury cannot be excluded and other exemptions have to satisfy a test of reasonableness. However, Schedule 1, para 1(c) provides that these provisions do not extend to:

'any contract so far as it relates to the creation or transfer of a right or interest in any patent, trade mark, copyright, registered design, technical or commercial information or other intellectual property . . .'

The wording of this paragraph does not appear to be appropriate for licences of intellectual property rights, because by definition a licence does not create or transfer a right or interest, but merely makes lawful that which would have been unlawful[1]. However, since it is difficult to conceive of a contract to create a right or interest in an intellectual property right other than a licence, presumably, that is to what the paragraph is intended to refer. Nevertheless, given the semi-punitive view of tort law which still seems to linger in the minds of some judges, it cannot confidently be asserted that the paragraph might not be interpreted literally. The safest course is to include a recital to the effect that the exemption is inserted to apportion insurance risks[2]. Such an exemption clause may be backed up by a reflexive[3] indemnity clause, but it must be remembered that such clauses are regulated by section 13 of the Unfair Contract Terms Act 1977. The effect, it can be argued, is that where section 2(1) *prevents* the exclusion of liability, section 13 prevents the indemnity clause from being enforced. Where however the Act merely subjects the exemption clause to a test of reasonableness, the situation is less clear. If the clause were held to be unreasonable, the Act would appear to apply, but what if the franchisor chooses not to rely on such an unreasonable clause, or the agreement does not contain a clause at all? The *Act* is not now preventing the exclusion of liability. This may provide an argument for inserting only a reflexive indemnity clause where it is desired to exclude the franchisor's liability to the franchisee.

1 See *Federal Comr of Taxation v United Aircraft Corpn* (1943) 68 CLR 525. However, for VAT purposes for example a licensee of intellectual property is regarded as a supply, and in tax law it can be regarded as a transfer—see paras 4.08 et seq.
2 See Adams and Brownsword [1982] JBL 200 and [1988] JBL 146.
3 Ie a clause which requires B, who has successfully sued his fellow but defaulting contracting party A, to indemnify A—see Adams and Brownsword, loc cit. See also [1988] JBL 146 for an update of this article.

Franchisor's liability to third parties for acts and defaults of the franchisee

5.44 We have already pointed out that there is a real danger that the franchisor could be held liable to third parties[1]. To the extent that such liability can be insured against, this does not matter although all forms of professional indemnity or third party liability insurance for traders are becoming increasingly expensive and less comprehensive in scope. The real danger is contract liability: if a franchisee goes bankrupt or goes into liquidation, the franchisor might find himself having to foot the bill. Exemption clauses exonerating the franchisor which are included in the contracts made by the franchisee with his customers are likely to be of very little use. In the first place the franchisor is a third party to that contract and whatever criticisms may be made of the rule that third parties may not shelter behind an exemption clause[2], the courts are likely to apply it with little compunction in this case. To argue that the franchisee is the franchisor's agent for the purposes of making that contract[3] is to run the risk that the court will accept that the franchisee *is* in fact the franchisor's agent, and not merely just for the purposes of negotiating exemption from liability, strike down the clause under the Unfair Contract Terms

5.45 *Setting up the franchise business: some other considerations*

Act 1977, and hold the franchisor liable as principal. However, to some extent the Business Names Act 1985 may have come to the rescue in this context[4].

1 Paras 1.28 et seq, ante.
2 *Scruttons Ltd v Midland Silicones Ltd* [1962] AC 446, [1962] 1 All ER 1, HL.
3 *New Zealand Shipping Co Ltd v AM Satterthwaite & Co Ltd* [1975] AC 154, [1974] 1 All ER 1015; *Pao On v Lau Yiu Long* [1980] AC 614, [1979] 3 All ER 65, PC.
4 See para 6.24 et seq.

Ways of protecting the franchisor

5.45 The real danger then for the franchisor, is that in the event of the bankruptcy or liquidation of the franchisee, it may be liable for the franchisee's debts. One possible strategy is to require the franchisee's status to be declared by a notice on the premises, on order forms and on other stationery[1]; the disclosure requirements of the Business Names Act 1985, require that all proprietors of the business shall be disclosed on orders and invoices issued by the business, if the name of the business is other than the name(s) of the proprietor(s) or the name of the limited company if that is the proprietor. Whilst those obligations do not require disclosure that the business is merely a franchised outlet and not a branch of a large chain, at least the customer should have no doubts as to the identity of the trader with whom they are dealing[2]. For many kinds of business, this will be adequate as contract debts owed to customers are unlikely to be significant. If they are, it will probably be worthwhile to consider insulating the franchisor by splitting the franchisor's business between a number of different corporations. A structure which may be worth considering, and which certainly fits quite well with our review of the relevant tax laws is to set up a company to own the trade marks and other intellectual property which, in turn, licences a subsidiary company, which will employ the staff who will supervise and exercise control over the franchisees. Provided the licence is revocable, this would not appear to endanger the marks[3]. The marks holding company will perform and charge for services to its supervisory subsidiary, which are in relatively low risk areas (such as administering the advertising fund), while the supervisory subsidiary will provide all the franchise services to the franchisee. In this way, it is unlikely that the franchisee or the subsidiary will be entitled and/or obliged to deduct tax at source from the franchise fee payments and the subsidiary will be exposed to any risks arising from the exercise of its functions. The arrangement may be represented diagrammatically as shown below. Needless to say, neither of the franchisor's companies will have assets other than in the case of the marks owning company, the marks themselves. The theory behind this structure is that the mere licence of a mark, itself, is unlikely to result in liability to third parties, otherwise the implications for marks licensing and celebrity name licensing would be quite far-reaching. Nor is control, of itself, likely to be enough (unless there were held to be a master and servant relationship.) For the normal franchise arrangement, it is the combination of holding out and control which is the danger and likely to be emphasised by a court. In the present arrangement, the two are separated. The arrangement will be suitable for United Kingdom resident or foreign resident trade mark holding companies if, in the latter case, the relevant double taxation agreement permits the payment of royalty without deduction[4]. It may be advantageous to alter this arrangement so that the marks holding company grants a licence to the franchisee to use the relevant intellectual property and, also, manages the advertising programme. The subsidiary enters into the franchise agreement with the franchisee and exercises the supervisory and control functions.

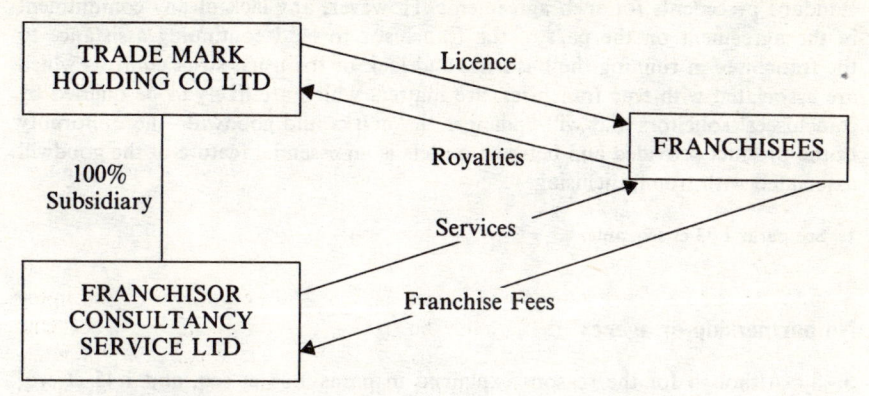

```
┌─────────────────┐                    
│  TRADE MARK     │    Licence         
│  HOLDING CO LTD │◄──────────────┐    
└─────────────────┘               │    
         │                        │    
         │              ┌────────────────┐
  100%   │   Royalties  │  FRANCHISEES   │
 Subsidiary ◄───────────│                │
         │              └────────────────┘
         │      Services       ▲          
┌─────────────────┐            │          
│   FRANCHISOR    │            │          
│   CONSULTANCY   │◄───────────┘          
│   SERVICE LTD   │  Franchise Fees      
└─────────────────┘                      
```

1 The Unfair Contract Terms Act 1977 would not appear to be applicable in such a case vis-à-vis third parties.
2 Business Names Act 1985.
3 See para 1.20.
4 For example US/UK Double Taxation Convention 1975. See paras 4.146 et seq, ante.

Indemnity clauses as a protection for each member of the network

5.46 Although there may be an implied right of indemnity, it is certainly advisable to insert an express clause in the agreement. The use of such clauses confined to indemnity in respect of the franchisor's liability arising as a result of the franchisee's acts, defaults, or business activities generally should not give rise to problems[1]. However, it is possible that franchisees could become liable for the acts or omissions of the *franchisor*. It is also possible, in a high profile franchise chain that the franchisor and all its franchisees may become liable for claims against one of the franchisees. Both of these suggestions may appear absurd, until one considers that the raison d'etre of franchising is to create substantial goodwill for the network, as a result of the activities of all franchisees. Efforts on the part of the franchisor to make each franchised outlet indistinguishable from its fellow may cause and is intended to cause the public to assume that each outlet is a branch of a chain under single ownership. If enhanced goodwill is enjoyed as a result, there is no economic reason why those outlets should not all compensate the public for any loss suffered when dealing with the franchisor or any franchisee. The authors consider that this may become a problem in the future for franchises and that franchisors must ensure that the public are on notice when dealing with a franchisee, that the person with whom they are dealing is separate from the franchisor. That is in the interests of the entire franchise chain.

1 See Adams and Browsworth [1982] JBL 200 and [1988] JBL 146—see Franchise Agreement precedent 1, clause 7.44, (Ch 8, post) and see para 5.44, ante.

Franchisor as lessor

5.47 Where a lease is involved to the extent that a court might base a distinction between petrol filling station 'solus' agreements, and tied house agreements on the fact that these can involve a landlord and tenant relationship (though, of course,

5.48 *Setting up the franchise business: some other considerations*

not always), it may be possible for the franchisor to escape liability to third parties[1]. The agreement should, in this respect, be modelled as closely as possible on the standard precedents for such agreements. However, any lack of any commitment in the agreement on the part of the franchisor to lend continuing assistance to the franchisee in running the business, and lack of the usual strict controls which are associated with true franchises, are matters which are likely to be queried by franchisees' solicitors and will endanger the marks and goodwill—the uniformity of the product provided and between outlets is an essential feature of the goodwill associated with true franchising.

1 See paras 1.33 et seq, ante.

No partnership or agency

5.48 Although for the reasons explained in paras 1.38 et seq, and 1.45 et seq, ante, there is no certain way that a partnership or agency can be prevented from arising, at the borderline a no partnership or agency clause may be effective and should be inserted[1].

1 Ch 8, Franchise Agreement precedent 1, clause 9.25, post.

Liability of the franchisor to third parties for his own acts and defaults

5.49 It is quite possible that a court may treat the relationship of the franchisor and franchisee as that of independent businesses, and conclude from this that the franchisor is not liable to third parties for the acts and defaults of his franchisees, but it is nevertheless to be remembered that the franchisor may become liable to third parties by virtue of its own acts. It would be liable if it were itself in breach of its duty to care. Thus a misrepresentation by a franchisee to a client in a consultancy franchise, which was caused by wrong information being supplied to the franchisee by the franchisor, could lead to the franchisor being held liable under *Hedley Byrne & Co Ltd v Heller & Partners Ltd*[1] to third parties suffering damage as a result. Where no negligence can be proved however there would seem at present to be no direct liability in respect of defective goods, since the Sale of Goods Act and Supply of Goods and Services Act warranties do not run to third parties. A franchisee held liable for selling a defective product supplied by the franchisor, might in turn however sue the franchisor or join the franchisor as another defendant in the action.

1 [1964] AC 465, [1963] 2 All ER 575, HL. It is believed that this statement is correct notwithstanding *Caparo Industries plc v Dickman* [1990] 1 All ER 568, [1990] 2 WLR 358, HL which is distinguishable.

5.50 Where the franchisor leases premises to his franchisee, he will owe a duty to the franchisee and third parties for injuries resulting from his failure in his duty to maintain the premises[1].

1 See Defective Premises Act 1972, s 4. He may also incur liability in respect of works executed by his direction at the commencement of the franchise—ibid, s 1. See generally Woodfall *Landlord and Tenant* (Sweet and Maxwell) §§1.1465 et seq.

Consumer Protection Act 1987

5.51 This Act is supposed to implement the EEC Product Liability Directive[1], by imposing upon manufacturers and certain other persons in the distribution chain, strict liability for defective products. Whether it actually does implement the intentions of the drafters of the Directive, and indeed, whether it introduces simply a species of negligence liability[2], is a matter of some debate. At all events, our principal concern here is how it might apply in the franchising context. Liability is imposed by the Act upon the following persons:

(a) the producer of the product;

(b) any person who, by putting his name on the product or using a trade mark or other distinguishing mark in relation to the product, has held himself out to be the producer of the product;

(c) any person who has imported the product into a Member State from a place outside the Member States in order, in the course of any business of his, to supply it to another[3].

Subsections (a) and (c) are clear enough, (b) is the problem. A person whose name is put on a product, whether by himself or by a licensee, is clearly within subsection (b), but it then goes on to refer to 'using *a* trade mark' [emphasis supplied] ie not *his* trade mark, and could be read as imposing liability on the proprietor, the licensee, or both. Arguably the former is the right interpretation, since the licensee who manufactures goods and applies the licensor's mark, would in any case be liable under subsection (a), and the section clearly contemplates joint liability[4]. Suppliers of products, other than persons falling under the above subsection, can also incur liability, if they fail upon a reasonable request to do so to identify their own suppliers[5]. Liability under the Act is for death or personal injury, or damage to property exceeding £275 caused by the defective product[6]. It is unclear whether or not negligence principles of remoteness of damage apply to liability incurred under the Act. The moral of the above is, that where the franchise involves the distribution of goods, whether supplied by the franchisor, or by the franchisee under the franchisor's marks[7], both parties should carry product liability insurance.

1   85/374.
2   At least negligence in the Learned Hand sense—see *United States v Carroll Towing* 159 F 2d 169 2d circ (1947). Strict liability properly understood is a species of loss distribution—*Goldberg v Kolloman Instruments* 191 NE 2d 81 (1963).
3   Section 2(1).
4   Section 2(5).
5   Section 2(4).
6   Section 5.
7   The Act does not, apparently, require the mark to be applied to the product, simply to be used in relation to it—s 2(2)(b). By contrast, a trade name apparently has to be on the product itself—(ibid). No doubt the draftsman chose the wording to echo the Trade Marks Act 1938, and the Trade Descriptions Act 1968, but in the present context the choice was hardly felicitous.

Insurance

5.52 There is no safe way in which double insurance can be avoided. The problem is the unsatisfactory state of English contract law. If the franchisor maintains insurance against public liability on behalf of himself and his franchisees, strictly speaking the franchisees cannot recover on that policy in the event of their being held liable to third parties. They have no privity of contract with the insurance

5.53 *Setting up the franchise business: some other considerations*

company. Another scheme sometimes suggested whereby the franchisees insure for the benefit of themselves and the franchisor is open to the same objection. The only safe course is either to have the franchisor made a party to the policy (which has the advantage that the franchisor will be notified if the premium is not paid), or for both parties to carry insurance[1]. No doubt the franchisor will be able to negotiate suitable policies with an insurance company, and thereby reduce the costs.

In the case of individual franchisees, the desirability of insurance to cover the expenses incurred on the incapacity of the franchise, should be considered[2]. Where the potential premium value in the lease of the franchise outlet will pass to the franchisor but the franchisee wishes to participate in any such value, the franchisor may wish to set up some life insurance linked pension plan which will cover the franchisee and to which he will make contributions subsidised from royalties due to the franchisor. In this way, the franchisor and the franchisee may be able to establish a tax-effective compromise which resolves the thorny problem of who benefits from the rise in property values generally.

1 See Franchise Agreement precedent 1, clauses 6.18 and 6.63, Ch 8, post.
2 See para 5.69, post.

Minimum turnover clauses and minimum royalty payments

5.53 These are useful as a way of ensuring that the franchisee puts the maximum effort into running his outlet[1]. In the case of distributorships, however, the possible application of Article 85(1) and of the Competition Act 1980 needs to be considered[2]. Minimum royalties are useful in areas where the franchisee is able to manipulate his books and take part in the so-called 'black' economy, to the detriment of both the franchisor and the Inland Revenue.

1 See Franchise Agreement precedent 1, clauses 3.18 and 3.20, Ch 8, post.
2 Paras 2.53, 2.69, 2.126 et seq, ante.

Goodwill

5.54 The problem as to whether, in the absence of agreement, the goodwill in the trade name, or 'house-style', would accrue to the franchisor or the franchisee was dealt with above[1]. It was concluded that it should accrue to the franchisor. However the agreement should contain a clause under which all goodwill generated by the franchisee is held by him as bare trustee for the franchisor[2]. The concept of holding an asset such as goodwill as trustee in such circumstances would not appear to give rise to difficulties[3].

1 Para 1.23, ante.
2 See Franchise Agreement precedent 1, clause 7.25:14.
3 See para 1.27.

Licence under the Consumer Credit Act 1974

5.55 The Act is very complex, and it is beyond the scope of this work to consider the possible application of all its provisions. The purpose of this section is merely to alert the franchisor's legal advisers to the probability of needing to apply for a licence.

5.56 Franchisors by virtue of the fact that they arrange finance for their prospective franchisees through finance houses and the like, or introduce them to sources of finance, will be deemed to be carrying on a consumer credit business[1] or credit brokerage[2]. They may also carry on a consumer hire business in respect of equipment hired[3]. In consequence they will need a licence. Consumer credit businesses require Category A licences, consumer hire Category B and credit brokers Category C. The address to write to for the forms is:

Office of Fair Trading,
Consumer Credit Licensing Branch,
Bromyard Avenue,
Acton,
London W3 7BB.

1 Sections 8 and 189.
2 Section 145.
3 Section 15.

5.57 The licence should be applied for on Form CC 1/86 (standard licence).

Fees

For an application relating to one category of business	£150
For an application relating to two or more categories of business: each additional category of business	£ 10
One business category plus canvassing off trade premises[1] (to the extent that this is allowed[2])	£160

1 See section 23(3).
2 See sections 48 and 49.

Data Protection Act 1984

5.58 Where it is proposed to keep customer records and other such details, on computer data bases, it will be necessary to register under the Data Protection Act and provision for this needs to be inserted in the agreement[1].

1 Practice and procedures under this Act should be included in the Manual. See precedent 1, clause 10.10, Ch 8.

Training

5.59 The training to be provided by the franchisor is perhaps from the franchisee's point of view the most important part of the franchise agreement[1]. The type of training to be provided will obviously vary greatly with different types of franchise. The franchisee will expect to learn any special skills involved in the particular business, e.g. the operation of special equipment, as well as basic business management skills such as staff selection and supervision, particulars of the accounting procedures to be used, dealing with problems which commonly arise in that type of business. In short, the franchisee expects to have imparted to him all the skills necessary to operate his business satisfactorily from the outset (albeit with the franchisor looking over his shoulder).

5.60 *Setting up the franchise business: some other considerations*

1 See Ch 8, Franchise Agreement precedent 1, clauses 6.7, 6.8 and 6.9, and Franchise Purchase Agreement, Form 9, clause 3.4, post.

5.60 The requirement that the franchisee is properly trained is not merely in his own interests but, also, in those of the franchisor. It is advisable to make the grant or commencement of the licence conditional on such training having been completed to the satisfaction of the franchisor[1].

1 See Ch 8, Franchise Agreement precedent 1, clause 7.1, and Franchise Purchase Agreement, Form 9, clause 5.3:1, post.

5.61 It is difficult to generalise about how much detail needs to be included in this section of the agreement. Certainly the persons to whom training is to be provided in addition to the franchisee should be stated—in the case of corporate franchisees this will obviously have to include directors and some employees.

Consideration should also be given to the desirability of specifying:

(1) the minimum period of training;
(2) place or places of training;
(3) hours of attendance;
(4) whether the franchisee will incur any additional costs such as necessary travel and subsistence.

The friction caused by franchisees finding that they have to pay for items they might reasonably have assumed to be included in the fee must be avoided at all costs. If the franchise is based upon a manual and sight of that manual is permitted after signature by a franchisee of a confidentiality agreement, then full details of training will be set out in the manual, thus removing the necessity for a full disclosure in the franchise agreement itself.

Further periods of training

5.62 It is quite likely that the franchisor will develop new systems during the course of the agreement which will require additional training[1], or it may simply be that 'refresher courses' are felt to be a good idea[2]. In either case, it should be declared expressly whether or not such training is to be provided by the franchisor free of charge. Quite probably, the course, itself, will be provided free of charge by the franchisor, but attendance will be at the franchisee's own expense. However, where the training comprises more than a brief refresher or introduction to new products or systems the franchisor may charge a fee to cover costs. The franchise agreement should contain an obligation on the part of the franchisee to attend further training when required by the franchisor.

1 See Ch 8, Franchise Agreement precedent 1, clause 6.9, post.
2 See Ch 8, ibid, clause 7.3, post.

Advertising

5.63 The uniform image presented by the chain is a key feature of franchising. Consequently individual franchisees must be restrained from unauthorised advertising[1]. Advertising at both a national and local level needs to be firmly under the control of the franchisor[2].

Subject to this, advertising must be paid for. The franchisor may, simply, pay for the advertising out of the royalties he collects. Alternatively, it may be charged as a separate item. In this case, it is important that the sums so collected should be strictly accounted for. Some American franchises have used advertising funds, not merely to promote the existing network, but to recruit new franchisees. A further refinement might be to separate advertising of the network generally from advertising of particular outlets, and with regard to the latter to charge the individual franchisee concerned. The advantage of this would be that any outlet would bear any extra cost due to the need to promote it heavily. Furthermore under such a system no franchisee is likely to feel aggrieved because he thinks his outlet is not being given sufficient publicity. He can be given as much as he wants. He is paying for it.

Each franchisee should be obliged to co-operate in advertising and promotional schemes, and to bear the costs of free offers, discounts etc[3].

It is essential that the franchisor be entitled to recoup excess expenditure on advertising in any year from the total advertising contributions of his franchisees in previously or subsequent years. This means that the franchisor can accumulate those contributions for a later major campaign or act as banker to the general advertising fund by lending it money, for example to counter a campaign launched by a competitor. The franchisor's own outlets should contribute to the fund on the same basis as each franchised outlet.

1 See Ch 8, Franchise Agreement precedent 1, clauses 7.9 and 7.56, post.
2 See Ch 8, ibid, post.
3 See Ch 8, ibid, clause 7.11, post.

Annual meeting and franchisees' club

5.64 The opportunity for the franchisees to attend an annual or more frequent meeting where discussions with the franchisor about problems, future plans, and advertising and promotion, can take place, is most important. Consequently, a clause may be inserted requiring the franchisor to arrange such a meeting at appropriate intervals, usually annually[1]. It should also be considered who is to bear the expenses of both the meeting, the travel and subsistence involved, and whether or not it may be desirable to state this expressly. Franchisees will wish to meet the branch managers of the franchisor at these events.

Consideration should also be given to the formation of a franchisees' club. A very valuable function of these can be to apply 'peer pressure' to help prevent individual franchisees letting standards slip. Some franchisors worry about the danger that these may turn into a 'trade union'. This must in part depend upon the identity of interest between franchisees, which will vary in different kinds of business. A news-sheet is a safe alternative.

1 See Ch 8, Franchise Agreement precedent 1, clause 6.11, post.

Minimum wages provisions

5.65 One of the advantages of franchising is that it is the franchisee who generally has the responsibility for hiring and firing labour. Moreover, there are likely to be fewer labour disputes in a small unit where each employee knows the person for whom he is working, than there might be were the franchisor to operate an enterprise of the same size directly. Nevertheless, in some types of franchise business, especially those involving catering, wages are generally low and hours of work

5.66 *Setting up the franchise business: some other considerations*

long and unsociable. From time to time disputes break out which get extensive, and from the employer's point of view, unfavourable press coverage. There is always the danger that an individual franchisee may get involved in such a dispute, and because most of the public at large in this country do not yet appreciate the nature of franchising, the effect might be to bring the whole chain into disrepute. It may therefore be advisable to insist on franchisees operating with standard terms of employment, laying down either minimum wages (so that the benefit of local labour conditions may be passed on by the franchisee in the form of lower prices), or simply specifying wages for the chain. One danger of this last might be[1] that the network as a whole would get involved in disputes with the chain's employees as a whole, if the employees belonged predominantly to one union. In view of current levels of national insurance contributions by employers for their full-time employees, franchisees may wish to consider employing part-time labour as much as possible. However, the franchisor may not be happy for the business to be entrusted to part-timers.

1 Another danger is that the further the franchisee's autonomy is reduced, the more likely is it that the franchisor may become liable to third parties for the acts and defaults of the franchisee—see para 1.28 et seq, ante.

Vehicles used in the franchised business

5.66 Many types of franchise business require the use of special, or specially equipped, vehicles. These may be sold outright to the franchisee, the price being included in the initial fee, acquired by the franchisee under a credit arrangement with the franchisor or a finance house, or simply hired to him during the term of the agreement.

5.67 If either of the two former arrangements are adopted, it should be considered whether or not to insert a provision specifying the conditions on which the franchisor or his named supplier will buy back the vehicle at the end of the agreement. Specially equipped vehicles may well have no general market, but be of use to the franchisor. A provision whereby the vehicle is written down each year will help the franchisee arrange his accounts, and should prevent argument about the price to be paid for the vehicle at the end of the term, subject to it having been properly maintained.

In the case of hired vehicles, the franchise may benefit from the owner's write down allowances being reflected in the rentals, and thereby achieve a more beneficial position than under either of the two former arrangements[1].

1 See *Adams Commercial Hiring and Leasing* (Butterworths) (1989) para 5.02 et seq.

5.68 One matter of potential difficulty in the case of franchises involving the use of vehicles is the liability of the franchisor under road traffic legislation. It is clear that even if it is the owner of a hired vehicle it incurs, in general, no liability as such because 'owner' is defined as the person in possession of the vehicle for the purposes of the Acts[1]. However it could be argued that by virtue of rights of inspection and control it could become liable for causing or permitting the use of the vehicle, eg in breach of the construction and use regulations. The best course here may be to provide that the franchisee shall enter into a service contract with an approved garage.

1 Road Traffic Act 1988, s 192(1); Road Traffic Regulations Act 1984, s 142(1).

Death or incapacity of the franchisee

5.69 The agreement should contain provisions dealing with either the death or illness of the franchisee. Some arrangement needs to be made for carrying on the business in either event. The precedent given suggests a convenient method[1]. The desirability of the franchisee taking out insurance cover should also be considered. It is in the interests of the dependants of the franchisee, the franchisor and the other franchisees that an outlet does not cease to trade because the franchisee is personally incapable of continuing the business. Public confidence in the network will be undermined if closures occur for whatever reason. The franchisor must be capable of assigning management to cover in the event of the death or sickness of the franchisee. That service will be charged, usually on a per diem basis, to the business of the franchisee. The availability of management to cover for him in emergencies is part of the security sought by a prospective franchisee.

1 Ch 8, Franchise Agreement precedent 1, clause 10.3, post.

Sale of the franchised business

5.70 Sale of a franchised business is different from the sale of an ordinary business: the proposed purchaser will need to be approved by the franchisor. This should therefore be regulated by the agreement[1]. The possible sale of a franchised business can create friction between a franchisor and the franchisee who wishes to sell. First, the highest bidder for the business may not be acceptable to the franchisor as a prospective franchisee. Second, the franchisor must retain the right to impose his latest form of franchise agreement upon an incoming franchisee and any changes made between the new and old forms may reduce the value of the franchisee's business, to his chagrin. Third, the franchisor may have a waiting list of persons wishing to become franchisees who are acceptable to him but who for some reason cannot agree terms with the selling franchisee. Fourth, the franchisor may exercise his right to purchase the business himself, but in practice, however well drafted that option clause, it can give rise to much haggling. Fifth, the franchisee may object to the franchisor's commissions on the sale. Sixth, the cost of vetting and training the proposed new franchisee may prove so expensive that the franchisor's charges for undertaking those services may materially reduce the sale proceeds for the selling franchise.

1 See Ch 8, Franchise Agreement precedent 1, clause 10.4, post.

Pre-printed replies to preliminary enquiries

5.71 At para 6.03, post. We suggest a rigorous form of preliminary enquiries. It may be a good idea when the marketing stage is reached, to consider pre-printing these as far as they are material, together with replies (so far as possible), so that prospective franchisees and their advisers are given the information they ought to request at an early stage.

Chapter 6
Acting for the prospective franchisee

Introduction

6.01 The role of the franchisee's adviser is limited by one circumstance peculiar to franchising: the possibility of negotiating alterations to individual clauses in an agreement, as is done in ordinary, commercial contracts, is much more limited. The reason for this is the nature of the operation. Franchising involves strict uniformity between outlets. If a franchisor is prepared to make substantial changes to an agreement at the request of the franchisee's solicitor, the franchisee's solicitor for this reason should be wary. First it could indicate that the concept has not been very well thought out, second it could suggest that the franchisor may be prepared to enter into different agreements with different franchisees with obvious dangers for the uniformity of the outlets, finally it could suggest market weakness on the part of the franchisor. The franchisor should require a strict and comprehensive franchise agreement to be entered into to enable him to operate the franchise network successfully. That will probably be in the long-term interests of the franchisee and the whole network.

Preliminary enquiries

6.02 The form of preliminary enquiries set out below may seem lengthy, and obviously not all questions will be relevant in a given case. However, bearing in mind that there is no United Kingdom disclosure statute, enquiries are the only alternative[1]. The list should, also, serve to alert the franchisee's advisers to potential problems. Vague and noncommittal replies of the sort commonly made to enquiries before contract in the case of the purchase of land, should not be accepted. The practitioner acting for the franchisee must clearly distinguish between the roles of the franchisor. Much of the information and advice required by the franchisee to compile his business plan and to evaluate the franchise prospects must, of necessity, be supplied by the franchisor. Insistence by the franchisor upon an unaltered franchise agreement may be an indication of strength and responsibility. Failure to provide adequate information and to respond fully to questions should be seen as a major flaw. Whilst the franchisor may be in an advisory capacity during his negotiations with a franchisee, the professional advisors of a prospective franchisee should not rely upon testing the relationship between the parties in the courts[2], at a later stage, if the information and advice provided by the franchisor is proved to be incorrect.

1 Part of this form is based on the Federal Trade Commission Rule which came into operation on 21 October 1979 TRR, 1978 December ¶38.029 — See para 7.56 et seq, post.
2 See para 7.09 et seq, post.

6.03 Form of Preliminary Enquiries

(1) (a) What is the address of the principal place of business of the franchisor (include telephone number, fax, telex, etc)? Is it resident in the UK?

(b) State address to which correspondence should be addressed if different from the above. Is this a permanent establishment branch or agency of the franchisor?

(c) If the franchisor is not resident in the UK, what is its address for service in England or Scotland?

(2) What is the franchisor's parent or holding company (if there is one)?

(3) Is the franchisor or its holding company a member of the British Franchise Association ('BFA') or the International Franchise Association?

(4) If the franchisor is a member of the BFA, please confirm that it complies with the code of ethical franchising promoted by the BFA.

(5) In what ways (if any) does the draft Franchise Agreement intended to be used by the franchisor in its proposed relationship with the franchisee differ from the recommendations or standards of the BFA?

(6) Has that draft been disclosed to the BFA? If not, please set out all deviations from the draft actually disclosed to the BFA.

(7) Give details of the intellectual properties which will form the subject matter of the licence to the franchisee.

(8) Does the franchisor own all such rights? If any are used by the franchisor under licence, who is/are the licensors? Please produce evidence of the franchisor's right to grant this proposed franchise. When does the franchisor's right to use those rights expire? Please provide a copy of all relevant documents.

(9) If those rights are used under licence please state what will happen if the licence is terminated or expires.

(10) What will be the result (in respect of that licence or any other document, agreement or arrangement) of the insolvency of the licensor or the franchisor?

(11) If that licence contains provisions whereby the rights of the franchisor under the franchise agreements, to which it is a party, shall automatically revert to the licensor, upon termination or expiry of the licence, please obtain replies to these enquiries separately from the licensor.

(12) Which, if any, of the intellectual properties mentioned in your reply to question 7 above are protected by registration? Give details including date and place of registration.

(13) Has any opposition been lodged or proceeding been taken against the registration or use of any of the intellectual properties mentioned in your reply to question 7 above?

(14) Is the franchisor aware of any actual or potential claims or proceedings involving other entities in which allegations of invalidity or infringement of those intellectual properties are or might be made?

(15) Are the intellectual properties mentioned in your reply to question 7 above subject to any agreement or arrangement with any other party which in any way limits or controls their use other than by any licence disclosed in reply to question 8?

(16) If the franchise includes the name of a well known person, has his consent and licence to use that name been given to the franchisor? Please produce evidence of this.

(17) If the franchisor has provided a statement of the projected earnings of the business to be franchised, what is the source of information on which that information was based? In particular, please state:

6.03 *Acting for the prospective franchisee*

    (a) Have those figures been calculated with reference to the actual performance of franchised or company-owned businesses?
    (b) Over what period?
    (c) Of similar size and location (both in terms of size and demographic characteristics) as the proposed location of the proposed business of the franchisee?
    (d) Whether those figures represent trading once the business has achieved maturity or take into account start-up and development time?
    (e) How accurate have the projections of the franchisor been in the past?
    (f) How many and in what circumstances have franchisees been obliged to put more money into their businesses due to shortfalls between actual and projected performance? What has been the average additional injection?
    (g) If any franchisees have achieved projected performance later than anticipated in their projections, please state the average delay.
    (h) Has the franchisor any evidence of performance by franchised or company-owned business after the period covered by the projections? If so, please confirm:
        (i) In no case, has any reduction in performance occurred.
        (ii) That any changes in management have had no adverse effect upon performance.
    (i) That no actual franchised or company-owned business is trading unprofitably or below its current targets.
    (j) If the significant regional variations or trends have appeared.
    (k) If the assumptions upon which the projections are based are not clearly stated in them, please set out those assumptions.
    (l) The risk factors which the franchisor and its advisors would consider appropriate to draw to the attention of potential investors as if the projections formed part of a prospectus.

(18) (a) Will the franchisor provide an audited set of his latest accounts relating to the franchise business?
    (b) What portion of the gross income of the franchisor was derived from payments made by actual or potential franchisees?
    (c) What part of such portion was derived from:
        (i) Royalties on franchisees' gross takings?
        (ii) Initial fees received from franchisees or potential franchisees?
        (iii) Sales of tied items from the franchisees?
    (d) What amount was spent on advertising the franchise business and its outlets (exclude from this figure any sums spent advertising for new franchisees)?

(19) Have there been any material changes since those accounts were prepared?—if so, give details.

(20) Who are the directors of the franchisor company and what business experience have they had?

(21) Who are the senior management responsible for the day to day running of the franchise operation, and if different from the persons mentioned in 20, ante, what is their business experience?

(22) How long has the franchisor: (a) conducted a business of the type to be operated by the franchisee? (b) offered or sold franchises for such business?

(23) Has the franchisor or its participators directors or managers at any time operated any other business in which the property rights set out in 7, ante, have been used? If yes, is such a business still in operation—give details?

Preliminary enquiries 6.03

(24) Does or has the franchisor or its participators directors or managers ever operated any other franchise business? If so, give particulars.

(25) Have any of the persons mentioned in 20 and 21, ante, been convicted of an offence involving dishonesty during the last ten years?

(26) Have any of the persons mentioned in 20 and 21, ante, ever been declared bankrupt?

(27) Have any of the persons mentioned in 20 and 21, ante, ever been parties to a civil action in which allegations of fraud or misrepresentation have been made against them?

(28) Have any of the persons mentioned in 20 and 21, ante, ever been involved in carrying on a business, in whatever capacity, which has ceased trading by reason of insolvency?

(29) Have any of the persons mentioned in 20 and 21, ante, ever been disqualified from holding office as a director or other officer of a company for any reason?

(30) The information and advice provided by the franchisor contains many representations which will materially influence the judgment of the franchisee in his decision whether or not to proceed with his proposed arrangement. Presumably, that information and advice will have been compiled by some of those persons mentioned in 20 and 21, ante? Please provide the names of those persons who are, were or will be responsible for:
    (a) the projections;
    (b) site selection;
    (c) size of territory.

(31) Please confirm that, notwithstanding the corporate veil, if it is proved subsequently that any material misrepresentations or omissions shall have been made by the franchisor in its provision of information and advice to the franchisee, those persons actually responsible for making those misrepresentations or for compiling the information upon which those misrepresentations were based shall hold themselves personally liable to the franchisee for all loss or damage and expense suffered by him as a result of those misrepresentations or omissions. If not, why not?

(32) Has the franchisor been convicted of any offence during the last ten years?

(33) Has the franchisor ever been a party to a civil action in which allegations of fraud or misrepresentation have been made against it?

(34) Has the franchisor ever been involved in litigation with present or former franchisees (action taken by the franchisor under summary judgment procedure may be ignored)?

(35) Provide a full factual description of the franchise business including:
    (a) the historical development of the business;
    (b) the reasons why the franchisor considers its franchise package to be superior to other franchises (if any) in the same business currently on offer in the United Kingdom;
    (c) in the case of new franchise business please provide full details of pilot schemes operated by the franchisor.

(36) What payments of any kind are required to be made by the franchisee in order to obtain and commence the franchise operation (including initial fees, deposit, price or rental of equipment)?

(37) Under what conditions are any such payments returnable?

(38) What recurring payments of whatever kind will the franchisee have to make in order to continue to operate the franchise business?

(39) (a) Will the franchisee need to purchase any services from the franchisor

6.03 *Acting for the prospective franchisee*

or any other person affiliated or wholly or partly owned by the franchisee?—if so, please give details.

(b) Is the franchisee required to acquire any specialist equipment from the franchisor in respect of the franchise business? If so, what are the terms of such acquisition? In the event that such equipment is hired or rented to the franchisee during the term of the franchise, what happens on expiry or earlier termination of the franchise agreement?

(40) Is the franchisee required or advised to hire or purchase any other equipment or materials needed to operate the franchise business from the franchisor or other specified supplier?—if so, please specify the materials and provide a list of the names and addresses of any specified suppliers.

(41) Are any such suppliers affiliated or owned wholly or partly by the franchisor?

(42) Will the franchisor or any person connected with the franchisor receive any payments or other consideration in respect of goods, services, property or finance supplied to the franchisee by persons other than the franchisor itself?—if so, please give details including the basis on which such payments will be calculated.

(43) What advertising policy does the franchisor pursue:

(a) with regard to the business as a whole?

(b) with regard to the opening of new outlets?—if there will be any material departure from this policy in relation to the present outlet, please specify.

(44) Will the franchisee need to acquire any freehold or leasehold property from the franchisor or any other person affiliated or wholly or partly owned by the franchisor?—if so, please give details, and, in particular:

(a) Will any lease of such premises expire or terminate on expiry or termination of the franchise agreement?

(b) What will be the permitted use of the premises under such lease?

(c) What rent review provisions are included in that lease?

(d) Is the valuation for rent review purposes limited to any restriction on the use of the premises, or is that restriction specifically excluded from consideration in such valuation?

(e) What is proposed in respect of any fixtures and fittings installed in the premises as part of the franchise package?

(45) What training in the business is provided by the franchisor to new franchisees? Is this included in the fees payable by the franchisee? What additional training facilities are made available by the franchisor during the term of the agreement and at whose expense? Is the franchisee obliged to attend further training when required by the franchisor?

(46) Will the franchisee be subject to any restrictions:

(a) as to the goods or services he may offer?

(b) as to the persons to whom he may sell or supply such goods or services?

(c) as to the geographic area in which he may offer for sale such goods or services?

(47) (a) In what way will the franchisee be protected against competition from all or any of the following:

(i) business operating under the same trade name and/or marks whether in the same or in different fields of activity?

(ii) business operating in the same or similar fields of activity which are connected with or affiliated to the franchisor or wholly or partly controlled by the franchisor?

(b) What will be the territorial extent of such protection?

(c) In the case of border areas dividing territories, does the franchisor insist

Preliminary enquiries 6.03

on strict adherence by the franchisees to the lines on the relevant maps or will it permit franchisees to make arrangements between them which are convenient to themselves?

(d) What is the attitude of the franchisor to orders from customers in one territory made to a franchisee in another territory if the goods or services are supplied by that franchisee to that customer:
   (i) in the territory of the supplying franchisee?
   (ii) in the territory in which the customer is located?

(e) How does the franchisor resolve territorial disputes between its franchisees?

(f) If the franchisee is permitted or obliged to undertake its own local advertising, what is the attitude of the franchisor to advertising by a franchisee in one territory in media which cover not only his territory but adjoining territories as well (eg local press or radio)? Does the franchisor permit joint local advertising by adjoining franchisees?

(48) Does the franchise agreement contain the right on the part of the franchisor to reduce any exclusive or other territory granted to the franchisee? If so:
   (a) In what events may that right be exercised?
   (b) Has it been exercised in the past?
   (c) If so, for what reasons?
   (d) What was the effect of that reduction as regards the gross turnover of the business whose territory was reduced?
   (e) Does the franchise whose territory is to be reduced have the right of first refusal to open a further franchised business in that part of his territory which is about to be split from the part retained by him?

(49) (a) If the franchisee is not granted an exclusive area, will there be a maximum number of franchisees within an area specified by the franchise agreement?—if so please give details.
   (b) Please confirm that, in the event that the franchise business deals in the supply of goods, the franchisor does not operate a mail order service.
   (c) Will the franchisor confirm that any enquiries from potential customers located in an area close to the proposed business outlet of the proposed franchisee, will be referred to the proposed franchisee as soon as possible after receipt?

(50) Will the franchisee be permitted to operate only within a specified area or from a specified location?—if so, please give details. In the event that the proposed franchisee is only permitted to operate from a specified location, please advise what criteria are applied by the franchisor in the selection of such a location.

(51) (a) Will the franchisee be required personally to participate in the franchised business, and to what extent?
   (b) What are the usual business hours of a franchise business?
   (c) Is the franchisee obliged by the franchisor or by practical considerations to work longer than the hours mentioned in the above?
   (d) May the franchisee use the premises from which he undertakes the franchise business for any other business venture?

(52) (a) If the franchisee is to receive financial assistance from the franchisor or any person connected with the franchisor, please confirm that the franchisee will be provided with all information which would be required to be provided if the provisions of the Consumer Credit Act 1974 applied to the agreement, *whether or not* that Act in fact applies to the agreement.
   (b) Does the franchisor have a particular relationship with any bankers or

6.03 *Acting for the prospective franchisee*

finance houses which may assist the franchisee with loans or other financing for the proposed franchise business?
(c) If so:
  (i) Which banks or finance houses? [Note: This may not be answered if no confidentiality agreement has been signed by the franchisee.]
  (ii) Upon what terms are loans usually made as to percentage of total funds required; security; interest rates; duration; capital repayments?
  (iii) Do those banks or finance houses usually require the personal guarantees of directors of company franchisees?

(53) Please confirm that the franchise departments (if any) of the potential lenders mentioned in 52(c)(i) above have received a copy of the current version of the draft franchise agreement.

(54) (a) What is the duration of the agreement to be?
(b) Is it renewable, and if so upon what conditions?
(c) Under what conditions may the franchisor refuse to renew or extend the agreement?
(d) In what circumstances may the agreement be terminated or varied unilaterally by the franchisor?
(e) When is the franchisee entitled to terminate the agreement?
(f) What will be the obligations of the franchisee (including obligations under any lease or rental agreement entered into with the franchisor or any person connected, affiliated or wholly or partly controlled by the franchisor) following the termination of the franchise agreement by the franchisor itself?
(g) Under what conditions may the franchisor repurchase the franchised business and how will the price be calculated?
(h) Under what conditions may the franchisee sell or assign all or any interest in the franchise business, or of the assets of the franchise business?
(i) Under what conditions may the franchisor assign in whole or in part its interest under such agreements?
(j) What steps to carry on the business will the franchisor take in the event of the death or incapacity of the franchisee?
(k) What rights will accrue to the franchisee's next of kin, or estate in the event of his incapacity or death?

(55) If the franchisor is to approve the site of the franchise business, how long a time usually has elapsed between the signing of the franchise agreements and other agreements relating to franchises and site selection during the past twelve months?

(56) If the franchisor is to provide the operating outlet, how long has elapsed between the signing of the franchise agreements or other agreements relating to the franchise, and the commencement of the franchisee's business under the agreements of other franchisees entered into during the last twelve months?

(57) What are:
(a) The total number of franchised outlets at present franchised by the franchisor in the United Kingdom?
(b) The total number of company-owned outlets operated by the franchisor in the United Kingdom?

(58) What are the names, addresses and telephone numbers of all the franchisor's franchisees operating businesses near to the proposed franchise business?

(59) What are the addresses of company-owned outlets adjacent to the proposed franchised business?

(60) Give details of:

Preliminary enquiries 6.03

    (a) The number of franchises voluntarily terminated or not renewed by franchisors within the last two years.
    (b) The number of franchises acquired by the franchisor within the last two years.
    (c) The number of franchises otherwise acquired by the franchisor during the last two years.
    (d) The number of franchises which the franchisor has refused to renew during the last two years.
    (e) The number of franchises which the franchisor has cancelled or terminated during the term of the agreements during the last two years.
Please give reasons for such termination.

(61) Will the franchisee be restrained from carrying on any similar business after the termination of the franchise?—if so, give details.

(62) Provide the names and addresses and telephone numbers of at least four other franchisees, and confirm that the franchisee may discuss with them and adjoining franchisees the proposed franchise.

(63) If the franchisor requires a franchisee to make payments to an advertising or marketing services fund controlled or administered by the franchisor:
    (a) Who will be responsible for deciding what advertising or promotional programmes will be commenced or maintained?
    (b) If the franchisor is responsible for such decisions who will receive advertising discounts or commissions?
    (c) If the franchisor administers the fund what management fees (if any) does it charge for so doing?
    (d) How is such a fund audited?
    (e) Will the fund be maintained in a separate bank account?
    (f) Please confirm that no advertising for franchisees will be charged to the fund.
    (g) Will the franchisor be entitled to recoup excess expenditure on advertising from the fund?
    (h) Please confirm that, if advertising expenditure in any period by the franchisor exceeds the amount then in the fund, there will be no additional levy on franchisees.

(64) Is there an association of the franchisees of the franchisor? If so, who is its secretary and his/her address? Please confirm that the proposed franchisee may contact him/her.

(65) If there is no such association does the franchisor hold regular meetings with all or groups of its franchisees? When is the next such meeting?

(66) If the franchisor has company-owned outlets:
    (a) Are they profitable?
    (b) Do they pay:
        (i) The standard franchise fees?
        (ii) The normal advertising contribution?
    (c) Are their managers freely permitted to attend any meetings of franchisees to discuss business or problems?

(67) What is the policy or requirements of the franchisor for the alteration refurbishment or updating of franchise outlets or equipment during the term of the agreement or on renewal? Are all its franchisees subject to the same obligations in this respect?

(68) How does the franchisor ensure that all its franchisees maintain high standards in their business?

6.03 *Acting for the prospective franchisee*

(69) Does the franchisor supply its franchisees with an operations manual? If so, is it updated? Who owns it? Has each copy a serial number?

(70) Is the franchisee required to conduct his business subject to standard accountancy and book-keeping practices stipulated by the franchisor? If so, are these methods acceptable to the Institute of Chartered Accountants (or its equivalent in Scotland or Northern Ireland) for audit purposes? Are these methods set out in detail in the operations manual?

(71) Has the franchisor the right to nominate the auditors of the franchisee? If so, which firm will be so nominated?

(72) Are those auditors chartered accountants?

(73) What is their charge-out rate and the anticipated amount of annual fees for a franchisee?

(74) If the franchise business comprises or involves the production of goods or any process or any method of altering or amending products, please confirm that all steps in such production process or alteration comply in all respects with any government or other regulations relating to the same?

(75) Please confirm that all wage rates recommended by the franchisor comply with any minimum wage regulations in respect of the franchise business and that the profit projections supplied by the franchisor in respect of the franchise business take such regulations into account. To what extent is the business dependant on part-time or casual employees?

(76) (a) Has the franchisor effected an insurance in respect of employers' and public liability?
    (b) Will the franchisee be obliged to insure against employer's and public liability with an insurance company nominated by the franchisor under the terms of a policy agreed by the franchisor with such insurance company?
    (c) If so, will the franchisor be covered by that policy?
    (d) In what way is the franchisee covered against claims by third parties against the franchisor?

(77) Is the franchisee required to offer credit to his customers? If so, how is this financed? Is there any special relationship with any finance house? Who receives any commission payable by such finance house upon the introduction of business?

(78) Please confirm that the franchisor has received written clearance from the Inland Revenue that none of the fees payable to it by its franchisees are liable to deduction of tax at source under section 349 of the Income and Corporation Taxes Act 1988.

(79) What is the VAT number of the franchisor? Are any part of the sums payable by a franchisee to the franchisor subject to VAT?

(80) Please confirm that the franchisor has submitted the draft of the Franchise Agreement to the Office of Fair Trading. What was the result?

(81) In the event that the proposed franchise business does not perform satisfactorily (or the franchisee or its key director is incapacitated or dies), does the franchisor have the right to install its own management? If so,
    (a) In what circumstances?
    (b) Who pays?
    (c) If the franchisee, what is the current charge?
    (d) What management resources has the franchisor to cover emergencies and poor performance?
    (e) Has the franchisor installed its own management in a franchised business in the past?
    (f) If so, why?

(g) What was the result?

(82) If the franchised business depends upon the performance of specialist employees, does the franchisor assist in recruiting them:
  (a) At the start of the business? Or
  (b) Throughout the duration of the franchise agreement?
  (c) Is recruitment charged to the franchisee?

(83) Is employee recruitment advertising a charge on the advertising fund?

(84) In the event that the franchisee wishes to dispose of his franchised business please advise:
  (a) Whether it is now the policy of the franchisor to purchase the business of franchisees who wish to sell?
  (b) If so, have any been purchased by the franchisor in the last two years?
  (c) If so, was the price reached by agreement or valuation?
  (d) If by valuation, on what basis was the valuation made by the accountant?
  (e) If the franchisor was the lessor of the location, did the franchisor claim a discount because of the terms of lease?
  (f) Have any franchises been assigned to a new franchisee in the last two years?
  (g) If so, what were the charges for vetting prospective assignees?

Replies to preliminary enquiries

6.04 Obviously all the replies need to be studied carefully. The following general principles should also be noted.

The territory

6.05 For the obvious reason that they do not want to under-exploit the potential market, franchisors may not be prepared to grant exclusive territories. This should not necessarily warn off a prospective franchisee. Some of the most successful American franchises give no area protection at all. Obviously however, territorial protection will be needed quite frequently to protect franchisee investment. For example, deliberate underselling by company owned outlets with a view to driving unwanted franchisees out of business, has been complained of in the United States[1]. Where exclusive territories are granted, the potential application of the various competition law provisions to the particular class of business needs to be carefully considered[2].

1 See, eg *Rea v Ford Motor Co* 355 F Supp 842 (1972); *Coleman v Chrysler* 525 F 2d 1338 (1975).
2 See checklists at paras 2.76 and 2.144, ante.

6.06 A strategy often adopted to avoid having to furnish particulars of agreements under the Restrictive Trades Practices Act 1976 by virtue of an area grant to the franchisee, is for the franchisor simply to undertake not to operate, or license any person to operate, under the same trade name in the specified territory[1]. This will provide adequate territorial protection for many kinds of franchisee business, though not where the subject matter of the business is more important than the name under which it is carried on. Another strategy sometimes adopted to avoid the need to furnish particulars under the Restrictive Trade Practices Act is to make

6.07 *Acting for the prospective franchisee*

the franchisor and franchisee interconnected bodies corporate[2]. The Restrictive Trade Practices Act however is in many ways the least problematic of the competition laws in operation in the United Kingdom and is likely to be replaced in the near future. Furnishing particulars of agreements is quite straightforward, and from the franchisor's point of view may be advisable in any event, rather than running the risk of the restraint of trade covenants being rendered void. EEC competition law causes greater difficulties. Any area grant, more importantly, should conform to the EEC block exemption[3]. Otherwise agreements may need to be notified to the European Commission. Undoubtedly, the category of franchise agreement most likely to give rise to problems in relation to Article 85(1) is an exclusive distributorship or dealership which is not within the block exemption. These need to be scrutinised with the utmost care to ensure that the franchisee's investment will be adequately protected without the danger of tthe protecting provisions being declared void (and of course other penalties being imposed). Otherwise, provided the franchise business is of a sort which is inherently incapable of affecting trade between Member States of the Common Market, the franchisee should have little to worry about.

1   Ch 8 precedents 7 and 8, post.
2   See para 1.02 n 1 et seq. We do not recommend this strategy.
3   See para 2.18 et seq.

Term of the agreement

6.07   The usual arrangement is a single term with one option to renew it. The length varies very much according to the type of business. The franchisee is looking for a term long enough for him to be able to recoup his investment, and get the sort of return he expects on top of it. Unless he is, also, the lessee or owner of the business premises and, thus, will benefit from any increase in their value, the profits made by the franchisee during the term are, usually, all that he will get out of the transaction. Normally, he will receive no payments of any sort when the agreement finally comes to an end[1].

1   See Ch 8, precedent 1, clauses 3.10, 3.27 and 6.22, post. Capital items will normally be written down over the term.

Write down and renewal

6.08   Part of the franchisee's initial investment is in the fitting out of premises, and equipment. It is common to write down this investment during the term of the franchise[1]. It is not usual for the franchisor to make any payments to the franchisee in respect of such things at the end of the term[2]. This is the case also where the business premises are leased to the franchisee. The franchisor is not usually willing to make a payment in respect of tenant's improvements[3]. In the case of most types of consumer franchise, regular redecoration and renewal is essential for the image of the network. The agreement should make adequate provision for this[4]. The franchisee must consider what will happen to equipment which may be installed in the franchised premises, especially if the franchisor is the landlord of those premises.

1   Ch 8, precedent 1, clause 3.10, post.
2   Ch 8, precedent 1, clause 9.0, post.
3   For the application of the Landlord and Tenant Act 1954, Part II in this respect see para 5.29 et seq.

4   Ch 8, precedent 1, clause 7.42.

6.09   The write down period should, in all cases, be appropriate: generally, it is better to err on the side of too short a period than too long. Some shady American franchisors have deliberately 'built in' cash flow problems by having capital items written down over too long a period—to enable them to re-acquire outlets cheaply.

Death and illness

6.10   All well drafted agreements involving individuals should have provisions for death and illness[1]. A common arrangement is for members of the franchisor's staff to come in and help run the business until the franchisee recovers, or a successor is found. In some kinds of family business there will be provisions for the members of the franchisee's family to take over the franchise. The agreement should also contain provisions to cover the event of the business needing to be sold. The sale of a franchised business is different from the sale of an ordinary business because the proposed purchaser will have to be approved by the franchisor. The franchisor may have a right of first refusal on any intended sale. He will, usually, require a sale's commission, if he assists in the sale process[2]. Franchisors of successful networks have lists of persons wanting to buy existing franchised businesses. A training fee will be payable by the purchaser of the business which may reduce the net sale price of the business. The sale of the business may be the only way out for a retiring franchisee. He must be sure that he will receive a fair value for it. This may be difficult if the franchisor is, also, the landlord of the business premises.

1   See Ch 8, precedent 1, clause 10.3, post.
2   See Ch 8, precedent 1, clause 10.4, post.

Termination

6.11   The circumstances in which the franchisor may terminate should be perused very carefully[1]. Whilst the present trend in the courts is against allowing contracts to be terminated for minor breaches[2], clearly the franchisee does not want to find himself in a position where the franchisor could even begin to argue about terminating the franchise for trivial breaches. A well drafted agreement distinguishes clearly between terms which go to the root of the contract, and more minor terms. However, it is essential that the franchisor should have effective sanctions against his franchisees, otherwise the network could disintegrate through lack of discipline. The ultimate sanction is termination. Of more concern to a prospective franchisee is what happens when the franchisor is in breach of his obligations or becomes insolvent. The natural reaction is to demand reciprocal rights of termination[3]. Past experience has shown that this may not be in the best long-term interests of franchisees. They will have invested considerable time, effort and money in entering the franchise and in contributions to the generation of public recognition of and goodwill for the business. Franchisors have failed but franchisees have remained trading successfully. Where franchisees have reciprocal rights of termination, the network has often broken up. Where there are no such rights, a rescue bid can be made by a consortium of franchisees or a third party and the whole retained as greater than the sum of its parts.

1   See Ch 8, precedent 1, clause 8.0, post.

6.12 Acting for the prospective franchisee

2   See especially *L Schuler AG v Wickman Machine Tool Sales Ltd* [1974] AC 235, [1973] 2 All ER 39, HL
3   See para 7.09, et seq, post, concerning misrepresentation.

Deposits

6.12   As we have already noted, the use of deposits and other initial payments to finance the sale of other outlets has been a major abuse in the United States, ie the franchisor's main concern, like the pyramid seller, has been selling franchises rather than operating businesses. Even less unscrupulous franchisors may assist their cash flow in much the same way as some mail order firms have done, by sitting on deposits for unreasonable lengths of time. Where a preliminary agreement is signed, because suitable premises have yet to be found, ideally the deposit should be paid to a stakeholder[1]. However, it is most unusual for a franchisor to agree to this because he will have incurred expense in assisting the franchisee with his business plan, funding arrangements and property search. If the proposed relationship aborts, he will wish to retain some money to compensate him for that expenditure[2]. This is a risk which the prospective franchisee must face. Probably, the cause of most failures to progress beyond a franchise purchase agreement[3] is the unavailability of suitable premises. In practice, to minimise the risk, the franchisee should search for suitable property in his chosen area, before making a deposit, if the deposit is a significant sum to him. Most franchisors, once they have provisionally approved a prospective franchisee, will allow him to choose a new area (if it is not already taken) if he cannot find a property in his first-choice area. In other cases, it is important to try to find out as best may be, whether in fact the franchisor has been delaying—see preliminary enquiries, Nos 55 and 56, ante, para 6.02.

1   Usually a solicitor.
2   See Ch 8, Form 9, post.
3   See Ch 8, Form 9, post.

Consulting existing franchisees

6.13   This is very important. It is quite possible that the franchisees may in general paint too rosy a picture—human nature being what it is and people being unwilling to admit that they have made a bad bargain. Questions should be addressed to specific matters on which the franchisee should be prepared to help. It may well be for instance that the franchisor does not, in fact, enforce many of the restrictions imposed in the agreement, eg enforce ties contained in the agreement. This may be a good thing, but it may also indicate a poorly managed chain. The franchisees should be asked about the helpfulness of the manual and the franchisor's initial and follow-up training programmes and other assistance given in starting and running the business. Franchisees should also be asked about the prices they have to pay for tied items. If possible, a prospective franchisee should try and work in a franchised outlet.

Streetwise franchising

6.14   Streetwise Franchising has been started inter alia, with a view to helping and supporting franchisees (as well as counselling franchisors). It supports the Code of Ethics of the BFA, and of the IFA. It will research a franchise on behalf of a prospective franchisee, and produce a report giving detailed information to enable the prospective franchisee to determine whether or not he or she is making a sound investment. The address of Streetwise Franchising is:

Lincoln House,
661 High Road,
London N12 0DZ.
Telephone: 081-445-7161
Fax 081-446-5065

Advertising and promotion

6.15 This is one of the most important aspects of the arrangement. Well drafted agreements will, usually, contain clauses requiring the franchisor to allocate contributions from franchisees to a specific fund for advertising and promotional purposes[1]. The franchisee should also find out whether or not he will be expected himself to finance discounts, free offers and the like associated with promotions[2]. He will, usually, be required to spend a minimum additional amount on his own local advertising. A prospective franchisee should study how effective has been the public relations of the franchisor both in relation to customers of the franchised business and the city pages of national newspapers. The latter form of exposure is helpful in the search for financial sources. The franchisee must check what advertising is to be charged to the fund. If the fund was constituted in the early days of the franchise and there is a power to charge back excess expenditure in earlier years[3]; the franchisee may discover that his own contributions are, merely, paying back the franchisor for earlier campaigns, which may not have been cost-effective or beneficial to the franchise network in any way. The fund should be paid and kept in a separate bank account. The franchisee should check what promotional literature and management expenses will be charged to the fund. Groups of local franchisees may wish to cooperate in local advertising campaigns, especially in media which penetrate several neighbouring territories. The franchisee should be wary of any requirement that the franchisee should use a nominated advertising agent or public relations consultant in its own local campaigns. Those specialists generally prove to be expensive and economies in scale are difficult to achieve on low budgets. An obligation that all advertising or promotions must be approved by the franchisor in advance is essential because it will prevent advertisements by some franchisees which are not of a standard which enhances the image of the chain[4].

1 See Ch 8, precedent 1, clause 6.4.
2 See Ch 8, precedent 1, clause 7.11, post.
3 See Ch 8, precedent 1, clause 6.4, post.
4 See Ch 8, precedent 1, clause 7.56, post.

Franchisees' associations and conferences

6.16 These can be very important, especially for businesses involving smaller outlets[1]. They provide a forum for the exchange of views, problems, technical information, and business trends. They help the franchisor by giving him additional feedback. They help to ensure conformity between the franchisees by 'peer pressure'. One bad outlet can affect the rest of the chain. The public at large are not, usually,

6.17 *Acting for the prospective franchisee*

aware of the nature of the arrangement, and tend to associate poor standards at one outlet with the standards of the chain as a whole. A club can be a useful institution for helping to maintain standards.

1 See eg Ch 8 precedent 1, clause 6.11 requirement that franchisor hold an annual conference.

Training and getting started

6.17 One of the main items which should be covered by the initial fee (subject usually to the franchisee paying travel and subsistence), is initial training. This should be a proper programme, and clear statements should be made about this and the amount of assistance the franchisee will, actually, receive in the few weeks before trading starts and for the first week or so afterwards[1]. The franchisee should check that training covers all aspects of the manual. Franchisors, because of their familiarity with their own business, can forget how much has to be learned by a new franchisee. The most elementary matters should be covered and particular emphasis should be placed on the accounts systems stipulated by the franchisor for the business.

1 See, eg precedent 1, clauses 6.7, 6.8 and 7.1 to 7.6 (inclusive) in Ch 8, post.

Insurance

6.18 The franchisee should be fully insured against public liability. The franchisor will, probably, have negotiated a suitable policy at favourable rates. The policy should be in the franchisee's own name[1]. The system whereby the franchisor insures on the franchisee's behalf is open to the objection that the franchisee is a third party to the contract. However, 'professional' indemnity insurance of almost any type is becoming increasingly difficult to obtain at anything other than punitive rates. If the franchisor has negotiated a standard policy, the franchisee must check the cover and conditions carefully. He should, also, check the claims record of the franchise network.

1 See eg Ch 8, precedent 1, clause 6.18.

6.19 In the case of an individual franchisee or the key director of a family company, insurance against sickness and death should be taken out. The sum insured will need to cover payments which may have to be made in respect of the franchisor's personnel who run, or assist in running the business in such cases[1]. The franchisor may well have negotiated a suitable policy and require the franchisee to use it. The policy should be upgraded to cover the daily charge rates of the franchisor for emergency management, whenever those rates rise. The operations manual should contain information on those rates and be updated when the rates rise. Health and sickness insurance should be a 'family' health insurance policy to enusre minimum inconvenience and anxiety for the franchisee if a member of his family falls ill.

1 See, eg Ch 8, precedent 1, clause 10.3, post.

Fees

6.20 There is a considerable danger here: if tax should be deducted at source by the franchisee and is not, he may be liable for it. This is dealt with in para 4.01 et seq, ante and must be watched with the greatest care[1]. Another matter to be considered is the true rate of royalty payment. An apparently low royalty fee may be deceptive. Some American chains have used the strategy of charging an apparently low fee, and recouping the balance from high profits on tied items. The replies to preliminary enquiries may elucidate this, but obviously this is something which existing franchisees should be asked about.

1 See Preliminary Enquiry No 78, para 6.03, ante.

Licence under the Consumer Credit Act 1974

6.21 If, as is almost certainly going to be the case (by accepting credit cards, etc) the franchisee is carrying on a consumer credit or hire business within the meaning of the Act[1], the franchisee must obtain a licence[2]. Application should be made to the Office of Fair Trading on Form CC 1/80. The franchisee must also be licensed to the extent that he acts as a 'credit broker' within the meaning of the Act[3]. He will be a 'credit broker' to the extent that he effects the introduction of customers to finance houses, insurance companies, building societies and the like. For these purposes the licence provisions apply irrespective of the amounts of the loans. The form is again CC 1/86. If the franchisee will be canvassing business off trade premises (to the extent that this is permitted)[4], this must be covered by licence[5].

1 Sections 8, 15 and 189(1). Some businesses may only enter agreements exempt under section 16(5) (SI 1977 No 326).
2 Section 21.
3 Section 145.
4 Sections 48 and 49.
5 Section 23(3).

Fees

6.22 See para 5.57.

Registration for value added tax

6.23 The franchisee will almost certainly need to be registered with the Commissioners of Customs and Excise for VAT purposes[1].

1 See enquiry 79, para 6.03, ante.

Business names: requirements under Business Names Act 1985

6.24 The Registry of Business Names was closed[1], and replaced by a requirement that any business carried on under a name other than that of its owner, display particulars of such ownership at the business premises and on business

6.24 *Acting for the prospective franchisee*

correspondence. The current provisions are in the Business Names Act 1985 which applies to a business carried on under a name which:

(1) In the case of partnerships does not consist of the surnames of all partners who are individuals and the corporate names of corporate partners (with any permitted additions).

(2) In the case of an individual does not consist of his surname (with any permitted additions).

(3) In the case of a company which is capable of being wound up under the 1985 Act, does not consist of its corporate name (with any permitted additions)[2].

The permitted additions are initials (including recognised abbreviations of names)[3] or forenames in the case of individuals, the addition of the letter 's' where individuals have the same surname (so that Smith and Smith can be called 'Smiths') and indications that the business is carried on in succession to a former business[4]. Section 2 prohibits the use without approval of the Secretary of State of certain names.

The disclosure requirements are contained in Section 4. Any persons to whom section 1 applies must state in legible characters on all business letters, written orders for goods or services to be supplied to the business, invoices and receipts issued in the course of the business and written demands for payment of business debts: (1) in the case of individuals their own names; (2) in the case of companies their corporate name; and (3) in either case an address within Great Britain for service[5]. Any business premises to which customers and suppliers have access must also display in a prominent position a notice in easily readable form containing this information[6]. Furthermore, this information must be supplied in writing to anyone 'with whom anything is done or discussed in the course of the business' who requests it[7]. The persons who may require information under this provision is somewhat unclear. It would seem to include anyone who has any contact however slight in the course of business, and to exclude a number of persons who, whilst they have had no contact in the course of business, may have a considerable interest in finding out who is running it.

As with the Business Names Act, these provisions are limited to persons having a place of business in Great Britain, thus excluding firms who merely have an accommodation address in this country.

Individuals and corporations failing to meet the Act's requirements are liable to a fine[8]. Policing the operation of the Act is the greatest problem, however. Whilst persons trading under invented words used as trade names will reveal themselves as it were ie the non-compliance within the Act's provisions will usually be manifest, in the case of Smith choosing to trade as Bloggs, this will not be the case. The Act also imposes disabilities in civil proceedings on persons failing to comply with the requirements of the Act[9]. Any legal proceedings brought may be dismissed if the defendant shows either that he has been unable to pursue a claim, or that he has suffered some financial loss by reason of the breach. The court may however permit the proceedings to continue if it considers that it is just and equitable to do so.

1 Companies Act 1981, s 119(5).
2 Business Names Act 1985, s 1(1).
3 Ibid, s 8(1).
4 Ibid, s 1(2).
5 Section 4(1)(a).
6 Section 4(1)(b).
7 Section 2(2). The Secretary of State may make regulations requiring the notices to be displayed or the information given in a specific form—s 4(5).

8 Section 7.
9 Section 5.

Warranty of intellectual property rights

6.25 Although a warranty will probably be implied, it is desirable that an express term be included in the agreement that the franchisor is entitled to the rights licensed, and will be throughout the term[1].

1 See precedent 1, clauses 6.17, 6.21 and 10.2 in Ch 8, post.

Guarantees

6.26 If the franchisor itself is prepared to give any guarantee required by the landlord as a condition of granting a lease, the form of the guarantee should attempt to reflect the points made at para 5.35, ante, in relation to franchisee guarantees generally.

Chapter 7
Control of unfair and fraudulent trading

Introduction

7.01 In this section we are concerned with measures which may help to prevent some of the abuses which can occur in connection with franchising. Sometimes the victim is the customer. In many cases, however, the victims are the franchisees themselves. Franchising can be an extremely good way of doing business for everyone concerned; it also, however lends itself to a number of frauds and sharp practices. Prospective franchisees and their advisers would be well advised to read *Streetwise Franchising* by Danielle Baillieu[1] which deals with the United Kingdom, and Harold Brown's books, *Franchising: Trap for the Trusting*[2] and *Franchising Realities and Remedies*[3], for an account of some of the misconduct which has occurred in the United States. In particular, it may be noted that such activities have not been confined to fringe operators. Some international names have on occasion been involved. Some of the practices have involved straightforward fraud. For example fictitious data has been derived from entirely or almost entirely fictitious pilot schemes in order to lure prospective franchisees. Projections as to the expected profits from an outlet have been provided which were based on no evidence whatsoever. Representations have been made that site selection would be based on the criteria established through the franchisor's skill and experience, when in fact it was based on the financial inducements offered by local estate agents. Other practices which probably just fall short of fraud have included disguising the true rate of royalty payments by the device of charging a low royalty and recouping the rest by extortionate profits on tied items. Accounting systems have been devised to make it difficult for the franchisees to obtain proper reimbursement for guarantee or warranty work[4]. Another fruitful use of misleading accounting has been to paint a healthier picture of the profitability of the franchisor than was in fact warranted. Under United States accounting rules it was possible for the franchisor to show as profits (1) sales of franchises, and (2) the total sums due under instalment sales, provided the purchaser was obliged to pay the total amount within a reasonable time and had a satisfactory credit rating. The result of this was that the profits of an enterprise which was failing to sell its ultimate product, and was therefore probably doomed to failure, could look very healthy[5]. It is by no means clear that under current British rules the position would be different, certainly there is no specific rule dealing with it. Certainly in the United Kingdom, operating leases (which under SSAP 21 do not appear as balance sheet items), and regional development grants etc, can help to paint an unusually rosey picture. Not infrequently the information imparted by the 'training programme' and the operations manual, which should represent two of the most important items covered by the franchise fee, have been minimal. The supervision and advice in starting and running the business has been given by inexperienced and poorly qualified staff. There are also some commonly made, but misleading assertions associated with advertising franchises, eg 'a business of your own', a statement which is misleading to the extent that the franchisee is controlled by the franchisor and is usually entitled to nothing by way of payments for goodwill, etc at the end of the relationship. Another notorious example is the statement that independent businesses have a 50 per cent failure rate and that franchise failure is less than 10 per cent. There would appear to be no valid statistical basis for this statement whatsoever[6]. Although it is true that good franchise operations do have a low failure rate, there would appear to be no reliable statistics for the industry as a whole. At the fringes of the business, firms have existed for the prime purpose of selling franchises and collecting fees rather than actually trading—ie they operate much the same trick as pyramid sellers. A practice on occasion indulged in by even more reputable operators is to use the money contributed by the franchisees for advertising the business, to advertise for more franchisees. Other dubious business practices have included selection of 'approved suppliers' and 'approved builders', etc on the basis of 'kick backs' and other incentives offered to gain approval rather than on merit. Company personnel, unnecessary and unrequested, have been installed at the franchisee's expense to assist and advise in the running of outlets—of course there is a real problem here that on occasions the franchisor may genuinely think that this is necessary and the franchisee refuses to believe that it is. There are also a range of practices which may raise unfair competition issues: 'full line forcing', discriminatory pricing, other discrimination against non-favoured franchisees. The competition law aspect has already been dealt with[7], and is not discussed further in this section. The scope for using competition law as a consumer protection device in favour of franchisees is much more limited than it was in the United States, which is probably just as well: it could be a clumsy and self-defeating strategy[8].

1 (1988) (Hutchinson Business).
2 (1969) (Little, Brown & Co).
3 (2nd edn, 1978) (Law Journal Press).
4 See H Brown 'A Bill of Rights for Auto Dealers' 12 Boston Coll Ind & Com LR 757 (1971).
5 Goodwin 'The Name of the Franchising Game is: The Franchise Fee, the Celebrity or Basic Operations?' 25 Bus Law 1403, 1409.
6 See H Brown *Franchising: Realities and Remedies* (revised edn, 1978) (Law Journal Seminars Press) 3.02[b] [2] [ii].
7 See Ch 2, ante.
8 See para 2.02 et seq, ante.

7.02 Termination is associated with a variety of sharp practices. Some networks have used franchising simply as a way of raising capital cheaply. Once the network is established, they want to recapture all profitable units, leaving only marginal units franchised. Termination is sometimes achieved simply under the terms of the agreement—even 30 days of termination without breach have been known. Termination can be 'built in', eg by writing down equipment over the full term which has a life of less than half of it, thereby creating cash flow problems for the franchisee who will either go voluntarily, grateful to be relieved of his obligations or accept a low payment to quit. Unfair competition through low pricing in company outlets may help to get rid of an unwanted franchisee[1]. Straightforward boycotts by withholding essential supplies have also been used. Of course such boycotts probably constitute a breach of the terms of the agreement, but the *ex post facto* remedy of damages for breach of contract has often proved worthless because the

7.03 Control of unfair and fraudulent trading

franchisor has been a subsidiary company with no assets. Trivial breaches of the agreement have also been seized on as excuses to terminate. Perhaps however the most invidious situation of all in this catalogue of horrors has been that where the franchisees have actually been forced into complicity in fraudulent business practices, by fear of termination[2].

1   *Rea v Ford Motor Co* 355 F Supp 842 (1972); *Coleman v Chrysler* 525 F 2d 1338 (1975).
2   See Brown *Franchising Realities and Remedies* (2nd edn, 1978) (Law Journal Publishing) p 143.

7.03 Although several countries now have regulatory legislation[1], there are as yet no specific franchising laws in the United Kingdom along the lines of the Federal Trade Commission Rule[2] or the Uniform Franchise Offering Code[3]. Regulation in this country therefore is through the British Code of Advertising Practice established by the Advertising Standards Association (ASA) and through the general law. In the following pages it is impossible to give more than a bare outline of some of the provisions, and to attempt to pinpoint possible areas for legislation. The problem is not so much straightforward fraudulent practices—the criminal law is capable of dealing with those. The real problem is the protection of the franchisees against sharp and unfair practices which fall short of fraud.

1   See para 7.56, post.
2   Trade Regulation Reports, December 1978, 91/38,029. See also interpretation guides Trade Regulation Reports, Number 396, 1 August 1979.
3   See H Brown *Franchising: Realities and Remedies* (2nd edn, 1978) (Law Journal Publishing), Appendix B.

British Code of Advertising Practice

7.04 Members of the British Franchise Association (BFA) give an absolute undertaking to subscribe to the Association's Code of Ethics[1]. Clause (1) of this Code states that the BFA's Code of Advertising Practice shall be based on that established by the Advertising Standards Association (ASA). However, since the ASA Code applies throughout the United Kingdom, any franchisor's advertising must be conducted in compliance with the Code even though it may not be a member of the BFA.

1   However, it must be stressed that the BFA provide no guarantee of the commercial success or viability of the franchise business.

7.05 The British Code of Advertising Practice is a self-regulating system supervised by the ASA. The Chairman is appointed from outside the advertising industry and about half its members must have no connection with advertising. The day to day administration of the Code is the responsibility of the Code of Advertising Practice (CAP) Committee and the CAP/ASA secretariat. The CAP committee is comprised of representatives of advertising organisations, agencies and the media. The CAP/ASA secretariat will give pre-publication guidance on copy. The object of the Code is to ensure that advertisements are legal, decent, honest and truthful, framed within a sense of responsibility to the consumer and conform to the principles of fair competition as generally accepted in business. Certain terms are spelled out, for example 'honesty'—advertisements should not abuse the trust of consumers or exploit their lack of expertise. Furthermore, all descriptions, claims and comparisons which relate to matters of objectively ascertainable fact should be capable of substantiation and advertisers must produce such substantiation on request. Testimonials must be genuine and related to the personal experience over a reasonable period of the person giving them.

7.06 Consumer complaints are investigated by the CAP/ASA secretariat, which reports to the ASA. The ASA publishes details of the complaints, when they have been upheld and the names of the advertisers involved. The media adherents of the Code have undertaken not to publish any advertisement found to be in breach of the Code, nor will they accept advertisements from agencies which defy the ASA's authority.

7.07 It is certainly arguable that statements such as 'a business of your own' or 'be your own boss', which as we have explained are misleading, infringe the Code. Foundationless statements about the rate of franchisee failure compared with independent business would almost certainly break the Code, as also would misleading statements about the true rate of royalty payments.

7.08 Television and radio advertising is monitored by the Independent Broadcasting Authority (IBA) constituted under the Independent Broadcasting Authority Act 1973. Standards and practice are set out in the IBA Code and are similar to those contained in the Code of Advertising Practice.

Remedies for misrepresentation

7.09 It need scarcely be said that if a misrepresentation is made fraudulently, the representer may be liable not only to a civil claim[1], but also to criminal prosecution. Misrepresentations which are not made fraudulently may also be actionable however. Not only is there a common law remedy for negligent misstatement[2], but also the statutory remedy under the Misrepresentation Act 1967. Contracting out is also regulated[3]. The Misrepresentation Act applies in England and Scotland.

1 *Derry v Peek* (1889) 14 App Cas 337.
2 *Hedley Byrne & Co Ltd v Heller &, Partners Ltd* [1964] AC 465, [1963] 2 All ER 575, HL. *Esso Petroleum Co Ltd v Mardon* [1976] QB 801, [1976] 2 All ER 5, CA.
3 By the Unfair Contract Terms Act 1977.

7.10 Section 2(1) of the Misrepresentation Act provides:

> 'Where a person has entered into a contract after a misrepresentation has been made to him by the other party thereto and as a result thereof has suffered loss, then, if the person making the misrepresentation would be liable to damages in respect thereof had the misrepresentation been made fraudulently, the person shall be so liable notwithstanding that the misrepresentation was not made fraudulently, unless he proves that he had reasonable ground to believe and did believe up to the time the contract was made that the facts represented were true.'

7.11 This provision is capable of applying to the written representations in advertisements, franchise kits, etc, as well as to oral representations by the franchisor or its servants or agents. It is to be noted that under this provision the basis of the damages award is arguably the fraud basis. It is thought unlikely, however,

7.12 Control of unfair and fraudulent trading

that if the representation were merely negligent, the literal meaning of the section would be followed[1]. More probably, the basis of the award would be the same as that at common law for negligent misrepresentation[2]. The principal difference between the two alternative claims is that under the Misrepresentation Act, the representer has the onus of showing that he had reasonable grounds to believe the facts represented were true up to the time the contract was made, ie it reverses the burden of proof.

1 Treitel, *Law of Contract* (7th edn) pp 268-9.
2 On which see *Hedley Byrne & Co Ltd v Heller & Partners Ltd* [1964] AC 465, [1963] 2 All ER 575, HL.

7.12 Representations are frequently made about the potential performance of an outlet. The case of *Esso Petroleum Co Ltd v Mardon*[1] is of particular relevance in this connection. The events which gave rise to this case preceded the Act, and it was therefore decided under the common law. Esso's representative told Mardon that the throughput of petrol on a certain site would reach 200,000 gallons in the third year of operation and so persuaded Mardon to enter a tenancy agreement for three years. This estimate failed to take into account the fact that because of a decision of the local planning authority, there would be no access from the main road. Mardon did all that he could, but could only achieve a throughput of 60,000-70,000 gallons. In July 1964 Mardon gave notice to quit, but Esso granted him a new tenancy at a reduced rent. Mardon continued to lose money and by August 1966 was unable to pay for petrol supplied. Esso duly brought an action against Mardon for the money due and for possession of the site. Mardon counterclaimed for damages in respect of the representation. He recovered inter alia on the ground of negligent misrepresentation. He recovered damages representing his capital loss, cash put into the business and loss and overdraft incurred in running the business. He also recovered for loss of earnings including a figure for loss of future earnings (a figure increased by the damage Mr Mardon had suffered to his health by virtue of his disastrous experience). A further ground of recovery in *Esso v Mardon* was contractual: the Court of Appeal held that the representation had become a term of the contract, a contractual warranty. The existence of alternative heads of liability did not however affect the quantum of damages recoverable[2].

1 [1976] QB 801, [1976] 2 All ER 5, CA.
2 In some cases it might however—see Treitel *Law of Contract* (7th edn) pp 276 et seq. The courts seem however to be increasingly reluctant to vary recovery according to the form of action where heads of liability overlap—see *H Parsons (Livestock) Ltd v Uttley Ingham & Co Ltd* [1978] QB 791, per Lord Denning MR at 804, and Scarman LJ at 806.

7.13 A material misrepresentation in reliance on which a party enters a contract, also renders the contract voidable in equity, even though innocent[1]. Damages may be awarded in lieu of rescission[2].

1 *Redgrave v Hurd* (1881) 20 Ch D 1, CA.
2 Misrepresentation Act 1967, s 2(2).

7.14 The attempt to avoid the consequences of misrepresentations by exclusion clauses is restricted by the Unfair Contract Terms Act 1977. Section 8 of the Unfair Contract Terms Act 1977 provides:

'If a contract contains a term which would exclude or restrict—

(a) any liability to which a party to a contract may be subject by reason of any misrepresentation made by him before the contract was made: or
(b) any remedy available to another party to the contract by reason of such misrepresentation.
That term shall be of no effect except in so far as it satisfies the requirements of reasonableness as stated in section 11(1) of the Unfair Contract Terms Act 1977; and it is for those claiming that the term satisfies that requirement to show that it does.'

7.15 The requirement provided by section 11(1) is that the term shall have been a fair and reasonable one to be included having regard to the circumstances which were, or ought reasonably to have been, known to or in the contemplation of the parties, when the contract was made. It is difficult to envisage circumstances in which a court would be prepared to hold a term fair and reasonable which sought to exclude liability for representations made during the negotiation of a franchise.

7.16 Terms which seek to confine the rights and liabilities of the parties within the 'four corners' of the contract are sometimes inserted, it is unlikely however that in relation to misrepresentations they will be of much use, although they may serve to prevent other matters which may have been mentioned in prior negotiations from becoming terms of the agreement even when they are not inconsistent with its terms. However, even where the written terms *are* inconsistent with matters mentioned in the prior negotiations the court may apply the collateral contract doctrine to give effect to the prior term[1]. If a court is satisfied that the written contract is the final expression of the parties' intentions, it will confine itself to the contract, if not it will consider prior matters, and the insertion of a clause expressly declaring that the contract is the full and final expression of the parties' intentions is unlikely to add much to the way in which the court decides this.

1 *City and Westminster Properties (1934) Ltd v Mudd* [1959] Ch 129, [1958] 2 All ER 733. How consideration for a collateral contract can consist in entering a flatly contradictory contract, is something which escapes the writers.

Trade Descriptions Act 1968

7.17 This Act is capable of applying both to goods and services supplied by the franchisor to the franchisee under the agreement (obviously it also applies to supply by the franchisee to the customers as well). The following sections merely provide an outline of the provisions likely to be of relevance.

Goods

7.18 The Act applies where goods are 'supplied'[1], not necessarily sold or even hired or leased. The Act may apply to any goods supplied, even if the supply is described as 'free'.

1 The term is not defined.

7.19 Section 1 of the Trade Descriptions Act 1968 provides that any person who in the course of a trade or business applies a false trade description to any goods, or supplies or offers to supply any goods to which a false description is applied

7.20 *Control of unfair and fraudulent trading*

shall be guilty of an offence. 'Trade description' relates inter alia to the following matters: quantity, size, method of manufacture production, processing, composition, fitness for purpose, testing by any person and the results thereof and approval of any person[1]. What amounts to applying a trade description is spelled out in section 4, in particular, it is to be noted that oral statements suffice[2]. Section 5 relating to trade descriptions in advertisements (including catalogues, circulars and price lists[3]) makes it easier to establish the connection between the description and the goods supplied.

1 Section 2(1).
2 Section 4(2).
3 Section 39(1).

Services

7.20 The equivalent provision in relation to services is contained in section 14. It provides:

'(1) It shall be an offence for any person in the course of any trade or business:
   (a) to make a statement which he knows to be false; or
   (b) recklessly to make a statement which is false;
as to any of the following matters, that is to say:
   (i) the provision in the course of any trade or business of any services, accommodation or facilities;
   (ii) the nature of any services, accommodation or facilities provided in the course of any trade or business;
   (iii) the time at which, manner in which or persons by whom any services, accommodation or facilities are so provided;
   (iv) the examination, approval or evaluation by any person of any services, accommodation or facilities so provided; or
   (v) the location or amenities of any accommodation so provided.
(2) For the purposes of this section:
   (a) anything (whether or not a statement as to any of the matters specified in the preceding subsection) likely to be taken for such a statement as to any of those matters as would be false shall be deemed to be a false statement as to that matter; and
   (b) a statement made regardless of whether it is true or false shall be deemed to be made recklessly, whether or not the person making it had reasons for believing that it might be false.
(3) In relation to any services consisting of or including the application of any treatment or process or the carrying out of any repair, the matters specified in subsection (1) of this section shall be taken to include the effect of the treatment, process or repair.
(4) In this section "false" means false to a material degree and "services" does not include anything done under a contract of service.'

'Knowingly' or 'recklessly'

7.21 Although section 14 requires the statement to be made 'knowingly' or 'recklessly' a person who deliberately refrains from making enquiries may be deemed to have actual knowledge[1], though subsection (1)(b) is likely to apply anyway. 'Recklessness' in this context is not to be taken to imply dishonesty. In *MFI Warehouses Ltd v Nattrass*[2], an advertisement offering louvre doors read 'folding doors gear (carriage free)' and offered folding doors sets on fourteen days' free approval. Two purchasers interpreted this to mean that gear sets could be bought separately from the doors at the stated terms. One of them found he had to pay carriage, the other that he had to pay for the gear set before it would be delivered to him. The chairman of the company offering these goods had not realised that it could be interpreted as offering gear sets as a separate item. It was held that it was sufficient for the prosecution to show that the advertiser did not have regard to the truth or falsity of the advertisement, it did not have to be shown that he deliberately closed his eyes or had any dishonest intention. The chairman had failed in his obligation to peruse the advertisements with sufficient care. One common type of statement which arguably infringes section 14 is 'a business of your own' or 'be your own boss', statements which we have suggested are misleading. Foundationless statements as to franchise failure rates, would also appear to infringe section 14.

1 *Knox v Boyd* 1941 JC 82 at 86; *Taylor's Central Garages (Exeter) Ltd v Roper* (1951) 115 JP 445 at 449, DC.
2 [1973] 1 All ER 762, [1973] 1 WLR 307.

Forecasts

7.22 It is to be noted that subsection (1) deals only with statements of past or present fact. Forecasts or promises do not fall within the provisions[1]. In *R v Sunair Holidays Ltd*[2] the appellants' holiday brochure had contained statements inter alia that a hotel possessed a swimming pool, and provided push chairs and special food for children. None of these statements turned out to be correct. The Court of Appeal held that section 14 related to statements of fact which were either true or false at the time they were made. A prediction or promise about the future could not be said to be true or false at the time it was made, and section 14 did not deal with forecasts or promises unless they contained by implication a statement of present fact. The jury should have been directed to consider whether the statement about the swimming pool related to the future, in which case they should have acquitted. The statements about children's meals and push-chairs could only relate to the future, and not to existing facts. If the jury had construed the statement to refer to the existence of a swimming pool at the time it was made or an arrangement having been made for children's meals and push chairs, and neither the pool existed, nor had an arrangement been made, then the defendant could have been properly convicted. McKenna J pointed out however that a promise or forecast may contain by implication a statement of present fact. The person who makes the promise may be implying that his present intention is to keep it. A person who makes a forecast may be implying that he now believes his prediction will come true or that he has the means of bringing it to pass. Such implied statements of present intention may well be punishable under section 14. This judgment was expressly approved by four of the Law Lords in *British Airways Board v Taylor*[3]. Arguably therefore if a statement is made about future services to be provided by the franchisor himself, such as training and assistance in running the business, and he has no intention in any real sense of providing those services, he could be prosecuted under section 14. He may also be guilty of obtaining a pecuniary advantage by deception[4].

1 Except where they relate to the effects of treatments, processes or repairs—section 14(3).
2 [1973] 2 All ER 1233, [1973] 1 WLR 1105, CA.

7.23 *Control of unfair and fraudulent trading*

3 [1976] 1 All ER 65, [1976] 1 WLR 13, HL.
4 Theft Act 1968, s 16.

Advertisements of goods

7.23 The Secretary of State can make regulations about the information required to be given in advertisements of goods[1]. There is no equivalent provision relating to services, and it would seem therefore that the information required to be given in advertisements for the sale of franchises cannot be regulated in the same way. This is unfortunate, as regulations might otherwise have been made requiring advertisements to disclose some of the information required to be disclosed by the Federal Trade Commission Rule[2], eg as to the training and other matters to be provided in return for the initial fee, as to revenue received by the franchisor from tied items.

1 Section 9.
2 Trade Regulation Reports, December 1978, ¶38,029.

Defences

7.24 Sections 24 and 25 provide as follows:

'24 (1) In any proceedings for an offence under this Act it shall subject to subsection (2) of this section, be a defence for the person charged to prove:
  (a) that the commission of the offence was due to a mistake or to reliance on information supplied to him or to the act or default of another person, an accident or some other cause beyond his control; and
  (b) that he took all reasonable precautions and exercised all due diligence to avoid the commission of such an offence by himself or any person under his control.
(2) If in any case the defence provided by the last foregoing subsection involves the allegation that the commission of the offence was due to the act or default of another person or to reliance on information supplied by another person, the person charged shall not, without leave of the court, be entitled to rely on that defence unless, within a period ending seven clear days before the hearing, he has served on the prosecutor a notice in writing giving such information identifying or assisting in the identification of that other person as was then in his possession.
(3) In any proceedings for an offence under this Act of supplying or offering to supply goods to which a false trade description is applied it shall be a defence for the person charged to prove that he did not know, and could not with reasonable diligence have ascertained, that the goods did not conform to the description or that the description had been applied to the goods.
25 In proceedings for an offence under this Act committed by the publication of an advertisement it shall be a defence for the person charged to prove that he is a person whose business it is to publish or arrange for the publication of advertisements and that he received the advertisement for publication in the ordinary course of business and did not know and had no reason to suspect that its publication would amount to an offence under this Act.'

7.25 It would appear that for the purposes of section 24, supervised shop managers and employees transacting business under their instruction are neither the ego nor the alter ego of the defendant[1]. It should therefore be possible for a franchisor to plead this defence where the proceedings result from activities of its representatives carried on without its knowledge or consent. The same defence should be available where the proceedings result from the franchisees' dealings with their customers.

1 See *Beckett v Kingston Bros (Butchers) Ltd* [1970] 1 QB 606, [1970] RPC 135; *Tesco Supermarkets Ltd v Nattrass* [1972] AC 153, [1971] 2 All ER 127, HL.

Penalties and compensation

7.26 The penalties for breach of these provisions are set out in section 18 which provides:

> 'A person guilty of an offence under this Act for which no other penalty is specified shall be liable:
> (a) on summary conviction, to a fine not exceeding two thousand pounds; and
> (b) on conviction on indictment, to a fine or imprisonment for a term not exceeding two years or both.'

7.27 In addition, the court can make a 'compensation order', requiring the defendant to pay compensation for any personal injury, loss or damage resulting from the offence[1]. In the magistrates' court there is a £2000 maximum in respect of any one conviction[2], but in the Crown Court there is no such limit. Although the words of the section are wide enough to allow consequential economic losses to be recovered, it is submitted that if these would not be recoverable in equivalent circumstances in a civil action they would probably not be recoverable under this section. In negligent misstatement cases, economic loss is recoverable[3] provided that the defendant owes the plaintiff a duty of care and provided that the loss is not too remote. Moreover, in the present context, false trade descriptions and contractual remedies are likely to overlap, and again economic losses are recoverable provided that they are not too remote. If the misrepresentation is fraudulent consequential economic loss will be recoverable, but the rules on remoteness may be more generous.

1 Magistrates Courts Act 1980, s 32, SI 1984 No 447.
2 Ibid.
3 *Hedley Byrne & Co Ltd v Heller & Partners Ltd* [1964] AC 465, [1963] 2 All ER 575 at 518 per Lord Devlin: *Esso Petroleum Co Ltd v Mardon* [1976] QB 801, [1976] 2 All ER 5, CA. In the latter case the measure was in part based on the plaintiff's loss of earnings—ie not on the shortfall in throughput.

Persistent unfair conduct

7.28 Under Part III of the Fair Trading Act 1973 the Director General of Fair Trading may take action against individual traders or companies who persist in a course of conduct which is 'unfair' and 'detrimental to the interests of consumers in the United Kingdom'[1]. Unfortunately, because the definition 'consumer' excludes persons who receive goods or services in the course of a business, these provisions can have little application to the relationship between the franchisor and the franchisee. They may have application in the fortunately infrequent cases when the franchise system involves a fraud on the ultimate consumer and the franchisee is compelled to follow the system for fear of termination. In the case of *Aamco Automatic Transmissions Inc*[2] for example, the franchisor's policy included deceiving the customer about the free reassembly of transmissions if no sale were made, and the non-disclosure of the fact that used parts might be installed during the

7.29 *Control of unfair and fraudulent trading*

repair. 'Unfair conduct' must involve breaches of the provisions of the criminal or civil law[3]. Franchise businesses which persistently fail to live up to the terms of 'guarantees'[4] or break the warranty provisions of the Sale of Goods Act 1979 or the Supply of Goods and Services Act 1982 may find themselves subject to scrutiny. The Director General in the first place is required to use his best endeavours to obtain a satisfactory assurance that the person/s concerned shall desist.

1   Fair Trading Act, 1973, s 34(1).
2   3 Trade Reg Rep ¶19,283 at 22,436, ¶19,425 at 21,536 (FTC 1970).
3   Sections 34(2) and (3).
4   There is of course the technical problem as to whether or not under English Law failure to honour a 'guarantee' given by a third party such as a manufacturer actually amounts to a breach of contract with the consumer.

Consumer Credit Act 1974

7.29 The application of this Act is complex, and it is beyond the scope of this book to give more than a bare outline of possible applications of it. An important feature of the Act however is that it may apply where an individual franchisee raises some or all of the capital to start the business through a loan. If the loan does not exceed £15,000, the agreement will be a 'consumer credit agreement' within the first of the Act's 'trigger' sections[1]. It does not matter that the loan is to be used for business purposes, so long as it is to an 'individual'. This includes a partnership but not a corporation[2]. A 'consumer credit agreement' is a 'regulated agreement'[3]. One consequence of this is that the agreement may be cancellable within the 'cooling off' period specified by the Act[4] and the effect of this could be to effect the cancellation of the franchise agreement as a linked transaction[5]. It is cancellable unless the agreement is secured on land (where other provisions considered below apply), or it is signed at the business premises of the creditor, owner, party to a linked transaction[6] or negotiator[7].

For operations directed at small investors (the most likely targets of fraud), this should cover some of the worst problems associated within 'pyramid selling' schemes[8]. Furthermore, antecedent negotiations are deemed to have been conducted by the negotiator, as agent for the creditor[9] who is therefore liable for misrepresentations, etc. Another consequene of the Act applying will be that the agreement will be terminable at any time by the franchisee under Part VII of the Act, in which case the franchise agreement may terminate as a linked transaction[10].

1   Sections 8(1) and (2).
2   Section 189.
3   Section 8(3).
4   Section 68.
5   Sections 19 and 69.
6   Section 19 as to meaning of this term.
7   Section 67.
8   See para 7.34.
9   These were frequently promoted in rooms in hotels, etc, around the country.
10 Sections 56(1) and (2).

7.30 To the extent that the purpose of the loan is to finance equipment supplied by the franchisor or approved supplier (and in the latter case the financing body has a pre-existing arrangement with the supplier as will almost certainly be the case), it will be a 'debtor-creditor-supplier' agreement'[1]. The same applies when the franchisor is supplying services to the franchisee. Ordinary bank loans raised by the franchisee will usually be 'unrestricted-use agreements'[2]. One significance of the loan falling within the 'debtor-creditor-supplier' definition is: that any claim the franchisee may have against the supplier for breach of contract or misrepresentation he has against the creditor also[3]. The cash price of the particular item must be more than £100 and less than £30,000, however[4] (and obviously the loan less than £15,000 otherwise it is not a 'consumer credit agreement' in the first place).

1 Sections 11(1)(a) and (b) and 12(a) and (b).
2 Section 11(2).
3 Sections 75(1) and (2).
4 Section 75(3).

7.31 The franchisor, whatever the amounts of loan involved will almost certainly be a 'credit broker'[1] and require a licence as such. If the franchisor is unlicensed, the credit agreement will be unenforceable against the franchisee without an order from the Director General of Fair Trading[2].

1 Sections 145(1) and (2).
2 Section 149.

7.32 In the case of the loan being raised on the security of a mortgage of land, as we have seen, there is no right of cancellation. Instead the Act contains special 'pause' provisions. These provide a formal procedure to be followed and provide a period of 'isolation' for the debtor during which he must not be approached[1]. The effect should be to protect prospective franchisees who are being pressed to sign mortgages or second mortgages of their house to raise the money.

1 Section 61.

7.33 The taking of promissory notes and the negotiating of cheques by the creditor is prohibited by the Act[1]. The Act also controls the form and content of the agreement and many other aspects of the provision of credit, but it is beyond the scope of this work to consider these. Reference should be made to the standard works[2].

1 Sections 123 and 124.
2 See Bennion *Consumer Credit Control* (Longman Professional); Goode *Consumer Credit Legislation* (Butterworths).

Pyramid selling

Introduction

7.34 In the United States it has been known for franchise business to become essentially traders in the sale of franchises, rather than traders in the product of the franchises. This has not always been due to fraud. Sometimes it has been due to over optimistic expansion. The Minnie Pearl Chicken System is a notorious example. When this collapsed in 1969 it had sold 1,800 franchises but opened only 161 outlets. The only Act dealing with this type of problem is the Fair Trading Act 1973. This Act regulates a particular form of it known as 'multi-level distribution' or, more popularly, 'pyramid selling'. This has been described as follows:

> 'The typical multi-level distributorship plan involves the manufacture or sale by a company, under its own trade name, of a line of products through "franchises" which appear to be regular franchise distributorships. These plans

7.35 *Control of unfair and fraudulent trading*

may include three to five levels of nonexclusive distributorships, and individuals may become "franchisees" at any level by paying the company an initial fee based on the level of entry. Once a member of the plan, the individual earns a commission by selling the company's products and attracting new members. Each distributor pays less for the product than the price he receives from the public and from those at lower levels in the distribution chain to whom he sells. Since one profits merely by being a link in the product distribution chain, the emphasis is on recruiting more investor-distributors rather than on retailing products.[1]'

1 61 Georgetown LJ 1257 (1973).

7.35 Pyramid schemes are lucrative for those at the top of the pyramid. Their inevitable tendency however is towards market saturation—they have the inherent instability of a chain letter[1]. Eventually participants will be unable to recruit further participants and the system will collapse.

1 61 Georgetown LJ 1257 (1973) at 1261.

7.36 For the reasons explained below, the legal controls over pyramid selling in operation in the United Kingdom are unlikely to affect franchise schemes, even those where a master franchise receives benefits for recruiting sub-franchisees.

Legal control over pyramid selling

7.37 The main legal control over pyramid selling schemes in the United Kingdom is exercised through the Fair Trading Act 1973 and the regulations made thereunder. The legislation is worth dealing with in a little detail since it could apply to the sale of business format franchises where there are master franchisees and area franchisees recruiting franchisees. It is certainly easy to envisage the same sort of selling techniques being used as have been used by 'pyramid sellers': a hotel room hired for a meeting with prospective franchisees in which they will be subjected to high pressure selling and told that only ten (or whatever) franchises are available to the lucky first few to sign up there and then.

The Act's strategy is essentially control of advertising, a 'cooling off' period and terms control. It does not make pyramid selling as such illegal. The Secretary of State has power[1] by statutory instrument to make provision with respect to the issue, circulation and distribution of documents, whether being advertisements, prospectuses, circulars or notices, which

(1) contain any invitation to persons to become participants in a trading scheme; or

(2) contain any information calculated to lead directly or indirectly to persons becoming participants in such a trading scheme, and may prohibit any such document from being issued, circulated or distributed unless it complies with such requirements as to the matters to be included or not included in it as may be prescribed by the regulations.

1 Fair Trading Act 1973, s 119.

7.38 The definition of 'trading scheme' is contained in section 118 of the Act. This requires that the goods or services be provided by the person promoting the scheme to other persons who participate in the scheme. The supply must involve

Pyramid selling 7.40

transactions by participants in the scheme other than the promoter, which are to be effected (or most of them are to be effected), other than at the premises where the promoter (franchisor/master franchisee) or particular participant carries on business[1]. Participants must be offered as inducement the prospect of receiving payments or other benefits in respect of one or more of the following:

(1) the introduction of other persons who become participants:

(2) the promotion, transfer or other change of status of participants within the trading scheme;

(3) the supply of goods to other participants;

(4) the supply of training facilities or other services for other participants;

(5) transactions effected by other participants under which goods are to be supplied to, or services are to be supplied for, other persons.

1 This provision should be noted, as it does provide a way of avoiding problems ie by having agreements executed on trade premises.

7.39 The present Regulations are the 1989 Pyramid Selling Schemes Regulations[1] and apply to schemes to which Part XI of the Fair Trading Act 1973 applies other than a scheme under which:

(a) the prospect of receiving payments or other benefits in respect of all or any of the matters specified in section 118(2) of that Act is held out to only one participant in the United Kingdom;

(b) the only prospect of receiving payments or other benefits in respect of the matters so specified is the prospect of receiving a sum not exceeding £30 in respect of the introduction by him of another person who becomes a participant[2].

Consequently a scheme may provide for one participant, eg a sole United Kingdom master franchisee, to receive payments on the introduction of other participants, to supply training facilities, etc[3].

1 SI 1989 No 2195.
2 Reg 3.
3 See Cunningham, *The Fair Trading Act 1973* (1974) (Sweet and Maxwell) s5.39.

7.40 The Regulations, inter alia, require advertisements and contracts used in relation to such schemes to contain the following 'health warning':

Warning for use in pre-contractual documents

> **STATUTORY WARNING**
> 1. Make sure that you understand what is being offered to you.
> 2. Do not be misled by claims that high earnings are easily achieved.
> 3. It is advisable to take independent legal advice before signing a contract.

7.41 *Control of unfair and fraudulent trading*

Warning for use in contracts

STATUTORY WARNING
Before you sign the contract:
 (a) Make sure that you have read it carefully and that you have seen a document which explains the scheme in detail.
 (b) Consider the following:
  1. It is advisable to take independent legal advice before signing a contract.
  2. Do not be misled by claims that high earnings are easily achieved.
  3. All businesses carry some risk. Do not purchase more stock than you believe you can sell in a reasonable period.

---

1 Regulation 4(1)(v).
2 Regulation 7(e).

7.41 The Act imposes criminal and civil sanctions for breach of its provisions. By section 120 distributing circulars, etc, is in breach of section 119(1). Contravention of the regulations made under section 119(2) is an offence. Payments made in contravention of the 1973 Regulations are recoverable, and any undertakings to pay are unenforceable. Recovery of other losses suffered by the participant, will of course depend on the general civil law. The court can order a pyramid selling company to be wound up on the ground that it is operating against the public interest[1].

1 *Re Golden Chemical Products Ltd* [1976] Ch 300, [1976] 2 All ER 543.

7.42 It has been suggested that an apparent weakness of the Act is that it covers only pyramid selling schemes where most of the participants' transactions occur away from the business premises of the promoter or particular participant, and this will confine its operation in the main to doorstep selling[1]. This is not correct. Indeed the Act defines its target rather precisely. Section 118(4) provides that in determining for the purposes of the sub-section[2] whether any premises are premises at which a participant in a trading scheme carries on business, no account shall be taken of transactions effected by him under the trading scheme. Consequently, premises from which a participant conducts his sales under the scheme and recruits other participants will not be a place of business, nor would an hotel room. On general principles the latter would not be a place of business anyway[3]. The same thing applies to convention halls or similar meeting places.

1 Cranston *Consumers and the Law* (1984) (Weidenfeld and Nicolson) p 345.
2 Section 118(1)(c).
3 *Re Norris, ex p Reynolds* (1888) 4 TLR 452, CA, per Lord Esher ' . . . if all a man did was to negotiate paper contracts at a room in a hotel, I should hesitate to say it was a place of business. Certainly, if he did it first at one hotel and then at another, it would not.'

7.43 The legislation does not actually prevent pyramid selling. Provided a promoter takes care to comply with the requirements of the Act he can operate a pyramid selling scheme.

7.44 When combined with the provisions of the Consumer Credit Act 1974, the Act has some of the worst abuses of the 1960s when a number of people were induced to take out second mortgages on their houses in order to become participants in doubtful schemes.

7.45 Another type of pyramid scheme which has been used in the United States is the 'founder member' plan. The legitimate object of the scheme is to raise capital, it differs from franchising however in that the outlets when opened are operated by the promoter, not a franchisee.

Financial Services Act 1986

7.46 This Act repeals the Prevention of Fraud (Investments) Act 1958. Like its predecessor, the Act does not apply to franchises as investments[1], and franchisors do not carry on an investment business within the meaning of the Act[2] unless they become involved in raising funds for their franchises other than by ordinary loans.

1 Section 1(1) and Sch 1, Part I.
2 Section 1(2) and Sch 1, Part II.

Companies Act 1985 and Insolvency Act 1986

7.47 The possibility of a franchisor incurring liability under these acts, in the event of a corporate franchisee's insolvency, has been dealt with above[1].

1 See para 1.62.

Protection against harassment

7.48 Where part of the franchised premises owned by the franchisor are occupied by the franchisee as a dwelling under a lease which is subject to a right of re-entry or forfeiture, it is not lawful to enforce that right without a court order[1]. Similarly, where premises have been let as a dwelling under a tenancy which is not a statutorily protected tenancy, a court order is required to recover the premises from the occupier[2]. The effect of these provisions could be that the franchisee will remain in occupation for some time after the franchise has been determined, and obviously this could cause problems for the franchisor wishing to bring in a new franchisee. The practical answer to this problem is, however, that so long as a new franchisee cannot be brought in, under the terms of the franchise agreement the business will have to be carried on by the franchisor's personnel at the expense of the former franchisee. This should provide some disincentive for lingering in the residential accommodation.

1 Protection from Eviction Act 1977, s 2.
2 Ibid, s 3. 'Occupier' includes any person lawfully residing in the premises at the termination of the former tenancy (s 3(2) and in this limited sense, a possessory licensee is covered by these provisions—*Ozer Properties v Ghaydi* (1987) 20 HLR 232, CA).

7.49 Control of unfair and fraudulent trading

Equitable relief

7.49 The relationship of franchisor and franchisee resembles that of partners, even if it is not a true partnership. The relationship of partners to each other in equity is a fiduciary one[1] as is that of agents and principals[2] directors and their company[3]. Certainly the franchisor/franchisee relationship is closely analogous to these, and it seems likely that it could be held to be a fiduciary relationship.

1 *Featherstonhaugh v Fenwick* (1810) 17 Ves 298; *Clegg v Fishwick* (1849) 1 Mac & G 294.
2 *De Bussche v Alt* (1878) 8 Ch D 286, CA.
3 *Regal (Hastings) Ltd v Gulliver* (1942) [1967] 2 AC 134n, [1942] 1 All ER 378, HL.

7.50 One consequence of this would be that franchisors would have imposed on them a duty of good faith in relation to their prospective franchisees: a duty not to misrepresent or wilfully conceal information[1]. Certainly an equitable right of rescission could arise from this, as well as a right to recover damages[2]. However, since the development of remedies for negligent misrepresentation[3] the importance of characterising the relationship as a fiduciary one is largely in relation to the duties of the parties during the continuance of the relationship. A person in a fiduciary position is not unless otherwise expressly provided allowed to put himself in a position where his interest and his duty conflict[4]. This rule could be applied to 'kick-backs' on tied sales. Where franchisees are permitted to purchase supplies only from 'approved suppliers', the franchisor's duty should be to select those suppliers on the objective commercial criteria of price, quality, ability to deliver on time, etc, and not on the basis of the 'kick-backs' they are prepared to give to the franchisor. Cases where a fiduciary obtains a benefit for himself at the expense of his beneficiary are the clearest cases for the application of the equitable principle[5]. The principle is applied even where the gain to the fiduciary has cost the beneficiary nothing. Thus agents must account to their principals for secret commissions received by them[6]. This rule applies even if there is no evidence that the agent was biased as a result of the payment[7], and notwithstanding any usage to the contrary[8]. It seems possible, on the analogy of these cases that a franchisor could be held accountable to its franchisees for sums of money received by way of 'kick-backs' and to hold such sums of money for them as trustee[9]. Certainly 'no agency' or 'no partnership' clauses ought not to affect the court's decision: it is the substance of the relationship which matters. The only safe way in which a fiduciary can accept such payments, is to make full disclosure, and obtain the consent of his beneficiaries. The consequences of doing this in the present context would obviously be disastrous.

1 The cases on company promoters would appear to be material here—see, eg *Central Rly Co of Venezuela (Directors etc) v Kisch* (1867) LR 2 HL 99.
2 *Nocton v Lord Ashburton* [1914] AC 932, HL.
3 See para 7.09, ante.
4 *Bray v Ford* [1896] AC 44 at 51, HL.
5 Hanbury and Maudsley *Modern Equity* (13th edn, 1989) p 565 et seq.
6 *Fawcett v Whitehouse* (1829) 1 Russ & M 132; *Beck v Kantorowicz* (1857) 3 K & J 230.
7 *Harrington v Victoria Graving Dock Co* (1878) 3 QBD 549.
8 *Bartram & Sons v Lloyd* (1903) 88 LT 286.
9 See *Jirna Ltd v Mister Donut of Canada Ltd* (1970) 13 DLR (3d) 645; revsd (1971) 22 DLR (3d) 639; affd (1973) 40 DLR (3d) 303. The views expressed by the first instance court in this case, and the two superior courts on this question are instructive.

7.51 Straight 'tie-in' sales by the franchisor to the franchisee are more problematic.

Where they are simply used as a convenient way of calculating royalties as in the brewing trade, they should be unproblematic, but where they are used as a means of disguising the true royalty payment, and enable the franchisor to represent the royalty payment as 'low' almost certainly they could come within the equitable principle[1].

1 See *Jirna Ltd v Mister Donut of Canada* (1970) 13 DLR (3d) 645; revsd (1971) 22 DLR (3d) 639; affd (1973) 40 DLR (3d) 303 appld *Patchett v Oliver* [1977] 5 WWR 299. See para 7.50, n 9, ante.

7.52 Another possible area where equitable relief might be granted is where the franchisor has constructed the accounting system in a way which will mislead the franchisee, eg where the franchisee is under-compensated for such things as repairs done to customers' goods by misleading him as to the true cost of the job[1].

1 This has occurred in motor dealerships in the United States—see Brown 'A Bill of Rights for Auto Dealers' 12 Bost Coll Ind & Com LR 757 (1971).

7.53 Equitable relief might also be granted to prevent a franchisor withholding supplies from a franchisee[1] or deliberately weakening a franchisee by unfair competition through company owned outlets. It might also be granted in cases of discrimination against particular franchisees[2], and against attempts to forfeit franchises for minor breaches, but there of course the tendency of recent years at common law has been against allowing a party to repudiate for minor breaches even where the term broken has been described as 'a condition'[3].

1 *Sky Petroleum Ltd v VIP Petroleum Ltd* [1974] 1 All ER 954, [1974] 1 WLR 576. The remedy of damages is inadequate in such cases, because the franchisee may well have to stop trading as a result of the boycott. An interlocutory injunction is therefore the most appropriate remedy.
2 See *Galloway v Hallé Concerts Society* [1915] 2 Ch 233; Finn 'Fiduciary Obligations' Law Book Co (1977).
3 See *Schuler AG v Wickman Machine Tool Sales Ltd* [1974] AC 235, [1973] 2 All ER 39, HL.

7.54 Another possible field for equitable intervention, but one in which admittedly there would have to be a significant shift from traditional views, is where the franchisor seeks to take advantage of a termination clause in the agreement providing an unreasonably short period of notice, eg 30 days as in some American agreements, or unreasonably refuses to renew the term. Certainly American courts have intervened in such cases[1].

1 *Cf*, eg *Division of Triple T Service Inc v Mobil Oil* 304 NYS 2d 191 (1969); *RLM Associates v Carter Manufacturing Corpn* 248 NE 2d 646 (1969); *Mobil Oil v Rubenfield* 339 NYS 2d 623 (1972), 370 NYS 2d 943.

7.55 For an adventurous court, the potential scope for equitable relief to remedy franchising abuses is quite considerable[1].

1 See Brown 'Franchising and Equity' 49 Tex LR 650 (1971).

Disclosure laws

7.56 At para 6.02 we set out a form of preliminary enquiries which attempts to extract from the franchisor the sort of information a franchisee will need to

7.57 *Control of unfair and fraudulent trading*

make an informed decision as to whether or not to invest his money in the particular franchise. The weakness of this strategy is that there is no obligation on franchisors to respond, and, in the absence of a general practice in the industry that such enquiries should be answered, there is no 'peer pressure' upon them to respond. For these reasons, a number of jurisdictions have enacted disclosure laws, requiring franchisors to disclose certain information. The thinking behind these laws is similar to that which underlies the requirements of the Consumer Credit Act 1974 that information eg about rates of interest be presented in particular ways to enable borrowers to make an informed choice between credit offers. The best known of these disclosure laws is the Federal Trade Commission Rule promulgated 21 December 1979[1]. The Rule only requires disclosure of material facts: it does not regulate the content of agreements.

1 See also the Model Franchise Investment Act — draft released 17 July, 1989.

7.57 The Rule covers two types of commercial relationship. The characteristics of the first type are as follows:

(1) the franchisee sells goods or services which meet the franchisor's quality standards (in cases where the franchisee operates under the franchisor's trade mark, service mark, trade name, advertising or other commercial symbol designating the franchisor ('mark')) or which are identified by the franchisor's mark;

(2) the franchisor exercises significant control over, or gives the franchisee significant assistance in, the franchisee's method of operation;

(3) the franchisee is required to make a payment of $500 or more to the franchisor or a person affiliated with the franchisor at any time before or within six months after the business opens.

The characteristics of the second type are as follows:

(1) the franchisee sells goods or services which are supplied by the franchisor or a person affiliated with the franchisor;

(2) the franchisor assists the franchisee in any way with respect to securing accounts for the franchisee, or securing locations or sites for vending machines or rack displays, or providing the services of a person able to do either;

(3) the franchisee is required to make a payment of $500 or more to the franchisor or a person affiliated with the franchisor at any time before or within six months after the business opens.

There are certain types of business excepted from the Rule, including horizontal chains of retailer owned co-operatives.

7.58 All franchisors within the above definitions must furnish to prospective franchisees a 'disclosure document'. It must contain the following:

(1) Identifying information about the franchisor.

(2) Business experience of the franchisor's directors and key executives.

(3) The franchisor's business experience.

(4) Litigation history of the franchisor and its directors and key executives.

(5) Bankruptcy history of the franchisor and its directors and key executives.

(6) Money required to be paid by the franchisee to obtain or commence the franchise operation.

(7) Continuing expenses to the franchisee in operating the franchise business that are payable in whole or in part to the franchisor.

(8) A list of persons who are either the franchisor or any of its affiliates, with whom the franchisee is required or advised to do business.

Disclosure laws 7.61

(9) Realty, personalty, services, etc which the franchisee is required to purchase, lease or rent, and a list of any persons from whom such transactions must be made.

(10) Description of consideration paid (such as royalties, commissions, etc) by third parties to the franchisor or any of its affiliates as a result of a franchisee's purchase from such third parties.

(11) Description of any franchisor assistance in financing the purchase of a franchise.

(12) Restrictions placed on a franchisee's conduct of its business.

(13) Required personal participation by the franchisee.

(14) Termination, cancellation and renewal of the franchise.

(15) Statistical information about the number of franchisees and their rate of terminations.

(16) Franchisor's right to select or approve a site for franchise.

(17) Training programme for the franchisee.

(18) Celebrity involvement with the franchise.

(19) Financial information about the franchisor.

7.59 The information must be current as of the end of the franchisor's most recent financial year. The document must be revised quarterly whenever there is a material change in the information contained in the document. The document must be given to the prospective franchisee at the earlier of either the prospective franchisee's first personal meeting with the franchisor, or ten days prior to the execution of a contract of payment of money relating to the franchise relationship. In addition, the franchisee must be given copies of all agreements which he will be asked to sign.

7.60 The Rule prohibits representations about the actual or potential sales, income, or profits unless reasonable proof exists to support the accuracy of the claim, and the franchisor has in its possession at the time the claim is made information sufficient to substantiate the accuracy of the claim; the claim is geographically relevant to the prospective franchisee's proposed location (except for media claims); and an earnings claim disclosure document is given to the prospective franchisee at the same time as the other disclosure document. The earnings claim document must contain:

(1) A cover sheet in the form specified in the Rule.

(2) The earnings claim.

(3) A statement of the bases and assumptions upon which the earnings claim is made.

(4) Information concerning the number and percentage of outlets that have earned at least the amount set forth in the claim, or a statement of lack of experience, as well as the beginning and ending dates of the time period covered by the claim.

(5) A mandate or caution statement, whose text is set out in the Rule, concerning the likelihood of duplicating the earnings claim.

(6) A statement that information sufficient to substantiate the accuracy of the claim is available for inspection by the franchisee (except for media claims).

Any changes to the above information must be notified to the prospective franchisee.

7.61 Failure to comply with the Rule exposes the franchisor to the risk of a

7.62 Control of unfair and fraudulent trading

substantial financial penalty. In addition, the Commission believes that anyone injured as a result of such non-compliance should have a right of action for damages.

7.62 States can have more stringent legislation than the Rule, but cannot attempt to modify the effect of it (it is Federal law). Thus, some States have registration requirements for franchisors and their salesmen (again, compare the Consumer Credit Act which has licensing requirements).

The following States have disclosure laws:
- California
- Hawaii
- Illinois
- Indiana
- Maryland
- Michigan
- Minnesota
- New York
- North Dakota
- Oregon
- Rhode Island
- South Dakota
- Virginia
- Washington
- Wisconsin

The Uniform Franchise Offering Code

7.63 UFOC is accepted in satisfaction of the disclosure requirements in the above fifteen States. The UFOC form is not, however, identical to the Rule. Nevertheless, the purport of the two is the same, and the Commission will allow a franchisor to use the UFOC format instead of that of the Rule, provided the UFOC form used is that adopted by the Midwest Securities Commissioners Association on 2 September 1975. The Rule nevertheless still governs who is required to make disclosure, the transactions requiring disclosure, the time of disclosure, and the types of documents to be given to prospective franchisees.

Other countries which have regulated franchising

7.64 Other countries have introduced regulations covering franchising. In Canada, Alberta has the Franchise Act 1980 which has registration and disclosure provisions, and in Quebec, the definition of 'Investment contract' in the Securities Act 1983 appears to be wide enough to bring franchise contracts within the scope of that Act. France passed a law in December 1989 which potentially could apply to most forms of licensing but, at the date of writing, no regulations have been made under it.

7.65 Other jurisdictions in which franchise disclosure laws have been considered include Australia, Belgium, Japan, Ontario and Sweden. However, the only laws actually to be introduced to date appear to be in the United States, Alberta and France. Some countries, including Germany, have rejected plans for legislation, at least for the present. In many countries voluntary regulation is operated along the lines of the British Franchise Association Code of Ethics.

7.66 In some countries, regulation of franchising is to some extent exercised through technology transfer legislation. Obviously, this only affects foreign franchisors, but where it applies, the terms of franchise agreements may require government approval, and matters which will be scrutinised can include the payments to be made in respect of individual items, tied items, and the duration of the franchises. Legislation of this type is in operation in Argentina and the Andean pact group of countries, and also the People's Republic of China.

7.67 Other legislation aimed at regulating business generally may impinge on the way in which franchises are offered. For example, until 1 September 1987 the disclosure requirements of the Australian Companies and Securities Code applied to franchising. The South African Harmful Business Practices Act 1988 regulates franchising as well as other types of business.

7.68 At an international level, the possibility of a model law or guidelines is being considered by UNIDROIT which circulated a report and draft questionnaire in 1986.

Conclusion

7.69 English law is probably better equipped to handle many of the abuses of the sort which occurred in the United States during the franchise boom of the 1960s, than the law of most States at the time. Obviously fraudulent persons are likely to enter the franchising field, but the criminal law is already capable of dealing with them, though quite a lot needs to be done to raise public awareness to the dangers. The greater risk however is that over optimistic selling of franchises will one day result in a disaster of the *Minnie Pearl* sort. Legislation similar in strategy to the Fair Trading Act's pyramid selling provisions might help here by mitigating the effects on high pressure selling. Regulation of advertising to prevent representations which while not actually false, are misleading to the ordinary person might also help. Probably the time and expense necessary to produce a comprehensive franchising statute would not at present be justified however, though an amendment to the Fair Trading Act to permit regulations to be made under it along the lines of the Federal Trade Commission Rule might be worth considering. It may be that the industry itself will be able to exercise effective controls over members of its own trade association, the British Franchise Association. That, however, will depend on how much pressure there is for franchisors to join that body. That in turn depends to an extent on public awareness that reputable franchisors ought to belong to it. The impact which Streetwise Franchising[1] may make, as an organisation representing franchisees generally, upon this, and the other problems discussed in this chapter, is something we will watch with interest.

1 See para 6.14.

Chapter 8
Precedents

Introduction to precedents

The object of franchising is to minimise the risk involved in any business venture for both the franchisor and the franchisee. Time is money, and a franchise programme should save time for both parties. Accordingly, a franchisor must set up systems for its franchise with this object firmly in view.

1 Franchise package. The package should be complete before any attempt is made to sell a franchise. The package should include the following:
1.1 Franchise Application Form[1]. This form is designed to obtain as much information as possible from prospective franchisees. The franchisor need not spend much time discussing the franchise with prospective franchisees until this information has been received. This saves the franchisor dealing with time-wasters.
1.2 Accompanying letter[2]. This letter softens the terseness of the application form. The draftsman must remember that franchising is a selling operation.
1.3 Confidentiality agreement[3]. This agreement is intended to enable the franchisor to release confidential information to the franchisee to assist with the preparation of the franchisee's business plan (see **1.4** below). Much of the financial information particularly margins, sales mix and projected volume will be of substantial interest to competitors. It is essential, therefore, to restrict the manner in which the franchisee may use that information. Directors and substantial shareholders of a private limited company franchisee should sign similar agreements.
1.4 Prospectus/Business plan[4]. Every franchisor will be aware that his franchisees may need to raise money. Some may be ideal prospective franchisees in every way, except that they have insufficient personal capital to comply with prudent debt/equity ratios for the franchise business. If that is the case, a responsible franchisor will seek to assist those franchisees, not only by introducing his franchisees to banks which he has already satisfied as to the prospects of the franchise business in general, but by trying to arrange marriages between those franchisees and equity funders. In this context, the franchisor should be licensed as a credit broker under the Consumer Credit Act 1974[5], and may also need to become a licensed dealer in securities[6]. The prospectus in this title is a framework or aide-mémoire to assist franchisors to standardise business plan presentations by franchisees to potential

1 For a Franchise Application Form see Form 2, post.
2 For a letter to accompany a Franchise Application Form see Form 3, post.
3 For a Confidentiality Agreement see Form 4, post.
4 For a form of Prospectus see Form 5, post.
5 See para 5.55 et seq.
6 See para 7.46.

Introduction to precedents

lenders and participators. A responsible franchisor will have made sample presentations to potential lenders and equity funders before commencing sales of franchises. Before using this form, practitioners must check very carefully current company and investment sales law and regulations.

1.5 Letter to the Inland Revenue[7]. Royalties for a bare licence of a trade mark or service mark, with no other services provided by the licensor, may be subject to deduction of tax at source by the payer. It is necessary that the franchisor obtains clearance from the Inland Revenue in order that his franchisees may pay the franchise fees to the franchisor gross. This includes any initial fees or non-refundable deposits. The Inland Revenue must be persuaded that that part of the franchise fees attributable solely to the use of the franchise trade name or marks is negligible in comparison to the element attributable to the other services provided by the franchisor. If such Revenue clearance is received, the franchise fees will be in the nature of services which are subject to VAT. Additional complications arise if patents are involved in the franchise or if the franchisor is non-resident for UK tax purposes[8].

1.6 Letter to Office of Fair Trading and relevant board minutes[9]. If the franchise agreement contains restrictions on the part of both parties, then those restrictions may fall foul of the Restrictive Trade Practices Act 1976 and its subsidiary instruments and regulations. The most common such restriction is the grant of an exclusive territory because the franchisor is bound not to trade or to grant other franchises in that territory and the franchisee is bound not to trade outside it. It is the practice of the Office of Fair Trading not to require registration of agreements containing mutual exclusive territory provisions, provided the restrictions on the part of the franchisor are limited to the conduct of the franchise business under the franchise trade name. If the franchisor may operate a similar business as the franchise business within the exclusive territory of a franchisee, but under another trade name, the Office of Fair Trading now takes the view that such a restriction is not one to which the Act applies. However, practitioners should always submit a final draft franchise agreement to the Office of Fair Trading to obtain confirmation that the agreement is not registrable, before any agreements are exchanged with franchisees[10].

1.7 Franchise Purchase Agreement[11]. This agreement binds both parties to enter into the franchise agreement on the conditions set out in the purchase agreement. It is intended to enable a franchisee to locate and convert suitable premises and to become trained in the knowledge that he will be granted a franchise.

1.8 Franchise agreement[12]. This should be in its final form. As a sales tool, it is better if the agreement is attractively printed, reflecting the high standard of presentation of all the promotional material and brochures used by the franchisor in its franchise sales programme (see **4** post for a detailed check list). If the franchisor wishes to become a member of the British Franchise Association, the recommendations of the Association as to terms and conditions of franchise agreements must be studied. The agreement should be compatible with those recommendations.

1.9 Directors' and shareholders' undertakings[13]. Many franchisees will be sole

7 For a letter to the Inland Revenue applying for clearance under the Income and Corporation Taxes Act 1988, s 349 (42 Halsbury's Statutes (4th edn) TAXATION) see Form 6, post.
8 See Franchise Agreement Checklist, p 313, post.
9 For a letter to the Office of Fair Trading and for board minutes relating to such a letter see Forms 7, and 8, post respectively.
10 See Documentation, p 312, post.
11 For a Franchise Purchase Agreement see Form 9, post.
12 For a Franchise Agreement see Master Form, Form 1.
13 For a letter containing undertakings by directors or shareholders see Form 10, post.

Precedents

traders or partnerships. In those cases, there is no need for further personal involvement on the franchisee's side. However, when the franchisee is a limited company, it is essential that its key directors and, in the case of a private limited company, its shareholders undertake to the franchisor in the manner set out in the undertakings. Franchising depends upon a strong personal relationship between representatives of the franchisor and the franchisee. Even if the franchisee is a limited company, the franchisor will rely upon the quality of the directors of the franchisee company. It would be unfortunate if any of those directors were able to set up in competition to the franchise business, using all the know-how acquired from the franchisor, after resigning their directorships in the franchisee company. The extent to which the covenants in these undertakings will be enforceable will depend upon the law relating to restraint of trade and practitioners must review this matter carefully before drafting the undertaking[14]. The possibility that particulars may need to be furnished to the Office of Fair Trade also needs to be considered[15]. The draftsman must be made aware of any particularly sensitive information or material in respect of which special covenants should be sought from franchisees and their directors and shareholders.

1.10 Deed of Guarantee[16]. This deed reflects the personal relationship between a franchisor and franchisee and is intended to make a director or directors liable to the franchisor, in the event of insolvency of the franchise company. This deed may be of particular importance when the franchisor supplies goods to his franchisees on credit (in which case a title retention clause can provide additional security—see precedent 1, Clause 10.15).

1.11 Lease clauses[17]. When a franchise depends upon property in good retail locations to trade successfully, in the present state of the United Kingdom retail property market, it is essential that good locations are not lost to the franchise, if a franchisee ceases to trade under the franchise agreement or becomes insolvent. The franchisor must ensure that, in those circumstances, he will be able to retain control of the property and make it available to another franchisee. Becoming the landlord of each of his franchisees is, perhaps, the most effective method of ensuring this, provided that the relevant lease or sublease is tied to the franchise agreement. Becoming the sub-lessor of a franchisee's outlet has its own dangers and the draftsman must keep abreast of the changes in business tenancy law and practice. Where relevant, the security of tenure of the franchisee under the Landlord and Tenant Act 1954 Part II should be excluded by an application to the High Court or the county court (depending upon the rateable value of the premises)[18]. However, it will be necessary to consult with prospective lenders to franchisees, because a large proportion of their security may depend upon any premium value in the lease of the premises. If no security of tenure is available to the franchisee, especially when the franchise may be terminated by the franchisor, lenders may require some form of protection for a proportion of the loans.

1.12 Sales reports[19]. One of the most important requirements in the relationship between the franchisor and the franchisee is the continuous periodic report by the franchisee to the franchisor on the progress of the franchisee's business. Sales report

14 See para 2.107 et seq.
15 See para 2.141 et seq.
16 For a Deed of Guarantee see Form 11, post.
17 For suggested clauses in a lease see Form 12, post. For alternative of a licence see Form 13.
18 See Forms 13 (Sch) and 14.
19 For an example of such a sales report see Form 15, post.

Introduction to precedents

systems are essential. Every franchise business will have its special characteristics which the franchisor considers he should monitor to assist him in assessing the performance of the franchisee. Increasingly, electronic communications are replacing paper, but the basis of any reporting programme will include the report form set out in these precedents.

1.13 Enquiries[20]. The franchisor should prepare replies to the various forms of franchise inquiries in anticipation of receiving some or all of them from prospective franchisees.

1.14 Manual. The operations manual which will contain all information (in the utmost detail) necessary for the conduct of the franchise business must be prepared by competent persons from all divisions of the franchisor. The practitioner must read the final draft manual carefully to ensure that the intellectual property rights of third parties are not infringed and that the information contained in it is correct. If in doubt, practitioners should require the franchisor to participate in a verification procedure involving all important divisions of the franchisor.

1.15 Stationery Text[21]. The relationship between the franchisor and the franchisee may not be apparent to customers or suppliers. The franchisor may become liable for the acts or defaults and debts of the franchisee on the basis that the franchisee is ostensibly part of the franchisor's business. This matter has not yet been resolved in the English courts[22]. Accordingly, without destroying the image of the franchise, it is essential that all persons dealing with the franchisee receive notice that the franchisee is trading on his own and not as part of or as agent for the franchisor. It will be necessary to draft a suitable text to appear on all stationery of the franchisee and in the premises used in the franchise business.

1.16 Brochure. The last part of the package to be prepared will be the brochure designed to sell franchises. The practitioner must check the drafts to ensure that neither misleading representations nor any material omissions are made.

1.17 Franchise Development Agreement[23]. It may not be the policy of the franchisor to permit the grant of several territories to one franchisee. If that is the case, the franchise development agreement will not be necessary. However, when a prospective franchisee wishes to secure an option to operate a number of franchised outlets, the development agreement will protect the franchisor by imposing strict time limits. The agreement contains both options and a right of first refusal.

1.18 'Core' Franchises. A fairly recent development in the UK has been 'core' franchises. The franchisor has developed a number of separate business systems, and licenses a selection of these to each franchisee. Characteristic locations for these are filling station forecourts, and a typical franchise might include a car-wash, shop, and service bays. Each element being in fact a separate franchise, requires separate treatment. The particular problem is that the 'package' of such franchises will differ according to each franchisee's requirements. A precedent is provided which attempts to meet the need on the part of the franchisor for a standard form whilst building in the necessary flexibility[24].

2 Franchise Package Preparation. Every franchisor should assess the individual needs of the franchise business and his prospective franchisees before embarking

20 See paras 6.02 et seq, ante, for various enquiries.
21 For an example of such a stationery text see Form 16, post.
22 See paras 1.28 et seq, ante.
23 For a Development Area Agreement see Form 17, post.
24 Precedent 19

311

Precedents

on sales of franchises. Each franchise will be different to others, even to its competitors in the same business area. However, the following is a brief checklist:

2.1 Analysis. The success of the business to be franchised should be analysed in detail.

Does it depend on:

    2.1:1   the flair of individuals involved;
    2.1:2   location;
    2.1:3   catchment area/territory;
    2.1:4   special products or services;
    2.1:5   promotion or advertising?

A realistic evaluation must be made of how simple it will be to reproduce those essential elements in a franchised outlet.

2.2 Finance. What finance will be required by franchisees? A detailed business plan, including projections, should be prepared. Those projections must be based upon the actual performance of the franchisor. Both prospective lenders and equity participators should be approached with a view to arranging credit and investment lines for franchisees.

2.3 Franchisee profile. The franchisor must decide upon the type of person or persons who will be most suitable to become franchisees. The various disciplines or qualities required in the franchise business must be considered and those qualities sought in applicants.

2.4 Territories. Consideration must be given to setting the boundaries of any territories to be granted to franchisees. Special consideration must be given to those businesses in which overlapping between territories may occur because of mobility of population, area advertising or Yellow Pages.

2.5 Properties. Estate agents in those towns which are considered by the franchisor to be suitable for the franchise business should be notified of the type and preferred location of its outlets. The franchisor should commence evaluation of and negotiations with architects and builders so that time and costs are saved for franchisees in the conversion of the property. If that conversion involves a change of use or works which will require planning consent, the franchisor must produce a full design brochure for production to members of planning committees, and because of the unpredictability of the planning process an appeal against a possible refusal of an application must be planned before the application is made and the application conducted accordingly.

2.6 Documentation. The documents in the franchise package must be prepared. It will be necessary:

    2.6:1   to write to the Inland Revenue to obtain clearance for payment of franchise fees gross;

    2.6:2   to submit the final form of franchise agreement, the board minutes and the relevant letter to the Office of Fair Trading;

    2.6:3   to seek confirmation, if the franchise agreement requires the franchisee to use auditors or accountants nominated by the franchisor, from the Institute of Chartered Accountants to the effect that such an arrangement does not breach the professional rules of the Institute. The accountants nominated in those circumstances must obtain written authority from their franchisee clients to enable them to disclose to the franchisor information obtained from franchisees during the course of an audit;

    2.6:4   to liaise with the design or marketing consultants or employees of the franchisor to produce an attractive documents package;

2.6:5 to check the replies made by the franchisor to the various forms of franchise inquiries which are in common use;
2.6:6 if required by the franchisor, to prepare and submit an application on behalf of the franchisor to the British Franchise Association;
2.6:7 to review all intellectual property used in the franchise by the franchisor and to apply for registration of appropriate trade marks;
2.6:8 to submit references to the Newspaper Publishers Association to ensure that the franchisor will be able to advertise in their newspapers for franchisees.

3 Procedures. Sales of franchises should be made by a set procedure. An example of such a procedure is:
3.1 Receipt of inquiry from prospective franchisee;
3.2 Initial telephone response from franchisor, establishing personal contact. No information disclosed at this stage.
3.3 Dispatch of franchise application form and accompanying letter together with franchise brochure.
3.4 Receipt of completed form from franchisee followed by assessment of information disclosed by replies.
3.5 If replies indicate that the applicant is unsuitable, personal contact again to discontinue process of evaluation in the nicest possible manner.
3.6 If replies indicate that applicant is worth investigating further, personal contact again to arrange interview and visits to outlets owned by franchisor.
3.7 Interviews with franchisor's assessment panel, including franchise manager, property specialist, sales manager and technical manager (this applies to a retail product franchise but any franchise will need to have each serious prospective franchisee vetted by each important division of the franchisor).
3.8 Establishment of franchisee's financing requirements.
3.9 Exchange of Confidentiality Agreement and payment of deposit. The deposit is non-refundable and will form part of the Initial Franchise Fee, if the Franchise Purchase Agreement is exchanged.
3.10 Disclosure by franchisor of confidential information to enable franchisee to prepare business plan. Issue of franchise documentation.
3.11 Introduction of franchisee to funding sources.
3.12 Evaluation of available properties in proposed territory.
3.13 When sufficient funding is available to the franchisee, the Franchise Purchase Agreement may be exchanged and the balance of the Initial Franchise Fee paid to the franchisor by the franchisee.
3.14 If the franchise business requires a site, it should now be acquired by the franchisor (conditional upon any necessary planning consent) and a lease or sublease agreed with the franchisee. The franchisee will work with the franchisor to convert the property to the house style of the franchise. An application for any necessary planning consent should be made.
3.15 The franchisee will attend training.
3.16 If the franchisee passes his training and is judged suitable by the franchisor, the franchise agreement will become effective on completion of the conversion of the property.

4 Franchise Agreement Checklist. When drafting the franchise agreement the practitioner should consider the following:

Precedents

4.1 Is the franchisee likely to be a limited company? If so, a deed of guarantee and directors' and shareholders' undertakings will be required[25].

4.2 What is the franchise business? If the franchisee requires the grant of an exclusive territory, the name of the business must include the franchise trade name to avoid complications under the Restrictive Trade Practices Act[26].

4.3 What will be the term of the agreement? The term should be sufficiently long to enable the franchisee to recoup his investment (based on the financial projections of the franchisor) and have a number of years left to make further profits. It is usual to include an option to renew on the part of the franchisee[27]. Usually, the larger the investment, the longer the term.

4.4 Will there be a territory? If so, will it be exclusive? If the territory is exclusive, it will be necessary to hold a board meeting of the franchisor to pass the board resolutions which will be submitted to the Office of Fair Trading[28].

4.5 Will there be a specific location where the franchise business will trade? If so, will the franchisor be the lessor of the property? If that is the case, the lease or sublease must be drafted and an application made to the relevant court for exclusion of security of tenure under the Landlord and Tenant Act 1954, Part II[29].

4.6 Does the franchise business depend upon the sale of goods? If so, does the franchisor sell those goods to the franchisee? Will the franchisor need to be the only supplier[30]?

4.7 Does the franchisor intend to make his profits from margins on the supply of those goods, rather than from franchise fees? If so, what would happen if competition law enabled a franchisee to obtain supplies elsewhere, if it were to his advantage? It will be necessary to include a franchise fee trigger clause in those circumstances[31]. What will be the size of the minimum order?

4.8 Does the franchisor need to supply all other equipment and materials used by the franchisee? If so, what is the minimum package to be taken and maintained by the franchisee[32]?

4.9-4.10 What are the amounts or percentages of the Initial Fee, the Continuing Fees, the Advertising Contribution and the Insurance Premium (if any) payable by the franchisee? What are the problems if the franchisor is not a resident of the United Kingdom for tax purposes? In those circumstances franchise fees may suffer deduction of tax at source.

4.11 How are fees calculated? Usually, recurring fees or contributions are calculated as a percentage of gross turnover (net of VAT)[33].

4.12 Is the franchisee required to achieve a minimum performance? If so, how much and by when and for how long?

4.13 If the minimum performance is not achieved, what happens[34]? Does the territory become non-exclusive (unlikely)? Should the franchisor be able to terminate the agreement or appoint his own management to run the business at the expense of the franchisee (probably)?

25 See Forms 10, and 11, post.
26 See for example Form 1, clause 6.28, post.
27 See for example Form 1, clause 6.22, post.
28 See for example Form 8, post.
29 See for example Form 13, clause 7.
30 See para 2.44 et seq, ante.
31 See for example Form 1, clause 7.14, post.
32 See Form 1, clauses 3.19 and 7.13:1.3, post.
33 See for example Form 1, clauses 3.6, 3.18 and 7.13, post
34 See for example Form 1, clause 8.3:2, post.

Introduction to precedents

4.14 What happens if a franchisee (or its key director in the case of a company) is incapacitated or dies[35]? Should the rights of termination or management appointment apply (probably)?

4.15 Should the franchisee be able to assign the agreement[36]? It should not be assignable without the franchisor's prior consent. What will the franchisor require upon a permitted assignment? Usually, a new agreement between the franchisor and the new franchisee, deeds of guarantee (where relevant), a commission calculated as a percentage of the sales price of the franchise business, depending upon how the business was sold, and fees from the assignee to cover the cost of training him.

4.16 Does the agreement comply with current British Franchise Association recommendations? These should be checked for each franchise, as changes in practice may occur from time to time.

4.17 What intellectual property is used in the franchise business? How (if at all) is it protected? Who owns it? If it is not the franchisor, is there a licence between the owner and the franchisor (trade marks, however, should *never* be sublicensed)[37]?

4.18 When are the Continuing Fees payable[38]? The more frequent the payment dates, the more control the franchisor has over the conduct of the franchisee's business, because any delays in payment will alert the franchisor to potential problems. In addition, the sales reports, which should be submitted by the franchisee at the same time as payment, will provide the franchisor with information concerning the state of the franchisee's business[39].

4.19 What are the obligations of the franchisee which are so important that any breach of them should be treated as fundamental entitling the franchisor to terminate immediately? The practitioner should discuss this in detail with the franchisor. Every franchise will have factors which are peculiarly important to it and will need to be protected against any harmful activities of the franchisee[40].

4.20 Does the franchisor require a block insurance policy or to be named on a policy taken out by the franchisee[41]? Should the franchisor nominate the insurer? Should the franchisor arrange a standard form of policy for all his franchisees? The question whether a franchisor is liable to third parties for the acts or defaults of his franchisees has not yet been answered under English law. In the United States of America, there have been cases where the franchisor has been held liable. The franchisor must arrange adequate insurance cover for himself and all his franchisees. Any policy taken out by a franchisee should cover the franchisor for the same risks. Detailed discussion with an insurance broker is essential. If insurance is arranged by the franchisor, in view of the probable changes in the law of regulations concerning insurance sales, the franchisor may need to take up the appropriate licence (if any) or make the appropriate disclosures as to commissions.

---

35 See for example Form 1, clause 10.3, post.
36 See Form 1, clauses 7.46 and 10.4, post.
37 See Form 1, clauses 3.14, 3.17 and 4.15, post. See Form 18 of Licence and Agency Agreement
38 See Form 1, clause s 3.22 and 7.13, post.
39 See Form 1, clause 7.29, post.
40 See Form 1, clause 8.8, post.
41 For examples of clauses dealing with insurance see Form 1, clauses 6.18, 7.44, 7.63, 7.64 and 7.65, post.

Precedents

1
FRANCHISE AGREEMENT—MASTER FORM

1 Parties

AB [plc] [whose [registered office *or* principal place of business] is at (*address*) *or* whose address for service within the jurisdiction of the courts of [England] is (*address*)] ('the Franchisor') (1)

CD [Limited [whose [registered office *or* principal place of business] is at (*address*) *or* whose address for service within the jurisdiction of the courts of [England] is (*address*)] ('the Franchisee') (2)

Notes
The full names of each of the parties should be set out with their respective addresses. If either of the parties is resident or registered outside England, an address for service in England should be included. The agreement is expressed to be governed by English law (clause 10.27). The agreement should not be used under any other jurisdiction, unless English law can apply (see more detailed discussion under clause).

2 Recitals

2.1 The Franchisor operates through [its own and] franchised outlets under the Trade Name a business of (*insert brief details only because a technical description of the franchised business will be included in the definitions clause*) according to the Method.

2.2 The Franchisor is the registered proprietor of the Trade Mark[s] [the [owner *or* licensee] of the [Copyright *or* Designs]] [the [patentee *or* licensee] of the Patents] comprised in the Intellectual Property.

2.3 The Franchisor is the proprietor of the [Copyright] [Design copyright] in the plans and designs for the [buildings] [structures] fixtures fittings including colour schemes pattern of furnishing dress styles of staff and the like used in the Method.

2.4 The Franchisee wishes to operate the Business.

Notes
The recitals should set out any material facts concerning the franchised business and any of the intellectual property which is capable of definition.

3 Definitions

The following terms shall have the following meanings:

3.1 'Accounting Reference Date': (*insert date*) in each year of the Term

Notes
It is, generally, more efficient administratively if all franchisees have the same year end for accounting purposes. This means that the performance of each franchisee can be compared against his fellows, without the need to make allowances for seasonal fluctuations or other influences.

3.2 'Advertising Contribution': [two point five per cent (2.5%)] of the Gross Turnover of the Business

Notes
The Advertising Contribution is the amount payable by the Franchisee to the Franchisor to fund an advertising and promotional programme (see clause 6.4 for further comment). The contributions are, generally, tied to turnover. Some franchisors agree to allocate a specific

Franchise Agreement—Master Form

proportion of royalties or franchise fees to advertising but this should be avoided, if possible. The contribution is in addition to an obligation on the part of the Franchisee to provide point of sale advertising.

3.3 'Business': commencing and undertaking a business of . . . . [at the Location] [within the Territory] in accordance with the Method

Notes
The definition of the 'Business' is one of the most important clauses in the entire agreement. The definition of 'Method' incorporates a reference to the Intellectual Property, and consequently the Grant, clause 4.1 need only be of the right to carry on the business in accordance with the Method.

3.4 'Commencement Date': [(*insert date*) *or* the date set out at the head of this Agreement]

Notes
The Franchise Agreement should commence when the Franchisee commences trading or immediately before. If a Franchise Purchase Agreement is used (see Form 9) the date can be left blank in the Franchise Agreement, pending completion of the property (if any) and training.

3.5 'Conditions': the provisions [contained in clauses [ ] *or* set out [overleaf *or* below] which shall be incorporated into this Agreement in their entirety]

Notes
If the format used is the facsimile printed form (see Appendix 1, post) it will be necessary to treat the definitions and clause 1.5 as the agreement and clause 6.10 as the conditions.

3.6 'Continuing Fees': Franchise fees of [five per cent (5%)] of the Gross Turnover of the Business net of VAT

Notes
The Continuing Fees are based, usually, upon the franchisee's gross turnover. There may be a minimum fee (see clause 3.18). Sometimes the Continuing Fees are low because the Franchisor will make profits from the supply of tied items (see chapter 5, paras 5.07 et seq). However, care must be taken in relation to competition law with such clauses (see para 2.44) a contingent fee provision must be included (see clause 7.14).

3.7 'Credit Limit':
    3.7:1 Time: [. . . days from date of [invoice *or* delivery *or* the restrictive periods for the Products set out in the Manual from time to time]
    3.7:2 Value: . . . [pounds sterling *or* units of the Currency] at any time in respect of [Products *or* Services] [invoiced *or* delivered]
    [or such other period or value limits as may be later agreed under this Agreement]

Notes
Time and Value Credit Limits will ensure that franchisees, who are supplied by the Franchisor, will pay for those supplies on time and will not run up large debts. If the Franchisee cannot get his supplies anywhere else, the Limits are a useful disciplinary weapon against a misbehaving franchisee (but see para 7.53). See also clause 6.25. Exclusive supply agreements require careful consideration in relation to competition law—see paras 2.44 et seq and 5.07 et seq.

3.8 'Currency': [pounds sterling]

Notes
This definition is only really necessary if the Franchisor and Franchisee are resident in different countries. Franchisees should beware of the withholding tax implications of payments to a foreign franchisor (see chapter 4, para 4.02 et seq, ante).

3.9 'Date': a day on which the banks are open for business in [England] or (if

Precedents

the banks are closed on that day) the next such day following and subject to this any reference to a particular date shall include that day itself

Notes
Bear in mind that England and Wales, Scotland and Northern Ireland have different statutory holidays.

3.10 'Expiry Date': . . . . . . 19 . . . or such later Date as shall result from any extension of the Term under clause [6.22]

Notes
The Expiry Date of the Term must be calculated by the Franchisor to provide a reasonable capital repayment and return on capital potential for the Franchisee. It is usual for the Franchisee to have an option to renew (see clause 6.22). The term is unlikely to be less than five years. Where substantial investment on the part of the Franchisee is required, the term will be much longer. The specimen business plan produced by the Franchisor should be based on franchisee borrowings of between 50% and 75% of the total investment including working capital. After projecting an interest rate of probably 3–4% above a London clearing bank base rate and capital amortisation on a straight-line basis commencing on the first anniversary of the Commencement Date, the number of years required to repay those borrowings can be calculated. The term should expire several years after that.

3.11 Gross Turnover: the gross takings of the Business in respect of the Products sold the Services supplied and business dealings entered into in each Accounting Month which shall be the gross sums receivable at the time of such sale supply or entering into in each Accounting Month and not solely the cash received or the cash banked and whether or not invoiced. In calculating the gross takings:
    3.11:1 there shall be included for the relevant Accounting Month all payments (if any) received under any insurance policy covering loss of profits
    3.11:2 the following shall not be included in the gross sums receivable
        3.11:2.1 all Value Added Tax (VAT)
        3.11:2.2 any benefit arising from or accruing to the Business solely attributable to any sale of Equipment permitted by this Agreement
    3.11:3 the following shall not be deducted so as to reduce the gross sums receivable:
        3.11:3.1 any customer refunds or allowances
        3.11:3.2 credit card discounts or charges suffered by the Franchisee
        3.11:3.3 the cost of any free offers or discounts made or given by the Franchisee as part of any special promotion unless required or authorised by the Franchisor.

Notes
Gross Turnover is the usual basis upon which Continuing Fees and Advertising Contributions are calculated. This means that the Franchisor is not concerned with the profitability of the Franchisee, merely his takings. This can lead to abuse, where the Franchisor is charging fees on high volume low margin sales. Many franchisees consider that the discounts achieved by bulk orders on behalf of the network, should match or even exceed the Continuing Fees and the Advertising Contribution. That belief ignores the probable increase in Gross Turnover arising from the goodwill of the franchised business.

3.12 'Initial Fee': as an initial fee the sum of (*insert initial fee*)

Notes
The Initial Fee should cover the expenditure of the Franchisor on (inter alia) vetting the Franchisee, training him and his staff, supervising the conversion of the premises (if any), pre-launch and post-launch assistance, pre-launch advertising and promotion, recruitment (if required), installation and testing of all accounts systems and equipment, electronic mail communications and any other matters requiring the involvement of the Franchisor in the

Franchise Agreement—Master Form

start-up of the Franchisee's business. There should also be a small profit. See also clause 7.13.

3.13 'Insurance Premium': the premium for the insurance arranged by the Franchisor described [later in this Agreement *or* in the Conditions]

Notes
If the Franchisor is concerned that he may be liable for claims made against the Franchisee, he may wish to arrange various types of cover for the Franchisee and ensure that the premiums are paid. The safest method of achieving this is to require the Insurance Premium to be paid to the Franchisor.

3.14 'Intellectual Property': all or any of the following:
    3.14:1 Mark[s] *(describe)* of which the Franchisor is the registered proprietor in the Territory [and which [is *or* are] applied to the [Products *or* used in relation to the Services] *or* brief details of which are set in Schedule . . .] and applications for registration of any such marks
    3.14:2 Trade Name *(insert name)* [or the names under which the Franchisor sells the Products]
    3.14:3 Patents of which the Franchisor is [patentee *or* licensee] in the Territory and [which relate to the Products or their manufacture *or* brief details of which are set out in Schedule . . .] and applications for the grant of any such Patents
    3.14:4 Copyrights and Design Rights held by the Franchisor in any written material plans designs or other work relating to the Products or the Method
    3.14:5 Designs whether or not registered or protected by copyright devised or acquired by the Franchisor and applied in the manufacture assembly and sale of the Products and Method
    [3.14:6 Permitted Name *(if different from the Trade Name)*]
    3.14:7 *(insert any additional or substitute intellectual property eg computer software)*

Notes
The Intellectual Property used in a franchise may range from a complete package comprising patents, various trade marks attached to different products, a trade name, know-how and designs, copyrights and design rights, to the other end of the scale which may comprise a trade name and very little else, except relatively non-specialist know-how. Every franchisor should analyse the component parts of his business and decide whether each of those parts is dependent upon or can be supported by some form of Intellectual Property. The Franchisor should always have the advice of patent or trade mark agents.

3.15 'Location': [*(describe premises to be used for the Business)* *or* a site approved by the Franchisor within the Territory] as described in clause [7.69]

Notes
The Location of the franchised business may be crucial. It may determine the success or failure of the business. Because the Franchisee must not trade except at the Location, its choice is very important (see clauses 7.36 and 7.37). It is essential that the Franchisee is aware of the site selection criteria of the Franchisor so that he can assure himself that the Location meets those criteria. The definition of the Location should exclude any other property which may be owned or let to the Franchisee, although care should be exercised when the Location is let to the Franchisee by the Franchisor.

3.16 'Manual': the Franchisor's standard operating manual as updated from time to time [serial number . . .]

Notes
The Manual is incorporated in the agreement. This means that administrative and even conceptual changes in the franchise may be made by the Franchisor within the agreement. As a result, the operation of the franchise is flexible and can respond to changing

Precedents

circumstances rapidly. In addition, much detail which may otherwise have had to be included in the franchise agreement itself can be set out in the manual in a factual manner.

3.17 'Method': a business conducted in accordance with the Manual using the Intellectual Property and any necessary know-how trade secrets methods of operating insignia identifying materials methods of advertising style and character of equipment and insurance arrangements specified in the Manual.

Notes
The Method is the aggregate of all the systems required to operate the franchised business in the manner concerned and developed by the Franchisor. It is largely know-how. Almost the whole of the Method should be set out in the Manual (see clauses 3.16 and 7.7).

3.18 'Minimum Fee': a minimum payment [to be set against the Continuing Fees] of [. . . . pounds]

Notes
Minimum Fees are often required by foreign Franchisors or in cases where it is difficult to police the activities of the Franchisee. The authors consider that Minimum Fees do not have much justification in business format franchising in the United Kingdom because the financial systems set up by the Franchisor should be able to cope with any tendency to cheat on the part of the Franchisee. Franchisees who, genuinely, fail to perform satisfactorily are unlikely to be helped by an obligation to pay Minimum Fees.

3.19 'Minimum Package':
    3.19:1 the equipment products stock of all types
    3.19:2 the minimum staff levels [at the Location]
stipulated in the Manual from time to time during the Term

Notes
Generally, Franchisors will require franchisees to carry a minimum amount of stock and or plant and machinery and a minimum number of staff in the business. This information will be set out in the Manual and will change as the business changes. These clauses can cause problems in relation to competition law, and need to be thought through carefully.

3.20 'Minimum Performance': . . . [pounds] of Gross Turnover of the Business in each [year] of the Term increasing by [the rate of increase of the Retail Price Index in the [Territory *or* United Kingdom] *or* the average of the rates of inflation according to the published government statistics of all the nations included in the Territory] [during the preceding year *or* since the last Accounting Reference Date]

Notes
Minimum Performance is a method of setting targets for the Franchisee and ensuring that he devotes his full time and attention to the business. It is more appropriate for use by foreign Franchisors or foreign Franchisees when the Franchisor may not be able to apply as much supervision as is his wont in his home territory. However, Franchisees should be suspicious of the possibility that the Franchisor may view the Minimum Performance clause as a means of insisting upon high performance, even if the Franchisor fails to provide the levels of assistance which may be required by the Franchisee. If the Franchisor requires a Minimum Performance clause, the Franchisee must ask the basis upon which it is calculated, check the levels required of other Franchisees and whether they have achieved it and study with care the consequences of any failure on his part to achieve those levels. They can be: termination (see clause 8.2); appointment of Franchisor's management (see clause 10.32; reduction in territory (see clause 10.32).

3.21 'Notice Period':
    3.21:1 for default notice [30] days
    3.21:2 for any other notice or termination [60] days

Notes
The Notice Period is crucial to the good management of a franchise, particularly in the case

of a termination notice. The period should be sufficiently long to be equitable but short enough to prevent a bad apple rotting for a long time. It should be noted that clause 8 contains provisions for immediate termination in certain events. The Franchisor must consider which events are likely to cause serious damage to the franchise chain and stipulate them in clause 8.3. However, there is a difficult period when the Franchisor may wish to terminate the agreement but the Franchisee has not committed any sufficiently serious breach to justify notice. This is when discussion and counselling by the Franchisor may be helpful and produce a sale of the franchise rather than termination.

3.22 'Payment Dates':
    3.22:1   for the Initial Fee: on the signing of this Agreement
    3.22:2   for the Insurance premium: within the relevant Notice Period
    3.22:3   for the Advertising Contribution and the Continuing Fees: [on [Friday] of each week in respect of the Business during the immediately preceding seven (7) days *or* on the [tenth] day of each calendar month in respect of the Business in the immediately preceding calendar month]
    3.22:4   for the Minimum Fee: every [Friday]

Notes
Regular and frequent Payment Dates for monies due to the Franchisor will keep his franchisees up to scratch with their accounts and give early warning of problems if a payment date is missed. Payment on the relevant dates is 'time of the essence' (see clause 8.3) so that franchisees are aware of the paramount importance of maintaining their payments.

[3.23 'Permitted Name': (*insert proposed name of franchised outlet*)]

Notes
The Permitted Name will be the trading name of the Franchisee. This definition is required only if the permitted name varies from the Trade Name eg by referring to a locality. The Manual must contain information concerning business names regulations (see para 6.24, ante) and the Franchisor should have standard stationery, invoices and brochure designs available which will have space for the necessary disclosures to be displayed (see also clause 7.53).

[3.24 'Products': the products briefly described in the Schedule *or* the Manual or other products substituted in accordance with this Agreement]

Notes
If the franchise depends upon the manufacture, processing or sale of products then those products should be listed somewhere. If the products are special to the Franchisor or the franchise, then it may be prudent that a description of them is incorporated in the agreement. If the franchised business is merely a retail operation, handling the products of third parties which are likely to change, then those products (being in effect the stipulated range of the franchised business) should be listed in the Manual which can be changed frequently. It is usual for franchisees to deal in all and only those products so listed. If the franchisee is to be restricted to products obtained from the franchisor or specified suppliers, it must be borne in mind that the block exemption clears only ties when it is impracticable, owing to the nature of the goods and as far as it is necessary to protect the franchisor's intellectual property, to apply objective quality specifications. Thus, a tie which is necessary to protect a secret formula would be permissible—see para 2.44

3.25 'Promotion Fund': the fund to be maintained by the Franchisor for advertising purposes in accordance with clause [6.4] [of the Conditions]

Notes
The Promotion Fund is the fund maintained by the Franchisor for advertising and promotional purposes. All Advertising Contributions from franchisees will be paid into it. The fund should be maintained in a separate bank account and held in trust for the franchisees. Audited accounts of the use of the monies in the fund should be produced to franchisees. (See question 63, para 6.02 and clauses 6.4, 6.5 and 6.6.)

Precedents

[**3.26** 'Services': the services forming part of the Business and described in the Manual]

Notes
The Services are those to be performed by the Franchisee for the general public (eg picture framing, chimney-lining, exhaust replacement, car maintenance, drain cleaning, plumbing and thousands of other franchised services). Once again, the Services should be capable of change by the simple method of changing the Manual.

3.27 'Term': . . . years starting on the Commencement Date and ending on the Expiry Date unless extended or earlier determined as provided by this Agreement

Notes
See the comments in clause 3.10. See also extension provisions in clause 6.22.

3.28 'Territory': the geographical area of *(insert description of area)* [and shown edged red on the map attached to this Agreement]

Notes
In a geographically small country like the United Kingdom, the Territory granted to a franchisee may be crucial to the success or failure of his business. He will, certainly, consider that it is vital to him. Accordingly, the Territory should always be defined by reference to a large scale map. At that time, difficult questions concerning border areas and procedures can be discussed, especially if there is an adjoining franchisee who has been trading for some time. If that is the case, the Franchisee should be informed of the proposed new Territory and should be given an opportunity of making proposals for dealing with customers in border areas. Some franchisors allow franchisees to liaise together and make their own arrangements for dealing with those customers as a matter of mutual convenience, especially in the case of a mobile service franchise (such as drain-cleaning). The Franchisee should be aware that any exclusivity relates to the operation of the franchised business under the trade name only and not to the business itself. This means that the Franchisor could carry on an exactly similar business within the territory of the Franchisee, provided that it traded under a different name (see clause 6.28). Some franchisors, especially those which have been franchising for a considerable time, do not grant an exclusive territory. The Franchisee is expected to trust the judgment of the Franchisor not to place another outlet of the franchised business too close to that of the Franchisee. As to what exclusivity is permissible under the block exemption see para 2.38.

3.29 'Trade Name': *(give details)*

Notes
The Trade Name of the business is the name which the public will recognise if the standards of the franchise network are strictly maintained by the Franchisor and the advertising and promotional campaign is successful, it will be the reason why more people patronise the Franchisee's business rather than the similar business run under his own name by one of the Franchisee's local competitors.

It is the goodwill attached to that name which, in many cases justifies the royalties or fees, irrespective of any other benefits arising under the franchise.

Reference to the Trade Name is used in the device suggested to avoid the need to furnish particulars under the provisions of the Restrictive Trade Practices Act 1976 (see para 2.141). When drafting the description of the business the practitioner should ensure that it is sufficiently exact as not to preclude the Franchisor from engaging in some other field of business under the same name (eg the manufacture and wholesale of software when the franchised business is the *retail* sale of computer products including software).

The Franchisee must check that the Franchisor owns or is authorised to use the Trade Name in the business and in franchising that business. In the case where the Franchisor's right depends upon a head licence granted to the Franchisor to use the Trade Name, the Franchisee must be satisfied that such licence exceeds the term of the franchise agreement and any renewal option. Sub-licences of registered trade marks or service marks should never be accepted (see paras 1.20 et seq, ante). The Trade Name forms part of the intellectual property of the Franchisor and he should covenant to maintain it (see clause 6.21). If there is no evidence of ownership of the Trade Name (for example if it is not

Franchise Agreement—Master Form

registered as a trade mark in some class of goods used in the franchise in the name of the Franchisor or as a service mark) the Franchisee should ask for a warranty of title from the Franchisor. It will be necessary for the Franchisee to indicate its own name as required by the Business Names Act 1985 and article 4(c) of the block exemption—see para 2.22 and 6.24.

4 Grant [and Reservations]

4.1 In consideration of the payment of the Initial Fee [the Minimum Fee] [the Insurance Premium] [the Advertising Contribution] and the Continuing Fees by the Franchisee to the Franchisor [on the Payment Dates] and of and subject to the agreements on the part of the Franchisee in this Agreement the Franchisor grants to the Franchisee the right to carry on the Business
    4.1:1 at and from the Location
    4.1:2 within the Territory
    4.1:3 for the Term
    [4.1:4 under the Permitted Name]
    4.1:5 in accordance with the Method

Notes
The essence of a licence is the grant of rights to use intellectual property in a defined manner, subject to restrictions. To that extent a franchise is a licence. However, it is not confined to the grant of rights to use Intellectual Property but extends to every aspect of the means of operation of a business, as a clone of the original business format conceived and/ or developed by the Franchisor. Thus, clause 4.115 by referring to the Method contains a grant of rights subject to restrictions (see clause 3.16).

4.2 The Franchisor reserves power:
    [4.2:1 to decline to accept any order from or through the Franchisee]
    [4.2:2 to [continue to] sell direct to customers in the Territory [by mail order only] [or to service national accounts even if the head office of the customer is located in the Territory or if the Products are delivered to offices of the customer in the Territory]]
    [4.2:3 to vary the specification and the price of the Products]
    [4.2:4 to vary Schedule ... either by the withdrawal from that Schedule of Products which the Franchisor proposes to withdraw from its product range or by the addition to that Schedule [after consultation with *or* with the agreement of] the Franchisee of further Products]

Notes
Clause 4.2:3 and 4 are more relevant to franchises dealing in products rather than services. However, if the Franchisor makes any of these reservations, the Franchisee must question him carefully as to the existing extent: to which orders are declined or not fulfilled by the Franchisor (clause 4.2:1), mail order business is conducted by the Franchisor and especially amongst customers resident in the proposed territory of the franchisee (clause 4.2:2), and the extent to which the price and specification of the Franchisor's products have been altered in the past (clauses 4.2:3 and 4.2:4).

5 No competition

In the consideration of the grant of a franchise under clause 4 the Franchisee agrees:
5.1 neither during the Term nor for [12] months[1] after the termination of this Agreement to be concerned or interested either directly or indirectly in any business which is involved in the supply of goods or services which are similar to the Products

Precedents

or the Services [either] [at the Location or within the territory] [within a radius of [ ] miles of the location] nor to damage the goodwill of the Business or the goodwill of the Business which survives termination in the other way[2.]

1 This period should not exceed one year—see block exemption article 3(1)(c) and para 2.41, ante.
2 See ibid.

5.2 Not during the Term to be concerned or interested either directly or indirectly in any business which is involved in the supply of goods or services which are similar to the Products or the Services in a territory where it would compete with any member of the [. . . . . .][1] network[2].

1 Insert name of network here.
2 See block exemption article 2(e) — para 2.43, ante.

5.3 [Not within [12] months[1] after the termination of this Agreement to be concerned or interested either directly or indirectly in any business at the Location which is involved in the supply of goods or services which are similar to the Products or the Services or to damage the surviving goodwill of the Business in any other way[2]][3].

1 This period should not exceed one year—see block exemption article 3(1)(c) — para 2.41, ante.
2 See ibid.
3 Use this sub-clause only when variant of clause 5.1 referring to radius of the Location is used.

5.4 Not at any time within [12] months after the termination of this Agreement:
   5.4:1   to solicit the customers or former customers of the Business with the intent of taking their custom or
   5.4:2   to employ or offer to employ any person who immediately before such employment or offer of employment was employed by the Franchisor or who immediately before such employment or offer of employment was employed by any person (including a franchisee of the Franchisor) who was at that time operating a business according to the Method or to employ or offer to employ any person who was so employed at any time during the twelve months preceding such employment or offer of employment and not directly or indirectly to induce any such person to leave his or her employment.

5.5 To procure that all directors and shareholders of the Franchisee (in the case of a company being the Franchisee) enter into direct covenants of similar content to those contained in sub-clauses 5.1 - 5.4 above with the Franchisor.

Notes
If this sub-clause is included, particulars of the agreement should be furnished pursuant to the Restrictive Trade Practices Act 1976—see para 2.141 et seq.

[Signed by [. . . . on behalf of] the Franchisor
Signed by [. . . . on behalf of] the Franchisee]
[*Conditions which should be renumbered separately from the Agreement*]

Notes
Signature block can appear here, in which case remaining conditions must be incorporated (see clause 3.5).

6 Franchisor's obligations

The Franchisor agrees with the Franchisee throughout the Term:

6.1 To permit the Franchisee to carry on the Business
To permit the Franchisee to [:]

[6.1:1 operate the Business under the Permitted Name or such other names or styles as may be specified or approved in writing by the Franchisor]

[6.1:2 promote the Business [under the Permitted Name] in accordance with the terms of this Agreement [particularly in the periods of [14] days either side of the Commencement Date] [at the expense of the Franchisee]

Notes
If clause [4.1:4] is included then 6.1.1 will be superfluous. Clause 6.1:2 may be superfluous if the Trade Name and the Permitted Name are the same. For example if the Trade Name is 'Bloggs' and the Permitted Name is also 'Bloggs', this will be the case. However, the Permitted Name may be 'Bloggs Mayfair' or some other geographical qualification. In that case, it will be necessary for the Franchisor to promote 'Bloggs Mayfair' specifically, especially in the pre and post-launch periods.

6.2 Not to derogate
Not to derogate from the Grant [and in particular not itself to operate nor to grant any other person the right to operate a business using any part of the Intellectual Property [and other insignia and identifying materials, methods of advertising and publicity forming part of the Method][1] in the Territory [not itself to supply the products to third parties operating under the Method][2]

Notes
A covenant against derogation should not prevent a franchisee checking the Franchisor's title to its Intellectual Property. In addition, the Franchisee must be satisfied that the inclusion of the restrictions relating to the Manual in the Grant (see Clause 3.16, 3.17 and 4) which, in itself, is capable of change, does not entitle the Franchisor effectively to reduce the extent of the Grant.

1 This would not appear to entail a relevant restriction for the purposes of the Restrictive Trade Practices Act 1976—see para 2.141 et seq.
2 See block exemption article 2(a). The territorial protection may alternatively be included as a separate clause—see clause 5, above, and para 2.38, ante.

6.3 Manual and update
To lend to the Franchisee for the Term a copy of the Manual and to update the Manual from time to time

Notes
The Manual is of crucial importance in a business format franchise. Updating of the Manual in response to changes in legislation, product development, competition and administrative changes is a sign of an alive and flexible Franchisor. The Franchisor should limit the extent of changes, so far as possible, except in the case of new products or services which will improve the business of the Franchisee. Where alterations are to the detriment of the Franchisee (for example, reductions in credit periods or increases in prices of products or services which are 'tied' items) the Franchisor must act equitably (see chapter 7, paras 7.49 et seq).

6.4 General advertising[1]
Subject to the performance of its obligations by the Franchisee:

6.4:1 to promote the Trade Name and Method in [the British Isles] or such areas of [the British Isles] as it considers appropriate in such newspapers, magazines, radio, television, directories, pamphlets or other media as it may

Precedents

from time to time consider suitable [in consultation with the Franchisee and other franchisees]

Notes
The Franchisor should be questioned about its advertising policy. It may be that the franchise network is too small to fund a national campaign and must restrict itself to local or regional advertising. The cost and impact of advertising is a strong argument for the cellular development of franchises: penetrating one area and covering it, before moving elsewhere. The Franchisor should have discovered the most cost-effective advertising method for its business and be able to demonstrate the effect of that advertising on its business in the past. It may be that the business is not suitable for promotion by media advertising but only by other methods, such as mail shots or competitions. If so, the level of Advertising Contribution should reflect this reduced expenditure.

1   See block exemption article 3(1)(g).

6.4:2   for this purpose to pay the Advertising Contribution paid by the Franchisee and all other franchisees of the Franchisor into the Promotion Fund [in a separate bank account solely for this purpose] [on trust for the franchisees of the Franchisor] provided that if at any time the Franchisor's promotional expenditure exceeds the money in the Promotional Fund such excess expenditure may be set off as a first charge against any prior or subsequent money received by the Promotion Fund from any source

Notes
The object of this clause is to create a type of trust or client's account which is outside the personal funds of the Franchisor. Franchisees should know that their contributions are safe from incorporation within the general assets of the Franchisor. However, it is debatable whether this arrangement, even if the contributions are paid into and maintained in a separate account, will be proof against creditors of the Franchisor, if it becomes insolvent. However, any more restrictive arrangements will not be acceptable to Franchisors, because they will limit the discretion of a Franchisor in the use, for advertising purposes, of the funds. It may be that in large and successful franchises, a promotions committee on which representatives of the franchisees serve and participate in advertising and promotional decisions, should be encouraged. However, the Franchisor will retain its discretion to overrule that committee.

6.4:3   annually to provide the Franchisee with an audited account of the income and expenditure of the Promotion Fund.
[Provided that expenditure of the Promotion Fund by the Franchisor shall be deemed satisfactory compliance with such promotional obligations]

Notes
Properly audited accounts with heads of expenditure clearly listed should be insisted upon by a franchisee. As the franchise grows and the turnover of each franchised business also grows, large sums can be amassed in the advertising fund. The Franchisor must demonstrate that it is dealing with those funds in a fair and efficient manner. The failure on the part of a Franchisor to advertise cost-effectively is one thing, failure to behave honourably (such as by using the fund to advertise for franchisees, charging unjustifiable management charges, not passing onto the fund commissions and fees from advertising agents, not passing on discounts for block bookings and many other abuses) is quite another.

[6.4:4   to charge the amount of the Advertising Contribution to each of its own [stores *or* outlets] and to pay the same into the Promotion Fund]

Notes
Each trading outlet owned by the Franchisor contributes to the advertising fund, as if it were a franchisee. Any projections supplied by the Franchisor based upon the performance of its own outlets should include the relevant contribution (as well as

Franchise Agreement—Master Form

national franchise fees). The contribution of the Franchisor's stores should start when the Promotion Fund is set up.

[6.5 Point-of-service advertising
To make available to the Franchisee [free of charge *or* at cost *or* at the prices then charged to other franchisees of the Method] point-of-service advertising material for issue to customers or potential customers (including the places of business and telephone numbers of other franchisees)]

Notes
It will be in the interests of both the Franchisor and the Franchisee if all necessary promotional and literature and display material is available from the Franchisor. This will save the Franchisee from having to design it himself and obtain the Franchisor's approval. Except for, perhaps, the initial launch supplies, the Franchisee should pay for it. However, the costs should not be exorbitant but reflect the cost of printing or manufacture and reasonable design and copywriting fees.

[6.6 Initial advertising
In due time for the Commencement Date to advertise the Business and the date of such commencement in such newspapers, magazines, radio, television, directories, pamphlets or any other media as it may consider appropriate [devoting to such a purpose a sum of not less than [£ . . . .]]]

Notes
This obligation is, usually, confined to local advertising, although in a growing network, announcements of new openings should be carried in all existing outlets. The launch package of advertising and promotion should be discussed fully between the Franchisor and the Franchisee. It will, usually, follow a standard format developed by the Franchisor during previous launches. Franchisors are reluctant to commit to specific expenditure, unless the franchise network is substantial and has a standard launch package which is not subject to change. Control by the Franchisor of the advertising by the Franchisee would not appear likely to create competition law problems.

6.7 Initial training
    6.7:1 To provide within . . . .days of the date of this Agreement at a place chosen by the Franchisor training [free of charge] in the Method during a period of not less than . . . . days for the Franchisee [and (*list other persons who will receive training*)]
    6.7:2 To discuss with the Franchisee the performance of all such persons during training.

Notes
Initial training (and any subsequent training) is very important. The quality of training often distinguishes a successful from a poor franchisor. The training should be comprehensive and capable of turning a willing person, who has no experience of any business, into a person who is capable of operating the franchised business and all the administration necessary for its efficient conduct. Above all, it should provide a franchisee with confidence and faith in the abilities and experience of the Franchisor. Franchisees often state that the loneliest period for them is during the few days before trading starts and in the first week after start-up. All sorts of doubts assail them. If the training has been well conducted and comprehensive, the Franchisee will, at least, have the confidence that he knows how to operate all the equipment and systems in the franchised business and will be able to serve the public properly. That still leaves the question whether the public will become patrons of the business—that is enough for any new franchisee to worry about!

6.8 Training of substitute personnel[1]
In the event of any of the persons required under the terms of this Agreement to undergo a course of training ceasing to act in the Business after completing

Precedents

such training, to provide the persons who will act in the Business in their place with similar training [in case the Franchisee himself cannot give such training] at the expense of the Franchisee (such expense including travel and accommodation and the standard training fees of the Franchisor as set out in the Manual)

1   See block exemption article 3(2)(e).

Notes
Training of substitute personnel should always be at the expense of the Franchisee. Franchisors should state their charges for training in the Manual. It should, also, be made clear which grades of employees are required to be trained by the Franchisor. It is undesirable if all persons employed by the Franchisee are obliged to be trained by the Franchisor, unless all employees have to perform specialised functions upon the proper fulfilment of which the goodwill of the franchise depends.

6.9   Improvements to the Method
6.9:1   To improve and develop the Method and

6.9:2   to provide [free of charge] such further training [at the expense of the Franchisee *or* free of charge] to the Franchisee and other persons engaged in the conduct of the Business as may from time to time appear to the Franchisor to be necessary in the light of such improvements or developments [at reasonable fees based upon the length of and the number of employees of the Franchisor engaged in such further training]

Notes
It is in the interests of both the Franchisor and the Franchisee that the Method is subject to continuous scrutiny, improvement and development. The Franchisor may insist on a 'grant-back' clause. This must comply with the block exemption Article 3(2)(b) (see clause 7.43). The Method must be capable of change, by alteration of the Manual and all franchisees must be obliged to adopt those changes at the same time (see clauses 3.16, 3.17 and 7.7). Changes in the Method should not be unreasonably to the detriment of the Franchisee (see para 7.49 et seq).

6.10   Equipment[1]
To supply to the Franchisee in due time for the commencement of the Business the [equipment and other items specified in the Manual *or* the Minimum Package] [at the prices [and hire charges] specified in the Manual]

1   If the franchisee's acquisition of equipment is to be tied to the franchisor or designated supplier, regard must be had to the block exemption article 3(1)(b).

Notes
The Franchisee must be assured that he will receive all necessary equipment on time for his start-up, if the Franchisor is responsible for procuring or supplying it. The Minimum Package should include everything necessary for the proper conduct of the franchised business in accordance with the Method. Each franchisee should be equipped in the same manner as the others. The Franchisor should not undertake to supply replacement or substitute equipment later during the Term, because it may not be able to do so. However, the Franchisee should be obliged to up-grade his equipment when required by the Franchisor (see clause 7.42).

6.11   Annual conference for franchisees
To organise and hold at its own cost at least once annually at a place convenient to the majority of the franchisees a conference of franchisees to discuss the Method (including possible improvements in the Method) and the Business

Notes
Franchisors, usually, welcome an annual conference for franchisees, to congratulate and publicly reward the high performers and introduce new systems and products. The franchisees have an opportunity to complain and also exert 'peer pressure' on poor

Franchise Agreement—Master Form

performing franchisees, who may be letting down the network. Annual conferences are an opportunity for the Franchisor to shake the complacency of those franchisees who are on a 'comfort plateau'.

6.12 Consultation

6.12:1 To consult with the Franchisee

6.12:2 to give to the Franchisee the benefit of its knowledge and experience in connection with any problems relating to the Method

6.12:3 to make available (as promptly as is reasonably practicable) members of the Franchisor's staff competent to give such advice or assistance as may be possible or necessary to give at the request of or in response to the incapacity or death of [the franchisee *or* the key director of the franchisee] [or recommend such independent experts as may appear necessary] the Franchisee paying the standard per diem charge of the Franchisor for such staff [as set out in the Manual] [and for the fees and expenses of such experts]

Notes
The availability of management assistance and advice is of great importance to a franchisee and provides considerable security for him. If he falls ill or dies or the Business is not successful, he has the benefit of the knowledge that the resources of the Franchisor can be called on, even if those resources are only made available at the Franchisee's expense. That is an advantage over an independent businessman with a business of similar size. That facility considerably reduces the risk of failure and many reputable franchisors have and will devote substantial management time and effort in taking remedial action in the case of an under-performing franchisee or acting as locums in the event of illness or death of the Franchisee. Those efforts, usually, are not adequately compensated by the per diem charge. However, when the Franchisor is relatively new or itself undergoing rapid growth, its spare management resources may be insufficient to provide much benefit to a franchisee in need of assistance. The Franchisee must ask relevant questions at an early stage in the negotiations (see para 6.02, question 81) although circumstances may change during the term of the franchise.

6.13 Procuring supplies etc

6.13:1 To assist the Franchisee in procuring such supplies services and equipment in addition to those supplied by the Franchisor as may be required by the Franchisee to commence and operate the Business and

6.13:2 as far as possible to negotiate and obtain from suppliers discount rates for furnishing such supplies [for the benefit of the Franchisee as regards its own purchases]

Notes
The Franchisor should be able to introduce the Franchisee to supplies of necessary articles, wherever the Franchisee may be located. It may not be possible to negotiate discounts with those suppliers unless they are given the benefit of bulk orders. This is another argument in favour of cellular development of franchises. Some items required by the Franchisee may be such a small part of the Business and be so generally available that it is not worthwhile for either the Franchisor or the Franchisee to seek to negotiate special terms. However, many franchisees join franchises with the intention of obtaining supplies of products and equipment at discounts, because of the bulk purchasing ability of the network. If the success of the franchised business depends upon the competitive edge that this will provide or upon the resulting increased margins, the Franchisee must ask the Franchisor to confirm its continuing agreement to pass on those discounts to its franchisees.

6.14 Credit cards

[6.14:1 To promote charge and credit cards and plans in accordance with the procedures established from time to time in order to make the operation

Precedents

of the Method more convenient for customers and create new and reliable customers]

[6.14:2 if credit cards are used by customers of the business to permit all credit card charges and discounts suffered by the franchisee to be deducted from the gross turnover of the business]

Notes
Any refusal on the part of a franchisor to permit the use of credit cards by customers of the franchised business, may reduce potential sales. Therefore, the Franchisee must check where the acceptance of credit cards would be appropriate, that the Franchisor will allow and encourage the acceptance of credit cards and permit the consequential discounts and charges as deductions from Gross Turnover and, thus, fees or royalty calculations. Further, if credit plans are, also, important to the customers of the business, the Franchisor must make all necessary arrangements with suitable finance houses so that franchisees can sell with the benefit of those plans. If so, the provisions of the Consumer Credit Act 1974 and subsidiary regulations must be considered (see para 6.21).

6.15 Staff engagement service
To make available to the Franchisee its staff engagement service for the provision of trained and other staff for employment in the Business.

Notes
In some franchised businesses the recruitment of specialist high-performing staff is crucial to the future of the business. The Franchisor should be able to demonstrate a proven recruitment record. In addition, the Franchisee should check staff turnover statistics and ascertain whether staff are being recruited from competitors or vice versa. If the former, that may be a sign that those staff recognise that the franchised business offers better opportunities for their own success. If the latter is the case, then the Franchisee should check the recruitment records of any competing franchises.

6.16 No discrimination between franchisees
To make available to the Franchisee all services and facilities which the Franchisor makes available to its other franchisees [and company owned outlets] including improvements in and additions to the Method

Notes
Some early franchisees request a new franchisor to covenant that no franchises will be granted after their own, on terms more favourable to the franchisee, unless all previous franchisees receive the benefit of those more favourable terms. However, this clause seeks to deal with discrimination between franchisees during the term of the agreement. Such discrimination would be abhorrent to a reputable franchisor who will wish to deal even handedly with all its franchisees. This clause is useful in an agreement with a recent franchisor.

6.17 Indemnity
To indemnify and keep indemnified the Franchisee from and against any and all loss damage or liability whether criminal or civil suffered [and legal fees and costs incurred] by the Franchisee in the course of conducting the Business (including any loss incurred by the Franchisee on its subsequent investment in the Business) because of:

6.17:1 any act neglect or default of the Franchisor or its agents employees licensees or customers

6.17:2 the proven infringement of the intellectual property rights of any third party

6.17:3 any successful claim by any third party alleging libel or slander in respect of any matter arising from the [supply of the [Products *or* Services] *or* conduct of the Business] in the Territory provided that such liability has not been incurred by the Franchisee through any default by it in carrying out the terms of this Agreement

Notes
The Franchisee needs to be indemnified against the defaults of the Franchisor and, particularly, against infringements of the Intellectual Property rights of third parties. The franchise network will depend upon the identity created by those rights which it displays publicly. In addition, some of the systems incorporated in the Method are general or specialist know-how which will be valuable to the Franchisee and, in some cases, will be crucial to the continuing conduct of the franchised business. Therefore, the Franchisee must be assured that if he is forced to cease trading or has to pay large damages or is obliged to pay royalties to third parties in order to remain in business, the Franchisor will compensate him for those adverse consequences. However, clause 6.17 is general indemnity, not limited to intellectual property matters. Is the Franchisee liable for the actions or defaults of the Franchisor? It is possible (see para 1.28 et seq). The arguments concerning the potential liability of the Franchisor for the acts of the Franchisee are relevant to the reverse situation. An indemnity, as set out in this clause may not be sufficient to protect the Franchisee from successful claims by third parties. In addition, even if an indemnity was effective in law, the Franchisor may, by then, be insolvent and unable to make any contribution to the amounts claimed against the Franchisee. It is in the interests of the Franchisee, therefore, that his separate identity is clearly stated to the public (see clause 7.53) and that the Franchisor is adequately insured.

6.18 Insurance

6.18:1 To maintain [at its own cost *or* subject to prompt payment of the Insurance Premium by the Franchisee] a [comprehensive *or* specific] insurance policy [with an insurer of repute in the [British Isles]] to cover the liability of the Franchisor in respect of any default for which it may become liable to indemnify the Franchisee under the preceding clause

6.18:2 To arrange that the [minimum *or* total] cover [per claim] of that policy is (*insert sum*) on [each annual date *or* the Accounting Reference Date]

6.18:3 To increase such cover by the [rate of increase in the Retail Price Index in the [Territory *or* United Kingdom] *or* average of the rates of inflation according to published government statistics of all the nations included in the Territory] [during the preceding year *or* since the last Accounting Reference Date]

6.18:4 To procure that the Franchisee is a payee of and a party to that policy

[6.18:5 To arrange a comprehensive block policy [with an insurer of repute [in the British Isles]] to cover the Franchisee [and the other franchisees of the Franchisor] and the Franchisor for all [usual] risks associated with the Method [and the Business] subject to prompt payment by the Franchisee of the Insurance Premium]

Notes
Clauses 6.18:1 to 6.18:4 (inclusive) contain provisions for insurance by the Franchisor which is intended to protect the Franchisee (see para 5.52). In that paragraph the dangers of double insurance are discussed. Clause 6.18:5 seeks to overcome the problem of double insurance but then falls into the unavoidable trap that the Franchisee may be held to be a third party to the contract of insurance (see para 6.18). Unless there are essential reasons why the Franchisor should have absolute control over insurance, it is probably better if the Franchisee arranges his own insurance through the agency of the Franchisor and the Franchisor has its own policy or cover its own risk factors (see clause 7.63).

6.19 Support and information

To support the Franchisee in its efforts to promote the [Business *or* sales or other dealings in the Products *or* supply of the Services] and in particular [at its own expense *or* at the expense of the Franchisee]

Precedents

[6.19:1   to supply samples of the Products]
[6.19:2   to supply patterns of the Products]
[6.19:3   [to supply user's manuals for the Products] [in the language[s] used in the Territory]]
[6.19:4   to provide and promptly update information about the Products]
[6.19:5   to provide courses for the instruction of [the employees of] the Franchisee in the [demonstration of the Products *or* the supply of the Services] [and in the provision of proper after-sales service at (*address*)] [at the expense of [the Franchisee] excluding travel subsistence and salary]]
[6.19:6   to hold seminars for the Franchisor's [agents *or* representatives *or* brokers] [active in the Territory]]
[6.19:7   to notify the Franchisee of any improvements in the method approved and adopted by the Franchisor]

Notes
Regular seminars or training updates by the Franchisor are essential, if the franchise chain is to remain flexible, innovative and competitive. This clause highlights the need for the Franchisee to evaluate the importance of a particular product or service to the success of the franchise and to review the market position of competitors. Clause 6.19:7 is not necessary if clause 6.9 is included.

[6.20   Delivery of Products
Subject to availability to supply to [the Franchisee *or* the customers of the Franchisee] [in the Territory] the Products which:

6.20:1   comply [in all respects] with relevant government or other regulations [in the Territory]
6.20:2   are of merchantable quality
6.20:3   conform to sample
6.20:4   are at prices notified to the Franchisee by the Franchisor [monthly]
6.20:5   are delivered with all reasonable dispatch
6.20:6   are in accordance with the usual business terms of the Franchisor from time to time in force]

provided that the franchisee shall remain within the Credit Limit

Notes
Both the Franchisor and the Franchisee should be aware that the supply of the Products is 'subject to availability'. This means that the Franchisee is not guaranteed supplies. This clause should be read in the light of clause 10.12. However, provided supplies are available to the Franchisor, it must supply the Franchisee in accordance with the requirements of clause 6.20:1 to 6.20:6 (inclusive). The Franchisee must remain within his Credit Limit (see clauses 7.66, 6.25 and 6.26).

6.21   Maintenance of Intellectual Property
To maintain the Intellectual Property during the Term and not to cause or permit anything which may damage or endanger it or the Franchisor's title to it or assist or suffer others to do so

Notes
This clause is intended to oblige the Franchisor to pay all necessary fees and take all necessary action to preserve any patents, marks, design copyright or any other form of intellectual property for which formal registration and renewal procedures exist. In addition, the Franchisor must not do or omit to do anything the result of which may be loss of its title to the Intellectual Property. The blend of public goodwill arising from components of the Intellectual Property and management systems and supervision are the core of a successful business format franchise. Therefore, the obligations of the Franchisor to maintain the Intellectual Property, improve the Method (clauses 6.21 or 6.9) and provide

Franchise Agreement—Master Form

training (clauses 6.7 and 6.8) are central to the relationship between the Franchisor and the Franchisee.

6.22 Extension of Term

To extend the Term [at the option of the Franchisee] for [one] further period[s] of ... years commencing on the day following the expiration of the Term provided that the Franchisee:

6.22:1 has achieved [the performance targets set out in Schedule ... or otherwise required under the terms of this Agreement *or* the Minimum Performance throughout the Term]

6.22:2 has properly observed and performed his obligations under this Agreement [and the lease of the Location] throughout the Term

6.22:3 pays to the Franchisor a renewal fee of ... % of the Gross Turnover of the Business in the calendar year prior to the Expiry Date

6.22:4 serves a notice on the Franchisor requiring such extension not later than .... days before the Expiry Date

6.22:5 [accepts that the terms of this Agreement shall apply to any extension of the Term under this clause *or* executes a new agreement on the Franchisor's standard terms current at the expiry of the Term]

6.22:6 re-equips the Business with such new or improved equipment as forms part of the Minimum Package at the expiry of the Term

6.22:7 accepts a new lease of the Location at a rent revised in accordance with the rent review procedures contained in the present lease of the location

Notes
An option on the part of the Franchisee only to extent the Term once is usual in franchising in the UK. The conditions upon which the right to that extension depend vary. The conditions set out in clauses 6.22:1 to 6.22:7 (inclusive) are not intended to be exhaustive. Each franchise may have some particular obligations on the part of the Franchisee which, if not strictly performed throughout the Term may adversely affect the goodwill of the franchise network. If that is the case, the performance of those obligations should be set out as fundamental to renewal of the Term. The Franchisor must consider this matter carefully. It is only the most disciplined Franchisor which has not accepted persons as franchisees whom the Franchisor knew were only marginally suitable candidates. If those persons perform satisfactorily throughout the Term, they may be acceptable as continuing franchisees, even if other franchisees would, probably, achieve a much higher performance at the same Location or in the same Territory. It is essential that any lease of the Location, especially if the Franchisor is the lessor or sub-lessor, expires at the same time as the agreement itself. (See para 5.26 et seq, ante).

[6.23 Extension of Territory

6.23:1 To give to the Franchisee not less than [30 days'] written prior notice of the Franchisor's intention to appoint any person (other than the Franchisee) and of the terms of such appointment to conduct the Business in any place adjoining or within ... miles from the perimeter of the Territory or (*insert other relevant details*) and such notice may be treated by the Franchisee as an offer of an equivalent appointment and before its expiry the Franchisee may give written notice to the Franchisor that it will take up such appointment on such terms

6.23:2 Not to offer to any other person terms more favourable than those contained in the notice within .... days of the expiry of that notice]

Notes
This clause is not usual in a territorial franchise in the UK. It sometimes appears when, in the early days of a franchise, the bargaining power of a prospective franchisee is greater than that of the Franchisor, particularly when the Franchisee is a corporation. It is intended

Precedents

to provide the Franchisee with an option to take up a franchise of an adjoining territory. This will minimise competition for the Franchisee and enable him to achieve expansion near to his original outlet. A development area agreement (see precedent 17) is a more comprehensive method of securing an option for the Franchisee with time limits to protect the Franchisor.

[6.24 Extension of Products
To add to the Products the goods listed in Schedule . . . . provided that the Franchisee:

    6.24:1   has achieved [the performance targets set out in Schedule . . . . or otherwise required under the terms of this Agreement *or* the Minimum Performance] [throughout the Term] [so far]

    6.24:2   has properly observed and performed its obligations under this Agreement throughout the Term [so far]

    6.24:3   serves a notice on the Franchisor requiring that such addition be made not later than . . . . days before the Expiry Date

    6.24:4   executes a new agreement in respect of the addition on the Franchisor's standard terms current at the date of the notice]

Notes
Again, this is an unusual clause. It is of use in franchises (such as dealerships) where the quality of the Business will be upgraded as the performance of the Franchisee improves. The conditions listed in clauses 6.24:1 to 6.24:4 are not intended to be exhaustive. If the Franchisor wishes to control the progressive upgrading of its franchises, it must consider carefully the particular conditions and timetables which it wishes to achieve in this context. At the same time, the Franchisee will wish to be assured that the conditions or targets are achievable.

6.25   Credit Limit
Subject to the performance by the Franchisee of all its obligations to allow the Franchisee credit up to and in accordance with the provisions of the Credit Limit

Notes
In a product supply franchise, the Credit Limit is of importance to both franchisors and franchisees. Both the time and value limits can have a restrictive effect upon the growth of the business of the Franchisee. At the same time, the Franchisor must ensure that the time limit is less than the credit periods granted to it by its own suppliers. Those time limits may vary according to each component or supplier and it may be necessary to set out in the Manual the time limits for each product individually. Also, the Franchisor must ensure that its own value credit limit with any supplier does not exceed the aggregate of all its franchisees for the products of that supplier. Therefore each product may have to be covered by an individual value credit limit. It is essential that the Franchisor constantly upgrades the value limits, as each new franchisee commences trading. Suppliers should be aware, from the outset, of the probable escalation of value credit limits. They will, therefore, in turn, have made arrangements with their own suppliers, so that their cash flow can be properly managed. Where all products dealt in by a franchisee are 'tied' items, credit limits are a useful means of checking turnover against sales returns submitted by franchisees. It may be useful for a franchisee, if special start-up credit limits can be negotiated to assist with his working capital requirement. This may require the special cooperation of suppliers and is only feasible in an established franchise with existing substantial turnover. However, the pincer-like effect of the expiry of special limits and increasing turnover must be monitored. Once the Franchisee's business has demonstrated its achievement of targets, with the benefit of special credit facilities, his bankers may assist with additional stocking loans to finance increasing turnover. Where the Franchisor is the main supplier of a company franchisee and those supplies are on credit, the key directors of the franchisee must be aware of the impact of the Deed of Guarantee (precedent 11).

6.26   Credit review
To review the Credit Limit [monthly *or* quarterly *or* annually] [on the last day

Franchise Agreement—Master Form

of each month *or* on the usual quarter days *or* on each anniversary of this Agreement] and subject to the strict performance and observance by the Franchisee of all its obligations under this Agreement to increase the [value of the] Credit Limit [as set out in clause [3.7:2] of this agreement by the proportion by which the [turnover *or* sales] of the [Products *or* Services] of the Franchisee has increased since the last review [or the Commencement Date]

Notes
An increasing credit limit matched to increasing turnover is an essential requirement of most product-supply franchises. Both the Franchisor and the Franchisee must be aware of the demands that increasing turnover will impose on both of them in those circumstances. Where the trading patterns of franchised outlets have become established and reasonably certain to estimate, the creation of a projected cash flow for at least the first 24 month period of trading by a franchisee will be important to both the Franchisor and the Franchisee in this context.

[6.27 Supply of services
To supply the Services stipulated in the Manual]

Notes
The Manual must specify in detail the Services. This clause is not 'subject to availability' but must be read in the light of clause 10.13.

[6.28 Exclusive territory
Not itself to operate nor to grant any other person the right to operate a business using any part of the Intellectual Property [and other insignia and identifying materials, methods of advertising and publicity forming part of the Method][1] in the Territory [Not itself to supply the Goods to third parties][2].
or
6.28 Non-exclusive territory
    6.28:1 Before granting to any person a licence [to use the Method *or* to conduct the Business] in the Territory, to offer the licence to the Franchisee[3] and
    6.28:2 If the Franchisee refuses it not to offer such a licence to use the Method in the Territory to any other person on more favourable terms
    6.28:3 If the Franchisee fails to send notice to the Franchisor of his acceptance of such offer of a licence within . . . of his being offered the licence, the Franchisee shall be deemed to have refused such offer]

Notes
This clause is important to both the Franchisor and the Franchisee. If it is desired to avoid the need to furnish particulars under the Restrictive Trade Practices Act 1976, it is essential that the grant of an exclusive Territory in the UK (in an agreement between UK residents) is limited to the business carried on under a particular name. The Franchisor, if it is a company, should ensure that board resolutions reserve and record its freedom to conduct a business similar to the franchised business in the Territory but under a different Trade Name (see precedents 7 and 8). If the definition of the 'Business' in the franchise agreement is carefully drafted so as to include reference to the Trade Name, then the term 'the Business' in this clause may be sufficient. Where exclusive territories are granted, even in this way, the possible application of other competition law and in particular the Treaty of Rome, needs to be considered.

1 See block exemption article 2(a). See as alternative clause 6.2 ante.
2 See ibid 2(a)
3 This clause appears to meet the concern expressed by the court in *Pronuptia* para 24.

6.29 To pay a commission of [5% of invoice value (net of VAT) on any [sales *or* supplies] to any leads introduced by the Franchisee to the Franchisor]

335

Precedents

Notes
This clause may apply when leads are very valuable (see clause 7.23 post).

7 Franchisee's obligations

The Franchisee agrees with the Franchisor throughout the Term:

7.1 Commencement conditional on training

Not to commence the Business until [the Franchisee *or* one senior director of the Franchisee] [and (*list other persons who will receive training*)] who will be responsible for the management of the Business [has *or* have] undergone the course of training provided by the Franchisor under clause [6.7] and been approved as competent by the Franchisor[1]

Notes
It rarely but sometimes occurs that an otherwise suitable franchisee proves himself so inept in training that the Franchisor cannot continue with the franchise. This can cause serious problems because, by then, the Franchisee will have acquired a Location, arranged all his finance and have prepared himself to take on the Business. Sympathetic counselling is required in these circumstances, usually followed by the acquisition and re-franchise of the Business by the Franchisor. As part of the vetting process, the Franchisor should have established that the Franchisee has attained a suitable educational standard to enable him to conduct the Business easily. This, usually, means reasonable levels of literacy and numeracy even where the systems included in the Method are designed for simplicity.

1 See block exemption article 3(2)(e).

7.2 No untrained personnel

Not to permit any person to act or assist in the Business in the place of persons trained in accordance with clause [7.1] unless and until such person has undergone a course of training by the Franchisor under clause [6.8] and been approved as competent by the Franchisor[1]

Notes
The goodwill of the franchise chain depends upon customer satisfaction. It is essential that all key persons engaged in the Business are fully trained and present a uniformly high standard to the consumer. Other employees may be trained by the Franchisee (see clause 7.6).

1 See block exemption article 3(2)(e).

7.3 Further training

To procure that [the Franchisee *or* the senior director of the Franchisee] [and the other persons mentioned in clause [7.1] and [7.2]] shall attend such further periods of training as may from time to time reasonably be required by the Franchisor[1] [at the expense of the Franchisee]

Notes
In view of the usual length of the Term of a franchise agreement (between 5 and 15 years), it will be necessary to introduce new products or systems in the Method from time to time. This may require further training and most franchisors wish to give their franchisees refresher courses to iron out the slovenly habits that inevitably afflict franchisees who have been trading for some time. It will be difficult to predict the future scope and amount of further training at the beginning of the Term. Franchisees who receive alterations to the Manual which they do not understand should contact the Franchisor and, if they are not confident about their own ability to absorb and act upon those changes, should request further training.

1 See block exemption article 3(2)(e).

Franchise Agreement—Master Form

7.4 Training expenses

To pay the travel and subsistence expenses of [the Franchisee *or* the senior director] [and of its employees and the salaries of any of those employees incurred during such training] [together with the Fees charged by the Franchisor for such training from time to time]

Notes
The introduction of new products or systems which necessitate further training often causes grumbling on the part of franchisees who have to pay for that training. However, franchisees should acknowledge their increased appeal to the consumer or competitiveness as a result of the changes and the amount of time saved by them because the Franchisor develops a training programme to acclimatise them to the new sections of the Method. It is fair that they should pay for that service. However, minor refresher courses do not justify additional fees and the Franchisee should only pay his expenses of attending those courses.

7.5 Engagement of staff

Within . . . . days of the commencement of the Business to [engage all staff and other persons required for the commencement and operation of the Business *or* engage the staff part of the Minimum Package] [in accordance with the recruitment criteria set out in the Manual] [subject to the prior approval by the Franchisor or any proposed employee]

Notes
The quality of employees in any business is fundamental to its success or failure. This is why so many franchises in the USA are designed to be operated as 'Momma and Poppa' businesses. This means that the family, whose livelihood and future directly depend on the success of the Business, are virtually the only persons engaged in it. In franchised businesses which require employees, the Franchisor must provide a profile of the most suitable candidate for each job in the Business. It may be that suitably qualified staff are so scarce or so specialist that the Franchisor must undertake recruitment for the Franchisee (see clause 6.15). The Manual should contain information about labour legislation, health and safety at work regulations and, most importantly, dismissal procedures. Unionised labour rarely becomes involved in franchised businesses, especially in the small service sector. The Minimum Package (staff part) should enable the Business to operate efficiently and with labour costs (including related costs such as National Insurance and employee 'perks' or benefits) within the levels projected in the business plan of the Franchisee. It is important that the Franchisor maintains good and close relations with senior employees of franchisees as they are good potential franchisees. It is better that, if they wish to leave a franchisee and set up on their own, they become franchisees of the Franchisor rather than joining another franchise whatever the employee undertakings signed by them may contain.

7.6 Training of staff

7.6:1 To ensure that its staff and their replacements and all persons required under the terms of this Agreement to undergo training in the Method and modifications to and improvements in the Method do so[1] and

1 See block exemption article 3(2)(e).

7.6:2 If and whenever required by the Franchisor to procure that they attend for the specified period at the place selected by the Franchisor for such purpose

7.6:3 To pay the travel and subsistence expenses involved of [the Franchisee *or* the senior director] [and of its employees and the salaries of any of its employees incurred during such training] [together with fees charged by the Franchisor for such training from time to time]

[7.6:4 To hold regular training and assessment sessions [at the Location] for all the employees of the Franchisee to ensure their competence in their allotted duties]

Precedents

[7.6:5 To report to the Franchisor any serious incompetence on the part of any employee after training]

Notes
The Franchisee must be obliged to attend (with his employees if appropriate) training sessions arranged by the Franchisor. The Franchisee should hold his own training sessions for his employees. The Manual should contain detailed information on employee training and assessment procedures. Training by the Franchisee should be confined to non-specialist and non-senior employees. It may be necessary for the Franchisee and his senior employees to be trained how to train their junior employees. Franchisees should be suspicious of any franchise on offer which does not require him to put considerable effort into being trained.

7.7 Conformity with the Method and other businesses[1]

7.7:1 To conform in all respects and at all times with the Method (as modified from time to time by alteration of the Manual)

1 See block exemption article 3(2)(f).

7.7:2 Not to do or suffer to be done anything additional to or not in accordance with the Method without the previous consent in writing of the Franchisor

7.7:3 To ensure that the Business conforms with other businesses operated in accordance with the Method in particular with regard to quality service and cleanliness[1] (the Franchisee acknowledges that such conformity is of the utmost importance to the successful operation of the Business and other businesses operated in accordance with the Method and the protection of the goodwill attaching to the Trade Name and Method)

1 See block exemption article 3(2)(g).

7.7:4 To adopt all changes in the Method as soon as required by the Franchisor

Notes
The Method is the main distinguishing feature between a full business format franchise and a bare intellectual property licence. Conformity with the Method should ensure that high standards are maintained and the outlets look and trade alike. Changes in the Method must be adopted immediately by all franchisees. There should be no deviations from it. Any improvements in the Method created or developed by a franchisee should be the subject of a 'feedback' arrangement (see clause 7.43). This may appear unfair to an innovative franchisee but he must accept that he is part of a team. Feedback (and no-challenge) clauses in patent licences can have anti-competitive implications and need careful consideration (see para 2.49 et seq).

[7.8 Minimum opening hours

To operate minimum opening hours for the Business as follows:

Mondays to Fridays inclusive (excepting statutory holidays) (*set out hours*) or other business hours that are usual in the area in which the Location is situated *or* To [open for the] conduct [of] the Business for the hours and at the times stipulated in the Manual]

Notes
The hours are best set out in the Manual. They can then be changed in response to changing circumstances and consumer habits. Opening hours are not an indication of the hours of necessary work required in the Business. Many franchisees, coming from secure employment, have been shocked by 70–100 hour weeks. Franchisors should ensure that franchisees are well aware of the amount of work involved in the Business (see chapter 6, enquiry 51). Any prospective franchisee must examine his own character to determine whether he is suitable material for the limited form of self-employment which is the substance of franchising. (see 'F is for Franchising' (by the same authors) (2nd edn) Alphabet Publications Ltd, pages 26 and 27).

7.9 Promotion of the Business

7.9:1 Diligently to promote and make every effort steadily to increase the Business by such advertisements signs entries in telephone or trade directories or other forms of publicity as may be approved by the Franchisor as provided by this Agreement and by distributing to customers and potential customers in the most effective manner point-of-service advertising material provided by the Franchisor[1]

1 See block exemption article 3(1)(f) and (g).

7.9:2 To expend not less than . . . % of the Gross Turnover of the Business [between each Accounting Reference Date *or* in each year of the Term] in such promotion[1].

1 See block exemption article 3(1)(g).

[7.9:3 [only] to use whatever promotional material or advertising copy is supplied by the Franchisor for local promotional or advertising purposes][1]

1 See block exemption article 3(1)(g).

Notes
Local promotion or advertising is important. A minimum percentage of gross turnover expenditure is necessary to prevent franchisees skimping in this vital area. The Franchisor should strive to achieve economies in promotional or advertising costs by supplying standardised material or copy which must be used by all franchisees.

7.10 Promotion of the Method

To use every reasonable means in the conduct of the Business to promote the Method and to co-operate with the Franchisor and other franchisees of the Franchisor in promoting and developing it.[1]

Notes
The Method is central to business format franchising (see clause 7.7, ante). It is essential that the franchise chain continually promotes the success of the Method in the Business. The customer must feel that he or she is dealing with a successful well-managed operation.

1 Block exemption article 3(1)(f).

7.11 Special promotions

To co-operate with the Franchisor and other franchisees of the Franchisor in any advertising campaign sales promotion programme or other special activity in which the Franchisor may engage or specify including the display of point-of-service advertising and the distribution of special novelties promotional literature and the like the costs of which shall be borne [in accordance with clauses [6.5 and 6.6] *or* by the Franchisee] [including the costs of free offers discounts and the like *or* notwithstanding which the costs of free offers discounts and the like shall be borne by the Franchisee] [provided all such costs free offers or discounts shall be deducted from the Gross Turnover of the Business for the calculation of continuing fees and the advertising contribution][1]

Notes
Some businesses, particularly retail and other consumer-orientated franchises, need to stimulate custom from time to time by special offers and promotions. It would be unfortunate and damaging to the reputation of the franchise chain if some only of the franchisees engaged in any special promotion. For the sake of uniformity and maximum impact all franchisees must join in the promotional programmes devised by the Franchisor. The cost of free offers and discounts should be deductible in fee calculations (see clause 3.11:3.3, ante).

1 Block exemption article 3(1)(g).

Precedents

7.12 Diligence
At all times to work diligently to protect and promote the interests of the Franchisor[1]

Notes
The interests of the Franchisor should be similar to the interests of the franchise network in relation to the Business.

1 Block exemption article 3(1)(f) and clause 7.15.

7.13 Payments
To pay to the Franchisor (or as the Franchisor directs) [without demand deduction or set-off] on the relevant Payment Dates (time being of the essence);
    7.13:1   The Initial Fee [which fee shall cover:
        7.13:1.1   initial training
        7.13:1.2   initial advertising [for the launch of the Business [at the Location *or* in the Territory]
        7.13:1.3   [supply of equipment and other matters specified in the Manual *or* that part of the Minimum Package stipulated in clause [3.19:1] of this Agreement]]
    7.13:2   The [Advertising Contribution[1] and the] Continuing Fees

1 See block exemption article 3(1)(g).

    7.13:3   The Minimum Fee
    [7.13:4   The Insurance Premium]

Notes
It may be that the description of what the Initial Fee will cover is better placed in the definitions section (see clause 3.12). It is essential that the Franchisee has no right or opportunity to withhold or deduct fees due to the Franchisor as a set-off or claim (see also clause 7.67). In addition, franchisees must be made aware of the fundamental importance of making payments on time. If there is a 'time of essence' provision for payments and the Franchisee is late in making payments despite being aware of the importance of making them on time, then that behaviour may indicate serious financial problems which are not apparent from the conduct of the Business generally.

7.14 Contingent payment
If for any reason the Franchisor is prevented by law from requiring the Franchisee to obtain [its supplies for the Business *or* the Products] from the Franchisor and the Franchisee ceases to purchase all or any part of [such supplies *or* the Products] from the Franchisor, to pay to the Franchisor [without demand deduction or set-off] a further fee of . . . % of the Gross Turnover of the Business [on the Payments Dates for the Continuing Fees]

Notes
When the Franchisor relies on margins on the supply of products or services to its franchisees rather than 'royalties' for its revenue, any statutory or other prohibition of 'tied' sales will cause it serious financial damage unless there is a facility in the franchise agreement whereby in that event 'royalties' will become payable by franchisees.

7.15 No competing products
    7.15:1   Not to manufacture sell or use in the course of the provision of services goods competing with the Products but nothing in this Clause shall be construed as extending this restriction to spare parts and accessories.[1]

1 See block exemption article 2(e)—see also clause 6.13.

    7.15:2   [to sell or use in the course of the provision of the services exclusively goods matching the minimum objective quality specifications laid down [in the Manual]][1]

[1] See block exemption articles 3(1)(a), 5(b).

7.15:3 [To sell or use in the course of the provision of the Services only the Products][1]

[1] See block exemption articles 3(1)(b) and 5(c)—as to when this clause is permissible see para 2.44 et seq. The franchisee must be free to obtain such goods from other franchisees, or authorised distributors (if any)—block exemption article 4(a).

Notes
This anti-competition clause is designed to prevent the franchisee competing with the franchised business in the Territory or elsewhere (see also clause 5). The definition of the 'Business' is set out in clause 3.3 and the scope of non-competition clauses throughout the Agreement must be considered with that definition firmly in mind. The Restrictive Trade Practices Act 1976 only applies to restrictive agreements in which both parties agree to accept relevant restrictions. The application of other competition laws, and in particular the Treaty of Rome, needs to be considered in relation to this clause—see paras 2.12 et seq. For restraint of trade issues, see paras 2.107 et seq.

7.16 Restriction on active sales
[Not to seek Customers for the Products [*or* the Services] outside the Territory][1]

[1] See block exemption article 2(d).

7.17 No change of location
[Not without the Franchisor's consent to change the location of the Business][1]

[1] See block exemption article 3(2)(i).

7.18 Interests in competitors
Not to acquire any financial interest in the capital of a competing undertaking which would give the Franchisee power to influence the economic conduct of such undertaking[1]

[1] See block exemption article 3(1)(d).

7.19 Customer restrictions
To sell the products only to end-users to other Franchisees of the Franchisor and to resellers within other channels of distribution supplied by the Franchisor or by others with its consent[1]

[1] See block exemption article 3(1)(e).

7.20 Good faith
In all matters to act loyally and faithfully toward the Franchisor

Notes
This is a form of 'uberrimae fidei' clause and is intended to cover those activities which do not infringe the letter but offend the spirit of the relationship between the Franchisor and its franchisees. As it is so general there is considerable doubt as to its effectiveness except in cases which should be caught by other more specific provisions. However, it is surprising how effective the intent of this clause can be in direct discussions between the Franchisor and a recalcitrant franchisee.

7.21 Compliance
[7.21:1 To obey the Franchisor's orders and instructions and in the absence of any such orders or instructions in relation to any particular matter to act in such a manner as the Franchisee ought reasonably to have considered to be most beneficial to the Franchisor][1]

Precedents

Notes
This clause can cause undue friction at the negotiating stage. It brings home to franchisees their dependent status.

1   See block exemption article 3(2)(f).

7.21:2   To conduct the Business in an orderly and businesslike manner[1]

Notes
This is again a general clause on which the Franchisor should not need to rely if the Agreement is otherwise well drafted.

1   See block exemption article 3(2)(g).

[7.22   Disclosure
On entering into this or any other agreement or transaction with the Franchisor during the Term or any continuation of it to make full disclosure of all material circumstances and of everything known to it respecting the subject matter of the contract or transaction which would be likely to influence the conduct of the Franchisor including in particular the disclosure of other agencies or franchises in which the Franchisee is interested directly or indirectly]

Notes
This clause may more appropriately be included in the Confidentiality Agreement (see precedent 4 et seq) although it should be included if there is no conditional period between conclusion of negotiations and provisional commitment as the first stage and final formal agreement as the last stage.

[7.23   Pass on information
7.23:1   Without prejudice to the Franchisee's right to supply such customers[1] promptly to refer to the Franchisor any inquiries from prospective customers or other leads outside the Territory

Notes
The franchise network should be a mutual aid marketing association. Most franchisees receive enquiries from potential customers who reside or operate outside the Territory of the Franchisee. It is essential that those leads are processed quickly. The Manual should set out procedures for dealing with extra-Territory potential customers. The Manual will include the names and addresses of all franchisees and a map showing the territories allocated. A franchisee should look up the franchisee in whose territory the lead resides or operates and contact him or the Franchisor. In this case the Franchisor must be notified. If franchisees are charged commission by the Franchisor for leads, this must be stated in the agreement and the Manual. The Franchisor may wish to share the commission with the Franchisee who passed on the lead to the Franchisor (see clause 7.23:4, post).

1   See block exemption article 5(g).

7.23:2   To supply to the Franchisor information which may come into its possession which may assist the Franchisor to effect sales or other dealings [for the Business *or* in the Products *or* in the Services] outside the Territory

Notes
This is a general information clause.

7.23:3   To pass on any information which may prejudice [sales of the Products *or* supplies of the Services *or* the Business] or reduce the Gross Turnover of the Business in any way

Notes
This clause is very important, especially if the franchised business is relatively new or subject to competition. Constant feedback from franchisees should assist the Franchisor. However, it is difficult to maintain a balance between useful information

and ill-founded criticism and some franchisees do not understand the constructive intention of this clause.

[7.23:4 To pay a commission of [ ]% of invoice value (net of VAT) on any [sales or supplies] to any leads introduced by the Franchisor to the Franchisee]

Notes
It is generally part of the ordinary role of the Franchisor to introduce business to its franchisees for no additional consideration other than the fees already payable. However, in circumstances where introductions are very valuable it may be appropriate that the Franchisor should receive additional remuneration for that service. If that is the case, to encourage franchisees to pass on leads it may be necessary for the Franchisor to pay a substantial proportion of that commission to the franchisee who introduced the lead.

7.24 Registered user

Where required by the Franchisor [to join with the Franchisor in making *or* to make] application to become [the registered user *or* the licensee] of any part of the Intellectual Property

Notes
The registration of users of trade marks and licenses of patents and designs is permissive. (See para 3.137, ante). This clause should always be included in a franchise agreement however.

7.25 Protection of Intellectual Property

7.25:1

    7.25:1.1 Not to cause or permit anything which may damage or endanger the Intellectual Property or other intellectual property of the Franchisor or the Franchisor's title to it or assist or allow others to do so

    7.25:1.2 To notify the Franchisor of any suspected infringement of the Intellectual Property or other intellectual property of the Franchisor[1]

1 See block exemption article 3(2)(c).

    7.25:1.3 To take such reasonable action as the Franchisor shall direct (at the expense of the Franchisor) in relation to such infringement[1]

1 See block exemption article 3(2)(c).

    7.25:1.4 To affix such notices to the Products or their packaging or advertising associated with the Business as the Franchisor shall direct

    7.25:1.5 To compensate the Franchisor for any use by the Franchisee of the Intellectual Property otherwise than in accordance with this Agreement

    7.25:1.6 To indemnify the Franchisor for any liability incurred to third parties for any use of the Intellectual Property otherwise than in accordance with this Agreement.

    7.25:1.7 On the expiry or termination of this Agreement forthwith to cease to use the Intellectual Property [save as expressly authorised by the Franchisor in writing]

    7.25:1.8 Not to apply for registration of the Trade Name or the Permitted Name as a trade mark but to give the Franchisor at the Franchisor's expense any assistance it may require in connection with the registration of the Trade Name or the Permitted Name as a trade mark in any part of the world and not to interfere with in any manner nor to attempt to prohibit the use or registration of the Trade Name or any similar name or designation by any other licensee of the Franchisor.

Precedents

7.25:1.9 Not to tamper with any markings or name plates or other indication of the source of origin of the Products which may be placed by the Franchisor on the Products

7.25:1.10 Not to use the Intellectual Property otherwise than as permitted by this Agreement

7.25:1.11 Not to use any name or mark similar to or capable of being confused with the Trade Name the Permitted Name or the Trade Mark

7.25:1.12 Not to use the Intellectual Property except directly in the Business

7.25:1.13 Not to use the Trade Name the Permitted Name or the Trade Mark or any derivation of them in its corporate name

7.25:1.14 To hold any additional goodwill generated by the Franchisee for the Intellectual Property or the Business as bare trustee for the Franchisor[1]

7.25:1.15 [To use the Permitted Name as its only trade name]

1 See *Scott on Trusts* (4th edn) 82.4.

Notes
These clauses are intended to protect the Intellectual Property from infringement and unauthorised use (See chapter 3). It is also essential that the enhanced goodwill attached to that Intellectual Property arising because of the favourable use of it by franchisees should ensure for the Franchisor alone. In this way, the franchise agreement may expire or terminate without the additional complication of arguments concerning the rights of the Franchisee to part of the value arising from the use by that franchisee of the Intellectual Property. These sub-clauses are similar to those which would be included in a bare intellectual property licence. As far as the intellectual property content of a business format franchise is concerned, this is the most formal and technical part of the Agreement. The protective intent of the clauses must be read in the light of EEC and UK competition regulations, restrictive practices and intellectual property law. It is an area where competition regulations may conflict with intellectual property law and even specialists treat extremely warily. See Chapter 2.

7.25:1.16 To display such notices concerning the Intellectual Property or the relationship between the parties on its stationery [and at the Location] as is stipulated in the Manual from time to time

Notes
This clause is intended to ensure compliance with the Business Names Act 1985 and to give notice to the public and all persons dealing with the Business at the Franchisee is an independent person or entity and not the agent or a branch of the Franchisor. This is not only necessary for safeguarding the Franchisor's interest in the Intellectual Property but an attempt to create a divide between the Franchisor and the Franchisee to prevent successful claims against the Franchisor arising from the activities of the Franchisee [see also block exemption article 4(c) which makes indication of the Franchisee's status a condition of exemption]. (See also para 6.24, ante.) (See also clauses 7.53 and 7.61).

[7.25:1.17 Not to register the Permitted Name as its trade name at (*insert name of business names registry*) without the consent of the Franchisor]

Notes
This clause will be redundant if as in England and Wales no form of business names registration is operative in the Territory (see para 6.24, ante).

7.25:2

7.25:2.1 Save that the Franchisee acknowledges that the Trade Name is well known and valuable nothing in this clause shall be interpreted as prohibiting

Franchise Agreement—Master Form

the Franchisee from challenging the validity of any part of the Intellectual Property[1]

1 See block exemption article 5(f)—as permitted by the block exemption however, the agreement can be made to terminate on such event (see clause 8.3:5).

7.25:2.2 *(Specify other)*

7.26 Secrecy[1]

7.26:1 Not at any time during or after[2] the Term to divulge or allow to be divulged to any person any confidential information[3] other than to persons who have signed a secrecy undertaking in the form approved by the Franchisor

1 See block exemption article 3(2)(a).
2 See ibid.
3 The block exemption uses the term 'know-how' but clearly does not mean this in the technical sense—see para 2.34.

7.26:2 Not to permit any person to act or assist in the Business until such person has signed such an undertaking

7.26:3 Neither during the Term nor at any time after its expiry[1] to use any confidential information provided to the Franchisee by the Franchisor under the terms of this agreement for purposes other than running the Business[2] but after the expiry of the Term this obligation shall cease if such confidential information becomes generally known or easily accessible other than by the Franchisee's breach[3]

1 See block exemption article 3(2)(d).
2 Ibid.
3 See block exemption article 5(d).

Notes

This clause which is widely drawn can cause difficulties for franchisees. It is usual for a Franchisor to permit confidential financial information concerning the Business to be disclosed to the bankers of the Franchisee and his auditors (see Confidentiality Agreement, precedent 4, post for covenant on the part of an intending franchisee). The employee undertaking is difficult to enforce and may not be necessary in the case of non-specialist employees engaged in low level tasks. However, a Franchisor must remember that every employee of its franchisees is a potential competitor learning the tricks of the trade whilst being employed by a franchisee. Therefore, the Franchisor must take care which of those employees (if any) should have access to trade secrets. Those that do so must be obliged to sign the relevant undertaking (see Undertaking, Form 4, post).

7.27 Sales reports

To supply to the Franchisor [by first class prepaid mail or by electronic means if required by the Franchisor] weekly *or* from time to time upon request *or* on payment of the Continuing Fees *or* on the Payment Dates sales reports and other information in the form stipulated by the Franchisor in the Manual concerning the Business.

Notes

It is usual that frequent regular reports are required from franchisees. A weekly report is common. (see Form 15 for a suggested form of report.) Even if the Franchisor is supplying all the goods or material required by a franchisee in the Business, it will be advisable to insist upon sales reports. These reports can be compared with the accounts reports and VAT returns to ensure that accurate and consistent reporting of the conduct of the Business is maintained. The sales reports provide a foundation upon which a supervisory and scrutiny system can be built by the Franchisor. That system may include random short-notice inspection, customer and supplier visits, the Franchisor's staff posing as customers and audits.

Precedents

7.28 Accounts

To keep accurate and separate records and accounts in respect of the [supply of the [Products *or* Services] *or* conduct of the Business] and:

    7.28:1   in accordance with good accountancy custom [in the Territory]

    7.28:2   have them audited by qualified auditors once a year during the Term

    7.28:3   submit copies [certified by such auditors] to the Franchisor within [90] days of the [Accounting Reference Date *or* end of the financial year of the Franchisee]

    7.28:4   keep them for not less than [3] years.

    7.28:5   within 14 days of submission or receipt to supply to the Franchisor a copy of each VAT return or assessment in respect of the Business

Notes

The keeping of accurate accounts is regulated in the case of corporations by statute. The present nervous state of the accountancy profession concerning possible negligence claims ensures that even small companies face rigorous audit procedures. However, in the case of individuals or partnerships between persons, the accounts are usually only prepared for the Inland Revenue and bankers. Thus a clear statement concerning the former and content of the accounts to be submitted by non-corporate franchisees should be inserted in the Manual. The submission of a VAT return or assessment is a further means of checking the sales reports and accounts (see clause 7.68).

7.29 Auditors

To appoint as the accountants and auditors of the Franchisee the [chartered] accountants nominated by the Franchisor

Notes

It will be necessary for any firm of chartered accountants to clear with their Institute their appointment under nomination. In practice the Institute raises no objection but warns that the firm must itself resolve questions of potential conflict of interest. This may be resolved by the Franchisee irrevocably and unconditionally authorising them to disclose to the Franchisor any matter which arises during the course of their audit investigations.

7.30 Customer list

To keep a list of actual and potential customers for the [Products *or* Services *or* Business] and to supply a copy of it to the Franchisor upon request

Notes

Many franchised businesses like most businesses rely upon recurring custom. Wherever possible a customer list should be established. This is the practical goodwill being generated by the franchisee's conduct of the Business. In the event that the franchise is terminated or expires, it will assist the Franchisor to keep the Business operational in the Territory whilst a new franchisee is appointed. As to the confidentiality of customer lists, see para 3.120.

7.31 Inspection of books and premises[1]

To permit the Franchisor at all reasonable times to enter the Location or any other premises used in connection with the Business for the purpose of carrying out checks on such premises [vehicles used in the Business] the Products sold and the Services provided and the inventory and accounts of the Business [and all other things material to the Business][2]

Notes

Random short-notice inspection is essential. Only in that manner can standards of the Business be maintained. The Franchisor must decide whether inspection should be permitted at any time or during normal business hours. If the Business is a retail business then it may be better if any inspection occurs outside its normal business hours. However, there may be times when inspection at any time is necessary to ensure that, for example, proper standards of hygiene are being maintained.

1   Block exemption article 3(2)(h).
2   This section in brackets goes beyond wording of article 3(2)(h).

Franchise Agreement—Master Form

7.32 Notice

To comply with the terms of any Default Notice (as defined by clause [9.3]) specifying a breach of the provisions of this Agreement and requiring the breach to be remedied so far as it may be but nothing in this clause is intended to require the Franchisor to serve notice of any breach before taking action in respect of it

Notes

The Default Notice is a last resort. It should only be used on occasions when all other possible means of persuasion have been exhausted. However, in the case of a damaging breach, it may be necessary to act quickly and serve such a notice immediately without prior consultation. Franchisors find it very difficult to deal with franchisees who behave in a manner which stops just short of a breach of contract. Further, a franchisee who is in financial difficulties but is not insolvent can cause problems without infringing any of the provisions of the agreement. Accordingly, the grounds for service of a Default Notice must be specified (see clause 9.3, post).

7.33 Best endeavours

7.33:1 To use its best endeavours to sell the Products [or to provide the Services] [and to offer for sale a minimum range and stock of the Products as specified in the Manual and to plan its re-ordering of such Products adequately in advance] and to procure the greatest volume of turnover for the Business consistent with good service to the public [or to achieve a minimum turnover of . . . .][1]

[1] See block exemption articles 3(1)(f). See also *Computerland* para 23(iv); *ServiceMaster* para 16

7.33:2 [To honour customer warranties in respect of the Products irrespective of the source of supply][1]

[1] See block exemption article 4(b). See also *Computerland* para 23(iv); *ServiceMaster* para 16.

Notes

This is intended to prevent a franchisee resting on his 'comfort plateau' for too long. The revenue of the Franchisor will depend on high levels of turnover in the Business. An underperforming franchisee can take up much management time and effort and the amount of fees being received may make the relationship unprofitable for the Franchisor. Where the Business depends upon the sale of goods, an adequate stock level is essential. If the Minimum Package method is followed, the Manual must contain a full stock list with minimum quantities of each item. The Franchisor must ensure that its response to orders from franchisees (in a franchise in which the Franchisor is responsible for supplying its franchisees) is efficient and helpful. Considerable problems can arise in an expanding network when the Franchisor is running up against the credit limits with its own suppliers and the turnover of its franchisees is expanding. This can lead to delays in supplies to the detriment of each franchisee's Business. Credit management by the Franchisor is then crucial to the survival of the network and it may be forced to alter its existing supply credit arrangements with its franchisees to provide a short-term respite from its cash-flow problems. If those credit terms are set out in the Manual, then an alteration in the Manual will be necessary. Franchisees may object and, if they are aware of the reason for the change, request the Franchisor to renegotiate credit limits with its suppliers. The Franchisor should alter both.

7.34 Protect goodwill

Throughout the Term to protect and promote the goodwill associated with the Method

Notes

This clause is a covenant to protect goodwill associated with the Method. To the extent that the Method includes intellectual property, the clause overlaps with clause 7.25, ante.

Precedents

However, the Method is more than its component intellectual property parts. This clause, although general, may be used to prevent behaviour which will cause the franchise network to acquire a poor reputation.

7.35 Foreclosing suppliers

Not to manufacture sell or use in the course of the provision of services goods competing with the Products but nothing in this clause shall be construed as extending this restriction to spare parts or accessories for the Products.[1]

1 See block exemption article 2(e).

7.36 No other business [at the Location]

Not to carry on or permit to be carried on any other business [at the Location] nor to extend the scope or range of the Business

Notes
This clause is not expressly cleared by the block exemption, and if used, the Agreement should be notified. It is usually important that the Business is not confused or associated with any other trade or business. It must operate in its own right independently. There is one class of exceptions. They are the so-called 'bolt-on' franchises which are intended to provide additional revenue for other businesses, using the staff and other assets of those businesses. They are often seasonal in nature and are busiest during the quietest season of the business on to which they are 'bolted'. The scope or range of the Business should be restricted so that innovative franchisees cannot add further trades to their conduct of the Business. This section of the clause must be read together with the territorial restriction. The combination means that a strictly defined and limited Business is only permitted to operate within specific boundaries.

7.37 Business not to be carried on other than from the Location

Not to carry on the Business or any part of the Business other than from the Location [without the consent of the Franchisor][1]

Notes
If the Location is important to the Business, then it is essential that the Business is always conducted from that Location and not, for example, from the Franchisee's home. This is especially so in the case of retail operations. The improvement in communications throughout the UK means that some franchisees may be tempted to stay away from the 'shop'.

1 Block exemption article 2(c).

7.38 Orderly conduct

To conduct the Business in an orderly and businesslike manner and strictly in compliance with all such policies and operating standards as may from time to time be specified by the Franchisor (particularly in the Manual) and generally to maintain the standards of quality of the Method[1]

Notes
This clause is intended to ensure that the Franchisee operates the Business in compliance with the standard requirements of the Franchisor. Unity of projected image and conduct are essential in a franchise network. It is, therefore, necessary that a franchisee should be obliged to conform.

1 Block exemption article 3(2)(f).

7.39 Compliance with laws

To comply with the conduct of the Business with all applicable laws byelaws and regulations of a governmental nature applicable to the Business or its conduct.

Notes
It is essential that if the Franchisee commits some breach of regulations or commits some

Franchise Agreement—Master Form

criminal offence in the course of his conduct of the Business, his conduct will be a breach of the agreement. This clause is widely drawn as it is impossible to foresee all possible forms of misconduct. Particularly damaging examples may be included in matters which are to be treated as fundamental breaches of the Agreement which cannot be cured (see clause 8.3:3, post).

7.40 Honour credit cards

To honour such charge and credit cards and plans as may from time to time be issued or approved by the Franchisor in accordance with the terms and conditions laid down by the Franchisor or in the manner from time to time prescribed by the Franchisor and to participate in and comply with the terms and provisions of a central billing programme and other credit plans programmes and procedures specified by the Franchisor

Notes
Credit card operators deduct a percentage fee from the payments due from their card holders to their participating retailers. This means that the gross profit of those retailers is reduced on credit card sales. Accordingly, although this is increasingly less common, some business owners refuse to accept credit card payment. If the franchised business relies upon increased sales levels encouraged by credit cards, the Franchisor will want to ensure that all its franchisees honour the cards which the franchised business generally accepts. The Franchisor may, also, wish to operate its own credit schemes, if the franchised business is suitable. Credit sales can generate useful additional profits for the Franchisor whilst encouraging increased turnover for franchisees. However, to be successful all franchisees must participate.

7.41 Pay suppliers promptly

To pay promptly all suppliers of the business in accordance with their usual terms and conditions

Notes
If the Franchisee obtains his supplies from third parties he may pay them promptly. The good name of the franchised business depends upon it. Further, if the suppliers are nominated by the Franchisor and participate in a group discount arrangement for all franchisees of the franchised business, the Franchisor must ensure that its franchisees are not late payers. A relatively low percentage of late payment averaged throughout each year among a group of franchisees may cause the loss of discount for all of them, even if there is no pattern of consistent late payment by any of them individually. This means that each franchisee must be obliged to honour agreed payment terms with his suppliers.

7.42 Repair decoration replacement and renewal

To keep the Location and furnishings in a good state of repair and decoration and to replace and renew equipment so as to enhance the reputation of the Trade Name the Method and the Business but in any event as required by the Manual or as may otherwise [on 24 hours' notice] be required by the Franchisor

Notes
Regular refurbishment of the Location is necessary in the interests of creating a uniform 'house-style' and of smartness.

7.43 Feedback[1]

To communicate to the Franchisor any experience gained in the Business which may improve the Method and to grant to the Franchisor and to other Franchisees of the Franchisor free of charge a non-exclusive licence to use any such improvements

1 See block exemption article 3(2)(b).

Notes
Sometimes franchisees invent or develop improvements to the Systems or other aspects of the Method or in other ways improve the Business. The Franchisor should have the right to

Precedents

pass on those improvements to its other franchisees without any liability to the Franchisee. They should, however, be fully tested first.

7.44 Indemnity

To indemnify and keep indemnified the Franchisor from and against any and all loss damage or liability whether criminal or civil suffered [and legal fees and costs incurred] by the Franchisor because of:

    7.44:1 any neglect or default of the Franchisee or its agents employees licensees or customers in connection with the Business or the Location

    7.44:2 any other reason so long as such loss damage liability fees or costs resulted from the Business and was not due to any default of the Franchisor

Notes

An indemnity is not of any value unless it is practically effective. An indemnity is not of any value if the person issuing the indemnity is a man of straw. Accordingly, even in the present difficult insurance markets, the Franchisor must protect itself against its potential liabilities arising from any act or default of the franchisee (see paras 1.28 et seq, ante for discussion of the liability of the Franchisor for the acts and defaults of its franchisees). The more successful the franchise network, the more likely is it that the public will consider it to be a single entity. The Franchisor may, therefore, face actions against it from customers of franchisees.

7.45 No Sub-licences

Not to grant any sub-licence of the Method or any part of it

Notes

The Franchisor and the Franchisee will have a close personal commercial relationship. The Franchisee must not be able to substitute someone else as Franchisee (see clause 7.46 for prohibition against assignment) or grant or allow anyone else to exercise his rights under the franchise agreement.

7.46 Assignment

    [7.46:1] Not to assign charge or otherwise deal with this Agreement in any way without the consent of the Franchisor[1]

Notes

The Franchisor must have control of all its franchisees through the franchise agreement and, it may be hoped, through the relationship of mutual trust and respect which will arise during the Term. That relationship will build up starting from the first interviews and will be greatly enhanced during training when the Franchisee will come to appreciate the value of the systems of the Method and the Franchisor will see the energy and willingness of the Franchisee responding to the challenge. That relationship is founded on the voluntary choice of both the Franchisor and the Franchisee to establish a business connection. The Franchisor cannot risk having a franchisee imposed upon it by way of an assignment of the franchise. Therefore, assignments should be prohibited.

1 See block exemption article 3(2)(j).

[7.46:2 In the case of an intended assignment by the Franchisee such consent shall not be unreasonably withheld in the following circumstances: (*set out particular circumstances eg*):

    [7.46:2.1 The proposed assignee is acceptable to the Franchisor]

    [7.46:2.2 The proposed assignee shall agree in writing directly with the Franchisor to be bound by the terms of this Agreement or the then standard franchise agreement of the Franchisor]]

Notes

An absolute prohibition against assignment may be softened by a 'consent not to be unreasonably withheld' provision. However, sub-clause 7.46:2.1 may re-establish the

Franchise Agreement—Master Form

absolute discretion of the Franchisor. See clause 10.4, post for procedure upon proposed sale by the franchisee.

7.47 Delegation
Not to delegate any duties or obligations arising under this Agreement otherwise than may be expressly permitted under its terms.

Notes
See comments concerning clauses 7.45 and 7.46, ante.

7.48 Director reliance
7.48:1 Because this Agreement is and all rights and licences granted to the Franchisee under this Agreement are personal to the Franchisee [and its [directors *or* shareholders]] not to assign them wholly or partly save in accordance with these provisions[1]

Notes
See comments concerning clauses 7.45 and 7.46, ante.

1 Block exemption article 3(2)(j).

7.48:2 Not to cause or permit any change in the number or identity of the directors and shareholders or the Franchisee (other than by death) without the prior consent of the Franchisor

Notes
If the Franchisee is a private limited company, the relationship between the Franchisee and the Franchisor depends upon the quality of the directors and, often, the shareholders of the Franchisee. It is, therefore, essential that no change in those directors or shareholders is permitted without the consent of the Franchisor.

7.49 No description as agent
Not to describe itself or act as agent or representative of the Franchisor except as expressly authorised by this Agreement

Notes
If the division between the Franchisor and the Franchisee in the context of third party liability is to succeed, the Franchisee must not be or act as the agent of the Franchisor. This clause alone may not assist either of the Parties in the event of a third party claim, the conduct of the Parties towards that third party will be more important (See paras 1.28 et seq, ante).

7.50 No pledge of credit
Not to pledge the credit of the Franchisor in any way

Notes
If the Franchisee is held out by the Franchisor as having its authority to pledge its credit then this clause may not protect the Franchisor against claims by creditors of the Franchisee. If the Franchisor has a network of suppliers who supply most, if not all, of the franchise network and is informed in writing that each Franchisee is a separate trader and not a branch or agency of the Franchisor, this potential problem should not arise.

7.51 Standard terms
To make contracts with customers for the [Products *or* Services *or* Business] on the standard terms and conditions set out in the Manual and not to take orders from customers unless they have assented to such terms

Notes
The Franchisor must ensure that all supplies made by the Franchisee are under the standard terms of trade drawn up by the Franchisor in the light of its experience. All pro-forma invoices or order confirmations should set out those terms or at the very least inform the

351

Precedents

customer where he can read a copy. Supplies made in the absence of those terms may expose the whole network to successful claims which the terms of trade may have prevented.

[7.52 Maximum prices[1]
Not to advertise or charge customers prices in excess of the prices specified by the Franchisor in the Manual from time to time [provided that the Franchisee shall be free to charge the public price less than such maxima at any time during the Term]]

Notes
Competition legislation in the UK (See para 2.150 et seq) prohibits resale price maintenance or agreements fixing sales prices between outlets (see block exemption article 5(e)). Accordingly, although the Franchisor may wish to impose uniform pricing throughout the franchise network, this is not permitted. However, it is permitted to recommend prices. It is unlikely that the Franchisee will charge less than those prices except when in financial difficulties. In that event, the Franchisor could step in and appoint its own management (clause 10.32) on the grounds that the Franchisee was not performing satisfactorily. In recent years, however, disparate prosperity levels in the UK have produced regional variations in pricing. Franchisors may have to accept such variations if its franchise network is to expand throughout the country.

1 Maximum price terms appear not to be permitted by the block exemption (article 5(a) and para 2.151).

7.53 Notice that the Business operates under licence[1]
7.53:1 To give notice in such places as the Franchisor may from time to time in writing require that the Business is operated under licence from the Franchisor [and is separate from the franchisor]

Notes
A framed notice in that part of the Location which is open to customers or suppliers stating that the Franchisee is a licensee of the Franchisor and independent of the Franchisor is essential. If customers or suppliers do not frequent the Franchisee's business premises, then that statement should be displayed on the Franchisee's vehicles or other plant or machinery. A statement such as: 'John Doe an independent franchisee of Richard Roe' may be sufficient to constitute actual notice to third parties that they are not dealing with a household name but with a small business which is authorised to use that name (see clauses 7.25:1.16 and 7.61). Notices should comply with the requirements of the Business Names Act 1985—see para 6.24.

1 See block exemption article 4(c).

7.53:2 To procure that all stationery quotations orders invoices promotional material and advertisements shall include a statement that the Business is operated under licence from the Franchisor and such other information as the Franchisor may deem necessary to inform third parties that it does not accept liability for the acts debts or defaults of the Franchisee

Notes
The Manual should contain a requirement that all orders or quotations made by the Franchisee are confirmed in writing prior to acceptance of supplies or custom on paper which makes clear that the Franchisee is independent of the Franchisor.

7.54 Staff gratuities

To ensure so far as practicable that staff pay gratuities into a common pool and that the total of such gratuities shall be divided amongst the staff of the Business equally irrespective of their standing but excluding [the Franchisee *or* [partners *or* directors] of the Franchisee]]

Notes
This clause may, more appropriately, be inserted as a direction in the Manual. However, in some franchises the goodwill and performance of staff employed is so essential to the proper conduct of the Business that it should remain in the agreement.

7.55 Staff dress and appearance

To ensure that all staff engaged in the operation of the Business dress in [accordance with the regulations in the Manual *or* in the manner required by the Franchisor from time to time] and at all times present a neat and clean appearance and render competent sober and courteous service to customers in accordance with the procedure laid down in the Manual

7.56 No advertisement etc

[To procure that any advertisement or information display concerning the Business or the Franchisee complies with the standards laid down in the Manual *or* To procure that no advertisements signs entries in telephone directories or other forms of publicity whether relating to the Business or not shall be used in connection with the Business or displayed on or at the Location unless the same have first been submitted to and approved as to content form colour number location and size by the Franchisor or a previous consent in writing by the Franchisor has been given][1]

Notes
To be safe, a franchisor should set out approved advertising copy in the Manual. A franchisor should check with each of its franchisees the future local advertising programme.

1 See block exemption article 3(1)(g).

7.57 No slot machines

Not to permit vending equipment or gaming machinery or any slot machine of any description on or around the Location [(except as specifically authorised in writing by the Franchisor)]

Notes
Again, this clause may be inserted in the Manual.

7.58 No credit

7.58:1 Not to extend credit to customers without the prior written consent of the Franchisor but to sell only on delivery against payment terms
7.58:2 In the event of the Franchisor authorising credit to be extended to any particular customer to acknowledge the right of the Franchisor to stipulate for such increase in the price of the [Products *or* Services] as it thinks fit

Notes
Many franchisees, being new to dealing with customers, are tempted to stimulate turnover by supplying on credit terms. This can lead to severe cash flow problems and, when bad debts mount up, real financial difficulties.

7.59 Pay expenses

To pay all expenses of and incidental to the carrying on of the Business

Precedents

Notes
This is self-explanatory

7.60 No warranties
Not to make any representations to customers or to give any warranties other than those contained in any standard terms and conditions set out in the Manual

Notes
All supplies should be made under the terms of trade formulated by the Franchisor. Problems can arise in cases where a franchisee has issued a guarantee to a customer which exceeds those terms of trade. This creates dangers for not only the Franchisee but for the Franchisor (see paras 1.28 et seq, ante). The Manual should set out those terms of trade and stipulate that all quotations, invoices or orders are made on paper which contains or refers to them (see clause 7.53:2).

7.61 Act as principal
In all correspondence and other dealings relating directly or indirectly to [the sale or other dispositions of the [Products *or* Services] *or* the Business] clearly to indicate that it is acting as principal

Notes
See clause 7.53:1.

7.62 Not to tamper with Products
To sell the Products in the same condition as that in which it receives them and not to alter or remove or tamper with them or any markings or name plates or indications of the source of origin on them or any packaging supplied by the Franchisor

Notes
A more detailed treatise on the handling of the Products may be set out in the Manual.

7.63 Insurance
7.63:1 To obtain and keep in full force and effect at all times a policy or polices of insurance covering public liability for injury to persons or property with policy limits and provisions conforming to such requirements as the Franchisor may from time to time prescribe

7.63:2 To deliver to the Franchisor copies of all applicable insurance policies taken out pursuant to the provisions of this Agreement [and to ensure that the Franchisor [and its other franchisees of the Method] shall be entitled to the benefit of such insurance]

Notes
The actual details of the required policy should be set out in the Manual. The Franchisor should have arranged a standard policy with an insurer which will give favourable terms to the franchisees of the Franchisor. Franchisees should check who gets the commission. As mentioned previously in these clause commentaries, insurance cover for the Franchisor against claims by customers of its franchisees may be difficult to obtain through the medium of a policy taken out by each franchisee. It may be easier for the Franchisor to obtain its own insurance covering the acts or defaults of its franchisees and any consequent claims against it. However, in the interests of the good name and stability of the franchise network, third party liability insurance should be taken out by each franchisee to protect itself.

7.64 No breach of insurance policies
Not to cause or permit any breach of any insurance policy maintained under the provisions of this Agreement

Notes
The Franchisee must comply with the terms of any relevant insurance policy. This is important if the Franchisor intends to rely upon that insurance for some of his own protection against the consequences of successful third party claims.

7.65 Insurer to notify late payment of premium
To note on all policies maintained by the Franchisee in accordance with the provisions of this Agreement [the interest of the Franchisor and] that the insurer shall notify the Franchisor in the event of the late payment of any premium by the Franchisee

Notes
If the Franchisee is responsible for maintaining his own insurance, the Franchisor must be satisfied that such insurance is in full force and effect.

7.66 Credit Limit
Not to attempt to exceed the Credit Limit in any way

Notes
Franchisees often attempt to exceed their own credit limits with the Franchisor, especially if they are insufficiently capitalised to cope with rapidly increasing turnover. The Franchisor must recognise this tendency and discuss with the Franchisee the problems of apparent success. The Franchisee or its bankers should be encouraged to commit more funds to the Business. In addition, it should be explained to the Franchisee that attempting to buck the system is both inefficient, time-wasting and unfair to the Franchisor and his fellow franchisees. The Franchisor should not be afraid to tell the Franchisee that it does not have unlimited funds to finance the expansion of the Franchisee. Capital resources are the responsibility of the Franchisee in his relationship with the Franchisor.

7.67 Set-off
Not to set off for any reason any money payable by the Franchisee to the Franchisor [for supplies of the Products *or* under this Agreement]

Notes
The Franchisor cannot risk any set-off claim by a disgruntled franchisee. This clause may entitle the Franchisor to obtain summary judgment against a franchisee for fees or other payments owed whilst defending other claims from that franchisee.

7.68 VAT[1]
7.68:1 Wherever applicable to pay to the Franchisor VAT or any tax or duty additional to or replacing the same during the Term charged or calculated on the amount of the Initial Fee [the Minimum Fee] the Continuing Fees the Advertising Contribution [and the Insurance Premium] or other payment made by the Franchisee to the Franchisor under the provisions of this Agreement

Notes
See para 4.08 et seq for discussion concerning VAT. A business format franchise will almost certainly be deemed to be a supply of services so that the fees payable by the Franchisee to the Franchisor will be subject to VAT.

1 The definition of 'Gross turnover' takes into account VAT—see clause 3.11.

7.68:2 Within 14 days of submission or receipt to supply to the Franchisor a copy of each return or assessment in respect of VAT or any other tax or duty additional to or replacing the same.

Notes
If the Franchisor suspects that its franchisee is sending it false sales returns, a comparison with the Franchisee's VAT return may show that the turnover of the Business is greater than the Franchisee has declared to the Franchisor. Filing false sales returns with the Franchisor may only entitle the Franchisor to its remedies under the agreement. Submitting

Precedents

false VAT returns to HM Customs and Excise is a criminal offence. Sight of any VAT assessments may also be illuminating for a Franchisor.

7.69 [Construction *or* conversion] of the Location

7.69:1 At its own cost and expense in accordance with the plans approved in writing by the Franchisor [to erect a building or structure on the site *or* to convert the premises] approved by the Franchisor for the carrying on of the Business

7.69:2 To take all reasonable steps to ensure that the works undertaken in accordance with the plans are completed within . . . [and if such works are not completed by that date otherwise than by force majeure or failure without fault of either party to obtain a necessary consent the Minimum Fee during the period of operation of the Business shall nevertheless be payable as from the expiration of that period without prejudice to the right of the Franchisor to terminate this Agreement for failure as stated above and to retain as liquidated damages all sums then paid by the Franchisee to the Franchisor]

7.69:3 Promptly to apply for and diligently to prosecute the obtaining of all necessary consents for [the construction of the building or structure *or* conversion of the premises] for the carrying on of the Business including consents for signs, hoardings, parking facilities, access ways and the like and to obtain the approval of police fire and any other relevant authority and all licences required to carry on the Business in a lawful manner

Notes

This clause may be more appropriate in the Franchise Purchase Agreement (see precedent 9, post). However, where the franchise is granted without such an agreement, clauses concerning the construction or conversion of the Location should be incorporated in the agreement. Most substantial franchises have a very detailed specification concerning design, construction, decoration, fitting and furnishing of the Location and a schedule of works should be agreed with the Franchisee.

8 Termination

This Agreement shall terminate:

8.1 Time

On the Expiry Date

8.2 Low orders

In the event that the Minimum Performance is not achieved [at any time *or* during the period stipulated in clause [10.32] of this agreement *or* these Conditions] *or* for [2] consecutive financial periods during the term. [provided that in such event the Franchisor at its discretion may require this agreement to continue and may treat such lack of achievement as an event to which [Clauses 10.3:2 to 10.3:4 (inclusive) shall apply *or* clause 10.32 shall apply]]

Notes

In a franchise in which reasonable turnover is crucial, the Franchisor may wish to impose a minimum performance obligation upon the Franchisee. This may be the case when the Products sold or Services supplied by the Business are fashionable or short life and have to be promoted vigorously. Franchisees should ensure that the period during which the Minimum Performance has to be achieved is sufficiently long to overcome slow start-up and any seasonal fluctuations. The proviso will apply if the Franchisor has the management capacity to take over the franchised business on a temporary basis.

8.3 Fundamental breach

On the occurrence of any of the following events which are fundamental breaches of this Agreement:

    8.3:1   failure to comply with the terms of any Default Notice (as defined by clause [9.3]) within the time stipulated

    8.3:2   failure to pay the [Minimum Fee *or* the continuing fees] on any of the relevant Payment Dates

    8.3:3   any breach by the Franchisee of clause [7.25 *or* 7.39] of this Agreement

    8.3:4   any assignment or other disposal of this Agreement [or the Location] by the Franchisee

    8.3:5   any challenge by the Franchisee to the validity of any part of the Intellectual Property[1]

1 See block exemption article 5(f) and clause 7.25:2.1, ante.

    8.3:6   (*specify other events*)

provided that the Franchisor may waive any breach of this Agreement by the Franchisee

Notes

This clause requires very careful consideration by the Franchisor and careful drafting by his solicitor. The Franchisor must set out a list of those acts or omissions on the part of any of its franchisees which may have a serious adverse effect upon the franchise business. For example, an adverse report by the health authorities concerning a restaurant outlet, or any wilful breach of copyright or disclosure of confidential documentation to third parties by an instant printer or dangerously faulty repairs to a vehicle in a vehicle repair franchise may warrant termination.

8.4 Insolvency

If the Franchisor goes into liquidation either compulsorily or voluntarily (save for the purpose of reconstruction or amalgamation) or if a receiver is appointed in respect of the whole or any part of its assets or if the Franchisee makes an assignment for the benefit of or composition with its creditors generally or threatens to do any of these things

Notes

Responsible franchisors try to avoid the liquidation or insolvency of a franchisee. That unfortunate state can arise because of circumstances not related to the Business, in which case it is virtually impossible for the Franchisor to assist the Franchisee except by arranging a speedy assignment of the Business. Where the Franchisee threatens or actually suffers insolvency because of matters arising in the Business, the Franchisor must try to assist the Franchisee for the good of the franchise network. A responsible Franchisor will meet with the creditors, bankers and customers of the Business. In many cases, the Franchisor will encounter hostility because the creditors and even bankers (who should know better) will blame the Franchisor and declare that they would never have supplied or lent to the Franchisee if he had not been a franchisee of the Franchisor. This hostility will increase if the Franchisor terminates the agreement and forfeits any lease or sub-lease of the Location, thereby depriving those creditors or lenders of some chance of recovering their money. The fairest procedure is to try to arrange a sale. This may not be possible if the Business has not traded successfully. If there is no prospect of a sale, the Franchisor may, after termination and forfeiture, trade from the Location itself. That is the time when creditors are likely to threaten action against the Franchisor on the grounds that they were unaware that they were dealing with an independent person (the Franchisee) rather than the Franchisor. The Franchisor will have to rely upon the actual notice given by the Franchisee to his creditors (ie the declaration that the Franchisee is independent on all notepaper, invoices and quotations and a notice to that effect on display in the Location) (see para 5.43 et seq, ante).

Precedents

8.5 Conduct prejudicial
If the Franchisee engages in any conduct prejudicial to the Business [or the marketing of the [Products *or* Services]] generally

Notes
This is a general clause. It may be too wide to be of much value in the case of a serious dispute but does provide an additional weapon when arguing with a franchisee.

8.6 Change of management or control
If any material change occurs in the management or control of the Business and in particular any change of directors [or shareholders] of the Franchisee save in accordance with the provisions of this Agreement

Notes
This clause is essential. However, even the Franchisor cannot prevent the Franchisee from dying! (See clause 10.3).

[8.7 Notice
If either of the parties gives to the other not less than . . . days' prior notice expiring [at any time not earlier than . . . years after the Commencement Date *or* on any Accounting Reference Date]]

Notes
This would be a most unusual clause in any business format franchise, although it does occur from time to time, particularly in badly managed franchises. If this clause is included neither party has any real certainty or security. The Franchisor cannot treat the asset of the franchise agreement as an addition to its balance sheet and the Franchisee may lose its investment in the Business if the agreement is terminated. Practitioners should advise their clients against the inclusion of this clause in the agreement.

8.8 Appointment of management
Whenever the Franchisor shall have the right to terminate this agreement it may act in the manner mentioned in sub-clause [10.32] until it actually so terminates the agreement

Notes
This refers to the appointment of management.

9 Termination consequences

9.1 Procedure
On the expiry or other termination of this Agreement the Franchisee undertakes:
    9.1:1   to dispose of all Products in hand in accordance with the Franchisor's directions
    9.1:2   to procure the transfer of the telephone [and telex and electronic mail] numbers of the Business to such person as the Franchisor directs
    9.1:3   to destroy all stationery used in the Business
    9.1:4   to return to the Franchisor all samples and publicity promotional and advertising material used in the Business
    9.1:5   to sign such notification of cessation of use of the Intellectual Property as is required by the Franchisor
    9.1:6   to return to the Franchisor all originals and copies of all documents and information in any form containing or covering in any way any part of the Intellectual Property
    9.1:7   immediately to cease carrying on the Business
    [9.1:8   to vacate the Location]

Franchise Agreement—Master Form

Notes
The procedure set out in this sub-clause is self-explanatory. The Franchisor must set out any other particular procedural matters which it wishes to include. If the Location is let by the Franchisor to the Franchisee, sub-clause 9.1:8 may be effective only if both parties have made an application to the relevant court to exclude the security of tenure provisions of the Landlord and Tenant Act 1954, Part II.

9.2 Financial consequences

... days prior to the expiry of the Term or ... days after the receipt of notice terminating this Agreement the Franchisee shall furnish to the Franchisor a complete and accurate up-to-date stock check with estimates of turnover of the Business to such date and not later than ... days after such date pay to the Franchisor any sums due under this Agreement

Notes
The Franchisor will wish to secure at least a reasonable proportion of the final fees due to it on expiry or termination of the Agreement. The last instalments of fees are often difficult to collect when a franchisee does not wish to renew the Term or the Agreement has been terminated. This clause may persuade the Franchisee to make some payment, at least enough to make litigation not worthwhile.

9.3 Default Notice

In the event of a breach by the Franchisee of any of the provisions of this Agreement other than a fundamental breach specified in clause [8.3] the Franchisor may serve notice (a Default Notice) requiring the breach to be remedied within the time stipulated in that notice at the discretion of the Franchisor [but nothing in this clause shall require the Franchisor to serve notice of any breach before taking action in respect of it]

Notes
It is important that a franchisor may take remedial action without serving notice of breach. For example, where counterfeit or printed products are being sold by a franchisee, the Franchisor must be free to obtain an Anton Piller order and/or a Mareva injunction (if appropriate) without alerting the Franchisee. This clause leaves the period of the Default Notice at the discretion of the Franchisor. Other standard clauses stipulate a minimum period. Flexibility has advantages for the Franchisor because the period stipulated can distinguish between minor breaches and those which require an almost immediate remedy. However, that discretion is open to abuse and franchisees' solicitors should ask searching questions as to the length of notice given in the past by the Franchisor. In a new franchise there may be no such track record.

9.4 Existing rights

The expiry or termination of this Agreement shall be without prejudice to any rights which have already accrued to either of the Parties under this Agreement

Notes
This clause preserves the rights of both Parties.

10 Miscellaneous

10.1 Warranty of power to enter Agreement

Each of the parties warrants its power to enter into this Agreement

Notes
If one of the Parties does not have power to enter into the agreement it may be that it will not have power to make this warranty. However, if it is a company, the signatory to the agreement ostensibly acting on its behalf, may become personally liable if it does not have power to enter into the agreement.

Precedents

10.2 Warranty of title to Intellectual Property
The Franchisor warrants that it is [entitled to the Intellectual Property *or* authorised by the beneficial owner of the Intellectual Property to make the Grant]

Notes
This is a most important warranty. The solicitors for a franchisee, especially when a foreign franchise business is involved, should investigate the title and extent of the relevant intellectual property. If the Franchisor is licensed by the owner of that property, a copy of the licence should be produced (if necessary omitting the financial information) to the Franchisee. Sub-licenses of trade marks and service marks should not be accepted—see para 1.20. The term and the termination provisions should be compared with those contained in the franchise agreement.

[10.3 Change of directors or shareholders
In the event of the [death or retirement of any director *or* change of shareholders] of the Franchisee [the appointment of a replacement *or* the transfer to another shareholder] shall be subject to the prior approval of the Franchisor [which shall not be unreasonably withheld] and such [replacement *or* transferee] shall enter into such agreement to abide by the terms and conditions of this Agreement as may be required by the Franchisor]

Notes
This clause is important because the relationship between the Franchisor and the Franchisee depends upon the personalities on both sides. If the persons owning and operating a company franchisee change, then the Franchisor is acquiring a new franchisee in the shoes of the previous one. Where there is a non-assignment clause in the agreement, this clause prevents a 'back door' assignment. The second alternative clause is more detailed and, also, reflects the responsibility of the Franchisor in the case of illness, accident or death of a franchisee. The Franchisor should have the management capacity to help a franchisee in any of those events. What will occur in the case of illness, accident or death is an interesting pointer to the attitude and responsibility of the Franchisor. If, as in the case of this clause, the Franchisor has the right to 'intervene' then both the family of the Franchisee and other franchisees will be protected by the rights of the Franchisor, if it ever exercises that right.

or

[10.3 Death or incapacity
    10.3:1 In the event of the death of the Franchisee the personal representatives of the Franchisee shall have . . . days from the date of the death to notify the Franchisor of their decision:
        10.3:1.1 to continue the Business or
        10.3:1.2 to assign this Agreement to any beneficiary of the will or intestacy or to a third party
and in either case the provisions set out in clause [7.46] shall apply
    10.3:2 In the event of the incapacity of [the Franchisee *or* . . . (*the key director(s) of the Franchisee*)] at any time or in the event of such incapacity or his death (but prior to any sale transfer or assignment in accordance with clause [7.46] the Franchisor shall have the right to appoint personnel to supervise the conduct of the Business to ensure that the Business is operated in a satisfactory manner to preserve the goodwill associated with the Business pending the recovery of [the Franchisee *or* . . . (*the key director(s) of the Franchisee*)] or such assignment
    10.3:3 In the event of the incapacity of [the Franchisee *or* . . . (*the key director(s)* of the Franchisee)] lasting for a continuous period of . . . days or a total period of . . . working days the Franchisor may require the Franchisee

Franchise Agreement—Master Form

to dispose of the Business whereupon the provisions of clause [7.46] of this Agreement shall apply

10.3:4 If so requested by the Franchisee or the personal representatives of the Franchisee the Franchisor may act as a non-exclusive agent for the sale of the Business and in such event shall be paid [a reasonable fee and its expenses *or* a fee of . . . % of the total sales price and its reasonable expenses] for the same]

Notes
The fee payable to the Franchisor for arranging a sale of the franchised business should not exceed five per cent. Two–three per cent would be more usual. When a compulsory disposal clause will operate depends on the nature of the business and whether it can be run economically by managers rather than the Franchisee personally. For example, a large service business may not depend upon the Franchisee (or its key directors) for day-to-day running. A small 'momma and poppa' restaurant cannot justify a manager on top of a living for the Franchisee. The smaller the business the more important a clause in the form of clause 10.3:2.

10.4 Sale of the Business

10.4:1 If at any time the Franchisee wishes to sell transfer assign or otherwise part with the Business or any part of it or the Location or any interest in it it shall immediately give notice of that desire to the Franchisor and offer by notice in writing to the Franchisor to sell the same to the Franchisor

10.4:2 If the Franchisor accepts such offer within 28 days the Franchisee shall sell and the Franchisor shall purchase the assets included in such offer for the consideration and on the conditions ascertained as set out below and the sale and purchase of such assets shall be completed within . . . . . . of the date of acceptance or the date on which the price becomes ascertained if later

10.4:3 The price and the conditions of such sale and purchase shall be as agreed between the parties the price representing the net market value of the assets to be sold [but without taking into account goodwill or any additional value arising from a sale of the Business as a going concern] and the conditions shall be such as in the circumstances would be normal and reasonable and in the event of a failure to agree on the price and conditions these shall be settled by a chartered accountant chosen by the parties or (in the event of a failure to agree on the choice of a chartered accountant within 14 days) by the President for the time being of the Institute of Chartered Accountants in England and Wales and such chartered accountant shall act as an expert and not as an arbitrator and his decision shall be conclusive and binding on the parties and the costs of such chartered accountant in certifying as above shall be shared equally by the parties

10.4:4 Upon sale or transfer by the Franchisee of any part of the Business or of the Location the rights of the Franchisee in so far as they relate to such assets so disposed of shall terminate but without prejudice to the existing obligations of the Franchisee

10.4:5 If within 28 days of the receipt of such notice the Franchisor has not indicated to the Franchisee its acceptance of such offer the Franchisee shall be free within three months of such notice to sell transfer assign lease or sublet or otherwise part with the Business or any part of it or the Location or any part of its interest in them as set out in the notice to the Franchisor [and clause 7.46 shall apply]

10.4:6 No third party who acquires the Business or any part of it or the Location or any interest in any of them shall have disclosed to him the contents

Precedents

of the Manual or any part of it nor shall he be entitled to operate under the Permitted Name the Trade Name or by the Method or any part of it unless such person has been approved by the Franchisor and has agreed to be bound by the terms and conditions of the standard franchise agreement used by the Franchisor at the time for a period not less than the residue of the Term (including any option to extend the Term) in accordance with the provisions of this Agreement

10.4:7 The Franchisee shall pay to the Franchisor the reasonable costs and expenses incurred by the Franchisor in the assessment of any and each person for approval under clause [10.4:6]

Notes
It is important that the Franchisor has the right to buy a franchised outlet if a franchisee wishes to sell. If the Franchisor is successful in generating cash surpluses, it may want to convert franchises into company-owned businesses. A first refusal clause (10.4:1) will provide the opportunity to do so. At the same time, the Franchisee may have the benefit of a quick and easy sale. The procedure set out in clause 10.4 for the valuation of the business may appear cumbersome. In practice both sides have a reasonable opinion of the value of the business, possibly because of sales of franchises in the open market or because of sales of non-franchised businesses in the locality. In a retail shop-based franchise, the value of the goodwill of the franchised business may not much exceed the bare premium value of the lease of the shop such is the present demand for retail outlets in favoured locations. The same now applies to restaurant franchises. Other franchised businesses, particularly those with very few fixed assets are much more difficult to value. The Franchisee should establish what the fees are of the Franchisor for vetting prospective assignees of the business. If the Franchisor is the lessor of the Location, the Franchisee should establish whether a discount will be claimed by the Franchisor because of the terms of the lease (see para 6.03 enquiry 84).

10.5 Cheques

The Franchisee shall be entitled to pay any cheques received in payment only of accounts rendered by the Franchisee in which the payee is (*insert name of franchised business*) into his own bank account and where necessary for this purpose only the Franchisee shall have the Franchisor's authority to indorse such cheques to the same extent as if the Franchisor were payee of them provided

10.5:1 that the drawer's name and address or cheque card number is recorded on the reverse side

10.5:2 The Franchisor shall not be liable for such cheques in the event of such endorsement

Notes
The Franchisee will have satisfied its bankers that it is entitled to receive cheques drawn in favour of the franchise trade name. Its bankers will wish to see a copy of the franchise agreement and, even with this clause included, may wish to hold a separate letter of authority from the Franchisor. It is essential that the authority to endorse cheques is limited solely to facilitating payments of cheques due to the Franchisee into the Franchisee's bank account.

10.6 Payment of fees

The Continuing Fees [the Advertising Contribution] and the Minimum Fee shall be payable notwithstanding that any of the intellectual Property of the Franchisor shall be invalid cease to exist or otherwise fail to protect the Franchisor or the Franchisee

Notes
Franchisees must satisfy themselves as to the validity of all necessary intellectual property and the title of the Franchisor to it. The impact of this clause will be only one of many serious implications for the Franchisee if any material part of the necessary Intellectual

Property is challenged. The consequences of a successful challenge could be: closure of the business; assimilation into a competing business run by the successful challenger; damages; possible criminal liability. The Intellectual Property will be one of the most important assets of the franchise. If all or part of it is lost, the Franchisee may face severe financial problems. It is, therefore, essential that all enquiries are made prior to commencing the business. This is especially important if the Intellectual Property is owned by an overseas holder (see para 6.03, enquiry 7 et seq).

10.7 Incorporation of Manual

All the provisions of the Manual (as amended or revised from time to time) or any new edition of it are incorporated into and form part of this Agreement as though fully set forth in it and in the event of any conflict between a term of this Agreement and a provision in the Manual this Agreement shall prevail

Notes

The Manual is the most valuable part of any franchise. It should contain the maximum assistance and advice to franchisees. It should also contain all the rules and regulations under which the franchise will operate. Much of the detail of those regulations is too complicated and too subject to change to include in an agreement which may have to endure for ten years. The Manual of an established franchise is almost unrecognisable in comparison to its Manual of a decade earlier. The house-style, the accounting procedures, employee regulations and a host of other subjects will all have been changed substantially. The Franchisee will rightly baulk at signing an agreement which contains this clause without first reading the Manual. The Franchisor will not wish to reveal the contents of the Manual until the Franchisee is, at least, bound by non-disclosure and non-competition covenants. The confidentiality clauses in franchise purchase agreements are important in this context (see para 3.118 et seq).

10.8 Franchisor's right to the Method

The Franchisee acknowledges the Franchisor's exclusive rights:

10.8:1 To the Method and all parts of it including without limitation all amendments and modifications to it and all advertising matter slogans and the like which may from time to time be used to promote the Method

10.8:2 To make such additions or modifications to the Method including the addition renewal or substitution of intellectual property rights as may from time to time appear to the Franchisor necessary to promote and improve the Method and to amend or revise the Manual accordingly

10.8:3 To use and license others to use the Method

10.8:4 To grant this licence

Notes

The Method will be set out in the Manual. It will be difficult to define the Method. Some parts of the business procedures of the franchise will be common to other businesses of its type or indeed common to all business enterprises. To that extent, the Method cannot be the exclusive property of the Franchisor. However, there will be parts of the Method which are exclusive to the franchise. The non-exclusive parts must be considered in the context of the exclusivity of the whole package of know how which forms the Method. It is important that the Method may be altered to suit changing circumstances. The Franchisor must be at liberty to license others to use the Method. At the same time the Franchisee must acknowledge the Franchisor's exclusive right to grant a licence to use the Method. This is intended to prevent the Franchisee claiming that others had rights to the Method. This clause should be read in conjunction with the 'feed back' clause (clause 7.43). The combination should prevent franchisees in concert cross-claiming that each other invented parts of the Method and that they have rights to part of it in priority to the Franchisor.

10.9 Other licences

10.9:1 The Franchisor may without liability to the Franchisee grant a licence to any entity in (*specify areas*) to [manufacture or sell the Products *or* provide

Precedents

the Services *or* use the Intellectual Property] or for any purposes except in direct competition with the Franchisee in the Business in the Territory

Notes
It is important that the Franchisor is at liberty to grant licences to third parties within the Territory to undertake work for the Franchisor without in any way infringing the territorial rights (if any) of the Franchisee. It is believed that this clause is consistent with the block exemption. See, however, para 2.46, ante.

10.9:2 The Franchisor (or any of its franchisees) using the Method may sell to customers through an outlet located outside the Territory without any liability to the Franchisee even if the supplies to any such customer are delivered into the Territory

Notes
This clause is intended to allow the Franchisor to operate a discretionary or flexible policy towards territories so that disputes can be resolved quickly. Franchisee neighbours can damage the goodwill of a franchise in an area if customers are subjected to competing claims and even threats from adjoining franchisees. The Franchisor must be able to impose its own views and not be faced with a franchisee strictly defending its territory.

10.10

10.10:1 The Franchisor and Franchisee mutually undertake and agree not to disclose to any unauthorised person any data the subject of the Data Protection Act 1984

10.10:2 The Franchisor and Franchisee mutually undertake and agree to apply for registration under the Data Protection Act 1984 either as 'data user' or 'computer bureau'

Notes
This clause will be required particularly when customer details are maintained on a computer.

10.11 Interest
All sums due from either of the parties to the other which are not paid on the due date (without prejudice to the rights of the Franchisor under this Agreement) shall bear interest from day to day at the annual rate of . . .% over the current . . . Bank plc daily base rate with a minimum of . . .% per year

Notes
The interest rate should be high enough to be a deterrent to late payers but not so high as to be extortionate.

10.12 Receipt
The receipt of money or payment by either of the parties shall not prevent either of them from questioning the correctness of any statement in respect of any such money

Notes
Both parties should have the right to adjust their accounts at a later date and not be bound strictly by any payment or receipt. This allows flexibility in the accounting and payment process and avoids strict liability being used as an excuse for late payment.

10.13 Force majeure
Both parties shall be released from their respective obligations in the event of national emergency war prohibitive governmental regulation or if any other cause beyond the control of the parties renders performance of the Agreement impossible whereupon:

10.13:1   all money due to the Franchisor shall be paid immediately and
10.13:2   the Franchisee shall forthwith cease carrying on the Business
[10.13:3   the Franchisor shall not be obliged to continue to [provide the Services *or* supply the Products stipulated in the Manual]

provided that this clause shall only have effect at the discretion of the Franchisor except when such event renders performance impossible for a continuous period of [364 days]

Notes
The Franchisor must ensure that the happening of an event covered by this clause does not give the Franchisee an automatic right to terminate the agreement. However, the Franchisee will be concerned, particularly when a Minimum Fee is payable, that the discretionary period is as short as possible. This is a matter of negotiation depending upon the nature of the business. In some circumstances, the requirement to cease the business may seem unnecessarily harsh but is essential so that franchisees cannot take advantage of a force majeur event by terminating the agreement and continuing to trade in the franchise name. Upon termination, the provisions of clause 9 will apply.

10.14   Severance

In the event that any provision of this Agreement [or these Conditions] is declared by any judicial or other competent authority to be void voidable illegal or otherwise unenforceable [or indications of the same are received by either of the parties from any relevant competent authority] [the parties shall amend that provision in such reasonable manner as achieves the intention of the parties without illegality or at the discretion of the Franchisor it may be severed from this Agreement and the remaining provisions of this Agreement shall remain in full force and effect unless the Franchisor decides that the effect of such declaration is to defeat the original intention of the parties in which event the Franchisor shall be entitled to terminate this Agreement by [30] days' notice to the Franchisee and the provisions of clause [9] shall apply accordingly]

Notes
The Franchisor must have the sole right to sever an offending clause to terminate the agreement. If the relationship between the Franchisor and its franchisees is good then it may be possible to amend the agreement to achieve what was intended. However, if the relationship is poor, the Franchisor will be faced with opportunistic attempts to amend the agreement to the advantage of the Franchisee. The Franchisee's advisers must ponder what parts of the agreement are most likely to be offensive to national or international regulations. The Franchisee should be advised which areas may be subject to attack and what changes may be forced upon the franchise chain as a result. If, for example, territorial rights become unenforceable, the Franchisee may have to face competition from other franchisees or even the Franchisor. If the Franchisor is foreign, the method of payment may become subject to deduction of tax or be subject to exchange control.

[10.15   Retention of title

10.15:1   The Products and any other goods delivered by the Franchisor to the Franchisee shall remain the sole and absolute property of the Franchisor as legal and equitable owner until such time as all money due to the Franchisor has been paid to the Franchisee but shall be at the Franchisee's risk from the time of delivery to it

10.15:2   The Franchisee acknowledges that it is in possession of all such goods as bailee for the Franchisor until such time as they are delivered to a purchaser under the terms of this Agreement

10.15:3   Until delivery to a purchaser the Franchisee undertakes to store such goods on its premises separately from its own goods or those of any other

Precedents

person and in a manner which makes them readily identifiable as the Franchisor's goods

10.15:4 The Franchisee's right to possession of such goods shall cease if it does anything or fails to do anything which would entitle a receiver to take possession of any assets or which would entitle any person to present a petition for the winding up of the Franchisee

10.15:5 The Franchisor may for the purpose of examination or recovery of its goods enter upon any premises where they are stored or where they are reasonably thought to be stored

10.15:6 The entire proceeds of such goods shall be held in trust for the Franchisor and shall not be mingled with any other money paid into any overdrawn bank account and shall at all times be identifiable as the Franchisor's money

10.15:7 The Franchisee warrants that it is not at the time of entering into this Agreement insolvent and knows of no circumstance which would entitle any creditor to appoint a receiver or to petition for winding up or to exercise any other rights over or against its assets]

Notes
There is some doubt concerning the extent of the effectiveness of general retention of title clauses. In the light of that doubt, this clause must be related to the specific business systems of the franchise. A solicitor for the Franchisor must become familiar with the supply side of his client's business. Only then may he attempt to draft a retention of title clause. In the case of corporate franchises, the charge created will usually need to be registered under section 395 of the Companies Act. Clause 10.15 is set out for illustration purposes only. The Franchisor must protect itself against the consequences of the insolvency of any of its franchisees. It is difficult to negotiate with a hostile franchisee when that franchisee owes money to the Franchisor for supplies and there is no retention of title clause.

10.16 Reservation of rights
[All rights not specifically and expressly granted to the Franchisee by this Agreement are reserved to the Franchisor]
or
[The Franchisor reserves the right notwithstanding anything to the contrary contained in this Agreement

10.16:1 to decline any order or to submit any quotation or tender on any inquiry transmitted to the Franchisor by the Franchisee

Notes
The Franchisee must be concerned to ensure continuity of essential supplies from the Franchisor. The Franchisor must not be strictly obliged to make supplies because any failure to maintain supplies may expose it to damages claims (see also clause 4.2).

10.16:2 to [continue to] sell and supply the Products [under the Trade Name] direct to [its existing] customers in the Territory [whose names and addresses are set out in Schedule . . .]

Notes
This clause will only apply if the Franchisor has already been trading in the Territory. Some care is needed in the use and application of this clause because whilst the territorial restriction contained in the agreement (clause 6.28) is limited to the definition of the Business (clause 3.3) which restricts the restraint on the Franchisor to the business as conducted under the franchise trade name, this clause may extend the restriction by implication beyond that limited restraint unless the supply of the Products is linked to the Trade Name.

Franchise Agreement—Master Form

[10.16:3 in the event of any delay in payment by the Franchisee to the Franchisor of any money due to the Franchisor to
   10.16:3.1 reduce the Credit Limit to whatever amount the Franchisor considers appropriate
   10.16:3.2 cease accepting orders from and the supply of [Products *or* Services] to the Franchisee or any of its customers]]

Notes
This clause is intended to prevent franchisees using the Franchisor as an unlimited banking facility. The power to cut off supplies in a product-based franchise is very important, especially if the franchise is part of a dealership or the franchisees obtain all their main products from the Franchisor. The power in this clause only applies to late payment by the Franchisee. Franchisees' solicitors should check that it will not apply in other circumstances (and see clause 10.31 post).

10.17 Whole agreement
The Franchisee acknowledges that this Agreement [and these Conditions] contain the whole agreement between the parties and it has not relied upon any oral or written representation made to it by the Franchisor or its employees or agents and has made its own independent investigations into all matters relevant to the Business

Notes
Franchisees' solicitors should question the scope of this clause. Where full enquiries have been made by those solicitors, they should insist that replies to those enquiries are not negated by the clause.

10.18 Supersedes prior agreements
This Agreement supersedes any prior agreement between the parties whether written or oral and any such prior agreements are cancelled as at the Commencement Date but without prejudice to any rights which have already accrued to either of the parties

Notes
This clause applies to the Confidentiality Agreement and the Franchise Purchase Agreement and any other arrangements between the parties prior to the Commencement Date. Franchisees' solicitors must ask their clients to provide all correspondence between them and the Franchisor and set out the contents of important negotiations between the parties. The effect of this clause can then be assessed.

10.19 Discretion
No decision exercise of discretion judgment or opinion or approval of any matter mentioned in this Agreement or arising from it shall be deemed to have been made by the Franchisor except if in writing and shall be at its sole discretion unless otherwise expressly provided in the Agreement

Notes
This clause should be noted by franchisees. Any variation of the franchise arrangements will be at the sole discretion of the Franchisor. This means that a 'reasonableness' test may not apply to decisions of the Franchisor except where expressly stated in the franchise agreement. The Franchisor will be able to exercise firm management of the franchise network but franchisees will have little influence over its decisions.

10.20 Change of address
Each of the parties shall give notice to the other of change or acquisition of any address or telephone, fax, telex [electronic mailbox] or similar number as soon as practicable and in any event within 48 hours of such change or acquisition

Precedents

Notes
In most franchises, the address of the franchisee will be the Location. Franchisees' solicitors should, when the Franchisor is a subsidiary of a foreign Franchisor, obtain confirmation that the Franchisor will not be moved abroad.

10.21 Notices
Any notice to be served on either of the parties by the other shall be sent by prepaid recorded delivery or registered post or by fax telex or by electronic mail and shall be deemed to have been received by the addressee within 72 hours of posting or 24 hours if sent by fax, telex [or by electronic mail] to the correct fax, telex number (with correct answerback) [or correct electronic mail number] of the addressee

Notes
The service of notice by the Franchisor should follow this clause strictly. Any notice not served in accordance with this clause but acted upon by the Franchisor may expose the Franchisor to a potential damages claim from a franchisee which may have suffered loss as a result of the cessation of supplies or other actions by the Franchisor. The staff of a Franchisor must be made aware of the importance of this clause and should not fire off notices without consulting its solicitors.

10.22 Headings
Headings contained in this Agreement are for reference purposes only shall not be incorporated into this Agreement and shall not be deemed to be any indication of the meaning of the clauses and sub-clauses to which they relate

Notes
This clause should be deleted if headings are not used. If the preferred layout of the printed document uses marginal notes, then the word 'headings' should be replaced with the words 'marginal notes'.

10.23 Joint and several
All agreements on the part of either of the parties which comprises more than one person or entity shall be joint and several

Notes
Franchisees should be made aware of the effect of this clause. If one of a partnership franchisee is a 'sleeping' or financial partner only, his potential liability under the franchise agreement and any related deed of guarantee must be explained. This is essential if the working partner has few assets and is unlikely to be able to meet his share of losses if the franchised business suffers problems.

10.24 Gender
The neuter singular gender throughout this Agreement shall include all genders and the plural and the successors in title to the parties

10.25 No partnership
The parties are not partners or joint venturers nor is the Franchisee to act as agent of the Franchisor save as authorised by this Agreement

Notes
Both the Franchisor and franchisees must be made aware that this clause may not protect either of them from the claims of third parties. A franchisor may find it difficult to defeat claims against it if the other protections suggested in this book are not implemented.

10.26 Franchisor's right to assign and novation
    10.26:1 This Agreement and all rights under it may be assigned or transferred by the Franchisor
    10.26:2 In the event of any such assignment in consideration of the Franchisor

Franchise Agreement—Master Form

procuring in favour of the Franchisee and other franchisees of the Method an undertaking from the assignee to be bound by the Franchisor's obligations under this agreement the Franchisee shall in favour of such assignee agree in writing to be bound by the terms of this Agreement

10.26:3 If required to do so by the Franchisor or the Assignee the Franchisee shall re-execute this Agreement

Notes
Franchisees may be reluctant to accept this clause. However it has proved of benefit when a franchisor has experienced financial difficulties. Because its franchise agreements have been assignable, the whole franchise network has been kept together and placed under the ownership of another. Provided the new owner is an experienced franchisor or has the benefit of the Franchisor's management, franchisees will benefit because their businesses can continue undisturbed. When no assignment is possible, often the chain breaks up causing losses to all parties. The novation provisions in 10.26:2 and 3 are necessary because an assignment only transfers the benefit of a contract.

10.27 Proper law and jurisdiction

10.27:1 This Agreement shall be governed by [English] law in every particular including formation and interpretation and shall be deemed to have been made in [England]

10.27:2 Any proceedings arising out of or in connection with this Agreement may be brought in any court of competent jurisdictions in [London]

10.27:3 The submission by the parties to such jurisdiction shall not limit the right of the Franchisor to commence any proceedings arising out of this Agreement in any other jurisdiction it may consider appropriate

10.27:4 Any notice of proceedings or other notices in connection with or which would give effect to any such proceedings may without prejudice to any other method of service be served on any party in accordance with clause [10.21]

10.27:5 In the event that the Franchisee is resident outside [England] its address for service in [England] shall be the address for such service nominated in clause [1] of this Agreement and any time limits in any proceedings shall not be extended by virtue only of the foreign residence of the Franchisee

Notes
The Franchisor will want the court to be located close to it. This can cause expense and inconvenience to franchisees who are located in Scotland or Northern Ireland, if the Franchisor is resident in England.

10.28 Survival of terms

No term shall survive expiry or termination of this Agreement unless expressly provided

Notes
Each clause in the agreement must be read in the light of this clause.

10.29 Waiver

The failure by the Franchisor to enforce at any time or for any period any one or more of the terms or conditions of this Agreement shall not be a waiver of them or of the right at any time subsequently to enforce all terms and conditions of this Agreement

Notes
This clause enables the Franchisor to be more flexible in the early years of the franchise, particularly in relation to extra-territorial trading by franchisees.

Precedents

10.30 Costs
Each of the parties shall pay the costs and expenses incurred by it in connection with this Agreement

Notes
The costs of the Franchisor should be covered by the Initial Fee.

[10.31 Payment not on time
In the event that the Franchisee fails to pay any money due to the Franchisor on time the Franchisor may:

10.31:1   cease immediately to take orders from and to deliver goods and services to the Franchisee

10.31:2   thereafter impose whatever credit limit it considers appropriate in respect of the Business of the Franchisee]

Notes
See also clause 10.16.

10.32 Low sales
The Franchisor may terminate this Agreement in the event that the Minimum Performance arising from the Business at the Location is not achieved within two years of the Commencement Date of this Agreement or for a continuous period of twelve months at any time thereafter during the term provided that the Franchisor shall have the right (but not the duty):

10.32:1   then to appoint management personnel to supervise the Business at the expense of the Business to assist the Franchisor to increase sales and

10.32:2   to reduce the area of the Territory in proportion to such sales

Notes
This is a very important clause. The Franchisor must provide evidence concerning the projections produced by it for the Business. If a Minimum Performance clause is included in the agreement, a franchisee must know that the mandatory performance is based upon reliable data and is achievable in the area of the Territory. The performance estimate should be conservative. The consequences for a franchisee of not achieving the targets may be serious. The appointment of managers by the Franchisor may increase losses or may reduce profits as a result of the fees charged. A reduction in Territory may reduce the value of the franchise and may make it more difficult for the Franchisee to sell.

Franchise application form**10.33   New outlets**

10.33:1   In the event that the Franchisor decides that the Territory is sufficiently large geographically and has a sufficiently large population to justify one or more further outlets for the Business in the Territory it may notify the Franchisee of such decision and on receipt of such notice the Franchisee shall have the right to open such further outlet elsewhere than at the Location (in an area of the Territory nominated by the Franchisor) provided that the Franchisee informs the Franchisor within [90] days of such notice of its agreement to do so

10.33:2   In the event that the Franchisee fails to notify the Franchisor of such agreement within [90] days or in the event of such notification fails to open such further outlet in the Territory within [six] months of such notice from the Franchisor the Franchisor shall have the right to reduce the Territory to enable it to provide an exclusive area in which a new franchisee may trade using the Method and the Intellectual Property without any liability to the Franchisee

Notes
Most franchisees want territorial certainty. In the early years of a successful franchise, the Franchisor may allocate territories which are too large and which cannot be serviced properly by franchisees. A Franchisor should be advised against allocating territories without a sub-division clause in the agreement. Otherwise the franchise will suffer from patchy cover throughout the country and from complacent franchisees. This clause is a compromise between the needs of both parties. It should be noted that the decision is at the discretion of the Franchisor. If the Franchisee in a large territory has been successful, he should have little difficulty in funding a second outlet, if requested to do so by the Franchisor.

10.34 Prior obligations
The expiration or termination of this Agreement shall not relieve either of the Parties of their prior respective obligations or impair or prejudice their respective rights against the other

Notes
Franchisees must be warned that the termination of the agreement will not necessarily close the book on their dealings with the Franchisor.

(If the Conditions are not a separate attachment the signatures of the parties should appear here)

SCHEDULE[S]
(Insert details as appropriate)

[Signed by [. . . on behalf of] the Franchisor
Signed by [. . . on behalf of] the Franchisee]

2
FRANCHISE APPLICATION FORM

CONFIDENTIAL
FRANCHISE APPLICATION FORM
SUBJECT TO CONTRACT

1 Name and address of applicant[s] . . . .
Telephone number . . . .
2 If the applicant is a company please provide a certified copy of the Certificate of Incorporation and of the Memorandum and Articles of Association of the company. (In the case of an applicant which is a company whose shares are freely traded on the London Stock Exchange or the Unlisted Securities Market, no replies need be given throughout this Form in connection with any of its shareholders.)
Please state:
2.1 Name and address of Chairman . . . .
2.2 Name and address and proposed role of all other directors . . . .
2.3 Name and address of all shareholders/investors and the proportions of their shareholding . . . .
2.4 What is (or will be) the issue share capital? . . . .
Enclose audited accounts of the company for the last three years (not required if company has been formed for this business).
3 Where is (or will be) the principal place of business of the applicant? . . . .
4 If this is different to the present correspondence address of the applicant, please provide details (including telephone numbers) of all business addresses of the applicant . . . .

Precedents

5   Please list all types of business in which the applicant has been engaged during the past five years. (If the applicant is a newly-formed company this question is not relevant) . . . .

6   Who will be in control of the day-to-day management of the franchised business? . . . .

7   Please provide a curriculum vitae for each applicant (or in the case of a company, for its directors and/or shareholders) and for any of the persons who will be in control of the day-to-day management of the company.

8   Please provide the names and addresses and a brief job experience résumé of all other management personnel or senior operatives who will be engaged in the business the subject of the Franchise.

9   Is the applicant or has the applicant been a licensee or franchisee of any other organisation? . . . .

10   Has the applicant (or in the case of a company, any of its directors, shareholders, subsidiary or affiliated or associated companies) ever applied for or achieved the registration of any design or trademark protection associated with the business the subject of the Franchise? If so, please provide full details . . . .

11   Please provide the names and addresses and references (if the applicant is a company, for the company itself and each of its directors and/or shareholders). (These references will only be taken up immediately prior to signature of a Franchise Purchase Agreement):

   11.1   Bankers . . . .
   11.2   Accountants . . . .
   11.3   Solicitors . . . .
   11.4   Three major traders (applicants only) (not necessary if company is newly-formed) . . . .

12   What funds (not borrowings) has the applicant available for this project? . . . .

13   Are the applicant's bankers (or other lenders) willing to make loans to the applicant? If so, how much? . . . .

14   Does the applicant require assistance with arranging finance for the project? . . . .

15   Has the applicant a suitable property for an outlet for the business? . . . .

16   In what geographical area is the applicant most interested? . . . .

17   Has the applicant (or if the applicant is a company, any of its shareholders or directors or managers) ever been made bankrupt or been a director or shareholder of a company which has been liquidated? If so, please provide full details of every case. . . . . . .

18   Has the applicant (or if the applicant is a company, any of its shareholders or directors) ever been convicted of a criminal offence involving dishonesty in any country? If so, please provide details of every case . . . .

Please note that all replies by the applicant[s] to inquiries made by the Franchisor in the course of discussions between the Franchisor and the applicant[s] will be treated by the Franchisor as representations which shall be important factors in any decision by the Franchisor whether or not to grant a franchise to the applicant[s] and, if any information disclosed by the applicant[s] to the Franchisor on this Form, or in the course of those discussions, is found to be incorrect or misleading, for any reason, the Franchisor will have the right to terminate any agreement between the Franchisor and the applicant[s] without any liability to the applicant[s].

Dated the . . . . . . day of . . . . . . 19 . . .

Signed . . . .

3
LETTER TO PROSPECTIVE FRANCHISEE ENCLOSING APPLICATION FORM[39]

To: CD of (*address*)

Dear. . . . . . .

Thank you for your recent inquiry. We have pleasure in enclosing our standard application form for completion by you. Please return it to us as soon as possible. Please note that this form is an application only and is confidential. Any information disclosed in the form will not be revealed to any other person outside our own organisation. Submission to you of a form is not to be taken to be any indication that this company will enter into any agreement with you.

We trust that this matter will proceed as quickly as possible and hope that we will be able to form a most satisfactory commercial relationship with you in the near future. Nothing in this letter or its enclosure shall constitute a contract.

Yours faithfully

(*signature*)
on behalf of AB plc

Note
The text of this letter could form a 'small print' section at the foot of a letter enclosing the franchise brochure and other literature, if its contents are considered to be too formal and reserved for an opening letter.

4
CONFIDENTIALITY AGREEMENT

Dated . . . . 19 . . . .

1 Parties

. . . . whose [registered office *or* principal place of business] is at (*address*) ('the Intending Franchisee') (1)

. . . . whose [registered office *or* principal place of business] is at (*address*) ('the Franchisor') (2)

2 Recitals

2.1 The Intending Franchisee wishes to become an actual franchisee of the Franchisor to engage in the Business

2.2 The Intending Franchisee needs finance to enable him to commence the Business

2.3 To raise that finance from third parties the Intending Franchisee requires to use the Information for incorporation in his business plan for presentation to potential financial sources for the Business of the Intending Franchisee

2.4 The Information is confidential and valuable and the Franchisor will not disclose the Information to any person other than its actual franchisees or persons

---

[39] See page 308, ante. For application form see precedent 2, ante.

Precedents

who have entered into agreements similar to this Agreement or financial sources who have been approved by the Franchisor
2.5 In addition to disclosure of the Information the Intending Franchisee requires the assistance of various members of the management of the Franchisor in the preparation of its business plan

3 Definitions

The following terms shall have the following meanings:
3.1 'Business': the business of (*insert description of the Business as in the Franchise Agreement*) to be carried on in the style and manner of the Franchise
3.2 'Deposit': (*state amount*)
3.3 'Franchise': the (*insert trade name*) Franchise
3.4 'Information': [Some of the] trade secrets and other confidential information concerning the Business and the Franchise which is the property of the Franchisor
3.5 'Term': [90] days from the date of this Agreement
3.6 'Territory': the geographical area of (*insert description of area*) [and shown edged red on the map attached to this Agreement]

4 Franchisor's obligations

In consideration of the payment of the Deposit by the Intending Franchisee to the Franchisor (receipt of which is acknowledged) and of and subject to the agreements warranties and undertakings on the part of the Intending Franchisee contained later in this Agreement the Franchisor agrees:
4.1 To disclose the Information to the Intending Franchisee immediately
4.2 During the Term to assist the Intending Franchisee to prepare his business plan
4.3 To check the business plan produced by the Intending Franchisee (but without any liability for its contents)
[4.4 Not to grant a franchise or open its own [store *or* outlet] in the Territory for the Business during the Term]

5 Intending Franchisee's obligations

In consideration of the agreements on the part of the Franchisor earlier in the Agreement the Intending Franchisee agrees with and warrants and undertakes to the Franchisor as follows:
5.1 Not to use the Information for any purpose other than for the preparation of his proposed business plan
5.2 Not at any time after this date to disclose any of the Information to any person without the prior written approval of the Franchisor
5.3 To make two copies of his business plan only unless permitted by the Franchisor in writing to make further copies
5.4 In the event that the Intending Franchisee fails for any reason to become an actual franchisee of the Franchisor.
    5.4:1 to destroy all records or copies of the Information and such business plan
    5.4:2 not to engage directly or indirectly in any business in the Territory

competing with the Business or likely to damage the surviving goodwill of the business for a period of two years from this date

5.5 That the intending Franchisee is not:
    5.5:1 directly or indirectly connected or associated in any way with any person or entity who or which is engaged or intends to become engaged in a business similar to the Business
    5.5:2 engaged in any discussions with or has an option to take up a franchise from such a person or entity

5.6 That the information disclosed by the Intending Franchisee to the Franchisor in his franchise application form and in any discussions with representatives of the Franchisor is true and correct

6 Further agreements

It is further agreed between the parties:

6.1 The Deposit shall not be repaid to the Intending Franchisee for any reason

6.2 In the event that the Intending Franchisee enters into a franchise purchase agreement with the Franchisor:
    6.2:1 the Deposit shall form part of the initial franchise fee (as defined in the franchise purchase agreement) then payable by the Intending Franchisee
    6.2:2 the franchise purchase agreement shall supersede this Agreement (except in the case of clauses [5.1 to 5.3 (inclusive) and 5.5, 5.6] of this Agreement which shall remain in full force and effect)

6.3 If the Intending Franchisee comprises more than one person their obligations under this Agreement shall be joint and several

6.4 Any description of the Intending Franchisee in this Agreement shall include the singular or plural and all genders

6.5 Any notice to be served on either of the parties by the other shall be sent by prepaid recorded delivery or registered post or by fax, telex or by electronic mail and shall be deemed to have been received by the addressee within 72 hours of posting or 24 hours if sent by fax, telex or by electronic mail to the correct fax or telex number (with correct answerback) or correct electronic mail number of the addressee
    6.5:1 Any proceedings arising out of or in connection with this Agreement may be brought in any court of competent jurisdiction in London
    6.5:2 The submission by the parties to such jurisdiction shall not limit the right of the Franchisor to commence any proceedings arising out of this Agreement in any other jurisdiction it may consider appropriate
    6.5:3 Any notice of proceedings or other notices in connection with or which would give effect to any such proceedings may without prejudice to any other method of service be served on any party in accordance with clause [6.5]

Signed by [. . . . . . on behalf of] the Intending Franchisee
Signed by [. . . . . . on behalf of] the Franchisor

Precedents

5

PROSPECTUS INVITING SUBSCRIPTIONS FOR SHARES IN A COMPANY FRANCHISEE

PROSPECTUS

.... (*name of Franchise*)
.... (*name of Company Franchisee*)

1 A copy of this Prospectus having attached to it copies of the documents referred to in this document has been delivered to the Registrar of Companies for registration.

2 This Prospectus is issued in respect of the shares described later in this document.

3 The directors of ..... (trading as [..... (*trade name*) *or* ..... Centrel]) have taken all reasonable care to ensure that the facts stated in this document are true and accurate and that there are no other material facts the omission of which would make misleading any statement contained in this document whether of fact or of opinion.

Those directors collectively and individually accept responsibility accordingly.

4 No part of this issue has been underwritten. Without prejudice to the Companies Act 1985 Section 83, if the share capital of ..... (*insert proposed share capital the subject of the issue*) is not subscribed in full the amount of that capital subscribed for in response to this offer may be allotted in any event at the sole discretion of the directors of ..... (*name of Company Franchisee*).

5 No application has been made to any Stock Exchange for the listing of the proposed shares in this document. The directors do not intend to make such application at present. The issue and transfer of those shares will be subject to the approval of the directors.

6 If you require advice on this document you should consult your Solicitor, Accountant, Stockbroker, Bank Manager or other professional adviser.

7 The procedure for acceptance of this offer is set out in Appendix IV of this document. The subscription list for the shares now being issued will open to the public at ..... (*address of* [licensed dealer or stockbroker]) [and at ..... (address of bankers)] on ..... 19 .. or at any time afterwards at the sole discretion of the directors of ..... (*name of Company Franchisee*).

8 A form of application for the shares is set out in Appendix IV. Further forms are obtainable from ..... (*name of licensed dealer*).

[9 The directors consider that the investment in shares in ..... (*name of Company Franchisee*) as a result of this prospectus may be eligible for tax relief under the relevant provisions of the [Finance Acts *or* Business Expansion Scheme]. Any potential investor seeking to take advantage of this relief should take professional advice before subscribing. The directors confirm that they will not knowingly undertake anything which may cause the investment in the shares to cease to qualify for that relief.]

1 Definitions

The following terms shall have the following meanings:

1.1 'BFA': the British Franchise Association

1.2 'Business': the business of [the retail sale of business equipment and systems as described in the Contract]

1.3 'Company': ..... (*name of Company Franchisee*) registered in [England] whose

Prospectus inviting subscriptions

registered number is ..... and whose registered office is at ..... (*address*) and which is incorporated [in England under the Companies Act 1985]
1.4 'Contract': the proposed Franchise Agreement between the Franchisor and the Company (See Section 7 Page . . .)
1.5 'Directors': the executive and non-executive directors of the Company described in this document (See Section 2 Page . . .)
1.6 'Franchise': the ..... (*name of Franchise*) Franchise
1.7 'Franchisor': ..... (*name of Franchisor*) whose registered office is at ..... (*address*)
1.8 'Issue': the issue of the Shares in the Company which is the subject of this document
1.9 'Premises': the premises set out in Section 9 Page . . .
1.10 'Shares': the ..... (*number of shares to be issued*) ordinary voting shares of [£1.00] each in the Company the subject of this document
1.11 'Territory': the geographical area in which the Company may conduct the Business under the Contract (See Section 8 Page . . .)
1.12 'Viewing': the inspection of the documents referred to in this Prospectus at ..... (*address of licensed dealer*) (See Section 8 of Appendix II) between ..... 19 . . and ..... 19 . . (inclusive) between 9.00 am and 5.00 pm

2 Directors

2.1 The following persons are the executive directors of the Company: (*give name and address, role in the Company, age, Shares in the Company and other relevant details*) ....
2.2 The following persons are the non-executive directors of the Company (*give above details*) ....
[2.3 Certain of the Directors have indirect shareholdings in the Company through companies in which they have a material interest (see Section 4 of Appendix II Page . . .)]
[2.4 All of the Directors are British Subjects *or* the following Directors are ..... subjects]

3 Professional advisers

(*Give names and addresses of the advisers*)
3.1 Bankers ....
3.2 Auditors [and Reporting Accountants] ....
3.3 Solicitors to the Company [and to the Issue] ....
[3.4 Licensed Dealers .....]

4 Secretary [and Registrar]

(*Give relevant details*)

5 Background information

(*Give general outline of market, Franchisor's specialist knowledge, existing competitors, potential sales figures etc*)

Precedents

6 General details relating to the Franchisor and the Franchise

(Give relevant details eg)
[6.1 On . . . . 19 . . the Franchisor was incorporated.
[6.2 A number of institutions have invested or arranged for their clients to invest in the Franchisor.]
6.3 The issued share capital of the Franchisor amounts to £ . . .
6.4 Since the Franchisor commenced trading it has opened:
    6.4:1 its head office, area sales centre, [main engineering department] and warehouse at . . . . *(address)*
    6.4:2 an outlet at . . . . *(address)* on . . . . 19 . .
6.5 The Franchisor intends to continue opening its own outlets at strategic locations throughout [the United Kingdom] in order to create centres which will cooperate with [stores *or* outlets owned by its franchisees].
6.6 Locations where stores are being fitted out are *(give addresses)* . . . .
6.7 The following franchised outlets have been opened *(give addresses and dates of opening)* . . . .
6.8 Franchisees are fitting out stores in the following area *(give addresses)*
6.9 A large number of other locations in the United Kingdom are considered of sufficient size to justify an [outlet].
[6.10 The Franchisor is a member of the BFA and subscribes to its code of ethical franchising]
6.11 In response to the demands of the market, the Franchisor has set up a retail business which [sells equipment and systems to multi-national corporations and to small businessmen *or (set out description of business)*] and which provides the following services to its customers *(set out)* . . . .
6.12 *(Set out other services, advantages etc eg product testing, training courses etc)*]

7 Contract

(Describe contract in detail eg)
[7.1 The parties to the Contract are the Franchisor and the Company.
7.2 In brief, the commercial terms of the Contract are:
    7.2:1 an initial franchise fee of £ . . (. . . pounds) is payable on signature;
    7.2:2 continuing franchise fees of . . . % of turnover (net of VAT) are payable monthly;
    7.2:3 a contribution to the advertising and promotional programmes of the Franchisor of . . . % of such turnover is payable at the same time;
    7.2:4 the term of the Contract is . . . years [with an option on the part of the Company to renew it for a further . . . years].
7.3 Some of the obligations of the Franchisor are:
    7.3:1 to train the personnel of the Company;
    7.3:2 to arrange the supply of products to the Company on the same terms as those products are supplied to the Franchisor itself;
    7.3:3 to advertise and promote the Business using the fund created by the advertising contributions (including those from its own stores);
    7.3:4 to supply and update from time to time an operations manual providing comprehensive information about and systems for the conduct of the Business.
7.4 Some of the obligations of the Company as franchisee are:
    7.4:1 not to compete with the Business;
    7.4:2 to trade only within its allotted Territory;

Prospectus inviting subscriptions

7.4:3 to conduct the Business only in the style and manner stipulated by the Franchisor.
7.5 The Contract contains strict and comprehensive reporting obligations on the part of the Company.
7.6 In addition, the Franchisor has the right to inspect the Premises and the books of the Company and to appoint its own management to run the Business, if the Company falls below reasonable performance standards.
7.7 The auditors of the Company are nominated by the Franchisor [and are the Reporting Accountants for this issue].
7.8 The Contract may be inspected at the Viewing.
7.9 Products are supplied by the Franchisor to the Company on [21] days' credit (subject to review).
7.10 The obligations of the Company to the Franchisor under the Contract are guaranteed by certain of the [directors *or* shareholders] of the Company. [The guarantee may be inspected at the Viewing].

8 Territory

8.1 The Territory in which the Company [alone] is permitted to trade under the Contract comprises . . . .
8.2 A map of the Territory is shown in Section . . . Appendix . . .

9 Premises

9.1 The Premises comprise:
    9.1:1 a retail shop on the . . . floor of . . . square feet; (or describe premises if any)
    [9.1:2 training, office and engineering space on . . . floor[s] of . . . square feet in total.]
9.2 The lessor of the Premises is [the Franchisor as sublessor *or* . . . .(*name of landlord*)].
9.3 In brief, the commercial terms of the [lease *or* sublease] of the Premises are:
    9.3:1 Rent: £ . . . (. . . pounds) per year [exclusive];
    9.3:2 Term: . . . years from . . . . 19 . . (*commencement date of term of lease*);
    9.3:3 Reviews: every . . . year[s] of the term, the first review will arise on . . . . 19 . .;
    9.3:4 Other: [the usual full repairing and insuring obligations on the part of the lessee are included];
    9.3:5 Surrender: in the event that the Contract is terminated the Company is obliged to surrender its lease of the Premises to the Franchisor and the security of tenure afforded by statute has been excluded in that event.
9.4 The lease of the Premises may be inspected at the Viewing.
9.5 The premises are located (*state eg near public transport facilities, parking etc*)
[9.6 The premium payable on assignment of the lease of the Premises is £ . . . (. . . pounds).]
9.7 The shop-fitting and other works will cost approximately £ . . . (. . . pounds) to complete (including professional fees) and will take around . . . weeks from commencement.
[9.8 The Premises have been valued by . . . . (*name of valuers or estate*

Precedents

agents) of . . . . (*address*) (on the basis of all proposed shop-fitting and other works being completed) at £ . . . (. . . pounds) for the [leasehold] interest.]

10 Management and Staff

10.1 The executive directors of the Company will be in day-to-day control of the Business.

10.2 Those directors have relevant experience as follows (attach curriculum vitae for each):
    10.2:1 Managing Director . . . .
    [10.2:2 Sales Director . . . .]
    [10.2:3 Finance Director . . . .]

[10.3 Other senior management are (attach curriculum vitae for each):
    10.3:1 Store Manager . . . .
    [10.3:2 Sales Manager . . . .]
    [10.3:3 Service Manager . . . .]]

10.4 The Company intends to recruit the following additional employees:
    10.4:1 . . . sales staff;
    10.4:2 . . . part-time trainees;
    10.4:3 . . . engineers.

10.5 The total salary and ancillary costs are estimated to amount to:
    10.5:1 Directors' salaries: £. . . (*insert total salaries*) per year;
    10.5:2 Other management salaries, sales staff salaries and engineers' salaries: £. . . (*insert annual salaries plus National Insurance for each category*) per year;
    10.5:3 Sales staff commissions and trainers' fees (based upon the median level of the projections in the Sensitivity Analysis (see Section 3 Appendix III): £. . . (*state for each category*) per year.

10.6 In addition to the above costs, the following staff-related expenses are expected to be incurred:
    10.6:1 Cars: £. . . per year;
    10.6:2 Private health insurance: £. . . per year;
    10.6:3 Travel: £. . . per year.

10.7 The Company will operate a sales-related bonus scheme for [the managing and sales directors].

11 The Issue

11.1 The estimated net proceeds of previous allotments and the Issue will be £. . . (*insert total proposed issued capital*) (after deduction of expenses and capital duty in the region of £. . . (*insert total of fees, capital duty, commissions and any other costs*)).

11.2 Planned capital expenditure projects will absorb approximately £. . . made up as follows:
    11.2:1 Premium for the lease of the Premises: £. . .
    11.2:2 Refurbishment of the Premises (estimated) £. . .
    11.2:3 Fees for those works: £. . .

11.3 Secured loan and overdraft facilities with a limit of £. . ., subject to the Issue being successfully completed, are available to the Company from . . . Bank plc upon normal banking conditions. A letter of . . . . 19 . . confirming such facilities is available for inspection at the Viewing.

Prospectus inviting subscriptions

[11.4 In addition, a proportion of the [store and office] equipment will be leased. Leasing facilities up to a limit of £... are available to the Company from .... (*name of lessor*) upon normal terms.]

11.5 The balance of the proceeds of the Issue will be used to provide working capital for the Company.

11.6 The Directors are satisfied that having regard to the net proceeds of the Issue and to the banking [and leasing] facilities available to the Company, the Company will have sufficient funds to enable it to achieve its projected operations.

12 Dividend policy

12.1 The Directors will not consider the payment of dividends until the Company has:
    12.1:1 achieved profitability;
    12.1:2 eliminated any deficit incurred in previous financial periods on the profit and loss account;
    12.1:3 profits available for distribution as stipulated in the Companies Act 1985.

13 Accounting and statutory matters

13.1 The accounting reference date of the Company is .... 19..

13.2 A copy of the report by the Auditors and reporting accountants is set out in Sections 1 and 2 of Appendix I.

13.3 Statutory and general information is set out in Appendix II.

13.4 A projected balance sheet of the Company on the date when it commences the Business is set out in Appendix III Section 1.

13.5 A series of these annual projected balance sheets for the first three years of the Business are set out in Appendix III Section 2.

13.6 Projections with sensitivity analyses for the first three years are set out in Appendix III Section 3.

13.7 Cash flow projections based upon the median level in those profit/loss projections in Appendix III Section 2 are set out in Appendix III Section 4.

13.8 A summary of the audited accounts of the Company for the [period *or* month] ending .... 19.. is set out in Appendix III Section 5.

14 Business start-up

14.1 The Company expects to commence Business on .... 19...

14.2 Business will only commence when:
    14.2:1 the Company has acquired the necessary lease of the Premises;
    14.2:2 the necessary shop-fitting and other works are completed at the Premises;
    14.2:3 the Premises are approved by the Franchisor; provisional approval was set out in a letter from the Franchisor of .... 19... That letter may be inspected at the Viewing.
    14.2:4 sufficient funds have been received by the Company to enable it, in the opinion of the Directors, to commence the Business.

Precedents

15 Financial projections

15.1 The figures set out in Appendix III Section 3 are subject to the following:
    15.1:1 the fact that there is not yet a fixed date for commencement of Business (see Section 14 Page . . .);
    15.1:2 the assumptions set out in Section 16 Page . . .;
    15.1:3 the risk factors set out in Section 17 Page . . .

15.2 Accordingly, the projections:
    15.2:1 are not forecasts;
    15.2:2 may not be directly comparable with the statutory accounts of the Company in each year;
    15.2:3 merely illustrate the pattern of income and expenditure which the Directors consider can reasonably be expected.

15.3 The projections do not take account of:
    15.3:1 any changes in the size of the Territory;
    15.3:2 any variation in the pattern of the Business.

16 Assumptions

16.1 The Financial Projections (see Appendix III Section 3) have been prepared in the light of, amongst other matters, the following Assumptions.

16.2 That the matters mentioned in Business Start-up (see Section 14 Page . . . ante) will be completed by the scheduled date.

[16.3 That the Company will be granted a . . . . [distributorship.]]

16.4 That current levels of margin will not decrease materially.

16.5 That prices for equipment will remain in the region of current levels, although power costs will increase substantially.

[16.6 That the demand for [training] at all levels will increase.]

[16.7 That current levels of [servicing] need will continue in line with the number of units of equipment sold.]

16.8 That the costs of shop-fitting and other works to the Premises (see Section 9 Page . . . ante) will not exceed those estimated.

16.9 That no further property will be required to house any part of the operation of the Company.

16.10 That current levels of interest on bank borrowings [and proposed leasing facilities] will not be exceeded.

16.11 That the projected management, staff levels and costs will be sufficient to conduct the Business (see Section 10 Page . . . ante) sufficiently and will not be materially exceeded.

16.12 That the present depreciation policies of the Company will not change. (*State policies*) . . . .

16.13 That present management and other accounting policies will not change.

16.14 That the basis and rate of taxation of companies in the United Kingdom will not change materially during the periods covered by the Projections.

16.15 (State other Assumptions relating to the specific Business).

17 Risk factors

17.1 A new venture of this type carries a number of attendant risks. The Directors consider that the following may be the most significant.

Prospectus inviting subscriptions

17.2 The Premises (see Section 9 Page . . . ante) may cost more to shop-fit and convert than estimated.

17.3 The Business may suffer from:

    17.3:1 technological changes which may adversely affect the nature of the Business;

    17.3:2 increasing competition from national chains (including franchises) and small local outlets;

    [17.3:3 increasing education in matters related to the Business may reduce demand for training;]

    17.3:4 (*state risks relating to the specific Business*).

17.4 The Company has not been involved before in the Business although some of the Directors have relevant experience and the Company has the benefit of the relationship with the Franchisor.

APPENDIX I

The following letters have been received by the Directors of the Company from . . . . (*name of Reporting Accountants*), Chartered Accountants, Auditors to the Company [and Reporting Accountants].

1 Accountant's Report

To the Directors of . . . . (*name of Company*)

Ladies and Gentlemen,

We report that we have reviewed the accounting policies, assumptions and calculations for the financial projections (which are not forecasts) of . . . . (*name of Company*) to trade as [. . . . . (*trade name*) or . . . . Centre] for which you, as directors, are solely responsible. In our opinion, those financial projections, so far as the accounting policies and calculations are concerned, have been properly compiled from the assumptions made by the Directors, as set out in the Prospectus, which you intend to issue, and are presented on a basis consistent with generally accepted accounting practices.

Yours faithfully,

. . . . (*signature of Reporting Accountants*)

2 Auditors' Report

To the Directors of . . . . (*name of Company*)   . . . . 19 . . .

Ladies and Gentlemen,

We have audited the accounts of . . . . (*name of Company*) for the period from . . . . 19 . . . (*date of incorporation*) to . . . . 19 . . . . A summary of the audited balance sheet is set out in Appendix III Section 2.

[On . . . . 19 . . . (*date(s) of previous issue(s)*) the Company issued [100] ordinary [£1] shares at par for cash.]

The Company did not trade during the period and the expenditure of £. . . (*state early expenditure*) incurred in preparation for the commencement of the business has been carried forward to be written off when trading commences. [At . . . . 19 . . . (*accounting reference date*) the Company had received sundry income of £ . . . against which formation expenses of £ . . . have been written off.]

Yours faithfully,

. . . . (*signature of Auditors*)

Precedents

APPENDIX II

1 Share capital and name change

1.1 The Company was incorporated in [England] on . . . . 19 . . . under the Companies Act 1985 as a [private] limited company, limited by shares with registered number . . . .

1.2 Until the [last day before previous issue] the authorised share capital of the Company was [100] ordinary shares of [£1] each ranking pari passu in all respects.

1.3 On . . . . 19 . . . the Company by [ordinary] resolution resolved to increase its authorised share capital by the sum of £. . . to £. . . divided into . . . ordinary shares of £. . . (*insert nominal value*) each, ranking pari passu in all respects with the original share capital of the Company.

1.4 Subsequently, on various dates, a total of . . . . (*insert previous allotments*) such shares were allotted to the present shareholders.

1.5 Accordingly, the present issued share capital comprises ordinary shares of £. . . each.

[1.6 On . . . . 19 . . . (*date of Extraordinary General Meeting*) by special resolution the Company changes its name from . . . . (*original name*) to . . . . (*new name*) to accord with its status as a public limited company (see Appendix II Section 3).]

2 Indebtedness

2.1 Save as disclosed in this document, at this date, the Company has no loan capital outstanding or created but unissued, no outstanding mortgages, charges, borrowings, or indebtedness including bank overdrafts [(other than those mentioned below)] and no liabilities under acceptance (other than normal trade bills) or acceptance credits, hire purchase commitments, guarantees or other material contingent liabilities.

[2.2 At the close of business on . . . . 19 . . . the Company had an outstanding bank overdraft with . . . . Bank plc of £. . . .]

3 Memorandum and Articles of Association

[3.1 At an Extraordinary General Meeting of the Company held on . . . . 19 . . . the Company resolved to become a public limited company and adopted new Memorandum and Articles of Association (available for inspection at the Viewing).]

3.2 The Memorandum contains provisions (amongst others) to the following effect:

    3.2:1   the main objective of the Company is to undertake all aspects of [the retail sale and servicing of business computers];

    3.2:2   the Company has broad powers to undertake other business in connection with its main objective;

    3.2:3   in addition, the Company has the wide ancillary powers usually contained in the memoranda of commercial limited companies;

    3.2:4   the Company is a public limited company;

    3.2:5   the registered office of the Company is in [England];

    3.2:6   the liability of the shareholders is limited in accordance with the

Prospectus inviting subscriptions

provisions of the Companies Act 1985 under which the Company was incorporated;

3.2:7 the authorised share capital of the Company is £. . . divided into . . . ordinary shares of £. . . (*nominal value*) each.

3.3 The Articles of Association contain provisions (amongst others) to the following effect:

3.3:1 the regulations in Table A of the Companies (Tables A to F) Regulations 1985 do not apply to the Company;

3.3:2 the Directors have the power:

3.3:2.1 to refuse to register any transfer of the shares of the Company without giving any reason;

3.3:2.2 to require any holder of any share of the Company to make a statutory declaration identifying the beneficial owner of that share;

3.3:2.3 if no statutory declaration is made, to preclude such holder from exercising any voting rights attached to such share;

3.3:2.4 to require the transfer of that share at a fair value to a person nominated by the Directors;

3.3:3 the number of Directors shall not be less than . . . nor more than . . .;

3.3:4 any of the Directors may contract with the Company, subject to declaring an interest and may vote in respect of any such contract provided at least [2] of the non-executive directors of the Company are present at the Board meeting at which any proposal concerning that contract is considered;

3.3:5 the Company may capitalise its profits.

4 Directors' and others' interests

4.1 None of the Directors has a beneficial or other interest in the shares at the date of this document other than in respect of the shares set opposite their respective names in Section 2 ante [(or as set out below)].

4.2 None of the Directors has or had any beneficial interest in any asset now belonging to or leased to the Company or in any asset which it is proposed the Company will acquire.

4.3 Save as disclosed in Appendix II Section 5 post, none of the Directors has any material interest, direct or indirect, in any contract in relation to the Business or the Company.

[4.4 Upon the Issue taking place, in accordance with their respective undertakings or irrevocable letters of commitment the interests of the Directors and their families through companies which they control will be (*give details of Director's name, proposed shareholder company and number of shares*) . . .]

5 Material agreements

All these agreements are available for inspection at the Viewing.

5.1 The agreements following, not being contracts in the ordinary course of business, have been entered into by the Company within two years preceding the date of issue of this document or will be entered into on the successful conclusion of the Issue and are or may be material.

5.2 The Contract and ancillary documents.

Precedents

5.3   The [lease *or* underlease] of the Premises (see Section 9 Page . . . ante).
5.4   A service agreement with the [Managing] Director as follows:
    5.4:1   Term: . . . years from . . . . 19 . . .;
    5.4:2   Salary: £. . . per year renewable annually;
    5.4:3   Car: annual value £ . . .;
    5.4:4   Profit share: . . . % of [net] profits.
5.5   (*Set out any further service agreements*).

6   General

6.1   Save as disclosed in this document:
    6.1:1   no share or loan capital of the Company has been issued or is proposed to be issued;
    6.1:2   no amount or benefit has been paid or given or is intended to be paid or given to any promoter;
    t6.1:3   there is no long-term service contract with the Company;
    6.1:4   no commissions, discounts, brokerages or other special terms have been or are to be granted by the Company to any person, in consideration for the subscribing or agreement to subscribe or the procuring or agreeing to procure subscriptions for any shares in or loan capital of the Company.
6.2   The Company is not engaged in litigation, nor, so far as the Directors are aware, is any litigation or claim of material importance pending or threatened against it.
6.3   The preliminary costs and expenses incurred by the Company in respect of the Issue, including printing and advertising costs, the fees of solicitors, accountants and bankers are estimated to amount to approximately £. . . (exclusive of VAT but including capital duty).

7   Consents

. . . . (*name of auditors*) [and . . . . (*name of reporting accountants*)], [Chartered] Accountants, have given and have not withdrawn their [respective] consent[s] to the issue of this Prospectus with the inclusion of the references to themselves and their reports in the form and context in which they [respectively] appear.

8   Documents available for inspection

8.1   Copies of the following documents will be available for inspection at the Viewing.
8.2   The Memorandum and Articles of Association of the Company.
8.3   The Contract (draft form) with possible amendments and ancillary documents.
8.4   The other material contracts mentioned in Appendix II Section 5 ante.
8.5   The [lease *or* underlease] of the Premises (see Section 9 Page . . . ante).
8.6   The report and letters from . . . . (*name of reporting accountants*) and . . . . (*name of auditors*) referred to in Appendix I Sections 1 and 2 ante.
[8.7   The audited accounts of the Company for the period from . . . . 19 . . . to . . . . 19 . . . (see Appendix III Section 5 post).]
[8.8   The valuaton of the Premises by . . . . (*name of* [*valuers* or *estate agents*]) of . . . . (*address*) provisionally approving the Premises.]

APPENDIX III

1 Commencement balance sheet

On completion of the Issue and at commencement of the Business the balance sheet of the Company may be (*set out projected balance sheet*) . . . .

2 Projected balance sheets

(*Set out projected balance sheets at end of Year 1, Year 2 and Year 3*) . . . .

3 Projections with sensitivity analyses

(*Set out three year projections with three levels of performance*) . . . .

4 Cash flow projections

(*Set out cash flow projections based on median level of projections in Appendix III Section 3*) . . . .

5 Audited accounts

(*Set out audited accounts for relevant period*) . . . .

APPENDIX IV

1 Procedure for applications

The procedure for applications in respect of the Issue is as follows:

1.1 Applications must be made on the form attached to this document;

1.2 Applications must be forwarded to . . . . (*name of licensed dealer*) of . . . . (*address*) by . . . . 19 . . .;

1.3 The minimum application shall be for . . . shares for which the total subscription price shall be £. . . payable in full on application;

1.4 Applications must be for multiples of the minimum application (ie multiples of £. . . (*insert minimum application*);

1.5 Each application must be accompanied by a cheque drawn on a United Kingdom authorised bank for the total amount due payable to . . . . (*name of Company*) and crossed 'not negotiable'.

2 Restrictions

The Issue and any application made in response to this document shall be subject to the following:

2.1 The Directors reserve the right to reject any application or to accept part

Precedents

only of any application and to give preference to some applicants over others at their discretion;

2.2 Any application for less than the minimum application shall not be eligible for allotment except at the discretion of the Directors;

2.3 The Memorandum and Articles of Association of the Company;

[2.4 All applications must conform to the requirements of the Business Expansion Scheme.]

3 Procedure on receipt of applications

On receipt of applications, the procedure will be as follows:

3.1 All cheques received with applications will be presented for payment immediately;

3.2 Applications will be checked by the Directors;

3.3 If any application is rejected by them for any reason, the amount subscribed will be returned in full to the applicant (without interest) by cheque through the post;

3.4 In the event that the Issue is oversubscribed, the Directors may allot part only of the application and the balance of the subscription money will be returned in full to the applicant (without interest) by cheque through the post;

3.5 Certificates for the shares will be posted to successful applicants as soon as possible after the allotments have been completed and shall be at the applicants' risk.

.... (*name of Company*)

APPLICATION FORM

Issue of ... (*number of shares the subject of the Issue*) ordinary shares of £... (*nominal value*) each (the Shares) at par payable in full upon application.

Notes

1 Applications should only be made on this form.

2 Applications must be forwarded to .... (*name of licensed dealer*) of .... (*address*) by .... 19 ...

3 The minimum application shall be for ... Shares for which the total subscription price shall be £... payable in full on application.

4 Applications must be for multiples of the minimum application (ie multiples of £... (*insert minimum*).

5 Each application must be accompanied by a cheque drawn on a United Kingdom authorised bank for the total amount due payable to .... (*name of Company*) and crossed 'not negotiable'.

6 No application will be considered unless the above procedure is followed.

7 The subscription list will be closed on .... 19 ... or at such later date as the Directors shall decide.

To: The Directors .... (*name of Company*)

1 Number of the Shares ... Total price £... (*amount of cheque*) subject to the provisions and conditions of Appendix IV of the Issue document.
2 I/We confirm that the enclosed cheque for the amount mentioned above will be honoured on first presentation.

Signed [for and on behalf of] .... (*applicant*) .... 19...

6

LETTER to Inland Revenue applying for clearance under the Income and Corporation Taxes Act 1970 Section 54

HM Inspector of Taxes
(*insert relevant district*)

Dear Sir,

Re: (*name of Franchisor*)

We act for the above [company] [which *or* who] is currently engaged in (*describe the business of the Franchisor*) through its own [stores *or* outlets]. However, in addition to that activity, it is also engaged in franchising and grants franchises to third parties to operate [stores *or* outlets] under the same name and in a similar style to its own [stores *or* outlets].

The [company] provides the following services to its franchisees:

1 Use of the trade name of the franchisor namely (*insert trade name*).
2 Training for the staff of the franchisee.
3 Advertising and public relations services.
4 Arranging competitive insurance for franchisees.
[5 Supply of goods to franchisees at competitive prices at a result of bulk discounts].
[6 (*Insert other relevant services*)]

Our clients charge a franchisee fee of ... % in respect of the provision of all those services. We shall be grateful if you will confirm that, in view of the fact that the fee relates to a number of matters, of which the use of the name is a relatively minor aspect, franchisees may pay all such fees gross to our clients, without deduction of tax at source.

For your information, we enclose a copy of our client's standard form of Franchise Agreement.

Yours faithfully,

AB & Co (*franchisor's solicitor*)

Precedents

7
LETTER to Office of Fair Trading concerning restrictions on franchisor relating to territory

The Office of Fair Trading, ... 19 ...
Field House,
Breams Buildings,
London EC4.

Dear Sirs,

Re: (*name of Franchisor*)

We act for the above company and enclose an extract from a board meeting of the company held on .... 19 ..., duly certified by the secretary of the company. On behalf of our client, we confirm that it is the possible intention of the company to trade on its own account in the territories which it is granting to its franchisees, under a different name to (*name of Franchise*). Accordingly, clause (*insert clause in Franchise Agreement which contains the agreement on the part of the Franchisor not to trade in the Franchisee's territory*) should not be read as a restriction upon the Franchisor.

Yours faithfully

AB & Co (*Franchisor's solicitors*)

8
BOARD MINUTES of Franchisor Company concerning letter to the Office of Fair Trading (Form 29)

1 It was reported to the board by [the solicitor of the company *or* ... (*director*)] that discussions and correspondence had taken place with the Office of Fair Trading.
2 It was reported to the board by [the solicitor of the company *or* ... (*director*)] that the Office of Fair Trading had been informed of the possible intention of the company to commence trading in territories which it had granted to its franchisees, using a different name and house style and in a different manner. It had been recorded that it was the intention of the company that the territorial restriction in each of its franchise agreements should only relate to the definition of the business in the franchise agreement which was specifically limited to trading under ... (*franchise name*) and that the company did not consider that it was, itself, precluded by the franchise agreement from trading under a different name within the relevant territories.
3 It was resolved that this intention be formally minuted by the board and that [the solicitor *or* (*director*)] be authorised to advise the Office of Fair Trading of the intentions of the company in this respect.

9
FRANCHISE PURCHASE AGREEMENT

Dated .... 19 ...

1 Parties

.... whose [registered office *or* principal place of business] is at (*address*) ('the Franchisor') (1)

.... whose [registered office *or* principal place of business] is at (*address*) ('the Franchisee') (2)

2 Definitions

The following terms shall have the following meanings:
2.1 'Confidentiality Agreement': an agreement between the parties of .... 19 ...
2.2 'Licence': the form of draft franchise agreement annexed to this Agreement
2.3 'Term': ... days from .... 19 ...
2.4 The terms defined in the Licence shall have the same meanings in this Agreement

3 Franchisor's obligations

The Franchisor agrees as follows:
3.1 (Subject as appears later in this Agreement) to grant the Licence to the Franchisee
3.2 To co-operate with and assist the Franchisee to find suitable premises to form the Location
3.3 In the event that such premises are not found prior to the expiry date of this Agreement to repay to the Franchisee (within fourteen days of demand from the Franchisee) the Initial Fee (less any sums which the Franchisor is allowed to deduct from the Initial Fee under the provisions of this Agreement)
3.4 To provide training for the Franchisee (or its relevant directors and employees) in the Business as soon as practicable after the Franchisee has acquired suitable premises for the Location

4 Franchisee's obligations

The Franchisee agrees as follows:
4.1 (Subject as appears later in this Agreement) to take up the Licence
4.2 To submit (or cause its relevant directors or employees to submit) to training as required by the Franchisor
4.3 On the signing of this Agreement to pay the whole of the Initial Fee to the Franchisor (less any deposit previously paid by the Franchisee under any other agreement between the parties)
4.4 To search diligently for suitable premises to form the Location

Precedents

4.5　If required to do so by the Franchisor to take a sublease of the Location from the Franchisor in the standard form used by the Franchisor for letting premises to its franchisees

4.6　To comply with sub-clauses (*insert relevant sub-clauses of Franchise Agreement*) of the Conditions of the Licence as if they were set out in full in this Agreement and the Franchisee shall observe and perform the same even if the Franchisee is not granted or fails to take up the Licence for any reason

4.7　In the event that the Franchisee obtains suitable premises during the Term and enters into the Licence to:

    4.7:1　apply for all necessary planning permissions and other consents certificates and licences in respect of such premises and all conversion and shopfitting works (including the display of signs) which the Franchisee shall undertake there

    4.7:2　convert and shop-fit the Location in accordance with those consents and the standard style of the Franchisor as stipulated in the premises design and equipment sections of the Manual

    4.7:3　to take all reasonable steps to ensure that such works shall be completed within . . . days of commencement of the same

5　Miscellaneous

The parties further agree as follows:

5.1　This Agreement shall expire on the expiry of the Term

5.2　In the event that no suitable premises for the Location have been found by such expiry date the Initial Fee shall be repaid to the Franchisee less:

    5.2:1　twenty-five per cent (25%) of it and

    5.2:2　The reasonable costs and expenses of the Franchisor incurred in searching for and assessing premises for the Location

5.3　In the event that such suitable premises are found prior to the date of such expiry and the Franchise fails:

    5.3:1　(or its directors or employees so fail) to attend for training not more than 28 days after such date of expiry or fails to take up the Licence within that period the Initial Fee shall not be so repaid and the Franchisor shall have no liability to or agreement with the Franchisee or

    5.3:2　to complete the works mentioned in clause [4.7] of this Agreement within the time stipulated in that clause the Initial Fee shall not be repaid and the Franchisor shall have the right to terminate the Licence on the expiry of that period without any liability to the Franchisee

5.4　Sub-clauses (*insert relevant sub-clauses of Franchise Agreement*) of the Conditions of the Licence shall be incorporated in this Agreement as if they were set out in full in this Agreement

Signed by [. . . . . on behalf of] the Franchisor
Signed by [. . . . . on behalf of] the Franchisee

10

SHAREHOLDERS'/DIRECTORS' COVENANT LETTER

To AB & Co [Ltd] (*Franchisor*) of (*address*)

Dear Sirs,

Re: .... (*name of Franchise*)

(All words starting with capital letters shall have the same meanings in this letter as in the Franchise Agreement already produced to the undersigned)

In consideration of your agreement to enter into a Franchise Agreement with .... (*name of Franchisee*) of (*address*) at my request I covenant agree and undertake to you that:

1 During the continuance of the Franchise Agreement (which I have read carefully and understand) and for a period of [two years] afterwards I shall not:

1.1 engage directly or indirectly in any capacity in any business venture competitive with the Business in the Territory except for the holding for investment purposes only of any security listed or traded on any Stock Exchange provided such holding does not exceed 5% of the issued share capital of the investee company;

1.2 engage directly or indirectly in any capacity in any business venture competitive with the Business in any other area which at the commencement of my engagement shall form part of the [United Kingdom] except for the holding of any security listed or traded on any Stock Exchange as mentioned in 1.1 above;

1.3 employ any employees or former employees who were employed in the Business by the Franchisee or by the Franchisor or any other franchisee of the Franchisor or any director or officer of any such franchisee;

1.4 solicit customers of the Franchisor or its other franchisees outside the Territory

[2 I shall use my powers in the Franchisee to procure that you are offered the exclusive right to acquire the Location at any time at your discretion during a period of [90] days from the date when the Franchisee notifies you of its desire to dispose of the Location at the price of one pound more than any offer received by the Franchisee for the Location from an independent third party (other than an entity in competition with the Business) or (in the absence of such an offer) the average of the market values of the Location as certified by two independent valuers (being members of the Royal Institute of Chartered Surveyors) one of whom shall be appointed by you and the other by the Franchisee]

3 For a period of [two years] after the expiry or termination of the Franchise Agreement I shall not solicit any customers or former customers of the Business in competition with the Business in the Territory

4 In the event that I become privy to or acquainted with any of your trade secrets or other confidential business information (particularly that contained in the Manual) I shall not disclose the same to any third party and shall not use any of it in any other business venture in which I am directly or indirectly engaged in the Territory or elsewhere

[5 On expiry or termination of the Franchise Agreement I shall use my powers in the Franchisee to procure that it honours its obligations to you [(and in particular that it shall vacate the Location as required by the proposed sublease of the Location between you and the Franchisee)]]

Yours faithfully

CD (*signature of* (*shareholder or director*))

Precedents

11
DEED OF GUARANTEE
Dated . . . . 19 . . .

1 Parties

. . . . [whose [registered office *or* principal place of business] is at *or* whose address for service within the jurisdiction of the courts of [England] is] (*address*) ('the Guarantor') (1)

. . . . [whose [registered office *or* principal place of business] is at *or* whose address for service within the jurisdiction of the courts of [England] is] (*address*) ('the Franchisor') (2)

2 Recitals

2.1 At the request of the Guarantor the Franchisor has agreed to enter into the Purchase Agreement subject to:
    2.1:1 the terms of both the Purchase Agreement and the Franchise Agreement
    2.1:2 the execution by the Guarantor of an unconditional guarantee and indemnity by the Guarantor of the obligations of the Franchisee under the Purchase Agreement and the Franchise Agreement as set out later in this Deed

3 Definitions

The following terms shall have the following meanings:
3.1 'Franchise Agreement': an agreement annexed to the Purchase Agreement and intended to be made between (1) the Franchisor and (2) the Franchisee subject to the terms of the Purchase Agreement
3.2 'Franchisee': . . . . [Limited] of (*address*)
3.3 'Purchase Agreement': an agreement of this date made between (1) the Franchisor and (2) the Franchisee (a copy of which is annexed)
NOW THIS DEED WITNESSES as follows:
1 In consideration of the agreement by the Franchisor to enter into the Purchase Agreement and (if appropriate) the Franchise Agreement at the request of the Guarantor the Guarantor agrees covenants and undertakes with the Franchisor:
1.1 To procure the strict observance and performance by the Franchisee of each and all of its obligations contained or referred to in the Purchase Agreement and the Franchise Agreement
1.2 To indemnify and keep indemnified the Franchisor from and against all and any costs claims damages and expenses whatsoever arising out of or as a result of any breach of non-observance or non-performance of those obligations or incurred by the Franchisor in the course of taking any proceedings or remedial action in relation to any matter the subject of the Purchase Agreement or the Franchise Agreement
1.3 In the event of any such breach non-observance or non-performance by or the insolvency or threatened insolvency of the Franchisee and written notice by the Franchisor demanding such action by the Guarantor:
    1.3:1 to procure the transfer to the Guarantor by the Franchisee of the Purchase

Agreement or the Franchise Agreement (as the case may be) subject to the provisions concerning assignment contained in them

1.3:2 thereupon to observe and perform strictly the obligations of the Franchisee under the Purchase Agreement or the Franchise Agreement (as the case may be) as principal

1.3:3 to accept liability fully as such principal and to indemnify the Franchisor from and against all costs claims damages and expenses whatsoever arising out of or as a result of any breach non-observance or non-performance by the Guarantor as such principal of the then obligations of the Guarantor under the Purchase Agreement or the Franchise Agreement

2 The Guarantor declares:

2.1 In the event that more than one person is the Guarantor in this Deed all obligations agreements covenants and undertakings of this Deed (or of the Purchase Agreement or the Franchise Agreement if the provisions of sub-clauses [1.3:1 to 1.3:3] (inclusive) of this Deed shall apply) shall be joint and several

2.2 Any description of the Guarantor in this Deed shall include the singular or the plural and all genders

3 Notices

Any notice to be served on either of the parties by the other shall be sent by prepaid recorded delivery or registered post or by fax, telex or by electronic mail and shall be deemed to have been received by the addressee within 72 hours of posting or 24 hours if sent by fax, telex or by electronic mail to the correct fax or telex number (with correct answerback) or correct electronic mail number of the addressee

4 Proper law and jurisdiction

4.1 This Deed shall be governed by [English] law in every particular including formation and interpretation and shall be deemed to have been made in [England]

4.2 Any proceedings arising out of or in connection with this Deed may be brought in any court of competent jurisdiction in London

4.3 The submission by the parties to such jurisdiction shall not limit the right of the Franchisor to commence any proceedings arising out of this Deed in any other jurisdiction it may consider appropriate

4.4 Any notice of proceedings or other notices in connection with or which would give effect to any such proceedings may without prejudice to any other method of service to be served on any party in accordance with clause [3]

4.5 In the event that the Guarantor is resident outside [England] its address for service in [England] shall be the address for such service nominated in clause [1] of this Deed and any time limits in any proceedings shall not be extended by virtue only of the foreign residence of the Guarantor

IN WITNESS etc

[(*seals of both parties*) *or*
(*signatures and seals of
both parties*)]

Precedents

12
LEASEHOLD COVENANTS in lease of premises to be used for franchisee's operations[40]

1 Qualified quiet enjoyment covenant

That subject to the Tenant performing and observing all its obligations under a Franchise Agreement made the ..... day of .... 19... between (1) the [Landlord *or* Franchisor] and (2) the Tenant and paying the rent reserved and performing and observing the several covenants conditions agreements and provisions contained in this Lease and on the Tenant's part to be performed and observed the Tenant shall and may hold the demised premises during the Term without interruption by the Landlord or any person rightfully claiming under or in trust for it provided that:
1.1 the exercise of any of the rights or duties of the [Landlord *or* Franchisor] (by it or any of its duly authorised employees or agents) under the Franchise Agreement shall not be deemed to be an interruption of the tenure by the Tenant of the demised premises or a derogation from the grant made;
1.2 this covenant on the part of the [Landlord *or* Franchisor] shall cease to have effect and shall not bind the [Landlord *or* Franchisor] further in the event that the Franchise Agreement expires or is determined for any reason whatsoever

2 Re-entry clause

Provided always that in the event that the Franchise Agreement shall expire or be determined (for any reason whatsoever) and notwithstanding that the Tenant shall have duly performed and observed its obligations under this Lease then it shall be lawful for the Landlord at any time afterwards to enter into and upon the demised premises or any part of them in the name of the whole and thereupon the Term shall absolutely cease and determine but without prejudice to any rights or remedies which may then have accrued to either of the parties against the other in respect of any antecedent breach of any of the covenants contained in this Lease

3 Rent review clause insertion

Any calculation or assessment of the open market rental at the rent review date shall ignore any restriction upon the use of the demised premises contained in this Lease

(*Include clause excluding Sections 24–28 of the Landlord and Tenant Act 1954 see precedent 13, clause 7*)

---

40 Because almost every lease of property is different, the clauses in this form are suggestions only and should not be taken as full precedents. They must be adapted to suit the particular circumstances and the text of each lease. See para 5.20 et seq, ante.

Licence agreement of site

13
LICENCE AGREEMENT OF SITE
Date . . . .

1 Parties

(the Licensor) (1)
(the Licensee) (2)

Notes
The licensor should be the franchisor's property company.

2 Recitals

2.1 The Licensee has entered into the Franchise Agreement and needs to be allowed to enter the Premises in order to perform its obligations under that agreement
2.2 The Licensor as occupier of the Premises [under the Lease] is willing to allow the Licensee to enter on to them for this purpose but for no other

3 Definitions

In this agreement the following expressions shall have the following meanings:
3.1 The Businesses: the businesses of supplying to end users [motor fuel, lubricants, parts and accessories, car washing and servicing facilities, as well as running retail shop(s) and restaurant(s)] in accordance with the terms of the Franchise Agreement
3.2 Franchise Agreement: an agreement dated . . . . between the Licensor and the Licensee under which the Licensee is granted the right to operate the Businesses
[3.3 Lease: a lease of the Premises dated . . . . made between . . . . (*Landlord*) and the Licensor]
3.4 Licence Fee: the Licence Fee specified in the Franchise Agreement
3.5 Licence Period: the period from the date of this Agreement until the date on which the Licensee's rights granted by clause 4 are determined in accordance with clause 6.1
3.6 Premises: the [fuel forecourt, associated buildings, parking areas and landscaping] situated at . . . .

4 Licence

Subject to clauses 5 and 6 the Licensor gives to the Licensee the right in common with the Licensor and all others authorised by the Licensor to use for the Licence Period the Premises for the sole purpose of operating the Businesses in accordance with the Franchise Agreement

5 Licensee's undertakings:

The Licensee agrees and undertakes
5.1   to pay to the Licensor
    5.1:1   the Licence Fee (together with VAT or any other tax imposed in addition to or in substitution for it) at the times specified in the Franchise Agreement

Precedents

[5.1:2 within fourteen days of demand by the Licensor a sum equal to the rates demand made upon the Licensor in respect of the Premises or within fourteen days of demand a sum equal to any other tax or charge substituted for or in addition to rates to which the Licensor may become liable by reason of its occupancy of the Premises]

5.2 to comply at all times with the terms of the Franchise Agreement such compliance being a condition of the Licensee's right to occupy the Premises under this Licence

5.3 not to do anything which would or might constitute a breach of any statutory requirement affecting the Premises or which would or might vitiate in whole or in part any insurance effected in respect of the Premises

5.4 to indemnify the Licensor and keep the Licensor indemnified against all losses claims demands actions proceedings damages costs or expenses or other liability arising in any way from any breach of the Licensee's undertakings contained in this Agreement or the exercise or purported exercise of any of the rights given in clause 4

5.5 not to do or permit or suffer any person exercising or purporting to exercise the rights given in clause 4 to do any act or thing on or in relation to the Premises which would or might cause the Licensor to be in breach of the covenants on the tenant's part and conditions contained in the Lease or which if done by the Licensor would or might constitute a breach of such lease

5.6 to pay to the Licensor on demand and to indemnify the Licensor against all costs and expenses (together with VAT or any other tax imposed in addition to or in substitution for it) of professional advisers and agents incurred by the Licensor in connection with the preparation negotiation and completion of this agreement

5.7 not to impede in any way the Licensor or its servants or agents in the exercise of the Licensor's rights of possession and control of the Premises and every part of the Premises

6 Termination

6.1 The rights granted in clause 4 shall determine (without prejudice to the Licensor's rights in respect of any breach of the undertakings contained in clause 5) upon termination of the Franchise Agreement for any reason whatsoever

6.1:1 The benefit of this licence is personal to the Licensee and not assignable and the rights given in clause 4 may only be exercised by the Licensee and its employees and customers

6.1:2 In the event of an assignment or re-franchising of the Businesses taking place in accordance with the terms of the Franchise Agreement the Licensor undertakes to grant a licence on similar terms to the present licence to the assignee or new franchisee

7 Landlord and Tenant Act 1954

Whilst both Parties intend to enter into a licence agreement and agree that nothing in this Agreement shall be construed otherwise than with regard to such intention both Parties recognise that it is open to a Court to hold that in the circumstances of the case a tenancy has been created and accordingly the Parties agree as follows:

Licence agreement of site

7.1 Sections 24 to 28 of the Landlord and Tenant Act 1954 shall not apply to this Agreement

7.2 Immediately to make to the Court an application in the form set out in the Schedule for a Court Order excluding the provisions of sections 24 to 28 inclusive of the Landlord and Tenant Act 1954 and diligently to pursue such application

7.3 The commencement of the licence granted by this Agreement therefore of Licensee's right to enter upon the Premises shall be conditional upon the Court making of such an order

7.4 If for any reason within the period of .... immediately following the date of the Agreement a Court Order has not been made either Party may at the end of such period or at any time subsequently before a Court Order has been made serve upon the other a notice invoking the provisions of the next following sub-clause

7.5 Upon service of notice pursuant to the previous sub-clause (and notwithstanding anything to the contrary contained or implied elsewhere in this Agreement) this Agreement shall (save for the next following sub-clause and without prejudice to any pre-existing right of action of either Party in respect of its obligations under this Agreement) immediately terminate and the Parties shall be released from further liability under it

7.6 If this Agreement terminates in accordance with the previous sub-clause the Licensee shall immediately pay to the Licensor the sum of £... as a contribution towards the professional charges of the Licensor's solicitors in respect of this Agreement and the application for a Court Order

8 Notices

All notices given by either party pursuant to the provisions of this agreement shall be sent by prepaid recorded delivery or registered post or by fax telex or electronic mail and shall be deemed to have been received by the addressee within 72 hours of posting or 24 hours if sent by fax, telex or electronic mail to the correct fax or telex number (with correct answerback) or correct electronic mail number of the addressee

Signed by .... (the Licensor)
Signed by .... (the Licensee)

SCHEDULE

IN THE .... COUNTY COURT   No of Matter .....
BETWEEN

[*The Franchisor*]
(*or property company*)

First Applicant

and

Second Applicant

Precedents

1. We [*Franchisor*] [*or property company*] (First Applicant) and .... (Second Applicant) jointly apply to the Court for an order pursuant to section 38(4) of the Landlord and Tenant Act 1954 ('the Act') authorising the inclusion in a licence made between (1) the First Applicant as licensor and (2) the Second Applicant as licensee in respect of .... (the Premises) of a clause excluding the provisions of sections 24 to 28 inclusive of the Act

2. The grounds upon which we claim to be entitled to such an order are that the Second Applicant will be permitted to enter the Premises for the sole purpose of operating businesses under the terms of a franchise granted by the First Applicant to the Second Applicant under an agreement dated .... and it has been agreed by us that the period of the licence shall be co-terminous with the franchise so that the Second Applicant's right to enter upon the Premises shall terminate with the termination of the franchise in order that the First Applicant may take over the running of the Businesses itself or appoint another franchisee to do so and this has been taken into account in negotiating the payments to be made by the Second Applicant to the First Applicant

3. Both Applicants have been fully advised on and informed of the provisions of and rights given by sections 24 to 28 (inclusive) of the Act and are willing to make this application

[4. The Premises comprised in the licence have a rateable value of £...]

5. The Applicants desire that this application be dealt with by post and not by personal attendance

6. It is not intended to serve any person with notice of this application

Dated the ..... day of ....

Signed etc.

14
LETTER TO ACCOMPANY APPLICATION TO THE COURT

To the Registrar,
.... County Court

Dear ....
We enclose herewith Originating Application for an order authorising the exclusion of sections 24 to 28 of the Landlord and Tenant Act 1954, together with a party of the agreement between the parties. Although both parties intend this to be a licence, and therefore outside the provisions of sections 24 to 28, it is not possible to be certain until the matter has been decided by a court that the effect of it is not to create a tenancy (see eg *Addiscombe Garden Estates v Crabbe* [1958] 1 QB 513). We would accordingly request that an order be made on the basis that the effect of this agreement might be to create a tenancy.

Yours faithfully,

15
SALES REPORT by franchisee[41]

Name of Franchisee:
Date of last report:

Period covered by this report:
From: . . . . 19 . . .
To: . . . . 19 . . .

List of Products sold	Average price	Total money for period

List of invoices of sales at more than 10% less than average price (attach copy invoices):

List of returns from this or previous periods (if returns made in this period)	Reasons for returns

Estimate of sales for next period:

Number of Products	Average price

Explanation why actual sales in this period are less or more than estimated in previous reports:

(*complete only if this is the case*)

Estimated sales	Number of Products sold	Reason for shortfall or excess

16
STATIONERY TEXT

. . . . (*insert name of franchisee*) [Limited] trading as (*insert Permitted Name*) is the franchisee of (*insert name of franchisor*) and (*insert Permitted Name*) is a principal (and not the agent of (*insert name of franchisor*)) in all its dealings with customers and suppliers [and any persons entering its premises].

1   See block exemption article 4(c).

41   See para 6.24, ante, and precedent 1, clause 7.53 ante.

Precedents

17
DEVELOPMENT AREA AGREEMENT

Dated .... 19 ...

1 Parties

.... whose [registered office *or* principal place of business] is at (*address*) ('the Franchisor') (1)

.... whose [registered office *or* principal place of business] is at (*address*) ('the Franchisee') (2)

2 Definitions

The following terms shall have the following meanings:
2.1 'Development Area': the area edged red [and green] on the Map
2.2 'Franchise Agreement': an agreement of even date between the parties in the same order
2.3 'Map': the map attached to this Agreement
2.4 'Outlet': a [retail computer store] trading in the style and manner stipulated by and under the provisions of the Franchise Agreement
2.5 'Term': the period commencing on the date of this Agreement and expiring on the ..... day of .... 19 ...
2.6 Other terms used in this Agreement shall have the meanings respectively attributed to them in the Franchise Agreement

3 Recitals

3.1 This Agreement is supplemental to the Franchise Agreement
3.2 The Franchisee wishes to open and operate in the Development Area more than one Outlet for the Business
3.3 The Franchisor is willing to permit the Franchisee the right:
    3.3:1 of taking up options to open and operate Outlets in that part of the Development Area edged red on the Map
    [3.3:2 of first refusal in respect of opening and operating additional such Outlets in the part of the Development Area edged green on the Map]

4 Option

In consideration of the payment of £... (... pounds) by the Franchisee to the Franchisor (receipt of which is acknowledged) and subject to the due performance and observance by the Franchisee of all its obligations under this Agreement and under the Franchise Agreement the Franchisor grants to the Franchisee:
4.1 The right and option for the Term to open and operate Outlets in that part of the Development Area edged red on the Map within the following time scale:
    4.1:1 First Outlet by .... 19 ...
    4.1:2 Second Outlet by .... 19 ...
    4.1:3 Third Outlet by .... 19 ...

Development area agreement

[4.2 The right of first refusal to open [an]] Outlet[s] in that part of the Development Area edged green on the Map]

5 Miscellaneous

The Option shall be subject to the following:

5.1 The Franchisor and the Franchisee shall execute a franchise agreement in respect of each exercise of the Option by the Franchisee for an Outlet in the Development Area

5.2 Each such franchise agreement shall contain the standard terms and conditions (including but not limited to the Term Franchise Fees [Advertising Contribution] and all other payments) incorporated in the standard franchise agreement then used by the Franchisor

5.3 The Option shall determine immediately:

> 5.3:1 on the expiry or determination of the Franchise Agreement (or any other franchise agreement between the Franchisor and the Franchisee arising from any exercise of the Option by the Franchisee at any time) for any reason whatsoever or
>
> 5.3:2 in the event that the Franchisee fails to achieve and maintain reasonable turnover at the Location or any of its Outlets in the Development Area as mentioned in the Conditions annexed to the Franchisee Agreement or
>
> 5.3:3 in the event that the Franchisee fails to open any of the Outlets within the time scale set out in clause [4.1] of this Agreement

[5.4 In the event that the Franchisor wishes to grant to a third party a franchise for a new Outlet in that part of the Development Area edged green on the Map during the term [(which the Franchisor undertakes shall not occur prior to the expiry of . . . months from the date of this Agreement)] the Franchisor shall notify the Franchisee in writing of such desire and thereupon the Franchisee shall have 90 days from the date of such notice in which to notify the Franchisor in writing that it shall exercise the Option in respect of such Outlet failing which the Franchisor shall be at liberty to grant a franchise to a third party for such Outlet]

5.5 In the event that the Franchisee wishes to take a franchise for an Outlet in the Development Area the Franchisee shall serve upon the Franchisor written notice of such desire together with particulars of the proposed Location whereupon the Franchisor:

> 5.5:1 shall inspect the proposed place from which the Franchisee desires to trade under the franchise within fourteen days of the date of such notice
>
> 5.5:2 if the proposed place is acceptable to the Franchisor and approved by it the Franchisor shall demand from and be paid by the Franchisee [one half *or* the whole of] the appropriate Initial Franchise Fee usually charged by the Franchisor of its franchisees at the date of such notice (less £. . . (. . . pounds)) and
>
> 5.5:3 on compliance with clauses [5.5:1] and [5.5:2] the Franchisor shall grant to the Franchisee a franchise for an Outlet at that place in the Development Area containing the standard terms and conditions (including but not limited to the Term Franchise Fees [Advertising Contributions] and all other payments) commencing 60 days from the date of such notice [whereupon the remainder of the then standard Initial Franchise Fee payable to the Franchisor by the Franchisee shall be paid]

5.6 During the Term the Franchisor shall not undertake on its own behalf nor

Precedents

grant any franchise to any other person or entity in respect of the Business in the Development Area [except under the procedures set out in this Agreement]

5.7 The Territory applicable in relation to each franchise agreement which may be entered into in respect of each additional outlet within the Development Area shall comprise of Areas A, B, C or D (as the case may be) marked on the Map within each of which areas an Outlet may be located

[5.8 The area marked 'D' is the area referred to in Clause [5.4] of this Agreement]

6 Further provisions

It is further agreed between the parties as follows:

6.1 [(*Set out relevant sub-clauses or* clauses .... of the Franchise Agreement are incorporated in this Agreement in their entirety]

Signed by [..........on behalf of] the Franchisor
Signed by [..........on behalf of] the Franchisee

18
LICENCE AND AGENCY AGREEMENT[42]

Date: .... 19 ...

1 Parties

[*holding company*]   ('Alpha') (1)
[*the franchisor company*]   ('Beta') (2)

2 Recitals

2.1 Alpha owns the Property set out in the Schedule attached to this Agreement
2.2 Alpha is exclusively entitled to licence Beta and third parties to use the Property
2.3 Alpha wishes to appoint Beta as its agent to grant Licences of the Property to Franchisees

3 Definitions

3.1 'Business': the negotiation and operation of Licences by Beta as agent for Alpha and all matters directly related thereto
3.2 'Commencement Date': the date set out at the head of this Agreement
3.3 'Conditions': the provisions set out overleaf which shall be incorporated into this Agreement in their entirety
3.4 'Franchise Agreements': agreements between Beta and franchisees for the operation of .... franchises entered into by Beta [pursuant to the terms

---

[42] This is a licence of intellectual property owned by a holding company for its use in franchised and company owned outlets. The Franchisor company is appointed agent of the holding company for the purpose of granting licences to franchisees. This preserves privity of contract between the holding company and the franchisees—this is important for trade mark purposes (see para 1.21).

of the Master Franchise Agreement] upon the terms of Beta's standard form current at the time of entering into such agreements

Notes
Is there to be a Master Franchise Agreement? It might also be a good idea to Schedule the form of the Franchise Agreements. If this is done provision needs to be made for variation

3.5 'Franchisees': persons who at the date of this Agreement have entered or who subsequently enter into Franchise Agreements with Beta
3.6 'Licenses': licences to Franchisees to use the Property in accordance with the terms of their Franchise Agreements
3.7 'Property': the intellectual property set out in the Schedule together with all copyrights designs trade names know-how and trade secrets used in the operation of .... businesses [pursuant to the terms of the Master Franchise Agreement] and any additional intellectual property which the Parties may from time to time agree [in writing] shall be used in such businesses under the terms of this Agreement
[3.8 'Master Franchise Agreement': an agreement dated ....]
3.9 'Term': the period starting on (and including) the Commencement Date and continuing until termination as provided by the terms of this Agreement
3.10 'Territory': [England Wales Scotland etc.]

Notes
The territory should be co-extensive with the territory as specified in the Master Franchise agreement if there is one.

4 Grant

Alpha grants to Beta for the Term the exclusive right to use the Property in its company owned .... businesses within the Territory and to negotiate and grant Licences of the Property within the Territory

Signed by ....
Signed by ....

CONDITIONS

Notes
Having regard to the relationship between the Parties, some of these clauses may be unnecessary: delete as appropriate.

5 Alpha agrees with Beta throughout the Term:

5.1 Exclusive agency
Not at any time during the Term to appoint any third party as agent for the negotiation or grant of Licences in the Territory nor itself to negotiate or grant any such Licence whether directly or indirectly
5.2 Support and information
To support Beta in its efforts to promote the Business and in particular at its own expense to supply transparencies or other copies of any item or items of the Property required by Beta
5.3 Indemnity
To indemnify and keep indemnified Beta from and against any and all loss damage

Precedents

or liability (whether criminal or civil) suffered and legal fees and costs incurred by Beta in the course of conducting the Business and resulting from:
    5.3:1   any act neglect or default of Alpha [or its agents employees or customers] which would amount to breach if committed by Alpha
    5.3:2   the proven infringement of the intellectual property rights of any third party
    5.3:3   any successful claim by any third party alleging libel or slander in respect of any matter arising from the conduct of the Business in the Territory
provided that such liability shall not have been incurred through any default by Beta in relation to its obligations under this Agreement

5.4   Maintenance of Rights
To maintain Alpha's rights in the Property during the Term and not to cause or permit anything which may damage or endanger it or Alpha's title to it or assist or suffer others to do so and to consult with Beta if Alpha's rights in the Property are or appear likely to be damaged or endangered

6   Beta agrees with Alpha throughout the Term:

6.1   Diligence
At all times to work diligently to protect and promote the Business and the interests of Alpha

6.2   No dealing outside the Territory
Not to deal directly or indirectly with any prospective licensee located outside the Territory

6.3   No representation of agency
Not to describe itself as agent or representative of Alpha except as expressly authorised [in writing] by Alpha

Notes
Because of the doctrine of undisclosed principal, it is not necessary for franchisees (other than those registered as users of marks) actually to know who owns the intellectual property.

6.4   No pledging of credit
Not to pledge the credit of Alpha in any way

6.5   No representations
Not to make any representations or give any warranties to prospective licensees other than those contained in the Franchise Agreements

6.6   Best endeavours
To use its best endeavours to induce Franchisees to use the Property and to ensure that it is used in a way which does not endanger it or bring it into disrepute

6.7   Protection of Property To protect the Property and in particular
    6.7:1   Not to cause or permit anything which may damage or endanger the Property or Alpha's title to it or assist or allow others to do so
    6.7:2   To notify Alpha of any suspected infringement of the Property
    6.7:3   To take such reasonable action as Alpha may direct at the expense of Alpha in relation to such infringement
    6.7:4   To compensate Alpha for any use by Beta of the Property otherwise than in accordance with this Agreement
    6.7:5   To indemnify Alpha for any liability incurred to third parties for any use of the Property otherwise than in accordance with this Agreement

Licence and agency agreement

6.7:6 On the expiry or termination of this Agreement forthwith to cease to use the Property save as expressly authorised by Alpha in writing

6.7:7 Not to apply for registration of any part of the Property as a trade mark or service mark but to give Alpha at Alpha's expense any assistance it may require in connection with the registration of any part of the Property as a trade mark or service mark in any part of the world and not to interfere with in any manner nor attempt to prohibit the use or registration of any part of the Property or any similar name or designation by any other person authorised by Alpha

6.7:8 Not to use the Property or the Rights otherwise than as permitted by this Agreement

6.7:9 Not to use any name or mark similar to or capable of being confused with any part of the Property

6.7:10 Not to use the Property except directly in the Business

6.7:11 To hold any additional goodwill generated by Beta or its Franchisees as bare trustee for Alpha

Notes
So far as the Franchisees are concerned, the effect of this clause is to create a trust of a trust (see clause [7.25:1.14] of precedent [1])). This is effective—see *Grainge v Wilberfore* (1889) 5 TLR 436 at 437 per Chitty J; *Grey v IRC* [1958] Ch 375 at 382. Goodwill can be held on trust—*Scott on Trusts* (4th edn) 82.4 (no English authority).

6.8 List of Franchisees
To supply upon request a list of actual and potential Franchisees

7 Registered users

To secure that at least one in ten of the Franchisees is registered as user of the Marks

8 Indemnity

To indemnify and keep indemnified Alpha from and against any and all loss damage or liability (whether criminal or civil) suffered and legal fees and costs incurred by Alpha resulting from any breach of this Agreement by Beta and Beta shall be responsible for:

8.1 any act neglect or default of Beta's employees customers or Franchisees which would amount to breach if committed by Beta

8.2 any successful claim by any third party alleging libel or slander in respect of any matter arising from the conduct of the Business in the Territory

provided that such liability shall not have been incurred through any default by Alpha in relation to its obligations under this Agreement

9 Termination

Without prejudice to the Licences already granted pursuant to it this Agreement shall terminate at the expiry of [four weeks] notice served by either Party in writing upon the other

Precedents

10 Termination consequences

Upon the termination of this Agreement Beta undertakes not to make any further use of nor to reproduce nor to exploit the Property in any way save in relation to its then existing company owned [. . . . .] businesses and in the then existing businesses of its Franchisees

11 Rights accrued

The expiry or termination of this Agreement shall be without prejudice to any rights which have already accrued to either of the Parties under this Agreement

19
CORE FRANCHISE[43]

1 Parties

. . . .   whose registered office is at
. . . .   ('Alpha') (1)
                                              ('Beta') (2)

2 Recitals

2.1 Alpha operates through [its own and] franchised operations businesses supplying to end users [eg motor fuel, lubricants, parts and accessories, car washing and servicing facilities], as well as running [a] retail shop(s) [and restaurant(s)], each operated in accordance with the system specially developed by Alpha for each kind of business

Notes
The expression 'end users' matches the EEC block exemption (Regulation 4087/88 1988 L359/88). Only a general description of Alpha's business is needed here. It is desirable to show that Alpha has run its own pilot schemes—hence the first reference in square brackets.

2.2 Alpha has expended time effort and money in developing the Systems
2.3 Alpha [and its associated companies are] [is] [are] the registered proprietor(s) of the marks and owner of the copyrights and analogous rights comprised in the Intellectual Property and Alpha is exclusively entitled to license those rights either on its own account or for and on behalf of its associated companies

Notes
The reference to 'associated companies' is to take care of the possibility that a holding company will be used for the intellectual property. A precedent for an agency agreement for the licensing of the intellectual property on the behalf of such company in favour of Alpha is provided in precedent 18.

2.4 Alpha is solely and exclusively entitled to operate and to license others to operate businesses in accordance with the Systems in the United Kingdom
2.5 Beta wishes to operate the Business at the Location and to be granted a licence for this purpose

[43] Under this Precedent, a package of separate business units is licensed. The particular package can be varied from franchisee to franchisee to suit the particular location.

3 Definitions

The following terms shall have the following meanings:

3.1 'Accounting Period': seven days expiring at [17.00 hours each Sunday] of the Term

3.2 'Accounting Reference Date': (*insert date*) in each year of the Term

3.3 'Advertising Contribution': . . . % of the Receipts

Notes
The definition of 'Receipts' takes care of special offers etc. The Receipts are the notional receipts of the Business.

3.4 'Business': the business or group of businesses listed in the Schedule supplying to end users all or any of the following: [motor fuel, lubricants, parts and accessories, car washing and servicing facilities; as well as running [a] retail shop(s) [and restaurant(s)]] each operated in accordance with the Systems

3.5 'Commencement Date': [. . . . .] [the date set out at the head of this Agreement]

Notes
Insert as appropriate words in square brackets.

3.6 'Conditions': the provisions set out overleaf which shall be incorporated into this Agreement in their entirety

Notes
'Small print' clauses will be incorporated.

3.7 'Continuing Fees': fees of . . . % of the Receipts

Notes
Do not call these 'royalties'. Royalties may be subject to deduction at source, and it is not advisable to invite problems with the Inland Revenue!—see precedent 6.

3.8 'Credit Limit':
    3.8:1 Time: . . . days from the date of [invoice]
    3.8:2 Value . . . [pounds sterling]

Notes
This clause may be advisable if Alpha is going to supply Beta with inventory.

3.9 'Currency': [pounds sterling]

3.10 'Date': a day on which the banks are open for business or (if the banks are closed on that day) the next such day following and subject to this any reference to a particular date shall include that day itself

Notes
'Date' will be used at various points in the Conditions.

3.11 'Deposit': 10% of the Initial Fee of which it shall be the first instalment

3.12 'Equipment': the equipment described in the Manuals or other equipment substituted for it in accordance with this Agreement

Notes
It is less cumbersome to specify equipment in the Manuals. Provisions for updating this from time to time is built into this agreement.

3.13 'Expiry Date': [. . .] or such later Date as shall result from any extension of the Term under clause [. . .]

Precedents

3.14 'Initial Fee': as an initial fee the sum of . . . thousand pounds (£. . .)
3.15 'Insurance Premium': the premium for the insurance arranged by Alpha described in the Conditions

Notes
Details of the insurance arrangements are spelled out in the Conditions.

3.16 'Intellectual Property': all or any of the following:
    3.16:1 The [United Kingdom] trade marks and service marks of which Alpha is the registered proprietor
    3.16:2 The Trade Name
    3.16:3 Copyrights and analogous rights held by Alpha in written material plans designs or other works building structures fixtures and fittings including colour schemes patterns of furnishings dress styles of staff and the like used in the Systems

Notes
It must be ensured that Alpha (or its associated companies) *is* the owner of the various intellectual properties, otherwise Recital 2.3 must be amended. 'Analogous rights' takes care of the changes the Copyright etc. Act 1988 has introduced.

3.17 'Licence Fees': the sum of £. . . per annum paid by Beta in consideration of Alpha permitting it to enter upon the Location for the purpose of carrying on the Business

Notes
In the present context, there is a good chance of a licence being upheld—see *Shell-Mex and BP Ltd v Manchester Garages Ltd* [1971] 1 All ER 841—see precedent 13.

3.18 'Location': [the fuel forecourt and associated buildings parking areas and landscaping situated at [. . . . .]]
3.19 'Manuals': the manual or manuals listed by their serial numbers in the Schedule being Alpha's standard operating manual for each kind of business as updated from time to time of which copies bearing these serial numbers have been or will be lent to Beta

Notes
It is possible to take care of changing and upgrading the Services etc by incorporating Manuals and providing for variation and updating.

[3.20 'Minimum Package':
    3.20:1 the equipment products stock of all types specified in the Manuals
    3.20:2 the minimum staff levels at the Location stipulated in the Manuals from time to time during the Term]
    3.20:3 the stock specified in the Manuals
3.21 'Notice Period':
    3.21:1 for a Default Notice (precedent 1, clause 9.3) [7] days
    3.21:2 for any other notice [30] days

Notes
Termination is automatic on certain events such as insolvency. Assignment and renewal are dealt with in the Conditions.

3.22 'Payment Times':
    3.22:1 for the Deposit: the date of the signing of this Agreement

Core franchise

3.22:2 for the balance of Initial Fee: the date of the commencement of each of the Businesses
3.22:3 for the Insurance Premium [ ] days [after demand]
3.22:4 for the Licence Fees Continuing Fees and Advertising Contributions: on or before 17.00 hours upon the day following the end of each Accounting Period
3.23 'Products': the products specified in the Manuals which are sold in the Business
3.24 'Promotion Fund': the fund to be maintained by Alpha for advertising purposes in accordance with clause [. . .] of the Conditions
3.25 'Receipts': for the purposes of calculating payments to be made by Beta to Alpha the gross takings of the Business arising directly or indirectly from the conduct of the Business during each Accounting Period (and for any period less than a complete Accounting Period) to include without deduction for or on account of and without limitation

3.25:1 all Products sold Services supplied and business dealings made by the Business or by Beta (whether or not invoiced) in each Accounting Period
3.25:2 all payments (if any) received under any insurance policy covering loss of profits
3.25:3 any customer refunds or allowances
3.25:4 credit card discounts or charges suffered by Beta

and the amount of Receipts shall mean the gross sums receivable in respect of Products sold Services supplied and business dealings entered into at the time of such sale supply and entering into and not solely cash receipts however there shall be disregarded

3.25:5 Value Added Tax or any similar tax or excise replacing it or in addition to it
[3.25:6 all free offers or discounts made or given by Beta as part of any special promotion required or authorised by Alpha]

Notes
Consider precedent 1, clause 3.11 as alternative.

3.25:7 any differences between till receipts recorded and cash banked
3.25:8 any benefit arising from or accruing to the Business solely attributable to any sale of Equipment permitted under the terms of this Agreement
3.26 'Services': the services provided by the Business as specified in the Manuals
3.27 'Service fee': a fee of £. . . for the use of the computer system or systems used in the Business as specified in the Manuals
3.28 'Systems': the operation of the businesses in accordance with the Manuals using the Intellectual Property and any necessary know-how trade secrets methods of operating insignia identifying materials method of advertising style and character of equipment [and insurance arrangements] specified in the Manuals
3.29 'Term': five years starting on the Commencement Date and ending on the Expiry Date unless extended or earlier determined as provided by this Agreement

Notes
There is always a potential problem matching termination of a franchise and termination of the franchisee's interest in the site—see p 310, para 1.11.

3.30 'Trade Name': the trade name or names under which each of the businesses is operated in accordance with the Manuals

Precedents

4 Grant

4.1 In consideration of the payment of the Deposit the balance of the Initial Fee the Licence Fees the Continuing Fees the Advertising Contributions and the Insurance Premiums by Beta to Alpha on the Payment Times and of and subject to the performance by Beta of its obligations under this Agreement Alpha grants to Beta the right to commence and carry on the Business for the Term

4.2 Alpha reserves the power to vary the Manuals from time to time including variation of the specification of the Minimum Package for each of the businesses

5 No competition [See Master Form precedent 1, clause 5]

Signed by . . . . Alpha
Signed by . . . . Beta

CONDITIONS
(*See Master Form precedent 1*)

Appendix 1
Franchise Agreement[1]

1.0 Parties	.... of *(address)* ('the Franchisor') (1) .... *(address)* ('the Franchisee') (2)
2.0 Definitions	The following terms shall have the following meanings in this Agreement:
2.1 Term	.... years from 2.1.1 The Commencement Date of the ..... day of .... 19 ... and expiring on 2.1.2 The Expiry Date of the ..... day of .... 19 ... (inclusive) unless sooner determined as provided in the Conditions
2.2 Location	The premises shortly described as .... or such other premises as are approved by the Franchisor during the Term
2.3 Territory	The area comprising .... and shown edged red on the map attached to this Agreement
2.4 Mark	The legend—.......... and the logos associated with the same and any additional or substitute marks which the Franchisor shall deem suitable for the Business during the Term
2.5 Know-How	The operational systems and methods of the Franchisor as divulged to the Franchisee from time to time during the Term
2.6 Permitted Name	The permitted business name of the Franchisee shall be: '..........'
2.7 Business	Using (for mutual benefit) the Mark and the Know-How in the business of trading under the Permitted Name in the style and manner stipulated by the Franchisor for: 2.7.1 retail sales of microcomputer and other associated processing products software and other communications and business equipment and furniture

---

1 Illustration of a suitable format—for text, reference should be made to Master Form.

Appendix 1

        2.7.2   training courses for users of any such equipment and products

        2.7.3   advisory and pre and post sales services only as listed in the Manual from time to time

2.8 Initial Fee   As an Initial Franchisee Fee the sum of .... pounds (£. . . . . .)

2.9 Advertising Contribution   ..... per cent (. . . %) of gross turnover (as defined in Clause ..... of the Conditions) of the Business

2.10 Continuing Fees   Franchisee Fees of ..... per cent (. . . %) of gross turnover (as defined in Clause ..... of the Conditions) of the Business

2.11 Payment Dates
- 2.11.1 for the Initial Fee on the signing of this agreement
- 2.11.2 for the Advertising Contribution and the Continuing Fees on the tenth day of each accounting month (as specified in the Manual from time to time) during the Term in respect of the Business during the immediately preceding accounting month

2.12 Manual   The confidential written systems of and regulations for the operation of the Business issued in several volumes and amended by the Franchisor from time to time during the Term incorporating part of the Know-How and deemed to form part of this agreement (Serial Number .....)

2.13 Minimum Package
- 2.13.1 the equipment products literature stock of all types and range of courses
- 2.13.2 the minimum staff levels at the Location stipulated in the Manual from time to time during the Term

2.14 Financial Year   Each Financial Year during the Term shall end on the ..... day of ....

2.15 Conditions   The Standard Conditions and Special Conditions (if any) annexed hereto shall be deemed to be incorporated in this agreement in their entirety

3.0 The Right   In consideration of the payment of the Initial Fee the Advertising Contribution and the Continuing Fees by the Franchisee to the Franchisor and of the subject to the agreements or the part of the Franchisee in this agreement and the Conditions the Franchisor hereby grants to the Franchisee the right of using the Mark and the Know-How only:

3.1 in the business
3.2 at and from the Location
3.3 within the Territory
3.4 for the Term
3.5 under the Permitted Name
3.6 in accordance with the Manual

Appendix 1

Dated this . . . . . . day
of . . . . 19 . . .

Signed by
for and on behalf of

. . . .
Authorised Signatory

Signed by
for and on behalf of

. . . .
Authorised Signatory

Appendix 1

Appendix 2
Guidelines laid down by the Trade Marks Registry, August 1984

Objections under section 28(6) of the Trade Marks Act 1938: trafficking

1 It might be helpful for practitioners to know the guidelines which were drawn up for Registry staff after the House of Lords decision on various applications to register HOLLY HOBBIE under section 29(1)(b) of the Act. This confirmed the Registrar's position of principle in taking objection under section 28(6) where he considers that the registration of certain user agreements would tend to facilitate trafficking in trade marks. Such trafficking may arise from, though not be confined to, user licences granted in the course of 'character merchandising'.

2 While all trade mark applications are considered dispassionately, the following indications will normally lead to an objection:—

(a) The application is made within the provisions of section 29(1)(b) *and*

(b) The application is made by a film or TV company outside Classes 9 and 16—it is reasonable to assume that eg a film company is not trafficking if it seeks registration under section 29(1)(b) in respect of records (the theme music of the film) or printed publications (the book of the film).

(c) The application is made by an author/publisher outside Class 16 for literary characters.

(d) The application is made for a famous trade mark for goods well outside the field in which the trade mark gained its reputation.

(e) Applications are made for identical trade marks for a range of unrelated goods.

(f) Applications are made by known character merchandising operators or organisers of major sporting events.

(g) Applications are for marks involving known fictional characters or well known personalities (sports, TV, films, etc).

3 If an application falls within heading (a) *and* any other heading, a trafficking objection will normally be taken.

4 Insofar as registered trade marks are concerned, if applications are made under Section 28 for registrations of registered users, to which any of headings 2(b)–(g) apply, objection will be taken. Objection may also arise if there are several registered user applications for one registered mark.

5 An objection having been raised, the onus rests with the applicant (for registration or for registered user) to satisfy the Registrar that it is not justified. The applicant may do this by explaining frankly the circumstances of the application and showing that he has a real trading connection with the goods. The decision will then depend upon the particular facts of each case.

6 If there is a reasonable doubt about an objection the benefit of the doubt

Appendix 2

will normally be given to the applicant. For example, if the owner of a famous trademark applies for registration of that Mark in a completely new field of trade and explains in a written statement made by a responsible officer that the applicant is considering entering a new field and wishes to use the reputation enjoyed through its trade mark, but first they wish to test the market through a registered user, then this may be accepted.

7 If a film or TV company applies *solely under* section 17(1) for goods outside Clauses 9 or 16, or the owner of a famous trade mark applies for goods very different from those for which he gained his reputation, there is no 'trafficking' objection. The applicant may however be invited specifically to satisfy the Registrar that at the date of application he either used the mark or had a firm intention of using it within the term of section 68. This type of objection is already taken and will continue to be taken. No significant enlargement of practice is envisaged; only a handful of known film or TV companies or famous specialist manufacturers should be affected.

8 These guidelines may be revised in the light of experience.

August 1984

Appendix 3
Commission notice of 3 September 1986

Commission notice of 3 September 1986 on agreements of minor importance which do not fall under Article 85(1) of the Treaty establishing the European Economic Community[1] (86/C231/02)[1]

I

1. The Commission considers it important to facilitate cooperation between undertakings where such cooperation is economically desirable without presenting difficulties from the point of view of competition policy, which is particularly true of cooperation between small and medium-sized undertakings. To this end it published the 'Notice concerning agreements, decisions and concerted practices in the field of cooperation between undertakings'[2] listing a number of agreements that by their nature cannot be regarded as restraints of competition. Furthermore, in the Notice concerning its assessment of certain subcontracting agreements[3] the Commission considered that this type of contract which offers opportunities for development, in particular, to small and medium-sized undertakings is not in itself caught by the prohibition in Article 85(1). By issuing the present Notice, the Commission is taking a further step towards defining the field of application of Article 85(1), in order to facilitate cooperation between small and medium-sized undertakings.

2. In the Commission's opinion, agreements whose effects on trade between Member States or on competition are negligible do not fall under the ban on restrictive agreements contained in Article 85(1). Only those agreements are prohibited which have an appreciable impact on market conditions, in that they appreciably alter the market position, in other words the sales or supply possibilities, of third undertakings and of users.

3. In the present Notice the Commission, by setting quantitative criteria and by explaining their application, has given a sufficiently concrete meaning to the concept 'appreciable' for undertakings to be able to judge for themselves whether the agreements they have concluded with other undertakings, being of minor importance, do not fall under Article 85(1). The quantitative definition of 'appreciable' given by the Commission is, however, no absolute yardstick; in fact,

---

[1] The present Notice replaces the Commission Notice of 19 December 1977, OJ No C313, 29.12.1977, p 3.
[2] OJ No C75, 29.7.1968, p3, corrected by OJ No C84, 28.8.1968, p14.
[3] OJ No C 1, 3.1.1979, p2.

Appendix 3

in individual cases even agreements between undertakings which exceed these limits may still have only a negligible effect on trade between Member States or on competition, and are therefore not caught by Article 85(1).

4. As a result of this Notice, there should no longer be any point in undertakings obtaining negative clearance, as defined by Article 2 of Council Regulation No 17[4], for the agreements covered, nor should it be necessary to have the legal position established through Commission decisions in individual cases; notification with this end in view will no longer be necessary for such agreements. However, if it is doubtful whether in an individual case an agreement appreciably affects trade between Member States or competition, the undertakings are free to apply for negative clearance or to notify the agreement.

5. In cases covered by the present Notice the Commission, as a general rule, will not open proceedings under Regulation No 17, either upon application or upon its own initiative. Where, due to exceptional circumstances, an agreement which is covered by the present Notice nevertheless falls under Article 85(1), the Commission will not impose fines. Where undertakings have failed to notify an agreement falling under Article 85(1), because they wrongly assumed, owing to a mistake in calculating their market share or aggregate turnover, that the agreement was covered by the present Notice, the Commission will not consider imposing fines unless the mistake was due to negligence.

6. This Notice is without prejudice to the competence of national courts to apply Article 85(1) on the basis of their own jurisdiction, although it constitutes a factor which such courts may take into account when deciding a pending case. It is also without prejudice to any interpretation which may be given by the Court of Justice of the European Communities.

II

7. The Commission holds the view that agreements between undertakings engaged in the production or distribution of goods or in the provision of services generally do not fall under the prohibition of Article 81(1) if:
— the goods or services which are the subject of the agreement (hereinafter referred to as 'the contract products') together with the participation undertakings' other goods or services which are considered by users to be equivalent in view of their characteristics, price and intended use, do not represent more than 5% of the total market for such goods or services (hereinafter referred to as 'products') in the area of the common market affected by the agreement and
— the aggregate annual turnover of the participating undertakings does not exceed 200 million ECU.

8. The Commission also holds the view that the said agreements do not fall under the prohibition of Article 85(1) if the above-mentioned market share or turnover is exceeded by not more than one tenth during two successive financial years.

9. For the purposes of this Notice, participating undertakings are:
(a) undertakings party to the agreement;
(b) undertakings in which a party to the agreement, directly or indirectly,
— owns more than half the capital or business assets, or
— has the power to exercise more than half the voting rights, or

4 OJ No 13, 21.2.1962, p 204/62.

Appendix 3

— has the power to appoint more than half the members of the supervisory board, board of management or bodies legally representing the undertakings, or
— has the right to manage the affairs;
(c) undertakings which directly or indirectly have in or over a party to the agreement the rights or powers listed in (b);
(d) undertakings in or over which an undertaking referred to in (c) directly or indirectly has the rights or powers listed in (b).

Undertakings in which several undertakings as referred to in (a) to (d) jointly have, directly or indirectly, the rights or powers set out in (b) shall also be considered to be participating undertakings.

10. In order to calculate the market share, it is necessary to determine the relevant market. This implies the definition of the relevant product market and the relevant geographical market.

11. The relevant product market includes besides the contract products any other products which are identical or equivalent to them. This rule applies to the products of the participating undertakings as well as to the market for such products. The products in question must be interchangeable. Whether or not this is the case must be judged from the vantage point of the user, normally taking the characteristics, price and intended use of the goods together. In certain cases, however, products can form a separate market on the basis of their characteristics, their price or their intended use alone. This is true especially where consumer preferences have developed.

12. Where the contract products are components which are incorporated into another product by the participating undertakings, reference should be made to the market for the latter product, provided that the components represent a significant part of it. Where the contract products are components which are sold to third undertakings, reference should be made to the market for the components. In cases where both conditions apply, both markets should be considered separately.

13. The relevant geographical market is the area within the Community in which the agreement produces its effects. This area will be the whole common market where the contract products are regularly bought and sold in all Member States. Where the contract products cannot be bought and sold in a part of the common market, or are bought and sold only in limited quantities or at irregular intervals in such a part, that part should be disregarded.

14. The relevant geographical market will be narrower than the whole common market in particular where:
— the nature and characteristics of the contract product, eg high transport costs in relation to the value of the product, restrict its mobility; or
— movement of the contract product within the common market is hindered by barriers to entry to national markets resulting from State intervention, such as quantitative restrictions, severe taxation differentials and non-tariff barriers, e.g. type approvals or safety standard certifications. In such cases the national territory may have to be considered as the relevant geographical market. However, this will only be justified if the existing barriers to entry cannot be overcome by reasonable effort and at an acceptable cost.

15. Aggregate turnover includes the turnover in all goods and services, excluding tax, achieved during the last financial year by the participating undertaking. In cases where an undertaking has concluded similar agreements with various other undertakings in the relevant market, the turnover of all participating undertakings

Appendix 3

should be taken together. The aggregate turnover shall not include dealings between participating undertakings.

16. The present Notice shall not apply where in a relevant market competition is restricted by the cumulative effects of parallel networks of similar agreements established by several manufacturers or dealers.

17. The present Notice is likewise applicable to decisions by associations of undertakings and to concerted practices.

Appendix 4
Commission Regulation (EEC) No 4087/88

of 30 November 1988
on the application of Article 85(3) of the Treaty to categories of franchise agreements

The Commission of the European Communities

Having regard to the Treaty establishing the European Economic Community,

Having regard to Council Regulation No 19/65/EEC of 2 March 1965 on the application of Article 85(3) of the Treaty to certain categories of agreements and concerted practices[1], as last amended by the Act of Accession of Spain and Portugal, and in particular Article 1 thereof,

Having published a draft of this Regulation[2],

Having consulted the Advisory Committee on Restrictive Practices and Dominant Positions,

Whereas:

(1) Regulation No 19/65/EEC empowers the Commission to apply Article 85(3) of the Treaty by Regulation to certain categories of bilateral exclusive agreements falling within the scope of Article 85(1) which either have as their object the exclusive distribution or exclusive purchase of goods, or include restrictions imposed in relation to the assignment or use of industrial property rights.

(2) Franchise agreements consist essentially of licences of industrial or intellectual property rights relating to trade marks or signs and know-how which can be combined with restrictions relating to supply or purchase of goods.

(3) Several types of franchise can be distinguished according to their object: industrial franchise concerns the manufacturing of goods, distribution franchise concerns the sale of goods, and service franchise concerns the supply of services.

(4) It is possible on the basis of the experience of the Commission to define categories of franchise agreements which fall under Article 85(1) but can normally be regarded as satisfying the conditions laid down in Article 85(3). This is the case for franchise agreements whereby one of the parties supplies goods or provides services to end users. On the other hand, industrial franchise agreements should not be covered by this Regulation. Such agreements, which usually govern relationships between producers, present different characteristics than the other types of franchise. They consist of manufacturing licences based on patents and/or technical know-how, combined with trade-mark licences. Some of them may benefit from other block exemptions if they fulfil the necessary conditions.

(5) This Regulation covers franchise agreements between two undertakings, the franchisor and the franchisee, for the retailing of goods or the provision of services

[1] OJ No 36, 6.3.1965, p 533/65.
[2] OJ No C 299, 27.8.1987, p 3.

Appendix 4

to end users, or a combination of these activities, such as the processing or adaptation of goods to fit specific needs of their customers. It also covers cases where the relationship between franchisor and franchisees is made through a third undertaking, the master franchisee. It does not cover wholesale franchise agreements because of the lack of experience of the Commission in that field.

(6) Franchise agreements as defined in this Regulation can fall under Article 85(1). They may in particular affect intra-Community trade where they are concluded between undertakings from different Member States or where they form the basis of a network which extends beyond the boundaries of a single Member State.

(7) Franchise agreements as defined in this Regulation normally improve the distribution of goods and/or the provision of services as they give franchisors the possibility of establishing a uniform network with limited investments, which may assist the entry of new competitors on the market, particularly in the case of small and medium-sized undertakings, thus increasing interbrand competition. They also allow independent traders to set up outlets more rapidly and with higher chance of success than if they had to do so without the franchisor's experience and assistance. They have therefore the possibility of competing more efficiently with large distribution undertakings.

(8) As a rule, franchise agreements also allow consumers and other end users a fair share of the resulting benefit, as they combine the advantage of a uniform network with the existence of traders personally interested in the efficient operation of their business. The homogeneity of the network and the constant cooperation between the franchisor and the franchisees ensures a constant quality of the products and services. The favourable effect of franchising on interbrand competition and the fact that consumers are free to deal with any franchisee in the network guarantees that a reasonable part of the resulting benefits will be passed on to the consumers.

(9) This Regulation must define the obligations restrictive of competition which may be included in franchise agreements. This is the case in particular for the granting of an exclusive territory to the franchisees combined with the prohibition on actively seeking customers outside that territory, which allows them to concentrate their efforts on their allotted territory. The same applies to the granting of an exclusive territory to a master franchisee combined with the obligation not to conclude franchise agreements with third parties outside that territory. Where the franchisees sell or use in the process of providing services, goods manufactured by the franchisor or according to its instructions and or bearing its trade mark, an obligation on the franchisees not to sell, or use in the process of the provision of services, competing goods, makes it possible to establish a coherent network which is identified with the franchised goods. However, this obligation should only be accepted with respect to the goods which form the essential subject-matter of the franchise. It should notably not relate to accessories or spare parts for these goods.

(10) The obligations referred to above thus do not impose restrictions which are not necessary for the attainment of the above-mentioned objectives. In particular, the limited territorial protection granted to the franchisees is indispensable to protect their investment

(11) It is desirable to list in the Regulation a number of obligations that are commonly found in franchise agreements and are normally not restrictive of competition and to provide that if, because of the particular economic or legal circumstances, they fall under Article 85(1), they are also covered by the exemption. This list, which is not exhaustive, includes in particular clauses which are essential either to preserve the common identity and reputation of the network or to prevent

the know-how made available and the assistance given by the franchisor from benefiting competitors.

(12) The Regulation must specify the conditions which must be satisfied for the exemption to apply. To guarantee that competition is not eliminated for a substantial part of the goods which are the subject of the franchise, it is necessary that parallel imports remain possible. Therefore, cross deliveries between franchisees should always be possible. Furthermore, where a franchise network is combined with another distribution system, franchisees should be free to obtain supplies from authorised distributors. To better inform consumers, thereby helping to ensure that they receive a fair share of the resulting benefits, it must be provided that the franchisee shall be obliged to indicate its status as an independent undertaking, by any appropriate means which does not jeopardise the common identity of the franchised network. Furthermore, where the franchisees have to honour guarantees for the franchisor's goods, this obligation should also apply to goods supplied by the franchisor, other franchisees or other agreed dealers.

(13) The Regulation must also specify restrictions which may not be included in franchise agreements if these are to benefit from the exemption granted by the Regulation, by virtue of the fact that such provisions are restrictions falling under Article 85(1) for which there is no general presumption that they will lead to the positive effects required by Article 85(3). This applies in particular to market sharing between competing manufacturers, to clauses unduly limiting the franchisee's choice of suppliers or customers, and to cases where the franchisee is restricted in determining its prices. However, the franchisor should be free to recommend prices to the franchisees, where it is not prohibited by national laws and to the extent that it does not lead to concerted practices for the effective application of these prices.

(14) Agreements which are not automatically covered by the exemption because they contain provisions that are not expressly exempted by the Regulation and not expressly excluded from exemption may nonetheless generally be presumed to be eligible for application of Article 85(3). It will be possible for the Commission rapidly to establish whether this is the case for a particular agreement. Such agreements should therefore be deemed to be covered by the exemption provided for in this Regulation where they are notified to the Commission and the Commission does not oppose the application of the exemption within a specified period of time.

(15) If individual agreements exempted by this Regulation nevertheless have effects which are incompatible with Article 85(3), in particular as interpreted by the administrative practice of the Commission and the case law of the Court of Justice, the Commission may withdrawn the benefit of the block exemption. This applies in particular where competition is significantly restricted because of the structure of the relevant market.

(16) Agreements which are automatically exempted pursuant to this Regulation need not be notified. Undertakings may nevertheless in a particular case request a decision pursuant to Council Regulation No 17[3] as last amended by the Act of Accession of Spain and Portugal.

(17) Agreements may benefit from the provisions either of this Regulation or of another Regulation, according to their particular nature and provided that they fulfil the necessary conditions of application. They may not benefit from a combination of the provisions of this Regulation with those of another block exemption Regulation,

---

3 OJ No 13, 21.2.1962, p 204/62.

Appendix 4

HAS ADOPTED THIS REGULATION:

Article 1

1. Pursuant to Article 85(3) of the Treaty and subject to the provisions of this Regulation, it is hereby declared that Article 85(1) of the Treaty shall not apply to franchise agreements to which two undertakings are party, which include one or more of the restrictions listed in Article 2.

2. The exemption provided for in paragraph 1 shall also apply to master franchise agreements to which two undertakings are party. Where applicable, the provisions of this Regulation concerning the relationship between franchisor and franchisee shall apply *mutatis mutandis* to the relationship between franchisor and master franchisee and between master franchisee and franchisee.

3. For the purposes of this Regulation:

(a) 'franchise' means a package of industrial or intellectual property rights relating to trade marks, trade names, shop signs, utility models, designs, copyrights, know-how or patents, to be exploited for the resale of goods or the provision of services to end users;

(b) 'franchise agreement' means an agreement whereby one undertaking, the franchisor, grants the other, the franchisee, in exchange for direct or indirect financial consideration, the right to exploit a franchise for the purposes of marketing specified types of goods and/or services; it includes at least obligations relating to:
— the use of a common name or shop sign and a uniform presentation of contract premises and/or means of transport,
— the communication by the franchisor to the franchisee of know-how,
— the continuing provision by the franchisor to the franchisee of commercial or technical assistance during the life of the agreement;

(c) 'master franchise agreement' means an agreement whereby one undertaking, the franchisor, grants the other, the master franchisee, in exchange of direct or indirect financial consideration, the right to exploit a franchise for the purposes of concluding franchise agreements with third parties, the franchisees;

(d) 'franchisor's goods' means goods produced by the franchisor or according to its instructions, and/or bearing the franchisor's name or trade mark;

(e) 'contract premises' means the premises used for the exploitation of the franchise or, when the franchise is exploited outside those premises, the base from which the franchisee operates the means of transport used for the exploitation of the franchise (contract means of transport);

(f) 'know-how' means a package of non-patented practical information, resulting from experience and testing by the franchisor, which is secret, substantial and identified;

(g) 'secret' means that the know-how, as a body or in the precise configuration and assembly of its components, is not generally known or easily accessible; it is not limited in the narrow sense that each individual component of the know-how should be totally unknown or unobtainable outside the franchisor's business;

(h) 'substantial' means that the know-how includes information which is of importance for the sale of goods or the provision of services to end users, and in particular for the presentation of goods for sale, the processing of goods in connection which the provision of services, methods of dealing with customers, and administration and financial management; the know-how must be useful for the franchisee by being capable, at the date of conclusion of the agreement, of improving the competitive position of the franchisee, in particular by improving the franchisee's performance or helping it to enter a new market;

(i) 'identified' means that the know-how must be described in a sufficiently comprehensive manner so as to make it possible to verify that it fulfils the criteria of secrecy and substantiality; the description of the know-how can either be set out in the franchise agreement or in a separate document or recorded in any other appropriate form.

Article 2

The exemption provided for in Article 1 shall apply to the following restrictions of competition:

(a) an obligation on the franchisor, in a defined area of the common market, the contract territory, not to:
— grant the right to exploit all or part of the franchise to third parties,
— itself exploit the franchise, or itself market the goods or services which are the subject-matter of the franchise under a similar formula;
— itself supply the franchisor's goods to third parties;

(b) an obligation on the master franchisee not to conclude franchise agreement with third parties outside its contract territory;

(c) an obligation on the franchisee to exploit the franchise only from the contract premises;

(d) an obligation on the franchisee to refrain, outside the contract territory, from seeking customers for the goods or the services which are the subject-matter of the franchise;

(e) an obligation on the franchisee not to manufacture, sell or use in the course of the provision of services, goods competing with the franchisor's goods which are the subject-matter of the franchise; where the subject-matter of the franchise is the sale or use in the course of the provision of services both certain types of goods and spare parts or accessories therefor, that obligation may not be imposed in respect of these spare parts or accessories.

Article 3

1. Article 1 shall apply notwithstanding the presence of any of the following obligations on the franchisee, in so far as they are necessary to protect the franchisor's industrial or intellectual property rights or to maintain the common identity and reputation of the franchised network:

(a) to sell, or use in the course of the provision of services, exclusively goods matching minimum objective quality specifications laid down by the franchisor;

(b) to sell, or use in the course of the provision of services, goods which are manufactured only by the franchisor or by third parties *designed* [*sic* ie 'designated'] by it, where it is impracticable, owing to the nature of the goods which are the subject-matter of the franchise, to apply objective quality specifications;

(c) not to engage, directly or indirectly, in any similar business in a territory where it would compete with a member of the franchised network, including the franchisor; the franchisee may be held to this obligation after termination of the agreement for a reasonable period which may not exceed one year, in the territory where it has exploited the franchise;

Appendix 4

(d) not to acquire financial interests in the capital of a competing undertaking, which would give the franchisee the power to influence the economic conduct of such undertaking;
(e) to sell the goods which are the subject-matter of the franchise only to end users, to other franchisees and to resellers within other channels of distribution supplied by the manufacturer of these goods or with its consent;
(f) to use its best endeavours to sell the goods or provide the services that are the subject-matter of the franchise; to offer for sale a minimum range of goods, achieve a minimum turnover, plan its orders in advance, keep minimum stocks and provide customer and warranty services;
(g) to pay to the franchisor a specified proportion of its revenue for advertising and itself carry out advertising for the nature of which it shall obtain the franchisor's approval.

2. Article 1 shall apply notwithstanding the presence of any of the following obligations on the franchisee:
(a) not to disclose to third parties the know-how provided by the franchisor; the franchisee may be held to this obligation after termination of the agreement;
(b) to communicate to the franchisor any experience gained in exploiting the franchise and to grant it, and other franchisees, a non-exclusive licence for the know-how resulting from that experience;
(c) to inform the franchisor of infringements of licensed industrial or intellectual property rights, to take legal action against infringers or to assist the franchisor in any legal actions against infringers;
(d) not to use know-how licensed by the franchisor for purposes other than the exploitation of the franchise; the franchisee may be held to this obligation after termination of the agreement;
(e) to attend or have its staff attend training courses arranged by the franchisor;
(f) to apply the commercial methods devised by the franchisor, including any subsequent modification thereof, and use the licensed industrial or intellectual property rights;
(g) to comply with the franchisor's standards for the equipment and presentation of the contract premises and/or means of transport;
(h) to allow the franchisor to carry out checks of the contract premises and/or means of transport, including the goods sold and the services provided, and the inventory and accounts of the franchisee;
(i) not without the franchisor's consent to change the location of the contract premises;
(j) not without the franchisor's consent to assign the rights and obligations under the franchise agreement.

3. In the event that, because of particular circumstances, obligations referred to in paragraph 2 fall within the scope of Article 85(1), they shall also be exempted even if they are not accompanied by any of the obligations exempted by Article 1.

Article 4

The exemption provided for in Article 1 shall apply on condition that:
(a) the franchisee is free to obtain the goods that are the subject-matter of the franchise from other franchisees; where such goods are also distributed through another network of authorised distributors, the franchisee must be free to obtain the goods from the latter;
(b) where the franchisor obliges the franchisee to honour guarantees for the

franchisor's goods, that obligation shall apply in respect of such goods supplied by any member of the franchised network or other distributors which give a similar guarantee, in the common market;

(c) the franchisee is obliged to indicate its status as an independent undertaking; this indication shall however not interfere with the common identity of the franchised network resulting in particular from the common name or shop sign and uniform appearance of the contract premises and/or means of transport.

Article 5

The exemption granted by Article 1 shall not apply where:

(a) undertakings producing goods or providing services which are identical or are considered by users as equivalent in view of their characteristics, price and intended use, enter into franchise agreements in respect of such goods or services;

(b) without prejudice to Article 2(e) and Article 3(1)(b), the franchisee is prevented from obtaining supplies of goods of a quality equivalent to those offered by the franchisor;

(c) without prejudice to Article 2(e), the franchisee is obliged to sell, or use in the process of providing services, goods manufactured by the franchisor or third parties designated by the franchisor and the franchisor refuses, for reasons other than protecting the franchisor's industrial or intellectual property rights, or maintaining the common identity and reputation of the franchised network, to designate as authorised manufacturers third parties proposed by the franchisee;

(d) the franchisee is prevented from continuing to use the licensed know-how after termination of the agreement where the know-how has become generally known or easily accessible, other than by breach of an obligation by the franchisee;

(e) the franchisee is restricted by the franchisor, directly or indirectly, in the determination of sale prices for the goods or services which are the subject-matter of the franchise, without prejudice to the possibility for the franchisor of recommending sale prices;

(f) the franchisor prohibits the franchisee from challenging the validity of the industrial or intellectual property rights which form part of the franchise, without prejudice to the possibility for the franchisor of terminating the agreement in such a case;

(g) franchisees are obliged not to supply within the common market the goods or services which are the subject-matter of the franchise to end users because of their place of residence.

Article 6

1. The exemption provided for in Article 1 shall also apply to franchise agreements which fulfil the conditions laid down in Article 4 and include obligations restrictive of competition which are not covered by Articles 2 and 3(3) and do not fall within the scope of Article 5, on condition that the agreements in question are notified to the Commission in accordance with the provisions of Commission Regulation

Appendix 4

No 27[4] and that the Commission does not oppose such exemption within a period of six months.

2. The period of six months shall run from the date on which the notification is received by the Commission. Where, however, the notification is made by registered post, the period shall run from the date shown on the postmark of the place of posting.

3. Paragraph 1 shall apply only if:
   (a) express reference is made to this Article in the notification or in a communication accompanying it; and
   (b) the information furnished with the notification is complete and in accordance with the facts.

4. The benefit of paragraph 1 can be claimed for agreements notified before the entry into force of this Regulation by submitting a communication to the Commission referring expressly to this Article and to the notification. Paragraphs 2 and 3(b) shall apply *mutatis mutandis*.

5. The Commission may oppose exemption. It shall oppose exemption if it receives a request to do so from a Member State within three months of the forwarding to the Member State of the notification referred to in paragraph 1 or the communication referred to in paragraph 4. This request must be justified on the basis of considerations relating to the competition rules of the Treaty.

6. The Commission may withdraw its opposition to the exemption at any time. However, where that opposition was raised at the request of a Member State, it may be withdrawn only after consultation of the advisory Committee on Restrictive Practices and Dominant Positions.

7. If the opposition is withdrawn because the undertakings concerned have shown that the conditions of Article 85(3) are fulfilled, the exemption shall apply from the date of the notification.

8. If the opposition is withdrawn because the undertakings concerned have amended the agreement so that the conditions of Article 85(3) are fulfilled, the exemption shall apply from the date on which the amendments take effect.

9. If the Commission opposes exemption and its opposition is not withdrawn, the effects of the notification shall be governed by the provisions of Regulation No 17.

Article 7

1. Information acquired pursuant to Article 6 shall be used only for the purposes of this Regulations.

2. The Commission and the authorities of the Member States, their officials and other servants shall not disclose information acquired by them pursuant to this Regulation of a kind that is covered by the obligation of professional secrecy.

3. Paragraphs 1 and 2 shall not prevent publication of general information or surveys which do not contain information relating to particular undertakings or associations of undertakings.

---

[4] OJ No 35, 10.5.1962, p 1118/62.

Appendix 4

Article 8

The Commission may withdraw the benefit of this Regulation, pursuant to Article 7 of Regulation No 19/65/EEC, where it finds in a particular case that an agreement exempted by this Regulation nevertheless has certain effects which are incompatible with the conditions laid down in Article 85(3) of the EEC Treaty, and in particular where territorial protection is awarded to the franchisee and:

(a) access to the relevant market or competition therein is significantly restricted by the cumulative effect of parallel networks of similar agreements established by competing manufacturers or distributors;

(b) the goods or services which are the subject-matter of the franchise do not face, in a substantial part of the common market, effective competition from goods or services which are identical or considered by users as equivalent in view of their characteristics, price and intended use;

(c) the parties, or one of them, prevent end users, because of their place of residence, from obtaining, directly or through intermediaries, the goods or services which are the subject-matter of the franchise within the common market, or use differences in specifications concerning those goods or services in different Member States, to isolate markets;

(d) franchisees engage in concerted practices relating to the sale prices of the goods or services which are the subject-matter of the franchise;

(e) the franchisor uses its right to check the contract premises and means of transport, or refuses its agreement to requests by the franchisee to move the contract premises or assign its rights and obligations under the franchise agreement, for reasons other than protecting the franchisor's industrial or intellectual property rights, maintaining the common identity and reputation of the franchised network or verifying that the franchisee abides by its obligations under the agreement.

Article 9

This Regulation shall enter into force on 1 February 1989.

It shall remain in force until 31 December 1999.

This Regulation shall be binding in its entirety and directly applicable in all Member States.

Done at Brussels, 30 November 1988.

For the Commission
Peter SUTHERLAND
Member of the Commission

Appendix 5
The text of the court's judgment in Pronuptia

Judgment of the Court
28 January 1986[1]

In Case 161/84

REFERENCE to the Court under Article 177 of the EEC Treaty by the Bundesgerichtshof [Federal Court of Justice] for a preliminary ruling in the proceedings pending before that court between

Pronuptia de Paris GmbH, Frankfurt am Main,

and

Pronuptia de Paris Irmgard Schillgalis, Hamburg,

on the interpretation of Article 85 of the EEC Treaty and Commission Regulation No 67/67/EEC of 22 March 1967 on the application of Article 85(3) of the Treaty to certain categories of exclusive dealing agreements (Official Journal, English Special Edition 1967, p 10),

The court

composed of: Lord Mackenzie Stuart, *President*, U Everling, K Bahlmann and R Joliet *(Presidents of Chambers)*, T Koopmans, O Due and Y Galmot, *Judges*,

Advocate General: P VerLoren van Themaat
Registrar: D Louterman, Administrator

after considering the observations submitted on behalf of the plaintiff in the main proceedings, by Dr Rainer Bechtold, the defendant in the main proceedings, by Dr Eberhard Kolonko, the Franch Republic, by S C de Margerie, acting as Agent, the Commission of the European Communities, by Dr Norbert Koch, acting as Agent.

after hearing the Opinion of the Advocate General delivered at the sitting on 19 June 1985,

gives the following

1 Language of the case: German.

Appendix 5

Judgment

(The account of the facts and issues which is contained in the complete text of the judgment is not reproduced)

Decision

1 By an order of 15 May 1984, which was received at the Court on 25 June 1984, the Bundesgerichtshof referred to the Court for a preliminary ruling under Article 177 of the EEC Treaty a number of questions regarding the interpretation of Article 85 of the EEC Treaty and Commission Regulation No 67/67/EEC of 22 March 1967 on the application of Article 85(3) of the Treaty to certain categories of exclusive dealing agreements (Official Journal, English Special Edition 1967, p 10) in order to ascertain whether those provisions are applicable to franchise agreements.

2 Those questions arose in proceedings between Pronuptia de Paris GmbH, Frankfurt am Main, (hereinafter referred to as 'the franchisor'), a subsidiary of the French company of the same name, and Mrs Schillgalis, who carries on business in Hamburg under the name Pronuptia de Paris and is referred to hereinafter as 'the franchisee', regarding the franchisee's obligation to pay to the franchisor arrears of royalties on her turnover for the years 1978 to 1980.

3 The franchisor's French parent company distributes wedding dresses and other articles of clothing worn at weddings under the trade-mark 'Pronuptia de Paris'. In the Federal Republic of Germany those products are distributed through shops operated directly by its subsidiary and through shops belonging to independent retailers under franchise contracts concluded by the subsidiary in its own name and in the name of the parent company.

4 By three contracts signed on 24 February 1980 the franchisee obtained a franchise for three separate zones, Hamburg, Oldenburg and Hanover. The three contracts are virtually identical in their wording. More specifically, they include the following provisions.

5 The franchisor:

(a) Grants the franchisee, in respect of a territory defined by means of a map attached to the contract, the exclusive right to use the trade-mark 'Pronuptia de Paris' for the marketing of her goods and services and the right to advertise;

(b) Undertakes not to open any other Pronuptia shops in the territory in question or to provide goods or services to third parties in that territory;

(c) Undertakes to assist the franchisee with regard to the commercial aspects of her business, advertising, the establishment and decoration of the shop, staff training, sales techniques, fashion and products, purchasing and marketing and, in general, everything which, in its experience, is likely to help to improve the turnover and profitability of the franchisee's business.

6 The franchisee, who remains sole proprietor of her business and assumes all its risks, is obliged:

(a) To sell the goods, using the trade name and trade-mark 'Pronuptia de Paris', only in the shop specified in the contract, which must be equipped and decorated mainly for the sale of bridal fashions in accordance with the franchisor's instructions, in such a way as to enhance the brand image of the Pronuptia chain, and cannot be transferred to another location or altered without the agreement of the franchisor;

(b) To purchase from the franchisor 80% of wedding dresses and accessories,

Appendix 5

together with a proportion of cocktail and evening dresses to be set by the franchisee herself, and to purchase the remainder only from suppliers approved by the franchisor;

(c) To pay the franchisor, in return for the benefits granted, a single entry fee for the contract territory of DM 15,000 and, throughout the duration of the contract, a royalty of 10% of total sales of Pronuptia products and all other goods, including evening dresses purchased from suppliers other than Pronuptia;

(d) To regard the prices suggested by the franchisor as recommended retail prices, without prejudice to her freedom to fix her own prices;

(e) To advertise in the contract territory only with the franchisor's agreement, and in any event to harmonise that advertising with the franchisor's international and national advertising, to distribute catalogues and other publicity material provided by the franchisor to the best of her abilities and in general to apply the business methods imparted to her by the franchisor;

(f) To make the sale of bridal fashions her main purpose;

(g) To refrain, during the period of validity of the contract and for one year after its termination, from competing in any way with a Pronuptia shop and in particular from opening a business of a nature identical or similar to that carried on under the contract, or participating directly or indirectly in such a business, in the Federal Republic of Germany, in West Berlin or in an area where Pronuptia is already represented in any way;

(h) Not to assign to third parties the rights and obligations arising under the contract or the business without the prior approval of the franchisor, it being understood that the franchisor will not withhold its approval if such an assignment takes place for health reasons and if the new contracting party shows that he is financially sound and is not in any way a competitor of the franchisor.

7   In the court of first instance judgment was given against the franchisee in the amount of DM 158,502 for arrears of royalties on her turnover for the years 1978 to 1980; the franchisee appealed to the Oberlandesgericht Frankfurt am Main, where she argued, in order to avoid payment of the arrears, that the contracts were contrary to Article 85(1) of the EEC Treaty and were not covered by the block exemption granted to certain categories of exclusive dealing agreement under Commission Regulation No 67/67. By judgment of 2 December 1982 the Oberlandesgericht upheld the franchisee's argument. It held that the mutual obligations of exclusivity constituted restrictions on competition within the common market, since the franchisor could not supply any other dealers in the contract territory and the franchisee could purchase and resell other goods from other Member States only to a limited extent. Since they were not eligible for exemption under Article 85(3) the contracts must, in its view, be regarded as void under Article 85(2). With regard to the issue of exemption, the Oberlandesgericht considered that it was not obliged to decide whether franchise contracts are in principle excluded from the scope of Commission Regulation No 67/67. In its view, the agreements in question in any event contain undertakings which go well beyond those described in Article 1 of the regulation and give rise to restrictions of competition not covered by Article 2.

8   The franchisor appealed against that judgment of the Bundesgerichtshof, arguing that the judgment of the trial court should be upheld. The Bundesgerichtshof considered that the outcome of the appeal depended on the interpretation of

Community law. It therefore asked the Court to give a preliminary ruling on the following questions:

'(1) Is Article 85(1) of the EEC Treaty applicable to franchise agreements such as the contracts between the parties, which have as their object the establishment of a special distribution system whereby the franchisor provides to the franchisee, in addition to goods, certain trade names, trade-marks, merchandising material and services?

(2) If the first question is answered in the affirmative: Is Commission Regulation No 67/67/EEC of 22 March 1967 on the application of Article 85(3) of the Treaty to certain categories of exclusive dealing agreements (block exemption) applicable to such contracts?

(3) If the second question is answered in the affirmative:

(a) Is Regulation No 67/67 still applicable of several undertakings which, though legally independent, are bound together by commercial ties and form a single economic entity for the purposes of the contract participate on one side of the agreement?

(b) Does Regulation No 67/67, and in particular Article 2(2)(c) thereof, apply to an obligation on the part of the franchisee to advertise solely with the prior agreement of the franchisor and in a manner that is in keeping with the latter's advertising, using the publicity material supplied by him, and in general to use the same business methods? Is it relevant in this connection that the franchisor's publicity material contains price recommendations which are not binding?

(c) Does Regulation No 67/67, and in particular Articles 1(1)(b), 2(1)(a) and 2(2)(b) therof, apply to an obligation on the part of the franchisee to confine the sale of the contract goods exclusively or at least for the most part to particular business premises specially adapted for the purpose?

(d) Does Regulation No 67/67, and in particular Article 1(1)(b) thereof, apply to an obligation on the part of the franchisee—who is bound to purchase most of his supplies from the franchisor—to make the rest of his purchases of goods covered by the contract solely from suppliers approved by the franchisor?

(e) Does Regulation No 67/67 sanction an obligation on the franchisor to give the franchisee commercial, advertising and professional support?'

The first question

9 Pronuptia de Paris GmbH, Frankfurt am Main, the franchisor, argues that a system of franchise agreements makes it possible to combine the advantages offered by a form of distribution which presents a uniform image to the public (such as a system of subsidiaries) with the distribution of goods by independent retailers who themselves bear the risks associated with selling. The system is made up of a network of vertical agreements intended to ensure uniform presentation to the public and reinforces the franchisor's competitive power at the horizontal level, that is to say, with regard to other forms of distribution. It makes it possible for an undertaking which would not otherwise have the necessary financial resources to establish a distribution network beyond the confines of its own region, a network which enables small undertakings to participate as franchisees while retaining their independence. In view of those advantages Article 85(1) does not apply where the franchise agreements do not include restrictions on the liberty of the contracting parties which go beyond those which are the necessary concomitants of a franchise system. Exclusive delivery and supply obligations, in so far as they are intended to

Appendix 5

ensure a standard selection of goods, uniform advertising and shop layout and a prohibition on selling goods supplied under the contract in other shops, are inherent in the very nature of the franchise contract and are outside the scope of Article 85(1).

10 Mrs Schillgalis, the franchisee, submits that the first question should be answered in the affirmative. The most significant characteristic of the contracts in question is the territorial protection given to the franchisee. They cannot be compared with agency agreements, since franchisees, unlike agents, act in their own name and on their own account and bear all trading risks. The system of franchise agreements at issue gives rise to significant restrictions of competition, having regard to the fact the Pronuptia is, as it itself asserts, the world's leading French supplier of wedding dresses and accessories.

11 The French Government states that Article 85(1) may be applicable to franchise agreements for the distribution of a product but should not necessarily be applied to such agreements, in view of their positive aspects.

12 The Commission emphasises that the scope of Article 85(1) is not restricted to particular types of contracts, and infers that in appropriate circumstances Article 85(1) applies also to contracts for the assignment of business names and trade-marks, registered or not, and the provision of services, as well as the supply of goods.

13 It should be pointed out first of all that franchise agreements, the legality of which has not previously been put in issue before the Court, are very diverse in nature. It appears from what was said in argument before the Court that a distinction must be drawn between different varieties of franchise agreements. In particular, it is necessary to distinguish between (i) service franchises, under which the franchisee offers a service under the business name or symbol and sometimes the trade-mark of the franchisor, in accordance with the franchisor's instructions, (ii) production franchises, under which the franchisee manufactures products according to the instructions of the franchisor and sells them under the franchisor's trade-mark, and (iii) distribution franchises, under which the franchisee simply sells certain products in a shop which bears the franchisor's business name or symbol. In this judgment the Court is concerned only with this third type of contract, to which the questions asked by the national court expressly refer.

14 The compatibility of franchise agreements for the distribution of goods with Article 85(1) cannot be assessed *in abstracto* but depends on the provisions contained in such agreements. In order to make its reply as useful as possible to the Bundesgerichtshof the Court will concern itself with contracts such as that described above.

15 In a system of distribution franchises of that kind an undertaking which has established itself as a distributor on a given market and thus developed certain business methods grants independent traders, for a fee, the right to establish themselves in other markets using its business name and the business methods which have made it successful. Rather than a method of distribution, it is a way for an undertaking to derive financial benefit from its expertise without investing its own capital. Moreover, the system gives traders who do not have the necessary experience access to methods which they could not have learned without considerable effort and allows them to benefit from the reputation of the franchisor's business name. Franchise agreements for the distribution of goods differ in that regard from dealerships or contracts which incorporate approved retailers into a selective distribution system, which do not involve the use of a single business name, the application of uniform business methods or the payment of royalties in return for the benefits granted. Such a system, which allows the franchisor to profit from

Appendix 5

his success, does not in itself interfere with competition. In order for the system to work two conditions must be met.

16 First, the franchisor must be able to communicate his know-how to the franchisees and provide them with the necessary assistance in order to enable them to apply his methods, without running the risk that that know-how and assistance might benefit competitors, even indirectly. It follows that provisions which are essential in order to avoid that risk do not constitute restrictions on competition for the purposes of Article 85(1). That is also true of a clause prohibiting the franchisee, during the period of validity of the contract and for a reasonable period after its expiry, from opening a shop of the same or a similar nature in an area where he may compete with a member of the network. The same may be said of the franchisee's obligation not to transfer his shop to another party without the prior approval of the franchisor; that provision is intended to prevent competitors from indirectly benefiting from the know-how and assistance provided.

17 Secondly, the franchisor must be able to take the measures necessary for maintaining the identity and reputation of the network bearing his business name or symbol. It follows that provisions which establish the means of control necessary for that purpose do not constitute restrictions on competition for the purposes of Article 85(1).

18 The same is true of the franchisee's obligation to apply the business methods developed by the franchisor and to use the know-how provided.

19 That is also the case with regard to the franchisee's obligation to sell the goods covered by the contract only in premises laid out and decorated according to the franchisor's instructions, which is intended to ensure uniform presentation in conformity with certain requirements. The same requirements apply to the location of the shop, the choice of which is also likely to affect the network's reputation. It is thus understandable that the franchisee cannot transfer his shop to another location without the franchisor's approval.

20 The prohibition of the assignment by the franchisee of his rights and obligations under the contract without the franchisor's approval protects the latter's right freely to choose the franchisees, on whose business qualifications the establishment and maintenance of the network's reputation depend.

21 By means of the control exerted by the franchisor on the selection of goods offered by the franchisee the public is able to obtain goods of the same quality from each franchisee. It may in certain cases—for instance, the distribution of fashion articles—be impractical to lay down objective quality specifications. Because of the large number of franchisees it may also be too expensive to ensure that such specifications are observed. In such circumstances a provision requiring the franchisee to sell only products supplied by the franchisor or by suppliers selected by him may be considered necessary for the protection of the network's reputation. Such a provision may not however have the effect of preventing the franchisee from obtaining those products from other franchisees.

22 Finally, since advertising helps to define the image of the network's name or symbol in the eyes of the public, a provision requiring the franchisee to obtain the franchisor's approval for all advertising is also essential for the maintenance of the network's identity, so long as that provision concerns only the nature of the advertising.

23 It must be emphasised on the other hand that, far from being necessary for the protection of the know-how provided or the maintenance of the network's identity and reputation, certain provisions restrict competition between the members of the network. That is true of provisions which share markets between the franchisor

Appendix 5

and franchisees or between franchisees or prevent franchisees from engaging in price competition with each other.

24   In that regard, the attention of the national court should be drawn to the provision which obliges the franchisee to sell goods covered by the contract only in the premises specified therein. That provision prohibits the franchisee from opening a second shop. Its real effect becomes clear if it is examined in conjunction with the franchisor's undertaking to ensure that the franchisee has the exclusive use of his business name or symbol in a given territory. In order to comply with that undertaking the franchisor must not only refrain from establishing himself within that territory but also require other franchisees to give an undertaking not to open a second shop outside their own territory. A combination of provisions of that kind results in a sharing of markets between the franchisor and the franchisees or between franchisees and thus restricts competition within the network. As is clear from the judgment of 13 July 1966 (Joined Cases 56 and 58/64 *Consten and Grundig v Commission* [1966] ECR 299), a restriction of that kind constitutes a limitation of competition for the purposes of Article 85(1) if it concerns a business name or symbol which is already well-known. It is of course possible that a prospective franchisee would not take the risk of becoming part of the chain, investing his own money, paying a relatively high entry fee and undertaking to pay a substantial annual royalty, unless he could hope, thanks to a degree of protection against competition on the part of the franchisor and other franchisees, that his business would be profitable. That consideration, however, is relevant only to an examination of the agreement in the light of the conditions laid down in Article 85(3).

25   Although provisions which impair the franchisee's freedom to determine his own prices are restrictive of competition, that is not the case where the franchisor simply provides franchisees with price guidelines, so long as there is no concerted practice between the franchisor and the franchisees or between the franchisees themselves for the actual application of such prices. It is for the national court to determine whether that is indeed the case.

26   Finally, it must be added that franchise agreements for the distribution of goods which contain provisions for sharing markets between the franchisor and the franchisees or between the franchisees themselves are in any event liable to affect trade between Member States, even if they are entered into by undertakings established in the same Member State, in so far as they prevent franchisees from establishing themselves in another Member State.

27   In view of the foregoing, the answer to the first question must be that:

(1) The compatibility of franchise agreements for the distribution of goods with Article 85(1) depends on the provisions contained therein and on their economic context.

(2) Provisions which are strictly necessary in order to ensure that the know-how and assistance provided by the franchisor do not benefit competitiors do not constitute restrictions of competition for the purposes of Article 85(1).

(3) Provisions which establish the control strictly necessary for maintaining the identity and reputation of the network identified by the common name or symbol do not constitute restrictions of competition for the purposes of Article 85(1).

(4) Provisions which share markets between the franchisor and the franchisees or between franchisees constitute restrictions of competition for the purposes of Article 85(1).

(5) The fact that the franchisor makes price recommendations to the franchisee does not constitute a restriction of competition, so long as there is no concerted

practice between the franchisor and the franchisees or between the franchisees themselves for the actual application of such prices.

(6) Franchise agreements for the distribution of goods which contain provisions for sharing markets between the franchisor and the franchisees or between franchisees are capable of affecting trade between Member States.

The second question

28   The second question, which was raised only in the event that the first question should be answered in the affirmative, seeks to ascertain whether Commission Regulation No 67/67 of 22 March 1967 on the application of Article 85(3) of the Treaty to certain categories of exclusive dealing agreements is applicable to franchise agreements for the distribution of goods. Having regard to the foregoing remarks regarding provisions which share markets between the franchisor and the franchisees or between franchisees, that question remains relevant to a certain degree and must therefore be examined.

29   Pronuptia de Paris, the franchisor, submits that the Court should reply to the second question in the affirmative. Regulation No 67/67 applies, it says, to exclusive supply and purchase agreements even where such agreements also involve the granting of licences to use an undertaking's trade-mark or other distinctive symbol. In a franchise agreement exclusive supply and purchase obligations present advantages of the kind referred to in the sixth recital in the preamble to Regulation No 67/67. Provisions other than those referred to in Article 2 of Regulation No 67/67 present no obstacle to exemption in so far as they do not restrict competition within the meaning of Article 85(1).

30   Mrs Schillgalis, the franchisee, argues that Regulation No 67/67 is not applicable to franchise agreements. First of all, that regulation was drawn up on the basis of the Commission's experience at the time, which extended only to exclusive dealing agreements. Secondly, the franchisor has much more power over the franchisee than a supplier has over his distributors. Thirdly, the restriction of competition inherent in franchise agreements also has horizontal effects, since the franchisor generally has subsidiaries which carry on business at the same level of distribution as the franchisees.

31   The French Government merely observes that Regulation No 67/67 does not seem applicable to this type of contract.

32   The Commission begins by admitting that it does not yet have sufficient experience to arrive at a satisfactory definition of franchise agreements. It adds that Regulation No 67/67 is not intended to provide exemption for restrictions on competition contained in agreements for the grant of a licence to use a business name or symbol or a trade-mark; the grant of such a licence, together with the provision of know-how and commercial assistance, seems to the Commission to constitute the initial feature of franchise agreements. However, where licensing agreements of that kind include agreements for the supply of goods for retail sale and where the supply agreements are separable from the licensing agreements, Regulation No 67/67 may be applicable to the supply agreements in so far as the conditions laid down in the regulation are satisfied. The exclusive distributor may not, as such, be made subject to restrictions of competition other than those covered by Article 1(1) and Article 2(1) of the regulation. In the contracts which have given rise to the proceedings before the Bundesgerichtshof the provision regarding the place of business creates such a close relationship between the exclusive

Appendix 5

dealership portion and the licensing portion of the franchise agreement that they make up an indivisible whole. The block exemption is therefore inapplicable, according to the Commission, even to the exclusive dealership portion of the contract.

33 Reference must be made in this respect to a number of points in Regulation No 67/67. First, the category of contracts covered by the block exemption is defined by reference to obligations of supply and purchase, which may or may not be reciprocal, and not by reference to factors such as the use of a single business name or symbol, the application of uniform business methods and the payment of royalties in return for the benefits provided under franchise agreements for the distribution of goods. Secondly, the wording of Article 2 expressly covers only exclusive dealing agreements, which, as has already been pointed out, differ in nature from franchise agreements for the distribution of goods. Thirdly, that article lists the restrictions and obligations which may be imposed on the exclusive distributor but does not mention those which may be imposed on the other party to the contract, while in the case of a franchise agreement for the distribution of goods the obligations undertaken by the franchisor, in particular the obligations to provide know-how and to assist the franchisee, are of particular importance. Fourthly, the list of obligations which may be imposed on the distributor under Article 2(2) does not include the obligations to pay royalties or the obligations ensuing from provisions which establish the control strictly necessary for maintaining the identity and reputation of the network.

34 It must be concluded, therefore, that Regulation No 67/67 is not applicable to franchise agreements for the distribution of goods such as those considered in these proceedings.

The third question

35 In view of the reply to the second question raised by the national court there is no need to reply to the third question.

Costs

36 The costs incurred by the French Government and by the Commission of the European Communities, which have submitted observations to the Court, are not recoverable. Since these proceedings are, in so far as the parties to the main proceedings are concerned, in the nature of a step in the action pending before the national court, the decision on costs is a matter for that court.

On those grounds,

The court

In answer to the questions submitted to it by the Bundesgerichtshof by order of 15 May 1984, hereby rules:
  (1) (a) The compatibility of franchise agreements for the distribution of goods with Article 85(1) depends on the provisions contained therein and on their economic context.
  (b) Provisions which are strictly necessary in order to ensure that the know-how and assistance provided by the franchisor do not benefit competitors do not constitute restrictions of competition for the purposes of Article 85(1).

Appendix 5

(c) Provisions which establish the control strictly necessary for maintaining the identity and reputation of the network identified by the common name or symbol do not constitute restrictions of competition for the purposes of Article 85(1).

(d) Provisions which share markets between the franchisor and the franchisees or between franchisees constitute restrictions of competition for the purposes of Article 85(1).

(e) The fact that the franchisor makes price recommendations to the franchisee does not constitute a restriction of competition, so long as there is no concerted practice between the franchisor and the franchisees or between the franchisees themselves for the actual application of such prices.

(f) Franchise agreements for the distribution of goods which contain provisions for sharing markets between the franchisor and the franchisees or between franchisees are capable of affecting trade between Member States.

(2) Regulation No 67/67/EEC is not applicable to franchise agreements for the distribution of goods such as those considered in these proceedings.

Delivered in open court in Luxembourg on 28 January 1986.

Appendix 6
SP 1/90 Company residence

9 January 1990

1   Residence has always been a material factor, for companies as well as individuals, in determining tax liability. But statute law has never laid down comprehensive rules for determining where a company is resident and until 1988 the question was left solely to the courts to decide. FA 1988, s 66 introduced the rule that a company incorporated in the UK is resident here for the purposes of the Taxes Acts. Case law still applies in determining the residence of companies excepted from the incorporation rule or which are not incorporated in the UK.

A   The incorporation rule

2   The incorporation rule applies to companies incorporated in the UK subject to the exceptions in FA 1988, Sch 7 for some companies incorporated before 15 March 1988. Paragraphs 3 to 8 below explain how the Revenue interpret various terms used in the legislation.

Carrying on business

3   The exceptions from the incorporation test in Sch 7 depend in part on the company carrying on business at a specified time or during a relevant period. The question whether a company carries on business is one of fact to be decided according to the particular circumstances of the company. Detailed guidance is not practicable but the Revenue take the view that 'business' has a wider meaning than 'trade'; it can include transactions, such as the purchase of stock, carried out for the purposes of a trade about to be commenced and the holding of investments including shares in a subsidiary company. Such a holding could consist of a single investment from which no income was derived.

4   A company such as a shelf company whose transactions have been limited to those formalities necessary to keep the company on the register of companies will not be regarded as carrying on business.

5   For the purposes of the case law test (see B below) the residence of a company is determined by the place where its real business is carried on. A company which can demonstrate that in these terms it is or was resident outside the UK will have carried on business for the purposes of Sch 7.

'Taxable in a territory outside the UK'

6 A further condition for some companies for exception from the incorporation test is provided by Sch 7 para 1(1)(*c*), para 5(1). The company has to be taxable in a territory outside the UK. 'Taxable' means that the company is liable to tax on income by reason of domicile, residence or place of management. This is similar to the approach adopted in the residence provisions of many double taxation agreements. Territories which impose tax on companies by reference to incorporation or registration or similar criteria are covered by the term 'domicile'. Territories which impose tax by reference to criteria such as 'effective management', 'central administration', 'head office' or 'principal place of business' are covered by the term 'place of management'.

7 A company has to be liable to tax on income so that a company which is, for example, liable only to a flat rate fee or lump sum duty does not fulfil the test. On the other hand a company is regarded as liable to tax in a particular territory if it is within the charge there even though it may pay no tax because, for example, it makes losses or claims double taxation relief.

'Treasury consent'

8 Before 15 March 1988 it was unlawful for a company to cease to be resident in the UK without the consent of the Treasury. Companies which have ceased to be resident in pursuance of a Treasury consent, as defined in Sch 7, para 5(1), are excepted from the incorporation rule subject to certain conditions. A few companies ceased to be resident without Treasury consent but were informed subsequently by letter that the Treasury would take no action against them under the relevant legislation. Such a letter is not a retrospective grant of consent and the companies concerned cannot benefit from the exceptions which depend on Treasury consent.

B The case law test

9 This test of company residence is that enunciated by Lord Loreburn in *De Beers Consolidated Mines v Howe* (5 TC 198) at the beginning of this century—

> 'A company resides, for the purposes of Income Tax, where its real business is carried on . . . . . I regard that as the true rule; and the real business is carried on where the central management and control actually abides.'

10 The 'central management and control' test, as set out in *De Beers*, has been endorsed by a series of subsequent decisions. In particular, it was described by Lord Radcliffe in the 1959 cases of *Bullock v Unit Construction Co* 38 TC 712 at p 738 as being—

> 'as precise and unequivocal as a positive statutory injunction . . . . . I do not know of any other test which has either been substituted for that of central management and control, or has been defined with sufficient precision to be regarded as an acceptable alternative to it. To me . . . . . it seems impossible to read Lord Loreburn's words without seeing that he regarded the formula he was propounding as constituting *the* test of residence.'

Nothing which has happened since has in any way altered this basic principle for a company the residence of which is not governed by the incorporation rule;

Appendix 6

under current UK case law such a company is regarded as resident for tax purposes where central management and control is to be found.

Place of 'central management and control'

11 In determining whether or not an individual company outside the scope of the incorporation test is resident in the UK, it thus becomes necessary to locate its place of 'central management and control'. The case law concept of central management and control is, in broad terms, directed at the highest level of control of the business of a company. It is to be distinguished from the place where the main operations of a business are to be found, though those two places may often coincide. Moreover, the exercise of control does not necessarily demand any minimum standard of active involvement: it may, in appropriate circumstances, be exercised tacitly through passive oversight.

12 Successive decided cases have emphasised that the place of central management and control is wholly a question of fact. For example, Lord Radcliffe in *United Construction* said that 'the question where control and management abide must be treated as one of fact or "actuality" (p 741). It follows that factors which together are decisive in one instance may individually carry little weight in another. Nevertheless the decided cases do give some pointers. In particular a series of decisions has attached importance to the place where the company's board of directors meet. There are very many cases in which the board meets in the same country as that in which the business operations take place, and central management and control is clearly located in that one place. In other cases central management and control may be exercised by directors in one country though the actual business operations may, perhaps under the immediate management of local directors, take place elsewhere.

13 But the location of board meetings, although important in the normal case, is not necessarily conclusive. Lord Radcliffe in *United Construction* pointed out (p 738) that the site of the meetings of the directors' board had *not* been chosen as '*the* test' of company residence. In some cases, for example, central management and control is exercised by a single individual. This may happen when a chairman or managing director exercises powers formally conferred by the company's Articles and the other board members are little more than cyphers, or by reason of a dominant shareholding or for some other reason. In those cases the residence of the company is where the controlling individual exercises his powers.

14 In general the place of directors' meetings is significant only insofar as those meetings constitute the medium through which central management and control is exercised. If, for example, the directors of a company were engaged together actively in the UK in the complete running of a business which was wholly in the UK, the company would not be regarded as resident outside the UK merely because the directors held formal board meetings outside the UK. While it is possibe to identify extreme situations in which central management and control plainly is, or is not, exercised by directors in formal meetings, the conclusion in any case is wholly one of fact depending on the relative weight to be given to various factors. Any attempt to lay down rigid guidelines would only be misleading.

15 Generally, however, where doubts arise about a particular company's residence status, the Inland Revenue adopt the following approach—

(i) They first try to ascertain whether the directions of the company in fact exercise central management and control.

(ii) If so, they seek to determine where the directors exercise this central management and control (which is not necessarily where they meet).

(iii) In cases where the directors apparently do *not* exercise central management and control of the company, the Revenue then look to establish where and by whom it is exercised.

Parent/subsidiary relationship

16 It is particularly difficult to apply the 'central management and control' test in the situation where a subsidiary company and its parent operate in different territories. In this situation, the parent will normally influence, to a greater or lesser extent, the actions of the subsidiary. Where that influence is exerted by the parent exercising the powers which a sole or majority shareholder has in general meetings of the subsidiary, for example to appoint and dismiss members of the board of the subsidiary and to initiate or approve alterations to its financial structure, the Revenue would not seek to argue that central management and control of the subsidiary is located where the parent company is resident. However, in cases where the parent usurps the functions of the board of the subsidiary (such as *Unit Construction* itself) or where that board merely rubber stamps the parent company's decisions without giving them any independent consideration of its own, the Revenue draw the conclusion that the subsidiary has the same residence for tax purposes as its parent.

17 The Revenue recognise that there may be many cases where a company is a member of a group having its ultimate holding company in another country which will not fall readily into either of the categories referred to above. In considering whether the board of such a subsidiary company exercises central management and control of the subsidiary's business, they have regard to the degree of autonomy which those directors have in conducting the company's business. Matters (among others) that may be taken into account are the extent to which the directors of the subsidiary take decisions on their own authority as to investment, production, marketing and procurement without reference to the parent.

Conclusion

18 In outlining factors relevant to the application of the case law test, this statement assumes that they exist for genuine commercial reasons. Where, however, as may happen, it appears that a major objective underlying the existence of certain factors is the obtaining of tax benefits from residence or non-residence, the Revenue examine the facts particularly closely in order to see whether there has been an attempt to create the appearance of central management and control in a particular place without the reality.

19 The case law test examined in this Statement is not always easy to apply. The courts have recognised that there may be difficulties where it is not possible to identify any one country as the seat of central management and control. The principles to apply in those circumstances have not been fully developed in case law. In addition, the last relevant case was decided almost 30 years ago, and there have been many developments in communications since then, which in particular may enable a company to be controlled from a place far distant from where the day-to-day management is carried on. As the statement makes clear, while the

Appendix 6

general principle has been laid down by the courts, its application must depend on the precise facts.

C Double taxation agreements

20   In general our double taxation agreements do not affect the UK resident of a company as established for UK tax purposes. But where the partner country adopts a different definition of residence, it may happen that a UK resident company is treated, under the partner country's domestic law, as also resident there. In these cases, the agreement normally specifies what the tax consequences of this 'double' residence shall be.

21   Under the double taxation agreement with the United States, for example, the UK residence of a company for UK tax purposes is unaffected. But where that company is also a US corporation, it is excluded from some of the reliefs conferred by the agreement. On the other hand, under a double taxation agreement which follows the 1977 OECD Model Taxation Convention, a company classed as resident by both the UK and the partner country is, for the purposes of the agreement, treated as resident where its 'place of effective management' is situated.

22   The commentary in Art 4 para 3 of the OECD Model records the UK view that, in agreements (such as those with some Commonwealth countries) which treat a company as resident in a state in which 'its business is managed and controlled', this expression means 'the effective management of the enterprise'. More detailed consideration of the question in the light of the approach of continental legal systems and of Community law to the question of company residence has led the Revenue to revise this view. It is now considered that effective management may, in some cases, be found at a place different from the place of central management and control. This could happen, for example, where a company is run by executives based abroad, but the final directing power rests with non-executive directors who meet in the UK. In such circumstances the company's place of effective management might well be abroad but, depending on the precise powers of the non-executive directors, it might be centrally managed and controlled (and therefore resident) in the UK.

23   The incorporation rule in FA 1988, s 66(1) determines a residence which supersedes a different place 'given by any rule of law'. This incorporation rule determines residence under UK domestic law and is subject to the provisions of any applicable double taxation agreement. It does not override the provisions of a double taxation agreement which may make a UK incorporated company a resident of an overseas territory *for the purposes of the agreement* (see 20 and 21 above).

Appendix 7
The Registration of Restrictive Trading Agreements (EEC Documents) Regulations 1973 (SI 1973/950)

Made 22nd May 1973
Laid before Parliament 4th June 1973
Coming into operation 25th June 1973

The Registrar of Restrictive Trading Agreements (in these regulations referred to as 'the Registrar') in exercise of the powers conferred upon him by sections 11 and 19 of the Restrictive Trade Practices Act 1956 (hereinafter referred to as 'the Act of 1956') and subsection (2) of section 10 of the European Communities Act 1972 hereby orders that the following regulations shall have effect:

1—(1) These regulations may be cited as the Registration of Restrictive Trading Agreements (EEC Documents) Regulations 1973 and shall come into operation on the 25th June 1973.

(2) The Interpretation Act 1889 shall apply to the interpretation of these regulations as it applies to the interpretation of an Act of Parliament.

2—(1) Where in relation to any agreement which is subject to registration under the Act of 1956 any such step or any such decision as is specified in paragraph (2) hereof is or has been taken or given under or for the purposes of any directly applicable Community provision affecting that agreement, there shall be delivered or sent to the Registrar by or on behalf of the parties to that agreement the information so specified in respect of that step or decision within 30 days of the taking or giving thereof or within 30 days of the coming into operation of these regulations, whichever is the later.

(2) The steps, decisions and information referred to are the following:
   (a) applying for negative clearance for or notifying the agreement to the Commission of the European Communities—a copy of the application or notification submitted to the Commission;
   (b) notification by the Commission to the parties to the agreement of the opportunity to be heard in relation to objections raised against them—a memorandum to that effect specifying the date of the notification;
   (c) a decision of the Commission giving negative clearance in respect of the agreement—four copies of such part of the decision as sets out the effects thereof;
   (d) a decision of the Commission pursuant to article 85(3) of the EEC Treaty given in respect of the agreement—four copies of such part of the decision as sets out the effects thereof;
   (e) a decision of the Commission finding infringement of article 85 of the EEC Treaty by the agreement—four copies of such part of the decision as sets out the effects thereof;
   (f) a decision of the European Court relating to any decision of the

Appendix 7

Commission hereinbefore described—four copies of such part of the decision as sets out the effects thereof.

3 The particulars of an agreement subject to registrations under the Act of 1956 to be entered or filed in the register shall include a copy of any such part of a decision of the Commission of the European Communities or the European Court affecting that agreement furnished in pursuance of regulation 2 hereof.

4 Anything required by these regulations to be delivered or sent to the Registrar shall be addressed to:

The Registrar of Restrictive Trading Agreements (Branch R)
Chancery House
Chancery Lane
London WC2A 1SP

Rupert Sich,
Registrar of Restrictive Trading Agreements.

22nd May 1973

Index

[In this Index, numbers in roman type, eg 4.08, refer to paragraph numbers in the chapters of the main text. Numbers in bold type, eg **216**, refer to page numbers of precedents and appendix.]

Accounting
  misleading, 7.01
Advertising
  British Code of Advertising Practice,
    application of, 7.04
    object of, 7.05
  British Franchise Association's code, 7.04
    consumer complaints, 7.06
    franchise agreements dealing with, 5.63, 6.15
  Code of Advertising Practice Committee, 7.05
  distributor having right to control, 2.73
  franchises, of,
    groups of franchisees, by, 6.15
    misleading, 7.01
    not regulated by Trade Descriptions Act, 7.23
  goods, of, Secretary of State's power to regulated, 7.23
  misrepresentation in, 7.11
  sale of franchise, of, 7.23
  television and radio, monitoring of, 7.08
  Trade Description Act 1968, 7.19
  unauthorised, 5.63
Agency
  advertising etc., use by third party, liability of franchisor, 1.42, 1.43
  definition, 4.149
  estoppel, by, *see* Estoppel
  franchise chains operating in new fields, 1.40
  holding out, by, 1.39
  liability, distinguished from vicarious liability, 1.31
  licence and agency agreement, **404–408**
  'no agency' agreement, 5.48
  ostensible authority, 1.40
  partner as agent of firm, 1.47
  third parties, liability of franchisor to, 1.38
Agreement. *See* Franchise

Anti-competitive practices
  Director General of Fair Trading,
    informal inquiries by, 2.137
    investigation by, 2.136, 2.138
    report of, 2.138
  exclusion of smaller operations, 2.135
  minimum advertised price maintenance, 2.132
  Office of Fair Trading Guide, 2.130
  patents, in relation to, 2.139
  'tie-ins', advice as to, 2.129
Artistic works
  design protection of, 3.79A, 3.79B

Berne Union, 3.132, 4.80
Borrowings, interest on, taxation, 4.62, 4.63
British Code of Advertising Practice. *See* Advertising
British Franchise Association
  activities of, 0.16
  aims and formation, 0.16
  applications for admissions to, 0.16
  Arbitration Scheme, 0.16
  Code of Ethics, 0.16, 7.04
  declaration to be completed by members, 0.11
  definition of franchise, 1.02
  reputable operators should be members of, 0.14
Business Expansion Scheme
  aim, 4.29
  breaches of spirit of scheme, 4.30, 4.31, 4.34
  business excluded, 4.32, 4.40, 4.42
  capital gains tax relief, 4.47, 4.48
  draft prospectus, 4.49
  franchises benefiting from, 4.35 et seq.
  husband and wife, relief for, 4.46
  introduction, 4.29
  investment policy, 4.30
  low-risk, high-asset companies, 4.34
  maximum limit, 4.33

449

Index

Business Expansion Scheme—*continued*
  relief for investment to incorporate trades, 4.36–4.39
  restriction on property-based assets, 4.40–4.45
  de minimis exemption, 4.44, 4.45

Business format franchising
  advantages to franchisor and franchisee, 0.12
  booms and failure, 0.13
  competition law problems, 2.08
  control exercisable by franchisor, 0.12
  distinctive feature of, 0.12
  distributorships, 2.15
  EEC competition law, application of, 2.15
  generally, 0.01
  heart of, 2.07
  information about, 0.15
  United Kingdom, in, generally, 0.14

Business names
  disclosure requirements, 1.53
  register of, search in, 3.05
  registration of, 6.24
  requirements as to, 3.08, 6.24

Business premises
  security of tenure, 5.26
  termination of tenancy, 5.26–5.28

Canada
  franchise regulations, 7.64

Capital gains tax
  generally, 4.71
  premium for lease, on, 4.20
  roll-over relief, 4.64

Character merchandising
  celebrity names, 3.09
  copyright, 3.14
  defamation in respect of, 3.15
  definition, 1.13n, 3.09, 3.10
  false trade descriptions, 3.17
  invasion of privacy, 3.16
  invented characters, 3.14
  name, right to use, 3.18
  passing off in, 3.72, 3.74
  'trafficking', 1.13, 3.12, 3.13

Close company
  interest payments, relief for investment in, 4.53
  tax disadvantages, 4.54
  taxation of, on transfer of assets, 4.97
  transfer of value, inheritance tax, 4.97

Community Patent Convention, 3.128

Companies Register
  search of, before choosing name, 3.05

Company
  close, *see* Close company
  controlled foreign, *see* Overseas company
  limited liability public unquoted, prospectus, 4.49, **308**, **376–389**
  residence, 4.105, **442–446**

Competition
  Act 1980,
    anti-competitive practices, 2.126–2.132
    checklist, 2.140
    competition as means of fighting inflation, 2.126
    definitions, 2.126
    equipment supply, agreements as to, 5.06
    exemptions from provisions of, 2.133–2.136
    investigation procedure, 2.126
    potential application of, 2.130
    practice, 2.137, 2.138
    Price Commission, abolition of, 2.126
  agreements, drafting of, 5.03
  American cases, 2.01, 2.03
  block exemption, *see* European Communities
  economic unit, meaning, 2.06
  forms approach, 2.04
  EEC law,
    generally. *See* European Communities
    objects of Treaty of Rome, 2.12
  laws,
    economic theories, in context of, 2.01
    types of, 2.01, 2.04
    unpredictability of, 2.05
  Pronuptia case, 2.15, 2.16, **432–441**
  resale price maintenance, 2.153, 2.151
  restraint of trade at common law. *See* Restraint of trade
  restrictive practice. *See* Restrictive trade practices
  'tie-ins',
    accounting system, as, 2.09
    American view of, 2.02
    effect of, 2.129
    manufacturing licences, in, 2.50
    royalty concealed by, 2.03
  White Paper, 2.92
  Yves Rocher case, 2.17

Consortium relief
  availability of, 4.110

Contract
  duties imposed by, 1.28
  preliminary, whether desirable, 5.36

Contract of service
  basic elements of, 1.34

Copyright
  Berne Union, 3.132, 4.80
  character merchandising, 3.14
  Convention countries, automatic protection in, 3.124
  designs, protection of. *See* Designs
  disposal of, taxation on, 4.94
  distinctive get-up, in, 3.04
  duration of protection, 3.84
  franchise features, protection by, generally, 3.77
  'get-up', protection of, 3.75–3.78

450

Index

Copyright—*continued*
  'house style' and 'get-up' dependent on, 4.80
  infringement, 3.82
  international, application to franchise business, 4.86
  licensing, 3.143
  meaning, 4.80
  must fit/must match designs, 3.79D, 3.105
  name, in relation to, 3.16
  operations manual, in, 4.80
  original drawings, protection of, 3.81, 3.85
    works, in, 3.86
  overseas protection, 4.80
  patentable articles, 3.106
  period of, 3.84, 3.87
  protection, steps to be taken to ensure, 3.85
  royalties, taxation on, 4.05, 4.06
  single word not 'original literary work', 4.80
  summary of protection, 3.88
  symbol used to denote, 3.132
  transitional provisions, 3.86
  Universal Copyright Convention, 3.132, 4.80
Corporation tax
  advance, 4.55, 4.56
  assessment and calculation, 4.55
  corporations chargeable to, 4.55
  examples of accounting, 4.55, 4.57
  franked payments, 4.58
  rent, on, generally, 4.22
Customer records
  data protection, 5.58

Data protection
  registration, 5.58
Defamation
  personality merchandising, resulting from, 3.15
Deposit
  payment by prospective franchisee, 6.12
  stakeholder, payment to, 6.12
Design right
  automatically arising, 3.85
  copyright, overlap with, 3.103
  design document for artistic work, 3.104
  design, meaning, 3.102
  disposal, taxation on, 4.95
  illustration of, 3.80–3.81, 3.105A
  must fit/must match features, 3.105
  transitional provisions, 3.86
Designs
  copyright protection of,
    generally, 3.79, 3.81
    original drawing protected, 3.81
    ownership of copyright to be stated, 3.53

Designs—*continued*
  copyright protection of—*continued*
    registrable designs, 3.89, 3.91
  doctrine of exhaustion of rights, 2.80
  functional and non-functional, 3.103
  meaning, 3.91
  overseas protection, 4.79
  registered, generally,
    advisability of registration, 3.89
    consent, form of, 3.98
    disposal, taxation on, 4.93
    extension of time for, 3.99
    licensing of, 3.146–3.148
    meaning, 3.91
    Paris Industrial Property Convention, effect of, 3.131
    procedure, 3.93–3.99
      application forms, 3.95
      documents to be submitted, 3.97
      forms and fees, 3.101
      patient agent, employment of, 3.94
      period of protection, 3.100
      plans, specimens, etc., 3.96
      search, 3.93
    qualifying articles, 3.92
    registration, 3.93–3.99, 4.79
    statement identifying features, 3.97
    time for, 3.90
    urgent cases, in, 3.96
Development area, agreement, **311, 402–404**
Directors
  shadow, franchisor as, 1.62
Directors' covenant letter, **309–310, 393**
Distribution franchise
  block exemption,
    application of, 2.48
  service franchise,
    assimilation of, 2.26
  ties in, 2.44
Double taxation agreement, 4.06, 4.103, **446**
Drawings, copyright in, 3.81, 3.85

Employees, wages provisions, 5.65
Equitable relief in dealings with franchisor, 7.49–7.55
Estoppel
  agency by,
    cause of action, 1.55
    English courts, and, 1.46
    holding out, 1.41
    principle, 1.39
    representation, 1.40
    third parties, expectations of, 1.42
    trade mark licensing, effect on, 1.46
  controls by franchisor taken into account where questions of, 1.43
European Commission
  approval of co-operation between small businesses, 0.06
European Communities. *See also* European Commission; Treaty of Rome
  abuse of dominant position, 2.89–2.91

451

Index

European Communities—*continued*
agreements not within block exemption, 2.48
Article 85(1), text of, 2.13
block exemption,
application, conditions for, 2.22
approach to, 2.28
benefit, withdrawal of, 2.25
black list, 2.23
definitions, 2.33–2.36
duration of, 2.25
franchisees, restraints on,
approved sources, 2.44
confidentiality, 2.45
contract premises, operation from, 2.40
customers, seeking, 2.39
exclusive dealing, 2.43
other members of network, not competing with, 2.41
persons with whom dealing, 2.42
quality control, 2.44
franchisor, restrictions accepted by, 2.38
guidelines, agreements within, 2.24
narrower scope, obligations with, 2.46
opposition procedure, 2.47
recitals, 2.29–2.32
restrictions, list of, 2.19
summary of, 2.18
unconditional clearance, clauses with, 2.21
white clauses, 2.20
Charles Jourden case, 2.27
Community Patent Convention, 3.128
disguised restriction on trade between states, 2.84
European Community trade mark, proposal for, 3.134
'exhaustion of rights' doctrine, 2.80–2.86, 2.88
franchise agreements, application to, 2.15–2.17, **423–431**
franchise agreements not considered in isolation, 2.57
manufacturing licences, 2.49–2.52
block exemptions, effect of, 2.51, 2.52
national intellectual property rights, insulation of markets,
cases, result of, 2.87, 2.88
exhaustion of rights, 2.80–2.86
limitations, by, 2.80–2.86
problem of, 2.77–2.79
notification of new agreement,
advertising, control of, 2.73
agreements excused notification, 2.62–2.66
Article 85(3), exemption under, 2.69–2.76
artificial division of market, 2.71
chain, restrictions to preserve, 2.74
comfort letters, 2.69

European Communities—*continued*
notification of new agreement—*continued*
conditions, 2.70
consequences of failure to notify, 61
exemptions, 2.69–2.76
Form A/B, 2.59
formal, 2.58
'free rider' problem, 2.72, 2.73
informal advice, 2.58
manufacturing franchises, 2.75
minor agreements, 2.68, **419–422**
negative clearance, 2.67
recommended prices, of, 2.72
small businesses, encouraging, 2.76
partition of markets, 2.85–2.87
promotion of inter-member trade, 2.12, 2.14
quantitative restrictions on imports between states prohibited, 2.12
restrictive trade practices, registrable agreements, 2.60
selective distribution agreements. *See* Selective distribution agreements
Servicemaster case, 2.26
undertaking, individual as, 2.14
European Company
draft statute for, 0.09
European Economic Interest Grouping
concessions, use for purpose of, 0.07
powers of, 0.07
use of, 0.06–0.08
European Patent Convention, 3.126
European Patent Office
applications to, 3.126
Exhaustion of rights
doctrine of, 2.80–2.86, 2.88, 3.107

Fair trading
Act of 1973, generally, 2.122, 2.123
credit card operations, 2.124
Director General of,
investigation and report, 2.137, 2.138
persistent unfair conduct, action as to, 7.28
powers, 2.122–2.124
franchises, in relation to, 2.125
monopoly situations, 2.123
Office of Fair Trading, letter concerning territorial restrictions to, **309, 390**
Board minutes concerning, **309, 390**
Fees
franchisor paid, 5.41, 5.42
initial, paid by franchisee to franchisor, 5.40
Fixtures
trade, 5.29
Franchise
agreements,
advertising, 5.63
annual meetings and franchisees' club, 5.64
application form, **308, 371–372**

Index

Franchise—*continued*
  application form—*continued*
    letter enclosing, **308**, 373
    checklist, **313–315**
    confidentiality agreement, **308**, 373–375
    Consumer Credit Act, licence under, 5.55–5.57
    death or incapacity of franchisee, 5.69, 6.10
    development area agreement, **311**, **402–404**
    formal notification, *see* European Communities
    goodwill, 5.54
    initial fee, 5.40
    insurance, 5.52
    lease of premises, *see* Lease
    linked transactions, 5.14
    minimum turnover clause, 5.53
    wages provisions, 5.65
    misrepresentation, attempts to avoid consequences of, 7.14
    precedent, **309**, 316–371, 413–416
    preliminary enquiries, 6.02, 6.03
    replies to, 5.71, 6.04 et seq.
    premises, who should own, 5.17
    problems of drafting, 5.03
    purchase agreement, **309**, 391–392
    quiet enjoyment, covenant for, 5.20, **396**
    renewal, 6.08
    rent review clause, **396**
    royalties, minimum payments, 5.53
    sale of business, clause covering, 5.70
    site selection, 5.15, 5.16
    term of, 6.07
    termination by unfair practices, 7.02
    territorial rights, 5.37–5.39
    training of franchise, 5.59–5.62
    vehicles used in franchised business, 5.66–5.68
  application form for, **308**, 371–372
  applications of, examples, 0.02
  basic ingredients, 1.05
  business, choice of name for, 3.03–3.05
    See also Name
  'business format' type, application of, 0.01
  businesses for which used, 0.02
  common law, technical meaning at, 0.01 n
  competition, laws against. *See* Competition
  confidentiality agreement, **308**, 373–375
  Consumer Credit Act considerations, 5.14
  'core', **311**, **408–412**
  corporate, relief for failure of, 4.50–4.52
  countries regulating, 7.64–7.68
  covenants in undertakings, **309–310**, **393**
  definitions, 1.02, 1.03
  development area agreement, **311**, **402–404**
  distinctive features of, 1.02–1.04

Franchise—*continued*
  documentation, **312–313**
  emergence of marketing form, 0.03
  features of, 1.03
  fees as consideration for grant of, 4.01
  Financial Services Act, effect of, 7.46
  franchisors, advantages to, 0.07
  individual agreements should not be negotiable, 5.02
  Inland Revenue letter, **309**, **389**
  kits, misrepresentation in, 7.11
  leasehold covenants, **396**
  legal concept, franchising as, 1.01 et seq.
  living accommodation provided, 5.31
  manufacturing,
    block exemption, application of, 2.48
    'tie-in', advantages of, 5.08
  marketing systems to which use of word related, 0.01
  minimum royalty payments, 5.53
  minimum turnover clause, 5.53
  network contract, operation as. *See* Network contract
  network, indemnity clauses for members of, 5.46
  object, **308**
  outlets for, 4.15–4.27
  patents, application of. *See* Patent
  preliminary contract for,, 5.36
  prospectus inviting subscriptions to shares, 4.49, **308**, **376–389**
  purchase agreement, **309**, **391–392**
  pyramid selling, *see* Pyramid selling
  quality control, 1.13, 1.14, 1.19, 1.20
  'rent-a-name', 2.03
  sale of, procedure, **313**
  sales reports, **310**, **401**
  service, 1.17
    block exemption, application of, 2.48
    distribution franchises, assimilated to, 2.26
  setting up,
    contracts, 5.36
    equipment, supply of, 5.06
    fees and royalties, 5.40–5.42
    generally, 3.01, 3.02, 5.01–5.03
    liability of franchisor, 5.43–5.51
    operating manual, 5.04, **313**
    site and premises, *see* site and premises, *below*
    territorial rights, 5.37–5.39, **314**
    ties, 5.07–5.13
    trade secrets and know-how, safeguarding, 5.05
    training, 5.59–5.62
  site and premises,
    evaluation, **312**
    finding sites, 5.15, 5.16
    guarantees, 5.35
    lease. *See* Lease
    licence agreement, **397–400**
    option to buy, taking, 5.34

453

Index

Franchise—*continued*
site and premises—*continued*
ownership of, 5.17
stationery text, **311, 401**
tax problems associated with franchise payments, *see* Taxation
territorial limits, **312**
letter to Office of Fair Trading as to, **390**
territory of, 6.05, 6.06
exclusive, 5.37–5.39
Unfair Contract Terms Act, application of, 5.38
uniformity of outlets, 5.02
VAT. *See* Value Added Tax
voluntary chains distinguished, 0.04
Franchisee
acts and defaults of,
estoppel, agency by, 1.39–1.44
franchisor, liability of, *see* Franchisor
partnership, relationship of, 1.45–1.54. *See also* Partnership
advantages available to, 4.28
business format system, of, 0.12
adviser to,
generally, 6.01
preliminary enquiries, 6.02–6.03
replies received to preliminary enquiries, 6.04, 6.05
advertising and promotion, 6.15
business names, registration of, 6.24
conferences and associations, 6.16
consulting existing franchisees, 6.13
death and illness, 6.10
deposits, 6.12
fees, 6.20, 6.22
guarantees, 6.26
insurance, 6.18, 6.19
licence under Consumer Credit Act, 6.21
pre-printed, 5.71
term of agreement, 6.07
termination for breach, 6.11
territory, as to, 6.05, 6.06
training and starting, 6.17
VAT, registration for, 6.23
warranty of intellectual property rights, 6.25
write down and renewal, 6.08, 6.09
annual meetings for franchisees, 5.64
associations and conferences, 6.16
bankruptcy or liquidation of, 5.44, 5.45, 6.11
capital, methods of raising, 4.28
risk taken by, 0.08, 1.03, 1.35
club, advantages of joining, 5.64
consultation with other franchisees, 6.13
contractual relationship with franchisor, 1.03
corporate,
relief in event of failure of, 4.50–4.52

Franchisee—*continued*
corporate—*continued*
tax to be deducted at source by, 4.02
death or incapacity of, 5.69, 6.10
deposit, payment of, 6.12
duty of care owed by, 1.28
exclusive territory granted to, 5.37–5.39
franchisees club, 5.64
initial fee payable by, 5.40
insurance of, 5.52, 6.18, 6.19
liability of franchisor to, 5.43
for acts and defaults of, *see* Franchisor
living accommodation provided, 5.31
loan raised by,
consumer credit agreement, 7.29
control of agreement, 7.33
credit broker, franchisor as, 7.31
debtor-creditor-supplier agreement, 7.30
mortgage of land, on, 7.32
no partnership or agency clause, 5.48
operating manual, should be required not to disclose contents, 5.04
outlet purchased by, 4.24
premium for short lease, payment of, 4.16–4.25
principal not agent, as, stationery text, **311, 401**
profile, **312**
promotions by, 6.15
prospective, application form by, **308, 371–372**
letter enclosing, **308, 373**
protection against unfair practices, 7.03
purchase agreement between franchisor and, **309, 391–392**
quiet enjoyment covenant, 5.20, **396**
relationship with franchisor, 7.49
inter se, 1.57–1.61
rent payments by, 4.22, 4.23
review, **396**
sales report by, **310, 401**
site selection by, 5.15, **312**
tax deductions, liability to make, 4.02–4.06
training of,
franchise agreements, clauses as to, 5.59–5.62
further periods, 5.62
generally, 5.59–5.61
Franchisor
acquisition of property by, 4.15, 4.16
acts and defaults of franchisor, liability for,
agency liability, 1.31
American cases, 1.32, 1.33
English case law, 1.34, 1.35
English courts, approach of, 1.36, 1.37
possibility of, 1.28–1.29
third parties, to, 5.44–5.48
vicarious, 1.30, 1.31
advantages of business format system, 0.08

454

Index

Franchisor—*continued*
  advantages of business format system—*continued*
    of granting franchise, 0.07
  advertising etc. by, effect on liability, 1.42
  agency liability, confusion with vacarious liability, 1.31
  annual fee as source of income, 5.41
  assistance to franchise, provision of, 1.03
  Consumer Credit Act, licence under, 5.55–5.57
  Consumer Protection Act, liability under, 1.56
  contractual relationship with franchisee, 1.03
  control exercised by, 1.03
  controls taken into account in questions of estoppel, 1.43
  corporation as, 1.49
  covenants in lease, 396
  deed of guarantee, 310, 394–395
  defective products, liability for, 1.56, 5.51
  directors' covenant letter, 309–310, 393
  disclosure by, 7.56–7.62
  equitable principles applied to dealings by, 7.19–7.55
  extent of liability to third parties, 1.55
  failure to maintain premises, 5.50
  finance and tax problems, generally, 4.28
  freeholds purchased by, 4.15, 4.16
  goodwill accruing to, 1.23, 1.24
  initial fee payable to, 5.40
  insurance, 5.52, 6.18, 6.19
  intermediate landlord, as, 4.16
  'kick-backs' received by, 7.50
  lease granted by, 4.15–4.25, 5.47
  leasehold covenants by, 396
  liability of,
    acts and defaults of franchisee, for, *see* acts and defaults of franchisee, liability for, *above*
    franchisees, to, 5.43
    own acts and defaults, for, 5.49, 5.50
  methods of arranging finance, 4.28
  non-resident, tax position of, 4.05, 4.06
  overseas trading, 4.60–4.64
  permanent establishment in UK, with, tax position, 4.06
  principal and agent, relationship of. *See* Agency
  protection from liability, 5.45
  protection of, indemnity clause, 5.46
    solus and tied house agreements, 5.47
  purchase agreement between franchisee and, 309, 391–392
  re-entry covenant, 310, 396
  relationship between franchisee and, generally, 1.29, 7.49
    master and servant, 1.30, 1.37, 1.57, 1.58

Franchisor—*continued*
  relationship between franchisee and, generally—*continued*
    partnerships, 1.45–1.54, 1.59–1.61
    principal and agent, 1.38–1.44
  relationship with franchisee inter se, 1.57–1.61
  residence for tax purposes, 4.06
  royalty payments to, 1.50, 5.41–5.42
  shadow director of corporate franchisee, as, 1.62
  shareholders' covenant letter, 309–310, 393
  short leases granted by, 4.16–4.19
  site selection by, 5.15, 312
  sub-lease granted by, 4.15
  territorial restrictions, 312, 390
  tied items, sale of, as income source, 5.41
  USA, resident in. *See* United States
  vicarious liability of, 1.30
    confusion with agency liability, 1.31
Fraud
  dealers in securities to be licensed, 7.46
  fraudulent practices generally, 7.01
  misrepresentation, generally, 7.09

'Get up'
  copyright, dependence on, 4.80
  protection, 3.04, 3.75–3.78
  distinctive, as part of franchise identity, 3.04, 3.47, 3.48
  goodwill attaching to protection, 3.76
  protection of, 3.75
Goods
  advertisement of, regulation of information in, 7.23
Goodwill
  agreements, clause dealing with, 5.54
  association with franchise, generally, 1.05
  consideration for transfer of, as capital gain, 4.21
  control of franchisor giving entitlement to, 1.23
  controls by franchisor designed to enhance, 1.36
  defunct business, surviving, 2.114
  exclusive territory, grant of, 4.14
  foreign franchisor, establishment by, 4.150
  franchisor, as property of, 1.23, 1.24
  franchisor, held in trust for, 1.25
  geography, questions of, 3.55, 3.61
  get-up, attaching to, protection, 3.76
  how arising, 4.85
  locality of, questions as to, 3.55, 3.61
  meaning, 3.54, 4.85
  outlets, attaching to, 1.23
  passing off action in relation to, 3.14, 3.55
  premium payments to be distinguished, 4.21

Index

Goodwill—*continued*
    purchase of company owned store, on, 4.24
    sale of, taxation on, 4.96
    trade mark assigned with, 1.08
        name, 1.24
    unregistered mark, in, 1.27

Group relief
    non-availability of, 4.110

Groupement d'intérêt économique,
    disadvantages of, 0.05
    European Commission, approval of, 0.10
    form and operation, 0.05
    introduction of in France, 0.04

Guarantee
    franchisor's deed of, **310, 394–395**

Holding out
    agency by, 1.39
    name, by use of, 1.41
    partnership by, 1.41, 1.48, 1.49

House style, dependence on copyright, 4.80

Improvements
    leasehold property, to, compensation, tenants entitlement to, 5.29
    exclusions, 5.30
    must add to letting value of property, 5.29
    'trade fixtures', exclusion of, 5.29

Indemnity clause
    franchisor protected by, 5.46

Inheritance tax
    close company, on transfer by, 4.97

Insurance
    double insurance, 5.52
    franchisor and franchisee, of, 6.18, 6.19
    incapacity of franchisee, cover for, 5.52

Intellectual property rights
    Community Patent Convention, 3.128
    'industrial property' as alternative devinition, 4.14
    licensing, procedural aspects of, 3.135–3.148
    meaning, 4.01 n
    national, insulation of markets. *See* European Communities
    overseas protection, 4.77–4.86
    Patent Co-operation Treaty, 3.127
    protection abroad,
        European Patent Office, applications in, 3.126
        generally, 3.124
        Paris Industrial Property Convention, 3.125
    taxation in respect of, generally, 4.01–4.07, 4.60, 4.77–4.86
    Trade Mark Registration Treaty, 3.133
    types of asset, generally, 4.77
    Universal Copyright Convention, 3.132, 4.80
    warranty of, 6.25

Interest
    definition, 4.154
    exemption of US resident from tax on, 4.154

International Franchise Association, code established by, 0.11
    definition of franchise, 1.02

Know-how
    consideration for disposal of, as capital gain, 4.21
    copyright in operations manual, 4.83
    disposal of, taxation on, 4.24
    franchise fees not to be treated as payments for, 4.24
    franchisor, as exclusive asset of, 4.83
    'grant back' clause, avoidance of, 4.84
    information and technique, 4.14
    licence granting right to, 4.84
    overseas company developing own, 4.84
    payment for acquisition of, 4.14
    protection, 3.118–3.123
    royalties in respect of, 4.02–4.07
    safeguarding of, 5.05
    specialised, rights in, 4.83, 4.84
    taxation in relation to transfer of, 4.91–4.93
    'tie-ins' preserving, 5.08
    undertakings not to disclose, 2.104, 2.105
    writing off of payment for, 4.14

Lease
    business premises of,
        residential property combined with, 5.31
        termination, 5.26–5.28
    checklist, 5.32
    compensation for improvements. *See* Improvements
    continuation of, after expiry of franchise licence, 5.26
    covenants in, 5.23, **396**
    grant by franchisor, 4.15–4.23
    grounds for refusal of new tenancy, 5.27
    Landlord and Tenant Act, exclusion of, 5.33
    liability for payment of rates under, 5.31
    licence distinguished, 5.18, 5.19
    premium payments for, additional rent, treatment as, 4.19
    franchise, by, generally, 4.16–4.20
        goodwill value to be distinguished, 4.21
        'long' lease, capital gains tax, charge to, 4.20
        'short' lease, 4.16–4.19
    problems to be considered, 5.25
    rent review, 5.24, **396**
    rent, tax on, 4.22
    security of tenure, 5.26–5.28
    surrender option in, 5.22
    term of, not to exceed term of agreement, 5.21

Index

Lease—*continued*
  user covenant, 5.23
Licence
  checklist, 5.32
  Consumer Credit Act, under, 5.55–5.57
  court, letter to, **400**
  lease distinguished, 5.18, 5.19
  liability for payment of rates under, 5.31
  licence and agency agreement, **404–408**
  Master Licence Agreement, **309**, **316–371**
  site, of, **397–400**
Licensing
  service marks, 1.15 et seq.
  trade marks, 1.13 et seq.
  unregistered trade marks and names, 1.22
'Limbo' trusts, 4.121, 4.143
Limited partnership. *See* Partnership
Liquidation of corporate franchise, 5.44, 5.45
Loan, franchisee, raised by, 7.29–7.33

Man, Isle of, trade marks in, 4.82
Manufacturing franchises
  block exemption, application of, 2.48
  tie-ins, advantages of, 5.08
Master and servant
  American case law, 1.32
  confusion between vicarious and agency liability, 1.31
  consequences of relationship between, 1.30
  contract of service, elements of, 1.34
  controls establishing liability of franchisor, 1.32
  degree of control as test of relationship, 1.31
  English case law, 1.34, 1.35
  franchisor and franchisee, relationship between,
    compared to, 1.30–1.37
    inter se, 1.57–1.58
  matters establishing non-liability of franchisor, 1.33
  owner-driver held not employee, 1.35, 1.57
  relationship not precluded by that of landlord and tenant, 1.37
  test of liability of master, 1.31
  vicarious liability, 1.30, 1.31
Master Agreement, form, **309**, **316–371**
Minimum wages provisions,
  advantages of, 5.65
  franchise agreements, in 5.65
Misrepresentation
  damages in lieu of rescission, 7.13
  exclusion clauses, attempts to exclude by, 7.14–7.16
  jurisdiction, generally, 7.09–7.16
  negligent, 7.11
  oral, 7.11
  potential performance of outlets, as to, 7.12
Monograms, registration of, 3.35

Monopoly
  common law franchise distinguished, 0.01*n*.
  Monopolies and Mergers Commission, references to, 2.122–2.124
  monopoly situations, 2.123

Name
  franchise business, of,
    celebrity names, 3.09
    choice, generally, 3.03–3.05
    common field of activity, businesses with, 3.76 et seq.
    consultation of specialist agencies, 3.03
    copyright, 3.14
    descriptive names, avoidance of, 3.04
    geographical, as trade mark, 3.29–3.32
    'get-up', distinctive, as part of franchise identity, 3.47
    invented or fanciful words, 3.04
    misspelled words, 3.04
    passing off, *see* Passing off
    proper names best avoided, 3.04
    protection,
      encroachment, from, 3.62–3.71
      generally, 3.52
      geography, problem of, 3.55–3.61, 3.76
    passing off, 3.52–3.61
    registration as trade mark, 3.26, 3.30
    representation to be distinctive, 3.05
    same name, use of, 3.04
    search in registers, 3.05
    service mark, registration as, 3.26, 3.33
    similar names, use of, 3.56
    symbol, combination with, 3.04
    trade mark and patent agents as specialists, 3.03
    unusual names to be preferred, 3.04
    use of names from other fields, 3.62–3.71
Netherlands, private resident companies incorporated in, 4.130
Network contracts
  management contract or licence, breach of terms of, 1.67
  master franchisee, actions against, 1.65, 1.66
  master franchisee and management company, between, action by franchisee, 1.64
  meaning, 1.63
  privity problems, 1.63, 1.68
Numerals, registration of, 3.35A

Operating manual, contents of, 5.04
Outlets
  checklist, 4.27
  franchise business, for, 4.15–4.27
  freehold premises, 4.16
  long lease, premium for, 4.20, 4.21
  purchase by franchisees, 4.24

Index

Outlets—*continued*
rent,
charge to tax, 4.22, 4.23
VAT on, 4.25
short lease of, 4.17–4.19
Uniform Business Rate, 4.26
uniformity, desirability of, 5.02
Overseas company
chargeable profits and gains, 4.99
controlled foreign company,
chargeable profits, 4.99
deemed, 4.99
exempt activities, 4.102
franchisor, subsidiary of, 4.100, 4.101
tax haven territory, subsidiaries in, 4.103
exempt activities, 4.102
double taxation agreements, 4.06, 4.103
guarantees by franchisor, 4.108
investment risks, methods of reducing, 4.109–4.119
partnerships, 4.113–4.119
'pilot' operations, 4.111, 4.113, 4.114
registration of trade marks, 4.106
tax havens, 4.103
taxation reliefs, 4.109 et seq.
UK, in, trading style, 3.07
whether resident in UK, 4.105–4.108
taxable on proportion of profits or gains, 4.98

Paris Industrial Property Convention, 3.125, 3.131
Partnership,
agency law, as branch of, 1.46
agreement as basis of, 1.49
codification of law of, 1.47
definition, 1.47
fiduciary relationship, 7.49
franchisor and franchisees, relationships between, 1.45, 1.59–1.61
generally, 1.45
holding out, by, 1.41, 1.48, 1.49
limited,
absence of English authorities, 1.53, 1.54
American view of, 1.52
limited partner intervening in business, 1.50
origin of, 1.51
rule relating to, 1.50
'no partnership' clauses, 1.49, 5.48
overseas companies, 4.113–4.119
partner as agent of firm, 1.47
partnerships between partnerships, 1.49
royalty, effect of payment of, 1.50
taxation, questions of, 1.60
test of, 1.46
Passing off
character merchandising, in, 3.72–3.74
common field of activity, 3.62–3.64

Passing off—*continued*
common law action for protection of trade mark or name, 3.52
confusion, must be possible, 3.64
proof of, 3.67–3.71
elements of tort, 3.53, 3.54
evidence of effect, 3.70, 3.71
genuine confusion, 3.64–3.71
locality, 3.55–3.61
general law of, 3.53, 3.54
goodwill, in relation to, 3.55
meaning, 3.54
'pre-launch' reputation of product, protection of, 3.59, 3.60
reputation of trader, protection of, 3.59, 3.60
survey evidence, 3.70
Patent
advantages of application for, 3.107
application for, 3.112–3.117
'black' clauses in agreements relating to, 4.84
challenge as to ownership of invention, 3.129
Chartered Institute of Patent Agents, 3.03
Community Patent Convention, 3.128
Comptroller-General of Patents, 3.129
Convention application, 3.125, 3.126
disposal for capital sum, taxation on, 4.89
European Patent Convention, 3.126
European Patent Office, applications to, 3.126
exhaustion of rights, doctrine of, 2.80, 3.107
generally, 3.106
infringement, action for, 3.130
International Search Authorities, 3.127
inventions, things excluded, 3.111
licensing of, 3.144, 3.145
lump sum, part disposal for, treatment as royalty, 4.89
maintenance of, 3.106
operations where used, 3.108
overseas protection, 4.78
Paris Industrial Property Convention, effect of, 3.125
patent agents, 3.109n
Patent Co-operation Treaty, 3.127, 4.78
'patent rights', meaning, 4.78
patentable articles, copyright protection of, 3.106
patentable invention, 3.111
pending applications, rights running from date of, 3.130
registration, 4.78
royalties, tax deductible at source, 4.02
split inventions, 3.129
taxation of receipts from disposal of, 4.78
'tie-ins' in licences for, 5.11–5.13
UK or European, 3.110
who may apply, 3.129

Index

Person
  association with another person, meaning, 2.128
  franchise chain treated as, 2.128, 2.136
  meaning, 2.128
Personality merchandising
  defamation in respect of, 3.15
  false trade description, 3.17
  invasion of privacy, 3.16
  meaning, 1.13, 3.09, 3.10
  name, right to use, 3.18
  'trafficking', 1.13, 3.12, 3.13
Preliminary enquiries, *See* Franchisee
Premises
  advantages of site ownership, 5.17
  business, termination of tenancy, 5.26, 5.28
  franchisee not having exclusive possession, 5.19
  harrassment, protection against, 7.48
  ownership by franchisor, advantages of, 5.17
  site selection, generally, 5.15, 5.16
Premium. *See* Lease
Price
  Price Commission, abolition, 2.126
  resale price maintenance, *see* Resale price maintenance
Principal and agent. *See* Agency
Privacy, invasion of by exploitation of name, 3.16
Product liability, 1.56, 5.51
Promotion, franchisee, by, 6.15
Public house, tied, relationship of parties, 1.37
Pyramid selling
  'founder member' plan, 7.44
  generally, 7.34, 7.69
  instability of schemes, 7.35
  legality, 7.43
  mechanics of, 7.35
  penalty for offences, 7.41
  regulations, 7.39–7.45
  statutory control of, 7.36–7.45
  'trading scheme', definition, 7.38

Quiet enjoyment, covenant for, 5.20, **396**

Rent
  arrears of, as grounds for refusal of new tenancy, 5.27
  review clause in franchise agreement, 5.24
  VAT on, 4.25
Resale price maintenance
  checklist, 2.151
  generally, 2.150
Restraint of trade
  agreement in, meaning, 2.94
  basis of doctrine, 2.101
  benefits received in return for, 2.101
  categories of agreement, 2.102

Restraint of trade—*continued*
  common law rules, 2.95
  contract unreasonably restricting, question of, 2.97
  disposal of business, provision as to, 2.101
  doctrine of, generally, 2.04
  effect of agreement in, 2.119–2.121
  employer and employee, covenants between, 2.103–2.105
  franchising, and,
    customers, soliciting, 2.116
    directors, covenants required from, 2.117
    effect on, 2.93
    goodwill, survival of, 2.114
    length of restraint, 2.113
    Prontaprint case, 2.108–2.113
    skill and information, franchisee using, 2.107
  geographical area of, 2.112, 2.115
  litigation, coming into play on, 2.118
  reasonableness, onus of proof of, 2.96
  'rule of reason' approach, 2.99, 2.100
  rules as to, 2.96
  sale of business, covenants entered into on, 2.106, 2.110
  solus agreements, 2.98
  tie, acceptable length of, 2.101
  time, reasonable period of, 2.111, 2.112
  trade secrets and know-how, undertaking not to disclose, 2.104, 2.105
    preservation of, 3.118–3.123
  trading pattern of similar agreements, 2.101
  unreasonable, 2.10
Restrictive trade practices
  checklist, 2.144
  generally, 2.141–2.142
  notification, 2.60
  particulars, failure to furnish, 2.145–2.149
  procedure, 2.143
  'restrictions', meaning, 2.147
Royalties
  copyright, payment of tax on, 4.05, 4.06
  definition, 4.146, 4.147
  disguising true rate, 7.01
  enquiries as to fees, 6.20
  fraud, guarding against, 5.41
  know-how, for, 4.07
  minimum payments, 5.53
  payment for supply of ancillary services, 4.147
  to franchisor, 1.50
  tax on,
    checklist, 4.07
    payment of, generally, 4.02–4.06
    when deductible at source, 4.02
  tied items, as profit on, 5.42

459

Index

Sales report
  precedent, **310, 401**
Selective distribution agreements
  Article 85(1), effect of infringement, 2.56
  effect of policy, 2.53
  price restrictions, 2.53
  termination provisions, 2.55
Servant. *See* Master and servant
Service franchise
  block exemption, application of, 2.48
  distribution franchises, assimilated to, 2.26
Service mark
  character merchandising, 3.12, 3.13
  colour, factor of, 3.35A
  container, shape of, 3.35A
  definition, 3.22
  device marks, 3.34
  distinctive in use, must be, 3.38–3.40
  foreign country, used in 3.39
  geographical names, 3.29–3.32
  invented words, 3.27
  licensing, 1.15–1.21
    permissible, 1.19
    quality control, 1.17, 1.18
    sub-licensing, 1.20, 1.21
  monograms, 3.35
  name, registration as, 3.26
  numerals, 3.35A
  personality merchandising, 3.12, 3.13
  register, 3.43, 3.44
  registered user provisions, 1.18
  registration, 1.15, 3.20 et seq.
    classes of service, 3.43, 3.44
    lack of, 3.24
    Part A,
      application for, 3.42 et seq.
      criteria, 3.25
    Part B,
      criteria, 3.36 et seq.
      rights conferred by, 3.37
    procedure, 3.41 et seq.
      advertisement of intention to register, 3.48
      application to register, 3.42 et seq.
      forms and fees, 3.51
      maintenance of register, 3.50
      objection to application, 3.49, **417–418**
      search, 3.05, 3.41
        computerisation, 3.41
      signature of application form, 3.46
      specification of goods, 3.44
      statutory definitions, 3.22
      who may apply, 3.45
  sub-licensing, 1.20, 1.21
    avoidance, 1.21
  surnames as, 3.33
  trade marks distinguished, 3.23
  'trafficking', 1.14, 1.20, 3.12, 3.13
  words not directly referring to service, 3.28

Services
  categories of, 3.43, 3.44
  trade marks, *see* Service mark
Shareholders' covenant letter, 309–310, 393
'Solus' agreement
  landlord and tenant relationship under, 5.47
  problems arising, 5.09
  relationship of parties, 1.37
  restraint of trade, application of doctrine of, 2.98
Statute of Monopolies, 2.01
Streetwise franchising, 0.17, 6.14
Surname
  trade mark, as, 3.33

Taxation
  anti-avoidance measures by Inland Revenue, 4.67
  borrowings, interest on, 4.62, 4.63
  capital gains, *see* Capital gains tax
  close companies, interest relief for investment in, 4.53
  commerce and tax avoidance, conflict of, 4.119
  controlled foreign company, 4.99–4.103
  copyright, disposal of, 4.94
  corporation tax and advance corporation tax. *See* Corporation tax
  double taxation agreements, 4.06, 4.103, **446**
  exchange controls, effect of, 4.120
  finance company funded by franchisor, 4.112
  franchise fees, on, 4.02–4.06
    checklist, 4.07. *See also* Royalties
  franchisor trading overseas, 4.60–4.64
  franked investment income, 4.58
  goodwill, sale of, 4.96
  investment companies, risk by, 4.59
  know-how, transfer of, 4.91–4.93
  Netherlands Antilles company, use of, 4.141–4.144
  Netherlands companies incorporated to receive royalties, 4.130–4.140
  overseas companies, *see also* Overseas company
    profits, methods of reducing, 4.65, 4.120–4.144
  overseas investment risks, reducing, 4.109–4.119
  overseas trading partnership, of, 4.113–4.116
  patent rights, receipts from, 4.78
  patents, disposal of, 4.89
  pilot operations, 4.111, 4.113, 4.114
  premium, position on payment of, 4.16
  problems of, generally, 4.01 et seq.
  relief where failure of corporate franchisee, 4.50–4.52
  rent, 4.22, 4.23
    deduction at source, 4.23

Index

Taxation—*continued*
  rent—*continued*
    paid by franchisee, on, 4.22–4.24
  tax havens, 4.82, 4.103
  trade marks, overseas grant of, 4.90
  transfer of property to overseas company, 4.68–4.76
  transfers overseas, actual or deemed, 4.87–4.97
  unilateral relief in respect of foreign taxes, 4.60, 4.61
  USA franchisors, 4.145–4.158. *See also* USA
  VAT. *See* Value Added Tax
  withholding tax, 4.120

Technology transfers
  regulation of franchising through, 7.66

Territory
  exclusive, granting of, checklist, 5.39
    legislation affecting, 5.38
    problems arising, 5.37
  restrictions, 5.37–5.39, 6.06, **312, 390**
  territorial grants generally, 6.05, 6.06

'Tie-ins'
  American view of, 2.03
  checklists, 5.10
  equitable principles applied to, 7.51
  generally, 2.02
  know-how and trade assets, preserving, 5.08
  linked transactions, 5.14
  patent licences, under, checklist, 5.13
    special provisions, 5.12
    void terms, 5.11
  problems arising, 5.09
  where justified, 2.02
  whether beneficial dependent on circumstances, 5.07

Tied house agreement
  landlord and tenant relationship under, 5.47

Trade descriptions
  advertisements of goods, 7.23
  compensation under Act of 1968, 7.26, 7.37
  defences to proceedings as to, 7.24, 7.25
  false, application to goods as offence, 7.19
    by use of name, 3.17
  forecasts, 7.22
  goods and services supplied by franchisee to customer, 7.17–7.23
  supplied by franchisor to franchisee, 7.18, 7.19
  oral statements suffice, 7.19
  penalties for offences as to, 7.26, 7.27
  services supplied by franchisor to franchisee, 7.20–7.23
  statutory provisions, generally, 7.17–7.27
  what amount to, 7.19

Trade marks
  assignment of, 1.27

Trade marks—*continued*
  assignment of marks in gross, prohibition against, 1.18
  Bowden Wire case, 1.08–1.11
  Channel Islands, 4.82
  character merchandising, 1.13, 3.12, 3.13
  colour, use of, 3.35A
  container, shape of, 3.35A
  commodity in own right, as, 1.13
  definition, 1.10, 3.22
    former, 1.07
  designs, registration as, 3.92
  device marks, 3.34
  distinctive in use, must be, 3.38–3.40
  doctrine of exhaustion of rights, 2.80–2.86
  European Community trade mark, proposal for, 3.134
  foreign country, used in, 3.39, 4.81, 4.150
  former view of use of, 1.07
  franchisees need not to be registered as users, 3.136
  generally, 3.19–3.23
  geographical names, 3.29–3.32
  goodwill associated with, 1.08, 1.23
  history of, 1.06–1.09
  infringement, action for, 3.20
  Institute of Trade Mark Agents, 3.03
  invented words, 3.27
  licence not conferring vicarious liability, 1.36
  licensing of,
    generally, 1.13 et seq.
    sub-licensing, 1.20, 1.21
    summary, 1.26
    where permissible, 1.13
    whether possible, 1.27
  Madrid Agreement on, 3.133
  Man, Isle of, 4.82
  monograms, 3.35
  names, registration as, 3.26
  numerals, 3.35A
  overseas use, grant for, taxation, 4.90
  Paris Convention, 4.81
  payments for use of, whether tax deductable at source, 4.02
  personality merchandising, 1.13, 3.12, 3.13
  priority protection in Convention countries, 3.05
  quality, as symbol of, 1.44
  register, 3.43, 3.44
    classes of goods in, 3.43, 3.44
    search, 3.05, 3.41
  registered user provisions, 1.18
  registration, 1.15, 3.20 et seq.
    classes of goods, 3.43, 3.43
    national, being, 3.21
    Part A,
      application for, 3.42 et seq.
      criteria, 3.25 et seq.
    Part B,
      criteria, 3.36 et seq.

461

Index

Trade marks—*continued*
  registration,—*continued*
    Part B,—*continued*
      rights conferred by, 3.37
      permissive, 3.137–3.139
      procedure,
        advertisement of intention to register, 3.48
        application to register, 3.42 et seq.
        forms and fees, 3.51
        maintenance of registration, 3.50
        objection to application, 3.49, **417–418**
      search, 3.05, 3.41
        computerisation, 3.41
      signature of application form, 3.46
      specification of goods, 3.44
      who may apply, 3.46
    statutory definitions, 3.22
  restrictions on, 4.82
  same mark registered in different countries, 3.21
  service marks distinguished, 3.23
    See Service mark
  sub-licensing, 1.20, 1.21
    avoidance, 1.21
  surnames as, 3.33
  tax havens, use of, 4.82
  'tie-ins', effect of, 2.02
  Trade Mark Registration Treaty, 3.133
  'trafficking', 1.13, 1.14, 1.17, 1.20, 3.12, 3.13
  types of, 4.81
  unlicensed, accrual of goodwill in, 1.27
  unregistered, licensing, 1.22
  users, registration of, 3.140–3.142
  Vienna Trademark Registration Treaty, 4.81
  words not directly referring to goods, 3.28
Trade name
  passing off action in respect of, 3.52–3.54
  protection of, 3.53 et seq.
  restriction on use of, after termination of licence, 1.24
  unregistered, licensing, 1.22
Trade secrets
  disclosure of, restraints on, 3.118–3.123
  names of customers, use of, 3.122
  safeguarding of, 5.05
  types of information subject to restraint, 3.119
Training of franchisees, 5.59–5.62
Treaty of Rome
  Article 30, 2.12
  Article 34, 2.12
  Article 85,
    equipment supply, agreements as to, 5.06
    franchise agreements, application to, **423–431**
    generally, 2.01
    text, 2.13

Treaty of Rome—*continued*
  Article 86, 2.89–2.91
Trusts
  'limbo', creation and effect of, 4.121, 4.143
  non-resident trustees, matters to be considered by, 4.122–4.127
Turnover, minimum turnover clauses, 5.53

Unfair contract terms, 5.43
Unfair trading
  accounting systems, 7.01
  generally, 7.01
  misleading advertising of franchises, 7.01
  persistent unfair conduct, 7.28
  pyramid selling. *See* Pyramid selling
  termination of franchise, 7.02
  Trade Descriptions Act, application of, 7.17–7.27
  withholding supplies to franchisee, 7.02
UNIDROIT
  model law, draft, 7.68
Uniform business rate, 4.26
Uniform franchise offering code, 7.63
USA
  franchisor resident in,
    double taxation agreement, effect of, 4.155
    Federal Trade Commission Rule, 7.56–7.62
    filing of tax form by, 4.157
    goodwill, 4.150
    interest, exemption from tax on, 4.154
    'permanent establishment',
      avoidance of, 4.149, 4.150
      disadvantages of, 4.153
      setting up of, 4.151
    profits accumulated outside US, 4.158
    royalties exempt from tax, 4.147
    subsidiary in UK, incorporation of, 4.154–4.156
    tax credit, UK tax payments as, 4.152
    taxation, generally, 4.145 et seq.
  tying arrangements, 2.01, 2.03

Value Added Tax
  account, example of, 4.10
  accounting periods, 4.09
  cash flow, 4.10–4.13
  enquiry as to registration and number, 4.13
  exempt supplies and services, 4.08
  franchise, in respect of, whether and how payable, 4.09
  generally, 4.08–4.13
  input and output taxes, 4.09, 4.10
  overseas franchisees, position of, 4.09
  penalty for delay in payment of, 4.12
  registrations for, 6.23
  rent for commercial property, on, 4.25
  security of borrowings, 4.12
  workings of system, 4.09

Value Added Tax—*continued*
  zero-rated supplies, 4.08
Vehicles
  provisions as to, in franchise agreements, 5.66–5.68
Vicarious liability
  agency liability distinguished from, 1.30
  franchisor, of. *See* Master and servant
  group unity as reason for acceptance of, 1.31
  trade mark licence does not confer, 1.36

Voluntary group or chain
  French equivalent, 0.04, 0.05
  idea behind, 0.10
  independent business of, franchise distinguished, 0.04

Wages
  minimum wages provisions, 5.65

Zero-rating
  VAT purposes, for, 4.08